THE MYTH OF THE NATION
AND VISION OF
REVOLUTION

THE ORIGINS OF
TOTALITARIAN DEMOCRACY

POLITICAL MESSIANISM:
THE ROMANTIC PHASE

THE MYTH OF THE NATION
AND THE VISION OF
REVOLUTION

*The Origins of Ideological Polarisation
in the Twentieth Century*

J. L. TALMON

SECKER & WARBURG
LONDON

UNIVERSITY OF CALIFORNIA PRESS
BERKELEY AND LOS ANGELES

Martin Secker & Warburg Limited
54 Poland Street, London W1V 3DF
University of California Press
Berkeley and Los Angeles, California

First published 1981

ISBN 0-436-51399-4 (UK)
ISBN 0-520-04449-5 (USA)

Library of Congress Cataloging in Publication Data
Talmon, Jacob Leib, 1916–
The myth of the nation and the vision of revolution.

1. Nationalism and socialism—History.
I. Title.
HX550.N3T35 *1981* 320.5'31   80-6167
70703

Printed in Great Britain

For Irene, my wife,
and Daniella and Maya, my daughters

L'histoire ne servirait a rien, si l'on n'y met les tristesses du présent.
Jules Michelet

PREFACE

While examining the interaction between the ideology of nationalism and the expectation of a total universal revolution in the last quarter of the nineteenth and first quarter of the twentieth century, the present book was composed to constitute also the concluding volume of a trilogy. The two preceding works, *The Origins of Totalitarian Democracy* and *Political Messianism—The Romantic Phase,* traced the origins and development of the tradition of revolutionary messianism, with its basic premises derived from the Enlightenment, its inspiration and model from the Jacobin totalitarian-democratic dictatorship and Babeuf's communits conspiracy, and its vision of the unfolding of a preordained and all-embracing pattern of historic inevitability leading to classless unanimity (totalitarian democracy) from nineteenth-century socialist thought. This book is concerned with the pre-1914 origins of the schism in the European, above all Russian socialist, movement, into reformism and revolutionary radicalism, which at a deeper level appears to have been the difference between an acceptance of the historic national community as the natural political-social framework and the vision of a socialist world society achieved by a universal revolutionary break-through. It probes then into the ways in which the Russian version of revolutionary and internationalist messianism emerged victorious out of its confrontation with the myth of the nation in the crucible of the Great War, and not as the inevitable end-product of social-economic development.

The Bolshevik Revolution came to serve as the new inspiration and model, and Russia as the Promethean guide—or patron power—to all the faithful of the religion of revolution, and above all to its practitioners outside Europe. At the other pole, the spectre of revolutionary internationalism combined with other stimuli to goad the resentful and frightened devotees of warring integral nationalism in the defeated or discontented nations into totalitarian Fascism and racist Nazism.

In the course of the long years which it took to write this work, and which were made the more difficult by a variety of impediments and predicaments, I was generously helped by a number of foundations and academic institutions. I wish to thank—in chronological order—the

Rockefeller Foundation for the research grant it accorded me at an early stage; St Catherine's College, Oxford, and its Master, Lord Bullock, friend and distinguished fellow historian, for the visiting fellowship awarded in 1962-3; the Intitute of Advanced Study in Princeton, where in 1967-8 I was fortunate to have as associates the then Head of its History School, Felix Gilbert, and fellow-members of similar interests Karl Dietrich Bracher and Carl Schorske; MIT for appointing me Ford Professor in International History in 1968-9; the Netherlands Institute for Advanced Study at Wassenaar for hospitality in 1971-2; St Anthony's College, Oxford, and its Warden, my friend Raymond Carr, for the spell spent with them; Woolfson College and its first President Sir Isaiah Berlin, an old friend, whose power to inspire and stimulate is never diminished, for the visiting fellowship held 1974-5; Yeshiva University for inviting me to give the Gottesmann Lectures of 1976, which task infused into me the energy to bring the work to completion after a period of near loss of nerve resulting from ill health; finally the National Humanities Center at the Research Triangle Park in North Carolina for enabling me to conclude the work in the Center's first year, which after the happiest of auspices had its closing days sadly clouded by the shattering death of its so dedicated and generous first President, Charles Frankel.

It would be difficult to name all who in one way or another aided me in carrying out the project in various, sometimes intangible and imperceptible ways. Special mention however is due to my direct assistants, in the first place to Mrs Lily Polliack, my long-time assistant who with characteristic loyalty insisted on typing out alone the whole book, on top of her important share in the work of research. Mr Amos Hoffman devotedly served me as teaching and research assistant in the final stage in 1977-8, another year of health troubles. I wish to thank Mrs Maya Asheri, whose researches on Mussolini and the rise of Fascism were of considerable assistance, and my other advanced graduate students, whose proficiency in languages was of great help, Mrs Rachel Heuberger, Mr Alex Dan and Mr Mordecai Zeldon, Mr Enzio Nepi. My colleagues Dr Hedva Ben-Israel, Professor S. N. Eisenstadt and Dr Jonathn Frankel, read parts of the manuscript and made helpful remarks. The discussions with Professor Zev Sternhell and Dr Baruch Knei-Paz were of great value. The books of Sternhell, *La Révolution Nationale 1885-1914*, and of Knei-Paz on *The Social and Political Thought of Leon Trotsky*, came out too late to be cited in this book, as much as they surely deserved. I profited not a little from conversations with my Jerusalem colleagues and friends Professors Joshua Arieli and Emanuel Sivan, and Dr Benjamin Kedar, and no less from contacts with Professors Perez

Zaprin and Norman Fiering at the National Humanities Center. My thanks to Mr Melvin J. Lasky, Editor of *Encounter,* for allowing me to reprint in this book the essay published in his journal on "The Legacy of Georges Sorel—Marxism, Violence, Fascism" and for permitting me to make extensive use of excerpts from the book by Professor M. Confino, *Daughter of a Revolutionary,* namely the Bakunin—Nechaev correspondence contained in it, published by the Alcove Press. Finally, I wish to express my deep gratitude to Mr David Farrer, the literary editor of Secker and Warburg, Publishers, and to my friend Miss Bernadette Folliot for their indispensable and faithful help in editing and polishing up the work. Needless to add that the author bears the sole responsibility for the views presented in the book.

CONTENTS

Part I

MARX, ENGELS AND THE NATION

CHAP.

Part II

THE EMANCIPATION OF THE PROLETARIAT AND THE NATIONAL DESTINY—WILHELMINE GERMANY

PART VI

LENIN—INTERNATIONAL REVOLUTIONARY AND ARCHITECT OF NEW RUSSIA

Part VIII

FROM GEORGES SOREL TO BENITO MUSSOLINI

Part IX

THE GERMAN REVOLUTION OF 1918 AND HITLER IN THE WINGS

INTRODUCTION

This book is the fruit of long reflection upon the evolution and the impact of the two most potent ideological forces of the last two hundred years, one might call them secular religions: the vision of a total social world revolution and the myth of the nation. The relationship between them has always wavered and undergone innumerable changes from alliance and even near-identity to ambiguity, rivalry and direct conflict to the point of mortal confrontation. This dialectic has been played out upon the local plane in accordance with place- and time-bound circumstances, and also upon a global scale.

The most momentous and all-determining encounter took place in the course and on the morrow of the tremendous upheaval of World War I. The unprecedented shock and sufferings produced by the war accorded awful significance to these two creeds: for they seemed to offer meaning to the catastrophe and hopes of a commensurate compensation in the form of a salvationist dénouement. Thus, from the methodological as well as the substantive point of view, we are here concerned with the dialectical interaction between ideas and historic realities.

The Great War and, before it, the rise and expansion of the global imperialist forms of racial-social oppression, put the religion of universal messianic revolution and totalitarian democracy on the agenda as containing a message of the utmost relevance and urgency; the more so, after they had come to fruition in the Bolshevik Revolution. At the same time, the idea of the nation as the source and focus of all values, as the most important vehicle of collective self-expression, had proved its incomparable potency in the greatest ever war of nations. In the defeated and discontented nations this idea became an absolute in the form of Fascism-Nazism and racism which also linked up with ideas earlier in origin, soaked by now in morbid passions.

(1) THE UNFOLDING OF A DICHOTOMY

The 'death of God' in the eighteenth century sent many people in search of focuses for collective identity, quite dissociated from the church and the confraternity of Christian believers. Such a substitute was found in the nation.[1] The break-up of the traditional ties which had been

maintained for so long by feudalism, the guild system and hierarchical
structures, combined with social mobility and urbanisation to turn men
into atoms—individuals comprised in one single whole, the national
community. This community was envisaged by those bred on the ideas
of the Enlightenment and the French Revolution as a society of free and
equal citizens participating in permanent deliberation on their common
welfare. To believers in organic wholes the nation assumed the shape of
a primary datum, prior to the individuals comprising it. Its own unique
possession, language, marked the nation off from all the other ethnic
entities. Not a deliberate contrivance of any single person or group,
putting consciously one and two together, but the fruit of infinitely slow
groping by countless human beings for expression, with words and
speech forms breaking forth like an elemental force, the collective
character of language seemed to demonstrate the primacy and superiority of the group over the individual. The marvellous cohesion of the
ripe product could also be taken as proof of a spirit that is a special
natural gift of the tribe and not merely a reflection of an abstract
universal reason. An unfathomable national spirit conditioned all the
responses of the members of the ethnic group. As such it determined the
historic tradition, fate and destiny of the collective entity. The first
version—we may call it Rousseauist—inclined towards rationalistic,
egalitarian and universalising patterns: endowed with freedom of
choice, men shaped their own lives on a contractual basis, always anew
as it were. The second version, which derived its inspiration from
Herder, was not easily reconcilable with the idea of the oneness of
mankind and objective truth. It contained conservative potentialities,
because of its tendency to consecrate the peculiar past and the unique
traditions of the nation, whatever their political and social content, as
expressions of a precious group-authenticity and group-integrity. In a
nation with a successful and expansionist past, such a conception of
nationhood has indeed often helped the ruling classes, nobility and
military castes to claim that they were the authors of its greatness and
that their own privileged status was therefore both a reward for historic
services and a condition of the continued greatness of the nation.[2]

  Historical experience has also shown, however, that in times of
national oppression and social stress the true nature of a nation may be
defined in an emphatically popular spirit. The masses are made out to be
the natural repository and faithful guardian of the national values. Their
pristine spontaneity and immediacy, their remoteness from contact
with the outer world, are held to immunise them against the contagion
of adulterating influences to which the upper classes are allegedly
exposed through whoring after alien gods. The unpretentious simplicity

of the lower orders and their staunch loyalty to native traditions and ancestral virtues are believed to foster uncompromising opposition to and insurrectionary resolve against foreign invaders and masters. The effete and sophisticated selfishness of the upper classes, on the other hand, easily tempts them into treasonable collaboration with alien masters who enable them to preserve their wealth and privileges. The national myth of the subjugated nations developed into a compound of nostalgia for past glories and a vision of a no less glorious restoration, made to last through a spiritual rebirth and a just social order.

Of the two alternatives, the French Revolution decidedly chose the rationalist one, when the National Assembly supplanted the Estates General, seized sovereign power from the divinely appointed King, who had for centuries been the focus of national consciousness (just as the Protestant cause was in England and in Holland, and crusading Catholicism was in Spain), and created a centralised regime on the ruins of provincial autonomy and particularistic institutions. The Declaration of the Rights of Man and Citizen does not mention France, nor does it refer to specific French traditions. Although its authors no doubt had the specific evils of their country and age before their eyes when composing it, the declaration, like its earlier American counterparts, was drafted as commandments of political and social principles applicable to all nations at all times. It was concerned with reconstructing society *per se*.[3]

The early French revolutionaries took no interest in foreign affairs, considering all rivalry and wars of the past as having been due to the ambition and rapacity of the ruling castes, kings and nobility. They believed that peoples as such had by nature no aggressive drives against other nations, only spontaneous sympathy, unless they were incited by vested interests playing on ancient prejudices. And so the French legislators of the National Assembly pledged France never to resort to war as an instrument of national policy. Nevertheless, a war which was to last twenty-five years and to change the face of Europe broke out between revolutionary France and old dynastic Europe. It was the result of the fatal incompatibility between the two.

Foreshadowing a situation which was to arise in the wake of the October revolution some hundred and thirty years later, each side was driven to deny the very legitimacy of the antagonistic form of government, and the very right of its representatives to speak on behalf of the nation. Regarding the popular will as the sole basis of political legitimacy, the French revolutionaries could not treat the dynastic kings as fathers of their nations, as if these were their wards. Nor did they consider themselves unconditionally obliged by the undertakings entered upon by the divine-right rulers of the French *ancien régime* towards other kings. The dynastic governments of old Europe, for their part, were under compulsion to treat the makers and leaders of the French Revolution as rebels and usurpers intent on spreading subversion all over Europe. The abstract principles underlying the unbridgeable differences were not at once obvious to kings and statesmen of the old school, who were not interested in mere theorising, still thought in terms of traditional diplomatic rivalries, and felt a certain *Schadenfreude* at the discomfiture of the Most Christian King of proud and powerful France, now so weakened by dissension and internal troubles. Writers like Burke and Gentz soon provided the ideological rationale.[4]

The French fear of foreign counter-revolutionary intervention, strengthened by the activities of the aristocratic émigrés, and the dynasties' dread of revolutionary contagion, were soon placed in direct and mortal confrontation. Revolutionary proselytism was given further impetus by the wish of the various French factions interlocked in bitter strife to break the impasse and to divert attention from internal difficulties. There developed a widespread exasperated determination in the radical as well as in the conservative camp to polarise the nation, and to force men to stand up and be counted, to choose irrevocably between king and revolution. Both tendencies appealed to the supremacy of the national interest and liberty. The Left was out to defend the newly won freedoms of the reconstituted French nation. The Right spoke of the immemorial traditions of eternal France.

By revealing and accentuating the social strains in a society torn by revolution and by the great travail of a total war for existence, the ordeal polarised the social forces into those which stood to lose from the revolution or felt threatened by instability and radicalisation, and those which fervently looked to the new regime, with its salvationist claims, to establish perfect social justice then and there, to make their formal liberty and equality real by securing to them well-being, work, social protection and economic equality. The exasperation of the latter was all the stronger when hopes like these were dashed by the hardships caused by war, and the scarcity, speculation, inflation and unemployment which are its unavoidable concomitants. A terrorist dictatorship emerged from that convergence of an external ideological war with internal class struggle and civil war. It found itself driven to impose patterns of forced unanimity, a rudimentary, inefficient and irksome economic dictatorship, and class policies which tended to restrict the concept of Frenchman to believers in the radical brand of the revolutionary ideology. Those policies were designed to make the poor patriots live, and conduct the war, at the expense of the rich. The latter became suspect of disloyalty to the national-social cause of the revolution. Some even envisaged—notably Saint-Just in the Ventose laws—outlawing, dispossessing and expelling whole classes in order to rid France of traitors, and accomplish a social revolution by the distribution of their property to the needy devotees of the revolution.[5]

Babeuf went a step further in concluding that real equality could not be maintained for long without a community of goods and the imposition of an appropriate *Weltanschauung*. This conclusion was fortified by extrapolating the experiences of the French Revolution into a vision of class war as the motive force of history, the doctrine of the historic inevitability of a revolutionary confrontation between the mass of the underprivileged and the overprivileged minority, and the necessity—and in Babeuf's view the proven feasibility—of a revolutionary dictatorship to carry out the social transformation and the total re-education of the nation upon the predetermined victory of the uprising of the oppressed classes. The result would be a nation one and indivisible, based on unanimous consent, which reconciled liberty with equality.[6]

The French Revolution bequeathed a colossal myth, which continues to have an incalculable effect as an inspiration and example all over the world: the vision of a people's revolutionary war, in which patriotism and ideological revolutionary ardour became fused. The defence of the native land then became identified with the struggle for a political-social ideal against a counter-revolutionary league of selfish traitors and foreign reactionary powers. *"Patrie"* became synonymous in France with "La Révolution", revolutionary "Liberté", "La République une et indivisible". Such slogans as "la patrie en danger", "levée en masse", and symbols like the tricolour, the "Marseillaise" and the red cap, came to evoke an almost religious response. In the cases of the Bolshevik, Chinese, Cuban, Vietnamese and other revolutions, the memory and legends of similar struggles have proved to be far more potent and more cohesive influences than social-economic doctrines and innovating aspirations.

Given the scant response to the French message of liberation from the peoples who were expected to be liberated, the urgent economic needs of bankrupt France and the fever of conquest which seized ambitious generals, the proselytising zeal of the Grande Armée evolved into sheer imperialism. The invaded nations then turned the democratic French principle of self-determination into a sacred right to defend (in the spirit of Herder) their national personality and particularity, as nature and history had shaped them, against rationalistic would-be-universal patterns, especially patterns imposed from above by domin-

eering and rapacious foreigners, even if that defence involved accepting
lack of political liberty, the rule of hereditary privilege and deeply
rooted social injustices. Paradoxically, it was the backward, ignorant
and brutally oppressed peasant masses of Russia and Spain who put up
the most tenacious, and most effective resistance to Napoleon, the heir
of the French Revolution. That form of nationalism was preached by
feudal and clerical writers all over Europe, such as Gentz, Adam
Müller, Arnim and others, but it was also espoused by racist populists of
a revolutionary hue like Arndt, Kleist, Jahn in Germany, between the
débacle of Jena and the patriotic awakening which contributed not a
little to the nations' victory over Napoleon at Leipzig in 1813. Of
ominous significance was the birth of the Teutonic myth—a radicalisation and universalisation of Burke's ideas on prescriptive tradition—
which portrayed the German resistance against Napoleon as a replica of
the defence of Germanic authenticity by Arminius against Rome's
attempts to impose uniformity in the name of universal natural law.[7]

More complicated was the position of French theocratic reactionaries, like de Maistre and Bonald. They had somehow to reconcile the
postulate of a final absolute moral sanction—Catholic universalism and
papal infallibility—as an answer to the rationalist apotheosis of abstract
reason—with the peculiarity of the national historic heritage, a
somewhat more relative proposition. Following Burke, they turned the
religious past into an essential part of the nation's historic personality.

The grand debate between the revolutionary and the counter-
revolutionary camps on the meaning of nation foreshadowed future
developments. The former implied that the true nation in its, as it were,
predestined form, could come into its own only as a community based on
equality and unanimity, after—anachronistically speaking—the elimination of class differences and class rule, and after all those who were
deprived of cultural sustenance had been enabled to participate in the
cultural endeavour of the nation. The latter presented the nation as a
pluralistic phenomenon: the historic differences had to be taken for
granted as articulations of an organic entity. Dialectically the rationalist theoreticians of liberty were driven into advocating coercive
imposition of ideological and social patterns, while the upholders of
privilege were enabled to claim that they were defending the freedom
of concrete individuality, even if hedged around with social inequality.

Of the two transformatory trends, originating with the French
Revolution—revolutionary radicalism and socialist ideology—the
former combined demands for social-political change with insurrectionary nationalism, while the latter remained indifferent, or even
hostile (at least in theory), to nationalism. The "forces of movement",

comprising Jacobins, Babouvists, Blanquists, radicals of various kinds, as well as the democratic patriots of Europe's subjugated nationalities, saw themselves after 1815 as a single camp pitted against the forces of authoritarian, reactionist "resistance" to change, under the guidance of the Holy Alliance. The common enemy, the progressives claimed, had created a single front against constitutional change, social reform and national aspirations. The leaders of the counter-revolutionary front were the very men who were responsible for the humiliation of France in 1815. France was therefore honour bound to try to wreak vengeance on them and, at the same time, to undo the work of the Congress of Vienna. By so doing she would continue her revolutionary mission of liberating the nations oppressed by the feudal-despotic Northern Empires. The oppressed nationalities were seen as the natural allies of a revolutionary, revitalised France: in the first place their patriotic elements, which were uncorrupted by collaboration with foreign invaders and unbribed by their favours, the popular masses in short, were yearning for liberty and aspiring to equality.

Even a nationalist like Mazzini, who was opposed to French tutelage and claimed the leadership of the oppressed peoples for Roma Terza— The Third Rome—and altogether thought of national revival more as a spiritual, religious rebirth than social-economic transformation, spoke in accents that were strongly radical, egalitarian, social and anti-capitalist. On the other hand, extreme natural-rights-inspired radicals and communists like Blanqui were passionate prophets of national liber-ation; indeed some of them saw no inconsistency between France's prophetic universal mission and the French claim for natural frontiers on the Rhine at German expense. Revolutionaries of various kinds, for example Michelet, who implored the French troops to keep their bright bayonets clean, since they were the only hope of European civilisation and liberty, or Mazzini, Blanqui and the rest, eventually became militarists, hankering for war; whereas feudal and liberal conser-vatives, like Louis Philippe and Lamartine (not to speak of the statesmen of the Holy Alliance) strove to maintain peace and prevent war because war was a threat to international and social order.[8] The pattern revealed itself strikingly in 1848.

Utopian socialists, Saint-Simon and his school, Fourier, Proudhon and many others, were all concerned primarily with the impact of technological change and industrial development. Saint-Simon regarded industrialisation and modernisation as the harbingers of the longed-for just and rational society, whereas Fourier and Proudhon saw them as a grave impediment. In either case, political institutions seemed of little importance. Saint-Simon hoped to replace government of men over men with an "administration of things" supported by a "New Christianity"—a revitalised pantheistic message of the brotherhood of men and the redemption of "the most numerous and poorest class" of proletarians. His disciples dreamt of a benevolent rule of technocrats-priests-artists over the souls and activities of men. Fourier and Proudhon, however, would have dismantled all states, and covered the earth with a loose federation of free *phalanstères* or communes. Saint-Simon and Fourier had no use for nationalism: Saint-Simon composed blueprints for a European federation and joint international gigantic development plans for Europe and the other continents, and was quite ready (like Robert Owen, incidentally) to collaborate with either the Western parliamentary regimes or the Holy Alliance.

The idiosyncratic Proudhon condemned all nationalist movements, even those of the Poles and the Italians, as diversions from the social issue and likely to promote the victory of *étatisme*; nonetheless like a good populist he extolled French provincial traditions and the mission of France as a light unto the nations (a mission—Proudhon thought—that would be threatened by the emergence of a powerful Italian state on France's doorstep). The later Fourierists, notably Considérant, became staunch pacifists and internationalists.

In one way or another, consciously or not, all French radicals and socialists thought of all the nations they wished to liberate or to guide on the path of social reform as eager and grateful candidates à *la civilisation française*, in their eyes the civilisation of all enlightened mankind.[9]

Marx and Engels continued the thread spun by utopian socialist thought on the decisive significance for history of technological and social-economic factors. But they remained to the end intensely responsive to the myth bequeathed by the events in France of 1789-94. The dialectic, with its message of historic inevitability and its vision of a final dénouement, easily harmonised both mental attitudes.

Doctrinally, there was no room in Marx's historic dialectic for the nation as a collective personality. The basic tenet of the primacy of technology and socio-economic changes in determining historic development and shaping spiritual phenomena was incompatible with the idea of the nation as an eternal datum; an unfathomable national spirit which was expressed in every facet of life; and with the notion of a national fate and destiny which affected all members of the nation, regardless of class, and which class structure influenced only incidentally. Moreover, implicitly or even explicitly, there was the assumption that history was relentlessly driving on towards a world-wide historic dénouement and a social transformation which would redeem man *per se*, whatever his race, religion or nationality, from all forms of alienation and bondage. Ultimately the desired, predestined total change was feasible only if it embraced the whole world, or what then counted as the world.

Finally, not only did Marxist materialism have no particular interest in nationhood and folk traditions and peculiarities for their own sake; it regarded them as archaic residues destined to be destroyed by universal civilising influences. Not that Marx and Engels wished for their suppression by alien national oppressors. They were deeply convinced that national oppression was only a form of social-economic exploitation. Once that exploitation had been done away with, all national oppression would disappear with it, and eventually so would national peculiarities and animosities too.

(2) SECT AND CHURCH

Heirs of the Jacobin tradition as they were, Marx and Engels were bound to see their age of incessant change, above all the Industrial Revolution and the sharpening social conflict, as proof that the great true revolution which Babeuf had proclaimed to be the inevitable completion and final act of the revolution in 1789 was now coming to maturity. The apocalyptic faith in the imminence of that second coming, so powerfully affected by the outbreak of the 1848 revolutions, gave considerations of revolutionary strategy a priority of importance. Activism appeared more immediately relevant than objective historic inevitability inherent in the workings of the social-economic dialectic. War in fact, began to be seen by them as the midwife of revolution. The facts of power replaced the vindication of right, and violence became a corollary of social-economic forces in action.

In the march towards the socialist breakthrough, the strong, advanced, industrialised and therefore also increasingly more democratised country, or the large nation striving to unite into a centralised state of this kind, seemed to emerge as a vastly more effective force in paving the way for the revolution than small backward, agricultural or pastoral ethnic groups, the unhistoric nationalities dominated by the great historic nations. There were no inalienable, eternal, natural claims to national independence to be granted unconditionally and fought for as an absolute goal. National aspirations were to be assessed by the contribution they were likely to make to the revolutionary global struggle—in the circumstances against the despotic monarchies, and above all Russia. Hence, for instance, the challenging validity of Poland's cause, whatever her actual social-economic structure or ethnic composition, as the cement of the Holy Alliance, and the denial of any national rights to the southern Slavs, the props of Habsburg dynastic rule, and later to the Balkan peoples, the puppets of Tsarism.

As with other apocalyptic movements, the failure of the messianic expectations to materialise, and the consequent dissolution of the sense of imminent fulfilment and that feeling of emergency which makes everything appear provisional, broke up the revolutionary brotherhood into its component parts. Marx's sights were gradually narrowed from a simultaneous international revolutionary breakthrough to the concrete situation of particular states. The local socialist parties for their part, now enjoying the concessions granted by a more self-confident and more prosperous bourgeoisie which was no longer haunted by the red spectre, began to feel more like members of a loose international federation than sections of a church militant—the socialist International. They were fighting the class enemy at home according to the parliamentary rules of the game, and were trying to become the national party which shaped the character of the nation liberated from class rule, instead of waiting for the call from a revolutionary GHQ to man a concerted assault laid down by an international proletarian strategy.

(3) TOWARDS CONFRONTATION

After the 1848 revolutions had brought home to men how intractable national conflicts were and how ultimately incompatible were the urge for national self-assertion and the democratic duty to respect the rights of other peoples, the movements of national liberation and unification broke away from the camp of general revolution.

By 1880 most national movements in Europe had gained their goals, achieving them not as a result of an international revolution, but by the pragmatic exploitation of diplomatic opportunities or of international war. This was especially so for Germany, with which Marx and Engels were deeply concerned. The pathetic exceptions were those unfortunate and heroic fighters for national freedom, the Irish, with no allies at a time when Britannia ruled the waves, and the Poles, left to the mercies of the all too powerful anti-Polish interests of the northern powers. Latter-day nationalism no longer found its characteristic expression in visions of cultural renaissance and social-spiritual regeneration but in imperialism, and consequently in the arms race, in the cult of vitality and power, and in self-idolatry disguised as integral nationalism or even incipient racism.

These developments led those radical elements, mainly Russians and East European Jews, whose actual condition and inherited messianic longings caused them to experience the universal revolutionary promise with a freshness and intensity unknown in the more fortunate West, to a passionate reaffirmation of the original monistic Marxist vision. Imperialism, they claimed, was riding on the wave of a second industrial revolution, uniting the world into a single economic unit, and combining social with national oppression, especially in the subjugated and colonial countries. It was polarising the world into international predatory capitalism on the one hand and a global proletariat on the other. It was extending the class struggle beyond the frontiers of the nation-state to the confines of the planet. War was inherent in imperialist rivalry, and an imperialist world war was destined to become the midwife of the international revolution. To some, Rosa Luxemburg for example, the struggles for national liberation appeared in this context a damaging and dangerous diversion and a surrender to bourgeois concepts of the primary and overarching reality of the national entity. Others, such as Lenin, decided that it was much wiser to sublimate nationalist resentment by legitimising it than to frustrate and therefore aggravate it into an irritant which would hinder international cooperation with the general camp of revolution, as happened in Austria. There the united social-democratic party, and eventually the trade union movement too, broke up into ethnic groups. The ethnic social-democratic parties often became spearheads in the struggle for national liberation, conceived as the basic condition of a socialist transformation, as in fact Marx and Engels came to think at the ends of their lives.

The wrath of oppressed nationalities could be used as a powerful weapon in the assault upon feudal absolutism in countries such as Russia and Austria-Hungary, where indeed racial oppression had almost always brought social oppression, and where the subject races were engaged in a sustained campaign of *reconquista* against the master nations which clung desperately to what they regarded as their national patrimony and were prepared for its sake to jettison all democratic procedures. Lenin urged the socialists of dominant nations to recognise the right of the oppressed nationalities to self-determination and secession. He hoped that this would secure a united proletarian front in the revolutionary struggle, and that these very things—self-determination and secession—would not be demanded by the socialists of the subjugated nationalities, once socialism had won and in so doing had abolished every kind of oppression. For the same reasons Lenin opposed Austro-Marxist theories of national-cultural-personal autonomy for nationalities in multi-racial empires. They tended, in his view, to perpetuate ethnic separatism at the expense of proletarian internationalism.

While colonial rivalries, the Russo-Japanese War and the Balkan imbroglio, seemed to be bringing world war closer and closer, influential circles in the various states which were harassed and worried by social unrest and the seemingly irresistible advance of socialism, began to speculate whether war might not be desirable as a means of uniting their nations, of silencing and even suppressing anti-patriotic elements as part of the national war effort.

The radicals among the socialists responded with a determined propaganda campaign against national and imperialist militarism. They proclaimed it as the bourgeois answer to socialism. Nationalism began to look to them like a very dangerous bait held out to the masses. Whether basing their revolutionary strategy on international war or not, they regarded anti-war agitation as a means of weaning the masses away from bourgeois spiritual tutelage, undercutting the power base and instruments of class rule—the military-industrial-feudal establishment—and preparing the masses to resist war, once it broke out, turning national war into civil war.

Such were the origins of the fatal schism in the European labour movement. Reformist social-democracy was torn between the deeply ingrained, almost instinctive habit of thought "my country right or wrong" when at war, no matter who happened to be its leaders, and the categorical imperative of international proletarian solidarity and class war. Hence the desperate efforts to conjure away the spectre of war and the passionate pacifism expressed in international rhetoric.

Far from being simply one of the characteristics of the ruling elite, nationalism became a vast mass movement once it was seized upon by the lower middle class, whom doctrinaire Marxism had written off too easily. Recruits of barricade brigades in the earlier times, petty-bourgeois shopkeepers, artisans, clerks and others began to feel squeezed out by a haute bourgeoisie which was changing the face of the earth and a proletariat which had developed organisational cohesion, a sense of purpose and a belief that it was destined to inherit the earth. Everybody was telling the lower bourgeoisie that it was a ludicrous and doomed class. The idea of the nation emerged as a lifebelt: the rich were selfish and effete, the workers were serving alien causes, the petty bourgeoisie was the core of the nation, had no other interest than the general national interest. Xenophobia strengthened the sense of equal brotherhood among the chosen and stimulated authoritarian attitudes towards foreign nations and lesser breeds, while fostering a hankering for hierarchical discipline at home.

Darwinism, racism, anti-rationalist and anti-liberal trends contributed to impart to imperialist nationalism the features of a scientific *Weltanschauung*. The unfathomable and elusive *Volksgeist* was made palpable with the aid of the quasi-scientific datum of blood: it was made to fulfil the role of matter in dialectic materialism. The ideas of the eternal struggle for survival waged by the different races were such as to drive out the premise of the oneness of objective reason, the postulate of human equality, indeed the doctrine of the unity of mankind. The promise of a Theodicea, the vision of an eventual triumph of universal justice, which had sustained Judaism, Christianity, liberalism, democracy and socialism, was proclaimed by Nietzsche to be the consolation and the cunning invention of the weak and the misshapen. He substituted for it the image of an eternal struggle, the crucible of the superior types and elites, who were nature's goal and pride.

This was the seed-bed of that type of racist anti-semitism which emerged around 1880 and strongly influenced most movements of integral nationalism in Europe. Overwhelmed by the incomprehensible workings of high finance, capitalism, commodity production and chain stores, on the one hand, and frightened by socialist teachings, the petty bourgeoisie identified all these evils with Judaism. Racist anti-semitism focused on the Jew as the solvent of the integrity of the nation (or race) and the destroyer of its unerring instinct. As capitalist or socialist, the Jew was the bearer of alien abstract values, the destroyer of national solidarity, fomenter of class war and internal strife, a cosmopolitan exploiter plotting world domination. The elimination of the Jews assumed the dimension of a social and national revolution and of a moral renaissance. On the universal plane, the Jew was made to appear as the eternal inciter, ever since Moses, of all the mobs of lower breeds against the national elites of the superior races.

The reactions to the age of imperialism thus gave a foretaste of what was in store for mankind on the morrow of the Great War.

(4) THE ORIGINS OF IDEOLOGICAL POLARISATION

The outbreak of the war in August 1914 was one of the most fateful events in history. A century of unprecedented progress in all fields of human endeavour—science, technology, economy, the art of living, the rule of law, control of the environment—was shattered by an orgy of carnage and destruction. These horrible events shook men's self-assurance and confidence, perverted all accepted moral values, and swept away inhibitions which had kept aggressive impulses in check. The most pathetic development was perhaps the collapse of the Second International. In spite of all vows and protestations, the working classes were swept off their feet almost to a man. They were overcome by instinctive patriotism.

Of all the messianic messages of redemption and compensation for the unspeakable agonies of the war which made themselves heard—such as "a war to end all wars", "to make the world fit for heroes", "a home for democracy"—the two most pregnant were the diametrically opposite responses to the catastrophe of 1914-18: the one given by Lenin and the other by Mussolini and Hitler.

Lenin (and Rosa Luxemburg) proclaimed that the war was the long-prophesied supreme crisis of bourgeois civilisation and the death agony of capitalism. It was the duty of the working class to transform the war of nations into an international civil war and to turn the bayonets against the civil and military leaders. The prophets of world revolution were not only convinced that the imperialism of the super-powers had deprived the nation-state of any reality and national sovereignty of any meaning. They held fast to Marx's idealised image of the 1871 Paris Commune as the model of a direct democracy that was to replace the state, and to Marx's description of the state as a superstructure of monopolist landowners, capitalists, generals, bureaucracy, army, police, church and intellectual time-servers imposed upon the mass of people, the mass of the nation.

Historic Russian realities and revolutionary ideology had contributed enormously to the engraving of those images upon Lenin's mind, and indeed completed the alienation of the whole intelligentsia and, in due course, large parts of the peasantry and proletariat from the historic Russian state and its leadership. For several generations revolutionary prophets had laboured to expose and loosen the spiritual chains which—to employ Marx's vocabulary—the myths of Tsar and the Orthodox church had laid upon the hearts of the masses, and to teach them to dare to rebel, for "once the realm of imagination has been revolutionised, reality can no longer hold out". Lenin's anti-war propaganda was intended not only to disarm and topple the establishment and its mainstay, the army, but also, as a preparatory task, to turn the defence of the country into a test case: who was for the existing order and who was for revolution? The question of national defence was intended to be the barrier of fear, the strongest inhibition which could not be overcome without total commitment. If anyone could not make the leap because he recoiled from treason this proved him guilty of petty-bourgeois obfuscation. But if he could make the leap he showed himself to be one of the citizens of the predestined proletarian heavenly city, indeed of a regenerated Holy Russia, conceived as the redeemer of a decadent Europe. The subsequent crises of conscience between loyalty to the nation, as represented by its ruling elite, and allegiance to an abstract ideal, also conceived of as the ultimate salvation of one's own country, were to re-create situations familiar from the time of the wars of religion.

At the other end of the spectrum, Hitler fell on his knees at hearing the news of the outbreak of the war to thank providence, as he tells us, for enabling him to be present at such a solemn hour for the German nation. Mussolini, the extreme socialist, anti-militarist and critic of patriotism, was shaken to his depths by the utter collapse of socialist internationalism and by the lie given to the most sacred principles of Marxism. He discovered the extraordinary potency of national sentiment and the supreme significance of the nation and its will to live. To a passionate revolutionary activist, the cowardly anxiety of the Italian Socialist party for Italy to remain a neutral onlooker, at a time when the fate of the world was being decided by millions sacrificing their lives, was an outrageous betrayal. And so Mussolini gradually transferred his revolutionary dynamism, as so many others were to do, to the service of the nation, its authenticity and its power and glory. The frustrated dream of a national revival, a social revolution and moral rebirth, which the Risorgimento had been able to think of as one, was to be realised in the struggle of the wronged, unfulfilled proletarian nation against the satiated plutocratic countries and that cosmopolitan Marxism, which was threatening to destroy the national nerve.

The Bolshevik Revolution was made in the name of revolutionary internationalism, and its very audacity was the result of the unshakable belief in the imminence of an international socialist revolution, which was indeed believed to be the very condition of the Russian Revolution's success. When that expectation failed, the truncated and ruined Soviet Union started its career by abject surrender to a German imperialist *Diktat*. Its next task was to prevent the rich border areas from seceding in accordance with the (Bolshevik) principle of the right to national self-determination and secession. The Bolsheviks invoked the sacred duty of rescuing an insurgent proletariat from falling under the yoke of a national-bourgeois class state and ally of imperialism, in the same spirit as they claimed that the Soviets had more progressive content than a constituent assembly elected by universal suffrage.

The doctrine of the higher, all-embracing and exclusive validity of the general will of the world proletariat, willing a socialist revolution, became the basis of the Third International. Its democratic centralism left hardly any mention of the national parties in the programmatic Nineteen (or twenty-one) Points, in contrast to the loosely built federal structure of the old and reconstructed Second International. Expressly barred from any membership of the Comintern were all social-imperialists, including socialists who advocated a Wilsonian peace without annexations and without reparations, a peace based on the principles of self-determination, international arbitration and disarmament; for to take such a stand implied acquiescing in the existing class state with its seeds of imperialism and war.

The Comintern was not to be a federation of national parties, but, like Lenin's own party, a mobilised force bent upon an imminent international breakthrough. But because the socialist revolution had been confined to one single, though enormously vast country, and because the GHQ of world revolution was set up in its capital, all those socialists outside Russia, whose dormant international messianism had been inflamed by the October revolution, found themselves in the position of nationalists of a foreign power. The bitter war for survival which the Bolsheviks were compelled to wage against the counter-revolutionary armies and foreign intervention—however half-hearted and ineffectual this proved in the long run—created a powerful revolutionary myth.

As Rosa Luxemburg had prophesied, in the new countries on Russia's doorstep, a desperate fear of the hereditary enemy and oppressor, now claiming to embody a universal message of salvation, became the source of morbid nationalism and a basis for authoritarian regimes.

In 1918-19 the German Social Democratic party (SPD) was faced with a choice: to carry out a social revolution while splitting the nation, or to take upon its shoulders the responsibility for restoring the shattered fatherland. In accordance with the overwhelming mandate it received from the workers to dissolve the Revolutionary Councils of Workers and Soldiers and convene a National Assembly, the SPD assumed the role of the national party of Germany. From that moment the Communists emerged as the chief danger. But the Weimar Republic became all the more dangerously exposed to inroads from the Right. Socialists, democrats, pacifists, Jews, Weimar in general were represented by Hitler as the willing or unconscious accomplices of the international Versailles conspiracy against Germany—a replica of his early obsession with a Slav-Socialist-Jewish plot in the name of the democratic principle of one man one vote against the hegemony of the racially superior German minority in an Austria fighting for its survival: "the life and death struggle"—as Theodore Mommsen called it at the time.

The latent war emergency on both the ideological and the political plane, sustained by the polarised ideologies, propagated and justified both kinds of totalitarianism—that of the Left and that of the Right. Politics based on faith in a single, all-embracing and exclusive truth raised Marxism on the one hand, the state and the race on the other, to the dignity of absolutes. They were epitomised in vanguard parties but also and above all in infallible leaders who alone were held to possess the ability to interpret the will of history, the destiny of the nation or race, the true interests of the universal proletariat.

The dictatorship of the proletariat was presented by communists as a provisional phase destined eventually to a special unanimity, which would realise at the same time both freedom and equality, make all coercion superfluous, and as a consequence cause the state to wither away. In Fascism and Nazism warlike self-assertion and competitive strife for superior status within society and within the family of races and nations were proclaimed as the eternal order of things.

(5) THE BLURRING OF LINES

In spite of their claims to exclusiveness, both trends gave rise to a bastard synthesis of nationalism and internationalism. Internal reasons, the dialectic of the ideology, and in World War II the supreme danger from outside, combined to accentuate a Great Russian nationalist mythology. But, as the official bearer of the most radical ideology of the day, Soviet Russia continued to attract the sympathies of, and advertise support for, all national liberation movements, especially in Asia and Africa, as part of the global struggle between the international proletariat and imperialism. For their part, national socialism and Fascism created a kind of Nazi-Fascist "international" against Judeo-Bolshevism. Hatred for the "international Jewish Marxist" thus became the cement of basically ultra-nationalist movements, and in World War II the road to national treason.

The post-1945 period saw the dismantling of all European empires by the imperial powers themselves, and thus posed the question whether the age of imperialism had really represented the climax of Western capitalism or had rather served to prepare the colonial peoples for independent statehood. Many of the latter have claimed allegiance to socialism, in the same way as in the first half of the nineteenth century European national liberation movements gravitated to the European camp of Jacobin revolution. But the signs are that the newly emancipated nations of Asia and Africa are more concerned with nation-building than with international proletarian solidarity. Socialist measures seem to be applied as instruments for shaping a cohesive nation out of congeries of tribes, for rapid industrialisation and state centralism and as elements of a national myth. The military confrontation between the new states in Africa and Asia make one wonder whether, after all, they are not retracing the history of the European nations.

At the same time the movement for European unity, still hampered by isolationist nationalism, seems uncertain about its destiny: is it to be a nucleus of genuine internationalism, or an enlarged self-contained political entity like the early modern nation-states, which were brought into being by powerful dynasties? Or an alliance against the communist bloc?

Perhaps more significant for our purpose are the fissions in the communist camp, which have been occurring just at a time when Soviet Russia seemed to have achieved the power to make a serious bid to incorporate the remaining class states into a single socialist world.

As is inherent in any doctrine which claims to offer a message of exclusive validity that is bound to obtain everyone's consent, unanimous consent is in the end imposed by superior force. But the facts of history, of geographic, economic and psychological diversity, which Marxists like to call the time-lag (and which they claim to be only a temporary inequality in the pace of development destined to be levelled out) have a way of sooner or later setting themselves against the unifying tendency. Before our eyes this takes the form of dissidence within a single country; on the global plane it takes the form of a nationalism which tries to defend itself against an all-levelling superior force.

The relationship between the myth of the nation and the vision of revolution at the present moment raises a host of questions, to some of which we shall return in the Conclusions. Is it no more than a lesson in ambivalence and in ambiguous relationships? Does it represent the unfolding of a dialectic leading to a dénouement? How does the problem look in the light of the view that history is the history of liberty? What perspectives are opened by the simultaneous emergence of the race problem as the most acute social question of our time and the rise of the international and cosmopolitan New Left on the one hand, and the growing white backlash on the other? Is schismatic Maoist China to be seen alongside Titoism and the unrest in the satellite countries as a force reasserting national uniqueness and separatism? Could China emerge as a potential focus for the coloured races against white racial and economic ascendancy? Finally, does Euro-communism signify a resurgence of nationalism in the form of a reaffirmation of democratic principles or is it to be seen as tactics? Is political messianism splitting into two camps: totalitarian democrats and pragmatists?

Part I

MARX ENGELS AND THE NATION

Chapter One

THE CHILIASTIC PERIOD OF MARX AND ENGELS

The main categories in the thinking of young Marx and Engels[1] were man, the individual and the species. The idea of nation as a primary phenomenon in its own right and with its own laws of development is wholly absent from their thought in the early 1840's. Social evolution is depicted by them as the story of man's alienation from his true nature, an estrangement from the essence of his species, its distinct vocation. These distortions were brought about by man's progressive subjection to his own creations. Instead of simplifying tasks and satisfying diverse needs, division of labour dehumanised the workers and subjugated man to dominant and exploiting classes. Instead of enhancing his dignity and making his existence secure and his freedom of movement possible, property and money became the sources of insatiable avarice on the one hand and unbearable deprivation on the other. They sowed general anarchy and strife. God, religion, the state, ideologies and perverse philosophies which spoke of impersonal essences and categorical moral imperatives, were harnessed to make oppression seem natural, and inequality and exploitation guarantees of law and order. All these pernicious institutions and false teachings joined together to pervert the natural and direct correlation between man and his species. They estranged man from nature, his fellow-men, the community, himself and the fruits of his labour. Communism was destined to restore man to his species, to enable him to realise his human destiny in all the manifold and diverse encounters with nature, society, work, enjoyment, to become an end in himself, instead of a slave, a mere tool, or a drugged and deceived creature, afflicted by a sense of guilt and unworthiness.

"The division of labour offers us the first example of how, as long as man remains in natural society—that is, as long as a cleavage exists between the particular and the common interest—so long therefore as activity is not voluntarily, but naturally divided, man's own deed becomes an alien power opposed to him, which enslaves him instead of being controlled by him. For as soon as labour is distributed, each man has a particular, exclusive sphere of activity which is forced upon him and from which he cannot escape. He is a hunter, a fisherman, a

21

shepherd, or a critical critic, and must remain so if he does not want to lose his means of livelihood; while in communist society, where nobody has one exclusive sphere of activity but can become accomplished in any branch he wishes, society regulates the general production and then makes it possible for me to do one thing today and another tomorrow, to hunt in the morning, fish in the afternoon, rear cattle in the evening, criticise after dinner, just as I have a mind, without ever becoming hunter, fisherman, shepherd or critic."[2]

What is the place of the nation in this scheme? The use of the word nation by our authors in their early writings seems to suggest that they employed the terms nation and state interchangeably: the nation was the population of the territory organised by and into the state as it existed or—a problem to be discussed later—deserving and destined to become organised into an emerging state. In so far as an ethnic group within a multi-racial state (without prospect or good claim to become an independent state, in the view of our authors) was concerned, it was merely a nationality, a fossil or an aborted embryo.

The state, which means the nation-state, is firmly characterised by Marx and Engels as the force of alienation and subjugation par excellence, emerging at a given moment in historical development, and thus destined to wither away together with, or indeed even before, the other forces of alienation and class exploitation have ceased.

"The crystallisation of social activity, this consolidation of what we ourselves produce into an objective power above us, growing out of our control, thwarting our expectations, bringing to naught our calculations, is one of the chief factors in historical development up till now. And out of this very contradiction between the interest of the individual and that of the community, the latter takes an independent form as the state, divorced from the real interests of individual and community. We are then faced with an illusory communal life, however much it is based on the real ties existing in every family or tribal conglomeration (such as flesh and blood, language, division of labour on a larger scale) . . . upon the classes, already determined by the division of labour . . . out of which one dominates all the others."[3]

Marx and Engels would have ceased to be believers in historical materialism had they continued to theorise without considering real circumstances, which differ from nation to nation. What distinguishes them from nationalists is that they accorded infinitely greater reality to the universal character of the process whereby the state emerges as a yoke, an illusory commonwealth and an instrument of class domination. The objective "national" aspects might influence the shape and the process of (class) nation building, but they had not the character, power

and dignity of a primary, eternal, formative influence. The cosmopolitan, universal, material, technological forces bred laws of development, which affected all nations and effaced or cancelled out the local
and national peculiarities, especially since the rise of the machine and
the capitalist mode of production.

"With the development of capitalist production," wrote Marx in
his *Theory of Surplus Value*, "there comes into being an average level of
bourgeois society, and with it of temperaments and dispositions in the
various peoples. That mode of production is as cosmopolitan as Christianity."[3a]

The universal bourgeois commodity economy was bound to leap all
borders, to sweep away all local, traditional, national modes of
production, forms of life and culture, to unify the world into one
workshop, a single market and a world culture. The universal
bourgeoisie could not help creating in its stride the universal propertyless proletariat, its grave-digger.

"The bourgeoisie has through its exploitation of the world market
given a cosmopolitan character to production and consumption in every
country. To the great chagrin of reactionaries, it has drawn from under
the feet of industry the national ground on which it stood. All old-
established national industries have been destroyed or are daily being
destroyed. They are dislodged by new industries, whose introduction
becomes a life and death question for all civilised nations, by industries
that no longer work up indigenous raw material, but raw material
drawn from the remotest zones; industries whose products are
consumed not only at home but in every quarter of the globe. In place of
the old wants, satisfied by the productions of the country, we find new
wants, requiring for their satisfaction the products of distant lands and
climes. In place of the old local and national seclusion and self-
sufficiency, we have intercourse in every direction, universal inter-
dependence of nations. And as in material, so also in intellectual
production. The intellectual creations of individual nations become
common property. National one-sidedness and narrow-mindedness
become more and more impossible, and from the numerous national and
local literatures there arises a world literature.

"The bourgeoisie, by the rapid improvement of all instruments of
production, by the immensely facilitated means of communication,
draws all, even the most barbarian nations into civilisation. The cheap
price of its commodities are the heavy artillery with which it batters
down all Chinese walls, with which it forces the barbarians' intensely
obstinate hatred of foreigners to capitulate. It compels all nations, on
pain of extinction, to adopt the bourgeois mode of production; it

compels them to introduce what it calls civilisation into their midst, i.e. to become bourgeois themselves. In a word, it creates a world after its own image."[4]

National histories are merged into universal history, no more nationals of this or that particular country, but men as universal individuals, interdependent for their fate, are engaged in world historical intercourse. We read in "The German Ideology"[5]: "Large industry makes competition universal . . . it establishes the means of communication and the modern world market. . . . It is this that creates true world history, to the degree that it makes every civilised nation, and every individual in that nation dependent for the satisfaction of their needs and destroys the exclusive character of diverse nations as was natural until now. . . . It is thus evident that bourgeois society—with its relationships—is the real focus, the real stage of all history" and not the pretended "great reverberating historic and political events. Upon the abolition of private property, the liberation of every individual will be realised exactly to the extent to which history will be transformed completely into world history.

"Only with the universal development of productive forces is a universal intercourse between men established, which produces in all nations simultaneously the phenomenon of the 'propertyless' mass (universal competition), makes each nation dependent on the revolutions of the others, and finally has put world-historical, empirically universal individuals in place of local ones."

When the indispensable conditions of the universal development of productive forces, and of the world intercourse bound up with them, have become a reality, how will communism be brought into existence in practice?

"The German Ideology" envisages it "as the act of the dominant peoples all at once or simultaneously", by which peoples Engels means England, the United States, France and Germany. The Communist Manifesto proclaims that "the united action of at least the civilised lands is one of the first conditions for its (proletarian) emancipation."[6] It may be presumed that the leading states will be able to carry the weaker brethren with them. The emphasis is upon the international character of the great social transformation and simultaneous action by the decisive countries. An isolated communist state would constitute a freak, and not part of a predetermined world process and universal breakthrough. Its communist regime could not hold out and retain its integrity in a world ruled by different sets of connections and relations. Such a "communism could exist only as a local event" not integrated into universal inter-course. The social forces in action would not bear the character of

universal, inevitable and irresistible powers, but of "home-bred superstitious conditions, and each extension of intercourse would abolish
[the] local communism."[7]

In 1858 Marx was still worried by these problems and wrote to
Engels on October 8: "The fundamental task of bourgeois society is the
creation of a world market . . . and [the shaping] of production upon that
case. Since the colonisation of California and Australia and the opening
of China and Japan, the difficult question for us is the following: on the
continent the revolution is imminent and it will also assume
immediately a communist character. Will it not inevitably be strangled
in this small corner, at a time when upon a much wider terrain bourgeois
society is still rising?"

This passage seems to suggest the conviction that unless communism
is world-wide it will not happen.

Would those states which had taken the initiative form a federation
of states with all those won over by them for the communist cause?
Would they merge into a single world state? Would the strongest
impose its will by force or carry others by example? We are not told.

We are given to understand that once universal communism is
established, all rivalry between nation-states and all national oppression
will come to an end. This conviction arises from the view that national
hostility and oppression are in effect the expression of the same
capitalist avarice which preys within the confines of a single country
upon the workers and other weaker classes. This same virus is then put
into operation against other, weaker nations.

"Is the whole inner organization of nations," asks Marx in his letter
to P. V. Annenkov of December 28, 1846—"are all their international
relations anything else than the expression of a particular division of
labour? And must not these change when the division of labour
changes? . . . The relations of different nations among themselves
depend upon the extent to which each has developed its productive
forces, the division of labour and internal intercourse." The end of
individual exploitation and of class war will also bring an end to
hostility among nations. "In proportion as the exploitation of one
individual by another is ended . . . so is the exploitation of one nation by
another ended too. With the end of the class war within a nation, the
hostile attitude of nations to one another disappears."[9]

There seems reason to believe that the relations between the nationalities in the multi-racial single state are also viewed through the same
prism. "The communist revolution," we read in the "The German
Ideology", "abolishes the rule of all classes with the classes themselves,
because it is carried through by the class which no longer counts as a

class in society . . . and is in itself the expression of the dissolution of all classes, nationalities, etc., within present society."[10]

The question is whether the dissolution of nationalities means that they would disappear through general amalgamation, lose their political relevance as say (up to recent times) the separate identities of the Bretons and Basques or the Welsh and the Scots were submerged in the unity of France and Britain; or whether Marx and Engels had in mind the gradual absorption of neighbouring principalities and semi-autonomous provinces by the great nation-states in the early modern era.

One may doubt whether Marx and Engels envisaged in their early writings such entities as nation, state and nation-state in the more or less generally accepted way. They proclaim that "even under the bourgeoisie, national divisions and antagonisms are disappearing more and more."[11] It is difficult to see what would be left of the nation and the nation-state as institutions in the socialist order. The institutions of central government, which had become an incubus, would disappear together with all the machinery of bureaucracy, the army and the police. The separation between town and country would be done away with. This vastly important step towards the liquidation of that division of labour which split society into classes and enthroned a ruling class over all the rest would, with the help of the machine—the erstwhile enslaver—create vast abundance and liberate men from degrading, deadening tasks. Satisfied men, free to realise their potentialities, to achieve all their legitimate desires, would no longer need coercive government to keep them from mischief, punish their offences and deter them from crime.

With all their abhorrence of anonymous government or tutelage, and prima facie, almost Fourierist predilection for small autonomous communities, Marx and Engels do not prophesy—as the anarchists do—the imminent liquidation of central government and of all its tasks: Yet its role seems to be reduced by them to a minimum. It is envisaged as the administration of things (à la Saint-Simon), a co-ordinating agency, and not as the government of men by men. Even if this implies the survival of the large, unified state, the local community appears nevertheless to be considered as the natural social framework. It is not easy however to reconcile these utopian expectations with the fact that Marx thought in terms of modern technology, the total mobilisation and co-ordination of resources, of planning, and the organisation of production and distribution on a vast, national and, as it sometimes appears, global scale.

Moreover, with all that emphasis upon the self-expression of the individual as a member of the species and the image thereof, to the exclusion of the stultifying collective patterns which had enslaved and perverted pure humanity, not only the organisational, institutionalised forms of the nation, but also its group distinctness, appear to be left hanging in the air.

It is at the same time theoretically possible to equate a classless society with the coming into being of the real nation, a nation one and indivisible of equals, instead of a class society riddled with inequality, antagonism and strife. This leads us to the famous passage in the Communist Manifesto about the proletariat without a fatherland, the workers as a universal class, and their task and destiny to become the national class.[12]

What the authors seem to suggest is that in so far as, like slaves, the workers lacked any share and stake in the fruits of the land, had no voice in administering the common weal, no active part in the culture of the country, enjoyed no protection of their rights by the state, they could not regard the country, in which they lived and toiled and suffered, as their fatherland. Deprived of the elementary rights and attributes of citizenship, the oppressed workers of one country were by this vital fact of deprivation, indistinguishable from those of another. They were in this sense a universal class, unattached, without a particular national imprint which would really single them out from the levelling universality of slavery.

"The proletariat," says Engels in 1847, "have in all countries the same interest, the same enemy, and the same struggle in front of them; the proletariat are, in the great mass, by their very nature without national prejudices, and all their education and movement are essentially humanitarian and antinational. Only the proletarians can do away with nationality, only the awakening proletariat may lead to the brotherhood of the various peoples."[13]

But unfolding capitalism, speeding to its collapse, and the simultaneous pauperisation of the masses and growth of their revolutionary consciousness, were bringing near the hour when, like the Third Estate in 1789, the proletariat would suddenly become a class called to inherit the earth, would sweep away the enfeebled and bankrupt parasites of the ruling class, and take over the helm of the ship, which the subjugated but now rising classes had for long been manning and keeping afloat under the tyrannical command of exploiting masters. They would become the nation-building or national class, not only fulfilling the vital social role, but also being recognised by all. When everyone had become a worker, the proletariat would cease to be a class, and become the nation. But that would not mean that a new nation, with a peculiar *Volksgeist* and destiny, had been born. The new national class and nation would, in so far as the workers of other states followed suit, continue to be a universal class. The salient feature of all of the reborn nations, or rather classless societies, would be universal justice, and not any particular national ethos. Would they therefore amalgamate and form a universal world state? This is not said in so many words by Marx and Engels. But it may be inferred.

Chapter Two

EUROPE IS PREGNANT WITH REVOLUTION

When on the eve of 1848 Europe began to look more and more pregnant with revolution, the problem of the concrete national situation vis-à-vis the expected international revolution assumed greater urgency in the thinking of Marx and Engels.

"The whole European social movement of today," proclaimed Engels, "is only the second act of the French Revolution, only a preparation for the finale of the drama which began in 1789 in Paris, and is now being played out in the whole of Europe."[14]

Polarisation into and direct confrontation on a European scale between the camp of revolution and the forces of counter-revolution were already a fact. The struggle appeared thereby simplified: only a single mighty blow was needed, with some country destined to be the first to take the initiative, to give the signal, and by its successful beginning set the other countries on the move.

In his speech at the memorial meeting of November 29, 1847, in London, Marx proclaimed: "Poland is to be liberated, not in Poland, but in England."[15] In England the class struggle was already at its most acute. The Chartist movement was thus sure to strike the first blow for international democracy, ("democracy—that is today communism")[16] and for the liberation of nations. "The victory of the proletariat over the bourgeoisie will at the same time mark the overcoming of the national and industrial conflicts, which cause differences and strife among nations," and will serve as a "signal for the liberation of all oppressed nations." Conversely, Marx ascribed to the term "fraternity of peoples" a social significance which absorbed the political aspects.[17]

Marx and Engels were not consistent in their views of the pioneering role of the English proletariat. Not that the national identity of the pioneering proletariat was all that important. The two young revolutionaries deprecated all claims to a special mission on the part of the socialist party of any single nation. The only thing that mattered was that some country should make the start. Germany in turn appeared as a likely candidate, not because it was in the forefront of the advanced countries but precisely because of its social-economic and political backwardness. For its backwardness was coupled and contrasted with a theoretical maturity exceeding that of all other nations.[18] There is little reason to suspect chauvinism behind this preference for Germany, the less so as the task of giving the first signal was actually assigned by Marx and Engels to Paris—the Gallic cock. The choice of Germany was in all probability determined simply by a livelier awareness of the German situation and keener responsiveness to its problems. But it was bound nevertheless to lead the two prophets to adopt extreme nationalistic attitudes, paradoxically as part of the global revolutionary strategy. They became indeed fervent champions of a Germany (more precisely a German Republic) one and indivisible.

"The workers should not only be striving to establish the *République une et indivisible* but should also try to realise in that republic the most absolute centralisation of power in the hands of the state," said Marx and Engels in their address to the Communist League in 1850.[19]

Federalism of any kind was associated in their minds with feudal particularism, divine-right rulers, dynastic traditions, social hierarchy, narrow horizons and interests, fragmentation, untidy asymmetrical residues of local customs, old privileges, immunities and inequalities of all kinds, finally with awe for superiors and respect for ancient aristocracy and old-established patriciate. In contrast to the United States, "in Germany, the struggle for centralisation and against a federal system was tantamount to the struggle between modern civilisation and feudalism." But also elsewhere, notably in Switzerland, "centralisation was the most powerful lever of revolution."[20]

A mighty broom was necessary to sweep away all those cobwebs and clear the ground for a total and rational reconstruction and radical modernisation of Germany. There was to be a single law, with all Germans equally subject to it, and participating on equal terms in shaping it and enjoying the same rights guaranteed by it. All the resources of Germany were to be mobilised for the establishment of a single modern industrial economy based upon maximum centralisation. In November 1847 Engels wrote in *Der Schweizer Burgerkrieg*: "Through industry, trade, political institutions, the bourgeoisie is working to tear away the small, lonely and self-enclosed localities from their isolation, to bind them together, to blend their interests . . . and to create out of the mutually independent localities and provinces a single nation, with common interests, habits and views. The bourgeoisie goes far in centralising. . . . The democratic proletariat will . . . have to go much further in that direction. During the short period, when the proletariat was at the helm in the French Revolution, under the rule of the Montagnard party, it carried out centralisation by employing all means, grapeshot and guillotine. The democratic proletariat will, upon reaching power, have to centralise as soon as possible not merely every particular country, but all civilised countries together."[21]

In the light of the weakness, timidity and political ineptitude of the German bourgeoisie, the bourgeois-democratic revolution was envisaged by Marx and Engels as being carried out by the German working class. Anticipating however the idea of the permanent revolution, which was to be propagated more than fifty years later by Parvus-Helphand and Trotsky, Marx and Engels were not resigned to seeing the German working classes relapse into passive and contented observers, after the new bourgeois liberal government had taken over the reins from their victorious hands and begun to create the conditions for free association, political activity and a conventional class struggle. The momentum of the revolution was to be maintained, and the passage from bourgeois liberal democracy to proletarian socialist society was to be made without an unduly long break between feudal absolutism and socialism, in a partly conspiratorial manner, within the mores of bourgeois society, and by methods of carefully graded sabotage and provocative action designed to undermine the position of the ruling petty bourgeois.[22]

That was the mission and great opportunity that history had reserved for the German proletariat. While the working classes of the other Western countries had long ago been relieved of the most obsolete, most onerous and humiliating burdens, history had left all these, undiminished and unmodified, upon the backs of the German proletariat. It vouchsafed at the same time to the German proletarian mind a fuller understanding of the present proletarian situation and of the absolute certainty of the eventual emancipation of the working classes. Meanwhile Europe had also advanced to a point where political democracy was relentlessly driving on to completion in the form of a social democracy, that is to say of communism. It was thus the destiny of the German proletariat—at the call of the Gallic cock—to shake off all the burdens in a single mighty heave and then to proceed to build a world of reason and justice.[23]

Chapter Three

THE REVOLUTION ONE AND INDIVISIBLE

Eighteen forty-eight seemed at first a marvellous vindication of revolutionary internationalism. And so was it seen by Marx and Engels.[24] As if to confirm the prophecies of the extreme revolutionary doctrinaires, the outbreak of the February revolution in Paris (not counting the earlier troubles in Italy) started a cascade of revolutions all over Europe. Their lamentable collapse once the tide was turned in June 1848, again in Paris, capital of the European revolution, showed up the indissoluble interdependence of all national revolutions. The fate of all was determined by the victory or defeat of the revolution in a single country, and the victory of the counter-revolution over one revolution was a triumph for reaction all over Europe. Europe seemed indeed polarised into two camps, and the revolution appeared to be one and indivisible. National, democratic and even socialist aspirations were fused into a single movement for the general liberation of men, classes and peoples. "The great decisive battle," wrote Engles, "has started . . . a single revolutionary period of long duration and full of alternatives, but a battle which can only end with a definite victory for the proletariat."[25]

While most revolutionaries were jubilant at the rapidity with which the old establishments capitulated, and at the ease with which the revolutions achieved in so many places an almost bloodless victory, the two most important representatives of revolution, Auguste Blanqui[26] and Karl Marx, were dismayed by the course of events. As was natural for true revolutionaries they were full of the worst suspicions of the defeated adversaries. An old-established ruling class could not give up so easily. Their quick surrender must have been a calculated tactical retreat, *reculer pour mieux sauter.* They were bound to do everything in their power, resort to any kind of ruse and violence, in order to return. The seeming acceptance of the changes was a trick to deceive the liberals, who so fondly believed in legality, give-and-take, contracts and compromises, abhorred mob violence and lawlessness, felt uncomfortable with their proletarian allies and feared their aspirations no less than their methods. Upon receiving their ministerial appointments from the kings, the liberal leaders were only too eager to leave the real levers of power, the army, police, courts and bureaucracy, untouched under the authority of the kings and their direct aides.

The extreme Right and Left shared the same mode of thinking and understood each other well. To both force was the final arbiter between classes and parties. Power was the decisive factor. If Friedrich Wilhelm IV, and with him men like Bismarck, believed that "gegen den Demokraten helfen nur Soldaten"[27] (soldiers are the only remedy for democracy), Blanqui was proclaiming the slogan, which Mussolini was to adopt when he came out against his own Socialist party in favour of Italy's intervention in the Great War, "qui a du fer a du pain" (the man with the sword eats). Neither Marx nor Blanqui was prepared to regard a parliamentary majority decision as the final verdict. Nor would they accept universal suffrage as a panacea and infallible judge. The question they put to themselves was how to prevent the come-back of the defeated class foe, how to stop the decline of the revolutionary momentum and the ebbing away of idealistic exaltation in the face of the growing readiness to come to an accommodation with things as they were before? Through a revolutionary people's war on the model of 1793—was their answer. There was a common revolutionary cause which could be turned into a national cause of every one of the insurgent peoples—a war against Tsarist Russia, the only country on the European continent to have been left untouched by the revolutionary wave. Russia was the implacable enemy and supreme danger to any revolution anywhere. So long as the Tsar, the self-proclaimed gendarme of reaction, was alive and at the head of his hordes, no revolution was safe. A pre-emptive strike in defence of the European revolution would also be a war for a positive and most sacred revolutionary cause, supported by revolutionaries of every hue—the cause of Poland.

Chapter Four

POLEN SCHWÄRMEREI

The case of Poland was *sui generis*. A great ancient empire—a free republic with an elected king—had gradually disintegrated under the weight of anarchy caused by a totally unrestrained, often downright treasonable abuse of the institutions of liberty by a most selfish nobility and an anarchical gentry. The latter had systematically squeezed out the middle classes, preferring the services of a poor, defenceless, politically harmless Jewish population, and had reduced millions of peasants, a large part of them of alien race and religion, to virtual slavery. It then destroyed every semblance of central government. Thus paralysed, Poland became the battleground for four virile and expanding powers—Sweden (up to the eclipse of Charles XII), Russia, Prussia and Austria. When its more patriotic elements woke up to the woes of their country and realised the urgent need of reform, the despotic rulers of Russia, Prussia and Austria declared themselves to be the defenders of the ancient liberties of Poland's nobility; they then dismantled the Republic of Poland as a dangerous nest of potential Jacobinism, and partitioned it between them.[28]

The astonishment and shock experienced by observers in the West at the sight of an ancient and once powerful nation wiped off the map of Europe was one of the factors in the emergence of the modern concept of a nation. They had no words to express their dismay and disapproval. No dynastic rights had been violated by the liquidation of the Polish elective monarchy, actually bearing the title of republic. Poland was not a city republic like Venice, Genoa or Hamburg. The possessions and privileges of the nobility were left intact by the partitioning powers. The victim who was deprived of sovereignty, juridicial personality and freedom was the nation. So the nation emerged as bearer of rights. The murder of Poland gave birth to the rise, or we should perhaps say, the re-emergence of that very ancient brand of nationalism, the Judaic mystique: "If I forget thee, oh Jerusalem." No sooner had the invading powers accomplished their occupation, than a legion of Polish volunteers was organised in northern Italy to fight for their country beside the French under the command of General Bonaparte.

34

Here was a nationalism based not on territory, but carried in the heart, not focused in a government, but riveted to a dream, not with a constitution as its point of reference, but with a vision of redemption as its guiding star. Consistently and cruelly deceived by Napoleon, the Poles never ceased to trust him. For generations they retained a mystical Bonapartist cult. In 1815, the fate of Poland was sealed for over a hundred years by the Holy Alliance. The European peace secured by the concord of the despotic partitioning empires turned Poland in the eyes of its patriots into a graveyard. The Poles became the knights errant of the European revolution, fighting on every barricade and battleground from Portugal to Turkey, from Chartist England to the Kingdom of the Two Sicilies. Their generals, Chrzanowski, Bem, Dembinski, Wróblewski, Dagbrowski, commanded insurrectionary troops in Italy, Hungary, the Commune. The revolutionaries of Europe took the cause of Poland to their hearts as their own, not only out of sympathy for a persecuted nationality and in gratitude for revolutionary dedication and valour. The fate of the European revolution depended on the cohesion or disintegration of the Holy Alliance.

The strongest link holding the northern powers together was the common interest in preventing the restoration of Poland. Once they fell out, the Poles were sure to rise as a free nation. A resurrected Poland was sure to bring their latent differences out into the open. In brief, here was a classic case of a nationalistic cause becoming the symbol and focus of revolutionary internationalism. In his letter of December 2, 1856, to Engels, Marx writes: "It is a historic fact that you can measure precisely the courage and vitality of all the revolutions since 1789 by their attitude to Poland. Poland is their external thermometer."[29]

The greatest Polish national poet, Mickiewicz, fervently prayed for a war of peoples against the Holy Alliance. The anniversary celebrations in memory of Polish insurrections and tragic defeats were platforms on which revolutionaries of every complexion and nationality sat together, and one such celebration gave the occasion for the rise of the First International.

Marx and Engels shared with Blanqui and all the other revolutionaries the special relationship to Poland. The unsuccessful insurrection of May 15, 1848, which marked the turning of the revolutionary tide in Paris,was undertaken by Blanqui and his followers in an attempt to force the National Assembly to declare war on behalf of Poland. In the eyes of the three revolutionaries, the only way to remove the standing Russian peril to the European revolution was to undertake a war of liberation on behalf of Poland. The country was to be restored to "at least its 1772 frontiers so as to comprise not only the area through which its great rivers are flowing, but also their mouths and large tracts of seashore along at least the Baltic sea",[30] which meant beyond the Dnieper up to Riga and down to the Black Sea. This would drive Russia out of the heart of Europe into the East, and also incidentally weaken hated Prussia (in the opinion of the German revolutionaries a satellite of Russia, nicknamed by them Borussia) and cut away substantial parts of its territories on its eastern border.

Polish society was still dominated by an aristocracy, most of whom preferred to stand aloof from the national struggle for fear of having their vast estates confiscated, and by an impoverished gentry, who could not bring themselves to emancipate their peasants for fear of bankruptcy. This unwelcome fact was hastily brushed aside by the revolutionaries with the argument that the leaders of the short-lived 1846 uprising of the Free City of Cracow (the last and only symbolic remnant of Polish independence left by the Congress of Vienna) against the encroachments of Austria and its allies had proclaimed the emancipation of the peasants and the lands cultivated by them. The insurgents had thus, in the words of the fathers of socialism, unfolded before the world the vision of a peasant national liberation movement and a peasant democracy, "steeling itself to put its hands upon the wheel of history."[31] A similarly flamboyant and far-fetched interpretation by Marx of an incidental matter turned the abortive Polish Constitution of May 3, 1791, into a historic pioneering attempt to abolish aristocracy and carry out an agrarian reform—a case according to Marx of a political revolution which also marked a social renaissance: "appears in the midst of the Prusso-Russo-Austrian barbarism as the sole act of liberty which Eastern Europe has ever made by itself . . . there is no similar example in world history of such nobility by a nobility."[32]

They did not care to examine more closely the disconcerting fact that in 1846 the Galician peasantry were actually playing into the hands of Austrian bureaucracy. In order to check the gentry's insurrection, the Austrian authorities had if not unleashed, at least connived at, the 1846 peasant *jacquerie*, which filled central Europe with dread, had a paralysing effect on the bourgeoisie in 1848 and put an end to the anti-Austrian attitude of Polish nobility for so long as the Danubian monarchy lived on.[33] The Jews were incidentally the main urban element, which, not unlike the peasants, looked upon the patriarchal monarchy as their protector.

A revolutionary war against Russia on behalf of Poland was bound to polarise Europe. It could not but bring the extreme revolutionaries to power, and forcce all the other elements in society to choose between revolutionary patriotism and pro-Russian counter-revoltuionary, and thus anti-national reaction. Such a situation would again enable, would indeed compel, the revolutionary governments to adopt the Jacobin dictatorial-terrorist methods of 1793, and use them as instruments of social revolution. "War against Russia," writes Engels "means a complete open and real break with our ignominious past, the real liberation and unification of Germany, the establishment of democracy upon the ruins of feudalism . . . the only possible way of saving our honour vis-à-vis our Slav neighbours, and notably the Poles."[34]

We know how tragically and how soon this enthusiasm for the Poles ended in a worse subjugation than before. When plans for greater territorial autonomy for the Polish areas were taken up, the German settlers in the Posen province raised an outcry against being sold out to an inferior race just when the liberated German nation had resolved to absorb all those privileged to belong to its stock and to speak its language, who had been torn away from it in the past by a cruel fate. As usual in such situations, it proved impossible to draw any satisfactory demarcation line in areas of mixed population, especially since to ethnic considerations were added economic, cultural and strategic calculations, notably in the case of the city of Posen, the capital of Prussian Poland.

The Polish-German conflict flared up into civil war, and the Prussian army put an end to all talk of special Polish territorial autonomy, to the accompaniment of voices in the Frankfort parliament mocking the mawkish sentimentality of those who bewailed the fate of Poland and expressed a sense of guilt towards the wronged Poles. The success of energetic conquering nations and the defeat of inept and indolent nations—proclaimed one of the the democratic deputies, Jordan—was the just verdict of history. This was a philosophical improvement upon the principle enunciated earlier in the Frankfort assembly by liberals and democrats, that German and Germany included any territory that throughout the centuries had ever been German.[35]

The *Neue Rheinische Zeitung* followed the great debates on the Polish question in the Frankfort assembly with bitter comments on the Germans' duty to do penance for their centuries'-old role as mercenaries to all the despotic regimes of the world intent upon subjugating foreign nations—in Italy, Switzerland, the American colonies, Austria and Hungary, revolutionary France, and Poland, and with elegies on the fate of Poland and prophecies of a coming day of judgment.[36]

Chapter Five

RIGHT AND FORCE IN GLOBAL REVOLUTIONARY STRATEGY

Before 1848, in their period of naive internationalism and undifferentiated monistic materialism, Marx and Engels simply ignored the existence of a nationalities problem. The "spring of the nations" forced the issue upon them, when they were hardly prepared to face it. They became entangled in seemingly unresolvable contradictions.

Their ardent support for Polish independence, for the struggle of the Hungarians, and for the causes of German and Italian unity stood out in glaring contrast to Marx's and Engels' utter condemnation of the national movements of the Czechs and indeed all the Slavs, except the Poles. Similarly disconcerting was the contrast between their severe judgement on the ignoble historic role of the Germans thoughout history as hirelings of oppressors of nations, and their verdict of doom upon the emancipatory aspirations of the Slav nations, coupled as it was with the glorification of the vigour displayed and the civilising role fulfilled by the Germans (and Hungarians) in subjugating and assimilating weaker neighbouring races. The key to this paradox is to be found in the fact that, as already suggested, Marx and Engels were anchored so firmly to dialectical historical materialism that they were unable to acknowledge the right of nations to self-determination as natural, inalienable, unconditional, eternal and in brief absolute. There were no natural eternal rights, not even of the individual. All rights were always conditioned by circumstances, time and place,and were a function of social-economic data, historic developments of the march of progress and most emphatically of the unfolding across history of the movement towards the inexorable ultimate dénouement—the global proletarian revolution.

In so far as they were unable to recognise the nationality question as a primary and independent issue, Marx and Engels may be said to have had no theory on the subject at all. They were in principle neither for unconditional national self-determination nor in all circumstances against it, neither for the preservation and cultivation of distinct peoplehood, nor for the amalgamation of races as ends in themselves.

They took the existing states for granted. There was no reason for them to embark upon an endeavour to abolish them and to cause them to merge into some united states or to link up in a European federation. National differences, animosities and rivalries were sure to be stilled, and frontier lines to be blurred in the wake of socialism. To undertake in the circumstances a struggle for the abolition of sovereign states as an issue on its own was tantamount to a diversion from the struggle for a socialist revolution; indeed to the creation of a rival cause. Let the workers of every country fight their own bourgeoisie, while acting with maximum co-ordination with the aspirations of the proletariat in other countries. The struggles in the individual countries were in the last analysis only parts of a universal confrontation between the proletariat and international capitalism.

Socialists were opposed to any kind of oppression, including national oppression. They were not however automatically quixotic about every movement of national liberation. This would mean pursuing a goal other than socialism for its own sake, in other words creating a diversity of aims. Every movement of national liberation should be weighed and tested for the contribution it could make or the difficulties it was likely to cause to the global strategy of revolution. Abstention from supporting or even opposition to one or another movement should be interpreted not as a denial of the right to national freedom, but only as a postponement. Since national conflicts were in essence a concomitant of social strife, the coming socialist revolution was sure to abolish all national oppression in its stride. What the oppressed nationalities would do, after their yoke had been lifted, with their ancestral language, their distinct cultural heritage and their institutions, was hardly a matter for theoretical consideration. It was the business of those directly concerned. Marx and Engels were not men likely to become sentimental about folklore and national dances, or to grow enthusiastic about the devotion to them of backward tribes and their stubborn resolve to win political independence. In his 1859 pamphlet on the Italian war of independence "The Po and the Rhine" Engels states that there was not a single great power in Europe which had not at one time or another incorporated parts of other nations: "No one will claim that the map of Europe has been definitively fixed. But any changes that may be made have to aim, in order to be lasting, to secure to the great European nations, possessed of vitality, natural frontiers, established in accordance with language and sympathies. At the same time the fragments of peoples, which may be found here and there, and which are no longer capable of leading a national existence, should remain incorporated in the great nations, either by dissolving, or by preserving themselves as simple ethnographic monuments, with no political significance."[37]

In contrast to Marx and Engels, Bakunin preached the absolute right of every ethnic group at any time and in every place to rise and achieve national freedom. But he was no believer in historical dialectic.[38] He believed there was a sacred right and duty to rise in revolt against any kind of oppression anywhere and at any time, and in any circumstances. There was no global strategy of revolution maturing throughout history in the thinking of Bakunin. Bakunin threw himself into the democratic Pan-Slav movement with his customary revolutionary passion. Marx and Engels had no use for Slavs, and bitterly condemned all except the Poles. Bakunin called for a peasant *jacquerie*, because such a movement was in his eyes spontaneous, unorganised, elemental, and thus deployed the greatest measure of revolutionary passion and destructive effect-iveness. Bakunin never tired of proclaiming that to destroy was also to create.[39]

Marx hailed the emancipated industrial proletariat as the architect of the most constructive of social-economic systems. Bakunin was moved by the fact that millions of peasants of the Slav (and Roumanian) race were bitterly exploited by landlords and townsmen of other races, and by the thought that their national liberation aspirations were at the same time a social movement for the liberation and the free flowering of peasant-nations living in peasant communes.[40] Marx and Engels despised what they called village idiocy and peasant obscurantism, and looked forward to the abolition of the peasants as a separate class and to an end to the separation of town and country. They had, as has been said, no sympathy for traditional folklore, but supported the higher cause of an advanced and more universal civilisation.

There is a repellant harshness in the curses which Engels heaped upon the Slavs. His contemptuous condemnation of all their past history strikes bewilderingly Darwinian accents, not to mention the Hegelian overtones. One may even call it cynicism. Yet a closer reading of the texts shows that Engels did not simply proclaim all Slavs guilty and deserving of punishment. They were indeed doomed, and sure to perish soon, but it was the Germans, the geopolitical situation and historic circumstances, that were responsible for their having become guilty. All the same, the sorry fate about to befall the Croats, Czechs, Serbs, Slovenes and other southern Slavs would be consonant with progress. It was a condition and would also be the result of progress.

In the early days of the revolution, Engels praised the "brave" Czech opposition to Habsburg rule, and just on the eve of it defended "Slav liberties".[41] In the very article in which the verdict of doom is pronounced, Engels still justifies the Czech refusal to send delegates to the Frankfort parliament or to associate themselves with the German bourgeois liberals, who were so timid towards their king and so chauvinistic and aggressive towards foreign nations. He understands the reasons of the Czechs for withdrawing support from the feeble, ineffective revolutionary government of Austria. Then abruptly Engels concludes the article with an astonishing purple passage: "Those who most deserve sympathy are indeed the brave Czechs. Whether they win or lose, they cannot escape their doom. Four hundred years of German oppression, of which the battles on the streets of Prague are now a continuation, drive them into the arms of Russia. In the mighty combats between the West and the East, which will break out in the immediate future—perhaps in a few weeks—a tragic fate places the Czechs at the side of the Russians, on the side of despotism against revolution. The revolution will win, and its wheels will crush the Czechs. The guilt for the ruin of the Czechs is once more with the Germans. For it is the Germans who sold them to Russia . . . The only solution now possible is a war of extermination between the Germans and the Czechs."[42]

Even after this harsh verdict of doom, in the June 25 and July 12 issues of the *Neue Rheinische Zeitung*, Engels found it necessary to rehabilitate the Czechs, by stating that the Prague insurrection had been "resolutely democratic" and had been supported by the mass of the people, workers and peasants, who rose against both the Czech nobility and the Austrian army. Moreover, it was the Macchiavellian design of German counter-revolutionaries to divert the lava of revolution into channels of "racial hatred" against the liberties of other nations.[43] But the Czechs and the southern Slavs might have, or should have steadfastly resisted such provocations. Had they chosen—says Engels elsewhere—to support the revolution, instead of exploiting an opportunity to promote their national claims by courting favour with Austrian absolutist feudalism, they would have earned the support of the revolution. But they chose to help the armies of Austria in crushing the revolution in Vienna, and lent a helping hand to the Austrians and Russians in their murder of Hungary. Had the Slavs at any moment of their history "started a new revolutionary history", they would have given thereby proof of their vitality, and "the revolution would have from that moment been interested in their liberation, and the particular interest of the Germans and Magyars would have lost all significance in face of the higher interest of the European revolution."[44] But while being oppressed themselves, they preferred (or were compelled?) to become the oppressors of all revolutionary nations—witness the misdeeds of the Croats and other Slavs in the service of Austria in Italy, in dispersing the Pan-Slav Congress in Prague in 1848, still earlier the atrocities committed by the Russian *muzhik* army in the conquest of Hungary.

The global strategy of revolution must take precedence over every and any particular national interest. And the fact was that "nationalism, that imaginary Pan-Slav nationalism, takes for all Pan-Slavists, including the democratic Pan-Slavists, precedence over revolution."[45] "The Pan-Slavists want to join the revolution on condition that they gain—without taking into account the most basic material conditions—the creation of independent Slav states for all Slavs without exception. The revolution does not allow men to put conditions to it. Either one is a revolutionary and accepts the results of revolution, whatever they are, or man is driven into the arms of the counter-revolution and will find himself one morning—maybe entirely unwittingly and in spite of himself—arm in arm with Nicholas and Windischgrätz."[46]

This had happened to the Slavs, and the revolutionary nations of Europe were now being asked to "guarantee to the counter-revolutionary hordes, hard upon our doorstep, an undisturbed existence, the right of free plotting and arming against the revolution; that we should in the heart of Germany create a counter-revolutionary Czech state, break the forces of the German, Polish and Hungarian revolutions with the help of wedges driven in between them by Russians leaning against the Elbe, the Carpathians and the Danube. This does not enter our heads. To the sentimental phrases about heroism offered to us here in the name of the counter-revolutionary peoples of Europe we answer: that hatred of the Russians was and remains the chief revolutionary passion of the Germans; that since the revolution the hatred of the Czechs and Croats has been added to it; and that together with the Poles and Magyars we can ensure the fate of the revolution only by applying to those Slav peoples the most decided terrorism . . . a pitiless struggle for life and death against the traitor to the revolution, Slavdom; a struggle to destruction, ruthless terrorism—not in the interests of Germany, but in the interests of the revolution!"[47]

How are we to explain such ferocious language and Darwinian terms about annihilation of races? True, no physical destruction is envisaged, only an end to distinct national existence. Yet the issue is put to nations: to be or not to be. Furthermore, similarly contemptuous abuse is heaped by the socialist prophets upon the wholly Western Danes, depicted as parasites upon German culture and puppets of the reactionary powers in the Schleswig-Holstein conflict. It is not surprising that the editor of the *Neue Rheinische Zeitung*, with his lamentable essays on the Jewish question behind him, and the vile anti-semitic abuse of Lassalle in his correspondence with Engels to come,[48] made no attempt to check the ravings of the Vienna correspondent of the paper, Müller-Tellering, about the "judaisation of European humanism" and the consequent loss of all "internal morality" drained by a million Jewish "leeches".[49]

In 1848 and for long after, Marx and Engels believed that they were living in the midst or on the eve of revolution. That revolution was to them a war, and the most pitiless of all wars at that—a European civil war. In that confrontation no quarter could be asked for or given. The forces were so polarised that no one could remain neutral. You were either a revolutionary or a counter-revolutionary. Whatever the causes, reasons, motives, intentions of the Czechs or Croats were, once they decided to support the Austrian monarchy, they chose to ally themselves, indeed to serve Russia in her crusade against the revolution. Once they decided to give preference to their nationality over the revolution, they had signed their death warrant. The revolution could not be expected to tolerate Vendées in the liberated territories, to be gracious to armies which were stabbing it in the back.

"In the first victorious uprising of the French proletariat . . . the Austrian Germans and the Magyars will liberate themselves and wreak bloody revenge upon the Slav barbarians. The general war, which will follow, will crush that Slav league, and not even the name will be left of those small, stubborn peoples. The next world war will wipe off the face of the earth not only reactionary classes and dynasties, but even reactionary peoples. And this too will be progress."[50]

There was however a dialectic within a dialectic. In a war between revolution and counter-revolution all "our" warriors were objectively noble and selfless heroes, and every soldier in the enemy army was a cruel barbarian; our troops were in all they did determined fighters, while the soldiers of the enemy invariably committed the worst atrocities. The dialectic leads Engels to proclaim that all the troops besieging Vienna and fighting the Hungarians were Slav troops, while in fact all their officers were German, and no German regiment outside Vienna ever made common cause with the revolution.[51]

Engels feels driven to set the revolutionary events of 1848 in the historic perspective of all history. And history is conceived in this case as nothing but a preparation for the ultimate socialist revolution. The historic role of the Slavs, he opines, in bringing the revolution close was nil: in fact it was harmful to it. They were therefore, in the spirit of Hegel, non-historical nations. The Slav nations of south-east Europe had never had a state of their own, and if one or two had achieved independence for a short while, they lost it soon forever. Statehood was the gateway to history, the way to contribute to the annals of man. The Slav nationalities lost their liberty to the more virile Germans and Hungarians. They remained pastoral, pig-keeping tribes without urban life, without developed social institutions and with hardly any cultural heritage. They became in fact an extension of oriental barbarism, in Engels' language, "abject dogs", "gypsies", "Slavonic beasts" of "animal idiocy", "canailles", "nations of bandits" and "brigands".[52] But then too, with regard to the German claims to Danish Schleswig-Holstein (in the name of the higher rights of historical development, of civilisation against barbarism, progress against stagnation) Engels uses the occasion to sneer at the enthusiasm for the ancient Nordic tribes, who were "brutal, dirty robbers."[53]

The virile, expanding nations, the Germans and Hungarians, wedged themselves into the Slav territories, cutting off the southern Slavs from their northern brethren and in certain regions surrounding them. It is they who saved a part of the Slav race from the Turkish conquest. Germans settled in the Slav countries in some parts as conquerors, wiping out or assimilating completely the native populations, in others as rural or urban colonists, teachers in the crafts, trades, professions, in brief as the middle class of the majority populations. By continuing for centuries the vegetative tribal existence of illiterate shepherds and ploughmen, the Slav peoples had proved their incapacity for statehood. In the mid nineteenth century, they were no more than rudimentary nationalities, relics and fossils of long-deceased and decayed nations. Consequently, they did not deserve the right to national self-determination.

Their alliance with despotic dynasties and their pretentions to independence threatened the nations to whom they owed their salvation from the Turks and the few blessings of civilisation which the Slav tribes were able to absorb. Possessed of a high degree of social-economic cultural and political development and a marked level of revolutionary consciousness and resolve, the great historical nations of Germany, Hungary and Poland were now in danger of being strangled by the despotic empires, supported by the amorphous Slav peasant masses. The great historic nations might thus be cut off from the Mediterranean shores of Illyria and deprived of other vital territories.

"Among all the nations and tribes of Austria only three were the carriers of progress, actively entered history and are still today capable of continued existence: the Germans, the Poles and the Magyars. This is why they are today revolutionary nations. The immediate destiny of all others, the big or small tribes is—to perish in the revolutionary world storm. This is why they are today counter-revolutionary."[54]

"The southern Slavs who have been subject to Germany and Hungary for a thousand years, have embarked in 1848 upon a campaign for their national independence only to strangle in the course of their struggle the German-Hungarian revolution. They represent the counter-revolution."[55]

No reactionary conservative could be so emphatic in treating history, the past "thousand years of history", as the ultimate proof, judge, sanction and irreversible reality as Engels appears to be when he lays down the law: "We repeat once more: apart from the Poles, Russians and at most the Turkish Slavs, no Slav nation has any future for the simple reason that all the remaining Slavs lack the elementary historical, geographical, political and industrial conditions for independence and development. Peoples which have never had an independent history, and from the moment of attaining the first, most elementary level of civilisation come under foreign domination, or are forced by a foreign yoke to enter upon the first stage of civilisation—such peoples are incapable of development, will never be able to reach any form of independence."[56]

It is not too much to say that in using such terms as "never, never", "irretrievably" and "inevitably" Engels sails dangerously close to racism, gives the impression of replacing social-economic determinism with quite another type of determinism, and seems to deny the basic tenet of materialism—that there was nothing eternal and unchangeable, and nothing was as permanent as change. In what can only be called his reactionary mood, Engels does not even stop to consider that those nations may wish for freedom for its own sake, may have reached the kind of maturity which makes them resent their subject status, abject circumstances and social backwardness, and aspire to freedom. Their new-fangled national ideology is to Engels nothing but a foreign import brought in by a handful of knaves and visionaries, with no relation to concrete realities.

Engels sometimes makes it sound as if it was only because of their malicious hatred of the historic nations and love for despots, that the Slavs had concluded that their social status, language, autonomous institutions and future development were safer under a tolerant and easy-going supranational empire than under the rule of such fierce, exclusive and enterprising nationalist governments as that of Kossuth, who was revolted by the fact that the Croats were refusing the gift of liberty offered to them by the revolutionary Magyars and preferred the yoke of absolutism, or—as was likely—of the Pan-Germans. The Slavs were not to be compensated for centuries of bondage and exploitation by the German nobility and bourgeoisie and the Magyar magnates and gentry, but in fact punished for having been humble for so long and become all of a sudden arrogant. Self-determination was not—one can only conclude—the right of the weak, who had not been given a chance, not a way of redressing a historic wrong, but a privilege for those who had proved to be strong and successful. The weak were doomed to subjugation and extinction if they did not subordinate their aims to the interests and aspirations of the more powerful and the more advanced nations, who represented the march of the revolution. It was hardly, in the last analysis, a question of right or wrong, but of power.

Painful experience had shown—writes Engels in "Democratic Panslavism" à propos Bakunin's slogans of a "European brotherhood of peoples"—that the goal will be reached "not with empty phrases and pious wishes, but through radical revolutions and bloody battles; it is not a case of a brotherhood of all European nations under one republican banner, but of an alliance of revolutionary nations against counter-revolutionary ones, an alliance which is not created on paper, but is hammered out on the battlefield."[57]

Engels mocks Bakunin's romantic, facile phrase-mongering about "justice", "humanity", "liberty", "fraternity", "independence" in the abstract, without taking into account concrete circumstances, differences between nations, their characters, histories and present condition. Engels has no patience with Bakunin's belief that it was enough to proclaim a crusade of the peoples against the despots to change history at a stroke and turn a Europe of predatory wars and diplomatic intrigues into one of total harmony and peace. But there seems to have been an additional reason, and one more closely connected with the materialist dialectic and the global revolutionary strategy of the age. Marx and Engels remained deeply convinced to the end of their lives that just as the bourgeois phase of historic development was impossible without industrialisation, so it was also "not viable without national independence" and unification.[58] The latter created the conditions for a large market and industrial progress. The break-up of large states, with capitalism forging ahead in them and bourgeois democracy in full swing, would be an entirely reactionary diversion, an attempt to abort a history pregnant with revolution. So while the liberation of great "nations" was a wholly progressive principle, the emancipation of backward, pastoral "nationalities" was a retrograde step, notwithstanding all the sentimental slogans of non-Marxist radicals and anarchists.

The fact that four million Hungarians had for centuries been ruling eight million Slavs should neither cause indignation against the Magyars, nor pity for the Slavs, because it went only to show that the former "had proved themselves more vital and more energetic." Together with the Germans, the Hungarians had rendered a great service to those peoples and to history in that they "brought together all those small, inept and impotent tribes in the framework of a single state, enabling them thus to take part in the historical development in which left to themselves, they would not have been able to take part!"[59]

Does not such a line of thought mean—to put the question once more—that might is right? Bakunin was not slow to point this out at a later date, condemning Marx's and Engels' advocacy of the superior rights of the civilised powerful nations over the barbarian or lazy nations to exterminate or exploit them as sheer Darwinism. Striking a Hegelian note, Engels admits that in the process the Germans and Hungarians had "violently crushed more than one national flower." "But," he goes on, "you cannot realise such things without violence. Without force and utter ruthlessness, nothing is achieved in history", as Alexander, Caesar, Napoleon showed.[60] The more so at present, when as a result of industrialisation and the development of communications, centralisation had become so essential. Just at this moment come the Slavs wanting to break up large centralised countries.

Nothing illustrates better the shifting, ultimately arbitrary nature of the dialectical revolutionary approach to the nationality problem than Engels' hair-raising letter to Marx on May 23, 1851, on the subject of Poland.[61] The full letter was published for the first time only in 1927, with an accompanying tortuous commentary in Vol. 27 of the Russian translation of the works of Marx and Engels, then rather surprisingly in full and without comments in the 1960 two-volume Polish anthology *Marx and Engels on Poland*, Vol. I, pp. 249-54: "The more I ponder over the question, it becomes clearer to me," writes Engels, "that as a nation the Poles are a *nation foutue* which can be used only until Russia has been swept into the agrarian revolution. From that moment Poland will have no *raison d'être* any more. The Poles have never done anything in history, except for foolish displays of bravery and querulousness . . . not a single deed signifying progress or having historical significance." In comparison with the "knightly indolence" of the Poles, Russia has, as far as the East is concerned, been an effective and progressive nation. With all its "meanness and Slavonic dirt", "the Russian rule has been a civilising force in the territories adjoining the Black Sea, the Caspian Sea, Central Asia, for the Bashkirs and Tartars". The Poles had never proved able to assimilate other nationalities, whereas the Russians succeeded in Russifying Germans and Jews in the second generation. "Even Jews acquire in Russia Slavonic cheek-bones." In the former eastern provinces of Poland the vast majority had made no move to resist

Russian domination. "A quarter of Poland speaks Lithuanian, another quarter Ruthenian, a small part is half-Russian, and Poland proper is, by at least a third, Germanised."

Two years later on April 12, 1853, Engels, writing to his comrade Wedemeyer, who had emigrated to America upon the failure of the German revolution, is waking up to the fact that since the peasants of the eastern provinces of ancient Poland were all of foreign stock, the restoration of Poland would in fact mean the restoration of the domination of the Polish nobility.[62] He refuses, he says, to hear of giving back to Poland the lands beyond the Dvina and the Dnieper.

These historical generalisations are made by Engels in the context of revolutionary German *Realpolitik*, which the Germans will have to resort to on the day when a revolution has taken place in Germany. France, Italy, the Czechs (to whom Mazzini had promised independence) and Poland will unite to strangle the revolution and to partition Germany, and Germany will be left with only two possible allies—the Hungarians and the Russians, who will have by then gone through their peasant revolution. Once she has had her agrarian revolution, Russia will become an infinitely more desirable ally than Poland. The Poles cannot be counted on raising more than an army of 20-30,000 soldiers out of its bankrupt, petty gentry. True, Marx and Engels had promised to support Polish independence, but—Engels adds—only on condition of an agrarian revolution.[63] It seems however pretty sure that such a revolution will occur earlier in Russia. Engels draws from that quite a far-reaching practical conclusion: "To take away from the Poles in the West all that is possible, to man with Germans their fortresses, especially Posen, under the pretext of defence needs, to permit them to administer [their economy], to despatch them to the firing line, to denude their country of food, to overwhelm them with promises regarding Riga and Odessa, but in the event of our success in getting the Russians on the move, to unite with the latter and to force the Poles to make concessions. Every inch of soil that we leave to the Poles on the borderline between Memel and Cracow weakens still further the already lamentably weak frontiers [of Germany] and exposes all the Baltic seashore up to Stettin."[64]

In the same spirit Engels writes in his "Revolution and Counter-revolution in Germany", in 1852, about the future of the Czechs. "The dying Czech nation made a last effort in 1848 to regain its old vitality, the failure of which is proof that independently of any revolutionary considerations, the Czechs can exist from now on only as part of Germany, even if a part of them continues for a few centuries to speak a non-German language."[65]

The relationship between the historical and unhistorical nations in Europe is paralleled by Marx's and Engels' conception of the relationship between the great colonial powers and the races of Asia (and to the extent that Africa is at all present in their thinking, Egypt and Algeria too). Engels also refers to the war between the United States and Mexico over Texas. Technically it was a war of aggression on the part of the United States, but the virile, brave, progressive Yankees were fully justified in wresting from the lazy, backward, inefficient Mexicans a country of vast mining and industrial possibilities, and they should go on and seize New Mexico and California.[66] They represented the cause of civilisation against turbulent barbarians. The same held true of the relationship between the progressive, revolutionary nations—the Germans and the Hungarians—and the Slav nationalities, whom "history had been dragging against their will", and who must inevitably be counter-revolutionary "as they have indeed been in 1848."[67]

In its inexorable march to realise the unity of the globe by intergrating the vast spaces, populations and natural resources of Asia into a single capitalist world economy, European imperialism was bound to break the immemorial Asiatic mode of production. The age-long stagnation of Asia was caused by the lack of commodity circulation, the consumption of most of the produce by the family or communal entity, the absence of any division of labour, and the appropriation of all surplus by the moneylenders and the despotic government, no matter what dynastic upheavals and changes occurred. The imperialist powers were committing untold crimes and inflicting horrible suffering, displacement and misery upon the subjugated races. But the price must be paid by the latter, because the former were acting as instruments of history and progress. Without either side realising it, the disruption of ancient frozen civilisations by arrogant and greedy invaders would become—especially in the case of China—the undoing of the intruders. This however would happen not through revolts, which would undermine, even destroy the might of the colonial powers and thus set the European proletariat on the move, but by the crisis which the effort to mobilise the wealth of the colonies would cause to the rival capitalist economies.

Victorious colonial uprisings were imaginable. But no more than the Russian commune could they become the starting points for local socialist transformation, still less serve as inspiration and models to the world at large. The subjugated peoples of Asia and Africa would be enabled to realise their own revolutionary potentialities only by being stirred up or offered effective help by victorious Western revolutions. The latter should not try to impose their own recipes for happiness upon the liberated colonial peoples, but should let them find their own way to socialism. They would however be in duty bound to offer a helping hand to revolutionary liberation movements outside Europe.[68]

In a remarkable letter to Kautsky, Engels writes in 1882 that while he believes that the British Dominions will gain independence whatever their social-political regimes, he expects India, Algeria, Egypt, the Dutch and Portuguese dependencies to be led to freedom by their proletariats, probably by way of revolution. Barred from conducting colonial wars, the Western proletariat will have to let the colonial revolutions have their share of the suffering and destruction, which is part of any revolution. "We shall have enough to do at home. A reorganised Europe and North America—that will constitute such a power and offer such an attraction that the half-civilised peoples will by themselves take up our example; their economic needs will by themselves make this necessary. As to what social political stages of development those countries will have to pass in order to arrive to a socialist organisation of their own, we cannot but engage in speculative hypotheses about that. One thing is certain: the victorious proletariat cannot impose any form of happiness on a foreign people, without undermining thereby its own victory. This does not exclude, naturally, various types of wars of defence."[69] The latter reservation may of course serve to legitimise any subversive effort by any minority and be taken to justify armed intervention by socialist countries.

Chapter Six

THE INCOMPLETE THEORY

Is it possible to detect a change and signs of evolution in the attitude of Marx and Engels to the national problem in the decades after 1848?

It has to be borne in mind that for most of the post-1848 period the two friends were not only keen and passionate observers of the international scene, but almost professional journalists. For quite some years the fees for his articles—487 in ten years, a quarter of them edited by Engels—to the *New York Daily Tribune* were Marx's main regular income.[70] Having to analyse and evaluate concrete events for the general public, and not as theoreticians or leaders laying down the line, Marx and Engels would become interested in them for their own sake, and tried to assess their contemporary significance. They sometimes give the impression of entirely ignoring the dialectics of world revolution. Still, never quite. The standpoint is always that of political radicals. All the same, for Marx and Engels so natural, indeed the compulsive manner of referring all political facts to social economic data almost disappears in the later period, or is reduced to perfunctory, superficial and often quite wrong-headed statements, as for instance in the case of Poland.

These were years of victory for the nationality principle such as the unification of Italy, and more important of Germany, causes in which they felt deeply involved, but which, frustratingly to them, were brought to fruition by factors and means not to their liking. In the Russian wars of 1853-4 and 1878, the nationality problem in the Balkans loomed very large, but again not in a way wished for by the two theoreticians. The Paris Commune of 1871 rekindled for a short while revolutionary internationalism and something of the pre-1848 polarisation into a camp of revolution (to some extent at least embodied in the International) and a seemingly revived Holy Alliance. But these developments were soon overshadowed by the fact that the Franco-Russian rapprochement on the one hand, and the stirrings of revolution in Russia on the other, were upsetting any speculations of a European confrontation between revolutionary and counter-revolutionary nations on the 1848 model.

51

(*a*) REVOLUTIONARY DIPLOMACY

The issue of international proletarian unity and national distinctness was put on the agenda of the First International.[71] Although the International was composed of associations which applied for affiliation or were co-opted, Marx's aim was to turn the International into a body composed of national parties. By nations he emphatically meant countries, and not nationalities as ethnic groups. Marx was very anxious for the International to keep clear of the nationality problem, and not to become a platform for debates between nationalities, or for the defence of particular national causes, the case of Poland being the signal exception.

Marx at the same time wished the International to become the sixth great power in Europe, ranged against all the other five. The working classes composing it were in duty bound to keep a watchful eye upon the doings of their respective governments, on international events in general, to "harrass them if necessary by all means at their disposal", and if unable to stay their hand, to unite for simultaneous denunciation. . . . "The struggle for such a foreign policy was part of the general struggle for the emancipation of the working class."[72]

Marx found himself hard pressed in the field of international policies, by Mazzini and his followers for one reason, by Bakunin for another, and the Proudhonists for still another. Very grudgingly, under protest, and with his tongue in his cheek, Marx agreed to the inclusion of Mazzinian phrases about the necessity of morality in international relations being the same as between individuals, about justice to all nations, in the declarations of basic principles of the First International. But he took care to keep nationalist prophecy out.[73]

Marx's insistence on the labour movement of the nation-state being represented by a single party and on the supreme duty of the proletariat in any country where it was organised as a political party to seize political power and establish itself eventually as a dictatorship; and of course the centralising tendencies of Marx as head of the International Council—both these scandalised Bakunin. They were to him another proof of Marx's incurable *étatisme,* which ran counter to his own deeply cherished ideas on universal and immediate liberation from all authority. The steady advance of German Social-Democracy, which had striven for so long for German unity in the form of a vast, centralised and powerful state, and the growth of its influence in the Council of the International, suggested to Bakunin a Teuton-Judaic plot to establish German hegemony over the international labour movement.[74]

The difficulties with the Proudhonists stemmed from their cosmopolitan opposition to national separatism, their desire for the "individualisation of mankind", which à propos his own son-in-law, Lafargue, Marx considered to be a form of inverted French chauvinism. To the French socialists France and the French language and civilisation stood as we have seen, for the civilisation of mankind *tout court*. These offended not so much the patriotic German in Marx, as his realism. The Proudhonists repudiated pro-Polish policies on the ground that it was a Russian Tsar and not the Polish gentry who had emancipated the Polish peasants. It was all wrong and contrary to revolutionary justice and to proletarian solidarity to prefer a querulous, self-centred nation like the Poles to the multitudes of Russia, and to put beyond the pale a great country which was straining to join the march of progress. Proudhon had exasperated many radicals by his warnings on the dangers held out by a nationalist exclusiveness in general, and the Italian Risorgimento in particular. The Proudhonist reproach that the International was degenerating into a "comité des nationalités à la remorque du Bonapartisme", concerned with the emancipation of nationalities, rather than with the liberation of the international proletariat, could not but rankle deeply with Marx.[75]

Although there is ultimately no basic change in Marx's and Engels' attitude to nationalism in the post-1848 period, there are signs of a stronger and more embarrassed awareness of the complexity of the problem, consequently a good deal of uncertainty and lack of firmness and consistency in tackling it. The supreme consideration remains the global strategy of revolution. It is that criterion which causes the two friends to proclaim Poland and Ireland necessary nations,[76] whose duty it was to be nationalist and who deserved every kind of revolutionary support in their national liberation struggle, even while they continued to repudiate the right of what they called relics of nations to national self-determination.

Ireland was a classic example of a blend of a national liberation struggle and a social problem of utmost gravity. Marx also held the exaggerated view that the lands owned by the absentee English landlords in Ireland were the economic basis of British Tory aristocracy, and that holding down the Irish by force necessitated a standing army which could at any moment be employed to quench social unrest and revolutionary action in England. The emancipation of Ireland was calculated to ruin the British ruling class and shake British capitalism to its foundations. The collapse of the most powerful and most advanced capitalist fortress was sure to cause an incalculable chain reaction throughout the world.[27] His intimate knowledge of British social-economic realities, however, forced upon Marx the embarrasing reflection that the Irish issue was having a most upsetting effect on the relations between English workers and their Irish comrades in England. The growing hatred between the proletariats of the two antagonistic nations was of course particularly disconcerting to a man, who had in his earlier days believed that the workers had already freed themselves of nationalist prejudices.

Marx and Engels continued to view Polish nationalism with sympathy and to offer powerful support to the emancipatory aspirations of the Poles, as part of their crusade against Russia's counter-revolutionary role and its allegedly set plans for "world domination" since the days of Peter the Great, the "heir to Ghengis Khan". Engels reserved his gnawing doubts for the privacy of personal cor-respondence.[78] Poland was absolutely indispensable for the revolutionary cause. When the tragic failure of the insurrection of 1863-4 led the extreme wing of Polish socialism to renounce policies of national liberation in favour of a common proletarian struggle with the Russian revolutionaries for international socialism, Marx and Engels hastened to restate the reasons for their continued support for the national liberation of Poland.

A new and striking argument is added by Marx and Engels (with greater elaboration) to the old arguments about the importance of Poland's geographic, military and political situation on the European chessboard and the role of the Poles as the knights of revolution all over Europe. The new argument is that lack of national independence was so strong an irritant and impediment that it made a nation incapable of devoting its attention and energies to a social transformation. Not only—says Marx—was there no contradiction between inter-nationalism and the national cause of Poland. "Only then, when Poland regains its independence, only when it is able to dispose of itself as an independent nation, will its internal development be resumed, and only then will it be able to participate in the social transformation of Europe. So long as a vital nation is subjugated by invaders, it directs of necessity all its efforts, all its energies to the struggle against a foreign enemy. Its internal life is then so paralysed, that it is impossible for it to work for socialism."[79]

Engels formulated his views on the same subject in an important programmatic letter to Karl Kautsky of February 7, 1882. He takes issue there with the anti-patriotic Polish socialist group "Równość", after having made his stand public in a letter he had sent to their 50th anniversary celebration of the November 29, 1830, uprising, which was held in Geneva.

"History shows that a great nation does not have the conditions even to discuss seriously its internal affairs so long as it lacks national independence. This was the case of the Italians before 1859, of Germany before 1870 ("where would our party be now, had the old Bundestag still been in existence?"), of Hungary before 1860. The international proletarian movement is possible only among independent nations . . . international co-operation is possible only between equals." So long as Poland was partitioned and subjugated, there would be no strong socialist movement there, and socialist parties would have relations only with Polish émigrés. "Every Polish peasant and worker, who wakes up from his torpor and begins to take part in general causes, is confronted first and foremost by the fact of national bondage as the first obstacle on his road. The removal of that obstacle is the first condition of any healthy and free development. . . . In order to fight, there is need first for ground under one's feet, for air, light and space." The reference to the nationalist feelings of the Polish peasants or workers was based on a misreading of the strongest sentiments of those classes in those days— the evil memories of *szlachta* oppression. The peasantry had hardly yet developed a national consciousness. Engels goes on to lay down the rule, which contradicts what he had been preaching in 1848 to the Slav nations: the question whether the restoration of Poland was possible before the revolution was irrelevant.

"At all events it is none of our business to hold back the Poles from efforts aimed at gaining the indispensable conditions for their further development or to tell them that national independence is from the international point of view something entirely subordinate." "There is no saying whether Poland will not be restored like other nations as a result of a sudden change in the diplomatic constellation, or like Germany, thanks to a war."[80]

Anticipating Kautsky's question, how was it that while sympathising so strongly with the national aspirations of the Poles, he had "devilishly little" sympathy for "the small Slav nations and remnants of nations, which had been scattered by the three wedges driven into Slavdom—the German, Hungarian and Turkish versus the Czechs, Serbs, Bulgars, Slovenes, Galicians, Ruthenians", Engels reiterates his conviction that those peoples had become the tools of "our greatest enemy—Russia", who had invented or was using the "fraud" of an "imaginary Slav nationalism".[81]

Engels would be prepared to consider the wishes of those "lilliput nationalities" after the fall of Tsardom, that is to say, only when their links with the Russian plans for world domination had been snapped. He was sure however, that after six months of independence, the Slavs of Austro-Hungary would be begging to be allowed to rejoin the Habsburg Empire.

What business, it may be asked, had Engels to ask whether the nationalism of the Slavs was genuine and deep or superficial and imaginary, if he felt that a foreigner had no right to tell the Poles not to put their nationhood before the revolution. Engels could sympathise with the desire of the Poles for national independence to such an extent that he justified their unwillingness and inability to think of any internal reforms before they had achieved political freedom. Why should he condemn the Slavs for trying to use an international situation, to find allies where they could, even embarrassing ones, to help them to gain independence, in the hope of getting out of their clutches eventually? But Engels remained adamant: as allies of the counter-revolution, the southern Slavs were enemies, and, as in 1848, their subjective feelings and rights did not matter and did not deserve any sympathy. To the end of his life Engels held fast to the axiom of the insoluble bond between the national aspirations of the southern Slavs and Russian Tsarism under the guise of Pan-Slavism. "I do not care to look for reasons why the small Slav peoples have come to regard the Tsar as their only liberator. It is of no importance, it is enough that they do so, and we can do nothing about it so long as Tsarism is not broken; in case of war, all those interested small nations will rally to Tsarism, the enemy of the whole west in its full bourgeois development stage. So long as that situation continues, I cannot be interested in their immediate and instantaneous liberation; they remain our enemies in the same manner as their ally and suzerain, the Tsar."[82]

But in fact Engels goes beyond these considerations. "We will not in any case accord to those nations the rights, which are claimed at present by Serbia, Bulgaria and West Rummelia—the right to put obstacles to the construction of a European railway network up to Constantinople",[83] which meant in effect support for expansionist German development plans for south-east Europe and Asia Minor. The nationalism of the Poles had to be satisfied because it was too powerful an irritant and thus capable of seriously holding up the march of revolution. The nationalism of the small, weak nations was incapable of doing the same harm, and of being an equally serious nuisance. It could and should therefore be ignored. It was too troublesome an undertaking to fight the nationalist aspirations of a developed nation. The fight against them would require too great a diversion from the main, the socialist, task. It would be an equally serious and much less justified distraction, to develop and cultivate the nationhood of decrepit or rudimentary nationalities, already allegedly in the process of disappearing.

The right of self-determination granted to relics of moribund nations seemed to Engels a licence to disrupt great existing nations and to restrict or even violate their right to untrammelled national self-determination. The whole idea was a Russian invention to justify the seizure and annexation to Russia of the Polish territories which were inhabited by Lithuanians, White Russians and Ukrainians. How the Poles and those nationalities would settle their differences after the revolution "does not concern us at the present moment", Engels concludes.[84]

(b) PREFIGURATION OF FUTURE REALITIES

This attribution of superior right to great nations raises the suspicion that Engels' unwillingness or inability to recognise the legitimacy, or even the reality of Slav nationalism—an imaginary invention of professors and bourgeois scribes or a Russian fraud—his indignation at attempts to try to undo the work of a "thousand years of history", his mocking references to the "oppression" suffered by the Slavs, the contemptuous rejection of Slav pretentions to interfere with the development plans of the great nations (outside their own borders and in Slav territory)—all these seem the reflexes of a member of a dominant nation which was behaving like a possessing class moved by indignation at the effrontery of a newly arrived claimant of whom nobody had heard. As proof of the bourgeois and imaginary character of Slav nationalism Engels invokes at the end of the letter the "magnificent solidarity of the German and Czech workers in Bohemia".[85] Little did he know what was soon going to happen in the multi-racial Austro-Hungarian Empire: the curious obtuseness of revolutionaries, who believed so unshakably that they knew and embodied the last word in historic development.

Marx and Engels watched the process of the unification of Germany with ambivalent feelings. It was something they had desired as a vital step in the direction of socialism. But—to say it once more—it was being carried out by men and classes whom they loathed and by methods which were abhorrent to them. Still, they could console themselves with the thought that unwittingly Bismarck was doing their work as if they had paid him for it. Although the Second Reich was not the *Gross-deutschland* they would have preferred, and was not emerging as the result of an uprising of the German popular masses, they felt that in his Bonapartist violation of dynastic principles and legitimacy, Bismarck was being a revolutionary in spite of himself, and was creating an atmosphere propitious to the spread of revolution. Furthermore, the victory of Germany over France sealed the victory of German Social-Democracy over French Proudhonism, thus enthroning the German movement as the leader of world socialism.[86]

But the Franco-German War had a very upsetting effect upon socialist revolutionary orientation. The manner in which Germany was united, just as a little earlier Italy had been, marked a definite divorce of movements for national liberation from revolution. The Paris Commune was a revolutionary flicker, blending Jacobin patriotism with social radicalism. It was hailed by Marx, who had originally opposed the idea of a proletarian uprising, as a promise of a new type of society, a direct democracy almost, without the coercive superimposed centralised state resting on army, police, church, permanent bureaucracy, separation of powers and the rule of capital. For a while it seemed as if the European bourgeoisie had rallied to another version of the counter-revolutionary Holy Alliance, this time against the European proletarian camp under the leadership of the International. After a while Marx had sadly to admit that in the last analysis the Paris Commune fell because its example was not followed by any other European capital. Worse than that: while the spontaneous revolutionary urge proved too weak, ominous signs were multiplying that chauvinist passion and nationalist mythology were developing into a highly effective rival to the myth of revolution. Marx and Engels realised with utter dismay that the annexation of Alsace and Lorraine had changed the character of the war for the Germans, from a war of defence which Marx had supported, although trying hard to stem any chauvinism in the proletariat of either of the warring nations, into a war of aggression.

It had made certain not only a Franco-Russian alliance across the gulf dividing bourgeois republicans from the Tsarist regime. It also made a militarist regime in Germany inevitable. These developments were sure to conjure away any prospect of an international ideological war. With conscript armies and armaments swelling to astronomic proportions, every future war would become for every country a war for its national existence: "a war of races, for Germany", a war of "allied Slav and Roman races".[87] This would place the working class of every country, above all Germany, in a desperately difficult situation. They would have to choose between loyalty to their country, right or wrong, on one side, and allegiance to international proletarian solidarity and the world revolution on the other. In his scathing *Critique of the Gotha Programme* for the united Social-Democratic Germany, Marx had lamented the weakness of the internationalist accents in the programme, and the influence of Lassallean nationalism on it.

"To what has the German working class party reduced its internationalism?" asks Marx..[88] To the consciousness that the result of its efforts will be "the international brotherhood of peoples"—a phrase borrowed from the bourgeois League of Freedom and Peace, which was meant to be taken as the equivalent of the brotherhood of the working class in their common struggle against the ruling classes and their governments. Thus not a word about the international functions of the German working class! And with this slogan it had to face its own bourgeoisie, already united with the bourgeois classes of all other countries, and the international policy of plots of Herr Bismarck. . . . Bismarck's *Norddeutsche* had every reason to announce that "in its new programme the German workers' party has renounced internationalism!"[89]

In the same spirit Engels writes to Bebel two months earlier and complains that even the barest minimum of international solidarity— aid to strikes and prevention of their violation by imported blacklegs, information about developments in the various parties, above all agitation against the threat or outbreak of wars hatched in Cabinet secrecy—had found no mention in the German Social-Democratic party programme. The decline of internationalism in the working classes and the blurring of ideological alignments in European diplomacy as a result of the new balance of power explain Marx's and Engels' own wobbling views on war and revolution in the closing period of their lives. Under the impact of the Commune, Marx wrote in his *Civil War in France*: "The highest heroic effort of which old society is still capable is national war, and this is now proved to be a mere governmental humbug, intended to defer the struggle of the classes, and to be thrown aside as soon as that class struggle bursts out into civil war. Class war is no longer able to disguise itself in a national uniform. The national governments are only one against the proletariat!"[90]

In 1877 in a letter to Sorge of September 27[91] Marx shows himself deeply impressed by the growth of the revolutionary movement in Russia, and the signs of the general disintegration of Russian society. Revolution was beginning this time in the East, which had been till now the invulnerable bastion and reserve army of counter-revolution. Marx believes Bismarck's feelings were ambivalent: pleasure at the discomfiture of the Russian colossus and fear lest it fall and left Austria and Germany face to face with revolution, without the Russian shield.

But this time Marx not only does not call on the Poles to rise, he enjoins them to keep quiet: should they provoke Bismarck into intervention, there would be an outburst of Russian chauvinism. The Poles must wait for the revolution to win in the two capitals of Russia. When this happens, and Bismarck intervenes as saviour, the Prussians will find their Mexico in Poland.

Marx and Engels seem to be recoiling more and more from the old doctrine of war as instrument of revolution. The vision of international war as the midwife of revolution still fascinated Marx at the time of the Crimean War. In 1853 he mocks Clarendon, Palmerston, Aberdeen and all foreign ministers of Europe who recoil with "fear and trembling" from the spectre of a world war. "But," writes Engels in one of his purple passages "he who has learned through the study of history to behold the incessant vicissitudes of human destinies, where nothing is constant but instability, where only change is invariable; he who has followed the iron laws of history, the wheels of which pitilessly crush great empires, and sweep away whole generations without compassion; he who, in one word, is able to understand that no demagogic slogan, no revolutionary proclamation will have the same profound effect as the simple facts of the history of mankind; he who realises the eminently revolutionary character of the present age, where steam and wind, electricity and the ink of the printing press, artillery and gold mines combine to produce in one year more changes and revolutions than a whole century in olden times; he will certainly not hesitate to pose this historic issue solely out of fear that the only right solution it offers may lead to a European war. But the governments, with their obsolete diplomacy, will never solve the difficulty. As with so many other problems, the solution of the Turkish problem lies in the European revolution. This affirmation has nothing shocking about it. Since 1789, the revolution has not ceased to gain ground and to widen its borders. It stopped at Warsaw, Debreczim and Bucharest; but it will push on to St Petersburg and Constantinople. These are the most vulnerable places from which it is necessary to attack the counter-revolutionary Russian colossus."[92]

The Italian war of 1859 brought to the fore considerations of German unification and revolutionary strategy. Lassalle supported the Franco-Piedmontese alliance in the hope that a war on behalf of the nationalities principle would revive democratic radicalism in France, and that an Austrian defeat would revolutionise Germany.[93] Marx and Engels could never bring themselves to say a good word for the Bonapartist usurper and murderer of liberty.[94] Austria was now in their eyes the German bastion against Russia, Slavdom and France. Napoleon

III was ready to grab the Rhine as France's natural border, and Russia was only waiting to fall upon Prussia. Before that happened Marx hoped the war would provoke a revolutionary conflagration across Europe, and unlike 1848, Germany might become the base from which the revolutionary forces, with Prussia as their spearhead, would mount their assault on Russia.

In 1870 Marx supported Prussia against Bebel and Liebknecht who refused to vote for war credits in the Prussian Landtag—because of his hopes of German unification, but also for fear that a French victory would consolidate Bonapartism for a long time, provoke a wave of nationalist passion in Germany, repulse the German labour movement, and put the French at the head of the European working class movement.

As we have said, the horror of modern warfare ("from ten to fifteen million soldiers will be facing each other") was strengthened for the two ageing prophets by apprehensions about the behaviour of the working classes in the warring countries. In his letter to Bebel of December 22, 1882, Engels says that he would consider a European war a misfortune. "This time it would be terribly serious; it would set chauvinism going everywhere for years, because every nation would be fighting for its existence." The present achievements by the Russian revolutionary movement would be wasted and France and Germany would be swept by a flood of chauvinism. The only good thing that might come out of it would be a little Poland. But such a Poland would come out of a Russian revolution in any case, and without war. A Russian constitution resulting from a defeat in war would be far less radical than one achieved by revolution. Yet Engels goes on immediately to say that such a war would delay the revolution by some ten years. "But," he adds characteristically, "a revolution (so delayed) would naturally go much deeper."[95]

Russia continued to be the keystone of the existing international system in Marx's and Engels' thinking. As a result of their contacts with Russian émigré revolutionaries, neither could ever shake off their conspiratorial view of Tsarist Russia, even when they began to speculate on the possibilities of a revolutionary upheaval in Russia. Their paranoiac Russophobia had reached a climax in the 1850's under the influence of the monomaniac Urquhart, leading Marx to proclaim Palmerston a Russian agent. It becomes impossible to distinguish whether they speak of Russia as the irredeemable embodiment of oriental Mongol barbarism or of Russia the spearhead of counter-revolution. Significantly Engels begins his analysis of the international situation in the famous *Foreign Policy of Tsarism,* written in 1890 by reassuring his readers that on this issue, too, he was speaking for his deceased friend. "I am only a successor; I execute what was not given to him to accomplish."[96]

After 1871 Russia, Engels argued, had again become the arbiter of Europe. The foreign adventurers who were steering its policies, exploiting the invulnerability of Russia to invasion, and compensating for Russia's inability to wage successful wars of aggression with unscrupulous intrigue, blackmail and cunning, were Germany's and Austria's guarantee against revolution. They were in a position to prevent France from employing in a future war her mightiest weapon— her international revolutionary appeal and Jacobin patriotism. This allowed Russia to spread her influence over the Balkan peoples, to sow discord and strife, while appearing as their liberator from the Turkish yoke; and to prepare systematically for the conquest of Constantinople. Only the elimination of Russia would release the revolutionary socialist potentialities of France and Germany, bring about the disintegration of Austria and allow her nationalities to sort out their territorial disputes and form a federal bond between themselves. Could the elimination of Russia be accomplished by war? Engels fears that the reactionary governments would prefer to save themselves from revolution by abandoning Constantinople, the Dardanelles and the Balkans to Russia. They might even send armies to save the Tsar's throne and restore him to it, if he were dethroned by revolution. Only a revolution in Russia could save Europe from a calamitous fate, prevent war, free the nations and unchain the revolutionary forces everywhere. "The noble Great Russian nation will then cease to chase the chimeras of conquests on behalf of Tsarism, and will devote itself to its true civilising mission in Asia, to co-operation with the West and to the development of its great intellectual potentialities."[97]

Engels expresses the hope that Europe will be spared a war in which the working classes could support neither side. Thus "a revolution in Russia at the present moment would save Europe from the disasters of a general war and initiate the universal social revolution". But only a few lines above, true to his unshakable conviction that in the end socialism must win, Engels says that terrible as the war may prove, "everything will in the end bring advantage to the socialist movement, bring nearer the victory of the working classes".[98]

Two years later Engels concludes his article on the foreign policy of Tsarism with the prayer: "Europe looks like sliding down a slope, and with precipitation, into an abyss of a world war of unheard-of dimensions and violence. Only one thing can halt the process: a change of regime in Russia. There is no doubt that it must take place in a few years. May it only come in time to forestall the events which are inevitable without that change."[99]

While clearly discerning that the myth of the nation had become the most potent rival and danger to the myth of socialist revolution, Engels does not reach a Leninist conclusion: the necessity of turning the war of nations into a civil war, into a general proletarian uprising. He is rather desperately preoccupied with the way in which the SPD ought to face the contingency of an attack by Russia, which would threaten Germany's very existence, and with it the leading position of the German Social-Democratic party in Europe. Engels concludes: the SPD will have to fight with the rest of the nation against any attacker "to the last man".[100] He adds somewhat incongruously that a war would so weaken capitalism that socialism would succeed it soon. Yet, he does not seem to hail the prospect.

When the French socialists protested against these views, Engels replied that if the Kaiser were to invade France, it would be the duty of the French workers to fight for their country.[101] In 1891 (October) writing to Bebel, Engels goes so far as to enjoin the SPD to vote for war credits in the Reichstag if a war breaks out, as was expected by the government of the Reich in 1892.

"If Germany is attacked from the East and West, every method of defence is good. . . . If, as the Prussian government says, there will be a war in early 1892, we could not on principle declare against voting credits now. This would be a rather *fatale Lage* for us. But what if there is really a war early in 1892? In this case we will have to vote for all credits tending to reinforce the *defensive,* and only those. In the perspective of imminent war, we cannot announce our army policy now (militia, democratisation of the army, new armaments, etc.—this army reform costs too much time), but must try to temporise and vote only those army credits which go to change the character of the army in the sense of a people's army."[102]

More than that, in case of a war with Russia—Engels says—it will be only the SPD which will be waging the war . . . in "a truly energetic spirit, since the Junkers and the cowardly bourgeoisie will be hampered by their class inhibitions".[103]

Chapter Seven

CONCLUSIONS

Marx and Engels never in fact came to grips with the phenomenon of nationhood. It is no accident that they never bothered to investigate how nations came into being at all, either from the anthropological, social-economic or cultural and political points of view. At most, they took it for granted as an epiphenomenon. Since they had great difficulty, as materialistic monists, in seeing the nation as a datum obeying its own laws and as an eternal phenomenon, they could consider it only in relation to the state, in other words to the historically evolved—but never explained—nation-state as it faced them or was about to become such, because of its having become a necessity to emergent bourgeois society. The right of ethnic groups to develop into nation-states was never regarded by them as a natural right to self-determination, but only as a function of the political strategy of world revolution—in weakening and destroying reactionary powers—or, differently put, as a concomitant of the march of universal progress—in securing a large market and a bourgeois democracy as a stepping stone to a socialist transformation. Hence the support for large and strategically situated nations, and the denial of the right of self-determination to undeveloped and parochial tribes, indeed the wish to see those spokes in the world's wheel, actual or potential Vendées, disappear and be absorbed by the great developed nation-states.

In so far as national self-determination was not granted as an unconditional right, and supreme reality was accorded to the inexorable march towards a world economy as a precondition of the unification of a revolutionised planet, the palm of leadership was handed over to the strong, energetic, enterprising nations. Of course, not out of a desire to increase their glory, but out of recognition for their role in promoting the ultimate goal of history: the realisation of the equality of all nations in a classless world community. If this meant the denial to relics or embryos of nations in Europe, of the right to free statehood, it entailed as far as the wider world was concerned the total rejection of the historic particularity and traditions of the allegedly stagnant, unhistoric civilisations outside Europe—the vast majority of mankind, subordinating them in practice to the conquering imperialist powers, and then subjecting them to the process of westernisation. The universal goal of the universal liberation of man *per se* took precedence over the irrational sentiments and attachments of the component parts. This again did not mean that the national values of the great nations became ends in themselves. There was just the fact that in a world of unequal development they had shot ahead and had become the effective instruments of history. In this—the idea of totalitarian democracy extended from the single society to the community of races and nations—they were carrying out the deep and true wishes of all members of the human species. If they did that in an unsentimental manner, that was unavoidable. It had to be done by those best equipped for the task. In a letter to Eduard Bernstein of August 9, 1882, Engels wrote: "I have the impression that in the question of Egypt you defend too much the so-called national party. We don't know very much about Arabi Pasha, but one can bet a hundred to one that he is an ordinary pasha who envies the financiers their pickings, because in the good oriental custom, he would like to pocket them himself. We are faced here with the eternal history of the peasant nations. From Ireland to Russia, from Asia Minor to Egypt, the peasant of a peasant nation exists to be exploited. He has been so from the days of the Assyrian and Persian empires. The satrap alias pasha is the principal type of the oriental exploiter, just as the merchant and the lawyer are in the modern West. The repudiation of his debts by the khedive is a very good thing, but the question is—what next? And we, the socialists of Western Europe, we should not easily fall into the trap as the fellahin of Egypt and all the Latins do. It is strange. All the Latin revolutionaries claim to have always made revolution for the good of others—it is very simple: they are always taken in by the slogan 'revolution'. And so, wherever some riot breaks out, wherever it may be, the Latin revolutionaries as a whole offer it their enthusiastic acclaim, without any reservation. In my opinion, we can very well demonstrate our sympathy for the oppressed fellahin, without sharing their momentary illusions (a peasant people has to be deceived for centuries before it can draw the proper lessons from experience), and show our opposition to the brutalities of the English, without having to take the side of their military adversaries at the time. In all questions of international politics, we have to use the organs of the French and Italian parties, soaked in political sentimentality, with the greatest distrust. We, the Germans are, on the contrary, called upon to exercise through a critical approach to these problems the theoretical superiority which we incontestably possess."[104]

And those who possess the most unclouded insight into the laws of history are of course called upon to give the lead, and to lead.

As the chiliastic expectation of an imminent proletarian uprising at the height of the predestined structural crisis of bourgeois capitalist society, and of the international revolutionary breakthrough by way of a chain reaction, began to be replaced by speculations upon international war as midwife of revolution, Marx and Engels continued almost compulsively to visualise the upheaval as coming in the wake of an armed confrontation between Tsarist Russia and the rest of Europe. Sometimes the accent was upon an ideological clash between the forces of progressive change and the bastion of despotic reaction; on other occasions the conflict was considered in terms of a struggle of the European states against a power incorrigibly set upon world domination. As this scheme appeared to become more and more complicated both by power alignments which made it unlikely, and by the spread of nationalist sentiment in the working classes, above all in Germany, Marx and Engels grew very apprehensive about, on the one hand, the position of Germany as the country with the most advanced civilisation and leading Social-Democratic movement, and on the other, the terrible position into which the workers' parties would in case of war be placed by the dichotomy of "my country right or wrong" and the principle of international proletarian unity and solidarity.

The only hope of escaping these predicaments was being offered to them by the prospects of a revolution in Russia itself. They never, however, envisaged the Russian revolution as taking the lead in unchaining revolutions outside its borders or offering a model to the Western countries. The very guarded admission that the old peasant commune might become a nucleus of a socialist transformation of Russia, once the revolutionary upheaval had got on the way there, was clearly conditional upon the outbreak and spread of revolution in the West and the aid and example given to the Russians by its more advanced working classes, which would have again meant Germany.

Part II

THE EMANCIPATION OF THE PROLETARIAT AND THE
NATIONAL DESTINY — WILHELMINE GERMANY

TWO CASTS OF MIND

The historian concerned with the confrontation between Left and Right, between internationalist revolutionism and the national sentiment in the Social-Democratic movement at the turn of the century, cannot do better than start his quest by bringing into relief the encounter between Rosa Luxemburg and Eduard Bernstein.[1]

It was the rise of the New Left that awakened popular interest in Rosa Luxemburg and released a flood of publications, some scholarly studies, much of it propaganda. Before that, she was an embarrassing subject to all parties, except for a few non-conformist Marxists who had befriended her and were deeply affected by her tragic end.[1a]

It was impossible to deny her on the morrow of her assassination the aura of revolutionary martyrdom, particularly after Lenin had eulogised her as an eagle of revolution.[2] Under Stalin, however, orthodox communists were not allowed to forget the strictures which she voiced as early as 1903, on the Leninist conception of a revolutionary party as a wholly centralised and elitist vanguard, nor her dire warnings in 1918 that the Bolshevik dictatorship was in danger of degenerating into an oppressive rule of the few over the many.[3] The Social-Democrats in the West remembered only too well Rosa's implacable condemnation of the Second International for its traitorous abandonment of the cause of proletarian internationalism in World War I. The German Social-Democratic party wavered between furious condemnation of Rosa Luxemburg's part in the fateful split of the German working class movement, and the growing sense of guilt for having connived in her murder by Right-wing freebooters in January 1919.

In her native Poland and in the newly created states around, Rosa's name was almost taboo between the two wars, due to her relentless struggle against nationalism and her staunch denial of the right of national self-determination. To Nazis and Fascists she was a most welcome addition to their rogues' gallery of Jewish-Marxist poisoners of Nordic life. Jewish Jews, as distinct from non-Jewish Jews—to use the late Isaac Deutscher's vocabulary—fought shy of a member of their race who was totally, and even contemptuously alienated from anything Jewish, and whose memory was grist to the mills of anti-semitic propaganda. Yet the socialists among them were not entirely free from a yearning pride and from that ancient hushed reverence for any true

believer who went to his death for the sake of the cause.
The standard of Rosa Luxemburg was symbolically raised in early
May 1968, when the rebel students at the University of Nanterre re-
christened one of the university halls with her name.[4]

That revulsion from the spectacle of a revolutionary creed
perverted into an oppressive bureaucracy which brought the New Left
into being, also revived the legend of Rosa Luxemburg as the
theoretician of revolutionary spontaneity and prophetess of a universal
revolution.

Chapter One

TWO CASTS OF MIND—ROSA LUXEMBURG AND EDUARD BERNSTEIN

What was it that moved Rosa Luxemburg, was the secret of her extraordinary intensity, her self-dedication and unflagging consistency;
made her a unique case and yet a representative of a wider tendency? It
seems to me that the key is to be found in a short passage in her early
pamphlet, "Social Reform or Revolution?", written at the turn of the
century against Eduard Bernstein's Revisionist heresy.

"The secret of Marx's theory of value, of his analysis of money, of his
theory of capital, of his teaching on the profit rate, and therefore of the
whole of his economic system, is [his faith in] the transitory nature of
capitalist economy, its [inevitable final] collapse, and thus—and this is
only the other side of the same coin—in the socialist final goal. Precisely
and only because Marx a priori approached capitalist economy as a
socialist from the historical point of view, was he able to decipher its
hieroglyphics; and because he made the socialist standpoint into his
point of departure for the scientific analysis of bourgeois society, he was
conversely in a position to prove socialism scientifically."[5]

This comes very close to saying that it was Marx's refusal or
inability to conceive that injustice and irrationality—capitalism—could
go on indefinitely, in other words his compulsive need for a rational and
just dénouement to the historic drama, that started him off assembling
evidence that this was sure to happen. The postulate pursued with
unabating zeal and rigour gained enough power to turn the pieces of the

puzzle into indispensable parts of a cogent, iron-clad whole, of a vision of a historical process moving in a preordained manner towards a final goal.

The debate between Rosa and Bernstein is one of those rare cases where the antagonists are not speaking at cross purposes, indeed address themselves to the same issues, make use of more or less the same data, yet are driven inexorably to reach opposite conclusions. The two represent two different worlds, two mutually exclusive casts of mind.[6]

Rosa is hypnotised by the *Endziel,* the final aim; Bernstein considers dwelling on the ultimate to be a form of madness. It was according to him the undoing of Marx. That great thinker suffered from a duality which he was unable to reconcile, or to overcome. He was an economic analyst and historian of unsurpassed genius. But his resolve and grandiose power of laying bare historical and social realities were vitiated by his prophetic, messianic urge to prove that the salvationist solution was an inevitable outcome of the historic process, of the iron laws of history. The scholar in Marx became aware that it was not in his power to provide that proof, and this, according to Bernstein, was why he never finished the third volume of *Das Kapital.* Colloquially speaking, he just could not make it, and this not for reasons of health or weariness of age.[7]

If to Rosa the dialectic was the key to all history and to the understanding of reality, Bernstein regarded it as a trap: "the perfidious element of the Marxist doctrine, the pitfall, the obstacle barring the way to every logical conception of things".[8] To cite his other much quoted saying, he was not at all interested in the inevitable end: all that mattered to him was the movement. To that Rosa replied that: "the movement as such, without reference to the *Endziel,* the movement as an end in itself is nothing to me, the *Endziel* is everything.... There was no more practical question than of the *Endziel....* it remains the soul of the struggle.... the conquest of political power."[9]

As we have said, the implications of the contrast between these two approaches are enormous. It is not only a question of whether the socialist revolution was the inevitable outcome of the historical dialectic or only a moral postulate, an ethical imperative. The fundamental divergence extends to the realm of epistemology and ethics, and—as we shall see presently—determines evaluations of concrete situations and shapes modes of action. Philosophers had for centuries been grappling with the question of whether the reality of the whole gave all their meaning to the component parts and fixed their place and significance, or whether the general concept was an inductive product of sensations, associations of ideas, the force of habit. In the case under review, the totality was not a reality in space, but a process of becoming which was strenuously driving to some climax, dénouement, final form. The parts and components were not entities or situations in themselves, fixed, stable and stationary. For there were no stationary things, all was becoming, and in permanent flux; every situation was a moment in the movement, in the evolution of the whole, which was in a state of incessant change. All events were acts in the drama of tension and struggle between forces rising and coming to replace over-ripe ones, soon in their turn to be overtaken by newcomers.

Where was authentic reality to the historian—and if it be agreed that all modern ideologies were at bottom philosophies of history—how will the historian, and for that matter the political leader, decipher the real, the significant in the welter of events? Should he cling to the idea of the drive towards a final goal, a dénouement, he would then be bound to regard the driving force as sweeping with it, swallowing up, assimilating, turning everything into grist to its mill; and to treat as unreal, irrelevant, insignificant those data and happenings which refuse integration, because of their, to his scheme, recalcitrant nature, accidental character, freakish uniqueness or arbitrariness. The last will be to him just refuse or scum, or he will assure us that at a closer look they were in fact, though only indirectly, a function of the substance. And as regards the seemingly unpredictable behaviour of wilful men, he will not deny that different men pulled in different directions, but will claim that since they were striving to take opposite courses, they will end by cancelling each other out. The dialectic alone will remain as the decisive force.

The historian or political theorist who eschews teleology will see historical reality as a confluence of an infinite number of heterogeneous factors, often sheer accidents, and of causes which were mostly unsurveyable in their interaction. The dialectic will be to him a deceiving simplification, a Procrustean bed, indeed a perverting influence.[12]

From a slightly different angle we find ourselves thrown back upon the ancient problem of the one and the many. The idea of the one, the absolute, the transcendental, is the begetter of asceticism and the seed-bed of mysticism. It is bound to treat the here and now, the concrete and the immediate, the contingent and the peculiar as ephemeral, indeed harmful to the pursuit of the goal that really matters. It will thus help to alienate the concrete man and the living generation from their real life, immediate needs, subjective worries: actual conditions of existence. Furthermore, where empirical data are not, for all their chaotic variety and incoherence, taken for granted, where trial and error procedures are denied overriding validity, and all is subordinated to the march towards the final goal, we are at once faced with the old moralistic casuistry about the end and the means, and in the case of determined revolutionaries such as Rosa Luxemburg we shall find ourselves enmeshed in the tension between the faith in historical inevitability, and the idea of revolutionary spontaneity and voluntaristic activism.

Chapter Two

REVOLUTIONARY ORTHODOXY AND REFORMIST HERESY

As we know, Bernstein concluded from the empirical data of the two or three preceding decades in German history that there were no signs that capitalist economy was heading towards a catastrophe. The phenomenal economic advance; the absence of the expected cyclical crisis; the steady improvement of the workers' conditions; the failure of the middle classes to shrink and to disappear, on the contrary their growth due to the emergence of new non-proletarian occupations; the dispersal of ownership through joint-stock facilities, instead of its alleged monopolisation by a handful of persons; the role of cartels and trusts in planning and regulating the economy; the role of the modern world-wide credit system and of the new revolutionary means of communication in averting or containing an incipient economic crisis—all these suggested to Bernstein that capitalism was not on the way out, but was learning to cope with and adjust itself to the difficulties which had beset it in its infancy.[13]

Rosa's rejoinder constitutes a lesson in the workings of materialist dialectics in history, and it contains the germs of all her future teachings. Rosa tries to put Bernstein to shame for his failure to understand the very nature of capitalism. By its very definition capitalism was being goaded on by an insatiable, never-ending drive to produce and over-produce through the exploitation of resources and labour. Owing to the gap between the ever growing pace of commodity production and the flagging capacity of the workers to consume (many of them being made redundant by advancing technology and the shrinking rate of capitalist profit), are created those gluts which engender unemployment, crisis and poverty in the midst of plenty. Bernstein—says Rosa—regarded crises not as tokens of the dysfunction of the basic structure, but as contingencies, mishaps, bad luck. He refused to see that the periodic crises were a necessity as well as a testing time for capitalism: an opportunity and a challenge to revitalise itself, to throw off obsolete habits and jettison failures, to overhaul its techniques and methods, to adjust itself to changing conditions. In brief, the crisis was an occasion for another leap forward through the seizure of new sources of raw

74

materials and the discovery of new classes and new regions and populations to exploit.[14]

With his narrow horizon confined to a single generation in a single country, in fact to that of an individual entrepreneur, Bernstein—Rosa claims—was unable to perceive that while the crises of the past were the infant illnesses of a still immature, fragmentary capitalism, history was in fact even then bringing near the final catastrophic crisis of capitalism. Having in the process of the international imperialist scramble reached the confines of the earth, capitalism had nowhere to go. No further resources and populations were at hand for it to refuel and to resume expansion. The exploitable world having become truly one, and polarised into global capitalist imperialism and a universal proletariat, the prophecies of Marx and Engels on the final dénouement of a world history that was a single whole, were coming to fruition.[15]

Rosa Luxemburg is concerned with the schema, and not with details and technicalities. So she does not bother for instance in all her writings to analyse the situation of German peasantry, or for that matter of peasants elsewhere except for the vaguest generalities about their eventual voluntary and enlightened renunciation of the private for co-operative modes of production, and about the abolition of age-old differences between agriculture and industry. The emergence of such new separate economic groups as technicians and white-collar workers remains unnoticed. Even social relations are not analysed by her. Purely economic determinism, or rather the allegedly preordained dynamics of industrial development, were all that mattered to Rosa Luxemburg. The division between Catholics and Protestants, to cite one example, never reaches her consciousness as having any significance. There were only a proletariat one and indivisible; and an undifferentiated bourgeoisie, just a single reactionary mass. No allowances are made for the peculiar interests, traditions, habits, preferences, prejudices, different political allegiances of the component parts of either. And the proletariat, or let us say the real proletariat, were industrial workers. When it came to the crunch, all historic reality was distilled into the inevitable apocalyptic confrontation between capitalism and socialism, each one of them swallowing up the respective fellow-travellers, the hangers-on, the interlopers, those elements suspended between different worlds.

Rosa Luxemburg remains glued to Marx's surplus value theory in its generalised form of the compounded body of capitalist employers appropriating the surplus produced by the compounded mass of hired labour. Bernstein is very much under the influence of the marginal utility theory.[16] He readily acknowledges that at all times some people exploit other people. But he refuses to speak of value determined solely by labour's effort to produce it, especially in Marx's universalised form. That is an abstraction. Use value, market value, which is all that matters to him, is determined by a great variety of factors: diverse kinds of land, therefore different rent rates, shifts of population, changes in social psychology, in consumers' preferences and tastes, pressure by guilds and trade unions and so on. As a confirmed reductionist Rosa Luxemburg focuses on the sole single factor—that of the profit motive which, as it were, could be cut away with one stroke. To this Bernstein replies: "When we deal with great masses of men such as the modern nations, with their life habits formed in course of millenarian evolution, it is impossible to expect either a profound revolution in the mode of property or a rapid metamorphosis in human nature; and the less so as the relations of production and property constitute only a part of the social milieu which has the determining effect upon human character."[17]

The postulate of the inevitability and the imminence of the global confrontation, of the collapse of capitalism and the arrival of revolutionary socialism, that a priori thinking which Rosa applauded in Marx, determines her repudiation of Bernstein's interpretation of recent economic developments.

Bernstein—as we have said—pinned his hopes on the expansion of joint stock, new credit facilities and cartels and trusts to prevent or stop crisis. On the contrary, those developments were calculated—argued Rosa—to hasten the collapse of capitalism, moreover on a global scale. They excited the passion for gambling and risk in wider and wider circles, and in all countries at the same time. Not only did the vast armies of small shareholders not become co-owners and participants in decision-making, but they were reduced to vassals and potential victims of the arch-speculators, the tiny oligarchy of heads of corporations, directors and managers. The result was not the dispersal of property, but its extreme concentration. The old contradiction between social forms of production and a system of private property had now received an additional twist: both production and property were growing more socialised, but distribution—of dividends—retained all the features of individual property. The latter was rendered all the more vulnerable for that. In view of the intricate connection between the various branches of the economy in what had become a single world economy and of the monopolistic character of highly advanced late capitalism, a crisis that broke out in one sector in a single country, was in the heightened atmosphere of gambling for quick and big profits sure to drag all other branches down with it. The tremors would develop into an earthquake.

The mass of shareholders and ordinary people would be seized by panic. The crash would have millions of victims all over the world. A succession of such failures was bound to pull the whole edifice down.[18]

Bernstein had been trying to show that in the democratic modern state it had become possible for workers' parties, trade unions, co-operatives, socialist representatives in parliaments and municipal bodies, to secure a steady improvement of workers' living conditions, social legislation, higher wages, the closing of social gaps. Europe was going through a process of transforming political into social democracy, of the gradual evolution of the capitalist economy into socialism—by way of objective developments, legislation, persuasion, moral pressure, appeal to long-term interest and to conscience. The liberal-democratic nation-state or national community had become the arbiter between the classes, a kind of overlord of the national economy, resisting and curbing the selfish greed of anti-social elements. Taxation, municipalisation, nationalisation, on top of the strict enforcement of fair play and the regulatory functions of the state—all these would gradually bring into being a socialist society as the inevitable fruit of genuine democracy.[19]

To Rosa Luxemburg the struggle for electoral success and trade union achievements had no other significance than that of being occasions for workers to become mobilised and activised. They were important only as injections of proletarian consciousness, means of political training, manifestations of strength. Their great value was precisely in offering convincing proof to the workers that none of these palliatives was capable of changing fundamentally their position as wage-earners, of securing to them their due share of the good things of life, of changing their condition as passive objects of the decisions and acts of the privileged. Through collective bargaining the trade unions had simply become allies of the mammoth enterprises in fleecing the consumers.

The greatest service rendered by non-revolutionary activities was in the frustrations they occasioned, in the lessons which they taught—that only the seizure of political power by a proletarian dictatorship was capable of effecting a genuine and lasting transformation. The whole value of the trade unions—which of course had no power to determine production, no share in fixing prices and no influence on application of technology—lay in showing that in the last analysis their labours were the exertions of a Sysiphus—a phrase which the bosses of the vast trade unions, proud of their membership of millions and their signal achievements in hard bargaining and in the painstaking husbanding of their assets, never forgave Rosa. Without the *Endziel* in view—and in sight—

as a definite and near goal, all those institutions and achievements were just props to ageing capitalism, tranquillisers designed to emasculate worker militancy, occasions for some intellectual careerists from the petit bourgeoisie to engage in parliamentary cretinism, and to capitalist interests acting from behind the scenes possibilities to manipulate proletarian consciousness and brainwash the workers.[20]

The reformist approach (according to Rosa Luxemburg) made the fatal mistake of believing and making others believe that voting and fair play were capable of causing a deeply entrenched class enemy to give up willingly its possessions, privileges and power. Only those who had lost all notion and all feeling for the reality of class war were capable of believing that, when it came to the crunch, and the haves saw their positions slipping away, they would not jettison all parliamentary democratic principles and resort to a Bonapartist (or what in the twentieth century has come to be called a Fascist) coup, in order to put the morally and materially disarmed and drugged workers into chains. Rosa recalls Lassalle's view on the futility of laws, decrees, formal resolutions and agreements as compared with the all-determining reality of social forces. If the former had some value in the feudal age, they had lost all importance in bourgeois society. Labour relations and class struggle found no mention in its codes, but they were all-pervasive. Even bourgeois victory over feudalism was not embodied in parchments, but in social-economic ascendancy.[21]

Reforms had value only as a function of the revolutionary resolve. It was wrong to consider revolution and social reforms as opposites. They were different phases and methods in the single revolutionary struggle. The reformist gains were not ends in themselves: only stepping stones, improvements in the combatants' position, or tokens of another victorious advance towards the revolution, and when revealed as nugatory—injections of class militancy. Ultimately social reforms were the way in which the revolutions with which all history was punctuated worked themselves out. Bernstein—Rosa argues—saw parliamentary democracy as the apex of history. But it was only a passing phase in the development of capitalism, a function of the needs of struggle against absolutism and feudalism. By now the bourgeois and the Junker had become bedfellows.

In the same way as Jaurès, Bernstein would not portray the struggle between the socialist proletariat and the liberal bourgeoisie as a war between the children of light and the sons of darkness. The coming of socialism was envisaged by him not as a knockout victory achieved by the proletarians over the capitalists, but as a gradual flowering, or rather as the ripening of a purified common humanistic tradition, cleansed of the squalor of backward barbarity. It was not to be the fruit of the workings of the iron laws of historic inevitability, but the result of an ethical resolve to will and do the good, in the spirit of Bernstein's famous dictum, "from cant to Kant", from Hegel's dialectic to Kant's categorical imperative.

Rosa argues back that the objective developments of late high capitalism had been accentuating the class character of the state, instead of the bourgeois state gradually evolving into a social state. The government did not regulate the cartels: the cartels were manipulating the political establishment. Capitalist exploitation had shed all the patriarchal personal features it might once have had and become wholly impersonal. In the past high tariffs, national wars and labour protection were to some extent influenced by the desire to create and protect a nascent national economy for the sake of the nation. But the customs barriers and armies in the age of imperialism were the weapons of rapacious, selfish capitalist interests and feudal landlords. Neither democratic parliamentarism nor social legislation were of any use to predatory imperialist capitalism bent no longer upon building a modern nation state, but upon imperialist expansion.[22] Rather they were an impediment: "The relations of production of capitalist society are coming closer and closer to socialist forms; its political and legal forms however are erecting a steadily higher wall between capitalist and socialist society. That wall is not being pierced by the development of social forms and democracy, but is on the contrary growing more impregnable and firmer. The only thing by which it can be torn down is the hammer blow of revolution, that is to say the conquest of political power by the proletariat."[23]

Rosa Luxemburg never tires of emphasising the total and absolute abyss separating the proletariat and the bourgeoisie "in the domain of human relations, in the field of ethics, artistic conceptions, education". While each camp invokes democracy, the same words "hide a total divergence as to contents and political action."[24]

Bernstein spoke with contempt of revolutionary romanticism. Far from being the great fulfilment, revolutionary violence was a regression into archaic barbaric ways of resolving conflicts. He depicted the dictatorship of the proletariat as the advent of demagogical adventurers, cliques with no political experience or sense of respon-sibility. Rosa was incensed by Bernstein's rejection of the "spiritual axis of crystallisation"—the guidance offered by the "organic totality of a consistent Weltanschauung"[25]—the dialectical idea of the oneness of history and the inevitable unfolding and dénouement of the historic drama of class struggle. Bernstein's teachings were tearing history to pieces. There was no purposeful, rational direction, no coherent striving, no terminal. There were just rich and poor, people who had good luck and failures with bad luck, good times and evil days, all a matter of chance. He did not believe in the organic, indivisible totality of capitalism. He did not believe in an objective historic process, there were only pious wishes; no iron laws of history, merely arbitrary fanciful hopes of individuals. Bernstein was taking away all hope from the disinherited. He was also slandering the working classes and their leaders. He was above all, depriving history of its grandeur and majesty. He was preaching capitulation, accommodation with capitalism, acceptance of the eternal reign of evil, irrationality and falsehood. Through his advocacy of reconciliation and his renunciation of class struggle, Bernstein was turning Social-Democracy into a left-wing liberal party, and degrading the SPD from the agent of a historic destiny into a bastard child of German reaction.[26] "The discussion with Bernstein has become a reckoning between two world views, two classes, two social systems. Bernstein and Social-Democracy stand now on entirely different planes."[27]

There is grandeur in Rosa Luxemburg's faith in anthropromorphic history. "*Au fond* the things which act and force a decision," wrote Rosa to Luise Kautsky on April 15, 1917, "are the great invisible forces of the great deep, and finally everything falls into its proper place of its own accord. . . . History always knows better than anyone how to get out of a situation which seems to be an impasse."[28] A year earlier she wrote to Klara Zetkin of the objective logic of history, which indefatigably accomplishes its work. "Madame History" was mocking the German trade union bureaucrats who "stood guard at the gates of trade union happiness".[29] "History, which knows how to sweep away the heaviest rocks from its course will also know how to lift our present burdens."[30]

Rosa Luxemburg is unimaginable without the call for strenuous voluntary activism and at the same time insistence on mass spontaneity. One can only speak here of a Calvinian temper, which combined faith in predestination with ardent and incessant activity. The unfolding imperatives of history must, according to her, first penetrate human consciousness, fire the will of men in order to be fulfilled in a spirit of irresistible élan and in an inevitable manner. If Rosa denies the possibility of arbitrary modes of action, she is also emphatic about Marxism not being a dogma laid down forever and for all situations. It was always necessary to consider the concrete circumstances and act accordingly. We shall return to this topic. What matters to us at this moment is to emphasise not merely the vision of the oneness, continuity and rationality of history as world history, but also Rosa's indignant realisation that Bernstein's revisionism was denying this all-important idea: more precisely that it pitted national local histories against universal history. This meant a relativisation of the ideal of the final single historical dénouement. The myth of the nation was being put above the universal dialectic. The hidden spring of the revisionist heresy was thus nationalism. Ergo, the latter was the real enemy. The question may however be put differently. Was not precisely Rosa's passionate aversion to nationalism the mainspring of her vision of the oneness of history, of the dialectic, of the world revolution, instead of her anti-nationalism being the function of her total commitment to revolutionary internationalism?

Writing in 1904 against Lenin, Rosa Luxemburg said "the more we discover the same fundamental traits of social democracy in all the variety of social milieux in which it dwells, the more conscious we become of the essential, fundamental principles common to the whole of the social-democratic movement.[31]

Such was the supreme reality of the oneness and identity of the all-embracing issue between capitalism and socialism all over the globe. As we have said, Rosa Luxemburg was not interested in and had no patience with the details, the special local circumstances or technicalities of the revolutionary breakthrough, of the passage from the capitalist to the socialist economy, nor for instance in the organisational sides of the general strike. The conceptual framework, the basic principles and the inevitable subjective disposition resulting from an 'objective' ripening of conditions were all that mattered to her.

Chapter Three

THE PORTRAIT OF AN INTERNATIONALIST REVOLUTIONARY AS A YOUNG WOMAN

What kind of person was the remarkable woman with that cast of mind, drunk with faith in an *Endziel*? What was the background from which she came and the people whom she was so strenuously endeavouring to goad into action? What was the latter's response and how did the encounter affect her stand and shape her attitudes in later days?

Rosa Luxemburg was born in 1870 to Jewish parents in the little Polish town of Zamosc, the cradle of the powerful and enlightened Counts Zamojski. The most famous member of the family, the Chancellor of King Stephan Batory, had in the late sixteenth century turned the dependency into a lovely Renaissance show piece. In the nineteenth century, Russian-dominated Zamość was in a sense a border town. It lay between the kingdom of Poland set up by the Congress of Vienna and the old Polish provinces which, on account of their Greek-Orthodox Ukrainian and Byelo-Russian majority, had been incorporated into Russia proper on the one hand, and Polish-Ukrainian Galicia under Austrian rule on the other. By the standards of the poverty-ridden mass of Jewish petty bourgeois, who formed the bulk of the town's population, the parents of Rosa were middle class and rather assimilated to Polish culture. They were also tinged by strong German influence, to which Jews, especially those, whom—like Rosa's father—trade in timber and wheat would take to Danzig or even Berlin, were highly susceptible. When Rosa was still a child, the parents moved from Zamosc to Warsaw. There the family's ties with the Jewish environment were loosened still further. Rosa went to a Polish Catholic *gymnasium*, receiving no Jewish education and being kept away from Jewish religious traditions and practices. All the Luxemburg children attended college and took up free professions. With all her later cosmopolitan existence, bitter hatred of nationalism and disdain for anything Jewish, Rosa retained throughout her life, in spite of long separation and only very occasional short meetings with members of her family, close affectionate ties with them. In a typical Jewish way she remained very concerned about their health and fortunes, feeling a strong sense of duty to help them financially when in need, though she herself was very seldom free from financial worries.

While still a student in the girls' high school, Rosa was swept into revolutionary activities. After having finished school, she decided to go west. She was smuggled out across the German border in a cart, hidden under a heap of straw, aided by a Catholic priest, who was told that the Jewish girl was running away from home in order to get baptised. Rosa made her way to Switzerland and embarked there upon her university studies. She also joined the hive of Eastern European students, émigrés and revolutionaries, Poles, Russians and Jews, with their endless meetings, disputations, controversies, splits and clashes, and the mass production of revolutionary journals, brochures, leaflets and other literature to be smuggled into the Tsarist Empire.

Rosa was an industrious and brilliant student, gobbling up whatever she could from her teachers and reading all she could lay her hands upon, but measuring everything with the Marxist yardstick. She wrote a learned doctoral dissertation on the industrial development of nineteenth-century Poland. In spite of being already up to her ears in the anti-patriotic Polish Socialist group, Rosa decided to make Germany her home in order to be active in the most powerful, most advanced and in every way leading Social-Democratic party of Europe, in the mightiest state of Europe. For that purpose she had to become a German citizen. She did that by contracting a marriage of convenience with the (unwilling) son of a German Social-Democratic couple who befriended her. And so she became Frau Lubeck, although husband and wife departed separately from the registry office and, it seems, never met again. Years after, a formal divorce was arranged.

Rosa was of short stature, and when speaking from the floor in large assemblies would stand on a chair so that she might be seen. She also had a slight limp, as a result of an unsuccessful operation in her childhood. She was not good-looking, had strong Jewish features, especially the nose, a very mobile face and very expressive eyes. With all her intellect-ualism and socialist ardour, she was by no means indifferent to how she looked and how she dressed. Her letters to her lover, Jogiches, abound with details about the frocks and the hats she was acquiring and with worries about the effects of overwork and ailments on her appearance. She could also describe a meal with every detail and boast of her own culinary feats. There was nothing bohemian about her tastes. She liked her home to be orderly, clean and well furnished, kept regular hours and was very meticulous in her accounts of income and expenses.

Rosa Luxemburg was a woman of extraordinary talents and attain-ments, a dynamo of nervous energy and a person of a phenomenally rich and complex nature. She was at home in three cultures, Polish, German and Russian; spoke French well; could read English and manage Italian;

and had of course studied the ancient languages at school. She could recite poetry by the yard in several languages, and was familiar with all the major literatures of Europe; and her letters, writings and her German speeches contain quotations from Goethe, Heine, Möricke and other poets. She translated Korolenko's autobiography into German and she loved Polish poetry. She drew and painted with skill. She was passionately fond of music, and had a discerning taste for opera. She was deeply interested in botany and geology, collecting flowers, plants and stones whenever and wherever she could. From her prison cell she would watch birds, and her letters from holidays are full of detailed, tender and poetic descriptions of nature and the changes of seasons.[32]

She was at the same time a political animal to the very core of her being. She would describe herself as an economist. Her longest and most ambitious book, in a sense the only one she wrote—as distinct from pamphlets and collected lectures and articles—was indeed her opus on *The Accumulation of Capital* published in 1913.[33] She was first and last a publicist. Marx, as she put it, took her breath away by the gigantic power and dimensions of his theorectical achievement in all three: philosophy, economics and political thought. Rosa wrote with great verve, and picturesquely, arguing her case with much force, consistency and skill. She had wit, and she excelled in turning out a fine aphorism and striking a felicitous phrase which could serve as a slogan or motto. Everything she wrote is suffused with passion, in both its poetic and rousing eloquence as well as in its mordant irony and invective.

No wonder that before she reached the age of thirty, only a year or two after she had settled in Germany, and notwithstanding her foreign accent, she became a household member of the upper crust of the SPD leadership—August Bebel, Karl Kautsky, Paul Singer, Franz Mehring, not to mention the lesser, but very influential men such as Ignaz Auer, Schönlank, Stadthagen, Haenisch and others—and a publicist and orator known and appreciated all over Germany.

The German Social-Democratic party suffered from a scarcity of intellectuals. Its press, above all the leading organ the *Vorwärts*, was irretrievably dull. Engrossed in practical politics, the party had long ago forfeited all intellectual curiosity, not to speak of creative originality, although it continued to enjoy the tremendous prestige not only of the largest, best-organised working class party in Europe, with the brightest prospects of reaching power in the foreseeable future, but also as the movement with the best claim to guide all other Labour parties in Europe in elaboration of theory as well as in practical politics. Against such a background Rosa Luxemburg rose like a meteor, at first employed as an election speaker in the Polish-speaking areas, being in this particularly welcome to the German party leadership for her anti-separatist and anti-nationalist stand and for her fierce partisanship of a unified super-national Labour party. Very soon she emerged as the most eloquent and keenest warrior against reformist revisionism.

From the very start she faced the veteran leaders as equals. Not only was she not overawed by elderly men with famous names and a lifetime of service and achievement, but in her letters, especially to Jogiches, she poked fun at them and had hardly a good word for any of them, grumbling at the waste of time and boredom caused by their noisy parties and unexpected visits.[34] Did she not by way of repartee say to a company of top leaders that the only two men among them were she and Klara Zetkin?[35] Rosa Luxemburg, in fact, disliked Germany and the Germans, although she revered their literature. It never seemed to have bothered her that there was something incongruous in the fact that she, only a recently naturalised alien, with a foreign accent, was agitating in a country seething with nationalist passion, for extreme socialist ·policies and taking up what was by very many held as anti-national stances. She was not as it were conscious of acting in a distinct country—Germany. She was serving the cause of socialism in a certain branch of the international working class. Her fatherland was the world revolution, which recognised no territorial divisions.

More than that, and we shall return to the point in another context, she does not seem to have been in the least bothered by the thought of her Jewishness in this respect. There is hardly a single reference to German anti-semitism in all her writings and even confidential letters. On the eve of the Hanover party conference, after she had lived for only two years in Germany, she reports to Jogiches about the agenda of the conference, and remarks thst no speaker had as yet been designated for the subject of militarism. In reply, Jogiches suggests to her that she should come forward as a candidate. She rejects his idea impatiently, sensibly pointing out that she was too recent a recruit and was not sufficiently familiar with the matter.[36] But she does not give a thought at all to any possibility that eyebrows might be raised and people complain that the inevitable tirade against the militarism and the expansionism of official Germany was being delivered by a foreign Jewess.

Quite early, the young woman gained a terrific sense of her powers and ascendancy. There are in her letters to Jogiches expressions, which very much recall the words written by Disraeli, after his first visit to the gallery of the House of Commons, that he felt sure he could outshine them all.[37] Rosa was indeed soon hailed as the most prominent exponent of Marxism, as a second Marx, as the best public speaker of the party, with a clear and strong voice. She attracted overflow audiences. They listened with rapt attention to her close but very clear reasoning, reacting enthusiastically to her flights of passion and with hilarity to her witicisms and quick repartees. "That small slight woman," wrote Max Adler, "did not cease to hold her listeners at the party congress under her spell. . . . Never did her intelligence lose control over her temperament, and so the fire of revolution which she always expressed was mixed with cool reflection."[38] The highly sophisticated Emile Vandervelde remembered Rosa's appearance at the Zurich congress of the International in 1893, when she was only twenty-three: "She defended her case with such magnetism in her eyes and with so much fire in her words that the whole congress was captivated and spellbound."[39]

There are Promethean accents in her utterances. Soon after the outbreak of the February revolution in Russia, she writes from her prison to Luise Kautsky of her regret not to be in a position "to assemble the sparks which are bursting forth there, to help direct things in Russia and also elsewhere. . . . As soon as the possibility is offered, I will hasten to put my ten fingers upon the world's piano and there will be some fine resonance."[40]

But there was another side to her contacts with people. She was twice appointed editor, first to the *Sachsische Arbeiter-Zeitung*, an important organ in a socialist stronghold, the second time at the *Vorwarts*. She lasted in the former for one month, in the latter for two months.[41] Her co-editor, the learned biographer of Marx and author of the history of the German socialist movement, Franz Mehring, a man of high moral principles who did not hesitate to brand Marx's treatment of Bakunin as cruel and mean, one of the very few top spokesmen of the SPD to join the Communist party later, wrote to Karl Kautsky to complain of Rosa's "boundless lust for power and filthy greed".[42] She never held a position of executive authority, never sat in GHQ taking decision to act then and there, at least not before she was free to plunge for a brief spell into Spartakist activity after her release from prison at the collapse of Germany in November 1918. The tone of her instructions, reprimands, words of command to her comrades in the tiny Polish splinter party concerning the preparation, transportation and distribution of literature, the stand to be taken up at conferences and in polemics, is that of an unmistakably domineering female who will brook no nonsense and despises irresolute Hamlets. She did not act on impulse, her conviction and ardour were too firm and steady for that. It would however be unfair to cavil and censure her cool calculations and mode of tackling people and situations as sordid scheming.

In addition, and indeed apart from the public, feverishly active Rosa Luxemburg, there was another Rosa, a private, an almost hidden and disguised person, determined to preserve the secret of her private life at all costs. That second Rosa emerges in the correspondence with her comrade and for many years lover, Leon Jogiches, and in her letters, especially from prison in wartime written to Luise Kautsky, Martha Rosenbaum, the Seidels, and her much younger friends—*amitié amoureuse*—Kostia Zetkin, son of her bosom friend Klara, and Hans (Hannes) Diefenbach.[43]

The decisive influence in the life of Rosa, private Rosa, was certainly Jogiches, whom she met in Switzerland when she was twenty-one and he twenty-four, in 1891. Their secret intimate relationship, in all but name marriage though they lived most of the time in different countries, and even when living in the same town, never together in the same apartment, continued until 1906. But the political collaboration and correspondence went on until Rosa's death in January 1919. Jogiches or Tyszka—the most frequently used of his numerous revolutionary pseudonyms—is the model international revolutionary.[44] He came from a wealthy and very cultured Jewish family in Vilna. His father descended from a line of Orthodox *grand bourgeoisie* and his mother was a noted pianist. He devoted all his life and inherited fortune to the cause of revolution. He started his noviciate in the middle 1880's as a leading member of the remarkable Narodnaya Volya circle in Vilna, which was the nursery of prominent revolutionaries of all hues, such as Martov (Cederbaum), at first close comrade[45] and later antagonist of Lenin, the founding fathers of the "Bund" Josif Mill and Arcady Kremer; and Charles Rappaport, the future grand old man of the French Communist party, early friend of Jaurès and Guesde.

From a distance but in close touch with the Vilna group, above all in connection with the abortive plans for an attempt on the life of Tsar Alexander III in 1887, were also Lenin's elder brother, Alexander Ulianov, who paid with his life for his part in the plot, and Josef Pilsudski, the PPS leader and eventually dictator of Poland, and his elder brother Bronislaw. Jogiches was charged with organising the flight of those compromised in the plot whom the police had failed to seize, and he himself escaped to the West in 1890, after a prison term and before being despatched into exile in Turkestan. He had in the meantime come close to Marxism and established contact with the Second "Proleta-riat" in Warsaw.

Jogiches was a born commissar and an obsessive conspirator, with a passion for secrecy, and an artist's love of plotting, underground activity and manipulation from behind the scenes. He never wrote anything. He never appeared in public as a leader or spokesman. Changing his pseudonyms, moving secretly from place to place, he strove to hold in his hands the threads of the political activities of several parties at once. He offered the proud and very egocentric father of Russian Marxism, Plekhanov, a considerable sum of money to start a journal, on condition that he himself would lay down editorial policies—a stipulation which was of course indignantly rejected. The whole plan was therefore given up. After having been a leading activist in the Polish anti-patriotic Socialist party, taken part in the 1905 revolution and worked in the various Russian revolutionary groups, Jogiches ended up as the virtual leader of the conspiratorial Spartakist movement during World War I, and was shot in Berlin "when trying to escape arrest" shortly after the murder of Rosa.[46] Upon Rosa's death, he still managed to send a telegram to Lenin announcing in a single laconic and monumental sentence that "Rosa has terminated her assignment".[47]

This faceless or rather many-faced conspirator is described in Charles Rappaport's memories of the Vilna days[48] as follows: "Jogiches was not liked in revolutionary circles in Vilna, because of his exaggerated conspiratorial behaviour and because of his disdainful manner. I too shared this view of him at first. Jogiches noticed this, and he once told me that he would like to have a special talk with me . . . about his character." "Strong-willed, keen but stubborn, he dedicated himself passionately to revolutionary activity and was truly an excellent conspirator. He established good relations with the smugglers and knew all the ins and outs of border smuggling. Pent up in himself, he was really not so hard as he appeared to be, and he could also be very witty when he wanted to. True, his wit was always sarcastic and venomous. . . . Once all the manuscripts of Lyuba Axelrod ("Orthodox") were nearly burned. Jogiches commented wrily: 'There was really no need to fear. There is enough water in her writings to put out the greatest conflagration'."[49]

The victim of that witticism describes Jogiches in her memoirs as a romantic revolutionary, relishing having broken away from his bourgeois surroundings, in love with the life of the eternal protestor and rebel. Because of his aloofness and lack of intimacy in his contacts with comrades he was nicknamed "Jupiter". Lyuba Axelrod praises Jogiches' subtle brain, great power of observation, love and knowledge of music, his insights into human nature, his oratorical ability and organisational talents. "He was a great conspirator and like every romantic, loved secrecy and conspiracy for its own sake."[50]

Jogiches and Rosa kept their relationship a deep secret. She never even hinted at it, let alone confessed it to, Luise Kautsky, probably the person closest to her after Jogiches, especially after the disastrous end of the intimate relationship with the latter, when Rosa discovered in 1906 that he had betrayed her with another woman. The early period, that of personal intimacy, is covered by 574 out of the total of 776 letters to Jogiches from March 1893 to November 1905. His letters seem to have been irretrievably lost.[51] There were no letters between them in the period when they were both active in the revolution of 1905-6 in Poland and were both arrested on March 4, 1906. When after fourteen months they came together in May in 1907, their relationship broke down. The remaining two hundred letters up to Rosa's death are wholly impersonal and purely political exchanges.

What strikes one most in her letters to Jogiches as well as to her other close personal friends is Rosa's insatiable thirst for life, and the intensity, diversity and changeability of her feelings and moods, so seemingly at odds with the iron tenacity of her political purpose. After having gone through every line of Rosa's correspondence with Jogiches, we still don't know why after all they did not settle down as husband and wife. That in comparison with her own ardour and passion, he was a rather reluctant lover seems certain from his procrastinations, pretexts for delaying meetings, cancelling journeys to her. "Why are you so bad?" is a phrase that recurs quite often in Rosa's letters. "And you could be so good." A "bad" letter makes her bitterly despondent, a good one elicits a flood of gushing affection and sends her spirits soaring.

It is impossible not to be deeply moved and often dismayed by the sentiments of a woman pining for love, uncertain, indeed in her heart of hearts aware of the lack of real reciprocity, dreaming of an idyllic togetherness away from it all in a lonely spot, spinning plans to make their abode a cosy little home, whispering wistfully "Shall I never have a little baby?", while recording an irresistible urge which had seized her the day before to snatch a little child. She kept relating to her lover every detail of her existence, her oratorical triumphs and her migraine and stomach troubles, exaggeratedly lauding his advice, but also often scolding him for his crazy ideas, and above all for his hopeless dithering with his studies and his doctorate. This dynamo of fiery energy, the domineering self-opinionated female, appears terribly vulnerable in her health and in her moods. The fact is, as already hinted, that she was living on her nerves.

What also makes one wonder in that correspondence and letters to other friends is the frequent reflection that she was not really meant for the bustle and noise of politics, but for lonely study and contemplation; the most longed-for thing was a little happiness, a soothing contentment. From letters written on her holidays and in her prison cell there

breathes a capacity and perhaps a strenuously self-conscious determination to savour to the full every possible variety of sensation,
impression, experience, the murmur of the water of the little stream,
the breeze shaking the trees, the shape of the cloud, the sound of a
distant song, the piercing cry of a wounded dog, the literary reminis-
cences, the free association of ideas, images, intimations, from the
quietist pantheistic loving embrace of all creation to ecstatic élan and
also searing indignation.

But there appears in all this anguished will to live a regretful feeling
that real happiness, perhaps reality altogether, was where she was not.
It was out of her reach, somewhere else.[52] Was it a fundamental
uncertainty about her own identity? Was it a lack of ability to take the
immediate and concrete naturally for granted? Was it the result of a
cosmopolitan rootlessness, which came from not being instinctively
anchored to a stable tradition and fixed mode of life? It is hard not to
begin to wonder about the hidden connection between her feeling that
happiness was always somewhere else and that her actual life was not
quite the real one, and the intensity of the passionate faith in a
revolutionary breakthrough, in the salvationist destination where time
would come to a stop, and a timeless reality would be inaugurated.

Chapter Four

THE RESPONSE TO A PROPHET

The truth of the matter was that Rosa Luxemburg was an outsider in Germany, even in the German Social-Democratic party, and an outsider she remained to the end. On one occasion Rosa wrote to Bebel that she realised that she was not regarded as *de la maison*. In 1904 after rejecting an article on Russian terrorism by Rosa, and inviting Plekhanov instead, Kautsky remarked that Rosa Luxemburg was not considered in Germany as genuinely German.[53] The party leadership and still more the rank and file, whom she never really got to know in their normal work and in their daily life, in their modes of reaction and their ideas, lived in a quite different world from hers. The leaders with whom she did establish contact, were quite uncongenial to her, except perhaps for the women like Klara Zetkin and Luise Kautsky. She repeatedly complained or spoke disdainfully of German arrogance and philistinism. It is doubtful whether she felt at ease with any of her comrades, except the Eastern European Jewish exiles or émigrés like Jogiches, Parvus (with whom she had also a brief affair), Warszawski and one or two Poles of her own Polish faction who were active in the German party, and in the international socialist arena, such as Julian Marchlewski and Cezaryna Wojnarovska. Matilda Wurm and Martha Rosenbaum were both Jewesses.

She was at first welcomed with open arms for the services which her freshness, youth and enthusiasm could lend to a movement which was growing but had no longer the vitality of youth. But she soon made herself an awkward customer, to many an embarrassment, to some a pain in the neck. This became clear at the time of the revisionist controversy.

Most of the SPD just did not share, and could hardly sympathise with Rosa's sense of revolutionary urgency.[54] They did not feel so terribly uncomfortable, they certainly did not regard themselves as persecuted outcasts and disinherited paupers. They did not feel their own type of existence was all that provisional. German economy was, as we have said, booming, its industry rapidly overtaking that of the workshop of Europe, old England. Wages were mounting, and the

91

social services and legislation, whatever the counter-revolutionary motives of Bismarck and the others who had initiated them, were the most beneficial to the workers in all Europe.

The population of Germany increased in the years 1870 to 1910 from 26 million to 65 million, and the urban population, which at the beginning of the period formed no more than 36 per cent, constituted on the eve of World War I more than 60 per cent of the total. There was the phenomenally fast growth of large cities: Germany had 48 of them with more than 100,000 inhabitants by 1910. Berlin alone grew from 800,000 in 1870 to over three million inhabitants in 1900.

Early in the period, textiles were still the most important branch of industry, some two-thirds of all German industry; in 1913 metallurgy and mining replaced textiles in that role. Coal production advanced from 34 million tons in 1870 to 290 million in 1913. The production of iron grew from 1,500,000 tons to 19,000,000, which means that by 1914 Germany produced twice the iron of Britain and four times that of France. By 1905 German industry was concentrated in 253 large cartels, of which 92 embraced heavy industry. In 1880 Germany was the fourth largest exporter in the world, in 1913 the second after the United States. The machine industry alone employed, in 1907, 1,120,000 workers, of whom in 1912 68,000 worked for Krupps. Karl Helfferich calculated that the national wealth of Germany increased from 1895 to 1912 from 200 to 300 billion marks, while the national income rose from 21.5 to 40 billion marks in the same years. From 1900 to 1913 the money wage index rose to 133.0 and the index of subsistence to 125.7. It seems, however, that while money wages continued to increase up to the outbreak of the war, real wages and the standard of living were showing some signs of decline by 1910.[55]

The Junker hegemony might be irksome, but it was not unbearably oppressive, after the anti-socialist laws of the Bismarck era were abolished. It was certainly not lawless and arbitrary. Moreover, in the 1890's the Reichstag consistently rejected government motions designed to curb the opposition press and the right of combination and strike.[56] Above all, fortified by the prophecies of the aged Engels,[57] the SPD felt sure that a socialist victory at the polls was inevitable and within sight, since its parliamentary representation was increasing by leaps and bounds at every election to the Reichstag. In 1893 Bebel told a conference that only a very few of those present in the hall would not live to see the final victory.[58] The same Bebel wrote some years after to Kautsky that Parvus, the ally of Rosa, who was agitating so fiercely against Bernstein, did not have the faintest notion of what went on in the minds of the German working class, nor of German realities:

"imagine, he wants us to come out in favour of a violent social revolution".[59] Rosa, whom he admired and liked at first in a kind of fatherly way became "that terrible woman" who could be such a nuisance. He wrote to Kautsky that the Gamaliel of the party could hardly imagine how widespread the dislike of Rosa and Parvus was among the rank and file. "That should not weigh with us. But it was not possible to ignore the fact altogether."[60] There was much sneering in the party about the male and female imports from the East, and a delegate at the Lübeck party conference complained, or should one say menacingly warned, that the strange methods and arrogant aggressiveness of Parvus were likely to spread anti-semitism. It was not the German way to strip old respected leaders naked before the world.[61]

The plain truth is that Alexander Israel Helphand (Parvus) was cast for the role of the sinister Jew in anti-semitic demonology.[62] Born and raised in deep misery in the Russian pale as a child of a family pursued by pogroms and hunger, he succeeded in making his way to the West, finishing his studies in Switzerland, and settling in Germany—if the life of a passportless unwanted alien, without permanent domicile and with no permit to reside, expelled from Land to Land, and with no steady income and with periods of starvation, could be called settled. In spite of these disadvantages, and notwithstanding his repulsive appearance, nervous and noisy restlessness, reckless behaviour towards people and carelessness about money, and venomous tongue and pen, Parvus gained soon the reputation of the best brain of the Second International and its finest economist, best informed expert in international affairs and discerning connoisseur of world literature. He was dreaded and abhorred, and yet held in very high esteem.

This most radical of revolutionaries then emerged overnight as a millionaire, when he was sent as war correspondent to cover the Balkan wars and took the opportunity to launch out as a supplier of arms to all belligerents. With the outbreak of World War I, the prophet of revolutionary internationalism turned into a fanatical German nationalist. He started an ultra-chauvinist publication called *Die Glocke*, obtained a virtual monopoly of the trade with the neutral Scandinavain countries and became the confidential and much listened to adviser of the Wilhelmstrasse and the High Command on Russian affairs; he was also in charge of channelling secret funds to Russia and fomenting defeatist propaganda, strikes and disturbances there. Parvus had an important share in securing Lenin's passage to Russia in the famous sealed train across the German lines. But Parvus, who did so much to take his revenge on his persecutors in Russia and to bring Tsarism down with German help, in the hope of hastening the longed for revolution in

Russia, refused to acknowledge the October revolution as the fulfillment of his dreams. He developed an implacable hatred for the Soviet
Union and drew close to Ebert and Scheidemann, becoming a kind of
grey eminence of the Weimar Republic.[63] Some ten years after his
death, his sumptuous villa, with its art treasures, was turned by the Nazi
government into the private residence of Dr Joseph Goebbels and his
large family.

The raising of doubts about Marx's prognosis by Eduard Bernstein
and the hue and cry made by Rosa and Parvus were both highly
unwelcome to the party. At first the party leaders failed to grasp the
gravity of the case made by Bernstein. They did not take theoretical
hairsplitting seriously. They were too engrossed in practical and constructive work which was both absorbing and immediately more
effective and successful. Kautsky, the official theoretician, was at first
content to praise Bernstein's learning. A little novelty was all to the
good. Kautsky later admitted that it was Rosa and Parvus who shook
him out of his slumbers, and that they had been the first to understand
the seriousness of the heresy and to raise the alarm. When the storm
broke out, Kautsky grew irritated enough to complain of Bernstein's
schoolmaster manner. As a result of the many years spent abroad as
exile, especially in England, his friend was out of tune with the mood of
the party.[64] Ignaz Auer, one of the most powerful members of the
central committee and its secretary, who was the first leading figure
with whom the newly arrived Rosa had established contact and received
his blessing, told Bernstein, "but my dear Ede, these are things which
one thinks, but does not talk about".[65]

It was irritation with people who would not let sleeping dogs lie. It
is surely no accident that Bernstein himself was a Jew, albeit rooted in
German culture, coming from a family of craftsmen in the half-Polish
province of Posen. Different in background and temperament as
Bernstein was from Rosa, and contrasting as their views were, they
were both disturbers of the peace and of the smug self-contentment of
the SPD. In both cases it was the non-conformism of the outsider, and
the inability of "fanatics" to accept humbug and lazy unconcern with
the gaps between pretence and reality.

With his appearance of an Orthodox rabbi, Bernstein was a self-
taught scholar and thinker, the party's oldest and perhaps most
deserving publicist. At the beginning of the emergency legislation
against the socialists, Bernstein was charged with editing the party
paper abroad, first in Switzerland, then in England. He became a very
close and favourite collaborator of Engels, who also appointed him to be
his literary executor. Bernstein was deeply influenced by his stay in

England, in particular by Fabian socialism, but also by the British constitutional tradition. He was a man of shining integrity and moderation, addicted to facts and figures, and he was very gentle and consderate even in polemics with pugnacious opponents.[66]

Thoroughly reformist, law-abiding and patriotic as the SPD had become in practice, its official vocabulary not to say phraseology, remained radical and revolutionary. Men like August Bebel and Wilhelm Liebknecht could not very well shake off the forms of speech and habits of mind bequeathed by 1848 radicalism and the early days of socialist militancy. In a vague way the party continued to be committed to the idea of some radical breakthrough. Bernstein's brand of reformism had as a matter of fact been practised and even preached for quite a while by the Social-Democrats in the relatively liberal atmosphere of the Länder in the south-west by men like Wolmar, an ex-officer and veteran of the 1870-71 war and also an ex-radical, and by leaders such as David who were concerned with agrarian policies, neglected by most party members whose attention was entirely absorbed by the industrial proletariat.[67] Yet it was one thing to pursue pragmatic policies and to defend them, and quite another to generalise them into expressions of a system of principles. In doing precisely that, Rosa and Parvus maintained, Bernstein had in fact taken leave of Marxist socialism, abandoned the fold and embraced a kind of eclectic social liberalism.

Gumplowicz summed up the situation neatly by saying that what Bernstein was now preaching, the party had been doing all along unreflectingly and in a shame-faced manner.[68] From now on it could do it with a good conscience. Perhaps the wisest reaction came from the undisputed leader of Austrian Social-Democracy, the Jewish Victor Adler, who was wont to confess that he had no head and no taste for theory. Adler was a supreme practitioner and, as we shall see, regarded it as his mission in life precisely to keep an extremely fissiparous multi-national party together by preventing all polarisation, confrontations and stretching matters of principle to breaking point. In spite of disagreement on many points of principle—tempered by approval of many others—and notwithstanding his views on the tactical harm caused by Bernstein, Adler entreated Bebel not to drive Bernstein out of the party, and not to create a situation where "there would be no room in it for a man like Ede". There was in all or in most of what he was saying a stimulus to a permanent "examination of conscience" which was altogether very beneficial. "Do we not all have attacks of doubt?" "And if we had the peace of mind to let them develop, and if we were not being constantly tossed about, who knows, how strong they might not become?" Bernstein's misfortune was that he suffered from an "obsessive sense of responsibility . . . he is a fanatic of justice and a sceptic . . . who never has enough of self-examination." But whatever the fine points of economic doctrine, there was the undeniable, stark reality of the division of mankind into haves and have-nots, capitalists and workers. "The proletariat", as Adler had written on earlier occasions, well before the outbreak of the controversy, "commences its world historic role not only in order to gain knowledge but also to will its goal . . . and the revolutionising of the minds is its real task . . . [it is vital] . . . to fill them with the confidence that they were destined to accompany the present social order to its grave, and to become the bearers of a new social ideal . . . a *Weltanschauung*. The proletarian revolutionary movement was at the same time only a part of that transformation of the minds which made the nineteenth century into an era of revolution."

Bernstein's scepticism about the *Endziel*, about the possibility of a fundamental reshaping of the capitalist social system into a socialist order, constituted in this respect a denial of any basic difference between Social-Democracy and the radical bourgeois parties. No less noble and sincere than the standard bearers of revolution as the preachers of class reconciliation indeed were, they were being driven to cut the socialist movement at its very roots. "He who is out to sow doubt about the proletariat, about its total justification, its right to its full inheritance; he who voices smug satisfaction at partial successes; he who advises [the proletariat] not to look beyond its immediate wants, to its roots, and to its distant goal, deprives it of its greatest strength." Adler goes on to say that "the conviction of the absolute right of the proletariat is inseparable from the conviction of the absolute wrong of its opponents . . . What dims that contrast, veils and obscures it . . . is a danger, a source of the paralysis of energy . . . a tendency to tame and to philistinise the party with a scepticism in regard to everything that shapes proletarian morality and proletarian heroism."

The myth was all the more necessary, when out of scepticism and as a result of analytical over-sophistication socialism was presented as no more than a categorical imperative. Without faith in its inevitability, there would be no rebellious opposition, no uprising against the existing order. Without the myth of the *Endziel*, the vision of the future, men would not be able to bear sacrifices, labour, strive day by day. "I am certainly no agitator, but the calm satisfaction which [the revisionists] call realism, turns me into a visionary."[69]

The SPD condemned the revisionist heresy at two conferences, and through the mouths of the leading spokesmen, above all Bebel, and in formal resolutions. But it would not listen to any demands to expel Bernstein from the party. All the same, although the myth was reaffirmed—in a language that even the reformists could live with and vote for—the practice of the party grew increasingly more reformist and opportunist.[70]

Chapter Five

A POLARISED NATION—THE SECOND REICH

Dim as the myth of revolution had become, diluted as its Marxism was and feeble as its socialist passion may have grown, it would be unfair to say that the SPD had become reconciled to the existing order and had lost all vision of and wish for a fundamental change. What the German Social-Democrats strove for however was to create a Weimar *avant la lettre.* And if that aspiration was not world-shaking enough, and did not deserve the name of a myth in the Sorelian sense, the SPD was nevertheless conscious of combating a powerful myth, and working for a vast social transformation when struggling against the authoritarian imperial class regime of the Second Reich, which stood out in such contrast to the advance of German industry, the sudden urbanisation of the country, the general democratisation of society, and the great flowering of German science and scholarship.

(*a*) THE PRUSSIAN MYTH

The imperial regime set up by Bismarck was based upon what may be called the Prussian myth.[71] It could be said that Robert von Puttkamer, whose services to the Wilhelmian Reich Eckart Kehr regards as second only to those of Bismarck, defined that myth as early as 1859 in a letter to his father. When viewing the complexities of European history he was unable—he wrote—not to feel that in the last analysis the peoples were only unconscious executors of a divine will, and that "Prussia is the special favourite of God, who had still great deeds for her to accomplish. He will not let her star wane."[72] That myth was accepted by all, or at least found little effective resistance on the part of any of the middle class parties. The reason for it was the fact that national unification,[73] which had for generations served for so many as a kind of *Endziel* of German history, had not been accomplished by revolution, not even by a new social contract entered upon by the representatives of the German nation one and indivisible, but had been imposed from above by the authoritarian servant of a king by divine right and a leader of the Prussian Junker class. The German liberal bourgeoisie was weighed down by memories of its failures in 1848, and by the parliamentary struggle against Bismarck on matters of highest principle, such as the exclusive right to grant and refuse supply by the Landtag, in the early 1860's. Having forfeited its self-confidence, it was overawed by and intoxicated with the tremendous saga of a divided nation which for centuries had not counted among the powers, and had become overnight the leading power in Europe; and so it was incapable of resolutely opposing those who had brought this about. This was signally symbolised by the retroactive approval of the unlawful budgets of Bismarck by the legislature. The fulfilment seemed so absolute a blessing—for instance to so convinced a liberal as the historian Sybel[74]—that anything that was calculated to dim or undermine it, smacked of treason. The true interests of Germany, its authentic spirit and traditions were officially identified with those of Prussia. Any tampering with the Prussian-dominated structure was interpreted as a mortal peril to the colossal achievement, with its delicately poised balance between social classes, special interests, division of powers and confessional differences. And so the social ideology of class war and international proletarian solidarity was just unthinkable.

The Prussian myth upheld the mystical belief that—as Puttkamer put it—Providence (or history) had in its inscrutable ways singled out the Hohenzollern dynasty and its faithful servants for the task of accomplishing the unification of Germany.[75] In the most unpropitious surroundings, upon the sandy plains of Brandenburg and the raw Baltic regions, a succession of highly gifted, utterly dedicated and singleminded princes had forged superb instruments of statecraft—an army and bureaucracy—out of a loyal nobility, a God-fearing and obedient peasantry and a caste of dutiful public servants. It stubbornly pursued policies designed to enlarge the territory of the state, and to increase its military power and treasury at the cost of the greatest sacrifices, even of private consciences. These forces had made Germany. They deserved well of the German nation. They were the core of the Reich. They were the guarantee of the survival and of the greater glory of the fatherland. It was necessary to preserve the position of the ruling class, including their possessions and privileges which enabled them to play that historic role. Without them Germany would not be the same. The conservative establishment remained at heart unreconciled to the principle of popular and parliamentary sovereignty—of the populace in their parlance—as against divine and hereditary right. The motion introduced by the Social-Democrat Heine in 1908 (reiterating earlier

SPD motions of 1900 and 1905) that the Chancellor who had lost the
confidence of the House must resign, was countered by the Free Conservative spokesman von Dirksen with the argument that if this happened
Germany would have abandoned the monarchical principle and would
have adopted "an extreme parliamentary regime". The Kaiser would
then—said Laband—become a puppet in the hands of the Chancellor,
and the Chancellor of the Reichstag.[76] In 1900 Chancellor Bülow, basing
himself on an 1882 law, stated that all government decrees were
"selbstständige Anordnungen" (independent decrees) of the monarch.
The Chancellor was responsible before the Crown, the country and
history. How far a Chancellor was prepared to go to in offering cover to
the Emperor's personal actions, expressions of opinion and sentiment
was a matter of discretion, sense of duty and expediency, and belonged
to the sphere of imponderables.[77] The authentic voice of the true diehard
conservative-militarist believer could be heard in the famous diatribe of
von Oldenburge-Januschau: "When I was an officer . . . I didn't care a
damn what the papers wrote about me; all that I cared for was what my
commanding officer thought of me . . . How is it now? When a
lieutenant jabbers in some corner, he is eager that it should be quoted in
the Reichstag . . . The King of Prussia and German Emperor should at
any moment be in a position to tell a lieutenant—take ten men and close
the Reichstag."[78]

   According to General Boguslawski, the social problem was not to be
solved in parliamentary ways and by legal methods, but by the sword.
"The constitution of the state does not bother us; *salus rei publicae suprema
lex*, the good of the Reich is the supreme law."[79] One of the reasons why
the German General Staff was allowed to become so powerful, indeed
formally exempt from control by the War Office, subordinate solely to
the Imperial Military Chancellery, was precisely the desire to keep the
army out of parliamentary control.[80]

   The conservative philosophy of some true, authentic national
tradition which had made the nation what it was, and the bearers of
which (in other words the historic ruling class) deserved privileged
treatment, since its decline would sap the vitality of the nation, was not
peculiar to Germany. Disraeli, and later Arthur Balfour, spoke in the
same vein when defending the House of Lords and the landowning aristocracy against Joseph Chamberlain's internal policies and Lloyd
George's people's budget.[81] In Britain those arguments were brushed
aside by a self-assured, powerful and liberal bourgeoisie which was
coming round to the view that not only were hereditary privileges as
reward for some past real or pretended services inadmissible, but that
the state budget should be used as an instrument of egalitarian social

policies and not merely as the financial means of maintaining the
government machinery and the armed forces. Britain was gradually
accepting the principle that liberty was inseparable from a measure of
economic security and equality. The British middle class was
sufficiently self-confident and too committed to British parliamentary
practice not only not to be overawed by landed aristocracy, but also not
to be frightened by the threat from the lower orders.[82]

In contrast, in Germany all the efforts of the SPD to obtain the help
of the liberal and progressive parties in its fight to change the out-
rageously anti-democratic franchise of Prussia or to reform the tax
system, based on high tariffs on agricultural produce and indirect taxes
failed, because at the last moment the bourgeois parties left the Social-
Democrats in the lurch—as shown for instance by the failure of the
liberals and progressives to honour agreements with the SPD on mutual
support in run-off elections in 1912, though the Social-Democrats
scrupulously fulfilled them.[83] In their heart of hearts, the former were,
as we have said, hypnotised by the Prussian myth, and lacked the
courage to assist an effort to undermine the political and social-
economic basis of the ruling castes. They were also afraid of opening the
floodgates to mass democracy.[84] So they bowed to Bismarck's cunning
arrangement: a popularly elected Reichstag representing the nation one
and indivisible, but a decisive role reserved for the Prussian Landtag,
which gave a crushing preponderance to a hereditary landowning aristocracy and acquired wealth, and hardly any representation to the
working classes; a federal authority with a permanent Prussian
majority, a Cabinet appointed by and responsible only to the Emperor;
special imperial prerogatives in foreign policy and military matters—
the soldiers' oath to the Emperor; a general staff subordinated only to
the Kaiser's military chancellery; finally, as already said, a budget based
mainly on indirect consumption taxes and high tariffs on imported
grain.[85]

The social fears were fortified by or rationalised in ways which
played no part in England. There was deep anxiety about Germany's
international position, threatened as it was universally believed by the
envy and ill will of rivals and by the precarious nature of Germany's
wide open borders. There was also the preoccupation with a dynamic
world policy as part of accomplishing an unfinished task, of fulfilling
Germany's manifest destiny by securing her rightful leading place
among the nations, and making good the historic failure of the Germans
to obtain their share, when centuries earlier the great nations of
Western Europe had brought whole continents under their domination.[86] In subtle and insidious ways these obsessions about the nation's

security and the incessant craving for safer and safer guarantees against the allegedly implacable French *revanchism*, the barbarism of the countless Russian multitudes and British monopoly imperialism, had an inhibiting effect on the more liberal and even on many socialist elements in face of the vociferous dynamism of German imperialists. In different degrees of intensity, these sentiments were shared by most of the nation, not entirely excluding the working classes, and even a good many card-bearing Social-Democrats. This basic attitude carried with it a deep reluctance to rock the national boat, the traditional military-political class which—as its apologists never tired of proclaiming—had been tried and had not been found wanting. There were men, for instance Friedrich Naumann and in his own way Max Weber, who were aware of the fragility of an archaic hierarchical regime confronted with dynamic social-economic changes, and of the close connection between economic power and political and military might. They called for a modernised people's Kaiserdom with a broad democratic basis, rational, utilitarian modes of thought and expansionist political and economic policies—backed by a modernised army and navy—in central Europe and overseas. While abetting or even strengthning imperialist sentiments, they failed to make a dent in internal policies.[87]

Class cupidity and conviction—whatever the proportions of uncon-scious rationalisation of the former with the help of the latter, and of downright deception or self-delusion—converged in the efforts to stigmatise Social-Democracy as anti-patriotic, anti-national, standing outside the national consensus: not a *staaterhaltend* party, but *Vaterlandslose Gesellen*. The fact that in every Reichstag election except 1907 (when the issue was a patriotic one—colonial policy) the SPD was increasing the number of its representatives, fed the temptation, as shown by Bülow in 1907, to use or engineer an international emergency, and thus to galvanise the right-thinking voters into rallying round the national flag against the faithless agents of cosmopolitan foreign interests.[88] All bourgeois parties acclaimed Chancellor Bülow when he lashed out against the SPD benches in the Reichstag: "This is the deepest abyss between you and us: lack of understanding for the conditions of our national existence, for those requirements, without which the nation cannot maintain its position in the world."[89]

Bülow accused the Social-Democrats of treason. Through their sympathies for the Russian revolutionaries they were prepared to turn the German people into mercenaries in the service of cosmopolitan alien causes. In every instance of international conflict they took the side of the enemies of Germany—the Chinese Boxers, the Hottentots and the Hereros in South-West Africa, the French in Morocco.

In the Reichstag on February 15, 1897, Bebel complained that one of the instruction courses in the army was on ways of combating Social-Democracy.[90] As late as 1913 the Minister of War, von Heeringen, while claiming that the army was apolitical, conceded frankly: "but there is a limit, and that is Social-Democracy . . . activity on behalf of SPD by an officer . . . cannot and will not take place".[91]

Not a few of those who identified the interests of Germany with their own class interests, shared the fatalistic view of the inevitability of armed confrontation between Germany and her conspiring jealous neighbours, and consequently contemplated preventive war, or even wished Germany to initiate a war of conquest. There was an additional incentive for that in the idea that a national war was calculated to stem the socialist flood, indeed to drive it back in the midst of patriotic fervour, or to serve as an opportunity to strangle the hydra of anti-patriotic Marxism.

One does not have to accept a conspiratorial view of history or the whole thesis that the German establishment consciously wanted and prepared for aggressive war for the sake of world domination or in answer to internal difficulties, to find plenty of evidence that such moods indeed existed, and that such speculations occupied the minds of people in high places.[92]

Friedrich von Holstein, the Grey Eminence of the Wilhelmstrasse, wrote: "Reactionary governments always try to divert the internal struggle to the foreign sphere."[93] Johannes von Miquel, the author of *Sammlungspolitik*, in 1897-8 advised Germans to turn their attention outwards, for in foreign affairs the sentiments of the nation could usually be united. "Only a successful foreign policy," claimed Bülow in 1897, "can help to reconcile, pacify, rally, unify", by which he meant *Weltpolitik*. The next Chancellor's close adviser, Kurt Riezler, wrote in his much quoted diary, "if war comes and the veils fall, the whole nation will follow, driven by necessity and peril".[94] The indecisive Bethmann-Hollweg saw through the mixed and muddled motives of the nation-alist expansionists, and on a late occasion in the July 1914 crisis brought himself to flail them: "The earlier errors: simultaneous Turkish policy against Russia, Morocco against France, the navy against England—challenge everybody, put yourself in everybody's path, and actually weaken no one in this fashion. Reason: aimlessness, the need for little prestige successes and solicitude for every current of public opinion, the 'national' parties which with their racket about foreign policy want to preserve and strengthen their party position."[95] But according to Fritz Stern, who quotes the statement, this awareness of the Chancellor was neutralised by his "curious blend of contradictory beliefs—social

Darwinism, misunderstood romanticism, and cultural pessimism—all pointing to German expansion as the only alternative to stagnation".[96]

(b) AN AUTHORITARIAN PHILOSOPHY OF STATE AND SOCIETY

It may be said that the official philosophy of the Second Reich was absorbed by the young scions of aristocracy and the upper bourgeoisie as they thronged to listen to the thunderous sermons of the historian-prophet Treitschke.[97] His idealisation of the state as "a lofty necessity of nature", "the outward form which the inner life of a people bestows upon itself", "the objectively revealed will of God as unfolded in the life of the state" did not however express the kind of national self-assurance which stems from long and unquestioned possession.[98] It represented the apotheosis of something that had been yearned for by a deprived nation, and an anxious straining to inspire, glorify, and hallow a state of mind which lacked roots as well as cohesion. Treitschke inveighed against the ultramontane and the Jacobin treatment of the state as the fruit of a social contract artificially entered upon by sinful men who viewed the state as a necessary evil, and against the utilitarian materialism of England (Gibbon) which looked upon the state as an insurance society that existed simply to protect property and to enable its members to buy cheaply and sell dearly. How could such an irreverent attitude to the state evoke a patriotic response, a readiness for the supreme self-sacrifice?

To Treitschke the aim of the state was to establish and guard "a permanent tradition . . . of successive generations . . . throughout the ages".[99] And such a political tradition the Germans precisely lacked. At a closer look that tradition was indeed not conceived by Treitschke as Burke's prescriptive constitution, but—in quaint contrast to Treitschke's anti-materialism and his worship of idealism—as embodied in "law of [property] inheritance": "the continuous legalised intention of the past, exemplified in the law of inheritance, must remain a factor in the distribution of property amongst posterity. In a nation's continuity with bygone generations lies the specific dignity of the state. It was consequently a contradiction to say that a distribution of property should be regulated by the desires of the existing generation."[100] This conviction derived from a far more generalised view of the universe and of society. In this finite world of ours, with its inexorably restricted resources—"the definite limits upon human endeavour set by the economy of nature"[101]—the millions were destined to toil for the few so that these should be able to cultivate a sample of culture and train themselves to rule the multitude. "To put it simply: the masses must for ever remain the masses. There would be no culture without kitchenmaids. Obviously, education could never thrive if there was nobody to do the rough work. Millions must plough and forge and dig in order that a few thousand may write and paint and study. It sounds harsh, but it is true for all time, and whining and complaining can never alter it. . . . It is precisely in the differentiation of classes that the moral [sic!] wealth of mankind is exhibited." But the poor may console themselves with their "virtues of vigour and sincerity . . . hearty joy of living . . . in simple conditions" which put "to shame the jaded victims of over-culture". Altogether—says Treitschke—"want is a relative conception". Governments should endeavour to "mitigate distress, but its abolition is neither possible nor desirable".[102]

This lofty treatment of material goods on the assumption that the assured haves are free of greed, and the have-nots have no reason to regret their deprivation, conditions Treitschke's attitude to war as the highest manifestation of the reality, vitality and moral destiny of the state. Adherence to the Manchester School is not a frame of mind that enables a state to wage war. "It is a false conclusion that wars are waged for the sake of material advantage. Modern wars are not fought for the sake of booty. Here the high moral ideal of national honour is a factor handed down from one generation to another, enshrining something positively sacred, and compelling the individual to sacrifice himself for it. This ideal is above all price and cannot be reduced to pounds, shillings and pence."[103] That ideal is hardly liberty or even a peculiar way of life, although Treitschke speaks of "ancestral achievements" transmitted to descendants; it is the concept of honour of a cavalry officer, who is motivated by the dream of cutting a fine figure, by the conviction that a slight to his honour can be redressed only by a duel, and that combat is a display of noble bravery and manly skill.

This mentality becomes intertwined with the Hegelian equation of power with vitality, and of virility with moral vigour: "the state as a person . . . is power, precisely in order to assert itself as against other equally independent powers".[104] There must therefore be a plurality of states. The "ideal of one universal empire is odious—the ideal of a state coextensive with humanity is no ideal at all".[105] Eternal peace would turn the world into a swamp, stunt the nations. The ideal of international arbitration to prevent armed conflict was an insult to the sentiment of national honour. In international relations, the state manifested its independence and won its place by the possession and display of power and the refusal to recognise any superior in matters of national honour, as shown by the case of Prussia vis à vis all other

German principalities. "The features of history are virile, unsuited to sentimental or feminine natures. Brave peoples alone have an existence, an evolution or future; the weak and cowardly perish, and perish justly. The grandeur of history lies in the perpetual conflict of nations, and it is simply foolish to desire the suppression of their rivalry."[106]

In internal affairs too, it was power and force that commanded that submission which was for fickle and unruly men the ordinary type of consent which their better selves might be induced by the show of force to grant. Small weak states like Holland, Switzerland, Sweden, Belgium were ludicrous creations in "the modern international system [which] assumes more and more aristocratic complexion". They existed on sufferance on the part of the great powers, and they elicited respect at home.[107]

War was the employment of concentrated force, was the lever of civilisation, and was sure to endure to the end of history. "The great strides which civilisation makes against barbarism and unreason are only made actual by the sword. Between civilised nations too war is the form of litigation by which states make their claims valid."[108] But war was also the powerful cement of nationhood. "Most undoubtedly war is the only remedy for an ailing nation. Social selfishness and party hatreds must be dumb before the call of the state when its existence is at stake."[109] The individual felt all his unimportance then. "It is a war which fosters the political idealism which the materialist rejects."[110] It creates the myth by which a nation lives: It throws out heroes to be worshipped by generations. It inspires writers "whose words ring like trumpet blasts". "To Aryan races, who are before all things courageous, the foolish preaching of everlasting peace has always been vain."[111] Pacifist lulling of Germany to an abhorrence of war would enable England and Russia to partition the globe.

"The historian who moves in the world of real will sees at once that the demand for eternal peace is purely reactionary. . . . All movement and all growth would disappear with war, only the exhausted, spiritless, degenerate periods of history have toyed with the idea."[112]

(c) WEIMAR AVANT LA LETTRE—SPD

The convergence of internal and external policy also played a decisive part in shaping the SPD attitudes. Those—the offical party leadership in fact—who rejected violent revolution, focused their aims on the task of effecting a peaceful democratic revolution. The programme of bringing down the ruling establishment and overpowering the classes upon which it was based could be presented to the liberal bourgeois parties as no more than the unfolding of the logical implications of the representative system which was established by the introduction of universal suffrage on the Reichstag level. In practical terms that involved establishing Cabinet responsibility to the elected representatives of the whole people, and replacing the outrageous Prussian class franchise by a democratic suffrage. All the desired changes were to be achieved by the SPD gradually and lawfully by means of the vote. And as matters were progressing, there seemed to be no need for any other measures.

SPD parliamentary representation in the Reichstag grew in the years 1893 to 1912 from 23.3 per cent (1,790,000 votes) to 34.8 per cent (4,250,329 votes), the only setback being in the 1907 "Hottentot" elections, when the number of its deputies was nearly halved. The membership of the party increased from 1906 to 1913 from 384,327 to 982,850 (it should be noted that the increase from 1912 to 1913 was disappointingly low—only 1.3 per cent compared with about 16 per cent annual growth in the two or three previous years). The trade union membership in 1913 had passed 2,500,000, while in 1891 it counted only 275,000 members. In 1914 there were 4,100 paid party functionaries and 11,000 salaried employees of the party. With a large pay roll and 20,000,000 marks invested in business on a profit basis, "the SPD was a nationwide corporation". Just before World War I the party owned 94 newspapers, and the party press had about 1,500,000 subscribers.[113]

It thus seemed imperative to remain on the plane of legality and not to offer the establishment any cause or pretext to strangle the workers' movement. Of course, there was the distinct possibility that once the ruling classes came to the conclusion that observing legality was threatening them with extinction—"la légalité nous tue"—they would resort to an illegal coup, curtail the Reichstag franchise and launch an attack on the SPD. But then the transgressors would be not the workers, but the government and the Junkers. The masses might then be called out into the streets to defend the constitution in the name of the sacred right of resistance to arbitrary oppression.

The problem of the Prussian franchise was in this respect regarded as a test case. The existing Prussian system was branded as illegal because of the crying contrast between it and the Reichstag franchise, and as a standing provocation and a glaring proof of class selfishness. The fight against it even by means of direct action such as mass demonstrations and strikes was not to be taken as subversive activity, whatever prudential abstention from such steps might be pursued in practice. As we have said, Engels brought his weight to bear in favour of parliamentary legality, confidently expecting a Social-Democratic majority in the Reichstag in the near future. From the point of view of strict Marxist orthodoxy a democratic revolution was a necessary stage and a stepping stone for the socialist revolution. The transition from political to Social-Democracy would be effected by a socialist Cabinet upheld by a SPD majority in parliament.

In line with the vagueness of the clauses of the Erfurt programme on the eventual transition from a capitalist into a socialist mode of production and the abolition of class privilege and class rule, the spokesmen of the SPD seemed to take the existing conditions in Germany for granted, in the hope of improving them. In the *Zukunftsdebatte* in the Reichstag in 1893 Bebel refused to be drawn into what he called immature speculations about the ultimate shape of things and a lesser light, Frohme, followed up by saying that all the party was interested in was evolution and self-adaptation—"the next phase of development, the next step of organic evolution, no more, no less".[114] The younger German historians Steinberg, Gerhard Ritter and Deman seem to be in agreement that the SPD had resolutely turned its back upon revolution in favour of democratic development.[115]

Since it was still a far cry to an SPD parliamentary majority, it was necessary for tactical reasons not to overemphasise the socialist policies which would be inaugurated on the morrow of the decisive SPD break-through at the polls, so as not to frighten away the potential middle class allies in the war of attrition which Kautsky preached against the feudal-absolutist establishment and for a genuine democracy.[116]

No less important, perhaps immediately more urgent, was the question of the image of an anti-national force pinned on the SPD by the conservative elements. In an effort to ward it off and to win over the liberals and the lower bourgeoisie, the socialists would try their utmost to destroy the equation of the establishment with eternal Germany, to highlight its class character, its parasitic exploitation of the masses, who were compelled to pay excessive prices for their daily bread, and to condemn the cynically selfish refusal of the propertied classes to agree to property and inheritance taxes, even when this became necessary for balancing the defence budget and for building a navy. The socialists then made the most of the reckless foreign affairs speeches of the Kaiser. Not only were they a menace to the country, they also revealed Bonapartist intentions, since Wilhelm II would condemn the Reichstag majority for binding his hands by curtailing the military budget. The Kaiser denounced the political parties for undermining national unity and destroying the credibility of German foreign policy. He would even throw out hints that an emergency might compel him to act as the real guardian of German destinies over the heads of the politicians and against sectional interests and party caucuses.[117]

As World War I was to show, nearly all the German workers and their leaders were deeply patriotic. Their attitude was aptly summed up in the slogan "not a penny to this regime, but we shall not abandon the fatherland in its hour of need". Should the country be invaded by a foreign enemy, exclaimed Bebel, he would take down his old gun, make it ready for action and march out to meet the enemy.[118] In their struggle against the Junker army and its militaristic spirit and for a citizens' army, the Social-Democratic spokesmen stressed the obsolete mentality of a conservative aristocracy officer corps, the narrowness of its social basis, the alienating effect of such a system upon the masses. Not only were they genuinely proud of German greatness, but the socialists could legitimately extol the progressive character and the mighty contribution of German philosophy, literature and classical humanism to the flowering of socialist thought. In fact, they claimed to be more national than the right-wing nationalists. They were eager to turn the masses, hitherto kept out of the cultural life and the creative effort of the nation, into active participants in the endeavour. They wished to make the sources, the inspiration, and treasures of German culture accessible to the totality of the nation, for the first time in history.

It is not likely that many German social-democrats at the turn of the century would have answered the question, where was their fatherland, as Rosa Luxemburg did: that it was the immense mass of toiling men and women the world over. Thus far had they travelled from the late eighteenth-century German humanism of Friedrich Schiller, who preached that "nur deutsch ist nicht deutsch sein"[119] (to be only German is not to be German at all) or of the young Jacobin Fichte who hailed revolutionary France as the fatherland of all progressive men in the world. It was in the forefront of the struggle for light, and the face of every lover of liberty was naturally turned to it, as to the sun. His fatherland should be chosen by the free man freely, and he should not be chained to it by the accident of birth in a certain valley near a certain river.[120]

Severing, the last Social-Democrat Minister of the Interior in Weimar Prussia, whose removal by von Papen in 1932 marked the beginning of the end of the republican regime, defined the fatherland as the "soil which feeds us, the economic base of our creative endeavour, the *Kulturboden* upon which we are linked by language and customs to our ancestors. And the fatherland is also ours, the workers', the fatherland which we love and shall defend, when it is attacked."[121] A less visceral, more spiritual definition of universalism is that by Engelbert Peraerstorffer. "In its highest form nationality is . . . an ideal good . . .

humanity's culture in a special, most particular and unrepeatedly unique form of radiation. It signifies the enrichment of mankind by a special form of its self-expression." It was the aim of socialism to give the proletariat access to the millenarian culture. "Every culture however is national. Its roots are in a particular nation and its highest forms—and above all these—display a decidedly national character." "Socialism and the national idea are not therefore contradictory [things], they belong by necessity to each other.... Socialism wants to organise mankind, not to atomise it. The organism of mankind is not composed of single individuals, but of nations as its components.... We [the German Social-Democrats] joyfully count ourselves as part of our nation, and take pride in its great ideas, since we also remember that theoretical socialism itself is a work of the German spirit.... And so as good socialists we are also the best Germans."[122]

When thinking of the fatherland the thoughts of the Social-Democrats almost automatically turned to the threat presented by Russia to Germany and to all it stood for. Moreover the great contribution which a powerful German Social-Democratic party based upon a highly civilised and mighty country was able to make to proletarian emancipation everywhere was menaced by "a country in which the vast majority is composed of ignorant peasants and is deprived of all political will".[123] It was therefore most important once war broke out, Bernstein insisted, to carry hostilities as swiftly as possible into enemy territory, "because in modern circumstances a war pursued on the national soil already marks a near-defeat".[124]

Bernstein's definitions seem to reach out to the conceptions of Lassalle, whose writings he edited. The head of the first Socialist party in Germany was an old Hegelian and was also deeply influenced by Fichte, in fact wished to appear as a latter-day Fichte. He was a great believer in the state as the lever of progress and guardian of impersonal moral values. He upheld at the same time the Fichtean brand of the *Volksgeist* idea. The conjunction of the eternity of the state and the uniqueness of the *Volksgeist* amounted to an affirmation of the imperishable and permanent nature of the nation-state. Lassalle became entangled in contradictions. He went so far as to envisage dynamic expansionist foreign policy as a token of the vitality of the state, dreaming of German cavalry horses washing their feet in the waters of the Dardanelles, and denying no less than Marx to embryonic or decrepit nationalities any raison d'etre and any right to independent statehood. The *Volksgeist* idea might have brought him perilously near to conservative approval of the feudal past. But he was both a socialist and a Jew. In what may be called, also in reference to Bernstein, a German-

Jewish way, he reconciled the contradiction by proclaiming that the true German *Volksgeist* was embodied in classical German humanism and universalism, in pure reason. It was the feudal and bourgeois selfish clinging to partial interests, old privileges and irrational obsolete particularism that vitiated the essence of Teutonism. A socialist Germany would enthrone the pure universalistic German *Volksgeist*.[125]

There were limits to which a person who was both socialist and Jew could go. It is no accident that Bernstein, the revisionist and patriot, felt compelled at the height of German chauvinism in 1915 to secede from the majority party and join the USPD, and on the morrow of the defeat to voice some home truths before a Social-Democratic forum on the German share of war guilt, to be shouted down by his incensed audience.[126]

"Although pledging that the SPD would oppose the attacking and invading foreign enemy just as any other party . . . defend the Fatherland, on whose soil we live, whose language we speak, whose customs we practise . . . because we wish to make this, our Fatherland, a land unexcelled in this world for perfection and beauty",[127] Bebel could not withhold his deep concern at the thought that "in a struggle for the integrity of the German soil" the SPD would willy-nilly be "helping to defend this infamous domestic system". The answer to this quandary was spelled out by the revisionist Schröder three years before World War I: "The SPD will in peace time apply the severest criticism to those in charge of national affairs. When however it comes to the crunch, when nation is ranged against nation, then the Social-Democratic workers will regard themselves as just a part of the national community. The SPD will then know no other interest but that of their nation."[128]

In other words, our country right or wrong, whoever happens to be at its helm.

Reformist revisionism, as Rosa Luxemburg perceived it, meant transforming the SPD from a section of the socialist International into a socialist, or rather left-wing liberal-social party of Germany, deriving its sustenance not from abstract universal doctrine, but from the life of the national community, its national spirit, past, traditions, needs, aspirations, in brief the concrete data of its existence.

Even on the very sensitive point of colonial policies, Bernstein and such followers of his as Schippel, Kampfmayer, David, Quessel, Hildebrand, eventually Lensch, the renegade radical, were—as we shall see—by no means opposed to peaceful German expansion and economic penetration into Africa and Asia. They considered such imperialism progressive, and beneficial to the natives. German workers stood to gain from the acquisition of free and easy access to raw materials by German industry and to new markets by German trade. The imperialist phase was after all a natural and inevitable stage in capitalist development, inevitably, indeed directly, preceding the socialist transformation. Finally, puritan abstention from having anything to do with colonial adventures amounted to leaving the field free for British monopolist imperialism.[129]

The gradualist reformist programme of the SPD required great self-restraint, which meant strict discipline imposed upon the masses by a strong centralised leadership: not mass spontaneity, but well-regulated behaviour; not militancy, but circumspection. It was important to build up slowly positions of strength, a network of institutions and organisations, to have full coffers, to exercise educational influence over the various component parts of the movement—the young, women, co-operatives, cultural ventures, in brief to form a state within a state, as Kautsky defined it. It was therefore most imperative to prevent too early a breakout, because waiting in the wings was a colossal apparatus of force and coercion, at the disposal of a determined ruling class, which had by no means lost its self-assurance and arrogance. All the same, there was to be no compromise on the principle of pure and consistent opposition to the regime and an unflagging war of attrition against it. But even this was not always easy to maintain. There was for instance strong temptation to pursue what Heine called a compensation policy, when the government's defence policy, especially its naval plans, necessitated taxing inherited wealth in the teeth of upper class opposition; the government was forced to court Social-Democratic votes in exchange for the alleviation of consumption taxes, on top of the 'socialist' measures against the rich.[130]

Chapter Six

THE LESSONS OF 1905 IN RUSSIA

For a while it seemed to Rosa that the alternative she had formulated in her juxtaposition of tempering or sharpening class antagonism, had lost its urgency: the revisionist heresy had after all been condemned by the party. Soon, however, her impatience with business as usual, her pining for activism, her need to feel that the revolution was being promoted, and not left to come in its own good time, made her realise that in fact opportunism had not been defeated, but had become the accepted practice. For this she could not but blame the leadership, the organisation, the party apparatus. It was not possible for her to bring herself to doubt the revolutionary instincts and will of the masses. Not only would her faith have been left in a void, if she had to admit that. Her materialistic creed taught her that the dynamic, phenomenal development of Germany's industrial economy was bound to be paralleled in the sharpening of class antagonism and reflected in proletarian revolutionary consciousness. Proletarian inertia had therefore to be interpreted as being artificially and deliberately maintained by the dead hand of a party bureacracy and an ignorant, narrow-minded trade union hierarchy, which feared change and abhorred stirrings from below.

This is incidentally the real background of Rosa's controversy with Lenin in 1904 and her condemnation of elitist centralism sustained by professional revolutionaries as propagated by the Bolsheviks, a subject to which we shall return. In the midst of her growing misgivings came the 1905 revolution in Russia and the movement of social and national rebellion in Poland. Although electrified by these events, Rosa, Jogiches and Parvus were somewhat late in setting out for the front, which delay earned them not a little sneering from the bourgeois press. With false papers (Rosa as Anna Maschke and Jogiches as Otto Engelmann) they crossed the border into Poland. After some weeks of not very effective activity, they were both arrested and identified. The German party helped with funds to get Rosa out on bail. She then travelled to St Petersburg and Finland, where she had frequent meetings with Lenin, and from there, after the revolution succumbed, returned to Germany,[131] to have her spirits soon badly lowered by the discovery that

113

Jogiches had betrayed her with another woman, and by the ensuing violent break, followed by the squalid quarrel about his retention of the keys to her flat, and made utterly painful by the resolve to continue their political collaboration on a strictly impersonal plane, symbolised by the change in the manner of addressing each other, not to speak of the wholly new tone and contents of their correspondence.[132]

The letters from Poland and from prison vibrate with revolutionary exaltation. Things were on the move. The unthinkable had been happening daily. The dams were broken. Deeds, every day more courageous and more daring, were multiplying. Whole historic epochs seemed to become telescoped into a few days, often hours. "The Revolution is great, long live the Revolution."[133] For the moment revolutionary dynamism allowed her to suspend her critical vigilance, and to blur the distinction, which she was always so apt to detect, between socialist revolutionary action, and social-patriotic romantic rebelliousness of the nationalist, separatist heirs to the Polish irrindentist tradition.

Rosa never mentions Henri Bergson, nor does she—rather surprisingly—refer to Georges Sorel. But her rapturous description of the *élan vital* released by the revolution, the new horizons opened, the creative capacity called into being and the historic leap precipitated by it, and her glorification of the general strike as the lever of the revolutionary breakthrough, suggest an inspiration from that direction rather than from doctrinaire adherence to economic determinism.

Ex oriente lux. Curiously, it was the pedestrian Karl Kautsky, who some time before the outbreak of the first Russian revolution and before Rosa, voiced the view that the next revolutionary outbreak which would set Europe on the move, was likely to come from the East, rather than from the West.[134] Of course, flashes of intuition or hope of that kind may be detected—as we saw—in some late utterances of Marx and Engels, after they had become acquainted with the Russian revolutionary movement and come into contact with some of its leaders in exile, such as Vera Zassulich and Lavrov. Rosa had not yet the word for it, but she seems to have stumbled upon the discovery of the phenomenon—the advantage of backwardness.[135] She was quick to sort out the lessons. As a by-product of the military defeat of the imperialistic adventure on the frozen frontiers of the earth, undertaken by a ruling caste of aristocratic speculators and an obsolete tottering regime anxious to secure foreign credit, win laurels and divert attention from feudal-monarchical despotism, the ignorant, backward, downtrodden masses in factories and in peasant cottages, without organisation, political experience, socialist consciousness, trade unions, strike funds, political parties or revolutionary preparations, rose spontaneously like lava, without any set plans or general staff to guide them, against the Tsar, with his mighty army, huge police force, secret services and centuries'-old oppressive bureaucracy, and brought the most redoutable despotism in Europe to its knees. Vast strikes swept across the whole of the colossal empire, paralysing state machinery and bringing bourgeois society to a standstill. A local and a nation-wide leadership sprang up from below overnight, without having been prepared or created by the existing parties. The industrial workers carried with them all the classes which were discontented and had any sort of grudge against the system, especially the peasants, who were awakened from their slumber by the urban proletariat, and together they forced the Tsar to grant a consti-tution and to dismantle an age-old despotism.

That such things happened in a backward country, and not in a highly advanced state, where over-ripe capitalism was reaching its pre-ordained structural crisis, and a highly organised working class party, possessed of long doctrinal formation, was firmly guiding the masses, as the accepted teachings had been foretelling, was due paradoxically to the fact that unlike their Western counterparts, the wretched, shivering, illiterate, unorganised masses of Russia did not suffer top-heavy organisation, bureaucratic conservatism, calculating, timid trade union bosses, possessions and funds, cherished gains or vested interests. They had nothing to lose but their chains.[136] Had not Marx in his pre-1848 period already looked to the German proletariat to make a leap forward as daring and as great as their backwardness in comparison with the working classes of the more advanced countries such as England and France; and to reach beyond them, in proportion to their disadvantages when compared with their Western comrades: in one heave to shake off their back the burden of absolutism, clericalism, particularism, feudalism, from which the Western workers had already been freed, as well as capitalist exploitation.[137]

The Russian events had confirmed Rosa in her fervent belief that the general strike was the modern revolutionary weapon par excellence, applicable not only to Russia, but still more to the new conditions elsewhere. The old idea of the Chartist pamphleteer, Bembow, the author of the "Grand Holiday", and still earlier of Owen, Doherty and the British proto-syndicalists of around 1830,[138] completely discredited by the lamentable failures when first propagated and tried, gained new relevance towards the end of the nineteenth century. It became clear to all that vast, highly disciplined modern armies, with their new weaponry, the new means of rapid transport and the introduction of urban planning had combined to make barricade fighting impossible, and had turned the spontaneous uprising of masses goaded on by student and underground activists into a chimera. The general strike did not call for a frontal confrontation with armed forces. It was intended to paralyse society by bringing to a standstill capitalist production, the workings of the state, and the movement of its armed forces. It was calculated to galvanise the striking masses into a sense of daring and fighting solidarity. The strikers were not to attack army and police, but to provoke them into lawless violence, which would arouse sympathy for the people among the more humane members of the armed forces. The establishment would thus be made to bear the responsibility for breaking the law, not the strikers. It would either totter from exasperated impotence, since it would also have lost bourgeois support, or would meet its defeat in armed clashes with the rebellious masses. For censorship reasons Rosa could only hint (and this too only by way of commentary upon the Russian 1905 revolution) at armed uprising as the climax of the chain of events to be released by the general strike. Out of her addiction to the idea of mass spontaneity, and deep distrust of the SPD leadership, Rosa rejected the Bolshevik idea of the technical preparations of such an uprising by the party. The masses themselves would break out, after they had received the proper education from the party.[139]

Rosa became the theoretician, indeed the poet, of the general strike, and earned thereby the deep and lasting loathing of the trade union leaders, who nicknamed the general strike "der Allgemeine Wahnsinn", and did not rest till they got the SPD formally to forbid any public discussion of the question. They went further, and bullied the party executive into giving a secret pledge that no political issue which in any way affected the trade unions would be decided without previous consultation and agreement with the general commission. This meant depriving the political party of any freedom of decision and ensuring the defeat of any notion smacking of radicalism.[140]

While the doctrinaires of the party regarded the trade unions as the handmaid of the political movement, its cadres and instruments in the political struggle for socialism and the revolution, the union bosses were not too squeamish to remind the party leaders where the party's funds and millions of voters came from. There was also the question of loyalty. They claimed that a large proportion of their members were not interested in politics, but relied upon the unions to defend their economic interests, and were unwilling to be used for political ends which they did not wish to support. They would not have their livelihood endangered by revolutionary adventurism.[141] As a matter of fact, the weapon of the general strike was at that time being used for a political purpose—the extension of the franchise—in quite a few countries, notably Belgium (very successfully), Sweden, Austria and Italy. Rosa also claimed that the events in Russia in 1905—a year which incidentally saw a vast number of large economic strikes in Germany— had shown the interdependence of economic and political factors in a general strike.[142]

The very slogan of a general strike was a provocation to the German authorities to initiate legislation against strikes of any kind, on the pretext of the need to defend workers willing to work, but cowed by militants. But the famous Zuchthaus motion was defeated in parliament with bourgeois liberal support. An actual outbreak of such a mass strike was however sure to strengthen the reactionary establishment's resolve to break the trade union movement and to throw it back for decades. It was sheer lunacy—the trade union leadership maintained—to embark upon such an adventure, without proper, meticulous preparation, strike organisation, funds, well-stocked granaries. Rosa could not but feel deep dismay and bitter disgust for petty-bourgeois timidity: "what shall we eat on the Day of Judgement". While she was singing hymns of praise to the Russian masses, the ordinary German worker could not but be incensed by the idea that the ignorant dirty *muzhiks* were to serve as their teachers, just as Social-Democratic activists would raise their eyebrows on being told that the querulous, hopelessly doctrinaire revolutionary émigrés from Russia, who were spending days and nights in hair-splitting disputations on verbal distinctions which meant nothing to the practical German working class mind, and lacked any political experience and responsibility, were to become the guides and mentors of the first, most advanced, most powerful Social-Democratic party in the most civilised country in the world.[143]

Chapter Seven

THE WORLD REVOLUTION ONE AND INDIVISIBLE — IN THE AGE OF IMPERIALISM

In her pamphlet "The Mass Strike", which summed up the Russian experience, Rosa made the significant, though cryptic, statement that the events in Russia were not a specifically Russian affair, but an event of the utmost importance to the German workers' movement, indeed a milestone in the history of Germany as such, transcending in its significance the local, parochial happenings in the Reich itself.[144] It was a symptom and token that international developments were about to overshadow and shape the fate of the national workers' movements. Rosa took great pains to present the events in Russia as incipient local expressions of a universal process. It had pleased Madam History to choose Russia as the starting point for her next dramatic leap.

World history as a whole had entered into a new revolutionary phase on the outbreak of the upheaval in Russia. As well as Rosa, Parvus, Trotsky, Radek and other Eastern European Jewish émigrés, socialist economists like the Austrian-Jewish economist Hilferding, were gripped (not of course uninfluenced by Hobson's famous book on imperialism) by an acute awareness of the primary and all-determining significance of what Parvus called *Weltpolitik* (the title of his new periodical publication). To him as well as to Rosa, the new state of ferment in international relations was only the political aspect of the new second industrial revolution. The new *Sturm und Drang* era of capitalism had been brought about by the industrialisation of Russia and the completion of the Trans-Siberian railway; by the joining of the two oceans by the transcontinental railway in the United States; the beginnings of intensive exploitation of the prairies in North and South America; the introduction of giant cargo ships equipped with refrigeration; the opening of China to international trade; the scramble for markets, for minerals, oil and other raw materials in the Asian, African and Latin-American continents; the technological advances in electricity and chemistry, the invention of the diesel engine, telephone, typewriter; the enormous expansion of joint-stock; the rise of giant national and international banking and industrial and commercial concerns. Those momentous technological-industrial developments were breaking down the last remnants of national and local autarchy and economic self-sufficiency, and creating a single world economy, a world market and a world workshop.[145]

Weary of German parochialism and SPD immobility, Rosa Luxemburg was finding in these developments convincing proof of the rapidly maturing polarisation of the world into universal capitalism and a universal proletariat, now consisting of the uncorrupted labour masses of the Western world and of the multitudes of the colonial races, mercilessly exploited economically and humiliatingly oppressed as subject nations, with their native economy and way of life shattered. She developed her economic theory of imperialism, which had a very mixed reception even from Marxist economists, when the ripe fruit of her cogitations and research, *The Accumulation of Capital*, appeared in 1913.[146] Briefly, returning to her favourite theme that capitalism, goaded on by an irresistible force, must go on overproducing and expanding through further and more intensive exploitation of resources, labour and consumers, she came to the conclusion that in the highly developed capitalist countries the possibilities of such exploitation had reached a limit—there were no new raw materials, no further labour reserve, no new consumers to be had. Capitalism would soon have also exhausted all possibility of further exploitation in the wider world. It was reaching the confines of the earth, as it had to, because no capitalism could for long restrict itself to a fixed limited market. The imminent closure of the new vistas was engendering frantic competition between the imperialist powers, which even before global capitalism had driven itself to a complete impasse and thus to inevitable collapse on a world scale, must lead to war. This view contrasted strongly with that held for a while by Kautsky, that imperialist exploitation might rather lead, through the growth of international concerns and international economic agreements, to a peaceful division of the globe and pacific international co-operation. Being in a frantic hurry to prove the inevitability of an imminent collapse of capitalism, Rosa ignored such facts as the growing volume of inter-Power commerce which dwarfed colonial markets. She tarred with the same brush industrial investments:[147] concessions in China and Latin America; Western, above all French, loans to Russia; and the exploitation of mineral deposits in Africa.

Rosa Luxemburg went on to prove that the bitter rivalry between imperialist interests had to be backed up with vast armies and huge navies and by invasions to forestall rivals and with punitive expeditions to hold down rebellious natives. Militarism and navalism were the inseparable companions of imperialism. They required enormous expenditure, mortal risks, and these could only be forced through parliaments by whipping up nationalist frenzy among the excitable crowds through a yellow press fraudulently presenting selfish rapacious ventures by capitalist concerns as vital national interests, and turning every dispute and incident in the far corners of the globe (such as the murder of a couple of white missionaries in China, a Fashoda confront-ation) into matters of national honour and prestige.[148]

Rosa Luxemburg may claim to have been the first to propose a theory of the military-industrial complex, without having actually coined the term. In Germany the close economic, social and even family ties between an almost hereditary military caste and heavy (especially armament) industry, made plausible the theory of a vested common interest in war and war preparations, which had to be kept going and indeed constantly widened.

The frequency of international crises such as Fashoda, the two Morocco disputes, the Bosnia-Herzegovina affair, wars like the American invasion of Cuba, American adventures in the Pacific, the explosions in the overheated Balkans, the Sino-Japanese, Russo-Japanese and Lybian wars, the revolutions in China, Turkey and Persia, the rumblings in India and the uprisings in Africa, not to mention the unabated general arms race and especially the Anglo-German naval rivalry on top of cut-throat economic competition—all these spoke of the danger of an imminent global armed confrontation between the great powers aided by their satellites, chiefly as a way of breaking out of internal social and political difficulties through wars that would rally all patriots to the flag, and give an opportunity to expose and liquidate anti-national elements at home.[150]

Hinting obliquely at Germany, Parvus-Helphand analysed the Russo-Japanese war as arising from the difficulties of a bankrupt despotism, frantically soliciting foreign loans. It needed to prove itself a credible debtor by displaying prowess on the battlefield, and by scurrying for the spoils of war so as not to have to come to the nation, like Louis XVI, to ask for money, show its accounts, and turn the Tsar's deficit into the nation's treasure. Parvus had prophesied earlier that in an international war the weakest link in the chain of capitalist countries would snap first, unable to sustain the colossal burdens of modern warfare, and devoid of mass support. Defeat on the battlefield would be followed by internal unrest, culminating in strikes, rebellions and revolution. Tsarist tyranny would be brought down by the united effort of all classes, with the working class acting as spearhead, and a bourgeois parliamentary democracy would be set up.

But that would not be the end of the story. The Russian proletariat was at that time unable to make the passage from a bourgeois liberal-democratic regime to a socialist society alone. Rosa for her part was also convinced that at the dawn of the twentieth century the bourgeoisie had neither the capacity nor the interest and the will which it had had in the previous century when confronting absolutism and feudalism, to fight for and maintain a parliamentary democracy. The masses would therefore be driven to go on from the bourgeois-democratic straight to the socialist revolution. They would thus act in a truly democratic manner as saviours of real democracy. Moreover, once the torch of revolution had been thrown into the West, it would—claimed Parvus and Trotsky—be seized by the socialist parties there. After accomplishing a social revolution against an over-extended class government, the victorious Western proletariat would hasten to help their Russian brethren to enthrone socialism by freeing them, first from the fear of interference by reactionary counter-revolutionary powers, and then by offering them their expertise and all other necessary material aid.[151]

The political prospect of an international imperialist war as lever of revolution was beginning to replace the expectation of a purely economic collapse of capitalism. This meant in fact linking up with an older revolutionary tradition in Europe, to which Marx and Engels had adhered before 1848 and for quite a while afterwards, too. But any such calculations were dependent on the behaviour of the masses in the belligerent countries on the eve of the war and once hostilities had started.

In flashes of intuition even the ageing Marx and Engels (but after them more clearly such socialist thinkers and leaders like Kautsky, Victor Adler and Karl Liebknecht) perceived that the myth of revolution was being confronted more and more dangerously by another powerful myth, the myth of the nation. The bourgeoisie, exclaimed Liebknecht, had found an answer to socialism in militarism, which was another word for nationalism and imperialism.[152] This was strikingly shown in the Hottentot election of 1907 which, as we have said, brought the only serious setback to the SPD since 1884. Still more clearly, and with her usual greater intensity, Rosa grasped that nationalism as such was the stumbling block and the enemy. The weaning of the masses from the compulsive grip of patriotic nationalism, and their re-education in the spirit of anti-militarism, were in her eyes calculated to cut the branch upon which the ruling castes were sitting, to undermine their raison d'être, discredit their moral authority, in short to prepare the conditions for the destruction of the existing governmental system and the class base upon which it rested.[153]

Under the impact of the failure of the mass campaign against the Prussian franchise to develop into a real uprising (because of the timidity of the SPD leadership, who became afraid of losing control over the mass demonstrations), and dismayed by the growing bureaucratisation of the party apparatus, Rosa concentrated more and more on militarism. Karl Liebknecht's demand for anti-militarist agitation among recruits and in the army, Rosa's speeches inciting proletarian soldiers not to shoot at the enemy, and not to obey their officers when war had broken out—which earned her a prison sentence at the end of the well-publicised trial of 1913—were not only acts of defiance of state authority and of the patriotic class enemies. They were also seen as actions calculated to split the Social-Democratic party from top to bottom and polarise the movement into a confrontation between the reformist wing and the left-wing radicals, forcing the centre to take sides or be squeezed out.[154] This was strikingly demonstrated when at the time of the Agadir crisis, Rosa Luxemburg got hold of and published the secret correspondence between the party secretary, Molkenbuhr, and the secretary of the Second International, Huysmans, in which the former asked the latter to soft-pedal the international dispute in order not to cause difficulties to the SPD in the forthcoming election campaign.

The loyal party men were incensed by Rosa's indiscretion, indeed from their point of view indiscipline, and in the eyes of some even downright treason. But she launched a counter-offensive against those who, she claimed, put a few parliamentary seats, and parliamentary idiocy in general, above their sacred duty to combat militarism and imperialism.[155] She thus emphatically placed loyalty to the cause of the international proletariat and revolution above obedience to the national party leadership, and implicitly above patriotic considerations.[156] Commitment to international revolution or loyalty to the nation was to become the shibboleth for the fateful split in the socialist movement of Europe in World War I. We can see how it was being prepared in the Second Reich in the confrontation between Rosa Luxemburg, Karl Liebknecht, Klara Zetkin, Franz Mehring on the one side, and the party establishment on the other, with men of the centre like Karl Kautsky, Haase, Hilferding, Ledebour and others, who never ceased to waver between revolution and parliamentary procedures, socialist internationalism and obligation towards the national community. There was no more delicate or more explosive issue.

Rosa had one safe and outspoken ally in Germany. Speaking out at the 1912 Chemnitz party conference on the world conflagration being prepared by the ruling classes, Karl Liebknecht invoked the old maxim: *si vis pacem, para bellum*: "If we want peace among nations, we must prepare and advance the class struggle, fomenting it more and more on an international scale."[157]

The Chemnitz conference adopted a resolution which pleased the centre and the Left, against chauvinism, imperialism and the threat of war and for international solidarity. The report of the Central Committee to the Chemnitz conference affirmed however that "no Social-Democrat thinks of leaving the Empire defenceless". It swore indeed to combat "the lust for conquest that is beginning to appear among our people", and went on to say: "We hold it self-evident that it is our duty to defend and protect our country and our culture against any thieving assault. . . . The accusation that the Social-Democrats are devoid of patriotism is absurd."[158]

The Jena party conference in 1913 was a milestone in the history of the SPD by its voting overwhelmingly (336 to 140) in favour of supporting inheritance taxes and graduated income and property taxes, because they hit mainly the possessing classes, in spite of the fact that they were designed to finance armaments, which to radicals meant supporting militarism. The conference rejected by a similarly crushing majority (333 to 142) Rosa Luxemburg's motion on reviving the issue of the political general strike as part of "an offensive, resolute and con-sequential tactic of the party in all fields . . . the form taken on by the proletarian struggle in the phase of revolution". Rosa did accompany the adverse vote with a prophecy that when war broke out, the flabby, hesitant, misguided leaders of the party "would be hustled along by the masses". Things turned out differently—as we know. Rosa was once more to prove wrong about the masses. "It is significant," writes Maehl, "that the minority was composed, with half a dozen exceptions, of the same persons who had voted against Wurm's resolution on tax policy. . . . Of the fourteen who later voted against the war credits in the SPD Reichstag delegation's session of August 3, 1914, all but three voted at Jena for Luxemburg's resolution. Further, of the thirty-two socialists who either voted in the Reichstag plenum against war credits or left the hall in protest on March 20, 1915, all but seven voted for Luxemburg's resolution."[159] The same comments are made by Carl Schorske.[160]

The polarisation in German Social-Democracy was brought about by the myth of the nation versus the myth of revolution.

Chapter Eight

NATIONALIST SEPARATISM OR REVOLUTIONARY CLASS INTERNATIONALISM IN POLISH SOCIALISM

In her uncompromising commitment to a brand of dialectical materialistic monism which flew in the face of all the lessons of history and sociology, Rosa was the most consistent and the most extreme of internationalists.[161] In her bitter arguments with the nationalist majority of the Polish socialist movement Rosa used to put the words "nation" and "national" into inverted commas. She was revolted by Social-Democrats who treated the nation as a primary and eternal entity above all class divisions, as if it were the only historic phenomenon which was not a function of changes in the modes of production or changing class relations, and had a prior existence, and would last forever, whatever social changes historic development engendered. "Patriotism and socialism are two ideas which can in no way be brought into harmony."[162] A socialist's fatherland was "the great mass of workers".[163] Echoing Marx's formulae, Rosa Luxemburg insisted at the Congress of the Second International in Paris in 1900 that the business of the proletariat was not to change the map of Europe as traced by history, but to organise itself for the struggle for a socialist republic.[164] She was aghast at the fact that people professing to be Marxists made the distinction "we" Poles and "they" Germans, Russians etc., instead of the distinction "we" proletarians, "they" the bourgeois: a German worker was closer to a Polish worker than a Polish landlord and entrepreneur. She never tired of insisting on the unbridgeable differences between the proletariat and the bourgeois in everything—interests, mentality, morality, *Weltanschauung,* aims and aesthetic views.[165] Conversely Ignacy Daszynski, the leader of the Polish Social-Democratic party in Galicia and head of the Austrian Social-Democratic deputies club in the Vienna Reichsrat, always identified himself as both a Pole and a socialist.[166]

Rosa was conscious that she was at odds with Marx's attitude to Poland, which entirely ignored the social-economic substratum of the Polish problem, in fact defended in spite of it the idea that the independence of Poland was a basic, unchanging postulate of the European revolution, whatever the social-economic conditions prevailing in

Poland. She said in her correspondence with Jogiches that, far from wishing to combat Marx, she desired to out-Marx him, to put him straight, and thus make Marx more Marxist and more effectively monistic.[167] In that spirit she set out to restate Marx's position in the light of changed historic circumstances. Hypnotised by the geopolitical importance of Poland in all plans for neutralising Tsarist Russia and the Holy Alliance, Marx let his image of Poland be entirely shaped by the romantic, insurrectionary revolutionism of the Polish émigrés and conspirators at home, soaked in the romantic patriotic tradition, who were almost exclusively sons of an impoverished gentry. They were products of a crumbling, if not already obsolete, natural, feudal economy. Since then, however, mighty changes had occurred. These were the abolition of the customs barrier in 1861 between the Russian Empire and the Russian-dominated Kingdom of Poland; the tragic failure of the 1863-4 guerilla uprising, led by the "red" elements of the nobility and its retainers and allies from among the petty bourgeoisie and the poor intelligentsia; the emancipation of the Polish serfs by the Tsar; and the ruin of the insurgent gentry as a result of decimation in the rebellion, exile to Siberia, punitive confiscation and loss of seigneurial dues, feudal lands and peasant services; the industrial development of Poland and the emergence of a new bourgeois middle class and of a native capitalism and thus also of a Polish urban proletariat; the rise of a dynamic revolutionary movement in a growingly industrialised Russia itself; finally, the altered positon of France, which from the spearhead of national liberation movements had become an ally of Tsarist Russia. All these developments had completely altered the setting of the Polish question and its relevance for international revolutionary strategy.[168]

Poland had entered into the era of money economy and had become one of the most important industrial workshops of the Russian Empire. The interests of the Polish bourgeoisie which had sprung up overnight were vitally dependent on union with Russia—that is with its unlimited market. So it had rationalised its class interest into a new version of Polish patriotism. The armed uprisings of hot-headed romantics having so dismally failed and brought untold suffering and ruin upon the Polish nation, the task was now—it claimed—to foster an "organic" development and a "positivist" orientation. The Poles were called upon to build up a modern economy, amass assets, develop resources, to modernise and to forget about conspiracy, terror and revolt. In other words, the selfish class exploitation of the proletariat was turned into a patriotic duty. The Polish bourgeois spokesmen never tired of using patriotic phrases, of vowing never to rest till a free Poland had been restored. Their sermons were however intended to bamboozle the workers into obedience to their employers in the name of the organic totality of the indivisible nation and of the national interest, which allotted to every class its proper necessary task. They enjoined brotherly co-operation upon all and forbade class war for its weakening effect upon a hard-pressed nation, which was trying to build up a healthy national economy—the true basis of a nation's strength.[169]

Polish independence, piously evoked day and night, was in fact relegated to doomsday. Not only was the bourgeoisie not interested in the secession of Poland from Russia. Notwithstanding class antagonism, the proletariat had the same need for union with Russia as Polish capitalism—the Russian market. Moreover, the Polish proletariat shared with the Russian working class the same needs and aspirations. Indeed, not only the defence of the class interests, but the abolition of Tsarism, were impossible without the closest co-operation between the workers of all the races of the Russian Empire. For its own reasons the Polish peasantry too had no interest in the restoration of the Polish state. Throughout the centuries, the ruling class of Poland, the nobles, had oppressed and exploited their serfs. The Polish peasants owed their emancipation to the Tsar. They were still altogether alien to any form of nationalism. Even the nobility, in the Russian-dominated part of Poland from fear of having their properties seized by the Tsar, in Galicia out of genuine loyalty to the Habsburgs—as well as the submissive Catholic hierarchy—had all abandoned irridentist dreams.[170]

So what were the social classes which were interested in an independent Poland? The dying petty bourgeoisie, with its narrow limited interests and horizons, the unemployed members of the intelligentsia and the remnants of the bankrupt gentry sunk into romantic regrets and mystical ideas about Poland's mission as saviour of the nations—in brief, solely the discontented groups about to be annihilated by the process of capitalist development.[171]

The ideology of a national resurrection was a utopian dream, if not a capitalist red herring and ruse: at all events an absurdity. The Polish question had already been solved by the capitalist development of Poland, solved negatively.[172] The Polish Social-Democrats who had espoused it, and who had become its leading spokesmen and vanguard, were now guilty of treason to the working class and the revolution, as agents of reactionary capitalism. This was most flagrantly demonstrated in 1905, when they refused to join in the general strike of all Russian workers, on the pretext that its failure in Poland would cripple Polish industry and harm the Polish interest. The followers of Pilsudski resorted to riot and terror against the Russian authorities in Poland, but they did so in the name of a national liberation struggle. Pilsudski betook himself to Japan in 1905 to negotiate with the Tokyo government about a diversionary action against the Russian forces in Poland.[173] The Social-Democrats indeed showed scant interest in securing an all-Russian constitution for fear lest a bourgeois nationalist Russia might—like the German and Hungarian bourgeois nationalists in 1848—prove a more effective national oppressor than inefficient Tsarism. A paper autonomy, which some expected to be granted by a reformed Russia to the border territories inhabited by national minorities, was calculated to blunt the patriotic insurrectionary ardour of the populations. Soon after the collapse of the 1905 revolution, Pilsudski started organising a Polish Legion in Austrian Galicia in preparation for armed action in the expected war against Russia, at the side of Austro-Hungary. In line with the traditional arguments of the Polish radicals throughout the nineteenth century, the Social-Democrats were at pains to discount the strength, significance and prospects of the revolutionary movement in Russia. According to them the half-Asiatic despotism was destined to last forever.

The Polish socialist movement had become polarised by 1880. An important date was the commemoration of the fiftieth anniversary of the 1830 uprising, called that year in Switzerland by a tiny group of left-wingers who had given up nationalist irridentism and the idea of the primacy of national independence, in favour of international solidarity with the Russian revolutionary movement. Marx and Engels had sent the customary greetings, with the ritual evocation of a free independent Poland as the aim of all socialists. The Polish speakers Stanislaw Mendelson, Samuel Dickstein and Warynski, made bold to dissociate themselves from the two prophets' benediction.[174] Rosa, Jogiches, Marchlewski and Dzierzinski carried on that tradition by setting up at the end of the century the splinter group which they called the Social-Democratic party of the Kingdom of Poland and Lithuania.[175] The PPS spokesmen sneered at the faction by saying that all its members could be seated on half a sofa. The PPS organ in Cracow, whose editor was the Jewish apostate Haecker, virulently attacked the hysterical, fanatical and treacherous female Rosa Luxemburg, its most articulate and inter-nationally best-known and most active representative. He ridiculed her alliance with the Berdichev "Russians", alluding to the Jewishness of most or many of the SDKPL (Social-Democratic party of the Kingdom of Poland and Lithuania) leaders, as well as of the Russian revolution-aries whom Rosa and her friends sought to win over as allies. It was even hinted that Rosa was a Tsarist agent.

If an agent of anyone, she was in a sense, though quite uninten-tionally, a tool of the SPD. Ignaz Auer, who as secretary of the party was the first to launch her upon her career, made no secret of his views on the solution of the Polish problem in Prussia: "The greatest service that could be rendered to the Polish workers was to Germanise them."[176] It is only fair however to add that though objectively she did serve the purpose of the hard-nosed SPD bosses and was warned about their real intentions, Rosa resolutely fought policies of Germanisation and national oppression. All the same, the SPD leaders liked her peroration at the 1900 Mainz conference of the party, which she concluded by proclaiming that it was necessary "to teach the Polish worker to renounce national utopias and to show him that the best way of defending the interests of his nationality was not by affirming his identity as a Pole through belonging to a nationalist party but by being a good Social-Democrat".[177] Those were the days of the Hakata, the nationalist German association with the aim of ousting Polish land-owners and peasants from their lands by every cunning device and chicanery. Forced Germanisation of schools was in full swing. In 1902 Rosa wanted with all her heart to believe not only that the Polish workers were quite immune to the virus of nationalism which sub-ordinated proletarian interests to national unity, but also that even Polish intellectuals had developed a healthy disgust for the rhetoric of social-patriotism.[178] But in the Junius brochure of 1915 she lamented the sway of "nationalist hypnosis" upon the German workers.[179]

Rosa bitterly fought the PPS ideology on the international scene and called for a halt to the traditional support given by the International to Polish irridentism. This also gave her an opportunity to universalise the issue into a sustained effort against the recognition of the right of national self-determination in general, and in particular by the Inter-national. She interpreted the resolution adopted by the London congress of the International in 1896 in answer to the motion by the PPS, asking the congress to reiterate the old Marxist principle that the restoration of a united and independent Poland was a socialist postulate and *sine qua non*, as in fact a rebuke to the nationalist Poles. Under her influence, the congress declined to pronounce upon that particular demand, limiting itself to a general declaration on the right of self-determination and against national oppression, and on the end of all racial and social oppression that the victory of socialism was sure to bring, thus securing to all subject nations the reality of self-determination which was impossible in the capitalist world, and enjoining the workers of all countries to labour for that goal.

According to Rosa there was in that declaration no recognition of any concrete right of any particular nationality to national self-determination. Ignoring the fact that the revolution spoke of peoples

"actually" suffering from national oppression by despotic governments, she went on to depict the revolution as an abstract general statement which contained no directives for concrete action in a concrete
case. And general principles were from the Marxist point of view
merely declaratory, and thus meaningless and inoperative. Socialism
was concerned with the right of self-determination not for nations, but
for the proletariat. And as to the bourgeois democratic principle of
national sovereignty, it was tantamount to declaring that the majority
of the nation had the right to decide. But Marxism rejected the fetish of
numerical majorities. Since when had socialists subordinated their aims
and policies to the decisions of a majority composed of class enemies?
The socialists, especially the conscious revolutionary socialists, were
still a minority in every country. Should they therefore subject themselves to the majority? The socialist revolutionaries owed allegiance to
their ideal, to the historic goal, to the future, to the predestined shape of
things, which was the immanent, albeit not always as yet conscious
"general will" of all working men.

Moreover, no single national Social-Democratic party could act as
spearhead of a nationalist movement. It was the general interest and
strategy, the general will of the international socialist movement that
counted. The same, and in a stronger measure, applied to separatist
socialist parties set up by racial minorities. They smacked of strike-
breaking, the perpetrators of which invoked the right to satisfy their
eagerness and their right to work. To put the right of separatist self-
determination unconditionally before the exigencies and imperatives of
Weltpolitic and global revolutionary strategy, was tantamount to sliding
into liberal idiocy.

The mission of socialism was not to erect a conglomeration of
separate nations, but to turn mankind into a single nation. Rosa
Luxemburg scorned the PPS hopes that an international war would
restore Poland, an idea cherished by all Polish freedom fighters
throughout the nineteenth century. In 1902, at a time when
Marchlewski, for instance, was still swearing never to cease protesting
against the partitions of Poland and to fight for its independence via
socialism, she wrote sneeringly that "the most fertile imagination of a
café habitué could not nowadays conjure up an independent Poland
emerging from a war between the German Reich and Russia".[180] Her
influence is visible in the insistence of the SDKPL early in the Great
War on the lack of any viable existence for a restored Poland or for any
other small nation between the imperialist superpowers.[181]

Rosa could only see imperialist powers devouring or rendering small
states obsolete, and turning their independence—"a transitional phase

of bourgeois class domination"—into a myth. Nor could she appreciate the role of imperialism in provoking national uprisings of the subject colonial peoples—in stark contrast to Lenin. Socialism could not be reached via national liberation struggles. National freedom could be obtained only through an international social revolution. The first and categorical imperative was therefore to sink all national differences and to unite into a common anti-imperialist front.[182] Not that she was entirely blind and deaf to the possibility, indeed heroism and glory, of an uprising against oppression from spiritual, religious and national motives, and not merely for economic interests. Far from it. She only maintained that solely revolutionary classes were capable of it, indeed as a result of their social-material situation.[183] And then, one may say, it was no longer really a national or religious uprising. Neither were autonomous impulses which could move different classes equally.

Part III

"THE WITCHES' KITCHEN" AND ITS BREW:
THE NATIONALITIES PROBLEM — AUSTRIA

At the Austrian Social-Democratic party conference in 1897 its leader Victor Adler called Austria "die Experimentierkammer der Weltgeschichte". It was, he said alluding to Goethe's Faust, the witches' kitchen where the brew of the nationalities problem was being cooked up. In no country, he exclaimed, were the proletariat of the different nationalities so dependent upon each other as in Austria.[1]

The "Austrian Internationale" was called upon, indeed compelled, to serve as an example of socialist internationalism by preventing or healing national strife. Its mission was to present a paradigm of the international socialist order of the future.

Chapter One

AUSTRIA AS THE HISTORIC TEST CASE

Austria had in the past been invoked as a test case of inter-racial relations both by followers of the French Revolution and by counter-revolutionary conservatives. To progressives of various hues the Habsburg multi-racial and patriarchal monarchy was an absurd monstrosity. It was "a prison of nations". The empire had been pieced together by conquest, dynastic marriage settlements and semi-private deals with magnates, without the inhabitants having been consulted or—after annexation—given a say in their own affairs. The local diets and ancient laws, charters and privileges, confirmed by the Habsburgs in every case of annexation in the old feudal-dynastic style, had become a mockery of self-government in the age of the rights of man and the sovereignty of the people. They were entirely out of tune with the new means of communication, rapid industrialisation and growing social mobility. The establishment and the privileged conservative forces continued to describe the ancient dynastic, feudal crown lands, with their mixed populations divided into master and subject races as historic entities at a time when sharply defined ethnic groups were already clamouring for the democratic right of national self-determination. This hypocrisy was made still more offensive by Viennese centralism and its obnoxious and squalid methods: intimidation, the fomenting of racial animosities, the cunning system of stationing army units recruited from the various antagonistic nationalities, censorship, spying, the bribing of pressure groups and dilatory muddling through.[2]

The reactionaries in their turn cited Austria as proof of the excellence of long traditions, and as confirmation of the potency of ancient institutions and of the strength of the conservative instincts of the masses. They admired the staying power of the venerable dynasty. It had survived invasions, terrible defeats, the loss of large armies, repeated expulsions or flights from its capital. It retained its territorial integrity and old institutions, seemingly unshaken by the agitations of clever, ambitious and restless intellectuals, so loathed by the Emperor Francis I, who had no use for clever people and always recommended Sitzfleisch above all. The House of Habsburg could safely rely on the unfaltering loyalty of a peasant army led by dedicated officers, recruited from the descendants of an aristocracy created in the Thirty Years War by the Habsburg emperors out of the motley of Catholic volunteers and mercenaries from all over Europe, rewarded with lands confiscated from Protestant nobles, above all in Bohemia and Moravia. The silent and dumb majority of Austria, the peasant millions of all nationalities, were tutored by an unflaggingly faithful church which taught them to love and venerate the apostolic kings and to obey their superiors.

The events of 1848-9 which rocked the Danubian Empire to its foundations, could certainly be regarded as a brew prepared in a witches' kitchen. It was a crucible of institutions, ideologies and aspirations, and in the final analysis all combatants were confounded by the events.[3]

On the surface the empire came out of these terrible ordeals with its territorial integrity intact and the system not only undamaged but to some extent strengthened. Schwartzenberg and Bach replaced the immemorial appeal to divine right with ruthless efficiency, stringent centralism and uninhibited authoritarianism. But in doing so, they undermined the ancient baroque edifice. They caused it to forfeit the principles and the mystique which sustained it. Business-like administration was no substitute for deeply rooted inner conviction or reflex responses by either rulers or subjects.

The revolutionary events of 1848-9 also administered a resounding blow to the naive liberal-democratic faith in the identity, or at least the close link between the democratic aspirations for self-government and the principle of national self-determination. The nationalities proved not to be just a citizenry fighting for the right to administer their own affairs. They emerged as collective personalities passionately desiring to assert their peculiar identity, their worth and power, and resolved, as the case might be, not to give up what they owned, to recover what they had lost, or obtain what they had for so long been denied. They would not prove unworthy of their glorious ancestors, or inadequate for their future tasks. These sentiments were passionate enough to still any whisper of conscience as well as promptings of friendly observers about fair play, equal justice to all and the duty to repair wrongs inflicted in the course of centuries upon weaker races. With Darwinian nationalism assuming the character of a religion, the Austrian idea of a family of nations amicably coexisting under a patriarchal dynasty was losing its credibility and its hold.[4]

The doctrine of the empire as an organic and historic entity as well as an economic unit was badly shaken by the loss of Lombardy and Venice. The Habsburg dynasty forfeited much of the proud and affectionate allegiance of the dominant nationality, the Austrian Germans, when it was so ignominiously defeated and driven out of Germany by the junior house of Hohenzollern. The latter was raised to the pinnacle of its glory as the imperial dynasty of a united Germany, which overnight became the greatest military, economic and cultural power on the continent of Europe. The compromise dual monarchy with Hungary in 1867 had a double effect upon the other nationalities. It showed them, above all the Czechs, that with perseverance and relentless pressure they too might become self-governing nations in a federal structure, and at the same time it embittered them by handing over several nationalities to ruthlessly oppressive Magyar rule.[5] The Hungarian ruling class of feudal magnates and gentry was animated by a wholly uninhibited, indeed passionately self-righteous determination to prevent the subject alien majority from diminishing, weakening or in any other way endangering the power and possessions of the lonely, isolated Magyar nation, surrounded as it was by Germans and Slavs. Less than twenty years after it had been crushed by the Austro-Russian armies, the Hungarian nation, more precisely its magnates, was placed in a position to exercise political ascendancy over a shaken, wobbling, buffeted Austria, and to frustrate or to impose at critical moments decisions of vital military or economic importance to the whole empire.[6]

The post-1867 constitutional structure of Austria was rightly called sham constitutionalism. It was designed to offer a semblance of popular participation, but it was in fact calculated to hold democracy at bay, and in the light of the symmetry of the racial and social cleavages in Austria, to secure the preponderant position of the historic nations. The quaint electoral system of the four colleges—landlords, chambers of commerce and capitalist potentates, the urban middle class, and peasants—gave the peasant masses and the petty bourgeoisie very little, and to the urban workers no say at all.[7] The original hope that German-Austrian liberalism would prove capable of preventing the excesses of class rule on the one hand and racial conflict on the other, by cushioning both social and ethnic antagonisms through latitude and mildness, proved illusory. German liberalism was soon undermined by the growing nationalism of the German population scared by the seemingly irresistible encroachments of the Slavs. It ceased to be the safe prop of the imperial administration. The turning point came when in 1879, Count Taaffe, a descendant of an Irish peer who had joined the Catholic cause in the Thirty Years War, was appointed prime minister and formed the 'iron ring' coalition of conservatives and Slavs, which ruled Austria for fourteen years, and was regarded by the German-Austrian nationalists as a feudal-clerical-Slav conspiracy against the historic, preponderant German position in the Ostmark. This was also the time when Slav, and above all Czech, nationalism became more and more militant.[8]

In these circumstances the awakening of the masses and the advance of democracy, culminating in the grant of universal suffrage in 1905, turned out to be not the hour of opportunity for securing civil liberties, establishing effective popular control, and carrying out long overdue administrative and economic reforms designed to narrow regional, race and class inequalities, but a time of nationalist self-assertion, rivalry and strife. The nationalities were ranged for war to defend threatened possessions and privileges, or to recover long-lost rights and gain a place in the sun.

It was difficult to shut one's eyes to the stark fact that the age of democracy was by no means inaugurating an era of civic and political liberty, popular sovereignty and equitable government based on consensus and universal goodwill. Rowdy obstructionism having rendered regular legislative action impossible, government had to be kept going by resorting to imperial decrees. The loss of faith in parliamentary government, which was being paralysed by nationalist passions, exacerbated racial susceptibilities still further. The national government was unable to inspire trust or allegiance, or a sense of common interests and joint responsibility, nor had it the power to act as impartial umpire and arbiter.

Chapter Two

CLASS OR NATION?

The Austrian Social-Democratic party was thus indeed forced to become a test case for the relationship between socialism and nationalism. When it came to the crunch, and nationalist conflicts degenerated into warlike neurosis, would it be possible for socialism to stem the destructive tide, with the help of the weapon of international class solidarity, and then to lead the masses, which had successfully passed the test of proletarian internationalism, to the revolutionary realisation of the universal socialist idea? Or would the nationalist obsession prove a stumbling block to international socialist unity, and grow still more intense from having faced and overcome the challenge of socialism?

It was in the last analysis really a question of which of the two rival ideologies would prove to be the more real, the more basic and the more potent creed. This was indeed a total confrontation. To the nationalists, the race or the ethnic entity was the primary datum, the community of communities, the all-determining collective fate and destiny. The national brotherhood was infinitely more significant than class distinctions, social cleavages or party alignments, above all, when the nation was oppressed by a foreign power or mortally threatened by it.

There could, on the other hand, be no Marxist socialist ideology without the basic tenet of class conflict. The state, even the nation-state, was an instrument of class domination. Its laws were not the expression of the general national will, interest or genius, but a means for rendering class exploitation easier and more effective. National conflicts stemmed from exploitative designs, and nationalist sentiments were red herrings used by the ruling class to divert attention from the social struggles or drugs to intoxicate the masses.

In spite of its warlike stance, revolutionary socialism, in so far as race relations were concerned, may be regarded as heir to the universalist or even cosmopolitan faith of original liberalism in the ultimate harmony of interests of all mankind. Adam Smith and his disciples, such as Cobden and Bright, firmly believed that once trade was allowed to flow freely, universal peace and concord would become

137

a blessed reality. It was only selfish, ignorant avarice, bent upon blindly grabbing what came its way, that was halting the natural circulation of goods and leading to crisis, shortages, international tension and war. Liberated from the virus of rapacious avarice, with which the ignorant possessing classes were irretrievably infected, the international proletariat, humanity itself, would, in the view of Marxist socialism, inaugurate the era of ultimate harmony. Politics was, in both original liberalism and Marxist socialism, a function of economics.

The concomitants of nationalism were inescapably some form of mercantilism and a Darwinian struggle for survival and power. Economics were in its eyes a function of politics, as List had thought.

Race conflict in a multi-racial state rent by strife inevitably tends to accord higher reality to ethnic origins than to class membership. The fear of being branded disloyal to one's group in distress and danger has always been a very powerful deterrent. Socialism cannot however function at all either on the political or on the economic plane, without inter-racial working class unity and solidarity. No struggle for the defence of working class interests, no strike, no wages policy, no trade union activity is practicable without a common organisation with an agreed policy, and without the axiom of equal terms for the workers of all ethnic groups. This is not just ideology, but pragmatic politics, and professional interest.

To admit therefore that nationhood had inherently greater power than socialist internationalism was tantamount to a renunciation of the great socialist vision. The principle of international proletarian solidarity and unity necessitated a single Social-Democratic party and, still more, a single trade union organisation throughout the Austrian Empire. However, it also militated against any idea of breaking up the multi-racial empire into ethnic states. Not only would this have been a retrograde step from the point of view of Marxist dogma on the need for larger territorial units capable of developing a large-scale modern industry and creating an urban proletariat. The dismantling of the Danubian Empire under the impact of nationalist separatism was sure to be taken to demonstrate the greater vitality of nationalism, and to prove that after decades of international socialism, proletarians of the various races were unable to remain under the same roof or to prevent their class enemies from disrupting the common home of the working classes of the different ethnic groups.[9]

As a result the Austrian Social-Democrats—ostensibly a party of revolution—emerged as the staunchest upholders of the indivisibility of the venerable monarchy, and as objectively the most reliable ally of the dynasty, and the state party of Austria *par excellence*.[10]

Victor Adler, the master of self-mockery, spoke of the Socialist party as Hofräte of the revolution.[11] The immediate aim of the socialists became not the revolution or seizure of power by the working class, but the modernisation of Austria, its restructuring and renovation in a manner that would enable it to withstand centrifugal forces. Although, as we shall see, the Austrian Social-Democrats were left as the sole genuine defenders of parliamentary procedures and democratic legitimacy for their own sakes, some of the socialist leaders became so disgusted with the savage obstruction practised in the Reichsrat and so horrified by the paralysis of all parliamentary action by warring nationalities, including legislation of the most innocent and urgent nature, that they were prepared to welcome a coup d'état by the Emperor in the form of an *octroi* of universal suffrage and a *ukase* regulating the nationalities problem.[12] The trouble was that the old Emperor could no more be expected to shed all the instincts and habits of thought of his hoary dynasty than Louis XVI had been. He was not equipped to become a people's king, in this case an ally of the till yesterday outlawed "anarchists". In their turn, the socialists were not a little hampered by the embarrassing recollection of the secret contacts between Lassalle and Bismarck at the time of the Prussian constitutional crisis, in the course of which the workers' leader suggested to the arch-Junker and royalist an alliance against the bourgeois liberals, with the concealed objective of outwitting and overwhelming the conservative allies, once universal suffrage had placed the proletariat in a position to do so.[13]

The Social-Democratic party in Austria only gradually came to realise that its success, indeed its very existence—at all events as a united party—depended upon its proper handling of the nationalities problem. For that it could find no recipe in Marx and Engels. The latter had simply not foreseen, or only very late begun timidly and most reluctantly to perceive, the possibility of socialism having one day to face the challenge and rivalry of nationalism. It was hardly conceivable to them that socialist strategy might have to be fundamentally reorganised to meet a threat which was extraneous to the scheme of the all-inclusive class struggle. Ready as Marx and Engels were to use the revolutionary potentialities of national grievances or to brush aside the nationalist pretentions of ethnic groups standing in the way of the national unification of a large territorial unit, if seized by a revolutionary ferment, they would never have agreed to halt or divert the general socialist advance in order to assure national independence to any claimant. They could never give up the faith that the eventual victory of socialism would, by putting an end to social conflict, solve all problems arising from national oppression. The belated admission that it was hard to expect a great enslaved nation to forget its bondage and devote itself to the universal cause of socialism, was not followed up by Engels with any constructive proposal.

While this admission was made in the secrecy of private correspondence, Marx's and Engels' harsh denial of the right of national self-determination to the fossilised reactionary remnants of unhistorical nationalities, and the hopes voiced by them about the eventual absorption of the subjugated peoples of Austro-Hungary into the stronger cultures of the dominant races were public property.

By the end of the nineteenth century, no ethnic group was prepared to acknowledge that it was so culturally insignificant, so hopelessly backward and irredeemably reactionary as to be excluded from the dictum which Engels had pronounced. Unprepared and unequipped to deal with the issue, the Austrian Social-Democratic party were at first naively unwilling to recognise its existence. They congratulated themselves that no nationalities problem existed for Social-Democracy and that questions of race, religion, language were irrelevant to fighters for the emancipation of the working classes. Not that all would be forced or even be expected to speak the same language and have the same culture. Allegiance to one's native culture, love for one's ancestral culture would be wholly respected and, if need be, accorded facilities for expression. But that was not expected to make any difference to the readiness of everyone to participate in the common revolutionary endeavour, which must be directed to the benefit of all mankind. It was a service which was more important and nobler than nationalist narcissism, arrogance and militancy. These views were embodied in the programme of the international Social-Democratic party of Austria, adopted by the foundation conference at Neudörfl in 1874, and four years later by the constitution of the autonomous Czecho-Slav party.[14]

Since Marx and Engels had committed themselves to the view that, unlike the bourgeoisie, the proletariat had freed itself from national prejudices, Engels was only too eager to instance the Danubian Empire as proof of that fulfilment: "While," he wrote in a message of greetings to the 1891 congress of the Austrian Socialist Congress, "in Austria, the possessing classes in the various crown lands are wasting the last remnants of their ability to govern, in blind nationalist strife, you are unfolding in the second congress of your party the picture of an Austria which no longer knows any national conflict, of an Austria of the workers".[15] Engels' words were echoed in his concluding speech at the end of the congress by the German Social-Democratic Reuman, when he solemnly proclaimed that in Austrian Social-Democracy there were "no questions of nation or race". Before him the Czech Burian hailed the idea of international Social-Democracy as "that of general brother-hood, a bond that embraces all mankind, love of all for all".[16] "Let us not emphasise the national [*Nationaltum*] or religious dogma, but humanity [*das Menschentum*]."[17]

The manifesto to the working people of Austria of May 5, 1868, spoke of "the age of national isolationism" as passed, and went on: "the nationalities principle is today on the agenda only for the reaction-aries".[18] *Der Radikale*, published in Reichenburg, was proclaiming: "we have only one nationality—mankind, only one fatherland, the earth".[19]

Chapter Three

THE BURDEN OF IRRATIONAL HISTORY VERSUS MODERNISATION

On a closer look, and indeed from the Marxist point of view, abstract internationalism with no reference to concrete situations was not very different from the platitudinous generalities of abstract democracy and the clichés of liberty, equality and fraternity with social contents entirely left out, which Marxists were always eager to ridicule. Not much more helpful was the blanket explanation that the inferior status of the non-German nationalities, the general division into master and subject races in the Danubian Empire and the consequent racial friction, were all due to the Habsburg policies of divide and rule, helped by clerical-feudal machinations. It is needless to add that equally vague and unhelpful was the general promise that the socialist revolution would at some future date abolish every kind of oppression and inequality.

In Austria, the postulate of the necessity of a single socialist party, with no differences of nationality, race, language or religion, steered by the best and most advanced and dynamic representatives of the proletariat on the model of the Western nation-state, was tantamount to taking existing German hegemony in the Social-Democratic movement for granted and natural, in the same way as it was in Austrian society in general. Moreover, for a long time Engels and Social-Democrats in Germany as well as in Austria had looked upon the single Austrian Labour party as merely an extension of the party of the Reich.[20] Austrian Social-Democrats participated in the Eisenach foundation conference. Bebel and Wilhelm Liebknecht, with their 1848 commitments, retained their *Großdeutschland* sentiments to the very end. Such were the views of Kautsky in his first attempts to analyse the nationalities problem in Austria. He still believed at that time that nationalism was altogether a passing phenomenon. Had the revolution of 1848 succeeded, the Czechs would have been absorbed into a democratic German culture already. Anyway, advancing capitalism and international trade were sure to reduce the Czech-speaking population to the two dying classes—the peasantry and the petty bourgeoisie.[21] In his preface to the 1896 edition of Marx's *Revolution and Counter-revolution in Germany*, Kautsky still believed that with advancing industrialisation, class conflict within the Czech nation had been steadily overshadowing the German-Slav antagonisms. "The latter are becoming cliques . . . imitating tradition, petty jealousies. . . . A truly revolutionary party will not be bothered with unilingual or bilingual street signs or the site of a school."[22]

It was flying in the face of reality to present the proletariat in Austria as consisting simply of workers, with no reference to ethnic origin, and to regard the division into ethnic entities as of no consequence for the class struggle. The facts were that history had predetermined the advantageous condition of the German-Austrian workers and had placed the Czech workers in an inferior position to their German counterparts; had kept Slovak, Rumanian and South Slav peasants in bondage to Hungarian landlords; had put Italians in Illyria and Dalmatia in towns, while leaving the Croats and Slovenes in the countryside; had enabled the Poles to hold down the Ukrainian rural and urban proletariat. Generations of poverty deprived most members of the subject nations of a vote for a parliament chosen on the basis of a steeply graduated census; and illiteracy, especially in the German language, barred their access to government posts and to most of the better-paid jobs. The vindication of rights by the ethnic groups as such was thus simultaneously a democratic aspiration, a nationalist postulate and a social vindication. Their inferior social-economic, and therefore political, status was largely the result of their racial origin.

The consistent Marxists welcomed the rush to towns caused by the agrarian crisis which resulted from the sudden lowering of agricultural prices in Europe in response to the opening of the vast prairies in the New World to the plough and to cattle, and the spread of railway communications, the steamship and refrigeration. The superfluous and landless villagers sought employment in the towns, and the capitalists saw their chance in the new abundance of cheap labour. Mushrooming industry was giving rise to a growing proletariat. All this meant a precipitate advance to socialism.

Equity in barter and exchange was in the eyes of the free traders the road to equality. Since Social-Democrats believed that all antagonism and oppresion arose from economic causes, they felt sure that fair and equal treatment for the workers of all nationalities was bound to take the sting out of nationalist animosities, and in due course to cure them altogether. Industrialisation would soon make the workers of different ethnic groups realise that equal pay and conditions and a single trade union organisation were essential for the prevention of competitive cheap labour and blackleg strike-breaking, for insuring mutual aid in case of strike and lockout, and for the establishment of a network of working class agencies and social services—such as old age pensions and sick funds. The Social-Democrats were confident that contacts between and mixing of workers of the various nationalities were bound to bring them closer to each other and to prove to them that social conditions had a more potent effect on their life than membership to their nationality.

Did the encounter result in rapprochement and friendship between the workers of different ethnic groups, or, on the contrary, in underlining differences and feeding animosities? The first outstanding fact was that the earliest industrial development and heaviest industrial concentration took place in regions either originally purely German, such as Vienna, Lower Austria and the Sudeten area in northern Bohemia, or in areas of mixed population such as the Prague district, Moravia and Silesia.[23]

The Slav newcomers were faced with employers, managers, clerks, foremen, skilled workers of different nationality and speech. They were inevitably thrown upon themselves, and became acutely conscious of the master-servant relationship, especially when their work required a measure of literacy in the dominant language. Moreover, the German industrialists could not withstand the temptation to employ cheap, non-unionised labour. They would keep them as guest workers in shacks in camps, exempt from inspection, and isolate them from the organised, predominantly German workers. The preference for cheap foreign over better-paid home labourers was rationalised into a patriotic desire to keep the Slav workers away from the city so as to prevent them from "changing the German character of the city".[24] Moreover, rapprochement between workers of the different races was made difficult by the fact that while the Slav ex-peasants had no tradition of professional organisation, a considerable proportion of the German industrial workers came from the pauperised artisan class, with long experience of closed guilds, and German miners and railwaymen who had a long tradition of membership of semi-secret confraternities.[25]

There were also the facts of unequal development and of time-lag. While Bohemia, Moravia and Lower Austria rapidly developed flourishing metal, textile and chemical industries, it took backward Galicia, Bukhovina and the Dalmatian coastal area a long time to become urbanised, to achieve tolerable communications and to begin to develop consumer goods by manufacturing processes. Had the development been more synchronised and less unequal, there would have been less migration, a larger measure of equality in wages and standards of living could have been achieved, and much friction and resentment might have been spared. As it was, while the workers of the more advanced nations were climbing a step or two higher on the ladder, the members of the less fortunate ones were only beginning their apprenticeship in the hardships of nascent industry.

In the early days of industrialisation and unionism, the membership of the trade unions came from the labour aristocracy, and the few Slav workers who belonged to it felt honoured to be the equals of the Germans. The rapid influx of large members of Czech and other, often illiterate, Slavs, without knowledge of German or any industrial training, made for their isolation and inferior status, even where employers were not deliberately trying to keep them apart.

The new conglomerations or ghettos of Slav workers were soon joined by shopkeepers, priests, teachers and artisans of their own nationality. In quite a few areas economic boycott under the slogan "buy your own only from your own", was added to the factors which operated to deepen ethnic solidarity and to intensify racial antagonism. To ignore a boycott regarded as a weapon in the defence of national interest was made to appear no less treasonable than strike-breaking.

As soon as backward workers of oppressed nationalities got through the barrier of totally stultifying poverty, degradation and ignorance and began to acquire a sense of dignity they usually developed feelings of resentment about the privileges of the workers of the dominant race. They became very susceptible to nationalist sentiment, because their human and class pride was easily channelled into it. Their acutely felt wish for literacy, and awakened desire for education could be satisfied in the immediate future only through the instrumentality of their native tongue and from the sources of their national culture. The road to general culture leads through national tradition, which again deepens and enriches national self-awareness.

In conclusion, industrialisation as such proved to be no panacea for human or even class brotherhood and against racial animosities. It would however be wrong to say that it was the root cause of nationalism and racial conflict. No doubt migration from village to town, improved communications, confrontation with other nationalities, unequal development and inequality of status made for the intensification of militant national consciousness. They did not however create it. Once nationalism has captured the minds and hearts of men, it will always find ways of pressing social-economic developments, tools provided by technology and newly awakened cultural interests into its service, "nationalising" them as it were, and turning them into instruments of the national struggle. Good arguments will always be found for presenting national militancy as the consequence of social injustice, as the awakening of a desire for human dignity and as a longing for self-expression.

Chapter Four

"A STRUGGLE FOR LIFE AND DEATH"

The Slav nationalities, which amounted to something like a half of the population of the Austro-Hungarian Empire, were very much on the move by the end of the nineteenth century. From zealous efforts by individual antiquarians, scholars, writers and publicists, dedicating themselves to salvaging remnants of dying folkloristic traditions, collating dictionaries, composing anthologies and trying to revive a national consciousness, the nationalist trends had developed into mass movements. These were bent on giving tangible and institutionalised expression to national distinctness, and asserting it in an all-embracing and integrated form.[26]

No longer was German the sole medium of the educated classes. The preservation, cultivation and recognition of the native tongue not only as the language of education, but as one of the official languages of the Empire, became a badge of honour and a proof of national achievement, power and prestige. Mass migration still further complicated the linguistic map of an empire in which races had always been intermixed and intertwined. The delineation of the language areas, the drawing of demarcation lines between them, became increasingly more difficult. Moreover, every nationality had a diaspora, often spread far beyond its homestead, and demands were made for rights, schools and other facilities for the mother tongue of their members in the dispersion, out of state funds. There was growing opposition to the principle of a state language, even when renamed *Verkehr-Sprache*—in other words to German as the official unifying language. The struggle was above all between German and the Slavonic languages, and it assumed the dimension of mass psychosis. The concession made to the Czechs to have notices in Czech in a miserable railway station in a mixed area produced furious demonstrations and street fights far away from the little town.[27] The decision to allow classes in Slovene as well as German in a town called Cilli, caused a wave of parliamentary obstruction which paralysed all legislative action for months.[28] Count Taaffe's agreement with the Czechs on the rights of the Czech language (concluded incidentally in violation of a promise given to the Germans of Bohemia not to change the status quo without their consent) was the signal for an outburst of savagery on the part of the German members of the Reichsrat which surpassed all rowdiness of the past. When the government was forced to rescind the agreement, the exasperated Czechs went into action and improved upon the Germans.[29]

Unable to get any legislation passed, the government had to resort to emergency decrees. This gave the Hungarians a pretext to refuse to deal with the Vienna government, because it had lost legitimacy and could not enter into commitments. The concessions originally made to the Czechs by Taaffe were incidentally the result of Vienna's need for the Czech vote in the Reichsrat to force through an arrangement with Hungary, which the Magyar magnates did not relish.[30]

There was an economic aspect to the conflict of languages, which turned the nationalist irritant into a cause of economic hardship and an occasion for discriminatory treatment. Many, if not most of the Slavs, at all events almost all Czechs, knew both languages, whereas very few Germans cared to learn a Slavonic language. The granting of official status to a Slavonic language thus gave preference to Slavs, above all Czechs, in regard to government jobs and public employment, in the first place, but not exclusively, in the mixed areas.[31] The ultra-chauvinist Hungarian government—to cite a particularly grave case—imposed upon all railwaymen of the Kingdom of St Stephen the obligation to speak Hungarian, even on remote local lines in purely Slavonic and Roumanian country. The matter became an issue affecting vital interests and inflaming uncontrollable passions.[32]

Of all the struggles of the nationalities in the Austro-Hungarian Empire the most acute and the most far-reaching was the Czech-German conflict.[33] The Czechs were not a nationality but a full-fledged ancient and advanced nation, which could face the Germans as near equals. Their history went back to the ninth century. For a while their Luxemburg dynasty (adopted but highly patriotic) provided emperors to the Roman Empire of the German nation. There was a time when Prague, housing the oldest university in central and Eastern Europe, outshone all cities over a very wide area.

The Hussite movement had heralded the Reformation and shook Christendom to its very foundations. It also bore all the characteristics of a national and social uprising against the Germans. It assumed on the morrow of the treacherous execution of John Hus at the Council of Constance, in violation of the solemn guarantee given to him by the Emperor, the dimensions of a vast social-religious cataclysm, giving rise to extremely radical heresies and most daring social theories. It unleashed a chain of wars, in which the Czechs displayed amazing valour and ingenuity, and nearly brought ruin upon the German Empire. Most characteristically, indeed in an anachronistic fashion, the defence of the Czech language against the encroachments of German was raised by the Hussite Czechs to the dignity of a crusade in defence of the true faith and the honour of the Czech common people, trampled by a German-dominated hierarchy.

The myth of Hus's teachings and martyrdom, of the Czech Maccabean struggle against German idolatrous tyranny, of the evangelical communism of the Taborites confronting Emperor and magnates, became a revolutionary inspiration of great potency. The dreadful catastrophe of the White Mountain defeat in 1620, the ensuing decimation of the Czech nation in the Thirty Years War and the two centuries of utter degradation and deep slumber which followed, were very reminiscent of Judaic martyrology.

Within decades the nineteenth-century Czech revival achieved astonishing results. A new rich, variegated and highly sophisticated culture sprang up, boasting writers, composers and scientists of world fame. A network of autonomous organisations and institutions came into being, some, like the famous Sokol sports movement, embracing a membership of tens of thousands. In no time the Czechs built up a very considerable modern industry. From having been a predominantly German city in the early nineteenth century, in the early twentieth century Prague's German population was only 25 per cent German, and by 1910 the Germans were no longer represented on the city council.[34] By about that time a quarter of Vienna's inhabitants were already Czech.[35] The Czechs looked upon their close kinsmen the Slovaks, who had for a thousand years lived under the yoke of the Magyars, and had never possessed a state of their own, as candidates for a federated Czecho-Slovakia. Of all subject races of the Habsburg Empire the Czechs, and to some extent the Slovenes, were the only nationalities who were wholly contained in the Danubian monarchy. The Poles, Italians, South Slavs, the Ruthenians, and the Roumanians of Hungary had brethren across the border, with whom they could and in one way or another and at various times, wanted to be, united.

To gain independence the Czechs had to dismember the Habsburg Empire. But they were also almost surrounded by Germans. The disintegration of the Empire into its ethnic components threatened for the Czechs a practically complete encirclement by a mighty German empire of vast expansive ambitions. The Czechs might flirt with the Russians from afar, but they had always very strong reservations about having the Russians inside or even near their border.

Until well into World War I, most Czech leaders could not bring themselves to espouse, and certainly not to advocate openly, the idea of the establishment of a wholly independent Czech or Czecho-Slovak state upon the ruins of a dismembered Austro-Hungary. On the eve of World War I, Beneš himself saw no economic reasons for the imminent collapse or dismantling of the Habsburg Empire.[36] In 1913 the highly respected Czech Labour leader, Smeral, warned his comrades against the dismemberment of the Empire. It would inaugurate another Thirty Years War and in the end the Czechs would find themselves under either German or Russian yoke.[37] But without daring to contemplate secession from Habsburg rule in the midst of some great upheaval, the Czechs were nevertheless consciously and strenuously engaged in a nationalist campaign within the confines of Austria.[38]

While the Slavs were fighting Germanisation imposed upon them by centuries of bondage, and continously enforced by the very survival of the old system, with its centralistic structure and methods, and indeed the facts of life ensuring the economic, social, political and cultural preponderance of the German element, the Germans grew more and more alarmed by the growing Slav element in Austria. The Slavs were streaming into the German strongholds. Mounting Slav strength and influence on the one hand, and the democratisation of Austrian government institutions, on top of linguistic concessions, on the other, were filling the Reichsrat, the regional diets and the administration with more and more Slavs. Cabinet after cabinet was composed of a Slav majority and was presided over by a Slav, and as we have said, purely German areas were being flooded with Slav newcomers, and formerly mixed regions were gradually changing into purely Slavonic preserves. In brief, the ancient German patrimony was being conquered by alien invaders or eaten away at its periphery. Even the most enlightened German was hardly free from the conviction that Germany represented a higher civilisation and superior values, and that the Slavonic advance was a menace to the ancient German, indeed European, heritage.[39] It is enough to mention the famous open letter of Theodore Mommsen to the Germans of the Ostmark, enjoining them to man the ramparts of Germany against the backward Slavs. "The brain of the Czechs," he wrote "does not understand reason, but it understands blows. This is a struggle of life and death."[40]

As old-established possessors the Germans did not feel they were expansionist chauvinists. On the contrary, the obsession of the Slavs with their parochial languages, their crusade against German, one of the leading languages of the world, with one of the finest literatures and greatest scholarly and scientific treasure houses of mankind, seemed to them absurd and aggressive. The petty stubbornness with which the

Slavs fought for recognition of the signs and tokens of their nationhood, for separate services and institutions, sometimes at great cost, and for seemingly no practical purpose, appeared to the Germans to be obsessive irrationality destructive of all businesslike government. Many a liberal and even socialistic German felt that the Slavs, especially Czechs, were asking the Austro-Germans to take up the cudgels for them in their fight for special privileges at the cost of their German compatriots.[41] The feelings of the Slavs about their cause were permeated with sentiments which animate shipmates on a ship in distress, defenders of a beleaguered city. To the Slav nationalists there was no worse sign of moral depravity than indifference to the national cause, no more ignoble sin than desertion of it, no more heinous crime than apostasy.

The Germans too felt menaced and beleaguered. Not only were they losing positions in the outer defences and being overrun in their heartland, but they were also forced to pay for the special treatment accorded to the Slavs. Although they constituted only 37 per cent of Austria's population, the Germans paid 63 per cent of the taxes.[42] Far from acknowledging the debt, the Czechs and others simply used the fact as proof of the privileged economic position which the Germans had gained over the centuries by exploiting the Slavs.

A tribal war thus became the supreme reality in Austria. It was waged with such weapons as economic boycott, street clashes, wild obstruction in representative assemblies, fights in the universities, scurrilous spitefulness in the popular press. The overriding reality of war was bound to subordinate everything to its imperatives. Considerations of rational utility gave place to calculations of the relevance and the importance of every step as weapons in the struggle. Economic interests, gains and losses were assessed as instruments of national power. Democracy came to be used not as an instrument to secure human rights but as an opportunity for recruiting fighters.[43] No wonder that this orgy of aggressive irrationality and mass psychosis awakened in psychiatrists like Alfred Adler and Sigmund Freud an anguished awareness of the hidden depths in the human soul and in the collective psyche,[44] the more so as the situation seemed entirely insoluble: reason appeared powerless to reconcile the warring tribes. All were convinced that Austria was doomed to disintegrate, yet none of the components was, for reasons already given, as yet prepared and ready to break away and stand alone. It has been said that Austria did not fall to pieces for so long because every nationality begrudged so much the prospect of liberty to its rival that it preferred to share the yoke of bondage with it.

Chapter Five

DEMOCRACY ERODED BY NATIONALISM

Social-Democratic strategy on the nationalities issue was, first, to give maximum reality to the common proletarian interest and to the class struggle of the workers of the diverse nationalities, and then to secure equality to all ethnic groups, more emphatically to their working classes, in the enjoyment of the gains obtained by the struggle.[45]
The former aim was facilitated by the existence of grave deprivations and hardships which hurt the workers of all races. Anti-socialist laws were in force from 1866 to 1881, and in 1884 the fear of anarchist action and of the agitation conducted by such radicals as Josef Peukert and Andreas Scheu and the anarchist Johann Most enabled the Vienna government to proclaim a state of emergency. Before that, although the right of association was nominally granted to the workers in 1866, the great labour demonstration in 1869 in defence of trade union demands evoked a series of severe reprisals. The government continued for years to harass socialist newspapers and to hamper party and trade union activities. Above all, the workers had no parliamentary vote and representation till 1897.
Victor Adler considered the struggle for universal suffrage the most vital issue. If in France the disillusionments of 1848 and 1871, caused by the reactionary preferences of the peasant voters, had dimmed the mystique of the democratic vote, and in Germany no such mystique ever developed, because universal suffrage was granted by Bismarck, in Austria the Social-Democrats believed that they could use it not only as a means and symbol of emancipation but also as an instrument for assuaging racial discrimination.
The electoral college system established in 1866 enabled the 5,402 landowning electors to send 85 representatives to the Reichsrat (1 deputy for 63 electors); 585 electors appointed by the chambers of commerce chose 21 representatives (1 deputy for 27 electors); all urban taxpayers had only 118 deputies (10,918 for one deputy); and more or less affluent peasants 128 (2,592 electors send 1 deputy). Given the racial composition of the aristocracy and *haute bourgeoisie*, here was not only flagrant social discrimination, but provocative national inequality, with

two-thirds of the population of Austria, mainly Slav, badly under-represented.[46] The 1882 reform which granted a vote to taxpayers of 5 gulden (included in the lower college) were of no help to the workers. It gave the vote to some members of the lower middle class, in fact to clerical anti-semites, without changing the proportionate strength of the existing colleges.[47]

When in October 1893 Count Taaffe proposed to abolish the property qualification for voters in the two lower colleges, and to grant them 246 seats while leaving the two upper colleges with their 106 deputies intact, he was denounced as a Jacobin who had donned the Phrygian cap and provoked another night of August 4. The leader of the Polish aristocrats, Count Stadnicki, violently protested against the shift in favour of the popular classes which had no feeling for the "spiritual possessions" of civilised mankind.

After Taaffe was overthrown, it was left to Count Bademni to carry out a much more modest reform in 1897 by creating a fifth college with 72 deputies out of a total of 425. Since the pre-existing four colleges retained their structure and quota of deputies, the newcomers had no chance of exercising any influence in the Reichsrat. Without power, they felt free not to show any sense of responsibility, and gaily joined in every orgy of obstructionism. The 1897 election enabled the Social-Democratic party to gain only 14 seats, and these were slashed in 1901 to 10.[48]

It was the 1905 revolution in Russia, and the grant of universal suffrage by the Tsar that made the victory of parliamentary democracy inevitable in Austria. In the 1907 election the Social-Democratic party gained 87 seats, distributed between 50 Germans, 24 Czechs, 6 Poles, 5 Italians and 2 Ruthenians. The achievement was marred by the fact that the anti-semitic Christian Social party obtained 96 members, and the Czech National-Socialist party 9. The composition of the house as a whole was 233 Germans, 108 Czechs, 80 Poles and all the others 95.[49]

The fight for the vote, and the methods employed in the course of it, had an indirect bearing on the nationalities issue and was influenced by it. In so far as it was waged by mass mobilisation, mass demonstration and strikes, it raised working class militancy, and made the workers of the various nationalities appear united in a vast common struggle on an issue which was vital not just to the working classes, but also to their nationalities. It also made them feel that they were not falling behind the bourgeois nationalists in radical opposition to the regime and in an aggressively dynamic assault designed to achieve an immediate break-through.

It was only to be expected that the struggle for universal suffrage would, as in Belgium, Sweden, Italy and elsewhere, bring to the fore the question of the general strike. It did so on two occasions in 1893, when Taafre came out with his reform proposals and was overthrown, and in 1905 shortly before the issue was decided in Russia.[50]

Austrian conditions were not the breeding ground for syndicalist ideas on the general strike as the weapon of revolution and the means of effecting the revolutionary breakthrough, in place of the obsolete street-fighting. Few in Austria played with the vision of the general strike evolving into an armed clash, escalating into general insurrection, bringing the barricades back to their honoured place. In the forefront of the class struggle were democratic demands.[51] Every issue was furthermore overshadowed and complicated by the nationalities problem. On the agenda was, in brief, the modernisation of Austria, its transformation from a predominantly agricultural, feudal-clerical-absolutist structure into a modern industrial state based on equal citizenship, parliamentary government and institutions of regional and ethnic self-government.

The general strike had relevance as a weapon in the struggle for a concrete aim, as a means of mass pressure and method of demonstrating the will of the popular masses fighting against privilege and irrational tradition. But even in the context of the franchise issue, Victor Adler never considered the general strike as a weapon that would paralyse the establishment, force it to its knees and extort from it universal suffrage. He envisaged it rather as the climax of a series of mass demonstrations. He had in mind a one-day strike, which would bring home to the possessing classes that the workers were capable of bringing the economic life and the machinery of the state to a halt. He feared a headlong clash between the strikers and the armed forces. Revolutionary romanticism was temperamentally alien to him. True, he deprecated Eduard Bernstein's disparagement of the myth of the apocalyptic collapse of capitalism preceded by the violent final confrontation between the proletariat and the possessing classes. But he did so because he felt that without it, the grey day-to-day struggle for better conditions and the sustained pressure for wider rights—which were his practice—would fail to satisfy the deeper yearnings of the workers and deprive the socialist ideology of its lustre as a great ideal. He was at the same time against heroics, and, above all, shrank from violent methods. He realised the relative weakness of the socialist labour movement in a country going through only an incipient industrial revolution. The paucity of its means and the rudimentary character of its organisation prevented any proper preparation and precluded the continuation of the general strike for any length of time.

The centrifugal forces of nationalism and the Christian-Social workers' movement not only put in doubt the possibility of mobilising the proletarian masses of all nationalities for direct, let alone insurrectionary, action. They raised the spectre of inter-racial clashes and confrontation with members of fellow unions, once armed violence had been given free rein. Adler was also acutely conscious of the loyalty of the troops to the Emperor. He knew equally well that the deeply conservative ruling classes had not yet lost their nerve to a point where they would be psychologically incapable of ruthlessly employing maximum force to crush an insurgent mob. But more than that, the attitude of the Social-Democratic leadership to the imperial government was not one of simple and implacable hostility. Taaffe's proposals were greeted by the socialists with jubilation as a victory of their cause and as a fruit of their pressure, though Taaffe's motives were not in the least of democratic conviction. He hoped to take the wind out of the sails of bourgeois nationalists and liberal intellectuals, and swamp them with the popularly elected men from outside their ranks.[52]

It was an awkward situation for socialists to take up the cudgels for policies promoted by a thoroughly reactionary regime, which had for so long been persecuting the working class movement. To proclaim a general strike, in protest at Taaffe's dismissal, could also have embarrassed the imperial regime. It did not want to be saddled with an ally who was proclaiming and resorting to "anti-social" methods. With his eyes glued to the nationalities problem, Victor Adler was very careful not to drive things to a bitter confrontation and polarisation. As language riots continued unabated, Social-Democrats began to feel totally helpless and became aware that they had no nationalities policy, only clichés and platitudes. On July 21, 1897, Adler laments in a letter to Kautsky, and similarly to Bebel a week later, that he would like best to bury himself till the storm had blown over. There were no difficulties yet in the party itself, but he dreaded a thorough debate on the subject. "It cannot be concealed that on this national struggle we have resounding slogans and oaths for home consumption, but no positive programme."[53] His whole philosophy and policy were aimed at accommodation, not coercion. Superior force was not to decide, but law, reason, fair play and give-and-take. Being so conscious of the irrational strength of mass sentiments, he feared to exacerbate them. It was only—he thought—by recognising their existence and their force and by offering them some satisfaction, that it was possible to take the sting out of them. Violence was a bad example, a bad educator and a contagious disease. Class suffrage was wrong and justified resistance, but lawlessness was no weapon against or cure for it. And so Adler let the aroused mass movement, heading for a general strike, fizzle out in 1893 and in 1905.[54]

The Czech Social-Democrats were incensed by these methods, and felt let down by the German leadership of the movement, particularly by its head, whom they accused not just of pusillanimity, but of not at heart caring for universal suffrage, since it was not in the interest of the Germans, and was calculated to destroy their dominant position.

It was not only that the Czechs were more militant than the Germans and were goaded on by the challenge and rivalry of their bourgeois nationalist compatriots, the Young Czech movement. The renunciation of the general strike, and the withdrawal from the struggle, just when it had reached a climax, deprived the common socialist struggle of its credibility. The fight for the universal panacea— universal suffrage— having been seemingly postponed *sine die*, and the class struggle having been reduced to slow and drawn-out pressure, the *volte face* looked like a renunciation of the idea of a rapid and decisive proletarian breakthrough and a Social-Democratic victory even on such a clear-cut democratic issue as universal suffrage.[55]

In comparison with the dynamism and zeal of the nationalist movements, the Social-Democrats appeared timid, ineffective and certainly incapable of thoroughly transforming Austrian realities. The Social-Democratic leaders of the nationalities, especially the Czechs, thus had their flank dangerously exposed to bourgeois nationalist criticism and rivalry. The Czech Social-Democratic deputies to the Reichsrat were placed in an invidious position at the time of the great obstruction initiated by the German faction in protest against the concessions made by Badeni to the Czechs on the rights of the Czech language and then by the obstruction practised by the nationalist Czechs upon the withdrawal of the concessions. The official stand of the all-Austrian party was one of neutrality. It approved the concessions, but disapproved of the manner in which they were granted—the breach of the promise made earlier to the Germans—and condemned all obstruction in principle.[56]

The bleak, disgusted despair, with which the "lunatic asylum" that was Austria, and its parliament in particular, filled Victor Adler could be borne by him only if it proved possible to keep the Social-Democratic party above the melée as the sole spokesman and guardian of sanity and humanity.[57] In anguished despair he clung to the hope that an enlarged franchise was capable of infusing a measure of rationality and fairness into Austrian politics by inoculating the socialists of the various races against the virus of irrational nationalist passion.

Chapter Six

THE FAILURE OF SOCIALIST INTERNATIONALISM

By the turn of the century, Adler had reconciled himself to the fact that Austrian Social-Democracy had become a federation of national parties joined in an overall organisation, its unity symbolised in common annual congresses, a joint central bureau and sporadic joint meetings of the executives of the national parties. It had proved impossible to maintain a single centralised party, with local branches, which pragmatically were accorded facilities out of common, but mainly German, funds to publish journals and propaganda material in their native languages. Nor was it enough to provide the ethnic partners with speakers who spoke to them in their own language, came from the same racial stock and had first-hand experience of the special local or ethnic needs and peculiarities.

The momentum of national self-awareness, strengthened by the challenge of bourgeois nationalism, soon turned pragmatic considerations into a matter of principle. Socialist internationalism came to be defined not as an indiscriminate unity of individual proletarians of all nationalities, but—in contrast to cosmopolitanism—as a confraternity of ethnic groups. No doubt a Vienna-directed centralised party was bound to perpetuate and highlight German hegemony, even if the executive could be made to comprise a fair number of non-Germans. The famous Brno programme of 1899 clearly and emphatically reinterpreted internationalism in terms not of individual sentiment and conviction, but of cooperation, solidarity and common aims of nationalities, or parties organised on the basis of nationalities as primary collective entities. While rejecting furthermore the crownland traditions, the programme insisted on territorial self-government of the nationalities wherever possible, on safeguards for national minorities in mixed areas and extensive autonomous rights, facilities and financial support for cultural self-expression. Foreign affairs, defence, economic policies were left to the all-Austrian parliament, which was also to solve the problem of the single official (*Verkehrs*) language. No mention was made in the programme of any right of secession from united Austria. Its unity was taken for granted.[58]

156

The desire for separately organised autonomous Social-Democratic parties and the cultural needs of the ethnic groups had already in principle been recognised by the Austrian government (without, however, clear guidelines and proper administrative machinery to turn recognition of principle into practical reality). Parliamentary representation was granted as a means for achieving just that. These measures were thought to go far in healing the frustrations, and in removing the grudges, of the under-privileged ethnic groups.

Instead however of doing away with national differences, modernisation appeared at that late date to accentuate them, and moreover to offer greater scope, and more effective instruments to nationalist separatism. In conditions of universal suffrage and of the newly constituted national, instead of class, electoral colleges, electioneering had to cater to nationalist passion, since the rivals of the Social-Democrats, especially in Bohemia and Moravia, were hammering away the nationalist theme incessantly and obsessively.

The Russian revolution of 1905 had an enormous effect on the peoples of the Danubian Empire. A new era seemed to have dawned. Everything appeared unfrozen. For so long the prison of nations, Russia was emerging not only as vanguard of revolution, but also the scene of the awakening of nationalities. As we have seen, in response to and in alliance with the colossal wave of working class insurgency, representatives of every nationality and national minority in Russia came out with loud demands for the recognition of its rights to wide autonomy and national status.[59] The international climate and the setting of the social and national struggles had changed over a wide area. The Czechs and others began to feel that the days of the Habsburg Empire might be numbered, and that a liberal or even socialist Russia might guarantee rather than menace future Czech independence.[60] To the Poles the prospect of a united Poland seemed no longer quite so hopeless. Polish socialists of the three occupied parts of Poland were feeling the urge to constitute a pan-Polish socialist party. This was to be soon facilitated by the exodus of the Polish socialists from the all-German party, and the break-away of the Polish party from the all-Austrain Social-Democratic federation.[61]

The South Slavs were deeply stirred by the events in Russia. The tendency towards a Yugoslav union of the South Slav nations received a most powerful stimulus, when the sudden formal annexation of the until now only "occupied" territories of Bosnia and Herzegovina—in answer to the Young Turk revolution—incensed the South Slavs to boiling point. A few years later the Balkan Wars, the prelude to World War I, were to release a flood of nationalist passion and to test both international proletarian solidarity and the resolve and ability of the socialist movement to oppose and stem it, and to prevent a war of nations from engulfing working class ideology. At the end of the road lay Sarajevo.

On the eve of that confrontation there came to a climax a fateful development, which went very far towards disarming the international labour movement. The federal Austrian Social-Democratic party ceased to exist, through the break-away of the component parts, first the Czechs, then the Poles, then others. The split was brought about by a dispute on a most vital issue, indeed a matter of "to be or not to be" to any Social-Democratic party. The Czechs broke away from the united trade union movement of Austria, with its central executive in Vienna.[62]

As we have already had an opportunity to point out, even the most conciliatory Austro-German Social-Democratic leaders, who had made their peace with the idea and reality of separate ethnic socialist parties, were unable even to contemplate the breaking up of the trade union movement. The working class struggle was unimaginable without such a single organisation directed from a single centre. Ethnic differences were by definition inadmissable in trade unionism. Moreover, in Austria the trade union movement was more closely linked with the political Social-Democratic party than elsewhere. In the years of illegality, then restrictive legislation and later of mass struggle for trade union rights, universal suffrage, political freedoms, it was the tens and hundreds of thousands of trade unionists who marched on the streets, went on strike, provided funds, flocked to meetings and often protected socialist gatherings and leaders from police and the physical violence of rowdy political opponents.

The Czechs set up a separate trade union organisation with a central bureau in Prague. This outraged the German trade unionists and party members and released their anti-Czech and nationalist German sentiments. Not all Czech workers joined the new separatist trade union. A substantial proportion, indeed in the beginning in certain places a majority, remained affiliated as a Czech section to the all-Austrian movement. They continued to be recognised by the German trade unionist and Social-Democratic rump as the Czech component. Against the wishes of Victor Adler, the Austrian trade union movement brought the matter of the split before the international Trade Union Congress in Copenhagen. The Germans accused the Czechs of the heinous crime of splitting the working class movement because of nationalist separatism. The Czechs replied by accusing the Germans of trying to overawe them, and of supporting a splinter body of national deserters against the parent organisation through interference in the affairs of an autonomous and equal organisation of a sister movement.

As was to be expected, the Czechs were overwhelmingly defeated. The main spokesmen for the majority were the Austro-Germans and the bosses of the powerful trade union movement of the German Reich, who thundered against nationalist deviation, and preached the necessity of stringent centralism. The dispute assumed the character of a clash between Germans and Czechs. It conjured up shadows of the Council of Constance and evoked Hussite accents in the pronouncements of the hard-pressed Czechs. The latter refused to yield. The break-away from the united trade union organisation was a fact. It was followed by the formal secession of the Czech Social-Democratic party.[63]

There was no common language between the Czechs and the Germans on this issue. To the Germans, the Czech exit from the united trade union movement signified, as Victor Adler put it, that the nationalist instincts of the Czechs had won a "brutal" victory over working class conviction and interests.[64] They were especially bewildered and incensed by the Czech insistence on ethnic Czechs resident in non-Czech territory in Austria belonging to the Czech trade union movement with its central commission in Prague.

Couched in traditional trade union arguments and language, the Czech case sounded indeed weak, hollow and almost hypocritical, not to say perverse. But no other language could be spoken between trade unionists. What was really behind their self-justification was something that few Czech spokesmen were yet able to think out to the end and still less to formulate, even to themselves. They were moved by a feeling that they were no longer a nationality, but were a nation on the move. It was no longer a matter of obtaining concessions or even rights, certainly no more a situation where Czechs were being, for pragmatic reasons, granted facilities by a supra-national body. The Czechs were striving to secure the attributes, conditions, resources, assets, institutions, instruments of a nation in the form of an integrated pattern. The Czech workers under the leadership of the Czech Social-Democratic party were out to assume the role of the national class of the Czech nation in the making. For the purpose of leading and moulding the nascent Czech nation, they needed to assume the powers, to play the part, to perform the tasks of the national class. For that a political organisation alone, without the powerful base and the economic power provided by trade unionism, was not enough.[65]

Chapter Seven

A SOCIALIST THEORY OF NATIONALITY

The Austro-Marxist theory of nationality was the fruit of the quest for a Social-Democratic answer to the challenge of nationalism. It was the work of Karl Renner,[66] who was destined to become the first prime minister of the post-1918 Republic of Austria, and then its first president after World War II, and the youthful Otto Bauer,[67] whose meteoric rise as theoretician in the last decade before 1914 was followed by a leading position as foreign minister in the government of the first Austrian Republic and a great role in the Second International, up to his death in 1938.

The inclination of Marx and Engels was, as we have seen, to regard the state's dominant racial, linguistic and cultural group as the nation, and to view the racial minorities as fringe elements continuing to employ doomed dialects or observe some local customs, but in everything else part of the nation, and destined to be eventually entirely absorbed by it, especially when class distinctions had been wiped out by socialism. Bauer and Renner rejected the territorial conception of nationality in favour of an ethnic-cultural conception. The nation was a distinct ethnic group stemming from a common ancestry, originally of the same blood. Its members having shared for a long time a common destiny, maintained uninterrupted close contact, co-operated, shared experiences, good and bad fortune, engaged in barter, co-ordinated consciously or unwittingly their economic pursuits, above all communicated with each other by means of common language; they could not but develop a national character.

Otto Bauer and Karl Renner were anxious to repudiate any worship of a national spirit, a *Volksgeist*, a mysterious germ or metaphysical substance, which inexorably predetermined the character, reactions, inclinations, the self-expression of all individual members of the race. In good Marxist fashion, they envisaged the individual as a social product, the sum and sample of the crossing of social endeavours throughout history, and not as an isolated, self-sufficient atom. The nation was to them an eternal becoming and evolving, a never-ending process, a history of social development, shaped by social-economic, techno-

160

logical, cultural and political changes. But, again, the evolutionary changes were not random developments, they were the function and result of the peculiar, historically conditioned way in which every nation reacted to stimuli from outside, as witnessed for instance by the distinct character of British, German, French capitalism.[68]

Although it was the material conditions which shaped the character of the nation at every juncture, the impact of being part of the national community was by far more real and more potent than membership of a social class. The proletariat included men who shared the same situations, but these were not so all-embracing as were the fate and destiny of the nation. The workers might be subject to the same living conditions, suffer the same disabilities, share the same aims, join in a common struggle. But they still did not share so many things, were not so permanently in communication with each other as they were with their co-nationals, including those of a different class.[69]

It is difficult to escape the conclusion that the Austro-Marxist theoreticians of socialism attributed more concentrated presence and more effective impact to the nation than to the class. It is hard to see a basic difference between the emphasis upon national history, quaintly called "national materialism", as the maker of distinct nations, and the romantic *Volksgeist*, a kind of ghost in the machine, an ineluctable and ineffable soul behind that history, if we discard the lunatic obsession with inexorable race determinism and race purity. The fundamental and important difference lies in Bauer's primary interest not only in the right and freedom of the individual to express himself through the medium of the collective cultural personality, but also in his not being bound to it indissolubly by ties of blood. The individual could choose membership of, or find himself a participant—for instance the Jews—in a cultural group of different ethnic origin. This possibility of as it were migrating from one culture to another was facilitated by the evolutionary development of the nation.[70]

It is interesting to follow up the historical analysis of the changing character of the nation. At its most real and most concentrated the national community appeared at the stage of the tribal Germanic horde when it lived in isolation and its members shared all things. With growing numbers, settlement on the land as an agricultural population, and the inevitable dispersal, some fragments of the horde developed dialects and eventually a life of their own. Others fused with other tribes, absorbed much of their blood, language and character and in the end became part of alien nations. The feudal-seigneurial monarchy in the Middle Ages split the nation into the dominant upper class of barons and knights, which in fact became the real nation, the only part of the nation that mattered, and the subject classes, which were relegated into the background, were cut off from an active share in the national culture and endeavour, and often evolved dialects of their own. The rise of money economy, the emergence of towns, and the unwritten alliance between absolute monarchs and the bourgeoisie against the feudal lords combined to broaden the nation to embrace the educated and culturally active members of the middle classes. But the peasantry and the pro-letariat were still kept in the background. They had not yet become part of the nation.[71] It was the aim and destiny of socialism to enable the lower orders, for so long kept out of the national community, to join the national culture, to become co-heirs of the national heritage. Far from being anti-national, from working for the disintegration of the national community and for the effacement of its distinctness, socialism was aspiring to raise the nation to much loftier heights. All would at last be partners in it. The partnership would embrace all aspects of life and endeavour, political democracy, common ownership, an infinite variety of values and experiences, with the workers bringing into the pool their peculiar experiences and characterisitics, overflowing with originality and youthful vigour.[72]

The reader is at times taken aback by the conclusion which forces itself upon him that the Marxist theoreticians of nationality wished to appear as the real defenders and standard bearers of a truly genuine and potent nationalism, rather than to accommodate socialism with nation-alism. Their socialist doctrine of "evolutionary nationalism" bears the imprint of revisionist reformism. The socialist realisation of the idea of nationhood is not conceived in terms of a revolutionary breakthrough, a violent dethroning of a class enemy, but as an evolutionary process. The finished product is presented not as a repudiation and denial of a dis-carded past by a rebellious heir, but as the fruition, an extension, a puri-fication, a vindication and apotheosis of an idea which was always there and immanent, in the same way as Bernstein and Jaurès depicted socialism as the purified product of the endeavours of European liberalism and democracy, and the crowning achievement of an ancient common European heritage.

Give a nation an equal status and the means of cultural self-expression, and the national urge will be satisfied and all aggressiveness will be stilled.[73] Bauer and Renner were not so crude or naive as to claim that all nationalist conflicts were the result of feudal, clerical or bourgeois manipulation and incitement. They were realistic enough to understand the exposed position of the social-democratic leaders of the national minorities and their vulnerability to the nationalist accusation of being deserters to their hard-pressed peoples. Bauer and Renner were however still enough of rationalists to fail to grasp the demoniacal, obsessive character of nationalist passion. They genuinely believed in the possibility of drawing and maintaining a line between the legitimate urge for collective self-expression and the passion for ascendancy, power, prestige and domination. A socialist nation could not by definition become imperialistic. With private property abolished, the acquisitive spirit and the will for dominion were bound to die out.[74]

This process would be facilitated paradoxically by the fact that the socialist nation would be a people in arms. The armed forces would no longer be a separate and superimposed factor, at the exclusive disposal of single or collective masters of the nations, to be used for the subjugation of other nations. It was unimaginable that in modern times peoples would wish to go to war in order to conquer territory and exploit other nations. And as to unequal development causing economic differences between nations, and poverty and scarcity goading the deprived to try to conquer resources and *Lebensraum* or markets, the fraternity of socialist societies could be counted upon to plan in a truly international spirit international well-being. There would be a wise distribution of tasks between nations, and a permanent and equitable give and take, in accordance with the needs and possibilities of all concerned. The socialist community of nations was likely to organise mass migrations from one country to another, without denationalising the migrants and without turning them into defenceless subjects of master nations or foreign conquering invaders.[75] The socialist society of the future would be based upon a personal and not a territorial conception of nation.

This leads us to consider very briefly the concrete measures proposed by Renner and Bauer for the solution of the nationalities problem in the Habsburg monarchy. Opposed to the feudal dynastic and reactionary regime of crown lands, and despairing of any possibility of drawing an acceptable demarcation line between the ethnic groups of the Empire, the Austro-Marxist writers were determined to reject the territorial principle of nationality, the idea that a country was the exclusive possession of the majority race and the dominant nation, with other ethnic groups living there on sufferance as tolerated guests or a nuisance, and expected or harassed to become assimilated to the master nation, and advised to make haste with it. Such a state of affairs was a corollary of the idea of monopolistic property and feudal privilege.[76] The Austro-Marxists insisted that a country belonged to all its inhabitants, seen not as individuals, but as members of cultural ethnic groups and collective bodies.

Renner saw nationalities as a variant of religious denominations, and so he regarded the territorial principle as a variant of "*cuius regio eius religio*". A nationality comprised all who felt and declared themselves to belong to it, and registered accordingly—something like members of a Jewish community—wherever they might be living. So conceived and identified, a nationality was to become a juridical person, properly constituted and endowed with rights, duties and powers to cater for the cultural, educational and social needs of its members. As such it would have the power to tax its members, represent them and act on their behalf vis-à-vis the government of the Austrian Empire. Austria was to become a federation of nationalities. Wherever the territorial and personal principles could be accommodated simultaneously, the confines of the nationality would be identical with the territorial autonomous division, with claims and rights to jurisdiction over its members who were living in other areas of Austria as migrants or national minorities.[77]

We need not be detained here by the division of tasks and powers between the institutions of the autonomous nationalities and the centralised state authority and its organs, which would take care of the needs and the interests of all the inhabitants of the Empire—such as defence, foreign policy, economic affairs, communication, social legislation.

What matters to us here was the conviction of Renner and Bauer that while being a question of the will to belong, nationality was a primary and indestructible datum. To what lengths they were prepared to go is shown in the way they argued against the upholders of the territorial principle of nationality. While bent on subjugating foreign ethnic groups, the territorial nationals were prepared to renounce lightheartedly whole groups belonging to their own ethnic culture but settled outside their "national" territory.[78] The other point that stands out is the insistence on the juridical recognition of nationality. The gravamen of their argument was that while the Austrian constitution had formally recognised the nationalities and promised them the satisfaction of their legitimate claims and needs in such matters as the use of their national language in official dealings, schools, cultural activities, access to jobs, the nationality was never formally and bindingly identified as having a clear and unmistakable address and as represented by a competent and legally established and universally recognised body. The vagueness of the promises, and the absence of bodies to define them in an obligatory way and to work for their fulfilment, were the cause of the chaotic and aggressive forms assumed by the conflict of races.[79] It became a scramble for positions, privileges, prestige and power pursued in the spirit of bitter war, fought out in the streets, in student brawls, in provocative demonstrations, economic boycotts, parliamentary obstruction and violent abuse and incitement in a yellow press and in meeting places, until all orderly government had come to a standstill and the parliamentary institutions had completely collapsed, leaving the reactionary aristocratic governments to govern by decree or with the aid of concessions under the counter which were indistinguishable from bribery.

The Social-Democrats were desperately anxious to reconcile disparate and conflicting aims, to ward off accusations of disloyalty to their nation and at the same time to prove themselves good internationalist socialists, to secure national identity and self-expression and simultaneously to maintain international unity in the struggle for socialism. The nationalities conflict was an unconquerable irritant on the way to socialism and democracy. But it was a gordian knot which could not be cut. From the narrow pragmatic point of view it was impossible to draw lines and proclaim the independence of all the severed nationalities. Such a victory of the territorial principle was calculated to saddle every new state with perhaps still more envenomed ethnic conflict. The break up of the monarchy would put most of the Austrian nationalities at the mercy of Russia, end Polish hopes of reunion and independence and turn the Czechs into vassals or hostages of Russia or Germany.

Part IV

THE JEWISH DIMENSION

Chapter One

THE ALIEN FERMENTING INGREDIENT AND THE MOUNTAINOUS SHADOW

Is there any valid reason for dwelling on the Jewish origins of revolutionaries, socialists, radicals, or for that matter of scientists, scholars, writers, artists, politicians, indeed people in any walk of life, who though of Jewish extraction did not practise the Jewish religion, were not active in Jewish life, maintained no Jewish associations, in some cases indeed had deliberately severed any ties with the world of Judaism? Should any significance be attached to the disproportionate number of men and women of Jewish ancestry among the theoreticians of socialism, revolutionary leaders, activists in radical movements, above all among the makers of the Soviet Union, the builders of the post-1945 communist regimes in Eastern Europe, finally in the New-Left? Can one find any "Jewish" common denominator, between Marx, Lasalle, Rosa Luxemburg, Trotsky, Radek, Kamenev, Zinoviev, Swerdlov, Uritsky, Litvinov, Kaganovitch, Anna Pauker, Slansky, Jacob Berman, Hilary Mintz, Rakoszy, Leon Blum, Harold Laski, Cohn-Bendit, other than the mere accident of their Jewish birth? Did they display characteristics of a group mind and represent a style or a temper, which would differentiate them from any score of revolutionary and socialist leaders thrown together out of a national or international sample?

These have become horribly charged and tormenting questions. Hitler has made it most painful, well-nigh impossible, even to pose them, let alone discuss them dispassionately. There is the horror of anything remotely reminiscent, even if only by association, of racism. Hitler singled out the international Jewish-Marxist revolutionary as his main target, as the prototype of Jewish evil-doer, as the microbe destructive of all Aryan civilisation. The punishment that he meted out to the Jewish people as a whole has been so terrible that even to raise the question sends a shudder through the spine. It becomes a demonstration of bad taste, an act of impiety, an unforgivable transgression, if not a sign of morbid masochism.

The problem has not been made any more amenable to discussion by the baffling change that has come in the relations between Jews and

169

revolution over the last two or three decades, with the emergence of
Soviet anti-semitism, and the alignment of the forces of communism,
the Third World, the New Left and, of course, the Arabs against Israel,
which is now alleged to be the moving spirit of contemporary
imperialism. Indirectly, and often directly, at all events objectively, this
common front has been assuming all the features of an anti-semitic
crusade, since the future of the Jewish people as such has become so
inseparably bound up with the fate of the Jewish state, after the
destruction of the centuries-old Jewish civilisation in central and
Eastern Europe, and in the light of the growing atomisation of Jewish
life in the West and in the USSR, whatever the pros and cons of the
tragic conflict between Jews and Arabs. The present author is not one to
deny that the latter too have a case.

The point about revolutionaries of Jewish extraction may be
considered as only one aspect of the much wider and still more
challenging and no less explosive issue—the Jews in the modern world.
How can we account for the strange phenomenon of a numerically
small, marginal, dispersed group, without any central authority,
seemingly in a permanent state of dissolution, until only yesterday an
almost hermetically closed and ostracised sect, becoming almost overnight so mightily effective an ingredient in the fortunes of Europe, not
to say the world? It developed into so problematic and controversial a
factor by the fact of its very existence, and infinitely more so by the
gigantic shadow it cast, the fierce reactions its image stirred up. What
awful power did that spectre possess to madden and goad men to plan
and carry out that crime which makes the imagination boggle?

We are here in the sphere of highly elusive imponderables, of things
which can neither be measured nor weighed, neither proved as in a
laboratory nor quantified in statistical data. More than that, we are
faced by a bewildering contradiction between ethereal intangibles and
awesomely real, crushing, irreversibly "final" consequences. The more
tenuous and meagre the bonds between Jews became in modern times,
and the more rapid their assimilation with the general environment, the
vaster grew their image in hostile eyes as a compact and decisive force.
Was it a case of obsession affecting a peculiarly unbalanced and isolated
group? The awful truth is that the astonishing derangement had very
deep and ancient roots and could become operative only in a richly
propitious context.

Liberals and people of rationalist and humanist persuasion in
general, people who believe in the primary reality and in the self-
determination of the individual, are inclined to raise eyebrows at so
much ado about nothing. But most Gentiles who are neither sworn anti-

semites nor devoted philosemites, and not doctrinaire individualists either, and certainly most Jews, suffer from an unconquerable malaise on the subject of Jew and Gentile.

In one of the earliest sessions of the Jerusalem court which tried Adolph Eichmann, the defendant's counsel, Dr Servatius, asked the eminent American-Jewish historian who had been called to unfold the historical background of the "final solution" to explain why "if they had done so much good" the Jews became in all ages and nations a problem and anti-semitism in them was so rampant.[1] There must be something in the Jews that placed them in such equivocal and complex situations and evoked so much animosity. This is the sort of question that drives a good many Jews to distraction. A British historian, who can by no stretch of imagination be called an anti-semite, got into trouble some years ago, when he voiced the same reflection in a review of a book on the French Enlightenment and anti-semitism. The Jewish over-reaction to a question of this nature may be exaggerated and neurotic. It may suggest lack of self-assurance and a paranoiac disposition. Yet, as history has so amply shown, we are faced here with a matter that does stimulate a rush of blood, unleashes irrational aggressiveness and may produce an uncontrollably contagious effect. The Jewish-Gentile relationship in Christian civilisation has been bedevilled by a fundamentally neurotic impediment, by a trauma which has been working itself out over centuries, becoming on the way more inflamed by disastrous encounters, unforeseen hitches and untoward accidents. Jewish history is a lesson in the hold of the dead upon the living, in the power of the past to determine the fate of a nation for all time, and to shape its fortunes by way of, it seems, inescapably recurrent patterns. It is also a lesson in the power of traumatic experiences, enduring memories, and compulsive images to become more effective than the realities, to overshadow, to distort them by surrounding them with compulsively assumed qualities and disproportionate dimensions. Pre-determined fate vanquishes as it were the conscious, deliberate resolves of actual men facing immediate choices. It is enough to consider the position into which the state of Israel has been placed of being "the Jew among the nations", the very fate which the Jewish state was conceived and created to escape. This may sound altogether too mystical, too fuzzy and too old-fashioned in an era of quantitative history. But it is a conclusion which only goes to confirm the immense potency of history, and the reality of the facts of psychology and sociology.

The "neurotic" reactions of Jews to the kind of question which Dr Servatius put to Professor Salo Baron remind one of the demand of blacks in America not merely to be accorded formal equality of opportunity, but to be compensated for centuries of bondage, deprivation and humiliation, which have left them so underequipped for the rat race. The Jews are implicitly asking to be spared the aggregate of obloquy and the effects of that load of calumny, which makes them so vulnerable, indeed presumed guilty from the start.

Granted that militant, murderous anti-semitism is a terrible disease, how, nevertheless, shall the historian as a clinical analyst and anthropologist steer a clear course between those rocks and shoals, between the dreadful shadows and the facile generalisations, however well-meaning or ill-intentioned, which in their platitudinous sweep explain nothing: that mankind is evil, that xenophobia is always with us, that the authoritarian, aggressive instincts need a target, that minorities are always at a disadvantage, that it was all the fault of Christianity and of capitalism? How finally could one guard oneself against trivialising an enormous issue by simply juxtaposing innocent lambs and ravenous wolves? What should then the researcher do in order not to appear the Devil's advocate, and avoid sliding into the attitude of "superior wisdom" of *tout comprendre tout pardonner?*

We have said that the relationship between Jews and Christians has been bedevilled by a millenarian neurosis. Louis Namier described neurosis as a way of reacting which is out of proportion to the stimulus. He was wont to add that neurosis was the normal state of mankind.[2] The neurosis in our case was due principally no doubt to the image of the Jew as deicide. Before elaborating the point, however, one must preface any exposition focused on that fact with a flashback to a still more distant past and still earlier complications.

Of all the races, peoples, religions, tribes conquered by Alexander the Great and the Romans, the Jews alone remained unabsorbed, however strongly influenced by the Hellenistic and Latin civilisations. All others, at least the urban elites, were wholly assimilated, whatever the impact which the subdued traditions, especially the oriental cults, succeeded in making on their conquerors. At the time of Christ, the Jews of Palestine and of the far-flung Jewish dispersion, which embraced a good proportion of proselytes who in varying degrees identified themselves with the Judaic faith, constituted some 10 per cent of the population of the Roman Empire.[3] Without them the work of St Paul and other missionaries of the new faith would—humanly speaking—never have achieved the success it eventually had.

Although they represented the third civilisation among the civilisations of the Mediterranean, the Jews stood apart.[4] They were intensely self-aware, recoiled from intermarriage, refused to join with others in meals. They stuck together. They were therefore charged with misanthropy, with enmity to mankind. As they stubbornly fought against being compelled to participate in the cult of Caesar, because their sovereign was God himself, and they would not worship idols nor bow to mortal men, they were looked upon as disloyal and rebellious. The invisible and incomprehensible God of the Jews, revealing himself only once a year on the Day of Atonement to the High Priest in the Holy of Holies, to which no one else was ever allowed access, suggested to the uncomprehending observers that the Jews had much to hide. Hence the absurd stories related by Tacitus, Appion and others that the Jews worshipped a pig or an ass in the Holy of Holies.[5]

The peoples of antiquity, especially those of the Middle East who gradually adopted Christianity, were thus already disposed to view the role attributed to the Jews in the Crucifixion in a particular way. The prejudice and animosity were there already. The Jews were already considered different, alien, strange, contemptible, suspect, often sinister. This had been highlighted by the momentous encounter between Jews and Greeks in Alexandria. The polemics between them read uncannily like the debates between anti-semites and Jews in modern times. The Jews, like Philo, claimed to be fully fledged citizens. The Greeks by blood or culture, notably Appion, denied them equal status, and built up a whole philosophy to rationalise this denial.[6] The astonishing fact is nevertheless that the new message out of Judaea was adopted by the Hellenistic world in the form of a synthesis of Jewish theology and Greek philosophy, although at an earlier date, the translation of the Bible into Greek, the Septuagint, failed at the time it appeared to evoke any response from Greek and Latin authors. There is much to be said for Nietzsche's extraordinary perception that the Gentile acceptance of Christianity was made possible only by the fact, or the belief, that the Jews, out of whom the Saviour emerged, had also killed him. Nietzsche's insight is marred by his suggestion that this was a breathtaking act of revenge by the Jews upon the Gentile world. They could succeed in achieving indirect dominion over the world and to inject man with their slave morality and priestly asceticism only by this devious means.[6a] It is no less paradoxical that the universal creed would never have come into being, had it not been for the retrograde rebellion of sectarian fanatics, the Maccabees, to halt the process of assimilation to pagan Hellenism: a paradigm of the recurrent pattern—tribal exclusiveness acting as lever of universal developments.

Why should the Jews, in the first place, have adopted the attitude which made them so obnoxious to the world around them? Although the outline of the misunderstanding seems fairly clear, the beginnings of the stimulus which evoked so disproportionate a response remain a mystery.

We have in mind the way in which the Jews as a people, and not just individual thinkers among them, came by flashes of insight into possession of the tremendous truth of the existence of a single, wholly transcendental deity, the creator of the universe, the source of all knowledge and goodness, the regulator of the destinies of men, the supreme judge of all. The truth discovered seemed so all-embracing that it was held to explain everything. It appeared not only to enable the initiated to dispense with the search for any further grounds and reasons for reality but even to forbid it to them. It came to constitute so full, so detailed and complete a *vade mecum* of laws and regulations that attempts to look for any further reasons or to try other experiments in living assumed the character of impious recalcitrance. God's omnipotence also made it an offence to obey any sovereign but him. Hence the Jews' obsession with right action, in contrast with the Greek passion for right thinking. Here is the clue to the abyss between Greek insatiable curiosity, the desire to try out every mode of existence, and the paralysing Jewish fear of transgression.[7]

The striving for rectitude and righteousness stifled the scientific quest as well as aesthetic needs. Its fanatical, incomprehensible and impoverishing single-mindedness repelled the Hellenised and Latinised environment. No wonder that the claim of a people culturally so insignificant to be the chosen, superior nation seemed a sign of sheer arrogance and incurable fanaticism. This was the more so, because militarily and politically the Jews were not only wholly unimportant, but the victims of every strong power: defeated, humiliated and eventually expelled and dispersed.

That they were able to bear the obloquy of neighbours, to survive disaster and degradation, and yet to remain steadfast, indeed emerge strengthened in their faith, and to retain an unsurpassed group cohesion was due to a number of factors. The Covenant was believed to have been concluded between Yahveh and the Children of Israel as a collectivity, a people. It was not an esoteric mystery imparted to an individual prophet or saint, not put into the keeping of a chosen priesthood, a monopolistic church. There was no suggestion of a division into perfect servants of God and imperfect believers, of a distinction between a minority designated to teach, to offer an example, guide, to whom more was given and from whom more was expected, and a majority of simple, rather passive believers who as it were stood on the receiving side, and from whom therefore less was expected. The service to God was performed not by individuals as such, but by the people as a whole. They were collectively responsible, and were to reap reward and punishment as a group. Hence the dignity of each individual as well as the strong bond uniting them, and as a concomitant the implication of fundamental equality. Hebrew prophecy thus focuses equally on the two: the collective duty towards God and the righteousness to be observed towards every individual, within the fold, especially the weak, the deprived and the injured.

When defeat at the hands of the heathen and social evils within raised the question, why do the righteous suffer and the wicked prosper, the answer was found in the messianic faith. The suffering was both a punishment and a trial, a purifying test and an atonement. And the final account would be settled and redressed at the end of time in a total reparation and final restoration. Although the messianic expectation became the cornerstone of the Jewish creed and the inspiration that enabled the Jews to survive and brave persecution and degradation, no binding canon has ever been laid down by the sages about the form its realisation would take. In periods of martyrdom and stress it was seen as a dreadful punishment meted out to the heathen in revenge for the injuries they had visited upon the remnant of Israel, and of a glorious reward to the faithful restored to prosperity, power and righteousness. In more relaxed periods, the last days were depicted as the coming together of all the nations on Mount Moriah to worship the father of all creation, to jettison all instruments of war and to shake off all aggressive intent and all greed for possessions and dominion.[8]

The salvationist hope was desperately needed by the Jews to explain to themselves and to others why the chosen people had been abandoned by God. The very idea of providential justice hinged upon it. The Jewish stubborn will to retain its uniqueness and the refusal to merge with the peoples around lacked all rationale without the sustaining vision of choice, sin, trial, atonement and salvation.

The idea of the messianic dénouement was the great bone of contention between church and synagogue. Jewish rejection of Christ as Messiah appeared as provocative defiance to Christendom. The Church Triumphant was driven to degrade and persecute the Jews in order to demonstrate that it was the true Israel, and that the Jews had forfeited their birthright as children of God.[9] This is why St Bernard of Clairvaux, still earlier the Fathers, and Papal dogma throughout the ages, laid down that it was forbidden to exterminate the Jews because their wretched existence was the most tangible witness to God having transferred the dignity of the chosen Israel to the Christians. Their degraded state must be preserved as a sign of Cain on their foreheads and a constant reminder to the faithful of the triumph of the church.[10]

Whatever the obloquy, condemnation and abuse heaped upon the perfidious Jews, official Christianity could never bring itself to adopt

Marcion's irretrievably damning verdict that the Old Testament and with it Judaism and all its works were nothing but the work of the Devil.[11] The doctrine that the Old Testament was the preparation for the Christian message, that it prophesied and promised the coming of Christ, and that Christianity was as it were the fulfilment and a purified form of Judaism—all these assumptions remained basic to the Christian faith. They came to constitute an additional and insoluble twist in the neurotic attitude of Christianity towards the Jews. For two millenia the Passion remained the central mystery of the Christian creed. For centuries and centuries myriads of humble and illiterate worshippers, who had no spiritual sustenance except the imagery of the mass and the sermons of the priests, were made to listen with sacred indignation to the story of the misdeeds of the murderers of the Saviour and the perfidy of Judas. But the same congregations had throughout the ages been intoning hymns to Zion and Jerusalem, invoking the God of Abraham, Isaac and Jacob and learning about the prophecies of Isaiah and Daniel. For over a thousand years, indeed as late as the late seventeenth century, so much political thinking and political conflict in Christendom was articulated in the form of a commentary upon the story of Samuel, Saul and David, the battles of God waged by the Maccabees. Jewish messianism provided the Western world with a basic and potent ingredient, one that confronted with other great civilisations, was perhaps one of the most distinct. It inspired the vision of the Second Coming, of the apocalyptic and millenarian movements, throughout history, and at one remove gave rise to the concept of infinite progress, of socialism and revolution as salvationist dénouements. The idea of Theodicea in its sacred form as well as in its secular versions, Hegelian and related variants, is unthinkable without it.

And so Christian feelings about Jews came to be a compound of rage, horror, hatred, revulsion and contempt on one side, and a sense of indebtedness, of awe, of deep, inscrutable mystery on the other. Aggressive urges and feelings of malaise alternated with one another. Hence the fundamental ambivalence which had persisted up to our own time, although mainly in a secularised form.

This Christian neurosis could not fail to produce a corresponding reaction—a Jewish neurosis vis-à-vis the Christian world. The Jews could answer the Christian challenge that they had lost their birthright only by an uncompromising denial of the truth of the Christian message and by assimilating the Gentiles to the heathen. The parent religion was able to bear persecution and humiliation solely by means of its sense of superiority towards its illegitimate offspring. Such a relationship, dominated by traumatic memories and images, with the here and now constantly and compulsively blurred and distorted by obsessive residues, made every Jew look like a Judas to the Christian, and in the course of time a Shylock, as every persecuting Christian was seen by the Jew as another child of Amalek, another heir to the Edomites, destined to be smitten by the Lord.

Chapter Two

THE PIONEER AND THE USURPER

The Jews were held up to derision for their literalness and neurotic ritualism. They were feared for their clannishness. So compact and hermetic a group evoked demoniacal suggestions of plot and conspiracy. Little did the Christians realise that those very qualities had been an essential condition of the triumph of early Christianity, as a Judean sect.

"The nations and their gods": all ancient tribes, Israel and its neighbours, the Greek *polis* and the original Romans of the eternal city, just as much as primitive tribes in other continents, had their lives prescribed by codes of belief and behaviour which made no distinction between faith and practice, church and state, the sacrosanct and the expedient, the individual and the collectivity, prescribed ritual conduct and free, deliberate choice. The conquests of Alexander the Great, the vast Greek migrations into Asia and Egypt and the arrival of the Romans all combined with social and intellectual solvents to bring about the decline, disintegration and demise of the *polis*. The conditions of life in large empires left no room for free self-governing communities. The vast multi-racial states had to be governed by despotic rulers and centralised bureaucracy. Torn away from the closely knit exclusive group, the individual was thrown upon his own resources. Individualism produced those cosmopolitan philosophies, which fostered the cultivation of the inner light and of personal perfection, and also opened up the whole universe as fatherland to the enlightened. Contemplative man was kept away from political pursuits, and he became alienated from and indifferent to unregenerate society. Given the abysmal gap between the minority of the educated on one side, and the mass of alien stock and language, sunk in superstition, on the other, all common social bonds, all sense of joint responsibility, were lost. The educated minorities came to dwell in an ethereal kingdom not of this earth.

The Jews, on the other hand, wherever they went and settled, would immediately set up a network of institutions of self-government, though they never really tried to create territorial units of their own in the countries of emigration, as Greek and Phoenician colonisers had done. The Jewish migrants might cease to speak their original tongue and adopt much of the culture of the new environment, but they maintained their communal cohesion. They had no choice but to give up the monopoly of the Jerusalem Temple as the place of worship; and so they created the *Minyan,* the congregation of ten (male) worshippers who wherever they came together were held to attract the presence of God by invoking his name.[12] Communal cohesion, strict and equal observance by everyone of the minute prescriptions, the absence of differentiation between doctrine and ritual, between a leading hierarchy and simple, passive believers, the sense of being chosen—all these continued to preserve that unity of life, and that measure of equality and joint responsibility, which constituted the earliest milieu of and then moulded the original Christian groups. Judaic prophecy developed a much greater power of attraction for the masses than the vastly more sophisticated philosophies of antiquity, because it touched the layers of the collective soul to which the pagan teachings found no access.

Treated with reserve or contempt, tolerated or persecuted as Jews might be, they continued to be Roman citizens, and to form an ingredient more or less taken for granted in the pluralistic Roman Empire.[13] They found themselves in a different situation, once they came face to face with the Germanic and other barbarians who established themselves upon the ruins of the Roman Empire. They were of a much older and higher culture than the invaders. The two groups were utterly alien to each other. In the eyes of these new rough and illiterate converts to Christianity, the Jew bore also the stigma of Cain on his forehead. He was abhorred and feared. He evoked bewilderment as an uncanny, sinister, threatening, demoniacal alien.

In Christian Europe, the Jews were not only the non-conformist group par excellence, indeed for centuries the only one from the religious and cultural point of view; they were also made to assume a special social-economic role. Not a few Jewish and other historians, deeply influenced by Marxist dialectical materialism, have tended to play down religious differences as the cause of Jewish persecution and anti-semitism, and to put all the emphasis upon the social-economic aspects as the root cause. They overlooked the fact that the original causes of the peculiar social role and the legal status of the Jews were psychological and religious.

In his famous work on the beginnings of urban life in eleventh- and twelfth-century Europe, Henri Pirenne[14] propounded the thesis that its earliest pioneers were human flotsam, fugitives from the law, serfs who had run away from their villages, men without name, occupation, standards or reputation. He went on to offer the generalisation that, in great social transformations and new ventures, it was precisely people of this kind who served as pioneers. The long-settled and the well-established clung to their patrimony and privileges. They shunned novelty, since it entailed displacement, risk, and had something disreputable about it. It was therefore men who had no ties, no reputations to lose, and were not permanently and safely rooted, who flocked into the new occupations.

Pirenne's observation can almost be taken as a constant recurring law of Jewish history in the Middle Ages and in modern times. In the Middle Ages the Jews chose or were driven to fill a vacuum and to play a necessary pioneering role. They were at first invited, welcomed and granted privileges by the princes, the great builders of towns, as money-lenders and international tradesmen. Usury, filthy lucre, was forbidden and despised by Christians (as well as Jews) in accordance with the Scriptures. The segregated Jews developed what Max Weber called a system of dual ethics, one code for their conduct towards one another and another for the outside world. They had no compunction about taking interest from Gentiles. The services of the Jews were indispensable, much as they themselves might be despised and hated. In time, and given the example of the papal bankers, the Lombards, who spread their net all over Europe to collect St Peter's pence and other donations for God's representative on earth, the Christian populations lost their horror of usury and began to look upon trade and commerce with approval as both respectable and profitable. They also grew tired of the obstreperousness of their creditors, pariahs without rights, and enemies of Christ. They resorted to a well-tried expedient and expelled the usurpers and parasites who, though ostracised and defenceless, were able and had the audacity to hold the well-born by the throat. The Jews were thus driven out from all the countries of Western Europe in the later Middle Ages. They continued to exist in the Iberian peninsula for a considerably longer period than they did in England, in France and in some of the German provinces.[15] Their fall in Spain was all the more catastrophic because of their large numbers and the tremendous role they played in all walks of life in that country, including acting as a bridge between ancient Greek, Moslem and Christian learning.[16]

The Jews went east to the sprawling kingdoms of Poland and the Habsburgs, and to the Ottoman Empire. Eastern Europe was still the almost townless underdeveloped part of Europe. There they were again welcomed and enabled to play a vital, and in some ways pioneering role. It paid the Polish-Lithuanian nobility and the Hungarian aristocracy and gentry who had turned their countries into quasi-republics, which they ruled as confraternities of privileged equals, to prevent or to check the growth of a native (or Polonised, Magyarised, German) middle class as a potential political rival. It also served their purpose not to foster a native industry, since they stood to gain more by buying foreign industrial products in exchange for wheat and timber exported to the West. The Jews were politically harmless and useful as lessors of mills and breweries, as innkeepers and barkeepers, petty traders, craftsmen and pedlars. In many Polish towns, the Jews became the majority, often almost the sole inhabitants. In the Ukraine they suffered a terrible fate in the seventeenth century because they had been the instruments of the noble Polish-Catholic oppressors of the Greek Orthodox, Ukrainian-speaking peasantry.

Squeezed in between a relatively large but exclusive Polish gentry and an enormous mass of downtrodden and illiterate serfs, the Jews remained a civilisation apart, with its own religion, language, culture, a special set of occupations, institutions of self-government, aspirations and dreams. There was in fact no Polish nation as such and no class to which they could become assimilated. The nobility and gentry were too high, the peasantry too low. Once Poland began to decline because of internal disintegration and anarchy, and the terrible invasions by the Swedes, the Cossacks and the Russians in the middle of the seventeenth century, the Jews started their descent into wretched poverty and cultural backwardness; yet they remained indispensable all the same, though too numerous. The situation changed entirely in the latter part of the nineteenth century, when tens of thousands of impoverished gentry and hundreds of thousands of emancipated, but superflous landless peasants, began to flock to the towns. This migration created bitter competition and desperate tensions which were to end only at Auschwitz.

The last, and perhaps the most bewildering, illustration of the recurrent pattern, the passage from the status of indispensable pioneer to that of a usurping parasite, has been what may be called the reversal of alliances between Jews and the Marxist revolution in our own day. The contribution of Jews to the elaboration of its theory, to the spread of its gospel, the maintenance of its tradition; their services to the Russian Revolution, to the survival of the Bolshevik regime in its early and most difficult years, so hard pressed from within and from without, and deprived of the co-operation of the old civil service and most of the intelligentsia; and the part played by Jewish survivors of the Holocaust in establishing Soviet-dominated communist regimes in the satellite countries—the pioneering part of Jews in these momentous developments had been vital, in some cases possibly decisive. The gradual elimination of Jews from all positions of influence, in the USSR, Poland, Czechoslovakia, Roumania, Hungary, accompanied by waves of shockingly open and even racist, anti-Jewish propaganda, indeed expulsion (from Poland) coming on top of the sustained implacable enmity to the state of Israel, raises fundamental questions which transcend the Jewish aspects, questions about the relationship between an *ancien régime* and revolution, between perennial, massive sentiments and prejudices on one side, and the power of innovative ideas and intents on the other; questions about the opportunism of a messianic ideology which has become an establishment.

In a sense these vicissitudes of the Jewish collectivities repeat the pattern that can be observed in the fate of Jewish individuals in German and other courts in the pre-emancipation period, and still earlier in medieval Spain. The Jewish money-lender or banker (whatever expression is preferred) to the prince becomes his close, indispensable adviser, the architect of his financial and fiscal policies in peace and war, especially war. In his zeal to promote the interests of the prince, to prove his worth and to fortify his own position, he resorts to devices and means which are calculated to provoke, irritate and harm the prince's subjects. Deprived of the protection of law and public opinion, while growing immensely powerful, solely through the favours of the prince, who also ill-uses him, the court Jew draws on himself the execration and hatred of the injured, the envious, the ignorant, and the self-righteous. He is eventually cast down in ignominy by them, sacrificed or betrayed by the prince.[17] This is the measure of the ambiguities and ambivalences which beset Jewish history, the strange alternation of unprecedented rise and horrible fall, blinding splendour and utter misery: in brief, the extreme precariousness of Jewish existence.

There is in all this a persistent refusal or inability to take the Jew for granted, as he is, to recognise his existence as legitimate, as of right, not on sufferance. History has turned him into an eternal alien, as somehow always guilty, his claims and titles not naturally due to him. He has to atone for his sins, and earn his place by special exertion and merit. When tired of this position of eternal stranger, who is always held guilty and so often becomes, indeed, entrapped in guilt, Jews determined to create a home in the land from which they had set out on their millenial peregrination, and to which the curses of all the anti-semites of the world had been despatching them throughout the ages, they again landed in a situation of disheartening ambivalence and ambiguity.

Chapter Three

TEST CASE AND TOUCHSTONE

It is a commonplace that Jewish emancipation in Europe was made possible, in a sense was initiated, by the Enlightenment. The rationalist idea that all men were free and equal and each man at birth a *tabula rasa,* with the potential of a teachable and perfectible creature; the rejection of old prejudices, superstitions and institutions which tied men to a special status on grounds of religion, race, birth, occupation—all these were the pre-conditions for Jewish equality; indeed, made it imperative. But it is seldom remembered—and Professor Hertzberg[18] did well to remind us, although to the accompaniment of rather one-sided conclusions—that there was also another aspect to the age of rationalism, and one of a nature distinctly unfavourable to the Jews and their future. We may ignore the inveterate anti-semitism of Voltaire, who had had his fill of troubles with Jewish money-lenders, and that of Holbach, who just abhorred them. The *philosophes* as a group fought every kind of religious obscurantism and inhumanity, and in particular the superstition of church and Christianity, by juxtaposing, indeed contrasting, the light that was classical antiquity with the darkness and absurdity of the Asiatic world. This world included, was even largely epitomised in their eyes by Judaism. The Old Testament and the Jewish heritage were an essential part of Christianity. From the point of view of censorship and the susceptibilities of readers it was easier to attack Judaism than Christianity and, since the hint was sure to be taken, to discredit and ridicule the church all the more effectively.

The *philosophes*—certainly not Montesquieu, Helvetius, Rousseau or Diderot—never condemned contemporary and future Jews as not deserving to be considered men, not entitled to the dignity and rights of men. They advocated the rights of humanity, and not of race. Yet it had to be asked whether there was not something in the Jews that made them the begetters of the great imposters—the founders of religions, the breeding ground of all the stupidities and obsessions of the dark ages; whether the fact that the Jews had remained attached to them so obstinately for so long had not corrupted them beyond recall. At all events, some of the French rationalists, as well as some of the English deists, relished in stripping Judaism naked of all its aura of mystery, awe, unique destiny. The Jews became under their pen just a fanatical sect, a superstition-ridden, ignorant, but pretentious, arrogant, intolerant tribe, with an utterly pernicious influence upon countless generations. Without intending it, the *philosophes* were preparing the ground for future racism[19]. Although they were critical of and satirised Christian Europe by glorifying the excellent simple virtues of distant peoples and noble savages, eighteenth-century writers never dreamt of following Ephraim Lessing in the choice of a Jew as archetype of a righteous and wise man.

The basic difference between the *ancien régime* and the modern world, as it emerged from the Enlightenment and the French Revolution, was the difference between a society based on status and a society based on contract. The Jew emerged as a test case. To believers in the old ways, the emancipation of the Jews was a flagrant proof that the world was out of joint: the murderers of Christ, the enemies of the church, the despised pariahs of all time, until then an utterly different isolated and alien group, were to become by decree free and equal partners in the common weal, as if society was a stack of straw (an expression of Calvin's in a different context and not a propos Jews at all) where rats run back and forth. To the champions of the equality of man and of social mobility, however, to regard the Jews as an exception on grounds of religion, race and the irrational and residual prejudices of a dark past, constituted a direct denial of the most sacred principle. There was only one plausible way of making such an exception; if the Jews themselves continued to claim that they were not just loosely associated members of a religious denomination, but a chosen people, determined to live apart and hoping to become a nation at some future date through the miraculous intercession of God himself. This was the burden of the famous statement by Count Clermont-Tonnerre in the debate in the National Assembly on Jewish emancipation, "to the Jews as individuals—everything, to the Jews as a nation—nothing", but expulsion.[20] This alternative was paralleled by the one, between the conception of a nation as a contractual, plebiscitary creation of individuals—atoms joining together—and the one which regarded the nation as a pre-existent organic, indivisible entity, a collective personality, a rock, of which the members were just chips from the whole block.

The mass of the Jews, as distinct from those Jews of wealth and privilege who were already secularised and practically emancipated, found it extremely difficult to give a clear answer or to commit themselves either way. Their interests and future well-being hinged entirely upon the victory of society based upon contract; but the whole Jewish past, the teachings of Judaism, its historic position in the world, the very uniqueness and exceptional fate of the Jews, were a standing confirmation of the fact of the superior reality and demands of the collective entity. The Jewish Notables found themselves in a tight corner, when the *Sanhedrin* convened by Napoleon was being hard pressed on the political significance of the expectation of the messianic redemption and its vision of the ingathering of exiles in the original land of Israel. No less embarrassing was the question on the readiness and freedom of the Jews to marry fellow-citizens who were not of the fold. The Jewish leaders were meant to answer that they were not only anxious to become members of "la nation une et indivisible" but qualified to do so. They answered in fact by playing down the isolationist elements as of a purely religious or theoretical-declaratory and symbolic nature. Any other explanation which contained an element of hesitation was bound to be seized upon by both reactionaries and progressives; as a corroboration of their own stand by the former, as a disqualification of the right of the Jews to belong to the nation by the latter. Early revolutionary nationalism had no feeling for ethnicity. The French Convention, for example, condemned the linguistic separatism of the Bretons, Alsatians, Basques and Provençals. Herder's teaching on ethnicity was at the time taken up as a revivalist message by underprivileged nationalities only in countries in which individual citizenship was overshadowed by the feudal traditions of rank, and historic territorial units where no account was taken of ethnic composition.

Most of the Jews of Western Europe, including Germany, were passionately determined to obtain emancipation, many of them to the point of taking the final step in jettisoning every remnant of difference, the step of apostasy, as did the parents of Karl Marx and Benjamin Disraeli. At the other end of the spectrum were the ultra orthodox who, without daring to come out against emancipation, dodged the issue by continuing their seclusion and holding fast to their ancient practices. In Eastern Europe the question was hardly on the agenda. The minority of the wealthy and educated did their utmost to behave like the upper classes. But the masses were still deeply sunk in their age-old folk ways and wretched poverty. They obeyed and sought guidance from the Hassidic rabbis, and were only dimly aware of what went on in the West. During Napoleon's invasion of Russia, the rabbis of the region described the alternatives likely to face Jews: if Napoleon won, it would be good for the Jews, but bad for Judaism; if the Tsar won, it would be bad for Jews, but good for Yiddishkeit.[21]

As late as 1939, a French chief rabbi was celebrating in rhapsodic language the anniversary of the French Revolution as the second exodus from Egypt, as the Jewish resurrection from the dead: the "Declaration of the Rights of Man and Citizen" was the modern Tablets from Mount Sinai. That was six years after Hitler had annulled Jewish emancipation by a stroke of the pen; and three years after the Nuremberg Laws solemnly segregated the Jews from the body of the nation, and replaced—for the Jews—a society based on contract by one based on a wholly inescapable status, undoing a century and a half of modern history.[22]

The revolution of 1789 answered the needs of Jews in Western Europe, who were mainly middle class. It offered political equality, guaranteed freedom of worship, sanctified property, opened access to all occupations and proclaimed the principle of "carrière ouverte aux talents". There was theoretically no reason why Jews should wish to go beyond the bourgeois revolution. And yet, many soon strove to go far beyond. They did this partly out of humanitarian idealism, tinged by ancient Jewish messianism, partly because the formal equality which they had been accorded had not in practice freed them from hostility, contempt, ostracism, and had consequently failed to cure their malaise. Many began to feel that after all it had not been the real, the final, the all-solving and all-curing revolution. There must be a revolution beyond the liberal bourgeois revolution. As we shall still see, this sentiment became intense in the later part of the nineteenth century in central and Eastern Europe, when the pauperised Jewish masses woke up from their sectarian seclusion to a sense of their human dignity, and found themselves savagely oppressed by a backward and despotic regime and in bitter conflict with the majority of the population, who were sunk in prejudice and goaded on by acute social-economic pressures and ideological obsessions.

Chapter Four

THE ENCOUNTER BETWEEN JEW AND GENTILE
IN MODERN SOCIETY

Independently of the battle of principles, the burden of history proved just too heavy for both Gentiles and Jews to begin to treat each other just as individuals, let alone as brethren. When most German Jews were already pining to be recognised and admitted as citizens and Germans, and acculturation, even mass apostasy, was already in full swing, left-wing Hegelians like Feuerbach and Bruno Bauer went to inordinate lengths to expose Judaism as fossilised, imprisoned in an impenetrable shell of superstitious ritual, away from the mainstream of history and progress and (naturally) the life of the nation. They revived the charge of Jewish hatred for mankind and the nations around them. They added for good measure the theory that the compulsive anxiety of Jews to fulfil the minutest prescriptions of their all-devouring religion, and their desperate resolve to survive, robbed them of all that playful spontaneity and immediacy, which were the pre-condition of any artistic creativity, and choked all disinterested philosophical curiosity and contemplation.[23] True, the left-Hegelian's real targets, not unlike that of the *philosophes* in pre-revolutionary France, were absolutist and feudal traditions, and the idea of the Christian state or more precisely its props—the principles of authority from above and of prescriptive tradition. For once the concept of God had been revealed as the result of social conditions, the creation of men who were bent upon subjugating themselves, and still more others who were exploited by them, to an omnipotent and perfect deity as a punishment for alleged unworthiness, no one will believe in the divine right of kings, in the hierarchy of the church or in hereditary aristocracy.

Still, the Jews were the first victim. And that they were singled out as a target, and not merely used as a ploy, is shown by the fact that decades later the same Bruno Bauer returned to the attack on Jews, but this time on the secularised Jews for their pernicious indifference to and alienation from their own heritage. The hatred of themselves felt by detribalised Jews on the one hand, he claimed, and their resentment of the hostility of the Gentile environment on the other, produced in them a rootless dryness of soul, ironic and sarcastic attitudes towards the myths of organic, deep-rooted cultures, a sterility of spirit and an urge for destruction. They alienated themselves from both their tribal environment and national society.

The discomfort experienced by the Jews who had been formally emancipated, but not really admitted into society, did indeed breed traits which it has been only too easy for unfriendly satirists to caricature. These characteristics arose from the perpetual feeling of insecurity and not belonging. Their common denominator was over-reaction. Their perennial uncertainty about what the tomorrow might bring had for generations driven Jews to amass possessions, and above all money, which could easily be carried from place to place. Their desire to prove their worth to themselves, and still more to others, made many of them over-ambitious, ostentatious and arrogant. Their lives and activities being so narrowly circumscribed by restrictive legislation, arbitrary chicanery and social ill-will, they had to learn to circumvent those obstacles by all kinds of devices and stratagems. Always on the alert, and fearful of sudden emergencies, they gave the impression of forever living on their wits. Sensing animosity and suspicion, anxious to please and fearful of causing displeasure, some would become too loud and effusive or fawning and furtive. It is commonplace that by way of self-fulfilling prophecy, anti-semites are driving Jews to behave and act in a way which conforms to their image—and to become as it were a clannish confraternity in a state of permanent alert.

From Börne and Heine to Walter Rathenau and Sir Lewis Namier, Jews of extraordinary talents and heightened sensibility, who stormed their way into the temples of national and world culture, and yet could never cease to feel themselves trespassers, gave eloquent expression to that anguished envy of what Namier called the unbought grace, the easy poise of the well-established, the deeply rooted, of old lineage, who never need to present credentials, display qualities and show worth. Yet while men like Rathenau suffered infinite regret at having negroid features, and a non-Nordic appearance, they were never quite wanting in that sense of superiority, almost condescension, which is felt by descendants of an ancient cultural tradition towards a society, still half-pagan, not very far from barbarism.[24]

Jewish responses to the half-open outside world display every aspect of polarity, from the idealising, romanticising love for the conservative traditions of Disraeli or Namier to the mocking outsider's eye for the absurd, the spurious, the hypocritical and the nasty of Karl Kraus or Kurt Tucholsky.

Both the sudden release from the ghetto and the malaise which resulted from the ambiguities encountered in their early contacts with the world at large triggered off an explosion of volcanic Jewish energies. To the Gentile world, conservatives and radicals alike, this looked like a sudden invasion, a flood. The emergence and the branching out of the Rothschild dynasty into five capitals, Frankfurt, Paris, London, Vienna and Naples, provoked the Fourierist, Toussenel, into writing his tract "Les Juifs—rois de l'époque"[25]; for the Rothschilds were more powerful and more ubiquitous than the Habsburgs. Already in the French Revolution clerical opponents of Jewish emancipation and Alsatian anti-semites had warned the National Assembly that the sale of confiscated church property would in no time make the Jews masters of Alsace, once they were granted civic equality.[26] Jewish participation in the Saint-Simonist movement inspired the ultramontane Polish poet Zygmunt Krasinski to compose a poetic drama with the significant title, the *Godless Comedy*[27], depicting the eccentric ideas and behaviour of the socialist fraternity as a Jewish plot to subvert Christianity, demoralise European society and spread Jewish dominion. At the turn of the eighteenth century German reactionaries and romantics were dubbing the universalistic ideas of the rights of man, natural law and social contract a Jewish import from France, intended to overcome the natural resistance of an organism to the transplant of a foreign body.[28] Some decades later the conservative ultra-patriotic critic Menzel raised the alarm against the insidious influence of poisonous Jewish writing upon the authentic German spirit.[29] In 1848 King Frederick William IV of Prussia would lament the disgrace which the circumcised ringleaders among the revolutionaries had brought upon Germany.[30]

In the "spring of the peoples" the Jews again served as a touchstone. The 1848 revolutions may be said to have brought to light for the first time the problem of Jews and revolution. In all of the revolutions the Jews played a prominent part: Cremieux and Goudchaux in France, Daniel Manin in Italy, Jacoby and Gavriel Riesser in the Frankfurt Assembly, the physician Gottschalk in the communist demonstrations in the Rhineland, Stephan Born heading the first all-German trade union movement, and of course Karl Marx—all in Germany, and Dr Fischhof as head of the Vienna University Students Legion in Austria.

It comes as something of a shock to discover that in 1848 the Jews, of all the peoples and tribes of Europe, were the only ethnic group not to be affected by nationalist sentiment. On the contrary, they greeted that year as the fulfilment of the promise of full equality and general fraternity. They believed it would see the last barriers between nations and religions falling. Some of them went so far as to call upon their co-religionists to show an example by shedding all separatist distinctness.[31] The most striking case was that of Fischhof, the prophet of the free and equal fraternity of all nationalities in the Habsburg Empire. This was not the way things looked to non-Jews. In 1848—the year of Revolution—a clerical paper in Vienna wrote sneeringly of the sorry sight of the Jew Dr Fischhof, the organiser of the Student's Legion, walking in procession under a canopy and holding a candle, as if he were the heir of His Apostolic Royal and Imperial Majesty. Was it an omen of things to come?—wondered the author.[32]

We may quote two highly eloquent Jewish reactions to the revolutions of 1848, one from Disraeli's *Lord George Bentinck,* published in 1852,[33] and the other from the German-Jewish socialist J.L. Bernays in the New York German-Jewish journal *Israel's Herald* in 1849.[34]

The prophet of British Toryism and imperial grandeur had achieved the astonishing feat of conferring an aura of exotic, historic romanticism upon his race, in spite of the image of prosaic or avaricious money-making normally associated with it. Immemorial antiquity, a wisdom that penetrated every mystery, uncanny yet benevolent, fabulous wealth and luxuries were showered by the novelist upon his Hebrew heroes.[35] At once a British patriot and a Jewish racist, Disraeli was not only not hypnotised by the appeal of equality, which intoxicated most Jews, but was full of disdain for all barbarous levelling and mob politics; at the same time, in contrast to his rival Gladstone, he detested insurrectionary nationalism. His predilection for multi-racial empires like Turkey and Austro-Hungary[36] was consciously motivated by his appreciation that such political entities like these were sure to offer Jews a future by accepting them not only as one legitimate ingredient among others but also as a unifying constructive factor. Disraeli sensed the dangers which were to face Jews as the only minority, and a rather awkward one at that, in a state founded upon an exclusive nationalism.

While Bernays glorified the Jews as the ferment of revolution, Disraeli was at pains to depict them as fundamentally a conservative force which persecution turns into a subversive factor. Bernays offers a not dissimilar evaluation, but in a spirit that he himself recognises will be considered by a large part of his readers as highly dangerous, namely that of joyous triumph, instead of the anxious regret felt by Disraeli.

Bernays is soaked in young Hegelian modes of thought, and often employs the same terms as Marx, only to reach the opposite conclusion. Both were agreed that the surest way of destroying political and social oppression was by destroying the faith in and respect for God and all religious authority—the fountainhead of all systems of oppression and alienation—what Gentile left-wing-Hegelians like Feuerbach, Fr D.

Strauss, Rugge and the Bauer brothers actually had set out to do. The Jews—Bernays claims—had succeeded in "galvanising the raw mob" against pope, bishop, kings and princes, feudal potentates and plutocrats. They "laid bare the human essence buried under the thick crust of intolerance", and "in the face of human worth, . . . there comes an end to priest and Rabbi". In order to obtain their emancipation, the Jews must first destroy the Christian state. "They criticised Christianity with great dialectical skill and with no pity", and by becoming "in the process atheists, radicals, they became truly free men, with no prejudices". And once they had shown that the Christian religion was nothing but a myth, the work was accomplished.

More than that, the Jews "have rescued men from the narrow idea of an exclusive fatherland, from patriotism. The Jew is not only an atheist, but a cosmopolitan, and he has turned men into atheists and cosmopolitans; he has made man nothing else but a free citizen of the world." Almost consciously contradicting Marx's famous dictum on the emancipation of mankind through its emancipation from Judaism, and of the Jews from Judaism, Bernays triumphantly proclaims: "In their struggle for emancipation, the Jews have emancipated the European states from Christianity." In other words, it is not the Christians who gave emancipation to the Jews, but the Jews who have enabled the Christians to obtain their own emancipation. "The Jews took their revenge upon the hostile world in an entirely new manner . . . by liberating men from all religion, from all patriotic sentiment . . . from everything that reminded them of race, place of origin, dogma and faith. Men emancipated themselves in that way, and the Jew emancipated them, and the Jew became free along with them. . . . They achieved the incredible, and historians of the people will in the future recognise their merit willingly and justly." It was not their religion or racial qualities that enabled the Jews to accomplish all this. It was their condition of existence, their fate: "Only as the result of a general emancipatory effort could they become free themselves." The Jews succeeded in forging for themselves mighty levers of power to help them in their work: "the power of mobile property represented by the Rothschilds"; the psychological, spiritually therapeutic influence of Jewish doctors whose very existence and sought-after activity defied religious taboos and differences of religion, race and tradition; and above all the press, "which fell into Jewish hands everywhere in Europe". And, when revolution broke out, the Jews were everywhere in the forefront. After all Christendom had now become atheistic and cosmopolitan; the Jews might as well leave the stage as a separate people. Their mission had been fulfilled. In a Hegelian manner, the highest assertion of their particularity marks their disappearance within universality.

Bernays concludes with a prophecy which he finds himself "unable to suppress". There will be more waves of anti-Jewish persecution. Attacks on the Jewish religion and the Jewish nationality will be turned into an assault upon radicalism and free thought. "Stand firm, Jews, bear that blow too, because it will be the last! He who will dare to attack the man in the Jew, will bring upon himself all mankind; and that this should not take its terrible revenge one day, of such a thing there is no example in history."[37]

This strange blend of near (Jewish) megalomania and *farouche* iconoclastic cosmopolitanism breathes a radically revolutionary hatred for all historic traditions upholding inequality, and building fences around themselves. We find the same spirit in the statement of Moses Hess, the communist destined to become the earliest prophet of Zionism in the West: "All life, every aspiration is bound to end in frustration as long as the aristocratic poison flows through all the arteries of society. I do not mean only the aristocracy of blood, nor solely the aristocracy of money. I mean every type of rule which is not based upon personal merit, but derives from blind chance, privilege of birth. In brief, I mean every so-called historic right"[38]—a rather strange attitude for a future Zionist.

Disraeli had set out to prove the superiority of the Jewish race. "The degradation of the Jewish race is alone a striking evidence of its excellence, for none but one of the great races could have survived the trials which it has endured." There was indeed no other race "that so much delights, and fascinates and elevates, and ennobles Europe, as the Jewish . . . the most admirable artists of drama . . . the most entrancing singers, graceful dancers, and exquisite musicians [including, incidentally, Mozart—J.L.T.] are sons and daughters of Israel", not to speak of the great bankers and advisers to great statesmen, like Friedrich Gentz, the Grey Eminence of Metternich. Moreover, the Jews were living proof of the nonsense of social and racial equality, of the "inexorable law of nature which has decreed that a superior race shall never be destroyed or absorbed by an inferior". The true Jewish values were the conservative values par excellence. "They are the trustees of tradition, and the conservators of the religious element. They are a living and the most striking evidence of the fatality of that pernicious doctrine of modern times, the natural equality of man . . . of cosmopolitan fraternity . . . [calculated] . . . to deteriorate the great races and destroy all the genius of the world." Now if "all the tendencies of the Jewish race are conservative . . . religion, property, and natural aristocracy, it should be the interest of statesmen that this bias of a great race should be encouraged, and their energies and creative powers enlisted in the cause of existing society".[39]

Instead, the Gentile world has chosen to oppress and persecute the Jews. See what has been the result. "In 1848 an insurrection takes place against tradition and aristocracy, against religion and property. Destruction of the semitic principle, extirpation of the Jewish religion, whether in the Mosaic or in the Christian form; the natural equality of man and the abrogation of property are proclaimed by the secret societies who form provisional governments, and men of Jewish race are found at the head of every one of them. The people of God co-operate with atheists; the most skilful accumulators of property ally themselves with the communists; the peculiar and chosen race touch the hand of all the scum and low castes of Europe! Had it not been for the Jews . . . imbecile as were the governments, the uncalled-for outbreak would not have ravaged Europe. But the fiery energy and the teeming resources of the Children of Israel maintained for a long time the unnecessary and useless struggle . . . everywhere the Jewish element. . . . And all this because they wish to destroy that ungrateful Christendom which owes to them even its name, and whose tyranny they can no longer endure."[40]

"THE SOCIAL QUESTION IS THE JEWISH QUESTION"— "JEWISH CAPITALISM" AND "JEWISH MARXISM" AS LEVERS OF NATIONAL SOCIALISM

The new era which was opened by the conjunction of the two revolutions, the French and the industrial—the open industrial society—seemed to be tailored to the needs, interests, above all the qualifications of the newly emancipated Jews, or those going through the process of emancipation. But in their eternally ambivalent situation, the exciting opportunities contained also mortal perils. In comparison with the initial disadvantages with which they had entered the arena, they did indeed seem to emerge as the main beneficiaries of the revolutionary changes. Their enemies and all those who were hurt, shocked or simply confused by the colossal transformation, proclaimed them its authors. It all had started, as it were, when they appeared from nowhere, having just emerged from the ghetto.

Bourgeois society sanctified the two attainments, in which Jews were able to excel—money and intellect. The same could be said about the Weberian marks of modernity—rationality, the utilitarian calculus, self-control. Whether the Jews, and through them the Calvinist Puritans, had received their training in the Protestant-capitalist virtues pinpointed by Weber from their strict reckoning with the Almighty and his precepts, acquired them as they became the spearhead of an international commercial confraternity by profiting from the exceptional tolerance and international trading opportunities offered to ex-Marranos by imperial Holland, as Sombart suggested, or developed them in their confined conditions, where they had to keep their wits about them, or in the study of the Talmud, it is enough that they possessed them to a high degree. Not being rooted in the soil, not being an integral part of a local tradition, regarding the Law as their government, their dispersed co-religionists as their national community, they fitted admirably into the wholly abstract frame of international finance, commodity economy and the exchange system. Already in the eighteenth century Addison called them the hooks and hinges of international economy: in themselves of no use, but indispensable in any edifice with parts joined together.[41]

With all these qualities and dispositions, their readiness to try out experiments and take chances, with no reputation to lose, no traditions to cast off, the suddenly emancipated and secularised Jews rushed into the new openings which the well-settled creatures of custom were too conservative, too careless, too squeamish, too timid, too little prepared, or not imaginative enough to avail themselves of. They made a vital contribution to building up the international economy. The financial linkage of Europe's governments and economies by Jewish banking was paralleled by Jewish enterprise in railway building: the Rothschilds, Pereiras and Foulds in France, the Rothschilds again in Austria, Bleichröder in Germany and Roumania, Baron Hirsch in the Balkans and Turkey, the barons Ginsburg and Poliakoff in Russia. Reuter, Havas, Wolff pioneered the great news agencies.[42] Jews became extremely active and prominent in setting up, editing and writing for newspapers: the "Jewish press" became synonymous with the "press". It was to a large extent the great department stores they established that made commodity production and standardised merchandise, and thereby industrial civilisation at all possible.

For good or for bad, Western society and in the course of time the whole world, became seized by an unconquerable urge to invest, produce and amass wealth, to consume, to try out all manner of experiment and experience, to bend nature to its uses, to dominate, reshape, change, alter the setting and conditions of life, with tangible, utilisable advantages—material, educational, hedonistic—as the overriding consideration and yardstick. Many existences, interests, values and susceptibilities were adversely affected by this. There were not only the painful displacement of large masses of people, the terrible living conditions in the new urban centres, the misery of the industrial proletariat, the impoverishment and ruin of independent artisans and craftsmen, the decline of the aristocracy and landed gentry, in many places rural overpopulation. Religious teachings, conservative attachments, old customs, inherited concepts of decency and decorum were brutally shaken and overthrown by the naked, ruthless, impersonal and repulsive cash norms, the worship of Mammon. The undeniably important part played by the Jews in all this and, to a far greater extent, the indelible images of the Jew, were at hand to suggest that it was all their work. Feudal ultra-conservatives, clericals, romantics hypnotised by medieval chivalry and feudal idyll, moralisers of all sorts, back-to-nature socialists like the Fourierists, anarchists like Bakunin and Proudhon, Marx himself in his two articles on the Jewish question, joined in lamenting the Judaisation of society and proclaimed the need to halt and throw back the Jewish invasion. In the jeremiads of nostalgia for lost innocence, in the pained expressions of people affected by a sense of some irreparable break and irreparable alienation, and in the rhetoric of advocates of injured classes and lost causes, liberation from the evils of capitalism and modernity became synonymous with de-Judaisation. Marx also proclaimed that only their liberation from Judaism would free the Jews themselves as men, since that was a precondition for universal liberation.[43]

Marx defined the fundamental lie of liberal-bourgeois society in a way which again evoked Jewish associations. That society had raised the banner of liberty, equality and popular sovereignty. It had at the same time declared the rights of property sacred, untouchable, because property was allegedly of no relevance from the point of view of civic equality and political principles.[44] Instead of becoming irrelevant to political life, property had emerged as the unacknowledged, and as it were illegitimate master of modern society, overshadowing and predetermining, when not mocking, the formal parliamentary democratic procedures. The socialists and radicals agreed with the liberals that only the possession of property made all other freedoms real. They added, however, that the lack of it turned all these freedoms into illusions and fraud. The power which money gave was infinitely more effective than were abstract rights on paper. In this very vein Bruno Bauer thundered about the paradox that the Rothschilds, who had no rights in Frankfurt and Vienna, were lording it over Europe, holding to ransom ancient dynasties and dictating terms to great powers.[45]

The Jewish pioneers of capitalism, and above all of finance capitalism, were placed in the great metropolitan nerve centres. There they were not only very powerful but also immensely conspicuous and therefore highly vulnerable. As bankers, railway magnates, floaters of loans, masters of the stock exchange, they manned the commanding heights of national and international economy. They had direct dealings with national governments. They could exercise great pressure and influence over parliamentary representation and public opinion. They were held to be in a position to affect the fortunes of very large numbers of people, shareholders, industrialists, consumers, indeed society as a whole. So long as the going was good, such magnates could ignore demagogic anti-capitalist agitation by cranks and rabble-rousers. In moments of crisis, failure and scandal, their position and, by the inevitable association in responsibility and guilt, that of the Jews in general, would become precarious and dangerous. This was suddenly and simultaneously shown in the years after 1870 in the leading countries of the Continent. That was the date of the rise of the type of anti-semitism which was to lead eventually to Auschwitz. Its emergence was marked by the convergence of many different developments: the arrival of the masses; the victory of parliamentary regimes, with universal suffrage established in the two most important countries, France and Germany; the sudden rise of capitalism in Germany, Austro-Hungary and Russia; the rapid intensification of nationalist sentiment everywhere: in triumphant, but anxious Germany, in bitterly resentful France, in the Habsburg Empire ridden by racial strife, and in Russia torn by the polar tendencies of a revolutionary terrorist ideology and a violent chauvinism abetted by a besieged government.

The coincidence of the triumph of the parliamentary system and of economic crisis administered a severe blow, above all in France, to automatic trust in a parliamentary regime: the panacea for all ills seemed to have failed in its main task. Worse, many deputies, and even ministers, were involved in the financial intrigues, machinations, scandals and cover-ups. There was the suggestion of occult forces and plotting to manipulate parliamentary decisions and government policies in favour of private interests. The mysteries of high finance, the vagaries of the stock exchange, the alternations of soaring expectations and sudden bankruptcies were altogether incomprehensible to most shareholders, and were witchcraft to the populace at large. In all the financial failures and scandals which shook the various countries in the seventies and eighties of the last century Jews were involved, or were believed to be involved. In Germany, it was Gerson von Bleichröder,[46] the private banker and the closest confidant of Bismarck, the wealthiest man in Germany after Krupp, who became the inevitable target; in France the guilt for failure of the Catholic Union Générale was placed at the doorstep of the Rothschilds and there was no denying that the wire pullers in the Panama affair, officially headed by the national hero of the Suez Canal, Lesseps, were the German Jew Reinach, the American Jew Cornelius Hertz and the Italian Jew Artom.[47] In the early days of the Wilhelmine Reich the Jews, who constituted no more than between 2 per cent to 3 per cent of Germany's population, formed half of the participants in the investment rush after 1870 which was triggered off by the vast sums of the French war reparations and came to grief in the great 1873 crash.[48] They were to be found among the greatest industrial magnates who pioneered the phenomenal development of the new and initially peculiarly German industries, in electricity—the Rathenaus; in the chemical industry—the Monds; in shipbuilding—Balin. They carried German enterprise and investment to other European countries and to still more distant lands. The banking, stock exchange and speculative activities of the Jews attracted however the greatest attention. Here were all the ingredients of the anti-semitic myth of a combined Judas and Shylock. The image of Jewish greed, deviousness and occult things seemed to be confirmed by the speculative nature of modern capitalism.

The overheated nationalist imagination of the post-1870 era was obsessed with a vision of power and glory and at the same time with the dangers threatening the nation. Financial scandals and bankruptcies, and the misdemeanour of public representatives and servants raised the spectre of treason. They provoked righteous indignation against corrupt men who had proved unfit to hold the destinies of the nation in their keeping, and, above all, to defend the power and honour of the nation abroad. Conspiracy and treason justified violent, direct action, a popular uprising led by a vanguard of the pure and the incorruptible against the Jewish purveyors of corruption, and their gentile accomplices, stooges and abettors. General Boulanger[49] was still too much of a product of the French revolutionary tradition to espouse anti-semitism as a political plank, and there were the Jewish anarchist senator Alfred Naquet and the Jewish convert, procurer of the movement's funds, Meyer, to hold the fort. The motley crowd of political entrepreneurs and agitators ranging from patriotic Blanquists and populist anti-semites to aristocratic Orleanists, who together built up the rather pathetic chocolate soldier into a national hero, the avenger of Sedan, and the social Messiah, were an expression of and set out to offer a response to the frustrations and the rages of great multitudes against the money-lenders in the Temple—the Palais Bourbon. They indeed pioneered an anti-parliamentary and proto-Fascist mass movement.[50]

The secular religion of militant nationalism seized upon the anti-capitalist and anti-socialist brand of anti-semitism as an antidote to proletarian cosmopolitan socialism, as the most effective means of weaning the working classes from the ideas of class war and Marxist internationalism. There was every temptation to proclaim the social problem to be the result of Jewish capitalism, and the social conflict a contrivance of Jewish socialists, working hand in hand to divide the nation the better to exploit it. Furthermore, nationalism as a mass religion needed the self-assurance of being "holier than thou". Anti-Jewish feeling satisfied the craving to believe the best of ourselves and the worst of others, to portray ourselves as we would like to be, and others when they are at their worst; to feel the inner light illuminating all our being, and to behold the impenetrable darkness in which the aliens dwell; to idealise Gentile pub-crawlers and dog-racing fans, and to caricature Jewish stockbrokers and pedlars; to attribute to ourselves all the lofty sentiments, all the higher needs, the Faustian idealism and Promethean heroism, all mankind's artistic sensitiveness and genius, and to damn the Jews as desiccated materialists, devoid of all the finer graces, instincts and longings. Renan said of this type of nationalism that it turned the nation into a union of those who were united by illusions about their own origins and by contemptuous hostility to all other nations. So there was an overriding necessity to guard one's own authenticity from contamination by lesser breeds.[51]

In the anguished post-mortem which the French conducted after the terrible defeat of 1870, the spokesmen of the Right clamoured that the French nation had been demoralised by the abstract, universalist, cosmopolitan teachings of the French Enlightenment and the French Revolution, and that its strength had been sapped in the service of foreign causes and revolutionary preaching. Charles Maurras blamed the Jews for importing the theories of the rights of man from Kantian Germany and for using them to destroy the resistance of the healthy organism to the transplant of the alien Jewish body. Not without wistful regret did Maurras call upon France, which had for centuries served as a model to all European nations, to retire into its own shell, mend its fences and fall back on its authentic ancient exclusive inspirations.[52] Barrès proclaimed that to Frenchmen the truth was the perspective of France's interests, and their compass sacred national egoism.[53] In Maurras' teaching, the monarchy, the French church hierarchy (rather than the ecumenical church), the army had been the life-saving social authorities of France. Out of fear of cosmopolitan solvents, the French extreme Right had developed a morbid dislike of industrialisation, liberalism, capitalism and socialism. It engaged in a cult of old cemeteries and extolled the beauties of rustic simplicity and ancient regional traditions. The cosmopolitan and un-French values were all centred in Jewry. And no Jew, even one wrongly condemned by a French military court like Dreyfus, could be right against the life-sustaining ideas and historic institution of France—above all the French army.

Sincerely or hypocritically deploring the vulgarity and savagery of rabid anti-semitic agitation, and at the same time telling the Jews that they had asked for it by their arrogance, Treitschke[54] frankly admitted that a strong dose of anti-semitism was calculated to deepen national self-awareness and pride in the newly united German Reich, which was so unsure of its identity, and the cohesion of which was kept weak by fissiparous traditions and interests. Adolph Stöcker[55], Kaiser Wilhelm I's court chaplain, a man of plebeian origins and an evangelical zealot, embarked upon a crusade to stem the tide of atheism, materialism and unpatriotic sentiments among the working classes, to convert them and lead them back to the good old Prussian traditions. He stumbled upon the Jews and he turned anti-semitism into the cornerstone of his Christian-Social movement. Jewish high capitalism was the ruin of the small man, and Jewish usury was a millstone round the necks of the German peasantry. The Jewish cult of Mammon and the ignoble selfish materialism of the Manchester School, preached by Jewish liberals and practised by Jewish interests, had put an end to the artisan's pride in work, contentment with one's station in life, patriarchal relationships between classes, the old traditions based upon Christian charity and sense of mutual obligation. Jewish scribes dared to mock God and church, abuse ancient pieties and national symbols, and inflame instincts of greed and insatiable self-indulgence. Jewish socialists were seducing the workers away from their loyalties to church, Emperor and fatherland.

Wilhelm I favoured his chaplain and shared his horror of Jewish arrogance and his desire to put a limit to the destructive influence of the Jews, but he had to withdraw his patronage when Stöcker got into trouble with working class audiences, especially on his missionary visit to London, and also fell foul of the law. Nevertheless, the espousal of militant anti-semitism by a court chaplain, and still more the famous pamphlet of Treitschke on the Jews as Germany's misfortune, lent respectability to the agitation which had been started earlier by such marginal figures and monomaniacs as the ex-radical Wilhelm Marr, Liebermann von Sonnenberg and Dühring, and had been continued by demagogues like Ahlwart, Böckl and Fritsch.[56] The Jews were appalled when the mass petition to abrogate Jewish emancipation—though rejected—gave rise to a long debate in which Conservatives, Liberals and Catholics vied with each other in warning the Jews to know their place in German society, to learn humility and to respect the interests, susceptibilities and decencies of the German nation. Indeed, in the grand 1879 debate on protectionism versus free trade, Bismarck himself hit the liberal Jewish opponents of the proposed agricultural tariffs, Lasker and Bamberger, below the belt, with hints about men who had never felt loving care for those who laboured on the soil, as they themselves neither hoed nor spun, but throve on speculation and felt no responsibility for the fate of toiling fellow citizens.[57] But all attempts, especially by Bleichröder, the manager of the Iron Chancellor's private investments and his political confidant, to make him and the Kaiser formally condemn anti-semitic agitation failed. In his magisterial book Fritz Stern says that, had they done this at the time when their prestige was at its zenith, by branding militant anti-semitism as immoral and anti-national, they might have inhibited the Conservatives as well as the National Liberals from making it respectable.[58] The Jews soon had the galling experience of being subjected to vile abuse from the tribune of the Reichstag by the dozen deputies elected on a platform which had anti-semitism as its main plank.[59] Bismarck had no liking for the big-mouthed cleric. He was not, however, bothered, he admitted, by Stöcker's anti-semitism. What did worry him was the thought that attacks on rich Jews were likely to lead to socialistic attacks on property in general, and thus endanger the social order.[60]

A Prussian police report of 1879 spoke of the help given by Jews to the Social-Democratic party. The help came from the ostentatious luxury they displayed, which provoked social protest among the poor, and from their open support to socialists in money and in the advocacy of socialism in the press organs under their control. "If we add the fact that the most prominent leaders of the revolutionary parties in the various countries are Jews, such as Karl Hirsch in Bruxelles, Karl Marx in London, Leo Fraenkel in Budapest and that the large party of Russian nihilists, who endeavour to spread their revolutionary teachings particularly in Galicia, Russian Poland and Switzerland, consists mostly of Jews, there is reason to justify the claim that Jewry is by nature of a revolutionary bent."[61] This and the fact of Jewish solidarity and cohesion made vigilance necessary. They had also manifested their lack of all patriotic feeling, "of which they like so much to boast", in their critique of the Reich's customs policy.[62]

In the early days after the débâcle of the last romantic uprising of 1863-4 in Poland, the idea of organic work and constructive achievement won the battle against Polish insurrectionary ideology. The Jews, especially the powerful captains of industry and founders of the Polish credit system, the Kronenbergs, the Blochs, the Natansons and others, were being lauded as contributors to and pathfinders of Polish prosperity and power. Soon Poles and Jews clashed as competitors, especially as the Poles lacked the experience and the resourcefulness which the Jews possessed, and a new spate of restrictive Tsarist legislation sent large numbers of Russified Jews into Congress Poland from White Russia and Lithuania, where the Poles were a minority consisting of landowners. The ensuing wave of fierce anti-semitism proclaimed the slogan of the necessity of building up a Polish middle class, a truly Polish economy, a healthy social structure, and it was proclaimed that the Jews were an alien exploiter, the fourth occupying power besides Russia, Germany and Austria, and the most tenacious and the most irremovable of the four.[63]

The programme of the National-Democratic party was built on the rock of anti-semitism. Its theoretician and leader Roman Dmowski propagated the idea of a special "vanguard of professional anti-

semites".[64] If it was not a replica of Lenin's idea of a party of professional revolutionaries, it was certainly meant as an antidote to the
"fighting units" of the Polish Socialist party. The National-Democrats
had no share in the generous and heroic, though often wrong-headed,
idealism of Pilsudski's followers. In fact, they put all their hopes on the
opportunities which international complications might one day offer
them, and in practice collaborated systematically with the occupying
powers, while preaching a brand of social Darwinism inappropriate for
a weak and subjugated nation. The Jews were an easy target for
nationalist militancy. No risk was involved. It comes as a shock, but not
as a total surprise, that in the days of Auschwitz, some Polish voices
blasphemously thanked Providence for solving an insoluble problem for
the Polish nation in a way that nobody could have imagined in his
wildest dreams.

It was Austria[65], the country of Hitler's birth, in which he lived till
1913, and where on his own admission he completed his political
education before settling in Germany, which revealed in a rudimentary
manner the frightening possibilities of modern anti-semitism.
Belatedly, but at a more precipitate pace even than Russia, the
Danubian Empire had made the leap from feudal-agrarian conditions
into industrialisation and capitalism, without the slow process of the
growth of a middle class. As well as the Germans, it was the Jews—in
certain regions even more prominently than the Germans—who
emerged as the leaven of modernisation, industrialisation and
capitalism. It was given to them to re-enact in the multi-racial
Habsburg domain, with its vast ethnic, cultural and social divergencies
and inequalities, the role of pioneers and "hinges and hooks".[66]

From a tiny community, the Jews of Vienna grew into one of the
largest Jewish centres in Europe, acting as a magnet to all the enterprising and dynamic young Jews from the remotest and most backward
corners of the sprawling Empire, Galicia and Bukovina. In Vienna most
banks were in Jewish hands; in Budapest, as it happened, all of the banks.
The Jews founded and edited most of the newspapers. They were the
first builders of railways.[67] Many of them set the tone in music,
literature, theatre and mass entertainment, especially in Vienna, to
mention only Authur Schnitzler, Hugo Hofmannsthal, Gustav Mahler
and Sigmund Freud; and this was even more so in Budapest. The
proportion of Jews in the student body of the universities and in the free
professions kept soaring.

All of this enabled the resourceful demagogue and rabble-rouser
Lueger to turn the Christian-Social party into an anti-semitic mass
movement, to sweep the boards again and again as candidate for the

mayorality of the Habsburg capital, and to compel the old Emperor to confirm him as mayor after several refusals. When the Rothschild concession of the leading Austrian railway came in for renewal by Parliament, Schönerer, formerly a liberal who had worked in close association with Jewish liberal leaders such as the eminent historian Friedjung and even Victor Adler (before Adler joined the Social-Democratic party) seized upon the issue as the great opportunity to appear as the defender of state rights and the people's interests against predatory Jewish finance capitalism, and to unleash a vast propaganda campaign.[68]

After the decline of the strong traditional loyalty which the ruling German nationality had felt for the Habsburg dynasty, as the result of the phenomenal rise of the German Empire and the rapprochement between the dynasty and the Slavs, it was the Jews who became the sole ethnic group which retained unreserved, indeed passionate allegiance to the Austrian idea. This did not endear them to Austria's pan-Germans. The Jews of Austro-Hungary realised that it was better for them to be one of the dozen or more ethnic groups in a large multi-racial state than to form the only minority in a self-conscious single nationality state. They were at the same time lovingly attached to the dominant German language and culture and this, again, alienated the non-German nationalities. But the Jews were also staunchly liberal and firm believers in democracy and pluralism. They were prominent in the leadership of the Liberal party as well as in that of the Social-Democratic party, since both upheld the principle of the unity of the Empire and racial equality. This excited the fury of the pan-German nationalists, like Schönerer. In their eyes the Habsburgs had sold themselves to the Slavs and betrayed the German mission in the Ostmark bastion. At the same time they were horrified by the thought that the principle of one man one vote, coupled with the growing insolence of the inferior breeds, threatened to swamp the Teutonic element with Slav hordes.

This gave rise to anti-democratic doctrines on the rule of the best instead of the many, charismatic dictatorial leadership and not parliamentary party majority, and the permanently mobilised nation with a single will. Jewish politicians and publicists who preached liberal democracy were said to be undermining German self-assurance and the German position. The individualistic, liberal, ironical attitudes of over-sophisticated cosmopolitan Jews towards old sanctities and ancient symbols were profaning the German national myth and having a distorting, pernicious, falsifying effect on German self-expression. The Darwinian images of the war of races, which Schönerer and his followers had taken over literally, carried with them overtones of biological racism. It led them to preach the subordination of class and party differences within the German nation to the need to fight the Slav siege from outside and the machinations from within of the begetter of all social evils—Jewish finance capitalism (as distinct from the constructive industrial capitalism allegedly practised only by Aryan Germans) and the Jewish socialists, who were calling for a united proletarian front of all ethnic groups, and were splitting the German camp.

The combined forces of the Christian-Social party under the charismatic demagogue Lueger[69] and of the pan-Germans, with the fierce Schönerer at their head, succeeded in turning Austrian anti-semitism into a mirror image of socialism and in the language of the aged Engels in making it into "the socialism of fools". "The anti-semites are now our most dangerous adversary, more dangerous here than in Germany," wrote Kautsky from Vienna to Engels in 1884, "because they appear as oppositionists and democrats, and respond to the workers' instincts."[70] He followed this up a little later in another letter to the grand old man of Marxism, informing him that anti-semitism was assuming colossal dimensions and was carrying with it a large part of the petty bourgeoisie—"among them very radical elements, which till now went with us. And the petty-bourgeois sentiments exist even among the workers . . . to such an extent that our leaders must take the greatest care to keep the masses from deserting to the anti-semites."[71]

In the overheated atmosphere of a Darwinian war of races, violence, as we have already noted, came to replace negotiation. Force and the display of it were substituted for argument. Here and there in the German-speaking areas and especially in the mixed or frontier areas, like the Sudeten, small fraternities or rather bands of nationalist militants were springing up calling themselves National-Socialists, under the leadership of charismatic leaders who exercised an irresistible spell upon and exacted absolute obedience from their followers and led them in the sustained struggle, often to the point of launching physical assaults against the tribal enemies, Slavs and Jews, in public meetings, on the streets and in the universities.[72]

Schönerer's fall came when he led a group of students in an assault upon the Jewish editor of the Vienna newspaper which had printed a premature report of the death of Emperor Wilhelm I, the idol of the Austrian pan-Germans. As a young student, the writer Herman Bahr witnessed the resistance of Schönerer to an Austrian police officer who came to break up an anti-semitic student political meeting: "a picture of truly Gothic wrath and Wagnerian fury—brandishing a sword . . .

seething with anger, elemental in its savagery! The picture of that uncontrollable fury remains unforgettable in my memory to this day, and when we hear people speak of the Gothic man, there always emerges that knight George.... That was the famous *Wagnerkommers.*"[73]

Chapter Six

THE ROAD TO AUSCHWITZ—RACISM

Not a few Jewish historians have tormented themselves with the question whether the "new anti-semitism", which emerged around 1880 and reached its terrible climax in Nazism, was "the same old thing", only an intensification of it, or a new and substantially different phenomenon. There is no need to tabulate the pros and cons of the respective views. Suffice it to say that even the believers in continuity and sameness will hardly deny that there was a quantitative change which amounted to a qualitative one.

There was a good deal of vacillation among the opponents of Jewish emancipation as well as among the later critics of undue and evil Jewish influence. The Jews were not yet ready to be absorbed into the body of the German nation, but continued to feel different even after the emancipation. Treitschke, and in a different spirit Mommsen, pressed upon them the need to make every effort to get rid of separateness.[74] Their more extreme adversaries insisted that the Jews would always remain aliens, because of their history and psychological make-up. They would never give up their expectations of a messianic national restoration to their ancient homeland, their dreams of one day ruling all nations. Their power and influence therefore bore the marks of harmful imposition and exploitative domineering. The upholders of this view despised the very desire of Jews to become Germans, the more so as German patriotism was being eagerly demonstrated by all German Jews. "The love of our German fatherland shall not cool." declared a Zionist pamphlet in 1897. The Prussian virtues—discipline, smartness, manliness, sense of honour and duty, bodily prowess and love of nature, finally the patriotic Turnvereine of 1813—all these were held up as a model to the lovers of Zion as well as to the great majority of Jews who only wanted to be Germans of the Mosaic faith.[75]

The wholly disproportionate contribution of Jews to the national culture, to German literature, science, scholarship, the press and the arts, and also their steadily growing share in the professions, caused by their being barred from the officer corps, from the higher echelons of the civil service, from the judiciary and from university chairs, were disparaged as gate-crashing by aliens who were nothing but "German-speaking orientals". It was treated as a kind of poisoning of the wells of the German spirit, especially when Jews displayed their analytical ability and critical acumen, let alone irony and wit. They were no more accepted, however, when they sincerely and fervently took part in the Teutonic cult. They were then ridiculed as pathetic, contemptible and ludicrous charlatans.

Keeping Jews at arm's length, warning against them, putting them in their place, erecting barriers against them, cruel, deliberate sneering—all this was checked by certain inhibitions which fell away in the "new" racist anti-semitism. In spite of all its share in arousing and sustaining anti-Jewish sentiments, Christianity could not wholly deny its Jewish antecedents and associations, or its teachings that all men were born in the image of God, about the oneness of mankind, above all "Thou shall not kill." More than that, doctrinally baptism freed the Jew from his stigma.[76]

Treitschke would thunder against the great Heinrich Graetz's use of the word *Volk* to describe the Jews and against his incautious remark that Gabriel Riesser was "accidentally" born on German soil: if the Jews felt alien, said Treitschke, let them pack off to Palestine. But he nevertheless deplored anti-semitic rabble-rousing, gave examples of "truly German" and "good" Jews and attributed most of the evil Jewish influence to newcomers from the East.[77] Nietzsche, for all his contempt for plebeian anti-semitism and for nationalist frenzy in general, and his glorification of the Jews as the best example of the good Europeans of the future, uttered warnings against the admission of any more Jews from across the Eastern border, since the weak German stomach would not be able to digest them. He also branded the stock-exchange Jew as the most execrable creature on earth.[78] Yet neither Treitschke, nor even Stöcker, would countenance any demand for the formal abolition of Jewish equality before the law. The old Emperor Wilhelm I had declared that such a thing was unthinkable. Jewish emancipation was laid down by the law, was part of the constitution.[79] And he had sworn to uphold the law, the constitution. A wholly new page was opened when race theory turned into ideology.

The Nazi philosopher Bäumler was to call the emergence of the race theory another Copernican revolution.[80] Anti-semitism may not have been Count Gobineau's inspiration, when he set out to speculate on the differences between races and their roles in history, but in the transformation of racist theory into ideology it certainly became that. There were no racial aliens in Europe other than Jews to "prove" the teachings and for the doctrine to be applied to. Although the theory of race was

more than mere Jew-hatred, the latter was not only the impulse of the
ideology, but became the focus of a whole *Weltanschauung*, a philosophy
of history and a political programme, which again reached out far
beyond the Jews.

It seems to me that the decisive moment in all this was 1850 when
Richard Wagner anonymously published his pamphlet *The Jews in
Music*,[81] only a year or so after he had fought alongside Bakunin on the
Dresden barricades and had declared that no man could be regarded free
so long as a single man anywhere in the world was left in bondage. In his
tract the composer juxtaposed the abstract imperative of liberal rationality that the Jews should be treated as equals with instinctive revulsion
from them. Which was more authentic? By deciding that it was the
latter, Wagner bade farewell both to rational, analytical reasoning, and
to the rights of man. He replaced what he and his followers would call
ratiocination with intuitive, instinctive modes of perception. Language,
poetry and art served as proof of the spontaneous and irrestible power of
those vital forces to create wholly original forms permeated by a logic
and cohesion all their own. In the efforts and achievements of
individuals in these fields of creativeness there worked the potency of
the race. The Jews, Wagner taught, lacked all inborn talent and feeling
for music. In this as well as in other creative endeavours they were
pitiful imitators, though skilful performers of the original works of
others. Being cut off from nature, its wholeness and its direct impact,
leading a fragmented and impoverished existence, with vital faculties
undeveloped or atrophied, they could not serve as the Aeolian harp of
nature.

Wagner is a first example of the baffling transition from the
atheistic, social radicalism of a barricade fighter in 1848 to extreme
racist anti-semitism and to poetry of the pagan Germanic myth. He was
strongly influenced by Feuerbach's preoccupation with the problem of
alienation and the view that the root cause of it was the idea of God, in a
social-psychological context. This gave rise to the resolve to roll back
the Christian heritage as a way of restoring man's authentic humanity
and freedom. It then led to the conclusion that both the Christian God
and the social conditions in a money-obsessed society were of Jewish
provenance. Mankind was to be liberated from both these Jewish
creations.[82] This as we know was also Marx's idea. But when Marx
spoke of the emancipation of mankind, and of the Jews themselves as
men, through the disappearance of Judaism, he meant liberation from
the Judaic spirit and its works. Under the influence of organicism,
Darwinism, racism, biological imagery, the decline of the idea of the
uniqueness of man in nature and the denial of the absolute sanctity of his

life, "disappearance" was gradually replaced by "destruction". The idea assumed a literally physical connotation.

On the spiritual plane, the rejection of Christian myth and symbolism led Wagner and others like him to glorify pre-Christian Germanic mythology and cults and to prophesy their revival through spontaneous art, above all music, no longer falsified by Jewish cerebral imitators, performed to Jewish tone-deaf snobs and commercialised by Jewish speculators.

Much of all this had been foreshadowed by German romanticism.[83] But it was then vague speculation. The concept of race, of blood, made possible the consummation of the marriage of science with mysticism, of biology with metaphysics, aesthetics, the philosophy of history, ethics, politics. It seemed to connect the measurable, quantifiable facts of race and blood with the remotest and most refined phenomena and achievements in history, philosophy, the creative arts, the modes of life and production and to create a deterministic and all-embracing totality. Here was as it were irreversible and unalterable trenchancy and finality: Aryans or Semites, Nordics or Jews, with their respective, peculiar and mutually exclusive myths, languages, aptitudes, attitudes, ways. The fact of the Jews being aliens in Europe for all time was thus irrevocably established.

Houston Stewart Chamberlain, the Teutonised son of a British admiral, and Wagner's son-in-law, built this cornerstone into a whole philosophy of history. In his widely read and extremely influential *The Foundation of the Nineteenth Century,*[84] the favourite book of Wilhelm II (who in spite of his friendship with some eminent Jews, spoke to Sir Edward Grey of the need to "eliminate the Jews"), the Jewish issue became the key to European, not to say world, history. The Jews, whether ancient or modern, were denied any metaphysical insights and any religious ethos whatsoever, apart from commerce with a tribal deity and an instrumental, magical ritualism. Jesus was therefore in fact a blue-eyed Galilean Aryan. The Dark Ages were the period of general mongrelisation, which resulted from race mixture and the deadly influence of Judaised Christianity. The turning point came about the year 1200, when the Germanic race entered the arena of history as the shaper of European destiny. Since then anything of original value had come from its descendants.

The Jews were then locked up in ghettos. They re-emerged on the morrow of the French Revolution, invaded all avenues of European life, and turned the nineteenth century into a Jewish century in the same way as the high Middle Ages were German centuries, the sixteenth was Spanish, the seventeenth French, the eighteenth English. It was not only the physical presence and doings of the individual Jews, but the spirit they embodied and then exuded that carried deadly contagion. Chamberlain therefore cautioned Aryans from ever touching a book or a newspaper article written by Jews. It was this that probably inspired his young disciple Adolf Hitler, who received the accolade from him before the revered sage departed to the Germanic Valhalla,[85] to agree with Eckart that the Jewish spirit could be exorcised only by the destruction of the flesh.[86]

Darwinism[87] was the justification for the transformation of racism into this murderous ideology. It not only dethroned the idea of providence, destroyed the vision of man's position as unique in creation, and did away with faith in the oneness of mankind. The theory of the eternal struggle for life and power between the races, and the concept of the survival of the fittest, implied not only the elimination of the unfit races, but also the denial of the universality and objectivity of reason and morality. Each race moulded its particular versions thereof in the course of struggle. The superior races had developed a well-coordinated mode of struggle, an unerring instinct. This gave them their fighting prowess. Thus it became supremely important to guard the organism from the debilitating effects of alien, inferior blood. In fact the failings and failures of the race had to be, could only be, explained by such dilution. The mood of *fin de siècle* must also be taken into account, the strange preoccupation with decadence, speculations about the causes of the decline and fall of civilisations, the spread of the sense of alienation, the onset of the crisis of identity, the weight of the growing relativity of values, of value-free science and scholarship, if the readiness of wide sections of educated and semi-educated people to absorb the new message was to be understood.

If not salvation, they seemed to be offered at least a key or a thread to the labyrinth of modern life. It was partly cultural despair, partly the need for defiant self-expression that made many people receptive to Nietzsche's denial, following Darwin, of the hitherto fundamental idea of the Western world, namely the idea of theodicy. As Nietzsche fully grasped, from Judaism through Christianity, the Reformation, the Enlightenment, the French Revolution, to liberalism, democracy and socialism—all these creeds were sustained by a faith in eventual reconciliation, the redress of wrongs, harmony, equality and rationality. The greatest revolutionary in two thousand years—as Nietzsche styled himself—was the first to dare to reject this consolation of the weak, the botched, the defeated, with its roots in the priestly morality of the Jews. The slave morality of Judeo-Christianity and its offshoots was to be replaced by the pagan cult of the winners in the eternal contest. History was not moving towards a unity based on the universality of reason, victory of rational truth, mutual acceptance in peace and concord. Its purpose was to serve as breeding ground for the strong, beautiful, superior specimen emerging out of common humanity in the crucible of struggle, rivalry, war.[88]

In the wake of this grim prophet, the counter-revolutionaries, who dared to proclaim a crusade against the legacy of the French Revolution and eventually to undo its work, presented themselves as revolutionaries. One does not have to be a sworn Marxist to see in this philosophy the inspiration of an ideology of imperialism. The crusade against Judaism paradoxically brought the standard-bearers of warring nationalisms together into an International as early as the 1880's, with international congresses, common platforms and campaigns launched to defend European or Aryan civilisation against the semitic solvent, exploiter and seducer.

The anti-semites had some difficulty in classifying the Jewish phenomenon. Seemingly a race of unsurpassed tenacity and cohesion, never intermarrying with others, braving all misfortune and persecution, springing up with such phenomenal resilience and increased energy after every disaster, it yet lacked all the attributes of a race or nation, and moreover preached cosmopolitan ideologies, and acted in bringing down the barriers between nations. The racists solved the enigma by proclaiming the Jews to be an anti-race. What kept them together was the plot to debilitate the national organisms in order to facilitate Jewish exploitation and pave the way for Jewish world mastery. Their pseudo-scientific imagery suggested the idea of a foreign body living in and upon another normal organism, in other words the idea of a microbe which was not an antagonist to argue with but a growth to be extirpated.

Racist anti-semitism provided a systematic refutation and also a mirror-image of socialist Marxism. Blood took the place allotted to matter in dialectical materialism, changes in the composition of blood replaced changes in modes of production, Jewish exploitation replaced capitalist oppression, Jewish-socialist incitement replaced class struggle, the elimination of Jews replaced the revolution, the confiscation of Jewish property, and its nationalisation and redistribution, replaced the social transformation.[89]

The growing strength of the proletarian parties, with Jews becoming prominent in their radical wings, led to a greater stress on insiduous, conspiratory Jewish manipulation. Dühring had already denounced Marxism as the spearhead of the Jewish grand design to gain world mastery. As early as 1879 when Jews were only beginning to join the revolutionary movement in Russia, Marr, the pre-1848 radical and also the inventor of the term "anti-semitism", warned that the Jews were determined to use Russia, "the only European country still to show resistance to the invasion of alien domination" to subvert the Western world. The Jews were pushing Russia into a "revolution, the like of which the world had never seen".[90] It was probably the influence of Nietzsche that was behind the famous dialogue between Hitler and his mentor Eckart, "From Moses to Lenin", on the historic role of Jews as inciters of mobs against ruling elites from Moses in Egypt through the early Christians, the Puritans, the Jacobins, socialists, up to the Bolsheviks, as a means of paving the way to Jewish world rule.[91]

A new spectre was haunting men's minds—the spectre of a Jewish plot to gain world domination. Ironically distorted, this vision appears in Nietzsche's *Dawn of Day*. It was calculated to have a tremendous impact. "The people of Israel—one of the spectacles which the next century will invite us to witness is the decision regarding the fate of the European Jews. It is now quite obvious that they have cast their die and crossed their Rubicon: the only thing that remains for them is either to become masters of Europe or to lose Europe, as centuries ago they lost Egypt, where they were confronted with similar alternatives. In Europe, however, they have gone through a schooling of eighteen centuries such as no other nation has ever undergone, and the experiences of this dreadful time of probation have benefited not only the Jewish community but, to an even greater extent, the individual. Now, however, that they unavoidably intermarry more and more year after year with the noblest blood of Europe, they will soon have a considerable heritage of good intellectual and physical manners, so that in another hundred years they will have a sufficiently noble aspect not to render themselves, as masters, ridiculous to those whom they have subdued. And this is important! and therefore a settlement of the question is still premature. They themselves know very well that the conquest of Europe or any act of violence is not to be thought of; but they also know that some day or other Europe may, like a ripe fruit, fall into their hands, if they do not clutch at it too eagerly. In the meantime, it is necessary for them to distinguish themselves in all departments of European excellence and to stand in the front rank. . . . Then they will be called the pioneers and guides of the European, whose modesty they will no longer offend. And then where shall an outlet be found for this abundant wealth of great impressions accumulated over such a long period and representing Jewish history for every Jewish family, this wealth of passions, virtues, resolutions, resignations, struggles, and conquests of all kinds—where can it find an outlet but in great intellectual men and works! On the day when the Jews are able to exhibit to us as their own work such jewels and golden vessels as no European nation, with its shorter and less profound experience, can or could produce, when Israel has changed its eternal vengeance into an eternal benediction for Euorpe: then that seventh day will once more appear when old Jehovah may rejoice in himself, in his creation, in his chosen people—and all, all of us, will rejoice with him!'"[92] One would give much to know whether Hitler ever read this prose poem and what impression it made on him. That the Führer knew and admired the poet of the superman is beyond doubt. When a Nazi commando rescued the imprisoned Duce in 1943, Hitler sent him a de luxe edition of Nietzsche's works as a gift.

It has been observed that the first wave of noisy and lunatic antisemitism which emerged around 1880 in central and Eastern Europe abated towards the end of the last century and in the years before 1914. But what is often overlooked is that while the savage tones and bloody excesses somewhat subsided, the more restrained forms of antisemitism became wholly respectable, and outside the Social-Democratic parties almost universally accepted. Association after association, from the free professions to alpinists, cyclists and municipal employees, not to mention student organisations, came to adopt the "Aryan clause" as a matter of course.[93] In the process, the liberal-democratic parties in central Europe were completely eliminated, or became reduced to Jewish members, depending on Jewish votes. The Jews were virtually sent back to the ghetto. Commenting upon the victory of the Christian-Social party, which was much milder in its anti-semitism than Schönerer's racist pan-German movement, in the 1897 elections to the Reichsrat, when it scored in Lower Austria 245,000 votes against the 123,000 cast for the Social-Democrats, an anti-semitic spokesman, Julius Patzelt, made a significant comment. Not all votes were from members of the party and sworn anti-semites, but "the party formed a crystallising point which attracted all anti-revolutionary elements. It proved itself fit and strong enough to draw to itself all the elements of law and order in the common fight against Social-Democracy." The election also demonstrated that "the bourgeois, so-called liberal progressive parties were dominated entirely by Jewish influence", "Jewish liberalism begot Social-Democracy and (now) hoped that Social-Democracy would rise to avenge liberalism".[93a]

Thus confrontation between bourgeois parties and the socialist movement was becoming identified with Christian or Aryan versus Jews.

Rosa Luxemburg was faced with a similar situation in Poland in the

years after the failure of the 1905 revolution. In both Russia and Poland
the socialist movement entered upon a period of deep crisis, demoralisation and in some places dissolution. The anti-semitic nationalists of
the Endecja under Roman Dmowski came out in loud condemnation of
the revolutionary policies in the years 1905-6 in Russian Poland and said
they were the result of an anti-Polish plot of the 'Jewish' internationalist wing of the socialist movement, the Social-Democratic party of the
Kingdom of Poland and Lithuania, with the cosmopolitan Jewess Rosa
Luxemburg as its head, a plot intended to destroy the distinct position of
Congress Poland in the Empire.[94] No notice of course was taken of the
prominence of Jews in the nationalist PPS—of Jews like Feliks Perl, at
one time the closest associate of Pilsudski, Diamant, Liebermann and
others.

While this was happening, there occurred a violent shift in the attitude of the progressive, radical and anti-clerical party, founded by the
old veteran of Polish radicalism, Swietochowski, and ably represented
by its spokesman, a writer, poet and journalist called Niemoyewski.
Suddenly, almost unnoticed, the organ of the party, edited by the
atheistic Niemoyewski, adopted a rabidly anti-semitic tone, which he
called progressive, digging up the hoary arguments against Judaism as
the source of every obscurantist superstition and immoral practice. Rosa
Luxemburg seems to have been deeply shaken, and came out in a series
of bitterly polemical articles against Niemoyewski in an obscure
ephemeral journal *Mlot*.[95] The articles do not however really deal with
Jewish matters, or with the defence of the Jews attacked. They are a
flaming phillipic against the betrayal of the cause of progress by an
erstwhile bourgeois radical. Rosa got busy and mobilised some of the
leading socialists in the West to speak out against anti-semitism, such as
Jaurès, Bebel, Mehring and Kautsky. The lesson she learned was not
about the peculiar *Judenschmerz*, however, but about anti-semitism as the
symbol of counter-revolutionary reaction. She became still more
confirmed in her view that all non-proletarian and non-Marxist parties
constituted a simple undivided reactionary mass. Anti-semitism was
becoming its cement.

While Rosa Luxemburg and her Jewish friends were labouring so
ardently for the cause of proletarian internationalism and the universal
brotherhood of redeemed humanity, in central and Eastern Europe, the
scene of their action, there was being prepared that ominous juxtaposition and opposition, Jews versus Aryans. In Austria, Poland,
Roumania, Hungary and elsewhere the epithet "Christian" or
"national" prefacing the name of an association, an enterprise, a shop or
a political party simply came to mean non-Jewish or anti-Jewish. Of

course not everyone became what Dmowski called professional anti-semites, permanently mobilised and active crusaders. Most non-Jews in central and Eastern Europe just had not enough inner conviction to resist the spread of the mood of embarrassed malaise, unfriendly indifference, suspicion, irritable hostility towards the Jews.

Charles Maurras told a young disciple, who voiced doubts whether anti-semitism could be much of a political programme that, on the contrary, it was as a function of the anti-semitic programme that all the rest of the nationalist programmes would be able to pass from conception to execution.[96]

Schönerer said the same thing still more pointedly: "We, the Germans in Austria, our mission is to serve as an outpost [of Germany] among the Slavs. . . . In contrast to the gentlemen of the [parliamentary] German and Austro-German clubs, we the nationalist Germans see in anti-semitism not a phenomenon which should be deplored, as a disgrace. On the contrary, we see it as the pillar of the national idea, as the chief instrument for promoting the true national spirit, and thus as the greatest national achievement of this century. We regard as a traitor to the nation anyone who knowingly supports Jewry, its agents and accomplices. . . . Our nationalist anti-semitism is not a token of religious intolerance, but unambiguous proof of the strengthened self-awareness of a nation, of the national sentiment, which has found a powerful means of self-expression. Every faithful son of his nation should therefore consider anti-semitism . . . as the expression of the greatest national advance of this century." Schönerer added that since the differences between Germans and Slavs were much smaller than between Germans and Semites, it was always right to accept "in the struggle against the Jewish solvent the co-operation of Slavs and Roumanians".[97]

At the end of World War I Hitler was to effect a transference of the conditions which he observed in Austria to the defeated, and in his eyes beleaguered, Germany, with the Jews constituting the spearhead within and outside Germany of the Versailles powers and Soviet Russia bent upon the destruction of the German nation.

Chapter Seven

THE ENCOUNTER WITH REVOLUTION

To religious and nationalistic Jews, and in a different way to anti-semites, Jewishness had become dreadfully meaningful and ubiquitous. To other Jews and Gentiles who had absorbed national-liberal and individualistic modes of thought, it became elusive, ghost-like, indeed much ado about nothing. For the detribalised Jews there was a discon-certing contrast between the omnipresence of the spectre and the paucity or even absence of any tangible Jewish contents in their lives. They failed to find a rational explanation for the obsession with Judaism by Jews and Gentiles alike. Yet, the rational, optimistic scheme of things was so disconcertingly and so often disturbed, shaken and even shattered by matters Jewish. This intractableness, flying in the face of all sensible needs and expectations, became an intense irritant and disturbance to those Jews who had been severed or had severed themselves from the Jewish heritage and had become convinced that they had done with it for good. Their irritation, on top of their total ignorance of Judaism and of their having absorbed the mental habits, images and views of a Gentile world, soaked in centuries-old anti-Jewish prejudices, made Judaism appear to them a tissue of superstitious beliefs and ritualistic compulsions, a fossil which had long ago lost all *raison d'être*, a delusion or neurosis, which nevertheless put them in a terrible predicament. The phenomenon became a symbol of that exasperating irrationality which prevented the world from becoming a reasonable place to live in.

There is a most striking pronouncement by Sigmund Freud on the matter, in his preface to the Hebrew translation of *Totem and Taboo*; "No reader of [the Hebrew edition of] this book will find it easy to put himself in the emotional position of an author who is ignorant of the language of the Holy Writ, who is completely estranged from the religion of his fathers—as well as from every other religion—and who cannot take a share in nationalist ideas, but who has yet never repudiated his people, who feels that he is in his essential nature a Jew, and who has no desire to alter that nature. If the question were put to him, "Since you have abandoned all those common characteristics of your countrymen, what is there left to you that is Jewish?", he would

216

reply: "A very great deal, and probably its very essence." He could not now express that essence clearly in words, but some day no doubt, it will become accessible to the scientific mind."[98]

Unlike the discoverer of the subterranean world in the human psyche, the doctrinaire Jewish revolutionary socialists from Eastern Europe active in Germany, people like Rosa, Parvus, Karl Radek, Leviné and others, imagined themselves to be just men, or, as Trotsky identified himself, socialists, in a social framework where only economic realities mattered, a framework, the development and future of which were predetermined by impersonal, objective, material iron laws. They would not—perhaps could not—give a thought to the impact and the weight brought to bear upon these laws by those massive forces hinted at by Freud.

To emphasise Rosa's inability to live with her Jewishness—the predicament of so many Jews from the days of the Enlightenment, when they first glimpsed the inside of the tents of Japhet, and forsook those of Shem—does not imply that that difficulty was the root cause of and the all-determining factor in a solipsistic idiosyncracy. It does however mean that it engendered a certain heightened sensitiveness, and was the source of that peculiarly obsessive quality of her thinking which has in various degrees been shared by many people. In brief, the fanatical and aggressive tone of her denial of the reality of nationhood and of her farouche condemnation of nationalism signifies a transference of her rejection of the Judaism which she could not accommodate in her life. Her all-pervasive revolutionary internationalism appears to me an expression of the Jewish malaise of an outsider. To repeat, a deprecating attitude towards nationalism and a commitment to internationalism are neither irrational nor freakish traits, but are defensible and not uncommon attitudes. With Rosa, however, they became furious obsessions bordering on the neurotic.

In a letter she writes from prison on July 8, 1917, she chides her correspondent and comrade-socialist Mathilde Wurm: "What do you want with the special Jewish sorrows? To me, the poor victims of the rubber plantations in Putumayo, the negroes in Africa ... in the Kalahari desert ... are equally near." She quotes the report of the German General Staff on the campaign in the Kalahari desert ... "and of the death rattles, the crazed cries, of those expiring from thirst, echoed by the sublime silence of infinity". She goes on: "Oh, that 'sublime silence of infinity' in which so many cries re-echo unheard, resounds in me so strongly that I have no special corner in my heart for the ghetto: I feel at home in the whole world, where clouds, birds and human tears exist."[99]

One is reminded of an aphorism by the Hebrew writer Chaim Hazaz in his tragi-comic novel on the impact of the Bolshevik Revolution on a Jewish townlet in the Ukraine. A Gentile Russian, Frenchman or German wants to redeem his nation, or the proletariat of his country; the Jewish revolutionary is out to save the whole of mankind at once. Since Rosa did not identify herself as a Jewess, had left Poland and fought Polish national aspirations, and never really felt at home in Germany, she could only think of herself as a member of suffering mankind and, like Trotsky, asked about his commitment to Judaism, reply that she was a revolutionary socialist.

In a letter of May 17, 1901, to her Polish-Christian woman friend and political comrade Cezaryna Wojnarowska, an exile in Paris, Rosa comments on the foolishness of their comrade, "the good fellow Zalewski", in not having "sufficiently warned her against the Jews in the Bund",[100] Arkady Kremer and Joseph Mill, who were about to visit Cezaryna. "These people are composed of two elements: idiocy and perfidy. . . . They are simply incapable of exchanging two words with you, of looking at you, without having the hidden intention of stealing something from you (I speak figuratively, of course). All the politics of the Bund rests on the same system." The reader feels the uncontrollable fury of the writer mount: "that Jewish cunning . . . I advise you therefore to administer a kick on the spot on which they sit, and to break off all relations with them, because they will implicate you in a situation which you will bitterly regret."[101]

Now Arkady Kremer and Joseph Mill were two veteran socialists. The former was the author of the famous pamphlet "On Agitation" which became a *vade-mecum* to Russian socialists of all hues, including the Bolsheviks and Lenin himself. Faithful, selfless servants in the vineyard, they dedicated their lives to straightening the backs of the hundreds of thousands of starving and hounded Jewish proletarians of Eastern Europe, to inspiring them with a sense of human dignity and to bringing the light of a new secular Yiddish culture and literature into their wretched dwellings—all to be wiped out forty years later by Hitler.

Writing to Jogiches, Rosa calls Victor Adler, "the arrogant Jew". True, there was no love lost between the two comrades: He thought her "a silly goose". But, in comparison with Rosa's superciliousness, Adler was a paragon of humility. Where she was all cleverness, he possessed deep wisdom. Where she spun facile syllogisms out of thin air and paraded them as iron laws of history, he was guided by a deep understanding of how things really worked and men behaved. She was a nervous exaltée, he had a sober, chastened, rather defeatist insight into the intractableness of things and the recalcitrance of people. Where she loved all mankind, but had a good word for very few living persons, and then only for people who gave way to her, Victor Adler was full of compassion for his fellow-men. He was a self-professed Jewish anti-semite. He did not hide the fact that he avoided employing Jews in the party headquarters for fear of having the party branded as full of Jews. Not that it helped him very much, since some of the greatest luminaries of the Austrian Social-Democratic movement were Jews: Otto Bauer, Hilferding, Austerlitz, Braun, Max Adler and others. Considering Jewishness a misfortune, Adler, a convinced atheist, let himself and his young children be baptised, although his beloved wife refused to follow him in that. By a stroke of irony his son Friedrich, a scientist and ardent socialist, who was moved in 1917 to shoot and kill the Austrian Prime Minister Count Sturgkh, in protest against the war, fell deeply in love with a ravishing Jewish student from a little town near Vilna. She reciprocated his sentiments, but uncompromisingly declared she could never do to her parents the injury of not having a Jewish wedding. Poor Fritz went to his father to whom he was very close. Old Victor was deeply touched by the filial feelings of the Jewish girl from Lithuania. "A Jewish heart is also a heart," he exclaimed. He agreed to travel with the whole family to Lida to celebrate a traditional Jewish wedding, surrounded by the numerous God-fearing, Yiddish-speaking members of the bride's clan. The girl then became the old man's favourite and mainstay.[102]

In 1903 there occurred the terrible pogrom of Kishenev, a turning point in Jewish history. It shook world Jewry to its depths and brought Jews out into the streets from Moscow to San Francisco. It inspired a vast literary output, in the first place the shattering epic poem of the greatest Hebrew poet Chaim Nachman Bialik on the "City of Murder". Karl Kautsky wrote an article on the massacre in the *Neue Zeit*, expressing his horror, and assessing the event from the Marxist point of view. In a single short passage and in an unexceptionable manner, he rejected the Zionist solution of the Jewish question.[103] Rosa wrote Kautsky a note on his article: not a word about the pogrom itself, only congratulations on the short shrift he had given to the Jewish (Zionist) *parches*—a particularly ugly Yiddish expression used by Jews among themselves, and with particular glee by anti-semites about Jews.[104]

In a letter to Jogiches, Rosa tells that Parvus-Helphand had added a subtitle "ai wai" to his article against Bernstein, and the Gentile editor refused to have it.[105] Upon which Parvus, in protest, broke with the paper. She makes no comment on the incident. Rosa and still more certainly Parvus must many a time have heard that sneering cry which the assailants of Jews gave as they struck their helpless and frightened victims.

In the nearly 900 letters written to Jogiches, her fellow-Jew and for so many years husband in all but name, there are Yiddish expressions here and there, but not a reference to, not a single reflection on Jewish matters, except for some vile invective against the Bund. Nor is there, as we have said, a word about German anti-semitism, as though she had never noticed or heard of it at a time when there was so much anti-semitic prejudice and agitation around. Was it that she just would not be bothered with irrational things, considering them beneath contempt, and for a believing Marxist of no consequence? Or was it an astonishing case of sustained repression, because what she was repressing threatened to topple the whole edifice of her beliefs? Again, in contrast to Rosa, Victor Adler in his old age summed up his experience with the sad reflection that the last anti-semite would be taken to the grave on the death of the last Jew.

Rosa and her Jewish comrades wished to forget that they were descendants of a people with a history of four millenia, with an exceptional degree of self-consciousness, with a religion which prescribed and dominated every minute of life, burdened with a collective fate which they could never escape, nearly all for many generations inhabitants of a well-delineated and not very large region, limited to very few occupations, subject to the same discriminatory legislation; ostracised, if not actively persecuted and actually massacred; with peculiar habits and modes of life and thought. How could they have shed all their genes, shaken off all heredity and heritage, become able to rid themselves of all the ancestral residuary reflexes and compulsions—and become nothing but pure products of and believers in dialectical materialism? Furthermore, no other people or class, not even the peasant masses, disinherited but once bound by tradition, who in the preceding century had flocked into the new industrial cities to become an unchronicled, unsung proletariat, had undergone such a radical change, had been so torn away from their moorings, as were the suddenly emancipated and secularised Jews. In their thousands and tens of thousands these made their way within a single generation from the little, almost purely Jewish towns and townlets, from sectarian isolation, a hermetically closed framework, into the whirlpool of metropolitan life, with its bewildering changes and soulless impersonal compulsions—and under the skin of deeply rooted, conservative, very compact societies which were fundamentally unfriendly to them.

Those Jews believed so deeply in the slogan of "carrìere ouverte aux talents" and in the feasibility, desirability, indeed inevitability of radical change and reform, or even more of revolutionary trans-formation, that they could not comprehend the aversion of their hosts to these too eager foreign agents of change. Much as the new arrivals might have wished to ignore that obtuse resistance, they were forced to become aware of it. The malaise of the unaccepted, unabsorbed outsiders, and the predicament of the displaced and uprooted, made reality in general and still more their own peculiar existence seem to them provisional, not quite real, incomplete. Moods such as these made them long for a shore, a destination and a new, wholly different world, where everyone would be welcome, made to feel at ease, freed from all alienation, where history would really begin: the leap from a world of necessity into a realm of freedom. And so the predestined revolutionary breakthrough into a reality where there would be neither Jew nor Gentile nor Greek, where all would be equal and receive their due, assumed the dimensions of a personal liberation within a universal redemption.

Moses Hess, called by Isaiah Berlin the first communist in Germany, (at a later date also its first Zionist), was an exalté always wanting a cause and a hero to worship. He divined the world-shaking genius of Marx when the future author of *Das Kapital* was a youth of only twenty, and Marx learned not a little from him, but ridiculed him as the "Red Rabbi". "So long"—wrote Hess—"as it [Christianity] has not yet become the truly universal religion . . . true entirely and solely to its founder, striving for the salvation of man in the fullest and most human sense, the Jew will be unable to espouse it". "The social revolution" was proclaimed by Hess to be his religion.[106]

Nervous impatience with the present, the urgency of the expectation of the new dispensation, the non-conformist's refusal to accept and to put up with the thoughtless conservatism or indolent toleration of irrational evil, and with irrelevant contingencies; the single-minded purposefulness and terrible reductionism of the messianic Jews from Eastern Europe—all these made their German and other comrades feel overwhelmed, imposed upon. Noske says that though he lacked any trace of anti-semitism, like other Gentile Social-Democrats, he could not but become aware of the compulsive inclination of the Jewish socialists from Eastern Europe to turn Marxism into a religious dogma.[107] There is a note in Lenin's hand, written in a moment of irritation, at the time of the famous Second Congress of the still united Russian Social-Democratic party: "What can be done at a conference where a third of all delegates are Jews?"[108] But Lenin also went out of his way on other occasions to praise the Jewish revolutionaries as the truest and best internationalists.

There was also a common denominator to the Jewish Eastern European socialists in their semi-religious, doctrinaire addiction to

totality, to abstract generalisation, and to dialectical thinking, and as
we have already seen with Rosa Luxemburg, in the neglect of concrete
practical detail and organisational exigencies. In his autobiography,
Trotsky says "that the feeling of the superiority of the general to the
particular, of theory to personal experience, arose within me early and
grew stronger with the years . . . I was looking for laws beyond the
facts".[109] "The final goal"—wrote Lucács—is "that attitude to the
totality (the totality of society conceived as a process), through which
every single moment of the struggle receives its revolutionary
meaning."[110]

The deeper common level, however, was the ancient Hebraic, more
precisely prophetic, legacy, already referred to in a different context:
the insistence on the equal rights and the equal responsibility of every
individual for the community, the "holy people" and "nation of priests"
chosen by God to hallow his name, accompanied by the persistent
question of why the righteous suffered and the wicked prospered, and
why the chosen people had been made to bear so much defeat, sorrow
and humiliation; and, as answer to those mysteries, the messianic
scheme of choice, sin, punishment and redemption and reparation at the
last end—in other words, the vision of history as inexorably moving
towards a salvationist dénouement.

The first, and perhaps most original prophet of socialism, Saint-
Simon, emphatically recognised, probably not without some influence
on the part of his Jewish disciples, the Judaic prophetic tradition as the
ancestor of his own message on the decisive turning point in history that
was imminent, and was destined to resolve the structural crisis, which
had gripped European society as a result of the vast technological and
industrial developments and the breakdown of the organic, tightly knit,
feudal, theological *Weltanschauung*. Saint-Simon invoked the Hebrew
prophecy on "the great epoch, to which it had given the name of
messianic, an epoch in which the religious doctrine would be presented
in all that general form (toute la généralité) of which it was susceptible,
would regulate equally the actions of the temporal as well as of the
spiritual power, and the human species would have but one religion and
the same social organisation . . . an essentially pacific organisation of
society", in which "all men will treat each other as brethren", a
solution "which no force on earth can prevent".[111] Saint-Simon's Jewish
disciple, Olinde Rodriguez, felt a direct call to face the crisis of political
and moral reorganisation, because of the tradition of Moses which, he
said, he carried in his blood. His Jewishness had caused him to become a
savant and an industrialist, and had thus given him a special insight into
the power of the capitalists as well as into the defects of their

morality.[112] D'Eichthal, another Saint-Simonist, a Jew baptised in early childhood, speaks of the language of the prophets, the word of truth, "which he derives from his race".[113]

Never having accepted the dogma of original sin, belief in which is the great impediment to any truly revolutionary disposition, and with no experience of practical politics, with their ambivalences, concessions and compromises, these heirs of the Judaic tradition, and with them the other Saint-Simonists, refused to recognise the distinction between theory and practice, between what is and what should be, between principles and pragmatic choices, spirit and flesh. They developed their eccentric pantheistic religion, with the doctrine of the rehabilitation of the senses and the flesh, the liberation of women, industrialisation, socialism and universal brotherhood.

As against the resigned Pauline view, "I know the good, but cannot help doing evil", Moses Hess, the Red Rabbi—who with the Pole Cieszkowski gave Marx the formula that it was not enough for philosophy to know reality, it was necessary to change reality—proclaimed: "Because I not only know what I want, but also want what I know—I am more of an apostle than a philosopher."[114]

The consciousness of being part of an ethnic tradition which clashed with the pagan Hellenic approach to life—essentially aesthetic, if not amoral—was not alien even to a man like Victor Adler, and indeed Rosa Luxemburg herself. After ecstatically recounting the joys he had got from a visit to Italy and Greece, the Austrian socialist confessed that in spite of himself, the semite in him was made to feel somehow uncomfortable.[115] Similarly, Rosa, returning from a visit to Italy, contrasts the Christian—so as to avoid calling it Judaic—attitude with that of the classical world.[116] Ernst Renan, Berdyaev in our own time, Ernst Bloch and many others, have detected the authentic voice of Hebrew prophecy in Marx's wrathful, terrifying resolve to strip away all the pretence, self-delusion, deceit, indolent thoughtlessness, and moral cowardice and evasiveness, which are used to conceal the root cause and core of all evil—cupidity; and in the flaming eloquence with which he described the inevitable dénouement, the collapse of Babel and the breakthrough of the oppressed and the exploited to inherit the earth.

What was Freud's epoch-making achievement if not the discovery of the subterranean springs of human conduct behind all pretence, external decorum and delusion? This work of unmasking, we are told, was undertaken in reaction to the arrogant, aristocratic posture of men of the establishment and out of a sense of wounded human and Jewish pride.[117] No wonder the targets of Marx's and Freud's revelations raged against such materialistic, impious insults to accepted decencies.

In the West, secularised Jewish messianism branched out into philanthropy, service to such causes as pacifism, civil rights, social justice, good works, education and international understanding, in short all liberal and humanitarian causes, rather than into a religion of revolution. In the small and economically prosperous communities of the West, it was the messianic heritage, the personal malaise they felt as of outsiders and, occasionally their experience of social-cultural anti-semitism or the awareness of Jewish persecution in more backward countries, that drove individual Jews into the camp of socialist revolution; but in Eastern Europe it was the condition of the Jewish masses that gave the relationship between Jews and messianic socialism its special complexion.

Although there were many rich Jews in the Austro-Hungarian and Russian empires who, as already noted, played a vital part in the belated but rapid industrial revolution and rise of capitalism, most Jews were miserably poor, and in Russia they were squeezed into the pale, the Western border regions, and fenced around with arbitrary and deliber-ately humiliating restrictions. They found themselves in the last decades of the nineteenth century and on the eve of World War I in a particularly explosive situation, above all in Russia. They had woken up from the fatalistic acceptance of discrimination and persecution, which the unshaken ancestral faith and sectarian isolation had enabled them to bear patiently for so long, and developed, especially those dynamic youths who against all odds acquired a higher education, an outraged resentment at the insult to their human dignity. They became natural recruits to the army of revolution. As a result, the hostility of the persecuting regime acquired a new rationale. In the early decades Jews were accused of being clannish, superstitious, unassimilable, obscurantist. Now they were enemies of the social order, a dangerous revolutionary leaven, godless inciters of the mob, moral nihilists.[118] But there was an additional factor, which was to grow in importance.

The awakening of militant nationalism among the backward and oppressed nationalities and tribes of the multi-racial empires made the situation of the Jews particularly delicate. In areas of mixed population the Jews normally inclined to the higher culture of the dominant nation-ality. They were as a result accused of being instruments of Russi-fication, Germanisation, Magyarisation, and in Eastern Galicia of Polonisation. This cultural antagonism became entangled with explosive social-economic conflict. Rising nationalities such as the Slovaks, the Ukrainians and the Baltic peoples had even smaller middle classes than the Poles. The arrival of dispossessed masses into towns and the rise of nationalist aspirations among them combined to place the

Jews between two attacking forces—social vindication and passionate nationalism. These acute and mounting pressures infused an additional intensity into Jewish messianic internationalism, and also gave rise to modern secular Jewish nationalism, Zionism. Some Jewish socialists were uncompromising international revolutionaries. The vast majority of the Jewish workers in Eastern Europe belonged to the Bund, the ethnic Jewish-socialist party. The Bund came into existence in Russia before the Russian Social-Democratic party, and was in the early days the larger and better organised, with a strong trade union following, and intense educational activity. At first it treated the national Russian party with some condescension, while extending help to it. On the other hand, even the Zionist movement soon acquired a socialist wing. This wing was determined to contribute to world socialism by freeing the embattled socialist parties of Eastern Europe from the Jewish irritant, which had become such an impediment to the class struggle and the revolutionary endeavour; and at the same time to offer relief to the hard-pressed Jewish masses, and enable them to engage in a normal class struggle without the strains of anti-semitism, in a national home, where they would simultaneously achieve national liberation and establish a socialist society. Some bourgeois parties tried to attach Jewish national aspirations to the general movement for personal cultural autonomy for the various ethnic groups. This endeavour was inspired by the idea that a country was not the property of any master-nation offering hospitality to minorities and tolerating subject nationalities, but belonged to all the peoples inhabiting it. Strong as their case appeared, it did not halt the vast exodus of Jews to the West, any more than the Bund's ideology of an international struggle for national and social liberation, and for that matter nationalism focused on Palestine. This exodus was heading in the main to the United States, unencumbered, it was said, by the evil legacy of religious animosities, national strife and prejudices of the Old World, the 'golden country' in the language of the new arrivals there. Those who had been left behind were waiting to join the more fortunate brethren who had preceded them.

    Almost all socialists of Jewish origin believed fervently at first that the universal revolution would solve the Jewish problem and that all proletarians, no matter what their religion or ethnic origins, should form a single camp. Many of these who went into the ghettos as propagandists to preach the general proletarian ideology to the Jewish masses in their own language gradually came to realise that they were dealing with a distinct collective personality and psyche, and a special Jewish grief, with which the most sensitive among them could not but deeply sympathise and become identified. There was for instance the case of Vladimir Medem, the son of a convert to Greek Orthodoxy and an army doctor with the rank of general. Medem was brought up as a Christian and did not know a word of Yiddish. He rose to be an advocate prophet of the movement of going into the (Jewish) people. Others, like Martov (Cederbaum), the future Menshevik leader and chief rival of Lenin, started off as activists within the Jewish fold, but soon began to look upon their work among Jewish workers as a dissipation of energy, and even denied the need to consider Jewish wrongs separately from the international revolutionary struggle.

In the 1870's the Jewish revolutionaries found their home in the Narodnaya Volya—the People's Will. They were filled with enthusiasm for the peasants, and much of their messianic fervour was shot through with Christian exaltation. Thus the Narodnik, Aptekman, described by Lev Deich as "a physically weak little Jew, a born revivalist preacher with the Gospel always in his hands", wrote about his "complicated and deeply disturbed mind" when under the impact of his encounter with Russian *muzhiks*, "the concrete universal aspiration of socialism fused with an evangelical Christian mood . . . I decided to adopt the Greek Orthodox religion . . . I felt as if I had been newly born. I go to the people, I thought, no longer as a Jew, but as a Christian. I have joined the people."[119]

Tscherikover, the historian of Jews in the Russian revolutionary movement, calls the astonishing testament of Wittenberg, the son of a poor pious Jewish artisan, written on the eve of his execution, the "most Christian document of revolutionary literature".[120] "Remember, the greatest example of love of man and of devotion was given by the Saviour; and he prayed, 'turn away this cup from my lips. . . . And I say to you as he said . . . if it is not possible otherwise, if it is necessary for the victory of socialism that my blood be shed, if the passage from the present social order to a better one is impossible without the road being strewn with our corpses, let our blood be shed, let us serve as a sacrifice for mankind. And that our blood will purify the soil, out of which the seeds of socialism will sprout forth, and that socialism will triumph and indeed soon—of that I have no doubt! And I remember again the words of the Saviour: 'I tell you in truth many of those here will not feel the taste of death, and the Kingdom of God will arise.' I am convinced of that as I am sure that the earth is turning round. And when I mount the scaffold, and the cord is around my neck, my last thought will be: 'And it moves, and no one in the world is able to stop it . . . and if you have any consideration for my last wish . . . then give up any idea of revenge . . . forgive them, for they do not know what they are doing.' For this too is a sign of time! Their reason is deranged: they see that different times are coming, and know not how to turn them back. I beg you once more, renounce any thought of revenge."[121]

As if that were not enough, there is a record of the last meeting between the condemned man and his old parents. The father was just able to stammer out the suggestion that perhaps the son should appeal for clemency to the governor-general. The son replied that it was being said that if a condemned Jew accepted baptism the punishment would be still further reduced. Upon which the mother broke in: "Die as what you are; your son will grow up and revenge your death."[122]

The Narodnaya Volya, the first great terrorist movement to which all those belonged, was a most uncongenial environment for Jews. Exalted and eager as they were to sink into the pure, unspoilt, collective soul of the peasant masses, the mission of Jewish boys and girls with semitic looks, a foreign accent and total ignorance of peasant life and mentality was often terminated by the peasant's astonished or indignant but unanswerable question to the child of the anti-Christ, "But you are a Jew", sometimes followed by a denunciation to the police.

Another factor gravely complicated matters: the presence of an anti-Jewish ingredient in Russian peasant socialism, and indeed socialism in general. In the first place there was the tradition to which Marx himself contributed so greatly in his lamentable writings on the Jewish high priests of the Moloch of Mammon; then there were vitriolic anti-semitic epithets employed by Marx and Engels, for instance when they belaboured Lassalle in their correspondence, although they did not hesitate to exploit him. They called him "Baron Itzig", "Gescheiter Ephraim", "Jewish nigger", "Jewish muck", "Jewish schemer".[123] Yet it could not be said that anti-semitism was an essential ingredient in their teaching. Marxist philosophy was too universalist to be really anti-semitic. It was too dominated by categories of thought which had no room for race mysticism and certainly not for biological racist determinism. Of paramount importance was the vision of a universal dénouement at the end of the dialectical historical process. Lacking the modernist ingredient, some utopian socialists of petit-bourgeois bent, like Fourier (bitter rival of Saint-Simon, incidentally) and Toussenel, the author of Les Juifs les Rois de l'Epoque and anarchists like Proudhon and Bakunin, the rival and victim of Marx, seethed with murderous hatred of Jews. They clung to populist notions of the healthy, primary instincts of innocent children, and they loathed the modern world. They shrank from its complexities, had no insight into the ambiguities and ambivalences of dialectical development, and identified the Jew with the evils of capitalism, centralisation and urban mass society.[124]

They looked back to the lost innocence of pre-capitalist society or some pristine state of nature. They extolled the virtues of independent craftsmen and peasants and glorified the instinctive nobility of the unsophisticated, primitive rebel. They dreamt of small communities, anarchistic groups held together by mutual aid. They looked forward to a utopian world of pure justice, to the abolition of all authority and the release of the passions. They detested credit, exchange, the market mechanism, modern communications, the international press: all this was incarnate for them in the Jew. Thus Toussenel: "The Jew is by temperament an anti-producer, neither a farmer, nor an industrialist, nor even a true merchant. He is an intermediary, always fraudulent and parasitic, who operates in trade as in philosophy, by means of falsification, counterfeiting [and] horse-trading. He knows only the rise and fall of prices, the risks of transportation, the uncertainties of crops, the hazards of demand and supply. His policy in economics has always been entirely negative, entirely usurious. It is the evil principle, Satan, Ahriman incarnate in the race of Shem, which has already been twice exterminated by the Greeks and by the Romans, the first time at Tyre, the second time at Carthage; the cosmopolitan Jew . . . Europe is heir to the domination of Israel. This universal domination, of which so many conquerors have dreamed, the Jews have in their hands."[125]

There surely is food for thought in the similarities between the morbidly inhibited and pedantic old bachelor Fourier and the volcanic arch-revolutionary but sexually impotent Bakunin. Any kind of convention, restraint, authority, organisation, seems to suffocate, to strangle them. The one dreams of the total gratification of desire, the other of the total release of spontaneous passion, and both rail against the Jew as the principle of repression and organisation.

Proudhon was enamoured of the French peasants and artisans and loathed all foreigners. Bakunin, to whom the authentic revolutionary was not a man who reasoned and planned but a creature of instinct, looked successively for salvation to the unspoilt spontaneous Slavs, the rebellious Russian peasants of Pugachev and Stenka Razin, primitive bandits, and finally to déclassé outcasts of all kinds, including criminals whose passion for destruction (the necessary condition for total reconstruction) was unhampered by possession or vested interests. For both Proudhon and Bakunin it was a short step from populism to racism, to the hatred of whole racial or national groups in defiance of the universality of the socialist ideal. Thus Bakunin could describe the Jews as "an exploiting sect, a blood-sucking people, a unique, devouring parasite tightly and intimately organised . . . cutting across all the differences in political opinion".[126] But no one could have gone further than Proudhon: "Jews—Write an article against this race which poisons everything, by meddling everywhere without ever joining itself to another people. Demand their expulsion from France, with the exception of individuals married to Frenchwomen. Abolish the synagogues; don't admit them to any kind of employment, pursue finally the abolition of this cult. It is not for nothing that the Christians called them deicides. The Jew is the enemy of the human race. One must send this race back to Asia or exterminate it.

"H. Heine, A. Weil and others are nothing but secret spies; Rothschild, Cremieux, Marx, Fould, malignant beings, bilious, envious, acrid etc., who hate us. By fire or fusion, or by expulsion the Jew must disappear.... Tolerate the aged who no longer give birth to offspring . . . what the peoples of the Middle Ages hated by instinct, I hate upon reflection, and irrevocably."[127]

Peasant populism, the mythology of the *jacquerie*, prophecies of fire and massacre, of a volcanic, formless upheaval, could not gain a real grip on the Jewish mind. That is why the Russian-Jewish revolutionaries like Martov, Axelrod, Dan and Lieber became the pioneers of Russian Marxism, especially its Menshevik brand, although other Jews such as Zhitlovski, Rubanowitch, Deich, Minor, Gershuni or Gotz of the fabulously rich Jewish family, who died as a martyr to his convictions, were among the founders and leaders of the socialist-revolutionary party. This party was the terrorist heir of the populist Narodnya Volya, and the standard bearer of peasant socialism, but also of a generous nationalities policy.[128] Russian populism, and to some extent even the Social-Democratic parties in the West, not only felt apprehensive lest a too conspicuous Jewish presence be used by the enemies to discredit them as Jewish parties or defenders of Jews. They also valued what they thought would be the good educational effect that popular propaganda against Jewish finance and capitalism could have. This was a curious inversion of Bismarck's objection to Pastor Stöcker's anti-semitic agitation.

The attitude of revolutionaries and socialists to early anti-Jewish riots and pogroms was by no means one of spontaneous, horrified and uncompromising condemnation. There is the famous proclamation published by the *People's Will* in the Ukraine on the occasion of the frightful wave of government pogroms inspired by the Tsarist government, after the assassination of Alexander II in 1881. "Good people, honest Ukrainian people! The damned police beat you, the landowners devour you, the Yids, the dirty Judases, rob you. People in the Ukraine suffer most from the Yids. . . . Wherever you look, whatever you touch, everywhere the Yids. The Yid curses the peasant, cheats him, drinks his blood."[129]

When the Austrian anti-semites first embarked upon their anti-Jewish campaign, the earliest reaction of Kautsky and Victor Adler was that however crude these excesses, they contained more than a grain of revolutionary potentiality: they were a sign that the masses were awakening from their fatalistic slumber and were daring to protest against social evils and the rule of their social betters. "They were unwittingly doing good work for socialism," wrote Adler "in radicalising the masses and goading them into rebellion."[130]

The Narodnaya Volya proclamation quoted above, no less than the pogroms themselves, shook many a Jewish revolutionary to his depths. Thus the saintly Narodnik, and later Menshevik Marxist, Pavel Axelrod, wrote in a heart-rending pamphlet: "The Jewish socialist intelligentsia suddenly realised that the majority of Russian society did as a matter of fact, regard the Jews as a separate nation, and that they considered all Jews—a pious Jewish worker, a petit bourgeois, a money-lender, an assimilated lawyer, a socialist prepared to risk prison or deportation—as Yids harmful to Russia, whom Russia should get rid of by any and every means. The Jewish student youth suffered their greatest disappointment, when they realised that the socialist-minded Russian students sympathised with the crusade against the Jewish masses and, worse still, exhibited their anti-semitic feelings towards their Jewish fellow-revolutionaries. Thus the pogroms made the Jewish socialist intelligentsia realise that the Jews as a people were in a unique situation in Russia . . . and that they . . . had committed an error in over-looking the actual condition of the Jews as a people different from the rest of the population . . . in forsaking the Jewish masses in the name of cosmopolitanism which was alien to the native masses no less than the idea of class solidarity among the poorer classes of Russia's nationalities."[131] Axelrod was prevailed upon by the party not to publish his pamphlet.

Still more moving was the reaction of the strong-minded and strong-willed Jewish wife of Plekhanov, the mainstay of her difficult husband in the long years of exile and tribulation, and afterwards the formidable defender of his memory, reputation and archives against the victorious rivals of the father of Russian Marxism. She spoke of the sudden urge of socialists of Jewish origins to atone, to go out to their injured, insulted brethren, forsaken by people like her, to "wipe away their tears and bind their wounds".

However mixed were the feelings of the social-democrats about Jews, they woke up at the end of the nineteenth century and realised that, like nationalism, militarism and imperialsim, anti-semitism had become a most dangerous challenge to socialism, indeed a powerful rival.

In the Dreyfus affair the French socialists found themselves compelled to choose between standing aside in the struggle of the different elements of reaction—Catholic, feudal, bourgeois, militarist—against the Jewish *grande bourgeoisie* and waiting till they had cancelled each other out and left the camp free for socialism, as Guesde preached; or coming out as socialists always should—as Jaurès insisted—in defence of any innocent victim of injustice and reaction and hastening to save the Third Republic from a nationalist *putsch*, and French society from a state of degeneration incurable even by socialism. The doctrinaire, tight-lipped Guesde was soon deeply stirred by Zola's heroic stand against the two most powerful pillars of French reaction, the army and the church, and called the novelist's famous article, "the most revolutionary act of the century". But as in the 1893 Brussels congress of the Second International, he wanted to keep clear of both anti-semitism and philo-semitism.[132]

The Social-Democratic parties emerged as the only parties unambiguously opposed to anti-semitism. Some leaders, like Bebel and Karl Liebknecht and of course Jaurès, came out emphatically against it in order to defend the Jews; others did so more to combat the dangerous rivals of Social-Democracy, which the anti-semitic parties preaching national-socialism were rapidly becoming.

While most Russian Jews were seeking salvation in Zionism and mass emigration, large numbers of them continued to swell the ranks of the socialist and revolutionary movements. Many of the Jewish recruits saw in it a way of fighting the oppressors of the Jewish people: "We are the oldest, the most intelligent people," wrote Abraham Magat from Vilna, "the best-educated and most energetic people, and we are deprived of all the rights possessed by the other subjects of Russia!... We have to fight for our rights and our equality, no matter what the cost."[133] Aharon Zundelevich joined the revolutionary movement and played a vital part as organiser, fund-raiser, and the man responsible for printing and transporting illegal literature because he felt an emphatic sense of obligation to those Gentile fighters for human rights, including the rights of the Jews. He professed to have no love for Russia, and little faith in the Russian people, and so, after yeoman service to the Russian Revolution, he decided that he had discharged his obligations and left for America.[134]

Important as was the work of the Jewish members in elaborating theory, proselytising and organisation, they also had their share of terrorists, like the legendary Deich and Gershuni; of provocateurs and traitors like the enigmatic Azef, at the same time head of the terrorist unit of the socialist revolutionaries, agent of the Okhrana, betrayer of his closest comrades and organiser of the assassination of his own chief Plehve, the Minister of the Interior; as well as of Dostoyevskian types like the early Narodnik, Grigori Goldenberg, an exalté terrorist who, in prison under sentence of death, lost his nerve, yielded to the blandishments of the highest dignitaries of state and in return for the promise of a constitution and a general amnesty, revealed all the secrets he knew, and then, realising the enormity of his deed and of the megalomaniac madness in imagining himself the saviour of Russia, committed suicide on July 15, 1880. "I consider it a piece of good fortune," he wrote, "and an honour to die on the gallows: may socialism be sown by my blood, just as once the blood of the early Christian martyrs made the Christian church sprout forth . . . socialism is a new revelation . . . a new religion, will usher in a new era . . . will sweep the whole world."[135]

The Tsarist regime had every inducement to present the revolutionary movement as a Jewish undertaking just as every government committee—composed of course of actual or former serf-owners—on the state of the peasantry had every interest in blaming the plight of the *muzhiks,* even in areas from which Jews were barred, on Jewish exploitation. The Protocols of Zion were circulated and avidly read in the highest circles, even by Tsar Nicholas II himself. The identification of Jews with revolution came to serve as a safety valve, a rallying cry for lumpenproletarian chauvinism and the Patriotic Leagues of an already distinctly fascist character, mobilised to carry out pogroms.

At his famous meeting with the "liberal" Tsarist minister Witte, Theodor Herzl was menacingly asked by Witte why the Jews, who constituted only 3 per cent of the population of Russia, supplied 50 per cent of all revolutionaries.[136] In the same year, Witte's colleague Plehve, the Minister of the Interior, treated a Jewish deputation to the following lecture: "Convey to your sons and daughters, to the Jewish youth, to your intelligentsia, that they should not think that Russia is a disintegrating and degenerating organism. Much is being said about Jewish cowardice. It is not true. The Jews are a most courageous people. In western Russia 90 per cent of all revolutionaries are Jews, and in the whole of Russia 40 per cent. I am not hiding from you the fact that the revolutionary movement worries Russia. At times of demonstrations here and there we get disconcerted. But we shall find a way. If you do not stop your youth from joining the revolutionary movement, your situation here will become impossible, and you will have to leave Russia to the last man."[137] The minutes of the famous Russian Cabinet discussion of August 4, 1915, foreshadow not a little of what was to happen to the Jews of Russia at the hands of the Nazi invaders some thirty years later. To quote from the explanatory preface written most probably by Iakhontov and added at a later date to the actual Cabinet discussion: " . . . GHQ became convinced that the Jewish population in the theatre of war was a focus of espionage and aid to the enemy. On this basis it developed the idea of the need to clear the battle front of all Jews. The application of this measure began in Galicia. The authorities in the rear began to send thousands and tens of thousands of Austrian Jews into the inner Russian provinces. All this took place, of course, not voluntarily, but by force. The Jews were driven out *en masse*, without regard for sex or age. They included the sick, the infirm, and even pregnant women.

". . . What went on is indescribable. Even the most irreconcilable anti-semites came to see the members of the government with protests and complaints against the outrageous treatment of the Jews at the front. . . . All kinds of crises occurred: in supplies, in housing, and so forth. Epidemics began. In various localities the atmosphere became more and more dangerous; the Jews were angry at everyone and everything, while the local inhabitants were angry at the uninvited guests who, moreover, were being denounced as traitors and were angered by conditions under which it became impossible to survive in their own homes."

The Minister of Internal Affairs, Prince N.B. Shcherbatov, opened the discussion, saying: "Our attempts to reason with GHQ have been in vain. All the means of struggle available to us against preconceived tendencies have been used. Together and separately, we have spoken and written and pleaded and complained frequently. But the all-powerful Ianushkevich thinks that national considerations and interests are not binding on him. It is his plan to maintain the army's prejudice against all Jews, and to represent them as responsible for the defeats at the front. Such a policy is bearing fruit, and a desire for pogroms is growing in the army. One does not like to say this, but we are among ourselves here and I will not disguise my suspicion that, for Ianushkevich, the Jews are probably one of those excuses about which A. V. Krivoshein spoke the last time. . . . At the moment the situation is as follows. Hundreds of thousands of Jews of all sexes, ages and condition have been moved, and continue to move, eastward from the war theatre. The dispersion of this mass within the pale of settlement is not only difficult but simply impossible. The local governers report that every place is filled to the brim, and that if further immigration is not stopped at once, they cannot be responsible for the safety of the new inhabitants, because the people are worked up and there is agitation for pogroms, particularly on the part of soldiers coming back from the front. . . . The leaders of Russian Jewry are firmly demanding general measures and a legal basis for ameliorating the situation of their compatriots. In the heat of discussion I was bluntly told that a revolutionary mood is growing irrepressibly in the Jewish masses, that people are being driven to the limit of despair, that every day it is becoming more and more difficult to struggle against the desire for active defence, that major unrest and disturbances are possible, and so forth and so on. It was pointed out to me that abroad, too, patience is wearing thin and that the day may come when Russia will not be able to borrow a penny."[138]

Throughout the deliberations the question was considered by the ministers almost entirely and exclusively from the point of view of the effect upon the circles in the West, Jewish and others, upon which Russia was dependent for her financial credits. A few years earlier Stolypin had submitted to the Tsar a strongly argumented memorandum in favour of lifting some of the worst features of anti-Jewish legislation on similar grounds. In his comments Nicholas II agreed with the reasoning, but explained that his heart was against it. The Prime Minister desisted.[139]

It can be no surprise that, although most Jews were thrilled by the February revolution, but not at all in favour at first of the October revolution, a great many began nevertheless to flock into the Bolshevik ranks, once the White Guards of Plehve's persuasion and the Ukrainian nationalists had embarked upon their campaign of pogroms, leaving the Jews no alternative.

It will not be irrelevant to refer here to a most interesting conversation between Arthur Balfour and Justice Brandeis, at that time leader of the American Zionist movement, held during the Versailles Peace Conference. Balfour expressed his deep concern about the prominence of Jews in revolutionary movements. And now, he went on, they had become not merely active members, but leaders of the Russian Revolution, and even Lenin was reported to be of Jewish ancestry. The reason for his ardent support for the idea of a Jewish national home, Balfour continued, was his wish to direct the talents and energies of this highly gifted people into constructive channels for the good of all mankind.[140]

Part V

RUSSIA — HOLY, PROFANED AND PREDESTINED

Chapter One

RUSSIA—HOLY, PROFANED AND PREDESTINED

Whatever the internal differences of opinion about the ways and means of putting an end to the war and about the shape of the peace settlement, in none of the belligerent countries was national unity in World War I—in spite of some strikes, hunger riots and incipient mutinies—so undermined, let alone broken by revolutionary internationalism, as it was in Russia. The revolutionary uprisings or insurrectionary stirrings in the various countries on the morrow of the armistice proved to be no more than passing events.[1] What was the reason for the victory of extreme international revolutionism, preceded by a sustained defeatist, indeed from the traditional point of view treasonous, agitation, in that country which seemed the least ripe for it, and for its failure in all other states?

Nowhere else, not even in the Austro-Hungarian Empire torn by racial strife, had alienation from the state and its governing elite become so widespread and so profound as it had in Russia, as the result of exceptionally grave economic, social, political and cultural dis-harmonies of very long standing.[2] Economic oppression and social injustices became quite intolerable when a corrupt and debilitated regime revealed its utter incapacity to wage a national war, and brought untold suffering upon the population. No less important a cause for the divorce between government and the popular masses in the midst of war was the impact of ideological revolutionary influences. Yet neither the crisis of confidence and the corresponding state of exasperation, nor the defeatist and subversive propaganda would have sufficed to sweep away, in an hour of national emergency, deep-seated instinctive patriotism to the extent it did, were it not for a special frame of mind which mitigated the horror of national treason. That particular disposition had for centuries been fostered by the vision of Holy Russia. Realities which seemed to belie the vision were presented as a profanation of the inner essence. The cleansing of the authentic core by removing the polluting accretions was a holy mission. The age-old concept of a restoration of pristine purity were replaced in the age of secularism by the image of some predestined future.[3] A purified and reformed Russia was called upon to fulfil the role of a Messiah.

237

Theocratic eschatology was transformed into revolutionary messianism.

Ideally, Tsarist Russia admitted of no division into spiritual and temporal spheres. This was part of the Byzantine legacy of Caesaropapism, with its total subordination of ecclesiastical affairs to the decisions of the God-anointed emperor-cum-head of the community of believers. The Russian church never achieved the modest measure of organisational autonomy which the Byzantine church had been able to maintain. The Russian state had no reason to stress the distinctness of the political realm. The long period of the Tartar yoke helped to cement the fusion of the religious and the secular. The fall of Constantinople and the subjugation of all Greek-Orthodox Slavs outside Russia by Turkey left Russia the sole independent Greek-Orthodox country in the world. It emerged as the heir to Byzantium—the Third Rome—and the pillar of fire to all the true believers under alien bondage. The sense of election was strengthened by the deep doctrinal faith that the Catholic church was not only heretical, but was by its organisation and its worldly activity a part of the ancient pagan Roman Empire. Protestantism, with its individualism, was not far removed from atheism.

The growth of urban life gave rise in the West to a dynamic and self-conscious bourgeoisie, with every member of it bent upon conquering for himself a recognised status and freedom of initiative. The burgher was watchfully jealous of his codified rights and proud of his personal worth and achievements. He began to aspire to throw off monarchical tutelage, and indeed to obtain a voice in the running of the commonwealth. During the end of the Middle Ages, the Renaissance, the Reformation and absolutism in the West, the Russian rulers were mobilising all their manpower and national resources for their prolonged effort to liberate themselves from Tartar rule and unite Russia under a single monarch. This was followed by the bitter struggle with the Poles, the Swedes and Turkey for the Baltic and the Black Sea shores, and the effort of colonising the newly acquired territories. This sustained endeavour forced the Tsars to keep a tight grip on the nobility and through them the peasants, who were always tempted to escape from their hard life on poor soil in a short growing season,[4] in conditions of virtual slavery, into the vast expanses of the Empire.

Gradually, all the ancient municipal traditions and representative institutions—like the Zemsky Sobor—were abolished or made to wither away under the sway of the divinely appointed Autocrat of all the Russias, whose claim to be carrying out the will of the Almighty seemed to be confirmed by signal successes.

It is impossible not to be struck by the stark contrast between the fundamental importance assigned to law and justice in the West and the insignificant place occupied by them in Russian thought from the early days of Tsarism up to the time of Slavophile ideology and revolutionary doctrines. The ancient Roman and then Western bourgeois way of drawing firm lines between mine and thine; the awed respect for written contracts; the addiction to the clear formulation of safeguards and sanctions; the principle of an independent judiciary and constitutional guarantees—all these were treated by successive Russian generations and schools of thought as the result of envy, selfishness, distrust, and avarice. The formative principle of Russian society was alleged to be not individual self-interest, but communal solidarity and loving trust. This was triumphantly demonstrated in the Russian village commune which recognised no private property, was based on unanimous consent, practised periodic redistribution of the land, and went on living without written laws and contracts. No pieces of paper, no written constitution should come between the Tsar and his children, the people of Russia: only loving care on one side, and trusting obedience on the other. The individual was to disappear in the living community, which was not regarded as an association of sharply contoured individuals joining together in pursuit of some clearly defined and limited common interest, but as a collective being, the vessel of an all-embracing peculiar tradition, and a Christian body.[5]

Claims so high pitched, and therefore unrealisable, are always bound to become the source of sustained and gigantic pretence, and eventually a cover for them. Loving unanimity in Russia came to mean the imposition of a single despotic will. Perfect social cohesion, without formal rules, turned into the bondage of a caste system. The unrestricted tutelary power of Tsar, landlord and bureaucrat bred unbridled arbitrariness and cruelty on one side, and servility, low cunning, total alienation from the state and the ruling elite, and finally seething rebellion on the other. In the more tender consciences the vast edifice of hypocrisy evoked protest, dissent, a sense of shame and guilt which gradually hardened into a resolve to punish and destroy the forces which had profaned Holy Russia and usurped the common weal. Upon their ruins there would be erected a purified and authentic Russia; true to its national destiny and universal mission; and with the allegedly uniquely Russian institution—the vilage commune—as its cornerstone.

In face of incipient threats to the regime from Western influences and social-economic changes, the nineteenth-century Russian establishment found it necessary to reassert most emphatically the theocratic basis and legitimation of the system. They were helped by grim doctrinaires, who justified brutal oppression by extolling the uniqueness of the

Russian way, and portraying the West as sunk in anarchy and selfish materialism, and by prophets of wrath who harped on the danger of total disruption from the slightest tinkering with the established order and depicted man as born incurably evil and only too easily swayed by anarchical ideas.

While the reactionaries equated social-political rebelliousness with godlessness, the revolutionaries raised the slogan "ni Dieu, ni maître". Absolutes were answered with absolutes: divine sanction with atheism; transcendental idealism with undiluted materialism; the doctrine of the superiority of spontaneous, direct, unhesitating faith over the debilitating treacherousness of analytical reasoning, and sophistication with teachings inspired by uncompromisingly doctrinaire rationalism and the crudest forms of utilitarianism. Caesaro-papism was confronted with anarchical freedom and a loose federation of communes; and the all-embracing ideology of pan-Slav Tsarism was mirrored in vast philosophical schemes of universal historical inevitability, in which a special place was reserved to Russia.

If in the ancient Russian tradition the individual was considered as giving his life to the Tsar and therefore performing a kind of religious duty, the revolutionary ideology presented its cause not just as an interest or political aspiration, but as a holy message, demanding the whole man, his implicit consent, his undivided dedication. The revolutionary movements in Russia became indeed monastic orders and religious fraternities, with heroes, martyrs and saints who perished on the gallows, wasted away their best years in dungeons or in the Siberian tundra, committed suicide or went out of their minds.

The establishment were afraid of the liberal influence of Western ideas, and were desperate to stop their infiltration. The revolutionaries, for their part, feared that bourgeois, liberal capitalism would delay or prevent the arrival of the perfect predestined order of their dreams. Both sides were in a hurry. Neither wanted readjustment, compromise, gradualness. Only total confrontation was possible: only war to the death. Salvation was now or never.

Doctrinaire theorising, due not a little to lack of practical political and administrative experience, coupled with the memory of the total change brought about by Peter the Great by *ukase*, sustained a faith in the sudden leap from unmitigated bondage to total freedom, and an eager, watchful readiness to exploit the hour of opportunity to the full or to create the upheaval which would create it. With its alienation from the class structure and political realities of Russia, its tender and painful conscience, and its messianic yearnings for certainty and salvation, the Russian intelligentsia displayed a fundamentally religious cast of mind, hardly paralleled in the West. The most influential early representative of that Russian religion of revolution—with its antecedents in the Decembrist movement, if not indeed in Radishchev—was Vissarion Belinsky, who may be seen as a paradigm of the spiritual pilgrimage of the Russian intelligentsia in the nineteenth century.

Chapter Two

THE BIRTH OF A REVOLUTIONARY IDEOLOGY—
BELINSKY AND HERZEN

(a) THE PORTRAIT OF A PILGRIM

Writing some six decades after Belinsky's death, Plekhanov, the father of Russian Marxism, had this to say on the famous critic: "To this day any new step forward in our social thought is a contribution to the solution of those basic problems of social development, which were detected by Belinsky with the help of the intuition of a sociologist of genius, but which he was not able to solve owing to the extreme backwardness of Russian reality in his day."[1] Evidence of the actual diffusion of Belinsky's ideas and of their sustained hold on the minds of men "who cared", whose business and passion it was to live by ideas and to transmit them is offered by Belinsky's Slavophile antagonist, Ivan Aksakov, who wrote eight years after the death of Belinsky: "The name of Belinsky is known to every thinking young man, to everyone who is hungry for a breath of fresh air in the reeking bog of provincial life. There is not a country schoolmaster who does not know and know by heart Belinsky's letter to Gogol. If you want to find honest people, people who care about the poor and the oppressed, an honest doctor, an honest lawyer not afraid to fight, you will find them among Belinsky's followers. . . . Belinsky's proselytes are on the increase."[2]

Belinsky was more of a wrestler with God than a discursive thinker. "To me—he says—to think and to feel, to understand and to suffer—means the same thing."[3] He is a pilgrim who can never feel that he has arrived, made peace with himself and come to terms with God, life, the world; an eternal protester.

Belinsky's obsessive preoccupation with the concept of reality, in other words with the meaning of life, his desperate efforts to obtain a key to the mystery of being, the way in which he would discard one all-embracing explanation to adopt the diametrically opposite one—all these betoken not only an inability to take concrete, actual, surrounding reality for granted, but also an intense crisis of personal identity. Belinsky is indeed most explicit and articulate about his eternal dissatisfaction with himself and his quest to find out what he is. Personal rootlessness and self-doubt should however also be seen as an example of the social and spiritual situation of his class, or rather non-class.

In his letter to Bakunin of September 10, 1838, Belinsky speaks of his feeling that he is in the process of achieving "a definition of the great word reality". He does not yet feel however that he is "real", and that he has "grasped reality". "At present I feel more than ever that I lack reality in my life and in my views." But he is on the way to "a total and rapid passage from one to the other".[4] Herzen and other contemporaries were made to feel very uncomfortable by the surly temper of the gifted, shy and gauche young plebeian, son of a provincial, drunkard doctor, and married to a dull unloved wife. There were rapid alternations of long, tormented, brooding silences and violent outbursts of rage, of spells of paralysing melancholy and fits of unbearable exaltation, of abject self-rejection and arrogant pose, of utter disgust with the world and blissful reconciliation with it.

Belinsky seems to have been unable to find a common plane of intercourse with people. There was "that bitter, tormenting feeling . . . that burns my soul as if with hot iron".[5] At another time he voices a hopeful sense of relief: he seems to be "no longer suffocated in practical people's company". They begin to interest him, "and my presence no longer weighs upon them". As a result of the easy contact, "all are pleased with me, and I am pleased with everybody".[6]

But not only suffering, even happiness, weighs upon Belinsky, everything: love and hostility, a new idea, new circumstances. Only in rare moments, when cheerfulness somehow breaks in, "do I breathe freely and gaily". "Poor, broken heart"—he laments—"which so passionately yearned for happiness and never experienced it." He wanted to give his whole self to society, to feel himself a fully integrated member of and partner in it, yet he knew he would remain forever an outsider.[7] Hence the permanent feeling of anxiety, the sense of a constant falling away from grace. A visit to the ancestral mansion of the Bakunins, Premukhino, releases a flood of contradictory feelings: awestruck yet anguished envy of the peace and harmony in a family of ancient lineage, self-assurance and inherited charm, and then utter disgust with his own behaviour, especially towards the venerable and highly civilised head of the house.[8] Belinsky cannot forgive himself the arrogant attitudinising pose he feels he had adopted when sporting a blood-stained Robespierrist variety of Fichteanism. He swears he spoke with sincerity; he was so taken up at the time with that defiant philosophy that he was "not free not to experience what I felt and voiced". All the same, "I was dishonest, trivial, repulsive. . . . I am a comedian, a phrasemonger, a clown." The "bloody views" he expressed came at that moment not from a concern for the truth, but from a desire to make an impression, and shock.[9]

Belinsky looks at himself from the outside. Like a person suffering from incipient insanity, his moods keep changing to such an extent that he can never be sure which Belinsky is the real, the authentic one. His spells of self-satisfaction alternate with a morbid urge for self-caricature, with a paralysing feeling of emptiness, fraudulence and sterility: "my own nothingness". "At times—writes Belinsky—"I found a true balm for my sick spirit in the self-respect which I achieved through momentary energetic impulses of love for the truth—those rare and brilliant flashes of emotion which would flame up in me. But sometimes I saw in all that . . . a certain apearance of brilliance without substance, a magnificent building without foundation, a tree of luxuriant foliage without roots; and I became repugnant to myself."[10]

(b) THE UNIVERSAL IDEA AND THE RECONCILIATION WITH IT

The personal misery of uncertain identity, the desperate need to be sure of his own authenticity goes together with the relentless quest for all-encompassing certainty about the universe. We observe in this the same violent swinging of the pendulum. "I break with an old idea with difficulty and pain, I reject it to the limit, and pass over into the new with all the fanaticism of a proselyte."[11] In his letter to D. P. Ivanov of August 7, 1837, Belinsky speaks the purest language of extreme transcendental idealism, and of total political submission to whatever political authority there may be. The only true and significant reality was the idea; everything else was illusion. Man was nothing but idea that was clothed in a body, and body was nothing but a shadow. Things partook of reality only in so far as they embodied a concept, were the focal point of meaningful connections which held the universe together. This was why only philosophy represented real knowledge, while the sciences and history, which were concerned with external, ephemeral accidental appearances, obscured them.[12] "The idea must explain the facts and not to be deduced from the facts. Otherwise matter could determine spirit and spirit would become the slave of matter. External objects only serve to give impulses to our ego and to inspire in it the conceptions with which those objects are then endowed."[13] In brief, the world was the creation of Fichte's thinking ego.

Philosophy based on experience was an absurdity, since facts were so diverse and contradictory, accidental and contingent. "To the devil with the French" who bury themselves with the "conditional appearances of a lifeless actuality"—"a game of jacks . . . a house built on sand". In contrast, the Germans were bent, with all their might upon the universal. Germany was "a house built on rock". It was "the Jerusalem of modern mankind", "Christ in glory". Virginal Russia, "the heir of all Europe and all European influences", should look for guidance to that German "philosophy which mathematically develops and explains the truth of Christianity as based on love and the elevation of man to divinity".[14] Belinsky's philosophy of art is wholly dominated by the universal "eternal idea" of transcendental idealism. All creation was nothing but the breath of the eternal idea, articulating itself in an infinitude of forms, creating to destroy, and destroying to create, incarnating itself in "the brilliant sun, in the magnificent plant, in the wandering comet; it lives and breathes in the stormy ebb and flow of the sea, in the savage hurricane of the desert, in the whisper of leaves, the murmur of the brook, in the growth of the lion, in the tear of the child, in the smile of beauty and in the free will of man", and above all in the creations of genius. The artist was like a harp played upon by the movement of the eternal idea " . . . its uninterrupted activity . . . the idea of the general life of nature". Literature was always and everywhere "a symbol of the inner life of the nation" participating in the life of universal humanity by reflecting a particular phase or aspect of it.[15]

In order to be able to contemplate, to gain consciousness and immerse himself in the universal idea, man must train himself unceasingly to throw off all selfishness, vanity and love of externals, like a Christian ascetic: "religion is truth in contemplation, while philosophy is truth in consciousness".[16] Thus he would be able to achieve selfless love and communion with the pure idea and to begin to feel that the whole universe was in him. Thus an ascetically chaste and mystical attitude ushers in a stern warning "above all jettison politics and beware of its influence upon your manner of thinking. In our Russia politics has no sense, and only empty heads busy themselves with it".[17] For a very long time to come the Russians would not be in a condition to shape their political existence and secure their liberty by themselves. Both would continue to be the gift of their monarchs as in the days of Peter the Great, the incomparable founder of new Russia. "Russia is still a child, which needs a nurse overflowing with love . . . with a whip in her hand." To give her a constitution in her present state would be like giving a child total freedom to ruin itself: "give the Russian freedom and he will rush to get drunk, to break windows and hang noblemen who shave their beards".[17a]

What Russia needed was enlightened guidance by benevolent despotism, "here loosening, there restricting our sphere of choice, on the basis of speculative and not empirical wisdom, true reason and not flat understanding". She required that inner freedom which comes from moral restraint. Belinsky thought he detected similar wise prudence and loving foresight in government policies on the peasant question and censorship. These were calculated to lead gradually to greater freedom and humanity without plots and rebellions.[18] "Absolute power gives us complete freedom to think and reason, but limits freedom of speech and interference with its affairs."[19]

It is the Platonic conception of true reality as contrasted with opaque appearance that causes Belinsky to condemn the French for mixing science, art and religion with politics, with ephemeral and changing matters, with "tracing everything to the social situation", and proclaiming "truths that last only a single day". A smug confidence that this was the best of all worlds, "that all is moving to the better, for only the good exists, and evil is only a negative idea and exists only for the sake of the good",[20] is anchored to faith in the eternal idea. From there Belinsky is able to call upon his educated contemporaries to become apostles of light, to learn to comprehend the essence of being, to imitate Christ who neither plotted nor organised political societies. "And so let us study, study and again study. To the devil with politics. Long live learning!"[21] Let us occupy ourselves only with ourselves, love the good and the true, with the help of knowledge and thus promote general perfection. Everyone should follow and cherish faithfully the vocation which had fallen to his lot, and guard himself against the error of trying "to fix a direction for society and interfering with providence that guides the world".[21a]

With all his *Weltfrömmtgkeit* and sense of a providential order, and with all his inability to admit the possibility of a world of irrational disorder, chaos and evil, Belinsky finds it hard to sustain the stark abstractness of the eternal idea and the assurances of God's justice offered by it. We see him trying hard to infuse vigour into his faith. A year after the letter to Ivanov, he writes to Bakunin[22] about the shock he experienced on making the marvellous discovery of Hegel's idea that reality and rationality were one: "nothing can be removed from it, nothing condemned in it, nothing thrown out". The seeming contradictions and opposites were the infinitely diverse elements making up life, the various hues of the same picture, facets of the same edifice. "Reality!"—he exclaims—"I repeat this word getting up and going to sleep, day and night, and reality surrounds me, I feel it in everything, even in myself."[23]

What explanation can be offered for the obvious evils, sufferings, injuries all around? "Reality is a monster with iron talons and immense iron jaws. Sooner or later she will devour everyone who does not yield to her and cannot live at peace with her."[24] Was there not a danger for the consistent idealist that the squalor in the actual world would turn him into a heartless cynic or a mystic who turns his back upon this vale of tears or rather world of shadows?[25] Should man resign himself to putting out the little candle of his own limited logic, in face of the "infinite phenomena of reality",[26] and just do his duty? Would he not soon discover that he was simply complying with "the orders of authority, which is civil society", doing some pretended duty? In brief, idealists somehow must fall into a trap.[27] Belinsky is nevertheless still roused to indignation by the abstract moralism of such "beautiful souls" as Schiller and Victor Hugo. In his letter to Stankewich of September 29-October 8, 1839, he fulminates against the subjectively moral stand, the terrible generalised idea of obligation, abstract heroism in the name of "an abstract social ideal, hanging in the air, unrelated to geographical and historical conditions of development . . . abstract love . . . empty, impersonal, insubstantial generality, with no special direction", general love for anonymous humanity. The latter showed personal, self-willed pride, and in fact was a kind of rebelliousness that absolved one from doing anything in particular.[28]

Hegel taught Belinsky that the eternal idea was not behind history as a system of pure, rational connections of which reality was a pale reflection, but was being unfolded in history itself—its ideas, institutions, laws in the historic process. All values, preferences, choices had therefore to be referred to the stages in the march of time. Pure, eternal principles were abstractions, indeed delusions. And yet Belinsky is deeply worried by the actual determinations of the unfolding idea and the situation of the concrete individual. Belinsky sums up his attitude: "I recognise personal, independent freedom, but I also recognise a superior will. Collision is the result of a clash between two kinds of will. This is why all is and will be as it is. If I hold out—well and good, if I fall—it cannot be helped. I am a soldier of God: he issues orders, and I march. I have desires and aims which God refuses to fulfill, although I think them just: I complain, I swear that I will not obey him, but in spite of that I obey and often I do not understand how it happens. I have no desire to peer into the future; my only concern is to do something, to be a useful member of society."[28a]

The saving formula was again found in Hegel.

"A new world opened before us: might is right, right is might; no, I cannot describe to you, with what feelings I received these words—it was a deliverance. I understood the idea of the fall of kingdoms, the lawfulness of conquests, I understood that there was no wild material might, there is no rule of bayonet and sword—there is no arbitrariness, no accidental things—and my deep worry about the fate of mankind came to an end. My own country appeared to me in a new light. I took leave of the rebellious French . . . the word 'reality' came to mean to me the same as 'God'."[28b] Instead of feeling crushed by the Hegelian idea of the world spirit and its antinomies, Belinsky experiences a sense of elation, an infusion of a consciousness of power and significance. As part of the historic process one should be able to feel happy even under a downcast sky and in a smoky kitchen: "away with the yoke of (abstract) duty, to the devil with that rotten (ascetic) moralising, that idealistic reasoning: man is the supreme reality, he may live without a sense of guilt or a feeling of only a shadowy existence, all belongs to him, and every minute of his life is great, true and sacred".[28c]

The deliverance afforded by Hegel turns out after a while to be not really a release, but once more a recognition of and a reconciliation with necessity, an acceptance of the superior judgement of history, society, God. We recognise here again the fundamentally religious fear of the sin of wilful pride. "The individual must renounce his subjective individuality, recognise that it is false and illusory, and put himself in harmony with what is universal and general, recognising that in the latter alone is truth and reality." The sin of the subjective person lay in being in eternal struggle with the objective world, and hence with society, which was much more coherent, much richer, much more rational than the individual and had superior rights over him. "Private [existence] is a reality and not an illusion only to the degree that it expresses society within itself."

Now where was society to be found? Who spoke for it? To this Belinsky offers a startling answer. Change the word Tsar for Stalin, and you would easily mistake it for a hymn to Stalin written in the thirties or forties of our century.

"For us Russians"—writes Belinsky in his famous article on Zhukovsky's poem "The Anniversary of Borodino"—"there are no national events which have not come from the living source of the supreme authority. . . . Yes, in the word 'Tsar' there is a marvellous fusion of the consciousness of the Russian people, for whom that word is full of poetry and mysterious meaning. And this is no accident, but the strictest, most rational necessity, revealed in the history of the Russian people. . . . In the Tsar is our freedom, from him will emerge our new civilisation, our enlightenment, just as it is from him that we draw our life. . . . Unconditional submission to Tsarist authority is not only useful and necessary to us, but it is the highest poetry of our lives—our nationality, if by the word nationality is to be understood the act of fusing particular individualities into a general consciousness of the personality and selfhood of the state."[28d]

(c) THE EDUCATION OF A REBEL

It did not take Belinsky long to become horrified by his "reconciliation with base reality, with all the fanaticism of passionate conviction". The revulsion from that hymn to Tsardom in the person of Nicolas I propelled Belinsky into Jacobin radicalism and eventually revolutionary socialism.

What led to that *volte face*? By his own admission Belinsky had come to realise the vital importance of the element of negation in the Hegelian scheme of history. Plekhanov seems to be right in pointing out that Belinsky was not enough of a historical or materialistic dialectician to make clear to himself the distinction between the element of negation inherent in the course of history and forming part of its very rationality, and the growth of a negating attitude among the enlightened observers, endowed with rational intuition and imaginative insight into the fact of the decay of the old forms and the necessity and possibility of replacing them with new alternatives. The slowness of change in a static, frozen Russia was not conducive to offering any understanding of the dialectics of historic change.

But above all, it was Belinsky's deep, passionate concern with the dignity of man, his boundless compassion with suffering to the point of feeling guilty for not sharing it with the afflicted that prevented him from accepting the Russian realities of his day. He became infuriated by despotic arbitrariness, callous inhumanity and the combination of sadistic bullying and cunning obsequiousness. He was gradually driven to proclaim the inevitability of total polarisation: "liberal and man mean the same, just as a follower of absolutism means a believer in the knout".[29] There was no middle way.

Suffering, deprivation, the injury of the living, palpitating individual assumed vastly greater reality for him than all the abstract universals. Hegel, he came to conclude, "made of the living phenomena shadows which hold each other's hands and dance in the air over cemeteries". He turned them into predicates of ideas, processes, laws of history, grandiose inevitabilities, deep forces. "The fate of the individual" should never be treated as a predicate, but always as subject; "it is more important than the fate of the whole world and of the health of the Emperor of China."[30] Belinsky asks Hegel to account for all the victims of life and history. Have not all the victims of evil and superstition always been made out to be the necessary price for some vast fulfilments? "I am told that disharmony is a condition of harmony. This may be all right by musical people, but is not quite so satisfactory from the point of view of those whose fate is to express in their lives the element of disharmony."[31]

The idea of delayed harmonies gave licence to Prussian Hofräte and German beer-drinking philistines to bask in smug self-satisfaction, in callous disregard of the actual suffering on their doorstep. "What does it matter that I am sure that reason will win, and the future will be beautiful, if fate has doomed me to be witness of the triumph of accident, irrationality, bestial violence? What does it matter that our children will be well, if I am unhappy and not from any fault of my own. . . . Words, words, words!"[32]

Belinsky becomes acutely aware of the fact of fundamental inequality, and therefore—in his eyes—of the iniquity inherent in the idea of a superior sphere of pure and lofty ideas reserved for the superior people. "What is it to me that something universal lives while the individual suffers, that solitary genius should live in heaven, while the common herd rolls in the mud? What is it to me, if I do apprehend the essence of art, religion and history, if I cannot share this with all these who should be my human brothers, brethren in Christ, but are in fact strangers and enemies because of their ignorance? What is it to me that happiness is accessible to the chosen, when the majority does not even suspect its possibility? Away with the happiness which I alone out of thousands can attain! I do not want it, if I cannot share it with my lesser brethren! . . . I cannot bear the sight of barefoot boys playing in the gutter, the poor in tatters, the drunken cab-driver, the broken soldier, the official padding along with a portfolio under his arm, the self-satisfied army officer, the haughty nobleman. . . . Has a man the right to forget himself in art and science while this goes on? And this is to be a society based on rational foundations and is to be a phenomenon of reality?[33]

Belinsky raises here a problem which never ceased to torment Russian thought in the nineteenth century, and to which we shall presently return: is evil a price to be paid for culture? And what if culture cannot be attained without injustice to the many and without approving the selfishness of the privileged few? The more he broods over the sights of human degradation, the more intense becomes his pre-occupation with the problem of the dignity of man, the human personality, in brief the individual. "I curse my odious effort of recon-ciliation with an odious reality! Long live great Schiller, noble advocate of humanity, bright star of salvation, emancipation of society from the bloody prejudices of tradition! . . . For me now the human personality is above history, above society, above humanity. . . . I have become completely absorbed in the idea of the worth of the human individual and his bitter lot—a frightful contradiction!"[34]

But this resolve to engage in "struggle against the actual", in place of "reconciliation with reality", opens up a new dialectic of far-reaching consequences. The sacredness of the independent human personality implied equality. "All men are to be brethren." And what if in their perversity, selfishness or sluggishness they want to persevere in their separateness, which nature, habit or circumstances, not to speak of hereditary privilege and exceptional talent have placed them in? In his "farouche, mad, fanatical love of independence and of freedom of the human person. . . . I understood Marat's bloody love for liberty, his bloody hatred of everything that tries to separate itself from human brotherhood. . . . I am beginning to love mankind à la Marat. In order to secure the happiness of the smallest part of it, I would be ready to exterminate all the rest with fire and sword."[35]

In his desire to find a way out of his dilemma of ends and means, Belinsky discovers socialism, notably of the utopian variety. "Socialism has become for me the idea above all ideas, the problem above all problems, the essence of essences, the alpha and omega of faith and knowledge. It is a problem and the solution of a problem. It embraces history, religion, philosophy. This is why I scrutinise my own life, your life, the lives of all with whom I have come into contact in the light of this idea."[36]

It is Belinsky's new religion—after Plato, Schelling, Hegel—which like all religions will not suffer any distinction between theory and practice, doctrine and conduct. There remains the dichotomy of ends and means, the postulate of total harmony and the necessity of a violent breakthrough. In his letter to Botkin of September 8, 1841, Belinsky dreams of a society without the guillotine and the stake. Criminals would simply beg for punishment. Goodness would become so spon-taneous that the word "duty" would disappear. There would be no need for contracts. "Man's will shall yield not to another's will, but only to love."[37] True to the Saint-Simonist prophecies, there will be no husbands and wives claiming rights upon each other, but lovers folowing the dictates of their hearts. "There will be neither rich nor poor, neither kings nor subjects, men will be brethren . . . in a new heaven and a new earth." It will be not an "old, unconscious, animal golden age, but one prepared by society, laws, marriage. . . . Reason and consciousness—that is the dignity and happiness of man."[38]

But it would be ridiculous to think that this could eventually come about by itself "without violent upheavals, without bloodshed". "Men are so stupid that they must be led to happiness through violence. And what is the shedding of the blood of thousands in comparison with the degradation and suffering of millions. . . . I am only beginning to understand revolution . . . men will never do anything better. The French are a great nation."[39] Belinsky thus emerges as a determined revolutionary: "negation is my God", and his heroes are Luther, Voltaire, the Encyclopedists, the terrorists, Byron, Béranger, and Schiller—so "deeply Christian, the most beloved of the disciples of Christ!"[40]

In his essay on a *Textbook of Universal History* by Frederic Lorenz, Belinsky firmly anchors his vision to a pattern of historic inevitability: "the present state of mankind is the inevitable outcome of a rational development and on the basis of the present state it is possible to form a hypothesis about the future state, that light will vanquish darkness, reason will overcome prejudice, free consciousness will make men into brethren in spirit and a new heaven and a new earth will arise".[41]

(d) A NEST OF REVOLUTIONARIES

Reflecting upon his spiritual pilgrimage, the see-saw development of his ideas, his vacillations, wild enthusiasms and dreadful revulsions, his indecision and feelings of emptiness and inadequacy, in short alienation and yearning for salvation, Belinsky begins to generalise his own experience and to see it as a sample of the predicament of his generation, or rather of that small group of idealistic intellectuals, the Stankevich circle, which comprised the best youth of Russia of the day: "Yes, this generation are the Jews wandering in the wilderness, condemned never to see the promised land."[42]

In a letter to Botkin of June 27-28, 1841, Belinsky writes: "We yawn, we busy ourselves, we gang up, we become interested in everything, but we do not get firmly attached to anything".[43] It came from inaction, from the lack of scope for action, which can be supplied only by the "substance of social life". But "we are men without a country . . . worse . . . whose country is a spectre". Their lives, aspirations, actions, loves and friendships were bound to assume a ghostly character. The fault was not in men, their natures, but in the "truly tragic situation of the disorder in Russian society" which twisted the souls of men, deprived them of unreflecting immediacy, filled them with hesitation and doubt. "School has deprived us of religion, circumstances of concrete education . . . we are in conflict with reality, we rightly hate and despise it, just as reality justifiably loathes us."[44]

Speaking of himself Belinsky laments: "By what zigzags has my development proceeded, what terrible price have I paid for discovering the truth and that bitter truth that all in the world, especially around us, is baseness itself",[45] while the exaltés of the circle were overflowing with ideas and sentiments for which society provided no channels and no forms. Hence their unassuaged thirst, their exaggerated demands upon life, and their idealistic ardour for sacrifice, but also their inadequacy as husbands and fathers.[46] The friendships within the circle fed on themselves, lacked stimulus from without: "Oh, if only we could add to it some fuel of external social interests!"[47]

This is the crux of the matter—"the base Russian reality, its officials, bribe-takers, licentious masters, onanist drawing-room society, obscurantism, willing servility . . . Chinese kingdom of materialistic animal life, cult of rank, class and money, kingdom of bribes, religious indifference, licentiousness, absence of any spiritual interests, triumph of shameless impudent stupidity, mediocrity, ineptitude, where everything human, intelligent, noble, talented is condemned to suffer oppression, torment, censorship . . . where all freedom of thought has so been completely annihilated",[48] "while the noble and gifted live in shameful idleness on a desert island".[49]

Belinsky and his friends feel strangers in their own land. "Are we really Russians?" he asks. "No, society regards us as some sickly excrescence, and we look upon society as a heap of stinking manure," without any of that sense of kinship which links perfect strangers into a confraternity, fighting despotism, defending the rights of man, struggling for bread or joining for a spiritual experience.[50]

Has Russia a national culture, a national spirit at all? Belinsky finds himself in an ambivalent situation. While Peter the Great had opened up Russia to the West, releasing vast spiritual potentialities locked up in the Russian soul—which came to such a wonderful flowering in Pushkin—he had also brought about the fearful social-cultural split in the nation, depriving the nation of national identity, creating an abyss between a Westernised elite and a half-Asiatic ignorant mass. "My love for all that is native Russia has grown sadder; this is no longer the enthusiasm of the beautiful soul, but a feeling of torment. All that is substantial in our nation is great, lofty, but the forms are miserable, dirty, base."[51]

The Russian nation had not yet come into its own. Despotism on one side and fearful class divisions on the other prevented its self-expression as a nation, made for its remoteness from Europe, and had delayed for so long its entrance into the family of nations and into the mainstream of humanity's creative endeavour.

HERZEN

Belinsky's astonishing conversion from a Schellingian-Hegelian reconciliation with existing reality, the glorification of Tsardom and the approval of serfdom and censorship, to extreme terrorist revolutionism à la Marat was made possible not only by an awakened awareness of crying human misery in a fundamentally unjust society, but also by his absorption of the Hegelian idea of negation as part of the evolving rationality of the World Spirit.

(e) "THE ALGEBRA OF REVOLUTION"

It was that concept of negation which caused Herzen, in *My Past and Thoughts*, to call Hegelian philosophy "the algebra of revolution".[52] This device is the cryptic message of Herzen's famous essay "Dilettantism in Science".[53] When read without knowledge of the author's real intent, the tract may appear a jejeune and trite piece of philosophising. It deals with the inadequacies of over-specialisation and the need for an overall view of mankind's intellectual endeavour on the one hand. It contains a condemnation of the sterility of Buddhist immersion in the abstract, general and formless on the other. It preaches the necessity of translating scientific findings into action, in the light of the clearly understood direction in which they both—as parts of an indivisible totality—were leading.

The idea that negation was not just subversive, destruction, but a condition for more constructive advance, and the affirmation of the importance of opposition, discontent, contradictions and conflict as instruments of progressive change, was in fact an answer to the reactionary, counter-revolutionary glorification of faith and tradition as pillars of stability, continuity and social cohesion. At bottom, it was a debate on the significance of the French Revolution generalised into the phenomenon of revolution in history.

Hegel's philosophy—wrote Herzen—"frees man to an extra-ordinary degree and leaves not a stone upon a stone of the whole Christian world, the world of traditions, which have outlived themselves".[54] The issue reduced itself for Herzen to "either Christianity and monarchy or science and the republic"[55]—a formula he found in 1842 in the *Deutsche Jahrbücher*, in an anonymous article by Bakunin, who had recently resigned his commission and embarked upon his career as the most stormy revolutionary conspirator of the nineteenth century.[56]

The forces of doubt, criticism, protest, rebellion, indeed the apparent disharmonies and injurious inadequacies were not just evil excrescences, disturbances of an established order, but were part of the rational pattern of history, which was by no means an emanation of the transcendental deity or a murky imitation of an abstract universal idea and its pure forms. The evils showed that the existing forms had outlived their usefulness, had become shackles instead of instruments of freedom and development, and that new forms were struggling to break out and to reshape reality in accordance with changed needs.[57]

The historic dialectic is still seen by Herzen in terms of changing and maturing consciousness, of comprehension, and not of objective social-economic evolution. But it was not only—as Plekhanov would have it—the stagnant state of pre-industrial Russian society that failed to impart to Belinsky and Herzen the Marxist type of awareness of impersonal, material social change. What impinged most upon Herzen's consciousness and filled him with fury was the outrageous lie behind the regime's claim to be preserving social stability against such "anarchical" forces as individual judgement and analytical reasoning. Indeed, under Nicolas I obscurantism had become the official policy to the point of banning the teaching of philosophy at the universities and barring children of the lower orders from even elementary education. Under Nicolas I, says S. M. Soloviev, education ceased to be a virtue and came to be regarded as a crime.[58]

"Christian teaching"—wrote the famous reforming minister Speransky in a letter to Alexander I in 1816—"should be at the basis not only of the social order, but even more so of education."[59] The Ministry of Public Education was consequently merged with that of Public Worship so that "Christian piety might always be the foundation of true education" . . . and "an enduring and blessed harmony between faith, knowledge and authority" could be brought about.[60]

"I know what these liberals, journalists and their accomplices want," declares Count Uvarov, Nicolas I's minister. "They will not succeed in planting their seeds in the field over which I stand guard. . . .

If I could succeed in turning Russia back fifty years, I would feel that I had fulfilled my duty and could die in peace."[61] Panic rather than robust self-assurance, fatalism rather than deep faith, a desperate anxiety to delay the evil day, rather than a triumphant sense of rock-like superiority, were behind these words. The minister was unable to pause and wonder whether such repressive ardour to stave off perils was not calculated to reveal itself as a self-fulfilling prophecy by driving the repressed into rebellion sooner than he feared.

In the 1830's Uvarov was campaigning against philosophy in his official organ *The Review of the Ministry of Public Instruction*. In the January 1836 issue a now forgotten book of a forgotten author comparing Hegel's philosophy with Christian philosophy is highly praised for "revealing fully the anti-Christian tendency of Hegel, in spite of his effort to hide it behind an obscure logic". German philosophy as a whole is condemned in the March number of the same year: "It has caused much evil, led many minds into error, and it is time to be rid of it." Kant is taken to task for having removed God from man, and thereby man from God. "His morality fails to satisfy the essential needs of the heart."

How could a young lively spirit like Herzen react to such exhortations in the light of his own experiences? He was thrown into prison in July 1834, kept there without trial or legal defence for nearly a year, and then sent into exile for over five years. He was being punished for consorting with young men with evil ideas who sang the "Marseillaise" and for having expressed rebellious thoughts in his private correspondence. The matter had been placed before the Emperor himself by the head of the political police (the Third Section), Count Benckendorf. Herzen had hardly settled down in St Petersburg as a government official upon receipt of a pardon in 1840, when he was exiled again for having shared some gossip with his father in a private letter, and added to the description of a trivial incident—a robbery committed by a policeman on a merchant—the remark "and such is our police". It was again the doing of the Tsar himself, who would not listen to his ministers' expostulations to relent. Once the case had come before the Tsar and he had put his foot down, there was nothing the ministers could do, as they ruefully and apologetically told Herzen.

In Novograd, his last place of exile, Herzen was put in charge of cases of political offenders and exiles, in other words he had to report on himself. No wonder that he developed an implacable hatred not merely for arbitrary despotism, but above all for the cant and humbug which opined that the individual found his expression and realisation in the national genius, history and destiny; for that matter, in any collective ethos and endeavour.[62] "The liberty of the individual is the greatest thing of all, it is on this and on this alone that the true will of the people can develop . . . with us the individual has always been crushed, absorbed, he has never even tried to emerge. Free speech with us has always been considered insolence, independence, subversion; man has been engulfed in the state, dissolved in the community. The revolution of Peter the Great replaced the obsolete squirearchy of Russia with a European bureaucracy, everything that could be copied from the Swedish and German codes, everything that could be taken over from the free municipalities of Holland into our half-communal, half-absolutist country, was taken over; but the unwritten, the moral check on power, the instinctive recognition of the rights of man, of the rights of thought, of truth, could not be and were not imported."[63]

Did this resonant *cri du coeur* of Herzen signify a repudiation of his country and all its works in the past and future? Not really. One of its targets was the Slavophile doctrine of the uniqueness of Russia, and its condemnation of the West. Herzen saw in that a *trahison des clercs*, if not an intended apologia of the Tsarist regime, a prop for its slogan "Orthodoxy, autocracy, nationality". In Herzen's eyes Slavophile patriotism would isolate Russia from the evolution of mankind, which was led by the West. "Slavophilism every day bears its luxuriant fruits; open hate of the West is open hate of the whole process of the development of the human race; for the West, as the heir of the ancient world, as the result of all general motion of all particular movements is the entire past and present of humanity . . . together with hate and disdain of the West go hate and disdain of freedom of thought, of all guarantees (of individual rights) of all civilisation. In this way the Slavophiles stand on the side of the government."[64]

(f) RUSSIA: THE NATION-MESSIAH

Both the concept of the oneness of history and the love of his native land made Herzen, like Belinsky, recoil from sectarianism. Only by joining the family of nations was Russia destined to become a great nation and deploy its immense potentialities. Without that, it was bound not only to remain a semi-Asiatic stagnant pool, but also to continue as a despotic society broken up into castes, without a common national identity. This was not a matter of pure speculation but of immediate urgency to Herzen, because of his messianic expectation of imminent great changes in the life of the European nations.

"Dilettantism in science" throbbed with a messianic faith in the imminent realisation of the "actual unity of science and life, of word and deed",[65] the enthronement of reason turned into full human self-consciousness. Who was called upon to shoulder that task, to act as the guide and saviour of mankind? The two obvious candidates were France and Germany. With all her heroic role in the struggle for liberation on the basis of assumptions similar to those proclaimed by German science, France "is not able to translate them into the language of the universal", and "Germany cannot render logic into the language of life".[66]

The reader is at this point staggered by the suggestion of a rather unexpected candidate. "On the other hand, we of the North might be called upon to contribute our share to the treasure-house of human reason. Perhaps we, who have hitherto scarcely lived, will come to be all the representatives of actual unity of science and life, of word and deed. In history, the late-comers receive not the leavings but the dessert. There is something in our character which combines the best sides of the French and the best sides of the Germans. We are far more fit for scientific thought than the French and we are decidedly averse to the philistine life of the Germans. There is something gentleman-like about us which the Germans lack. Upon our brow there is the imprint of grave thought which somehow evades the countenance of the French."[67]

Should one read into this astonishingly prophetic utterance sentiments of Russian nationalism or particular Russian messianism? Revolutionary writers of other nations—as we know—staked out similar claims for their own nation. The French would extol their pioneering role in the French Revolution. The Germans could invoke their idealistic philosophy of revolution. The Italians claimed the role of teacher for Roma Terza. The Poles saw themselves as Christ of the nations, crucified by the Holy Alliance. Herzen sees virtue in the Russians being a nation without a history. It was young, spontaneous, virile, innocently generous in comparison with old, over-ripe, too experienced and indeed decrepit Europe. It is thus in a position to turn its backwardness to advantage by absorbing and using all the knowledge accumulated by others. The last will be the first.

In an entry to his Diary of February 21, 1844,[68] Herzen spells out the contents of the message about the imminent practical reconciliation between theory and practice, and the reasons why Russia might be called before all. "But do we have the right to say that the coming epoch, on whose banner is written not the individual but the commune, not liberty but fraternity, not abstract equality but the organic division of labour, does not belong to Europe? In this is the whole question. Will the Slavs, fertilised by the West, realise its ideal and unite decrepit Europe to their existence, or will Europe unite us to her rejuvenated life? The Slavophiles decide such questions quickly, as if the matter had long since been settled. There are indications, but we are far from a final decision."[69]

(g) THE DISILLUSIONMENT WITH THE WEST

Herzen's encounter with the West resulted in lacerating disenchantment. In the wake of 1848 it then developed into utter despair. Soon after his arrival in the West and well before the perplexing events of that year of hope, Herzen began to write to his Russian friends letters which distressed them greatly as possible ammunition for Slavophile and other reactionary detractors of Western liberalism.

Why should the revulsion have been so violent? Herzen's criteria were not political, but religious. They were simply not applicable to the political traditions of the West. Politics in the latter consisted in muddling through, in distracted groping, in self-interest trying to concede to others as little as possible; not in making radical changes, but in avoiding or lessening trouble. Herzen however was glued to a vision of rationality, justice and high-mindedness coming at last to fruition in the immediate future. The anguish and scorn of the disenchanted lover may be heard in these following lines:

"When one seriously contemplates everything that is happening, one becomes disgusted with life. Everything in the world is nauseating, and stupid too, people run around in circles, work, don't find a moment's rest, and all produce absurdities. Others want to reason with them, to stop them, but are crucified and persecuted, and, all this is done in a kind of delirium, without any effort to understand . . . stifled for a moment, indignation mounts again, and one resents only one thing, that one hasn't sufficient power of hatred, of scorn for their indolent soullessness, their reluctance to rise higher, to be nobler. If only one could turn away from them, let them do what they wish in their cave, let them live today as they did yesterday bolstered by custom and ritual, with blind beliefs about what is right and what is wrong . . . and moreover at every step betraying their own morality, their own catechism!"[70]

Herzen was not quite unaware of the reasons for his disappointment. He was anything but a bigoted narrow-minded fanatic. Possessed of a passion for introspection, he could also be often paralysed by a sense of ambivalence and ambiguity. He speaks of the spurned and disillusioned prophet, who "acting as mankind's conscience . . . accepting the burden of its sins, wants to awaken its consciousness . . . because of a tendency to idealise, to judge everything from above, just as life is commonly judged in terms of some dead letter, or passions in terms of some legal code, or individuals in terms of their lineage".[71]

The events of 1848 seemed to Herzen an orgy of play-acting, make-believe, hypocrisy, deceit and finally ruthless cruelty. The liberal republicans had no wish at all to realise their promises of liberty and equality. All they wanted was to secure their property and hold the masses at bay. The revolutionary leaders lacked all conviction and passion. They were phrase-mongers, hypnotised into re-enacting the roles of the great heroes of the French Revolution. The proletarians took the message of the social republic seriously. When they realised that they had been duped, they rose to demand what had been pro-claimed to be their right. The frightened liberal bourgeoisie appealed to the naked sword to save them, and the revolutionary demagogues stood impotently by, making speeches.

"I feel ashamed of our generation, we seem mere soulless orators. Our blood is cold, only our ink is hot, our minds are in a constant state of ineffectual irritation, our mouths are filled with passionate words with no influence on action. When we should be impulsive, we are hideously rational and are haughty about everything, we endure everything, we are interested only in the universal, the idea, humanity. . . . We have wasted our spirit in the regions of the abstract and general just as the monks let it whither in the world of prayer and contemplation. We have lost our taste for reality, come out above it, just as the bourgeoisie came out below it. And what were you doing, revolutionaries, scared of the revolution? Political children, clowns of freedom, you played at republic, at terror, at government. You made fools of yourselves in the clubs, chattered in the chambers, rattled on in your parliaments. . . . You anticipated nothing, you foresaw nothing. . . . A whole world is dying."[72]

(h) CULTURE OR JUSTICE

As if jettisoning all faith in reason unfolding itself in history, Herzen reflected on the fact that Western civilization too, only in a somewhat slighter degree and more shamefacedly, or hypocritically, than Russia, was "a civilisation of a minority . . . made possible only by the existence of a majority of proletarians". European society had been and still was soaked in monarchical and feudal institutions, concepts and habits. These had bred a love of power on one side and a fear of freedom, a wish to obey on the other.

The liberal-democratic institutions designed to establish and to safe-guard freedom were at bottom transmutations of hierarchical power patterns. "The Republic, as they conceive it, is an unrealisable abstraction, the fruit of theoretical reflections, the apotheosis of the existing state organisation, the transfiguration of what already exists; their republic is the last dream, the poetic delirium of the old world."[73] The Republic one and indivisible, the centralised state, the absolute power of the legislative assemblies, the sovereignty of the people, Jacobin fanaticism forcing the people to be free—they were all different expressions of the urge for power, the will to dominate. Furthermore, the dominated masses were wholly indifferent to individual liberty; they were fascinated by the arrogant glitter of authority, they were hypnotised by the Bonapartes. "For the people, despotism was not a peculiarity of the Empire. For them all governments so far have been despotic."[74] But the masses themselves were of a despotic temper, they hated any sign of independence, of non-conformity.

The root cause of all the failures of all participants in the tragedy of 1848 was man's fundamental inner inability to be free, to obey his spontaneous inclinations, in brief to be truly himself. For too long man had been the victim of alienation, or in Herzen's favourite phrase dualism, the eternal tension between his own tendencies, concrete needs and wishes in his concrete situation, and the abstract standards and demands laid down from outside, from above, and claiming objective validity. Man was not living his own life, fulfilling his own self, he was obeying, conforming, sacrificing himself, whether to God and religion, the moral code, the national tradition, the state and its laws, idealistic philosophy or romantic illusions and delusions. Now and again there emerged revolutionaries who carried the masses with them in revolt against the suppression of their lives. Very soon they would grow frightened of their own courage, and would reinstate the old idols under different names. Luther and Calvin shook off the yoke of the papacy, but enthroned Holy Writ with greater severity, and set about persecuting the sectarians who took them at their word and began to interpret Scripture in their own way.

Modern man had discarded religion, but could not shake off the habits of religion. The ingrained, compulsive need to worship mystical beings, to sacrifice oneself, was so deep, had so much entered man's blood, language, images, metaphors that people would not stop to ask themselves in what way the nation was more real than the church, popular sovereignty more infallible than divine right, why it was silly to believe in paradise and noble to strive for utopia, why belief in God was wrong, and trust in humanity rational. The sonorous collective nouns and vague abstractions, like progress, the state, the party, society, were created by man to satisfy his need to run away from himself, his inner voice, his freedom or his need to make choices, so as to be able to obey in good conscience and to sacrifice themselves more readily.

"This is strongest of all the chains by which man is fettered; the strongest, because either he does not feel the violence it does to him or, what is worse, considers it to be absolutely just. The submission of the individual to society, to the people, to humanity, to the idea, is merely a continuation of human sacrifice of the immolation of the Lamb to pacify God, of the crucifixion of the innocent for the sake of the guilty. All religions have based morality on obedience, that is to say, on voluntary slavery. That is why they have always been more pernicious than any political organisation. For the latter makes use of violence, the former of the corruption of the will. Obedience means the transference of all that is most individual in man to an impersonal generalised sphere independent of him. Christianity, the religion of contradictions, recognised the infinite worth of the individual, as if only for the purpose of destroying him all the more solemnly before Redemption, the Church, the Father in Heaven!"[75]

The social-political patterns of the modern world were nothing but a variation on the Christian text: man was subjugated under the pretext of liberation. The individual who was the true, real monad of society continued even in secular civilisation to be sacrificed to some social concept, some collective noun, some banner or other. In a truly Nietzschean manner Herzen saw the root cause for that in what he called dualism: the division of man into body and soul, of reality into matter and spirit, things and ideas, nature and morality, the urge to live and ascetic self-constraint, the individual and the collective.

"As Christ tramples upon the flesh thereby redeeming the human race, so in dualism idealism sides with one shadow against the other, granting spirit the monopoly over matter, species the monopoly over the particular, sacrificing man to the state, the state to humanity."[76]

Dualism had penetrated into our language and gained a compulsive hold not only on our thoughts, but also our subconsciousness, our proverbs, metaphors and images. It seemed for a while at the end of the eighteenth century that some thinkers had at last seen through the colossal mystification and undertaken to set men truly free, make the individual an end in himself.[77] However, either through inner compulsion or from outside influence, Rousseau and Hegel soon came to speak like Christians, Robespierre and Saint-Just to behave like monarchists; German philosophy evolved into speculative religion, the convention became a church, civic dogmas were proclaimed as a creed, popular sovereignty turned into providence, and legislators into priests and prophets.[78] As for the masses, whose liberation was to be the final goal, "to govern themselves does not enter their heads". The most they dared to hope for was that a "social government" would govern for them, and not against them. All the socialist liberators were incensed by the only man among them, Proudhon, who had the courage to stand alone and to raise questions about the very reality and value of such abstracts as the state, central government or democracy itself. "They were terrified of his atheism and his anarchism."[79]

The consciences of men had been enslaved by the institutions, in which they had been reared for centuries, the family, the tribe and the church. Slavery existed only among mankind. Among animals the stronger, when hungry, devoured the weaker and the weak fought back, escaped or were devoured, they did not submit. Only man "introduces into the animal world of savage independence and self-assertion the element of loyal and humble service, the element of Caliban".[80]

Dualism was not only a source of servitude, but also the cause of unhappiness, hypocrisy, and demoralisation. Since human beings were not able to live up to the demands of idealism and asceticism, man became afflicted with a bad conscience. He either tormented himself, or became a hypocrite out to deceive himslf and others. In fact our whole civilisation, like the Catholic indulgences, was a Tartuffian fabrication. Nor were the ways of life commensurate with the dialectic of pure reason. So we began to lose our self-confidence.

In order to become truly free, man had to learn that life and every moment was an end in itself, and not a means or step to some higher, more abstract goal. The fragrance of the flower, the bird's song last as long as they last. We had to become used to the idea that there was no libretto behind the sights and sounds of the stream of history. There were infinite possibilities. History was an improvisation, knocking at many doors, some which opened, others which refused. To labour for a distant goal, like progress, the glory of the nation, the emancipation of the proletariat, and suffer deprivations in the process was tantamount to a refusal to live one's life. Mankind was afflicted with the fate of Sisyphus.

"If progress is the end, for whom are we working? Who is the Moloch who, as the toilers approach him, instead of rewarding them, only recedes, and as a consolation to the exhausted, doomed multitudes crying morituri te salutant, can give back only the mocking answer that after their death all will be beautiful on earth? Do you truly wish to condemn all human beings alive today to the sad role of caryatids supporting a floor for others to dance on some day . . . or a wretched galley of slaves, up to their knees in mud, pulling a barge filled with some mysterious treasure and with the humble words 'progress in the future' inscribed on its bows . . . and end that is infinitely remote is not an end, but, if you like, a trap."⁸¹

The conclusion of these acute observations was that men would never become truly free before they had swept away all those cobwebs, and torn out of their system deep-rooted, compulsive habits of thought, sentimental attachments or respectful awe for the inherited eternal verities and taboos. In what way? We are not given a consistent and unambiguous answer, except for the idea of abolition of central state government and its replacement by a loose federation of communes. Herzen seems to suggest that Western civilisation was disintegrating under the weight of age-long contradictions and was sinking like ancient Rome at the end of its days. He returns again and again to the vision of what Vico called *ricorsi*, of an uprising of fresh, unspoilt, virile, virginal barbarians, without a past and without a culture, to sweep away the old decrepit world, which had become incurable due to over-ripeness and a surplus of reflection, introspection and nihilistic self-doubt and selfishness. Herzen speaks at times of a moral fraternity such as socialism which was destined to redeem mankind; at other times he seems to pray for another invasion of fresh, unspoilt barbarians with powerful passions.

Herzen nowhere goes so far, as for instance Rousseau did, not to speak of Feuerbach and Marx, as to relate the spiritual chains on human hearts to a deliberate misuse of power by property-hungry exploiters, or indeed to social-economic realities and modes of production. He remains in the sphere of ideas and morality, above all of the imperatives of eternal justice. He stumbles in this connection upon a frightening moral dilemma: since all European civilisation was based upon the exploitation of the many by the few, and culture was made to flourish by and for the leisured classes by the slaving multitudes, was it not possible that culture and justice were in deep, insoluble conflict? It was, as with Belinsky, a dilemma that would never cease to plague the conscience-stricken Russian intelligentsia. And Herzen is deeply aware that he is a grand seigneur, a fastidious aesthete and a capitalist.

To bring real equality into being meant to put an end to existing civilisation, which was feudal and monarchical through and through, notwithstanding the superficial rhetoric or abstract philosophising. All intelligent conservatives such as Metternich and Guizot saw the injustices of the social order, "but they saw also that these injutices were so much part of the organism as a whole that it needed only a push, and the whole edifice would come tumbling down.⁸² They opted for the status quo.

"We may still regret the old order", Herzen says. "Who should regret it if not we? It was good only to us. We grew up in it, we are its favoured sons; we admit that it ought to go, but we cannot withhold a tear. The masses crushed by toil, weakened by hunger, dulled by ignorance . . . they were the uninvited guests at the feast of life . . . their suppression was a necessary condition of our lives."[83]

Herzen is very doubtful whether well-being can be within everyone's reach in the modern social order. He is not sentimental or puritanical enough to be sorry for the fact that twenty generations of Germans were wasted in order to produce a single Goethe, and that the feudal dues in the Pskov region made it possible to rear Pushkin. "Nature is merciless, like the notorious tree, she is at once a mother and a stepmother—she does not object to two-thirds of her creatures feeding the other third, so long as the other third does develop." Again, "A landowner's rent and a capitalist's profits were no doubt a form of cannibalism."[84]

In so far as the democratic principle had been imbibed by both the workers in revolt and the conscience-stricken liberals, it had become the cancer of existing society. If the later did not give up, naked force would become the arbiter which the haves would use with a bad conscience, and the have-nots with a defiant sense of right. But what would happen to civilisation? Would the virile barbarians, without history—the proletarians of the West—create a better one than the decrepit, history-laden feudal and bourgeois classes? Would they themselves, like the early Christians, become infected by the old world, and create a coercive Catholic church and a dominant class? Sometimes Herzen seems just to thrill at the idea of universal chaos and doom.

(*i*) SALVATION FROM THE SLAVS

It was a statement by Michelet that Russia's role in Europe was that of a barrier cast across the high road of human progress that stung Herzen to claim for the Russians the mission of redeeming doomed Western civilisation. "Europe is approaching a terrible cataclysm"—writes Herzen—"the world of feudalism is expiring. The religious and political revolutions are petering out under the weight of their own complete impotence. . . . They have stripped throne and altar of the prestige they once enjoyed, but they have not established the era of freedom. They have lit new desires in the hearts of men, but they have not provided ways of satisfying them. Parliamentarism, Protestantism—these are mere prevarications, temporary measures, attempts to stave off the flood."[85]

Doubt, sterility, sluggishness were paralysing Europe. In societies emptied of convictions, only mutual fear held sway, in other words—force. Salvation was beckoning from that part of Europe which had up to now been outside the mainstream of history, the Slav peoples, above all Russia. The paradox of Russia was that the rule of naked, tyrannical force embodied by the Russian government concealed from the world the fact that there was a total divorce between the people and the government of Russia. History-less, poor, unattached to any vested interests or happy memories, the Russian people was entirely free of the virus of the will to power. It had no understanding at all of centralised abstract power, or for any form of property. The Russian way of life was represented by the peasant commune, with its perfect equality, common ownership, periodic redistribution of land, perfect self-sufficient self-government: "an almost boundless good faith prevails amongst them: contracts and written agreements are quite unheard of".[86]

The commune had been a fortress which preserved genuine Russian life from Mongol barbarism, from imperial despotism, the Europeanised landlords and from the German bureaucracy, and indeed from Western civilisation, which would certainly have sapped its life through private ownership. It was equally fortunate for Europe, now on the point of taking the first step forward in a social revolution to be confronted with a country that could provide an actual instance of an attempt—a crude, barbaric attempt of a sort—in the direction of the division of the land among those who worked on it.[87]

"If the Slavs," writes Herzen—"are right in believing that their hour has come, then this element must necessarily be that which is in line with the revolutionary ideas of Europe"[88]—since that was *le dernier cri* of history. But Russia was not only an example of communal living, and the solution of the problem of the individual versus society. The Slavs were also called upon to show how to achieve genuine independence from the Moloch of abstract force within the centralised state and in the family of nations.

"Centralisation is contrary to the Slav genius; federalism, on the other hand, is its natural form of expression. Once the Slav world has become unified, and knit together into an association of free autonomous peoples, it will at last be able to enter on its true historical existence."[89]

Chapter Three

LOOSENING THE SPIRITUAL *ARCANA IMPERII* —CHERNYSHEVSKY AND DOBROLYUBOV

Brooding over the dilemma of culture versus justice led to a gradual relativisation of Herzen's revolutionary creed. The ruling classes were exploiters, but they were also the bearers of civilisation; the masses suffered from oppression, but they were also a coarse, savage mob. No one lived up to his professed standards. A little digging would always discover self-seeking, nastiness, thoughtlessness and hypocrisy in all idealistic postures. All mankind lived by deception and delusion.

Herzen had a sharp eye for the ignoble, hidden recesses, and he showed flashes of insight which were to be systematised by Marx, Nietzsche, Pareto, Freud and others. This had a good deal to do with Herzen's personally ambiguous situation. He was an illegitimate child of a rich and highly educated Russian nobleman and a much younger and utterly insignificant German mistress, whom his father installed at his home as lady of the household but never formally married. Alexander did not bear his father's name. He was ennobled through joining government service. He was legitimised and made sole heir, although there was an older half-brother in the house, the son of a serf-girl. Then there was a deaf-mute brother who perished with Herzen's mother in 1851 in a shipwreck. Herzen's own matrimonial experiences, so breath-takingly described in E. H. Carr's *The Romantic Exiles,* were just a tale of dreams of ideal love coming to grief because of both the inadequacies of the beloved and his own sorry lapses, and ending in terrible tragedies. Herzen's attitudes to his mother and father were most ambivalent. The passionate master of portraiture and incomparable analyst of the human heart does not have a single word to say about his mother in his voluminous recollections. Herzen admired his father's mind and political liberalism, was conscious of the price which his father took in him, but was maddened by the cruelly insulting treatment of his mother and old Yakovlev's generally neurotic and tyrannical capriciousness and fundamental indolence. The humiliating circumstances which he could do nothing to change strengthened the feeling of the irreparable intractableness of things, in other words fate. But the experience of indignities prevented his sense of ambivalence from developing into a Nietzschean pitiless scorn for the breed of man. There was no stronger sentiment in Herzen than indignation at the sight of human degradation. But again, this never moved him to liberate the serf "souls" who produced his wealth, just as his socialism did not prevent him from using the services of one of the Rothschilds to force the Tsar to disgorge the family property which the government tried to confiscate.[91]

Class background, personal experiences and ideological disappointments combined to heighten Herzen's consciousness of the dangers threatening civilisation, and especially of the danger of a *jacquerie* in Russia. Herzen's *Kolokol* rendered immense service as a platform from which the concrete evils of Tsarism were mercilessly castigated, but it also came out with the flaming warning to the young generation of revolutionaries in the 1860's under the ominous title "Dangerous!", for heedlessly resolving the dilemma of culture and justice in favour of the latter.

Chernyshevsky and Dobrolyubov appeared to be inviting a conflagration. Apart from disguised or indirect incitement, they were systematically endeavouring to undermine the very foundations of the existing social system by freeing men's hearts from the chains which centuries of indoctrination had laid on them. They were out to teach men to dare. They had decided to replace all inherited values with diametrically opposite ideas, sentiments and myths: a revolutionary challenge and a social utopia.

(a) THE TIMID BENEFACTOR OF MANKIND

Pisarev explains the tremendous importance of Chernyshevsky's novel *What is to be done?* by saying that "all those who are nourished by routine or stew in it" could not help feeling enraged by the way the novel "mocks their aesthetics, destroys their morality, demonstrates the fraudulence of their chastity and does not conceal its contempt for its own judges". The book became a banner to all "that is young and alive. . . . Never has the new trend declared itself so resolutely and strongly."[92]

Pisarev is suggesting that Chernyshevsky as it were fulfilled the task which Bakunin assigned to himself and to his followers: to destroy in order to build, destruction being a necessary condition for revolutionary creation. That *What is to be Done?* achieved that goal is testified by the painter Repin, who tells us how the book fired the minds of a whole generation: it was read with passion, in tattered, printed or hand-written copies and preserved together with other prohibited literature and pictures. In many political trials a defendant's possession of it was recognised as evidence of guilt. Not only was the book dissected and discussed endlessly by the young, "it became their confession of faith and code of behaviour".[93]

It was not for nothing that although only a publicist (admittedly the foremost contributor to the first periodical of the day) without any party or any organised underground movement behind him, Chernyshevsky was singled out by the regime for the exemplary punishment of a symbolic execution in the public ceremony of administering "civil death" in the pillory, before being banished for life to Siberia at the age of thirty-five.[94] He was considered so influential just before he was imprisoned and after he had withstood government pressure to step down from his editorial chair, that when in 1861 an epidemic of fires visited the capital, Dostoevsky came to beg him to intercede with the revolutionaries who were allegedly responsible for the arson.[95] After a series of abortive plans by his young admirers to rescue him from exile, Chernyshevsky was finally allowed to return to European Russia in 1883 as a result of a deal between the Tsarist government and the "People's Will" party who had just assassinated Alexander II. In exchange for the release of the author of *What is to be Done?*, its members promised to abstain from disturbing the coronation of Alexander III and the subsequent celebrations.[96] From Valentinov's conversations with Lenin in the second part of the first decade of this century,[97] it can be seen that, indeed like Plekhanov, the Bolshevik leader venerated Czernyshevsky as the earliest pathfinder of revolution, the first true materialist thinker and socialist economist in Russia, whose flair for revolution was comparable only to that of Marx: a model and inspiration to generations of Russian revolutionaries[98]—a fact which the author of *Das Kapital* endorsed when he called Chernyshevsky "a great Russian scholar and critic".[99] So the dream of Chernyshevsky's youth thereby came true.

On September 29, 1848, Chernyshevsky commits to his journal his innermost thoughts: "to be honest . . . my destiny . . .[is] . . . to cause mankind to advance upon a new road . . . to be one of the vessels chosen by God to bring happiness to mankind . . . a new view of life . . . a new orientation to be worked out by the generations to come, somebody like Hegel, Plato or Copernicus".[100] Chernyshevsky was by origin neither a conscience-stricken member of the landed gentry nor a child of downtrodden serfs. He came from a well-educated and relatively comfortable priestly family in the fair-sized city of Saratov on the Volga. There was little in his background, childhood and adolescence to leave scars, breed rancour or inspire dreams of self-asserting revenge. Bookish, priggish, externally very unprepossessing, terribly short-sighted and physically weak, young Chernyshevsky was inordinately shy and dreadfully afraid of being disliked and unwanted, in short, of being a nuisance. He speaks of his "abject, apathetic, timid and indecisive character".[101]

"I must marry, also because in that way from the child I now am I will become a man. Then my timidity, shyness, etc., will disappear"[102]—he says most disarmingly. In another place he says that he has "the kind of character which was made to be subordinate" and that he wants a wife to "govern" him.[103] Chernyshevsky's earliest abortive attempts to achieve such a breakthrough make one wince or smile. He finally picked up courage to persevere, and even to overcome the strong opposition of his mother to the match. His courtship had all the high-minded purity of sentimental idealism. He appealed to his bride to see herself as superior to him. All that he wanted was to be of help to her. When departing soon after the engagement to St Petersburg to study, he insisted that she should feel herself free to break off the engagement, while he would consider himself onesidedly bound to her. Also in the future, should her feelings cool off, he would give her freedom to choose the better man and he would, if told to, quit. He also wished Olga to address him as "thou", while he would stick to "you".[104]

After the wedding he felt triumphant. "I have become decisive, daring, my doubts, my hesitations have vanished. Now I have will, now I have character, now I have energy."[105] Later on he said that without Olga he would have degenerated into an apathetic Oblomov. She released the forces latent in him, gave him faith in man's goodness, reason and honour. The sad truth however is that the two never reached any true rapport, and that she was quite unsuited to be the partner of a thinker and prophet. Chernyshevsky's own anxious, indeed panicky, sense of duty towards wife and children never weakened, and in the days of difficulty and danger, and above all of exile, it was a source of constant torment to him. Rousseauist manic-depressive vacillation between a mood of devouring self-rejection and bursts of conquering self-assurance, the need to abase himself and dreams of surpassing glory, fill the pages of Chernyshevsky's *Journal*.

(*b*) THE METAPHYSIC OF REVOLUTION: MATERIALISM AND UTILITARIANISM

While harping on his shyness and timidity, Chernyshevsky never tired of repeating that in matters of conviction he was wholly unyielding. He would din into the ears of his uncomprehending and distracted bride that perhaps she should not consent to marry him, that if she did, she had to be ready for the danger that one day gendarmes would appear to take him away. A revolutionary conflagration was imminent, and he would certainly not remain aloof, since he was unable to bear the sight of human degradation and humiliation.[106]

We can see through his journal the way in which these sentiments crystallised into revolutionary conviction and resolve under the impact both of the events in Western Europe in 1848-9 and of the slow erosion of his religious faith in divine guidance. He was becoming, in his own words, an extremist, a Social-Democrat, a communist, a red Montagnard, a revolutionary terrorist and an ardent follower of Louis Blanc, Proudhon, Pierre Leroux, and, less decidedly, of Ledru-Rollin. His basic categories of thought, in particular on religion and the nature of man, had been taken over from Feuerbach, whom he adored unreservedly. Hegel's idea of the dialectics of historic development was another great formative influence, although Hegel's reluctance to draw the full political conclusions from his philosophy offended him. Fourier's cooperativism (but not the phalanstere as such) is implicit in *What is to be Done?*—notwithstanding Chernyshevsky's distaste for the mixture of realistic insights and bizzare devices in the writings of the half-mad utopian socialist. The man whom Chernyshevsky was most drawn to identify himself with, was Lessing, the eighteenth-century prophet of light, progress and broad humanity. Helvetius supplied the elements of associationist psychology, materialist epistemology and of course utilitarian ethics.[107] To these we have to add the contribution of John Stuart Mill, whose economic views impressed Chernyshevsky no less powerfully than his utilitarianism.

Thomas Masaryk called Chernyshevsky's message "a species of popular messianism".[108] In the spirit of Feuerbach, Chernyshevsky appears to have envisaged his liberating mission as the task of teaching the people that their subjugation was the result of submitting to erroneous ideas, which exercised a compulsive sway over their minds, but which were the projection of social conditions. It was therefore necessary, concluded Chernyshevsky, to lay bare those social conditions, or in more anthropological terms, to start by stripping naked the social superiors responsible for them and revealing the hollowness of their pretentions.[109]

Like the universe itself, we were all made of the same stuff—matter, and only matter: of quantities and combinations of matter, of physiological reflexes to external stimuli. We were all part of nature and natural evolution. There being no divine maker, nor any transcendental authority, there was no room for church, princes and their auxiliaries, aristocracy or governments. Man was his own master and legislator. The seemingly non-material phenomena which were ascribed to mind and soul, were due to a greater condensation or greater refinement of the particles of matter forming compounds, coming into contact or collision, joining or separating, or to a more highly developed nimbleness in performing certain psychological functions in response to stimuli: the same principle guided Newton in his discovery of the fundamental laws of nature as the hen picking out grains from a heap of rubbish.[110] Quantitative differences became qualitative differences, water became ice or was transformed into steam. In the same way the most elementary and crudest sensations and reflexes evolved into the most delicate and refined feelings and thoughts.[111] Will was not a manifestation of a spiritual force free from the determination of nature; it was "a mere subjective impression which in our consciousness accompanies the origination of thoughts, actions or external phenomena".[112] In brief, there was no place for a claim to innate superiority by an independently existing spirit or mind, and—the most important thing—there was no superior sphere of the spirit reserved for or maintained by a caste of guides and mentors, uniquely and exclusively endowed with higher attributes. "Philosophy sees in man what medicine, physiology and chemistry see in him . . . no dualism is discoverable . . . all human conduct and all human manifestations conform solely to his real (material) nature."[113]

With the help of their five senses all people were capable of knowing this knowable universe, of fathoming its laws and of controlling our environment. The view that treated our sensual impressions as illusions or murky perceptions, whose cognitive capacity was made operative by abstract concepts; which presented the world of the senses as a kingdom of hazard and chaos, into which reason alone injected meaning and regularity; which finally postulated the idea of some hidden superior long-range design—in brief all the pretended verities and ideals, above and beyond our concrete existence, needs, desires, capacities and objectives, were a libel on life. They were tantamount to damning this world as inferior, not worth bothering with, and to treating concrete events and human life as pale shadows; not ends in themselves, but caricatures of real superior things. Man was thereby deprived of the faith and will to improve the realities of the present, and was plunged into despair and resignation.

Every type of idealism carried with it the implication of a division into people who were earth-bound, who would always live in a world of shadows, and an esoteric part of mankind, alone able to commune with the pure ideas, free to pursue the search for them, destined to act as their spokesmen, and as guides to the less gifted or privileged. Culture became the exclusive domain of some, of a few, and the many were called to labour so that culture might be preserved by the chosen.

But the truth was that we were all motivated by the same forces— the consideration of utility, the desire for pleasure, the fear of pain. Chernyshevsky gave no quarter on this point, and brooked no deception or self-deception. Even the loving mother, or the grief-stricken widow, even the hero who sacrificed himself for an ideal, his country, honour, the good of his fellow men, did so because it gave him satisfaction, enhanced his worth in his own eyes or in the opinion of others, or because he was far-sighted and firm enough to distinguish between momentary gratification and long-term advantage, and to weigh the investment of effort against the profit to be achieved later.[114]

The implication was that everyone was an egoist of one kind or another, and any claim to any exceptional heroic nobility and purity was inadmissible. The very demand or expectation of self-sacrifice from others for pretended idealistic purposes was illegitimate, because the latter usually concealed monopolistic interests. We were all equal, we were all pursuing pleasure, and everyone had therefore an equal right to happiness. The tendency to differentiate between gross delights and refined pleasures, the former allegedly craved by the populace and the latter savoured only by exceptional people, was again a function and sanction of the wish to maintain inequality. And in so far as the distinction reflected actual inequality it was again the result of the social situation, of a system of class distinctions.

Utilitarianism offered a safe standard and an instrument for securing equality. It enabled people to measure the needs of men and assess the nature and degree of gratification, and it could thus serve as an instrument for securing justice: amounts of pleasure awarded for equivalent quantities of pleasure contributed to smaller or larger numbers of people. Moreover, egoism was calculated to become the most effective instrument of social cohesion because it taught us to be reasoning and calculating—rational, in the words of Chernyshevsky.[115] Rationality in this context means the recognition of the right of others to happiness, and the realisation that no one's well-being could be achieved or endured without others having their needs satisfied. A social system built upon these truths and presided over by enlightened and skilful men would succeed in coordinating egoistic endeavours, rewarding them and punishing them accordingly, in making the happiness of the individual depend on the welfare of society. This is what the novel *What is to be Done?* sets out to do, by proving how rational egoism was sure to lead to the noblest altruism, to self-sacrifice and to an ascetic self-discipline of the highest order.

Chernyshevsky would not hear of original sin. He was absolutely sure that "outside a few morally sick persons, all other men, both from among the common people and from among the enlightened, wish to do right; and if they do wrong it is only because the evil environment in which they live forces them to be wrong".[116] This is good Helvetius and Holbach. It shows the transformation of the quest for the free and spontaneous individual, into the view that man was entirely the product of his environment, and that the environment could be so manipulated that it would produce the socially desired type: "to improve man's conception of his obligation towards others, to make him a better person; to develop in him a sense of justice and honour".[117] Modern science was at hand to help us in rearing the desired type of man. "The natural sciences have already developed sufficiently to provide a great deal of material for the exact solution of moral problems."[118]

(c) SOCIALIST REALISM IN THE ARTS

Chernyshevsky had the triumphant feeling that his foolproof system represented a vindication of science, scientific objectivity and precision. All ideas which were not susceptible of being analysed and verified by scientific method were prejudices, superstitions, errors, delusions, fostered by vested interests, privileged groups and ruling classes to obfuscate the minds of the exploited and legitimise their dominant position and their claims for preference. Only the natural, exact sciences deserved the title of science. The humanities and the arts were suspect. They lacked the precision of the exact sciences, and they offered little possibility of verification. Above all, they were burdened with a bad past, because of their ancient association with the idea of the "liberal arts" with the conception of a higher pursuit by men who had the leisure, the freedom of mind, the finer taste to engage in them. This applied, in the first place, to literature and the other arts. Science was by its very nature egalitarian. Objective truths imposed themselves equally on all normal minds.

"As basis for its theories [modern learning] looks to the truths discovered by the natural sciences, using the most exact analysis of facts . . . to truths as credible as the earth's revolution around the sun, the law of gravity, the action of chemical affinity. From those principles which are beyond all dispute or doubt, modern learning arrives at its conclusions with the same care as that used to reach the [principles themselves]. It accepts nothing without the strictest, most inclusive proofs, and concludes from what it accepts nothing except that which necessarily follows from facts and laws that cannot be logically refuted. With such a character, the new ideas offer to man . . . no road to retreat, nor any kind of compromise with the fantastic errors of former times. . . . Thus the basic character of present day philosophical views is their unshakable validity, which precludes all vacillation of opinion."[119]

Chernyshevsky would have nothing to do with the Hegelian view of art as the initial stage in the human perception of the absolute spirit, alongside religion and philosophy, or, for that matter with Schelling's conception which assigned to art the task of initiating us into insights superior to the ordinary ones. Those approaches were a denial of the objectivity and self-sufficiency of reality and of its knowability. Art for art's sake would prove a snare for men who wished to escape the misery of existence. They were running away from the responsibilities of life and their duties towards their fellow men into an illusion and opium dreams. The cult of art for art's sake, with no reference to the problems of real life, the preoccupation with form with no regard to content, concealed callous indifference to the sufferings of mankind, indeed worse than indifference, since it constituted an approval of the status quo. That kind of romantic art, which expressed solipsistic obsession with idiosyncratic qualities, neurotic predicaments and deviations, tiresome self-analysis, fearful passions or sentimental melancholy, was another token of pride and arrogance, of unmitigated and unhealthy selfishness.[120] "Away with erotic problems," exclaims Chernyshevsky in his review of Turgenev's *Asya*: "the modern reader takes no pleasure in them, for he is concerned with the question of perfecting the administration and the judicial system, with questions of finance and with the problem of liberating the peasantry."[121]

Art must be concerned with life. It must profess humility towards nature. Any attempt to create a realm of beauty finer, loftier, purer than life stood condemned because it smacked of idealism, of a denial of the significance of life. It must be permeated by the faith that no artistic achievement was an improvement upon nature, upon the unsurpassable beauty of the real apple, the real orange, the real problems of life. Not that art was called on simply to copy, to imitate, to photograph life. It should be concerned with the significant things in life and above all with the human endeavour[122] to enhance life, to reflect and promote the never ceasing ascent to higher and nobler forms of life. In that task art should of course employ imagination and discernment in a creative and effective manner by judicious selection of theme and object, by isolating the most striking or potent aspects of life, by properly highlighting and dramatising what it wanted to convey, by inspiring enthusiasm and faith. Chernyshevsky condemned the traditional idea of tragedy as struggle against blind fate, because such a conception of fate was anathema to him. For him the tragic was simply the horrible in life, and the sublime was merely the quantitatively huge.[123]

Art should be mindful of the class character of aesthetic criteria. It was called upon to bring into relief and praise vitality in the way the common people responded for instance to the beauty of a healthy, hefty, ruddy, full-bosomed wench, in contrast to the aristocratic inclination to caress sickly pallor, frail bodies, dainty little feet. In brief, the object of art was not isolationist individualism, but society, the social endeavour—"humaneness and concern for the betterment of human life in the spirit of Schiller and Byron". "The artist became a thinker and guide, and works of art, while remaining in the sphere of art, acquired scientific significance."[124]

(d) TOTAL COMMITMENT

Chernyshevsky had started with a call to man to free himself from inhibiting fears, life-choking taboos; to dare to be himself, to live his own life, in brief to throw off the yoke of human bondage imposed by selfish interests and stultifying teachings. In the process he came to preach the imperatives of self-discipline, dedication to society, the virtues of a soldier in the service of progress. Human emancipation from shackles came to be seen as a collective endeavour for general emancipation and as a sustained mighty struggle. Instead of being set free, the individual was now faced with the challenge to prove his single-minded devotion to the general cause, to commit himself, never to look back or across his shoulder, never to bother about his allegedly lost originality or authenticity, but to become a new man. The proof of commitment was action. Any distinction between theory and action—what I should like to do and what I actually do, what I was professing and how I was actually behaving—was impious, smacked of hypocrisy. As in any true religion, service to the cause embraced faith and deed alike.

No wonder that Chernyshevsky was deeply suspicious of hesitations, vacillation and doubt, the inclination to see both sides of a question, to be impressed by the complexity and the relativity of issues. He had no patience with compromise, with regard for different opinions and interests, with happy mediums, gradualism, or above all liberalism. They all appeared to him to be proof of evasiveness, of lack of conviction, of selfish cowardice or of inability to part with the good things in life. Hence the self-righteous, denunciatory, scathing tone, the refusal to admit shades, indeed the crudity and often affected, defiant coarseness. Neither Chernyshevsky nor his younger friend, Dobrolyubov,[125] with the past and soul of a seminarist, who was always counting the sins of mankind and indeed of himself, could have any understanding for the all-pervading sense of ambivalence of a man like Herzen.

Herzen's sybaritism, his love of good things in life, his recoil from fanaticism, vulgarity, hysteria and shrillness, and Turgenev's fastidious aestheticism and reluctance to join causes were met by Chernyshevsky with the relentless and morbid "But I think."[126] Herzen was appalled by the "new men", with whose views he was of course in sympathy, whose devotion to the cause he deeply respected, but whose crude extremism alarmed him.[127] He called these men of the sixties "the superfluous men and the bilious ones", the "Daniels on the Neva" who hated people who ate without gnashing of teeth and whom no beautiful painting or lovely piece of music could cause to forget the evils of the world for a moment.

The contrast between the shuffling shyness and awkward external timidity of Chernyshevsky and that steely resolve, which made him view without fear "mire, drunken peasants with cudgels, slaughter",[128] the scathing arrogance together with the cunning displayed in the permanent hide-and-seek game with censorship—made Turgenev call Chernyshevsky "a snake", and Dobrolyubov "a cobra".[129] Chernyshevsky's arrest was unwittingly precipitated by Herzen, when his letter with the offer to help to publish *The Contemporary* abroad if it was closed down by the authorities, was intercepted by the police. The government was also convinced of Chernyshevsky's authorship of the inflammatory manifesto to the peasants—a matter that has never been settled conclusively.[130]

Kavelin, the prototype of a Russian liberal in the mid-century, wrote that he had a very great affection for Chernyshevsky, "but a more crude, tactless and conceited man" he had never met![131] Chernyshevsky and Dobrolyubov treated the liberals as actual or potential traitors. They were blunting revolutionary energy, while appearing as defenders of the rights of the people and adversaries of despotism. Like the liberals of 1848 in the West, they were sure to rally to the Tsar and hasten to the defence of the old order, as soon as the masses had entered the arena. They were spineless rhetoricians, indolent and self-indulgent Oblomovs.[132]

Dobrolyubov treats Russian liberals on a par with aristocracy as Oblomovians, "superfluous persons" satiated with culture to the point of morbidity. "None of the Oblomovians have transmitted into their own blood and marrow the principles that have been instilled into them; they have never carried them out to their ultimate logical consequences; they have never attained the boundary line where word becomes deed, where principle becomes fused with the innermost need of the soul, is dissolved into that need and is transformed into the single energy that moves the man. This is why such persons never cease lying, this is why they are so inconsistent in the individual manifestations of their activity. This is why abstract opinions are dearer to them than living facts, why general principles seem more important to them than the simple truths of life. They read useful books to learn what is written therein; they write well-meaning essays in order to luxuriate in the logical constructions of their own phraseology; they utter bold speeches in order to enjoy the sound of their own periods and in order to secure applause. But in all that lies beyond, all that is the goal of reading, writing and oratory, if not utterly beyond their ken, is at least a matter about which they are little concerned."[133]

It was the beginning of the fateful duet in Russian history preceding the 1917 revolution. The spokesman of liberalism, Kavelin was issuing anguished warnings not "to hasten the decay of the rotten traditional social forms . . . step cautiously, warily, not to pour oil on the flames, not to take a naked candle into a powder-magazine! Let turbulent thoughts calm down, let things crystallise . . . every new undertaking involves effort, great effort; have patience!"[134] To this "the founder of materialism and communism upon Russian soil"—in the words of Yuri Steklov, Chernyshevsky's leading biographer—answered with the statement that no great breakthrough was ever achieved in history without great convulsions.[135] Kavelin was alarmed by the Russian gentry "playing at a constitution".[136] It "frightens me so much that I cannot think of anything else. . . . Our historical fate is very much like that of France", where it was the nobles who on the eve of 1789 had incited the masses to revolution, "by their unreasonableness . . . doctrinaire attitude, or immaturity".[137] Chernyshevsky pointed to Turgot's failure as example of the futility of gradualness.[138]

As one might expect, Chernyshevsky always related a disputant's views to his social position. Every philosopher's views "have always been elaborated under the powerful influence of the social situation, as a philosophy of a given political party".[139] Kant was a follower of the French Revolution, but recoiled from terrorist methods. Fichte did not. Hegel was a moderate liberal, but extremely conservative in the application of his principles, ready to fight the outmoded reactionary past with revolutionary methods, but very anxious to curb the dynamism of revolution.[140]

The struggle against human degradation and for the autonomy of the human personality meant above all a struggle against class domination and class oppression, and in Russia against peasant serfdom and for peasant emancipation. His passionate belief in the paramount importance of the class issue made Chernyshevsky intolerant towards what he would call nationalist humbug, any idealisation of the peculiarity of Russian character, Russian past, the peculiar institutions of Russia or her unique mission. In comparison with the magnificent cultural achievements of the West, Russia had hardly had a history or a life worth living. She had contributed nothing to the sciences and the arts, but was just a colossal garrison and military machine, like the Huns of Attila.[141]

Since the social class issue was so basic to him, Chernyshevsky paid hardly any attention to political structure and institutions. Sometimes he toyed with the idea that a dictatorship, even a monarchical dictatorship, was the only way of realising the general good and of overcoming class selfishness and economic exploitation.[142]

It was not political forms but the social structure that was of decisive importance to Chernyshevsky. "It does not matter whether there is a Tsar or not," wrote the young man in his diary, "whether there is a constitution or not; what matters are social relations, whether one class exploits another."[143] "It will be best," he writes elsewhere, "if autocracy holds us in thrall until a democratic spirit has developed, so that with the onset of popular government power will *de jure* and *de facto* pass into the hands of the lowest and most numerous class—peasants and journeymen and workers, so that we can avoid any kind of provisional state."[144] Not unlike Herzen, Chernyshevsky was thus swept off his feet by Tsar Alexander II's first Rescript. "You love righteousness"—he quoted the Psalmist—"and hate wickedness. Therefore God, your God, has anointed you. . . . The history of Russia from this year will be as different from all which preceded it as the difference between Peter's era and early times. The new life which now begins for us, will be as much more beautiful, prosperous, brilliant and happy, in comparison to our former life."[145] Some historians believe they detect in this hymn of the Tsar's a piece of cunning Machiavellianism: Chernyshevsky had from the start no illusions about the outcome of the emancipation of the serfs. All he wanted was to heighten the eventual disenchantment of the peasant masses and bring revolution nearer.[146]

Whether Chernyshevsky was momentarily swayed by enthusiasm or acted on the principle of the worse the better, he never wavered in his theoretical stand that all the land, including the seigneurial domain, belonged to the nation, more specifically to the labouring peasants, and consequently in his insistent demand for emancipation with land.[147] Although he was prepared to concede compensation to the landlords, so as not to destroy a whole class by the stroke of the pen, he would never agree to it being paid by the peasants. At most it should come from the state. He would not of course hear of any services by the liberated peasants to the landlords: "to maintain obligatory labour, would be, in essence to maintain the bondage law. The people could understand this in no other way, and they would be right. There is no need to say what consequences would follow if the people were left with the conviction that serfdom remained intact."[148]

Chernyshevsky seemed almost to sigh with relief, when he was able to unmask the results of the great reform as a devious deal between the Tsar and the landlords to change the form, but to keep the substance, of serfdom. This he did in the famous "Letters without Address"[149] of February 1862, addressed in fact to the Tsar but forbidden by the censorship to be published. In some cases, he wrote, the "emancipated" peasant now had to pay 1.10 roubles for the one rouble he had been paying in the past.[150] Since events had shown that half-measures were intended to frustrate any hope of true reform, and to prop up the historic alliance of autocracy and aristocracy, the whole system had to be abolished root and branch.[151] This meant a reaffirmation of the importance of politics. In exile Chernyshevsky countered the argument that political reform could not feed a single hungry peasant by saying that political freedom was like air: you could go without food for days, but you would not survive without air for more than a few minutes.[152] Chernyshevsky's earlier underestimation of politics was also conditioned by his identification of constitutionalism with the rule of the bourgeoisie and the operation of the market mechanism.[153]

He began to realise that no effective struggle against the alliance of monarch and aristocracy was possible without political liberty, and no revolutionary change without the seizure of political power. Chernyshevsky was unable to put his trust in the working of economic forces alone to bring about a social-economic reorganisation of Russia.[154] Economics was not a problem of production and of economic growth, but of equitable distribution, and of doing justice to the real producers of all wealth—the labouring masses—by securing to them the whole net product of their labour. He defined economics as "the science of man's material welfare depending on the objects and situations of labour".[155] Like the Narodniks and their heirs the Social Revolutionaries, Chernyshevsky and Dobrolyubov preferred the division of mankind into toilers and parasitic idlers to the distinction between proletarians and bourgeois.[156] They were in fact inclined to identify man with toiler, treating the idler as in some way no-man, at all events as failing to assert his humanity and liberty in the tangible effects of labour—man's essential means of self-expression, his title to recognition and rights, and sole source of social wealth.

"Man is not an economic machine"—he wrote—"but a living being endowed on the one hand with various needs, and on the other with reason. They forget that in human society, over the blind, irrational, pitiless principles of the relationship of demand and supply, another principle should prevail—the law of the satisfaction of human needs and the rational organisation of economic strength. Supposing that the best system is formed without the interference of rational intention, by some instinct of the manufacturers, they deny the necessity of theory and accept the inviolability of practice."[157]

This explains why though not being a pure agrarian and while welcoming industrialisation as inevitable and desirable, Chernyshevsky was one of the first Russian thinkers to preach the imperative need to skip the stage of unrestrained *laissez-faire*, competitive capitalism and its inevitable consequence, a mass proletariat.[158] Without any idealisation of the commune, which he believed to have come into existence and to have been maintained because the peasants thought it advantageous to them, Chernyshevsky came to look upon it as a cornerstone of the future socialist organisation of production, along with the urban industrial cooperatives. It was above all a means of obviating the stage of capitalist organisation and centralisation; with all the squalor and injustices brought in their wake. He invoked the Hegelian "Trinity" to prop up his belief that the third, final stage was usually a restoration of the first, in a much higher and more differentiated form.[159] He also looked to the commune of the future to apply all the facilities supplied by modern technology and large-scale production. While free from the romantic idealisation of ancient institutions and customs, as well as of ascetic traditions, Chernyshevsky firmly rejected the passion for economic growth as an end in itself and treated as humbug the view that it was calculated to benefit indirectly all and sundry, including the workers.[160] "Our Siberia, where ordinary people enjoy well-being, is superior to England where the majority of the people suffer extreme want."[161]

(e) ELITE AND VIOLENCE

Chernyshevsky could not but view freedom as real only in so far as it secured well-being. Formal freedom unaccompanied by economic security was to him a mockery. Politics could not be divorced from the social problem. The peasant question was thus both at the same time the social and the political issue of Russia.

Already in the early fifties, but irrevocably under the impact of the disappointment with peasant emancipation, Chernyshevsky became convinced that salvation would not come to the peasants from government action or the objective workings of the economy or the enlightened self-interest and generosity of the nobility. The peasants could only save themselves by their own exertions, in other words, by a violent uprising, a revolution. In 1850 he was experiencing an "irresistible expectation of the revolution and a longing for it", feeling sure that it was a matter of only a few years.[162] Early enough he thought of a plan of issuing a forged manifesto granting the peasants freedom with land in the name of the Holy Synod.[163] The commotion caused by it would result in bloody uprisings. Although these would be suppressed, the masses would be sufficiently stirred up to try again soon after. He also speculated about tyrannicide. "Arise from your sleep"—he called upon the *muzhiks*, hinting at the great peasant *jacquerie* of the past.[164] He was fully conscious of the tremendous dangers he was conjuring up in rousing the deep-seated savage resentment of the peasant masses, their inveterate distrust and hatred of all the other classes and those passions of destruction, which would spare no monuments of art and no cultural values. But the "pathway of history does not resemble the pavements of the Nevsky prospect: it cuts now across dusty, dirty fields, now across swamps, now across wilds. . . ."[165]

It may have been not only the feeble reaction of the peasants to disappointment with the Emancipation Act—just a few scattered riots—but also precisely the fear of the masses running amok one day and destroying civilisation that directed Chernyshevsky's thoughts towards an elitist orientation and stern voluntarism. Chernyshevsky's elite, as it appears in *What is to be Done?*[166] is an elite of understanding and character, of a rational egoism which can be driven to purest self-sacrificing idealism and constructive social endeavour. Its ideal specimen, the athlete of socialism, Rahmetov, understands the course of history, the demands of the hour, the imperatives of science and social morality, and has the ability and strength of character and the freedom from selfish temptations and diversions, in brief all the virtues necessary to carry out in practice what he demands in theory: He lives the life of extreme asceticism. He sleeps on a bed of nails. He says to his comrades in the cooperative "my linen is your linen, my wife is your wife". Lopukhov, his comrade, withdraws when he feels that his wife has transferred her affection to another, and stays friends with both. His whole life is a preparation for the arduous task on behalf of the people.[167]

"Such persons are few in number, but through them life in general blossoms, and without them it would be choked; they are few in number but they enable all other men to breathe, for without them these would be stifled. Honest and good men exist in plenty, but those of whom I am thinking are rare specimens. They are like thyme in tea, like the bouquet of a fine wine, they are the source of the strength and the fragrance. They are the flower of the optimates; they are the primal source of energy; they are the salt of the earth."[168] In his tribute to Lessing,[169] Chernyshevsky quite explicitly attributes greater effectiveness to the role of a moral and intellectual elite than to economic and political developments. "Though politics and industry may move more noisily along in the foreground of history, history none the less bears witness to the fact that knowledge is the essential energy to which politics, industry and all else in human life are subordinated."[170] Chernyshevsky does not seem to be bothered by his own earlier statement that economic conditions "may be the fundamental causes of almost all the happenings in other fields and in the higher spheres of life".[171]

For Chernyshevsky it was still opinion that ruled the world. In that respect progress was the progress of enlightenment and understanding among the most enlightened, the most sensitive and daring. They were like the vanguard of the conquering army, the first to reach the destination. The rest were sure to fall in eventually and to join the vanguard. Guided by the will for knowledge and the desire for happiness, the masses could not fail to come up, and once they reached the peak, they would behold the uplands to the widest horizons and rejoice.[172]

No one probably contributed more to the creation of the myth and the ideal, indeed the living type of the servant of the people, the dedicated fighter for the salvation of the masses, as a member of a semi-religious, semi-monastic order than Chernyshevsky. The West can hardly understand the deep seriousness with which professional revolutionaries, in fact idealists of all kinds in Russia and Poland, treated their calling. Herzen said that the Russian post-1862 generation were almost all out of *What is to be Done?*[173] Berdyaev called it a sort of catechism of Russian nihilism.[174] Chernyshevsky was aware of it and full of anticipation. "This type sprang up not long ago and is growing rapidly. It was engendered by the times. . . . In a few years these people will be called upon . . . proud and modest, stern and kind . . . again this type will return and in greater numbers, for there will be more good in the world . . . eventually all people will be of this type . . . and they will find it difficult to understand how there ever was a time when it was considered a peculiar type, and not the general nature of all people."[175]

The test of belonging and acting as members of the vanguard was self-sacrifice, and not ascendancy over others as born leaders. It is no accident that in such stark contrast to Marx and Engels, Chernyshevsky sensed the dangers lurking in the Darwinist theory of the struggle for existence, natural selection and survival of the fittest to the ideas of socialist brotherhood and equality.[176]

Chapter Four

THE ANTINOMIES — BAKUNIN AND LAVROV

The Russian revolutionaries of the post-emancipation period were tormented by a whole series of dilemmas. They were determined to achieve the abolition of the whole Russian social order, indeed of the historic Russian state. They were at the same time most anxious to prevent Russia from entering upon the seemingly inevitable road of a capitalist-industrial revolution and a bourgeois-liberal regime. So they substituted human choice for their earlier reliance upon the historic dialectic. Extreme revolutionism went hand in hand with the apotheosis of Russian nationalism and with the imperative to by-pass the bourgeois-democratic revolution of the West in order to bring about a socialist revolution based upon the ancient Russian village commune. Time was however against them. Russia was beginning its industrial revolution, and capitalism was threatening to dissolve the peasant communes and to proletarianise the Russian masses. So it was a matter of utmost urgency: now or never. Either the revolution was made here and now, or it would be postponed *sine die*; at all events, the unique chance of establishing a wonderful Russian socialist society, without having to experience the frustrations and the miseries of the West, would be irretrievably lost.

(*a*) MASS SPONTANEITY AND REVOLUTIONARY VOLUNTARISM

Who was to make the revolution? Ideally, the peasant masses themselves, in the footsteps of the *jacqueries* of Stenka Razin and Pugachev. The Russian theoreticians had however no illusion as to their backwardness, apathy and lack of revolutionary consciousness and organisation. Even those who like Bakunin glorified the revolutionary and socialist instincts of the *muzhik* and prophesied a violent peasant uprising, made a clear distinction between an elemental insurrection and the constructive phase of rebuilding the social and political order.[177]

The revolutionaries abhorred the idea of putting themselves above the masses, of usurping the right of the people to decide and to act by itself, and to shape its own destiny. Yet, there had to be an elite, a vanguard, indeed a revolutionary dictatorship of one kind or another. The Russian thinkers resorted to infinite mental acrobatics to abjure the idea, while working out a scheme for it; and then to reassure themselves that the revolutionary dictatorship would not perpetuate itself, but fade away and let the masses themselves take over, and build a loose federation of free communes on the ruins of a centralised coercive state apparatus. In the process of educating the revolutionaries to immerse themselves in the popular soul, efface themselves and their distinctiveness, to the point of abandoning university studies, before the simplicities of the peasant's way of life, the prophets inevitably came to take the utmost pains in training cadres of elitist leadership.

Perhaps the most sincere and the noblest representative of this outlook was Pyotr Lavrov (1823-1900), a former artillery officer and a professor at the Military Academy. Deep concern with the dilemma of revolution led him late in life to socialism, exile, emigration and intense publicistic activity as editor of *Vperyod*. In the West, Lavrov developed close contacts with Western socialism, and enjoyed the friendship, among others, of Marx and Engels.[178]

Once the consciousness of the historic injustice inherent in a culture that was the exclusive privilege of the ruling classes and was being maintained at the cost of the labouring classes, had seized the public mind, especially the best among the privileged, they would not rest—taught Lavrov in his *Historical Letters* (1868)—until they had repaid their debt to the deprived and righted their wrongs. Out of a revulsion from mindless routine and indifference to evil bred by habit and tradition, and of course not without the influence of socialist thought, Lavrov came to put all the emphasis upon the vital role of critical thought, of an incessant re-examination of existing reality, its foundations, its premises and its consequences. At that particular moment the critical thought of the age was called upon to organise the campaign of united labour against monopolistic capital[179] by changing the docile submission of the toilers to their exploiters, the acceptance of a fate allegedly imposed by the decrees of providence and the laws of the universe as a punishment for their ancestors' sins—into pride in their productive capacity and in the virtues of labour.

In his essay on *The Definition of Progress* by N. K. Mikhailovsky, Lavrov says that in fact the ideal of justice had at all times been linked to the notion of human dignity. The man who violated another's human dignity was always considered unjust. Only the old criteria were faulty, vague or just wrong.[180] Now critical thought had found ways to accord to all members of society a recognition of their human dignity, of the right to equal enjoyment of goods, to equal conditions for everyone's individual development, and as full a participation in running the common weal as possible.[181] In Lavrov's own words "the physical, intellectual and ethical development of the individual, the materialisation of truth and justice in social structure—such is the brief formula which, I believe, encompasses everything that can be regarded as progress".[182]

Nikolai K. Mikhailovsky (1842-1904),[183] another populist spokesman of shining integrity, came up against a mighty difficulty which Comte and Spencer had discerned before him. As far as the individual was concerned, progress meant ever freer, fuller and more diversified self-expression, in short the breeding of an integral personality. In the social sphere however, progress signified growing differentiation, division of labour, specialisation—all needed for the achievement of greater output, more efficiency and economy of effort. In primitive simple society, with no division of labour, conditions had forced man to use, train and realise all his potentialities, because he had to provide all the needs of himself and his family by himself. In modern society man was becoming more and more a cog, at most, an expert in a tiny function, while all his needs were being provided by society, using innumerable experts. His personality was increasingly more stunted and atrophied, not to speak of all the restraints which complex modern urban civilisation imposed upon his freedom of choice and movement. So what was progress in modern society was regress for the individual. In contrast, the primitive ages were in fact a school of character and the seed bed of personality growth.[184] We are not concerned here with Mikhailovsky's remedies, like the distinction between simple and composite division of labour, with the former designed to salvage as much personal initiative and individual diversification as possible.[185] We give him as an example of the knots in which Narodnik thinkers became entangled in their preoccupation with the problem of the dignity of the human personality in an egalitarian modern society.

A sense of guilt towards the millions of serfs caused them to idealise the pristine purity and simplicity of the peasants and often to castigate themselves as parasites, as impotent talkers, hypocrites, ineffectual Hamlets. In some cases this led indeed to a form of populist anti-intellectualism: instinct, empiricism, ancient traditions and customs were extolled as a better school, and a safer guide than cogitation and ratiocination. But Lavrov was a thorough rationalist, who had no patience with gut thinking and acting from instinct and habit. The function which he considered most creative was, as we have already hinted, critical thinking, and what he feared most was a stagnant, unthinking society. In his polemic against Mikhailovsky, who was at such a loss to reconcile human diversity with equality, and justice with modernity, Lavrov pointed out that critical thought always emerged in the single brain of a non-conformist, often an eccentric individual, and never in all brains at the same time.[186]

Lavrov's philosophy was thus intensely activistic. In so far as it called for conscious effort and for the deliberate reshaping of reality and exalted the role of critical thinking as the instrument of change, it was bound to raise the intellectual elite to the pinnacle of society. Lavrov's very distinction between culture and civilisation amounted to giving preference to rational social engineering over instinctive, custom-ridden social existence in the organic society. Lavrov taught a "subjective type of sociology" and deprecated talk about iron laws or objective laws in history. In his view, the latter were rationalisations resorted to by existing establishments which felt endangered by efforts to change reality.[187] Similarly, he thought all significant history was subjective. A historian with a faith in an ideal and in a set of values in process of realisation, in brief a faith that history had a direction, was bound to attach decisive importance to those moments or events which seemed to him to have promoted (or retarded) the unfolding of the allegedly preordained course of history, and to treat the "indifferent" events, problems and epochs as of no consequence. Such a philosophy accorded paramount importance to enlightened guides and inspired prophets, that is to say to a conscious minority and a vanguard of activists. Without them, history would indeed become a stagnant pool.[188] The Russian village commune seemed to be the protection against impersonal centralisation and elitism alike.

Herzen, Chernyshevsky and the other theoreticians with a more lively awareness of economic problems, or a greater reluctance to yield to Slavophile romanticism, were inclined to put all the emphasis on the commune as an economic institution, a form of collective ownership and periodic redistribution of the land. Shchapov, The Populist publicist, was primarily concerned with the mir, the village assembly. He envisaged Russia as a vast panorama of direct democracies, the general assemblies of all members adopting unanimous decisions, maintaining contact with the mirs in the neighbourhood on a footing of equality, and viewing the distant central government as a superimposed alien power to which tribute—taxes—had to be paid and men for the army had to be supplied. The village meetings were the real Russia, and they had by their very existence—he thought, like Herzen—preserved authentic Russia from the Tartar yoke, Tsarist autocracy, from Peter the Great's reformed Russia, from German bureaucracy and from other forces of oppression and dissolution. In this respect the forthcoming revolution could be envisaged as a kind of restoration and renovation. The mirs would take over Russia: the masses themselves by themselves, for themselves, not only by doing away with Tsarist autocracy and bureaucracy but also by not receiving the state as a gift from an outside self-appointed revolutionary vanguard, with a claim to watch over the fruits of their work.[189]

The problems of political and social revolution, of leaders and led, of the *mir*, popular spontaneity and revolutionary organisation were also discussed in the early 1870's under the impact of the Paris Commune and the dissolution of the First International as a result of the Marx-Bakunin confrontation. The Paris Commune appeared as a new type of state, an anti-state in fact. It "personified the anti-state idea, the social revolution . . . the living negation of dictatorship and government!"[190] It was direct democracy, direct self-rule by the people in permanent assembly, the very negation of the rule of man over man, and—in Marx's words—of bureaucracy, church, army, police, in brief the whole superimposed state apparatus, the watchdog of the privileged classes. Bakunin and Lavrov shared the same views. The latter grew lyrical at the sight of a revolution without great names, made by unknown men, the people themselves, simple workers, "honest, intelligent, resolute", exploding the myth of the indispensable role of the bourgeoisie and officialdom. "The Commune had shown that a worker's government was possible."[191]

Then why had the Commune failed? The Bakuninists had their answer. The popular uprising had been taken over and frittered away by the Jacobins. Instead of simply releasing the people's energy and letting it do the work of destruction as instinct dictated, in preparation for the flowering of creative energy into small direct democracies immediately the ground had been cleared, Jacobin-trained leaders stepped in. They took over the helm and began to issue decrees from above designed to do away with bourgeois abuses through revolutionary dictatorship, that is to say another form of central government. As Rousseau had foreseen, the representatives of the people soon became its rulers and dictators. The people lost interest in the Commune, just as they had done in the French Revolution, and allowed their leaders to be guillotined.[192]

Lavrov is not very far from the Bakuninists in his analysis of the reasons for the failure of the Commune. He agrees on the fateful legacy of 1793, but puts the emphasis upon the lack of intellectual preparation, of a clear view and strong resolve to abolish the state by a socialist economic programme. The Commune failed to become the true workers' state and the nucleus of a socialist federation, because it lacked the courage and the clearsightedness to sever proletarian aspirations from bourgeois interests. What Lavrov seems to envisage is a syndicalist type of society, "the independent commune of the proletariat", consisting of a federation of syndicalist communes.[193] Seemingly speaking of economics, he is in fact envisaging the elimination of politics by a total social-economic transformation at a single blow carried out in the form of direct action by the masses themselves.[194]

"Never under any circumstances"—writes Lavrov—"have the socialists the right to forget that in the present state of the historical struggle, the economic problem dominates all others, and that until the economic revolution has carried out every one of its fundamental points, nothing has been done. . . . Today there is no field, neither religious, national nor political, in which the proletarian workmen have or can have the moral right to follow the path of the ruling classes in whole or in part."[195]

Lavrov's condemnation of centralised statehood is also visible in the reasons he gives for the failure of the First International. It floundered on the rock of centralised power: the General Council was aiming to become the centralised government of "a state without territory", composed of the national parties of the existing bourgeois nations. The component parts of the International resented dictation from above, lost interest in socialist internationalism and became deeply concerned with their own countries' political realities.[196]

With all their abomination of centralised power and their faith in mass spontaneity, even Bakuninist anarchists and Lavrovist anti-étatists could not help recognising the immaturity of the Russian peasants and the absolute necessity of a revolutionary vanguard.

(b) ANARCHY AND DICTATORIAL LEADERSHIP

In his famous letter to Nechaev of June 2, 1870, Bakunin refuses "to acknowledge the usefulness, or even the possibility of any revolution except a spontaneous or a people's social revolution. Any other revolution is dishonest, harmful, and spells death to liberty and the people. It dooms them to new penury and new slavery."[197] Any other type of revolution—such as a conspirational coup, barricades—had become impossible because of the proliferation of centralising forces such as railways, the telegraph, modern arms and new military organisation and administrative techniques—all techniques of the systematic enslavement and exploitation of the masses. Moreover, as a result of its ignorance and disunity—Bakunin goes on—the people were unable to formulate the programme, to systematise it and to unite for its sake. They needed helpers. "Where can one find these helpers? This is the most difficult question in any revolution."[198]

In Lavrov's view the masses always followed the banner which at the decisive moment proclaimed the most precise programme and fixed the clearest objectives. The masses followed those who were resolute and did not hesitate. If such firm guidance was not forthcoming from the most determined and the most sincere members of the intelligentsia, they would inevitably fall back upon the old traditions and follow their natural, traditional superiors. "And then even the most heroic actions, even the most disinterested energies will not be able to prevent a return to the old evils, though in somewhat changed form."[199]

All the Russian prophets of revolution, with the exception of Tkachev and Nechaev, took the greatest pains to seek reassurance that the revolutionary vanguard would never degenerate into an oligarchy, driven by ambition, vainglory, love of power, self-seeking. They must at all cost remain an elite of service, self-sacrifice, martyrdom. By their lives they should set an example of total dedication, ascetic self-denial, tireless exertion in the service of the cause. They were not out to lead, to foist their views and ideas on the people. They were called upon to elicit, make conscious, help to articulate and systematise what was slumbering in the unawakened or half-awakened thoughts, dreams and wishes, instincts of the people. They did not go to the people to teach them, but to absorb their spirit, to learn to decipher their sentiments, so as to be able to comprehend them, to attune themselves better to them and to learn how they could effectively lend a helping hand, put their knowledge and training at the disposal of the peasants. Bakunin, who was so sure that the masses of Europe were pregnant with revolution, had no doubt about what was the historic general will of the Russian *muzhiks* from the days of Stenka Razin and Pugachev to his own day. It was repeatedly expressed by them in chronic rioting, in forms of speech and proverb, in the deilberations of the *mir* and in their musings about a better day: common ownership of the land and liberation from state interference, officials, policeman, tax collectors and of course landlords.[200]

The revolutionaries came to the people to awaken their courage, liberate them from their fears and inhibitions; not to lead, but to unleash the masses' will. "He who wants to be at the head of a popular movement must adopt it [the "people's programme"] as a whole and execute it. He who tries to foist his own programme on the people will be left holding the baby."[201] Bakunin's recipe for a reconciliation of mass spontaneity with moral guidance from outside was an unacknow-ledged secret vanguard: the overthrow of the "so-called bourgeois civilisation by a spontaneous people's revolution invisibly led, not by an official dictatorship, but by a nameless and collective one composed of those in favour of total people's liberation from all oppression and everywhere acting in support of a common aim and in accordance with a common programme".[202]

The revolution breaks out spontaneously and it is led on by a secret confraternity which has prepared secret cadres of local leadership and subordinated them to a secret central committee.[203] All are acting in absolute secrecy and are subject to the most stringent discipline. Once a decision has been taken by the fraternity, all are bound to obey it uncon-ditionally. Appointments will be made from above with the help of trusted and tested comrades.[204] Bakunin's determination to hold the stick by both ends—popular spontaneity and secret dictatorial mani-pulation—is quite bewildering.

It is also difficult to see how Bakunin, the voluntarist, differs at all from those who had a more deterministic view and insisted on such conditions as the ripeness of historic development and hour of opportunity. "Thus the sole aim of a secret society must be not the creation of an artificial power outside the people, but the rousing, uniting and organising of the spontaneous power of the people; there-fore, the only possible, the only revolutionary army is not outisde the people. It is in the people itself. It is impossible to arouse the people arti-ficially. People's revolutions are born from the course of events, or from historical currents, which continuously and usually slowly, from under-ground and unseen, increasingly embrace, penetrate and stir up the masses, until the hidden forces emerge from the ground and their turbulent waters break all barriers and destroy everything that impedes their course."[205] Revolutions cannot be artificially induced, they can at most be hastened and facilitated by an organised revolutionary under-ground. There were historical periods when revolutions were simply impossible; there were other periods when they were inevitable. "In which of the two periods are we today? I am deeply convinced that we are in a period of a general, inevitable popular revolution . . . a popular social revolution is inevitable everywhere within Europe as a whole. . . . All secret societies who wish to be really useful to it must, first of all, renounce all nervousness, all impatience. They must not sleep, on the contrary, they must be as ready as possible every minute of the time, alert and always capable of seizing every opportunity. But, at the same time, they must be harnessed and organised, not with a view to an imminent rising, but aiming at long and patient underground work, taking as an example your [Nechaev's] friends the Jesuit Fathers."[206] The emphasis is thus put upon permanent mobilisation, and no less on the need to be circumspect and patient.

The secret organisation is not to constitute the army of the revolution. The people as a whole is the revolutionary army. The fraternity is its GHQ "an organiser of the people's power", a middle-man between popular instinct and revolutionary thought. "To strive to foist on the people your own thoughts—foreign to its instincts—implies to wish to make it subservient to a new state.[207] The organisation must accept in all sincerity the idea that it is a servant and a helper, but never a commander of the people, never under any pretext its manager, not even under the pretext of the people's welfare."

But let us see how this secret collective organisation or, as Bakunin himself calls it, "collective dictatorship of our organisation"[208] will act and what tasks it proposes to take upon itself. It is called upon not only to insure the success of the people's revolution through propaganda and the unification of popular power; not only to destroy totally the whole existing economic, social and political order, but after victory to prevent at all costs the imposition of any, even of their own revolutionary form of state power, over the people, "because any [such] power, whatever it called itself, would inevitably subject the people to the old slavery in a new form".[209] In a heavily underlined passage Bakunin defines the main task and purpose of the organisation: "To help the people to achieve self-determination on a basis of complete and comprehensive liberty, without the slightest interference from even temporary or transitional power, i.e. without any mediation of the state."[210]

Bakunin repeats again his protestation of bitter hostility to all "official power", to all "publicly acknowledged dictatorship", "even if it be ultra-revolutionary power".[211] But he himself is aware that the reader will wonder how can anarchists influence the people, without resorting to force and with no power? How will they direct the revolution? "An invisible force—recognised by no one, imposed by no one—through which the collective dictatorship of our organisation will be all the mightier, the more it remains invisible and unacknowledged, the more it remains without any official legality and significance."[212]

In other words, through manipulation. Significantly, the opponent of all state power, even temporary or transitional power, does not envisage at all the dissolution and disappearance of the secret dictatorial organisation after the people's victory. On the contrary, he fears that in the midst of a successful spontaneous revolution in Russia, after the people have chased away all their oppressors, abolished all state laws and powers, broken all dams, in the midst of general anarchy "the enormous quantity of mud which has accumulated within the people is stirred and rises to the surface".[213] Clever, ambitious and unscrupulous usurpers of power will then emerge in various places and fight each other. The collective secret dictatorship will step in to save the people from "struggling without purposes or plan".[214] Will their intervention not be usurpation? In what way is their title better than that of other anonymous pretenders to the right to guide the masses? If the people are to have the right to uninhibited self-expression, why should the secret organisation have to interfere at all and not let the people act as their good instincts dictated to them?

To small anonymous groups of the organisation, scattered over the whole territory of the Empire, "firmly united, inspired by a common ideal and a common aim which are applied everywhere" would pursue an ideal "which expresses the very essence of people's instincts, desires and demands", "strong in their solidarity which ties all the obscure groups into one organic whole . . . around themselves a circle of people more or less devoted to the same ideal and naturally subject to their influence".[215]

His characterisation of the secret organisation as not being really a party like any other party, with interests of its own, but the quintessence of the people, foreshadows Lenin's conception of the Bolshevik party. "This dictatorship is free from all self-interest, vanity and ambition, for it is anonymous, invisible and does not give advantage or honour or official recognition of power to a member of the group or to the groups themselves. It does not threaten the liberty of the people because it is free from all official character. It is not placed above the people like state power, because its whole aim, defined by its programme, consists of the fullest realisation of the liberty of the people. This dictatorship is not contrary to the free development and self-determination of the people, or to its organisation from below according to its own customs and instincts, for it acts on the people only by the natural personal influence of its members who are not invested with any power and are scattered like an invisible net in all regions, districts and rural communities and each one in his own place and in agreement with others, trying to direct the spontaneous revolutionary movement of the people towards a general plan which has been fully agreed and defined beforehand. This plan for the organisation of the people's liberty must firstly be firmly and clearly delineated as regards its main principles and aims in order to exclude the possibility of misunderstanding and deviation by its members who will be called upon to help in its realisation. Secondly, it must be sufficiently wide and human to embrace and take in all the inescapable changes which arise from differing circumstances, all varied movements arising from the variety of national life."[216]

The task was not just of propaganda and setting up the organisation within the people itself and uniting the "divided strength of the people" into a mighty force which could break the state, but was also "capable of remaining in being in the midst of revolution itself, without breaking apart or altering its direction on the morrow of the people's liberation".[217] Needless to say the secret organisation, particularly its basic nucleus, the executive committee consiting of three to five members chosen by the society—"the People's Fraternity"—and elected for an indefinite number of years, had to be obeyed unconditionally (except where their order contradicts the programme and rules adopted by the society as a whole); and the brothers or leaders (appointed by the central committee) of the regional groups must be composed of persons "who are most determined, most intelligent and as far as possible knowledgeable, i.e. intelligent by experience, who are passionately and undeviatingly devoted, who have, as far as possible, renounced all personal interests and have renounced once and for all, for life or for death itself, all that attracts people, all material comforts and delights, all satisfaction of ambition, status and fame. They must be totally and wholly absorbed by one passion, the people's liberation. They must be people who would renounce personal historical importance while they are alive and even a name in history after their death."[218]

Such people needed above all passion. The degree of self-denial demanded of them could not be arrived at by reasoning or external control and compulsion. Passion meant energy. Admittedly "energy without sensible guidance is fruitless and absurd. Allied to passion there must be reason, cold, calculating, real and practical, but also based on theory, educated by knowledge and experience, wide ranging but not overlooking details, capable of understanding and discerning people, capable of grasping realities, relationships and conditions."[219] But "passion alone can bring about this miracle within a man, this strength without an effort".[220]

Its source was not in cogitation, strong intellectual conviction, but stemmed from actual conditions which bred the most intense forms of indignation, protest, hatred, rage, so obsessive as to leave one with no choice, and with nothing to lose, but a craving for revenge and a vision of redemption. The great sources of such passionate energy were in Bakunin's view to be found among the brigands, the thieves, the tramps, the outlaws, the outcasts of Russian society. Distasteful as such an idea might be to beautiful souls, those forces had to be mobilised and utilised. It was a terrifying idea, Bakunin admits, but the Russian revolution was bound to be a terrible event.[221]

Lavrov's difficulties were still greater than those of Bakunin, and yet on the whole their views coincided. He was at one with the anarchist prophet in stating emphatically that "revolutionary socialists must give up their old ideas of being able to replace the state, after they have succeeded through a lucky stroke in destroying it, by introducing a new form of government through the processes of law and making a gift of this to the unprepared masses. We do not want a new constraining authority to take the place of that which already exists, whatever the origin of this new authority may be."[222] But as we have said, Lavrov was a thorough rationalist. He despised "fanatical religious revolutionaries".[223] He was suspicious of irrational exaltations and enthusiasms. He did not believe in the stability or durability of revolutionary changes which had not been carefully thought out, were not based upon data and statistics and were not carried out according to plan. Faith was no substitute for critical thought. Any kind of irrationalism and denigration of the intellect and study were abhorrent to him, condemn as he might academic careerism and claims to privilege by men with diplomas. Lavrov was concerned with the question how "to unite the proletariat with the intellectual part of the bourgeoisie which comes to join its ranks out of sincere conviction".[224]

His scenario for a revolution envisages a series of riots breaking out simultaneously after some grave local incident. The army, in part at least, refuses to come out against the people. The members of the social revolutionary union within the existing *mirs* and *artels* (organised groups of peasant industrial workers) who had been saturating their comrades with revolutionary propaganda emerge as organisers. Steps are taken at once to confiscate estates in favour of the peasant communes, to expel or kill the landlords and kulaks and to merge all property "into a single property of all the workers". Once the old authorities have been toppled, the social revolutionary union is transformed into the natural core of the new organisation of society. Lavrov hastens to add that "they will have nothing new or artificial to invent; they are already members of groups historically formed in the people, of peasant communes and artisan groups".[225] This fact would, in the eyes of Lavrov, prevent them from becoming a sharply delineated, centralised, super-imposed dictatorial authority, a revolutionary dictatorship. The revolution would be carried out by a majority at the inspiration and initiative and under the leadership of an organised minority of the people (including a small proportion of the intelligentsia). A national federation of Russian revolutionary communes and *artels* would rise from the ruins of the centralised Russian Empire and act as the creator of a new workers' socialism based upon common ownership and compulsory common labour, while receiving its inspiration from the socialist-revolutionary cells and thus escaping the dangers of extremism, faction and irresponsibility in a fluid situation.

(c) THE ABOLITION OF THE STATE

As for guarantees against party members becoming a clique, a bureaucracy or a state apparatus, Lavrov considered the most effective would be their staying on in the communes and *artels* and continuing to do their share in the common task, including physical labour. The vigilance and control exercised by the activists, but above all their purity of character and devotion to the common cause, would be the most effective guarantee.

In the dislocation and turmoil of revolution a "directing council, which would represent the rule of a minority", might be inevitable for organising and carrying supplies, for instance; but "the directors must remember that, however energetic their activities may be in the first moments, they have no moral right to preserve their dictatorship a single minute longer than is necessary". At the first opportunity they would step down and leave all power to the free associations of the people.[226]

While he understood the need to have a central organisation for essential services, Lavrov was again at pains to warn against a standing army and national police. He envisaged the danger of a coalition of capitalist states trying to strangle the revolutionary regime. He built his plans for defence upon partisan warfare and upon the aid of socialists and workers in the interventionist countries in sabotaging the war effort of their governments, "in the event of it falling to Russia to begin the struggle" before open (revolutionary) outbreaks occurred in other countries. The possibility of Russia becoming the spearhead of the European or world revolution threw Lavrov back most paradoxically upon the anti-intellectual attitude of Bakunin. On the centenary of the 1773 uprising of Pugachev he wrote an article in which he compared the significance of that *jacquerie* with the American Revolution, the French Revolution and the popular ferment in England in the late eighteenth century: "The manifestoes of an illiterate Cossack who followed an absurd religious faith, signed with the forged name of an idiot whom nobody knew [Peter III], contained more vital social principles, more solid promises, more threatening and certain prophecies for the future, than those contained in all the humanitarian 'codes' of Catherine II, and even in all the liberal and radical prophecies against throne and altar, that echoed along the banks of the Thames, the Seine and the Delaware."[227]

Bakunin wrote in the same vein: "From being rooted in the most cynical and brutal reality of the most absolute state, the Russians are now reaching out for the most daring human ideas and the most absolute negation of the state."[228]

Similarly the mildly socialist economist, Flerovsky, author of the *Alphabet of Social Sciences* (1873), and before that *The situation of the working class in Russia* (1869), while complaining of Russia being at the "tail end of civilisation", called upon the Russians to espouse "a great idea", by which he meant socialism, a social system based upon universal solidarity and cooperation, excluding the class war that was tearing the Western world apart. This would enable the Russians to play a great and glorious role in history, and put themselves at the head of civilisation and to guide mankind.[228a]

Lavrov was an educated man, too well versed in the history of the French and other revolutions not to be worried, in spite of all his faith in human nature and in the educational influence of good teachings and just institutions, by the danger of counter-revolutionary subversion, sabotage, intrigue, abuse of power by some revolutionary functionaries, and by the fact that these constituted the ultimate cause and rationale of terrorist revolutionary dictatorships. "Some might think it best to use the customary methods of the old society: to draw up a code of socialist laws with an appropriate section 'On Punishments', to select from among the most reliable persons (in the main naturally, from members of the social revolutionary union) a 'public security' commission for the dispensation of justice and retribution; to organise a communal and territorial police corps of detectives to snuff out lawbreaking and of guardians of propriety to look after 'order', to place 'evidently dangerous' people under socialist police surveillance; to establish the requisite number of prisons, and probably of gallows, together with a corresponding assortment of socialist gaolers and executioners; and then, to implement socialist legal justice and set into motion this whole rejuvenated machine of the old order in the name of the principles of workers' socialism."[229]

Lavrov abhorred such a development, and placed all his trust in "direct people's summary justice", in knowing how to undertake with regard to criminals such measures as they themselves regard to be most expedient: the way in which the vigilante associations in the Wild West of the United States had acted. "Mob rule," Szamuely calls it.[230]

No one understood better than Lavrov the danger of a minority revolution issuing in a minority dictatorship, as may be seen from his pamphlet against Tkachev, "To the Russian Social-Revolutionary Youth". "History and psychology both prove that any unlimited power, any dictatorship, corrupts even the best people, and that even men of genius, who wish to benefit their nations by decree cannot succeed in this. Every dictatorship must surround itself by forces of compulsion, by blindly obedient weapons. Every dictatorship has been compelled to suppress by force not only the reactionaries, but also the people who simply disagree with its methods. Every imposed dictatorship has had to spend more time, effort and energy in the struggle for power against its rivals than in implementing its programme with the aid of this power. The belief that a party, once it has seized dictatorial power, will then voluntarily renounce it can be entertained only before the seizure; in the struggle of parties for power, in the turmoil of overt and covert intrigues, every minute will create a new imperative for the preservation of power, a new insurmountable obstacle to its renunciation. Dictatorship is torn from the hands of the dictators only by a new revolution. Could our revolutionary youth ever agree to serve as the dais for the throne of a few dictators who—even with the best will in the world—can only become a new source of social distress, but who would far more probably be not even selfless fanatics, but men of vaulting ambitions, craving power for power's sake, craving power for themselves?

Let the Russian Jacobins fight the government. We will not hinder them. We wish them well, and shall try to make use of their successes. But the party of the people's social revolution will always be their enemy as soon as any of them takes a step towards seizing the power that belongs to the people and to nobody else. . . . The power of the state must be transformed directly into the self-government of people's communities, people's meetings, people's circles. This is a question not of secondary, but of primary importance. State power, whoever wields it, is hostile to a socialist system of society. Any minority power means exploitation, and a dictatorship can mean nothing else. We cannot accept a programme of a dictatorial revolution as the programme of the social revolution. Not only will we fight the adherents of dictatorship tomorrow—we cannot go along with them today."[231]

The question that forces itself is whether—given Lavrov's inability and unwillingness to hinder the Jacobins, though he disapproves of them, from preparing and making the revolution in their own way, and his readiness to make use of their successes—he would fight them, when they had won. Would he try to roll back the revolution, or would he accept it as the realisation of the will of history? And would he not behave in the same way, should his own followers—the revolutionary socialists—in spite of all adjurations and warnings, go Jacobin upon the success of their revolutionary endeavours?

Chapter Five

A RUSSIAN VERSION OF TOTALITARIAN DEMOCRACY — TKACHEV

The ambiguities, scruples, self-delusions and futilities of the anarchists and populists—full self-expression and absolute equality, perfect social cohesion and the absence of coercion, an elite and no subordination, a revolution and no central authority, a dictatorship without commissars—invited someone with a clear mind, impatient of humbug and cant, and delighting in confounding the confused thinkers, the high-minded moralists and the heaven-storming doctrinaires, to cut the gordian knot.

(*a*) THE COMMISAR

This role was fulfilled by P. N. Tkachev (1840-84).[232] He was born into a family of impoverished gentry and lived the life of a typical revolution-ary activist, in and out of prison, plotter and journalist, at one time companion of the unspeakable Nechaev—an assocation which he never repudiated—then an emigré in the West, and member of an extremist Russo-Polish group. There he edited *Nabat*, a journal with scant reader-ship, engaged in resounding polemics with such famous Nestors as Lavrov and Engels. He then allied himself closely with the French Blanquistes. He ended his turbulent life in a French lunatic asylum, leaving no school or organisation behind him.

A relentless seeker after consistency and with a quick eye for detecting the lack of it in others, he got himself not a little entangled in a maze of incongruities. Although one of the earliest Russian propa-gators of Marxist economics, he became the most conspicuous example of a Russian Jacobin of the Babeuf and Blanqui variety. Preacher of the primacy of economics, he turned them into the handmaid of politics, and replaced economic determinism with the crassest kind of voluntarism and with insistent agitation for a violent seizure of power. He con-sistently advocated the idea of a terrorist dictatorship. A minority was to force everyone to be free by becoming equal, indeed identical in all

301

their thoughts, sentiments and conditions, so that eventually, amid total universal unanimity, the state could wither away.

In brief, Tkachev may be regarded as the most consistent theoretician of the Russian version of the ideology of totalitarian democracy before Lenin. In the days when Nechaev was execrated, Tkachev his associate naturally became a *bête noire*. Yet as Plekhanov attests, he continued to be read, and after the failures of "going to the people" many minds were stirred by him.[233] At all events, Tkachev himself never doubted that his ideas were destined to win. There is reason to believe that he was not merely a precursor of Lenin, but had real influence on him. Writing on the Narodnaya Volya, the people's party, Lenin says in *What is to be Done?* that "the attempt to seize power, which was prepared by the preaching of Tkachev and [was to be] carried out by means of a "terrifying" terror that did really terrify, had grandeur".[234] More direct is the testimony of one of Lenin's closest associates, Bonch-Bruevich: "Vladimir Ilyich read through and examined most carefully all of this old revolutionary literature, paying particular attention to Tkachev and remarking that this writer was closer to our viewpoint than any of the others. . . . We collected articles that Tkachev had written and handed them over to Vladimir Ilyich. Not only did V.I. read these works of Tkachev, he also recommended all of us to familiarise ourselves with the valuable writings of this original thinker. . . . 'Begin,' V.I. would advise, 'by reading and familiarising yourself with Tkachev's *Nabat* . . . this is basic and will give you tremendous knowledge."[235] To which Bonch-Bruevich adds that "it is an irrefutable fact that the Russian revolution proceeded to a significant degree according to the ideas of Tkachev. The seizure of power was made on a date determined in advance by a revolutionary party organised on the principles of strict centralisation and discipline. And this party, having seized power, operated in many respects as Tkachev advised."[236] Tibor Szamuely also quotes the leading early Soviet historian Pokrovsky who gave Tkachev the title of "the first Russian Marxist", and called Tkachev's Jacobins the "Bolshevik wing" of the revolutionary movement. Tkachev's biographer Kouznin regarded his persistent advocacy of the establishment of a united centralised party as "a gigantic historical merit".[237]

Tkachev insists on objectivism. He will have no truck with the subjectivism which the ideal of personal fulfilment implied. In spite of his attribution of primacy to material developments, he would not admit of any historic relativism. A universal, eternal and objective criterion was capable of fixing infallibly "obviousness", and hence absolute truth. That criterion was made "certain by our physical identity, and consequently the same psychic make-up". "There exists therefore an absolute criterion of the truth . . . a possibility of an infallible *Weltanschauung*, that is to say of an absolute, universally binding criterion of progress."[238] An example of this was the premise that men joined together to form a society with the aim of securing "a happy life, happiness". A similarly safe axiom was that equality must by no means be reduced to political and legal or even economic equality. "It entailed an organic, physiological equality maintained by the same type of education and the same common living conditions. This is the final and only possible aim of human life; this is the supreme criterion of historical and social progress; anything that can bring society nearer this aim is progressive, anything that holds it back is retrograde. In this way the word progress gets a precise and specific meaning, and the party of progress obtains a fixed and unchangeable banner, a motto which cannot be adapted to double meanings and ambiguities."[239]

It is not surprising to find Tkachev unmasking individualistic ideas on self-expresion or self-perfection as narcissism, disguised bourgeois self-satisfaction, a claim to constitute a superior breed, and therefore to be granted special conditions for self-improvement and for the main- tenance of esoteric peculiarity. On Lavrov's critical personality Tkachev says scathingly, "it is we who decide what must remain and what must change . . . it is we who make progress, it is we who show humanity the way, it is we who give the tone to everything. Oh ingenuous self-adulation! If they carried you into a black pit and told you 'Sing the praises of the perfume of this miasma. Show that what is in black pits is the most healthy and excellent food', you would carry out these orders with cringing humility. You show the way to progress! In actual fact you go where you are driven, you are only the echo of life, the reflection of needs and dreams of practical action and daily routine."[240]

The guilty conscience, the sense of a debt to be repaid, was an excuse for doing nothing to change the situation. Sighing and noble sentiments were considered an adequate substitute for action, a token of the under- standing of the growing resentment of the underprivileged. The belief in popular spontaneity was a rationalisation of the unwillingness to commit oneself by acting here and now and in person.[241] Adoration of the commune and *mir* enabled the Slavophiles to defend the status quo. The *muzhiks* were such a happy, virtuous, contented lot, a model of Russian authenticity; why touch serfdom?[242] Insistence on the need to educate the masses, to prepare the revolution, was tantamount to postponing it *sine die*, and another pretext for doing nothing in the fore- seeable future, and for enjoying the role of educator and guide. Furthermore, the very idea of a revolution after thorough preparation, when the majority had been won over for the revolutionary cause, was an absurdity. The very notion of revolution implied an uprising by a minority. Once a revolution was willed by everybody or nearly everybody, there was no longer any need for it. In his "Letter to the Editor of *Vperyod*" (Lavrov), Tkachev complains that that was the mood which had come to prevail in the working class movement in the West. It was expressed in the German programme of the International concerning gradual peaceful progress.

"Do you not understand"—asks Tkachev—"that the difference between revolution (in the usual sense of the word) and peaceful progress is that the first is carried out by a minority, and the second by a majority.... A violent revolution can take place only when the minority is no longer willing to wait until the majority itself recognises its needs, and when it decides, so to speak, to impose this consciousness upon the majority, when it attempts to bring the people's muted but ever-present feeling of dissatisfaction to the point of explosion.... And when this explosion takes place, the minority tries to give it a sensible, rational shape, directs it towards certain aims."[243]

(*b*) ECONOMIC DETERMINISM AND HUMAN RESOLVE

The original and prophetic contribution of Tkachev was the cruious blend of economic Marxist determinism with extreme political voluntarism. Tkachev is said to have been the first writer to mention Marx in a Russian publication, in 1865 in connection with Marx's *Critique of Political Economy*, and in a manner suggesting that he took it for granted that any intelligent and honest person was sure to uphold the predominance of the economic factor.[244] But in what sense? At first sight Tkachev seems to regard the economic factor as determining all our attitudes.

There is a curious comment of his on the Peasant War in Germany in 1525. He describes it as a turning point in German history, indeed European civilisation. The panic which it evoked among the German burghers caused them to ally themselves with the nobility. They became subordinated to the feudal interest and their horizons were restricted to the narrow confines of the small principalities and free cities. The ensuing gap between daring theological thought and the meanness of concrete existence led them to sink into romantic philistinism and metaphysical system-building.[245] The strong ingredient of peasant realism, stemming from constant and direct contact with the exigencies and compulsions of the struggle with nature, was stifled and perverted into superstition and mysticism.[246]

Further, the changed position of the professional classes and the intelligentsia in nineteenth-century Russia is ascribed by Tkachev to the economic effects of the reforms in the sixties. The earlier primitive Russian economy gave them no scope, made their existence very insecure and caused them to feel outsiders.[247] The beginnings of industrialisation and capitalism created a strong demand for their services and offered them a crucial role and an important status. Their earlier self-identification with the cause of the revolution should therefore no longer be taken for granted.

What is missing entirely from Tkachev's Marxist economic materialism is the dialectic. Men, he thought, were in the first place moved by their economic situation and interests. But Tkachev knows of no predetermined unfolding of a pattern, of social contradictions working themselves out objectively to reach the dénouement of a classless society. He vehemently rejects—as we have said—any kind of social-historical automatism, out of fear that it would kill all revolutionary endeavour and help the status quo. He repudiates any analogies between an organism and society, between nature and history.[248] With a deep distrust of human nature, he can only visualise a Hobbesian war of all against all, once the principle of natural selection is allowed to function freely.[249] The whole aim—and by aim Tkachev means a conscious goal men set themselves—of history is to put an end to the struggle for existence, and to the rat race. His attitude to the communes and to peasantry in general is determined by this approach. Although he does appreciate the socialist features and possibilities of the peasant commune, he calls attention to its negative sides such as deep-seated veneration of the Tsar, superstitious religion, hopelessly narrow outlook, the dead hand of custom and tradition, the lack of any interest in and sense of solidarity with the peasants in other communes.[250] In itself, the institution was neutral. The forces of old might preserve it as a frozen stagnant pool, but in the hands of the revolutionaries it could become an instrument of socialist transformation.

There is in Tkachev's work only a very feeble attempt to present egalitarian communism as the function of changes in the modes of production. The machine was calculated to act as a vehicle of equality. By simplifying and facilitating labour, it was making equal demands upon all. By necessitating mental alertness it was bound to narrow the gap between blue- and white-collar workers.[251]

The truth of the matter is that to Tkachev economic interest, economic pressure and discontent were of importance only in so far as they fed or weakened the urge for change, and the revolutionary resolve. Deprivation and the lack of economic security appeared to him to be the most important forces goading the European proletariat. By themselves they were not likely to hasten the revolution.

"The historical process has created conditions such that the general sum of the needs of all individuals in the given society cannot be covered by the general sum of the means to satisfy them . . . some have gained the possibility to spend too much for the development of their personality, and others too little. . . . History has thus not brought us any nearer, but all the time removed society from achieving the desired goal (equality); in other words we have to consider the historic process not as a progressive, but as a regressive movement."[252]

(c) NOW OR NEVER

The intervention of the human conscious will was therefore necessary. This entailed planning and sustained purposeful action. As against gradualists and believers in peaceful and piecemeal progress, Tkachev insists that their view was much more utopian than the idea of a clean sweep and a complete revolutionary transformation. Like the laws of reasoning, the social development of a given system had to proceed by stages, none of which could be skipped. It was bound up with facts and interests which could not just be done away with. But it was far easier to sweep away an existing order and rebuild it from scratch. The hour to strike and the best chance of success was when one phase of development was visibly coming to an end, and the next stage had not yet made its arrival, or had not yet crystallised. That was the time to erect an utopia from scratch. In such a context Tkachev is not afraid of the word utopia. Utopia was a blueprint based upon a logic stretched to its extreme, a set of chemically pure syllogisms, as a plan for a social transformation should be.[253]

Clearly, such an endeavour to bring down enormous powers and interests, institutions and habits, could not be effected without violence and terror. A peaceful transition from one social form to the next was surely and precisely "one of the non-existent Utopias that humanity has always invented to quieten its conscience and to obscure its vision".[254] Such a breakthrough, however, could never be effected by the masses themselves, ignorant, inert, downtrodden as they were. It was incumbent upon the vanguard of the enlightened to take the initiative on behalf of the masses, in response to their inarticulate yearnings. What did taking the initiative mean? Not propaganda among and preparation of the masses. This would be a hopelessly drawn out business, and in fact a pretext not to take decisive action. The real task was to seize power, make a political revolution in order to carry out by force the social revolution. And this was a categorical imperative of supreme urgency in Russia.[255]

Tkachev sees the Russia of his day as a classical example of the danger of letting history take its course. *Nabat*, Tkachev's journal, was a call of alarm, a warning against the dangers of waiting. In his famous polemic with Engels, Tkachev formulated views which in the light of the Bolshevik Revolution strike one as truly prophetic.[256] Tkachev felt with greater intensity than anyone else the menace of bourgeois capitalism, already launched and threatening to delay the revolution or make it impossible for generations. In a schoolmasterish article Engels scolded the green student for his arrogance and ignorance of the ABC of socialism. He tried to din into his ears the orthodox thesis of the inevitability of a bourgeois-liberal phase, and the impossibility of a proletariat growing, maturing and becoming organised for a revolutionary breakthrough before that stage had come into being.[257] Political relations were a function of social economic forces. Tkachev retaliated in kind, accusing Engels of bureaucratic arrogance and of total ignorance of Russian conditions.[258] He was the first to resort to Marxist economic terms to prove the possibility of a political revolution, indeed the necessity of a revolutionary seizure of political power in a backward country, precisely before the social conditions and the political institutions accompanying them had matured—in order to carry out the social revolution by the *ukase* of a dictatorial political power.

In every normal country, the state and the government were the representatives and the defenders of a class interest. In Russia the Tsarist regime was suspended in air, existing in a social vacuum. The nobility was bankrupt and impotent, the peasantry was entirely alienated from the state, and there was no middle class. So there was no difficulty in toppling such a regime, after it had lost a war, become entangled in a grave economic crisis, and come under attack from popular rioting. Apart from the army and the bureaucracy, there was no social force faithful enough, interested, and ready to defend it.[259] A dictatorial revolutionary government would surely not have less mass support than the hated, decrepit and bankrupt Tsarist despotism. If the absolutism of the Tsar could maintain itself in ignoble isolation, why should the revolutionary dictatorship, the bearer of the deepest hopes of the masses, be unable to survive? To wait meant to give the Tsarist regime time to gain a firm base in a large middle class engaged in a frantic search for opportunities to exploit a growing proletariat and developing an interest in an alliance with the Tsarist army and bureaucracy against the working classes. The disintegration of the peasant commune by bourgeois individualism was advancing and with it the cult of private property and the growth of a rapacious class of *kulaks*. Russia was menaced by the loss of the most promising nucleus of a socialist reconstruction of society and the economy—the village commune.[260]

"Have we the right to wait? Have we the right to spend time on re-education? Remember that every hour, every minute separating us from the revolution costs the people thousands of victims; even more, it diminishes the very probability of success. At present the strongest enemy confronting us is our government, with its armed forces and its vast material power. As yet there does not exist any intermediate force between the government and the people which could for any length of time, stop the popular movement, once it had begun. . . . This is why we cannot wait. This is why we claim that in Russia a revolution is indispensable, and indispensable now, at this moment. We cannot permit any postponement, any delay. It is now or—perhaps very soon—never. Now the circumstances are in our favour—within ten or twenty years they will be against us."[261]

How could the Russian peasants and workers be educated and prepared for revolution in a country which had no freedom of speech, no free press, no freedom of assembly, no possibilities of legal organisation, of setting up a trade union or even of receiving guidance from the intelligentsia? Tkachev had no difficulty in pointing out the futility of the efforts of the "reactionary revolutionaries" to set up illegal cooperatives in towns and villages, to organise classes for adult education or conduct propaganda. Doomed to failure because of lack of an economic basis and of freedom of action, impotent as revolutionary cells because of dispersal and lack of a nation-wide organisation, any success that they might have would contribute to the introduction of Western models and to the disruption of the *mir*.[262] In these circumstances the initiative for any revolutionary change could come only from a self-appointed minority, a vanguard. None of the conditions of Russian life which were pressing for change, and none of the elements which contained socialist possibilities, could become operative without action by a determined minority. This applied in the first place, as suggested before, to the commune.

There was still a long way to go from the life forms conditioning the self-governing peasant commune—based on periodic repartition of the land and the subordination of the individual to the collectivity—to complete communism. "But they constituted as it were the seed of communism; that seed may blossom, but it may also dwindle and die."[263] Should the economy of Russia take a turn in the direction of bourgeois capitalism, the commune would meet with the same fate as the ancient West European communes: it would perish. "However should the revolution erect a dam in time to hold the fast moving waves of bourgeois progress, stop the trend and give it another, and contrary direction, then no doubt, with proper friendly care, our present peasant commune will evolve into a socialist commune."[264]

Without a push from outside, the commune would remain a fossil. "The social ideal of our people does not transcend the fossilised forms of its existence. Beyond the centuries old form of land tenure, beyond the patriarchal servility towards the bureaucracy, an obsequiousness which has entered its blood, beyond the passive subordination of the individual to the community, beyond the traditional family relations and the like— the people see nothing and do not want to know anything. Give them the possibility to arrange their life as they wish, and you will see, that they will make no changes in it . . . and will remain the same old peasant world with its obsolete, fossilised ways and immovable conservatism. And so the positive ideals of our peasantry are not yet revolutionary; they cannot be just adopted as the ideals of the socialist revolution."[265]

The commune must be revitalised and redirected by an infusion of modern ends and means from outside, "capable of throwing it off its stable equilibrium. . . . We shall search in vain in the popular ideal for any notion of those new elements and new factors . . . we shall find them only in the socialist programme of the revolutionary minority. This is why the ideal professed by that minority, as an ideal of wider horizons and more revolutionary, must at the time of the revolution dominate the popular ideal."[266]

(d) THE REVOLUTIONARY DICTATORSHIP OF THE MINORITY VANGUARD

It was impossible to expect the people to play a decisive role in building the communist society, declared Tkachev. "That part belongs exclusively to the revolutionary minority".[267] But if the people had no importance as a positive revolutionary force, they would be most effective as "a force of destruction, as a force of revolutionary negation".[268]

"Indeed, our people are the eternal foe of landlords and authorities. . . . Once that hatred finds a free outlet—the people will in one mighty effort destroy the present-day defenders and guardians of the status quo, will take back the land of which they have been deprived, will destroy everything which has until now stifled and oppressed the *mirs*, the communes, will wreak terrible vengeance on their enemies. But they will go no further."[269] Then the masses would return to their communes and families, freer and more content to cultivate their beloved old traditions.

That was why the minority must not step down as soon as the masses had destroyed the old order. It must carry its revolutionary action into the very heart of peasant life—must strive to remove from it the old forms, which were hostile to communist progress, and replace them with the ones most suited to its progressive needs and tasks. "Precisely in order to be able to continue its destructive, revolutionary activity in these areas, in which it is difficult to count upon the active support and cooperation of the majority of the people, precisely for that the revolutionary minority must have the strength, the power and the authority. The greater that strength, the more determined and energetic will be that power, the fuller and wider will be the realisation of the ideas of the social revolution and the easier it will be to avoid a clash with the conservative elements of the people."[270]

Without being able to count on active popular support for the revolutionary vanguard in this restructuring of the traditional forms, the revolutionary vanguard need not fear that "the people will refuse to the revolutionaries its passive support. On the contrary, they have every reason to count on precisely such support: after all, their revolutionary ideal is in its general outline the same conservative ideal of the people, only developed more fully. . . . In this way the revolutionary minority, taking advantage of the destructive revolutionary strength of the people will destroy the enemies of the revolution, and leaning on the general spirit of the positive ideal of the people, [that is to say] on the conservative forces of the people will build the foundation of a new, rational form of existence."[271]

Tkachev refuses to flatter the people by preaching like Lavrov that the people could save themselves. He refuses "to impose upon the people the whole burden of the cause of the revolution".[272] So long as the people found themselves in the present economic and political conditions, neither Lavrov's ideas, ideals, nor their own attitude to their environment could change, and therefore "the people will also in the future remain as helpless as they are today".[273] Tkachev concludes that all who preached to the people to wait and have patience were hypocrites.

"Neither now, nor in the future will the people left to themselves be able to make a social revolution. Only we, the revolutionary minority, can do it—and we have to do it as soon as possible."[274]

(e) THE SOCIAL REVOLUTION FROM ABOVE

And so the social revolution must be made from above in the wake of the political revolution, that is to say the violent seizure of power, and the sudden transformation of the state as the representative of the exploiters into a people's revolutionary state. The task must be carried out by the revolutionary vanguard with the greatest speed, determination and ruthlessness, in other words "violence . . . centralisation, severe discipline, speed, decision, and unity of action. Any concession or doubt, any compromise, multiplicity of command or decentralisation of the forces in the fight, can only weaken their energy, paralyse their work, and do away with any chance of victory. Constructive revolutionary activity, on the other hand, though it must proceed at the same time as the destructive activity, must by its very nature rely on exactly opposite principles. The first is based mainly on material force, the second is based on spiritual force; the first relies on speed and unity, the second on the solidity and vitality of the changes it has brought about. The former must be carried out with violence, the latter with conviction. The ultima ratio of the first is victory just as the ultima ratio of the second is the will and reason of the people."275

In this context Tkachev set out to settle his accounts with Bakuninist anarchism. Considering his low estimate of the capacity of the masses for revolutionary initiative and of their readiness for change, the organisation man in Tkachev had no difficulty in ridiculing Bakunin's idea of an anonymous secret dictatorship of three score people: if the people's revolutionary instinct was the paramount factor, what need was there for such a dictatorship, and if guidance from outside was necessary, how effective could that be without organisation; and if its role was vital, what was left of the people's spontaneity?276 The same arguments applied, and were, as we have seen, employed by Tkachev, against Lavrov. Furthermore, a good dose of Bakuninism was contained in Tkachev's evaluation of the elemental destructive role of the masses in the revolutionary upheaval. But there was more of it. Tkachev envisaged the ultimate withering away of the state. And that would occur sooner and in a more thorough manner the more stringent, dictatorial and thorough the action of the victorious revolutionary minority had been in uprooting the old order, the powers of yesterday, and in changing the social conditions and the mentality of man.277

Precisely in a revolutionary upheaval, where all restraints were gone, and free rein was given to all kinds of ideas, sentiments, ambitions and indeed perversities, chaos could be prevented only by a firm, clear-sighted and absolutely united minority overcoming all fractionalism, making its intellectual and spiritual superiority prevail over the majority, and turning the spiritual power so dear to Bakunin and Lavrov into material power.[278]

In the best tradition of Babeuf and Buonarotti, Tkachev envisaged a constituent assembly, not elected by all and sundry and in conditions of free discussion and propaganda, but summoned only after the masses had been weaned away from the old classes and the old fears and prejudices. After they had been liberated to will freely their own happiness and believe in its imminence, there could be no doubt how they would vote. An assembly so elected would approve the actions of the revolutionary minority dictatorship with the greatest enthusiasm as the fulfilment of their most cherished dreams.[279]

In other words, the first thing was to create *faits accomplis*, not to get a mandate to carry out reforms. The measures to be taken were, in the social-economic field, the transformation of communes based on family property into fully fledged communes built on collective ownership and collective work, and the nationalisation of all lands and means of production confiscated from the class enemy. Far more meaningful, and in the Russian revolutionary environment more daring and original, was Tkachev's Babouvist plan for effecting a total spiritual transformation of the people and his solution of the dichotomies of the integral personality and social cohesion, liberty and equality, spontaneity of instinct and the postulates of justice. Real equality was only possible by fashioning all men on the same model, by training all to will the same, without hankering after distinction, preference, peculiarity, individualism; without experiencing needs which not everyone had. That was a recipe for real anarchy in the sense of absence of government. Without that, anarchy was bound to mean chaos and a war of all against all.

"Society can only fulfil its task completely when: first, it unites into one (whole) the life aims of all its members, that is to say creates identical conditions of education and further activity, reduces to a (single) common denominator, to the same level the whole chaotic diversity of individuals, which is the result of the regressive historical process; second, leads to a harmony between means and needs, that is to say develops in its members only those needs which can be satisfied by the given level of labour productivity, or those which have a direct influence upon the growth of productivity or upon diminishing what is needed for the maintenance and the development of the individual; third, will guarantee the most equal and fullest possible satisfaction of all the needs of everyone of its members. . . . When all members of society find themselves at the same level of development, then their life aims are identical; that is in turn the necessary condition of the harmony between the individual aims and the goal of society. Where there is no such harmony, where society can fulfil the aims of some individuals only by doing injustice to others, where the diversity of individuals breeds diversity of and conflict between individual aims, there the fulfilment of the basic task of the state is logically impossible. Nor will the task of society be realised when everyone has the right to develop his individuality or the individuality of his children, with no regard to the quantity and quality of the means which are at society's disposal,"[280] not to mention a situation where everyone was free to take by force any quantity of things that he might desire.

Absolute "organic, physiological equality" through the levelling of all needs and satisfactions and a proper re-education—"that is the final, the only possible goal of human society".[281] This entailed inhibiting some urges and developing others by a compulsory system of civic and social education, the abolition of the family, and the enthroning of a spirit of solidarity and love in the collective institutions of self-government, or rather self-administration.[282] Not a vague federation of communes embodied in a congress of delegates with limited mandates, nor groups of enlightened individuals, nor unorganised secret inspirers of the people—but an extremely self-assertive dictatorship of a most closely knit and disciplined revolutionary minority party was postulated by Tkachev.

Fears that a revolutionary vanguard might after the seizure of power degenerate into an oligarchy were countered by Tkachev with arguments employed at a later date by Lenin. The revolutionary party was the quintessence of the people, neither above nor outside it. The party did not consist of politicians who were out to gain power and make a career for themselves. Why should "this minority—brought together partly through its social position, partly through its ideas— totally devoted to the people's interests suddenly change itself into a tyrant, after having conquered power?"[283] Those whom power corrupted had usually been corrupted before they got it—Napoleon, Caesar and such like. The others, Cromwell, Washington, Robespierre, retained their austere virtues and devotion to the cause of the people to the end. "Robespierre, a member of the Convention, the omnipotent ruler of the destiny of France, and Robespierre, an unknown provincial lawyer, were the same—the identical person. Power made not the slightest difference to his moral character or to his ideals and tendencies, his private habits."[284]

In these circumstances, the immediate and most vital problem was the education of the members of the revolutionary minority and the nature of their organisation.

"Their distinctive badge lies in the fact that all their activity, their whole way of life is dominated by one ambition, one passionate ideal: to make the majority of men happy and to invite as many as possible to the banquet of life. The bringing about of this ideal becomes the only purpose of their activity, because this ideal is completely fused into their conception of personal happiness. Everything is subordinated to this ideal, everything sacrificed—if one can at all use the word sacrifice."[285]

The closely knit, rigidly centralised, utterly disciplined confraternity would be guided by this supreme goal, which was the criterion of all values, actions, morality. They would not recognise any formal, abstract ethics. To them morality had meaning only in relation to that final goal, unlike those philistines who claimed to be guided by "do not steal", but who while preaching "the untouchability of other people's handkerchiefs . . . quietly remove the contents of their neighbour's pockets, when given a chance".[286]

Chapter Six

WHEN "CONSISTENCY REACHES THE POINT OF MONSTROSITY" —NECHAEV AND BAKUNIN

The Russian revolutionary in the nineteenth century never ceased to hear the call "Cain, Where is thy brother, Abel?" While enjoying the good things in life, he was agonising about the people who could not afford them, about not hastening to succour the oppressed and liberate the enslaved. He was brought up to see himself as the self-indulgent accomplice of a conspiracy, a nefarious system erected to exploit and hold down the larger part of the nation.

(a) "IS EVERYTHING PERMITTED AND NOTHING FORBIDDEN?" —
ENDS AND MEANS

While entailing total self-dedication, the revolutionary's mission was however also a self-appointed role, an usurpation of office. The mission required total self-denial and complete self-surrender, but it was incapable of realisation without emphatic self-assertion, without the revolutionaries feeling free and called upon to take audacious decisions, perpetrate deeds of vast import, and that without authorisation, counsel or control on the part of those who stood to be affected by those actions. In brief, the obverse side of self-sacrifice was self-will. And also the danger of immorality.

Theirs was a mission to rebel, to act against the law, against a legality which was evil incarnate. This invited, necessitated, and justified unconventional and lawless acts, ruse, deceit and violence. As only fanatical determination and ruthless action could be effective and succeed, the ability to command them became the test not merely of efficiency, but also of the strength and depth of conviction and devotion. The loathing for the existing kingdom of evil and the courage not to shrink from anything in the process of destroying it, demanded an equally deep and passionate belief in the absolute goodness, purity and salvationist quality of the world which the revolutionaries were destined to bring into being. The nobler the vision of the things to come,

315

the stronger seemed the justification of ruthless conduct here and now against the kingdom of the devil.

We are faced here with a world of moral ambiguities, ironically pitted against a philosophy whose simple, not to say primitive, axioms and alternatives were intended to deny their very reality, indeed the very possibility of relativism. No other episode in the whole of the revolutionary Russian tradition could be chosen to highlight those dilemmas so glaringly as the celebrated case of Nechaev.

(b) THE PROTOTYPE OF A REVOLUTIONARY

Born in 1847 and deprived early of his mother, S. G. Nechaev was brought up as a member of a large orphaned family by a severe father, an artisan in the drab, muddy, miserable town of Ivanovo, just emerging as an important centre of the textile industry. From the few data and hints about his childhood and adolescence, we can imagine an existence filled with experiences which leave lacerating memories, rancour and rage. Boundless grim energy enabled Nechaev to gain some education, but he failed in his first examination for a teacher's certificate. He persisted and managed at the age of nineteen to become a schoolmaster for a while and to continue his studies as an external student. He had a morose appearance and behaved like an uncouth, rancorous lone wolf, "not a product of our world, of the intelligentsia . . . a stranger to us"—as Vera Zasulich testifies.[287] On his arrival in Switzerland in 1869 to join Bakunin, Nechaev already had behind him quite a record of revolutionary activity, even if his story of being an emissary of a vast revolutionary organisation, headed by an all-powerful central committee and poised to strike out next year—1870—and of his own dramatic escapes from impregnable prisons were fantastic yarns based on insignificant grains of fact. Nechaev had been a member of a small band of ultra-revolutionary students, "Committee of the Russian Revolutionary Party", and had collaborated with Tkachev and the Bakuninist Ralli. He became intoxicated with the Bible of the revolutionary underground of the first half of the nineteenth century, Buonarotti's *Conspiracy of the Equals*, the story of Babeuf's plot. He also elaborated with Tkachev a revolutionary vade-mecum, *The Programme of Revolutionary Action*.[288]

Vera Zasulich speaks of Nechaev's inordinate, indiscriminate hatred of the world as he saw it. "This hatred was directed not only against the government and exploiters, but against society as a whole and against educated society . . . against the rich and the poor, against conservatives, liberals and radicals. . . . These children of that hated society, linked to it by innumerable bonds . . . and striving towards love rather than hatred, were for him only tools or means and definitely not comrades or disciples."[289]

"This reality without any refinement hits me so hard," wrote Nechaev, "that I have to leap into the air . . . so . . . it does not allow me to sink into apathy and settle down to contemplate the beauties of the world". . . a "Kingdom of the mad—so terrible and unnatural are people's relations to each other; so strange and unbelievable their attitude towards the mass of injustice, vileness and baseness that constitutes our social regime".[290]

Whether composed by Bakunin alone, or jointly by Bakunin and Nechaev or by Nechaev alone, *The Catechism of a Revolutionary*, the most famous statement of Nechaevism, is an unmistakable, though outsized, reflection of the image of the revolutionary and his calling which was current in the revolutionary Russian milieu from the day when Chernyshevsky drew the portrait of the new man (Rahmetov). Indeed it owed not a little to the various pronouncements and manifestos from the pen of Bakunin, and to Tkachev's article "The men of the future and the heroes of the bourgeoisie" (1868). A microscopic exegesis designed to decipher who used, repeated or failed to re-echo somebody else's favourite term may seem somewhat pedantic in the light of the eclecticism which prevailed in the circles of pre-Marxist Russian revolutionaries.

The *Catechism* is an anti-intellectual document *par excellence*, and its message is a call for total and absolute commitment.[291] It treats speeches, discussions, theoretical analysis, even study as harmful distractions, as a substitute for action, a rationalisation of inaction, as leading astray, diverting attention, weakening man's fibre and resolve, sowing doubt and uncertainty, and naturally as a lever of careerism and a licence for self-indulgence. Only studies bearing directly upon action, say the production of bombs, such as chemistry and physics are tolerated by it.

"To us an idea is of value only in so far as it can serve the great cause of radical and universal destruction. But in none of the books we read today is there a single such idea. He who teaches himself about the revolutionary cause through books will never be anything but a revolutionary sluggard. An idea able to serve the people's revolution can only be worked out in revolutionary action . . . practical trial and manifestations, all having one and the same unswerving aim—merciless destruction by any means. Everything that does not follow this course we regard as alien and hostile. We will not let ourselves be reduced to any of the revolutionary phrasemongering practised nowadays so lavishly by doctrinaire champions of paper revolution. We have lost all faith in the word; for us the word is of significance only when the deed is sensed behind it and follows immediately upon it . . ."[292]

In this Nechaev was in fact echoing Bakunin. "Go to the people," wrote Bakunin, "there is your way, your life, your learning. . . . Young men of education must become not the people's benefactors, not its dictators and guides, but merely an instrument for the people to free itself, the unifier of the people's own energies and forces. To gain the ability and right to serve the cause, youth must submerge itself and drown in the people. Take no notice of learning in whose name men try to shackle you and strip you of your power. Learning of this kind must die altogether with the world of which it is the expression. New and living learning will undoubtedly be born later, after the people's victory, from the liberated life of the people itself."[293] In another manifesto, "How the revolutionary question presents itself", Bakunin poured scorn on socialist conspirators, young doctrinaires, bookish revolutionaries, armchair revolutionary-statesmen and future dictators, who "play at revolution but are incapable of making it . . . university corruption . . . the only real school is the people".[294]

The members of the revolutionary underground should, according to Bakunin, acquire their necessary knowledge by the infiltration of their clever and practical men into the company of pedlars, bakers etc.; listening to gossip, consorting with prostitutes; by gathering and disseminating rumours; and by hobnobbing with police, old clerks and "the so-called criminal elements of society".

The revolutionary organisation envisaged by Bakunin and Nechaev's *Catechism* was a monastic order, not a political party. The person joining it took vows which amounted to an oath to assume a different nature, to retire from the world; to give up his own will; renounce his personal interests, natural inclinations, ties; abjure the customs and conventions, codes and standards obtaining in society; subordinate himself to one single aim—the revolution; to obey blindly the orders of those whose task and right it was to issue them; and to judge everything by the sole criterion, does it promote or hinder the revolution, and to act accordingly.

One cannot help being reminded of the Gospel story of the young man who asked Jesus for permission to bid goodbye to his family before following him and was rejected by him for looking back.

"The revolutionary is a dedicated man. He has no interests of his own, no affairs, no feelings, no attachments, no belongings, not even a name. Everything in him is absorbed by a single exclusive interest, a single thought, a single person—the revolution . . ."

The revolutionary was at war with existing society. Its laws, principles, conventions were anathema to him, and so he felt neither any obligation to them nor any sense of shame or guilt in defying them. Moral was what helped to destroy that reality, immoral what maintained and assisted it. "He despises public opinion. He despises and abhors the existing social ethics in all its manifestations and expressions. For him, everything is moral which assists the triumph of revolution. Immoral and criminal is everything which stands in its way."[295]

The revolutionary must learn to overcome and to refashion his own self. Hard towards himself, he must be hard also towards others. All the tender emotions of kinship, friendship, love, gratitude and even honour must be stifled in him by a cold and single-minded passion for the revolutionary cause. There existed for him only one delight, one consolation, one reward and one gratification—the success of the revolution. Night and day he must have but one thought, one aim—merciless destruction. In cold-blooded and tireless pursuit of this aim he must be prepared both to die himself and to destroy with his own hands everything that stands in the way of its achievement.[296]

"The nature of the true revolutionary has no place for any romanticism, any sentimentality, rapture or enthusiasm. It has no place either for personal hatred or vengeance. The revolutionary passion, which in him becomes a habitual state of mind, must at every moment be combined with cold calculation. Always and everywhere he must be not what the promptings of his personal inclinations would have him be, but what the general interest of the revolution prescribes."[297]

Not sentiments, but association for the pursuit of the common cause made men friends. The degree of friendship was determined by the use of the befriended to the cause. Those who possessed "the same degree of revolutionary understanding and passion"[298] should discuss matters together and aspire "to come to unanimous decisions" as much as possible, while in the execution of them each should as far as possible rely on himself. The attitude towards the less tested members of the movement should be that of a superior towards those "who are not completely initiated". Those were like capital which was to be spent economically. The revolutionary regarded himself too as "capital consecrated to the triumph of the revolutionary cause", and when faced with the problem whether to take risks and how much risk in order to rescue a comrade, he must be guided not by personal feelings, but by the calculus of revolutionary utility: what "amount of revolutionary energy" was the part of the revolutionary capital represented by the comrade worth?[299]

In his mission of destruction the revolutionary must not be

hampered by feelings of pity, consideration, liking for any part or aspect of the odious reality of this existing society: "all the worse for him if he has family, friends and loved ones in this world; he is no revolutionary if they can stay his hand".[300] At the same time, he was called upon to infiltrate into every class, milieu, institution in order to help to destroy it from within, or as need might be to use, manipulate them for the sake of the cause.

For instance politically ambitious persons and liberals of various hues were to be treated in somewhat the same way as Marx in his address to the Communist League wanted to treat the petty-bourgeois democrats: ostensibly collaborating with them, pretending that "we are blindly following them", but in fact manipulating and controlling them, "rooting out all their secrets and compromising them to the utmost, so that they are irreversibly implicated and can be employed to create disorder in the state".[391] Similarly "doctrinaires, conspirators, revolutionaries . . . given to idle peroration",[302] should be incited to make ultra-violent declarations.

The section of the *Catechism* called "The Attitude of Our Society towards the People" reads like a manifesto composed by Bakunin, and its anarchist character is in parts at variance with the Jacobinism ardently professed by Nechaev, the champion of Tkachev. It starts by proclaiming a policy of "the worse the better". The organisation did not see its task as bringing succour to the common labourers but as bringing about "the total emancipation and happiness of the people . . . by means of an all-destroying popular revolution".[303] To hasten that revolution would "promote an intensification and an increase in those calamities and evils which must finally exhaust the patience of the people and drive it to a popular uprising".[304] But it was not "a regulated movement on the classical Western model"[305] that was envisaged, a change of political personnel, with property and the traditional social order of so-called civilisation and morality left intact. "The only revolution that can save the people is one that eradicates the entire state system and exterminates all state traditions of the regime and the classes in Russia."[306]

Strikingly anarchist and non-Jacobin is para. 24;[307] the society will abstain from imposing upon the people any organisation from above, hoping that the victorious revolutionary people itself will shape the proper institutions for its happiness. "Our task is terrible, total, universal, merciless destruction":[308] there is not a word about the right and duty of the revolutionary vanguard to see the ship of the revolution through to its final haven.

Similarly Bakuninist is the paragraph which speaks of the necessity of an alliance with "the intrepid world of brigands" who are "the only true revolutionaries in Russia . . . ever since the very foundation of state power of Muscovy . . . against the nobility, bureaucracy, priests . . . merchants' guilds, the tight-fisted peasant profiteer".[309]

In the articles of Nechaev's *Narodnaya Rasprava* we are faced with a ferocious activism. The test of a revolutionary society is action, deed. "A modest and excessively cautious organisation of secret societies which show no outward, practical sign of activity at all is in our opinion nothing more than a ridiculous, abominable, childish game. We term "real" only a series of actions which destroy something absolutely: a person, a thing or an attitude which is an obstacle to the liberation of the people."[310]

A revolutionary society proved its worth by braving all dangers and difficulties by engaging in a succession of individual acts and sacrifices which followed a strictly ordered and agreed plan, "by means of a series of bold, nay, audacious ventures, burst into the life of the people to inspire them to faith in us and in themselves", thus goading them to accomplish the historic task. All thoughts and energies must be centred on action here and now, without bothering about theories and blue-prints for the post-revolutionary period. The earlier revolutionaries "were assiduously occupied with implementing irreproachably in their imagination plans for the future life of the people, and missed their chance of liberating the people from conventions of state and class . . . plunging into those local revolts and uniting them into a single, terrible, all-destroying popular uprising".[311]

The details for immediate action read like a programme for the Narodnaya Volya terrorist organisation or indeed of a present-day guerilla organisation. The people to be liquidated were senior government officials and army leaders displaying particular zeal—to be "exterminated absolutely": "people of great economic strength", selfish, or helpful to their class or state—to be dispossessed or otherwise rendered harmless: venal writers and publicists working for the establishment—to be silenced ("even if this means depriving them of their tongues").[312]

The execution of the Tsar was to be postponed for a considerable time so that he might go on drawing upon himself all the mounting rage of the masses "in a divine thunderbolt that will strike the aristocracy as it wallows in its depravity and foulness . . . on the day of the people's justice",[313] when they rise "from their long, agonising slumbers . . . to tear asunder the chains of slavery and smash with their own hands that head with its loathsome crown".[314]

(c) ABSOLUTE CONSISTENCY OR HUMAN PATHOLOGY?

It is in this context that we have to set the Nechaev-Ivanov murder case which shook Russian society, including its revolutionary wing, and was immortalised by Dostoevsky as a demonstration that once men tear themselves away from the rock that is faith in God, nothing can be held forbidden and everything is permitted.[315]

It remains uncertain whether Nechaev really suspected Ivanov of spying or of being capable of denouncing to the police the conspiratorial group to which they both belonged and of which Nechaev was the leader, and therefore arranging for his assassination. What seems beyond doubt is that Nechaev wished to turn the matter into a test case. The joint planning and execution of the murder were to serve as a stage in the education for ruthlessness, as shock treatment designed to liberate the accomplices from scruples and inhibitions, as a way of testing the measure of their resolve and commitment, as an act of leaping the barrier of fear, as a means of closing to the members any avenue of retreat, as a device to bind the group with collective guilt and fear of punishment, and finally to probe, assert and secure Nechaev's ascendancy as leader.[316]

The question arises whether given the philosophy of total revolution, of a mortal confrontation between children of light and children of darkness, there could be a rational, consistent and convincing argument against the crime, except prudential considerations regarding immediate risks or the danger of the disintegration of the confraternity itself from lack of mutual confidence, and from licence given to lying, cheating, treachery and murder.

An underground organisation which has embarked upon subversive, more precisely terrorist, activity develops a dynamic which can hardly be halted. The Narodnaya Volya movement of going to the people was motivated by the noblest urges and aims and certainly abhorred bloodshed. But upon the discovery of the futility of the effort, the lack of response on the part of the peasants, they began to see themselves as it were as a lonely besieged outpost and a commando. And so there ensued the escalation from Vera Zasulich's shot at General Trepov to punish him for the brutal humiliation of an imprisoned comrade and the earliest, almost improvised decision taken by revolutionaries about to be apprehended, to defend themselves with arms against arrest—to the policies and actions of rescuing prisoners or condemned comrades on the way to exile, to liquidating *provocateurs* and spies, to revenging the brutality of particularly obnoxious officials and gendarmes, to sowing fear and panic, to committing acts which would highlight government impotence and ridicule it while creating the impression of the omnipotence and omnipresence of the terrorist executive committee; finally to laying siege to the Tsar, to assassinating him, to aiming at the total disorganisation of government and society. Admittedly, neither the Narodnik terrorists nor their heirs, the SR, ever resorted to deeds of "spitting in the face of society", of taking revenge on society as a whole for its implicit complicity in general social evil by the indiscriminate use of dynamite in public places (and against crowds)—as was practised in the West by individual, often deranged, anarchists.[317]

The question may now be asked—given the commonly agreed premises, why do some become Jacobins and others Girondists, Bolsheviks or Mensheviks, Bakuninists or Lavrovists, in present-day parlance hawks or doves? Is it a matter of deeper or less deep conviction and fuller or shallower understanding of the doctrine, of stronger and weaker characters, more or fewer scruples and more or fewer inhibitions? Some may be able to go on to the bitter end. Others will stop at some barrier unable to scale it, for lack of strong enough conviction or of the strength of character either to commit the deed themselves or oppose determinedly those who are prepared to commit it. Since the end pursued by the fire-eaters as well as by those who shrink from the ultimate test is fundamentaly the same, will the waverers, once the common goal has been achieved, perhaps by means they disapprove of, try to unscramble the egg? Where does reason end and psychology, not to say pathology, begin? If rational differences offer no explanation, do social origins supply one? Lenin called all his moderate socialist rivals, the hesitant, vacillating, waverers—in contrast to the hard, consistent Bolsheviks—petty bourgeois. Should we not however dismiss this class epithet as just a metaphor, and look for an explanation in psychology, above all in experiences in childhood?

There seems to be in the wholly true and wholly uninhibited believer a demoniacal power that weaker, more inhibited natures (which means most men) are unable to resist. There is Nechaev's uncanny, unbelievable feat, when in solitary confinement, of turning his jailers in the most horrible prison in the Tsarist empire into accomplices, messenger boys, obedient tools, carrying messages to and from the executive committee of the Narodnaya Volya, ordering them to release him and then giving preference to their plot to assassinate the Tsar.

(d) THE SPIDER IN THE COBWEB—BAKUNIN AND NECHAEV

The controversy about Bakunin's part in the drafting of Nechaev's last *Catechism* is still unabated. As far as content, ideas, form and style are concerned, there is nothing in it to disprove that Bakunin had a hand in it, nor to prove it conclusively. Even in his famous letter of parting, Bakunin still insists that "our programmes" (by which was meant on Nechaev's side the "Programme of the Russian Revolutionary Party") were at first identical, and diverged only on the eve of the parting of the ways, as a result of young Nechaev's outrageous behaviour towards the Nestor of the international European revolution and martyr of the Russian one. He cheated him systematically. He wrote behind his back a threatening letter to a publisher, with whom Bakunin had a contract to prepare a translation of *Das Kapital*, demanding that the publisher should cease pestering the old revolutionary, who was too busy with more important things—the revolution.[318] The letter created an international scandal, and was one of the blows which hastened the rupture between Marx, the "Teutonic-Judaic worshipper of state power" in Bakunin's words, and the mad, barbarian Russian impostor, as Marx considered the Anarchist leader.[319] Nechaev then laid siege to Natalie Herzen in an attempt to obtain her money and control over her late father's paper, *The Bell*. When these attempts proved unsuccessful, he began to importune her with offers of marriage, regardless of her detestation of him as a person, in whom—as she put it strikingly— "consistency had reached the point of monstrosity".[320]

Michael Confino quotes the passage: "Do you remember how cross you were when I called you an Abrek and your catechism a catechism of Abreks. You said that all men should be such, that a complete renunciation of self, of all personal wishes, pleasures, feelings, affections and ties should be a normal, natural, everyday condition of everybody without exception. You wished, and still wish to make your own selfless cruelty, your own truly, extreme fanaticism into a rule of common life. You wish for an absurdity, an impossibility, a total negation of nature, and society."[321]

It is very curious that in his famous letters to and about Nechaev at the time of their break, there is no mention of the Ivanov affair in the list of reproaches and characteristics of Nechaev unfolded by Bakunin. Natalie Herzen was to claim that she did not know of it at the time, but the fact is that she did.[322] And so we have to conclude that neither was shattered or repelled by the *cause célèbre*.

It is hard to see how Bakunin, the seasoned and passionate plotter, practising secrecy, mystification, deceit in what he considered to be a part of the war against an evil all-powerful regime and, for the happy future of mankind, could reproach Nechaev with dissimulation and lies. It all comes down to the question of tactics, of effective or ineffective handling of people. Bakunin by no means rejected manipulation or misdirection on behalf of the cause. What else were all his attempts to create a secret alliance as a personal power base in his struggle for power over the International and against Marx? Or his fictitious lists of members of non-existent international revolutionary committees in order to create the impression of vast power?

When read carefully, Bakunin's mammoth letter of June 2, 1870,[323] to Nechaev and the other of June 20[324] to his closest friends, appear not as a condemnation, but as an apologia for Nechaev. Bakunin's bitter grudge against him flows not from disapproval of Nechaev's philosophy and methods as such. It is reduced to something like "how could you do this to me?", an older comrade, closest friend and collaborator, who loved and trusted you so much. He continues with a sermon on Nechaev's ignorance of human nature, his obliviousness to the Old Adam, his exaggerated expectations from flesh and blood—weak, sluggish, prejudiced, selfish and stupid humanity.

"This shows your inexperience, your ignorance of life and people, and associated with this, a fanaticism bordering on mysticism. Your ignorance of social conditions, customs, morals, ideas and the ordinary feelings of the so-called educated world renders you incapable of successful action within it, even with a view to its destruction. You do not yet know how to acquire influence and power within it."[325]

Coming from a prophet of unconditional hostility to this world, preaching its total destruction, with the certainty of the arrival of a new heaven and a new earth, these are rather astounding sentiments, more appropriate in a Herzen. "You demand too much and expect too much from people, giving them tasks beyond their strength in the belief that all people must be filled with the same passion which animates you. At the same time you do not believe in them and consequently you do not take into consideration the passion which is aroused within them, their orientation, their independently honest devotion to your aim. You try to subdue them, frighten them, to tie them down by external controls which mostly prove to be inadequate. . . . You wish for an absurdity, an impossibility, a total negation of nature, man and society. This wish is fatal because it forces you to spend your strength in vain, always missing the target. No man, however strong, and no society, however perfect its discipline and powerful its organisation, can conquer nature. Only religious fanatics and ascetics could try to conquer it. . . . I recognised in you a certain mystical, pantheistic idealism . . . an idealist, a prophet like a monk of the revolution, your hero should not be Babeuf, not even Marat, but some sort of Savonarola . . . nearer to the Jesuits than to us. This is your enormous and peculiar strength . . . your blindness . . ."[326]

Bakunin's pained letters abound with protestations not only of affection, but of admiration and to some extent envy for the utterly dedicated young conspirator. "I am not angry with you and I do not reproach you, knowing that if you lie or hide the truth, you do it without self-interest and only because you consider it useful to the cause. I and all of us love you sincerely and have a great respect for you because we have never met a man more unselfish and devoted to the cause than you are."[327] "I recognised (and still recognise) in you a great and, one might say, perfectly pure force, free from any admixture of self-love or vanity, such as I have never met in any Russian . . . you are still young and whole-hearted . . . you cannot long remain on the wrong path."[328]

Bakunin is even prepared to make allowances for Nechaev's lack of full confidence in him and his attempts "to use me as a means to immediate aims which were unknown"[328] to him. He approved Nechaev's caginess about the existence and nature of the alleged revolutionary organisation in Russia: "in such movements even the most trusted people should know only as much as is necessary for the success of their particular enterprise. . . . I never asked you indiscreet questions. . . . I believed and believe in you".[329]

Bakunin does not reproach Nechaev for having exaggerated the strength of his pretended organisation: "this is an objective often useful and sometimes bold gesture of all conspirators. . . . [But] you should have talked to me as an equal, person to person, and submitted for my [approval] your programme and [plan] of action . . . You were too fanatically devoted to your plan and your programme to subject them to criticism by anyone."[330]

The letter of parting also contains however an astonishing offer of renewed collaboration. "To make this union even closer and firmer", the old man insists that Nechaev should change his system entirely and make mutual trust, sincerity and truth the foundation of their future relations.[331] But while inveighing against Jesuitical methods, he goes on to say: "All nervous, cowardly, ambitious and self-seeking people are excluded from the society. They can be used as weapons by the society, without their knowledge, but on no account must they belong to its nucleus."[332] But Bakunin fails to state who will judge their qualities. Since in Bakunin's scheme coopting comes from above, it would be the individual leaders who would do this.

In para. 8 Bakunin lays down that "in principle each member has the right to know everything. But idle curiosity is forbidden . . . as is aimless talk . . . to find out details",[333] apart from the general programme and general direction. Bakunin abolishes his whole case against Nechaev as far as principles, and not the personal resentment of a trusting man who was duped and made a fool of, are concerned by characterising the proposed reformed society in the leadership of which he was prepared to collaborate with Nechaev as "one body, firmly united whole, led by the CC and engaged in unceasing underground struggle against the government and against other societies either inimical to it or even acting independently of it".[334] War against societies which were not hostile but independent carried with it in a nutshell claims to exclusive status, and indeed proscription of factionalism and opposition in one's own movement. Bakunin says in the same breath: "Where there is war, there is politics, and there inescapably arises the necessity for violence, cunning and deceit."[335] Furthermore, "societies whose aims are near to ours must be forced to merge with our society or, at least, must be subordinated to it without their knowledge, while harmful people must be removed from them. Societies which are inimical and positively harmful must be dissolved and finally the government must be destroyed. All this cannot be achieved just by propagating the truth; cunning, diplomacy, deceit are necessary. Jesuit methods or even entanglement are a necessary and marvellous means of demoralising and destroying the enemy, though certainly not a useful means of obtaining and attracting a new friend."[336]

Eighteen days after the mammoth epistle to Nechaev, Bakunin writes on June 20, 1870, a collective message to his closest friends, which in fact is an apology for Nechaev.

"I, at least, have not ceased to regard him as the most valuable man amongst us all to the Russian cause, and the purest, or (to use Serebrinkov's expression) the most saintly person in the sense of his total dedication to the cause and his utter self-denial . . . endowed with an energy, constancy of will and tireless industry the like of which I have never encountered before . . . a jewel, and one does not throw away jewels . . . while others dabble in dilettante fashion. He wears workman's overalls, the other white gloves; he acts while the others wag their tongues."[337]

Bakunin explains that he revolted against Nechaev's dictatorship because of his Jesuitical devices, and not out of pride or out of rejection of dictatorship in principle. "In my view, the man who best understands the job, who does more and is utterly dedicated, is—so long as he understands, dedicates himself and acts—a dictator by right, that is a guide, stimulus, encouragement and inspiration to all the rest, and the rest naturally follow him."[338] This of course sounds very much like an apotheosis of personal dictatorship, and a licence to Nechaev to manipulate, and inevitably also deceive, his closest collaborators, who have to be "handled" properly and led where they were not quite yet prepared to go. But even the Jesuitry of Nechaev was not "the result of some vice ingrained in his being—egoism, vanity, ambition, the thirst for glory, covetousness, the hunger for power. . . . At the heart of his entire being and all his aspirations there lies a passionate love for the people, an indignation for the people and a long standing hatred for everything that oppresses them . . . everything is subordinated to a ruling passion . . . to create an organisation or collective power capable of carrying out this great work of destruction—to hatch a conspiracy."[339]

What follows is a moving, despairing confession, indirectly an admission of the futility and bankruptcy of the revolutionary endeavour, bitter disappointment with men, and for an anarchist professing boundless faith in human goodness and spontaneity—a terrible apologia for coercion and ruse.

"What terrible disillusionment can be encountered along the road—the eternal disproportion between the grandeur of the goal and the wretchedness of the means, the insufficiency and ignorance of people—a hundred failures for one successful choice, one earnest man to a hundred garrulous and barren minds. And then too there is the perpetual play of vanities, ambitions great and small, grudges, misunderstandings, evasions, gossip, 'intrigue'—and all this in the face of a gigantic, superbly organised, oppressive and punitive power which one wishes to destroy. A hundred times a week one makes a gesture of despair and weariness."[340]

Equally despairing is the description of Russian society. "A country where there is little or no uniting passion, or where, instead of the passion of the heart there exists and operates the passion of the head, where the inclination is more to argument than to action, where Byzantine benediction still continues its corrupting influence, and where, on the other hand, scientific criticism, having successfully destroyed the old morality, has not yet succeeded in creating a new morality, where the scientific negation of free will means for the majority of the youth an indulgent and objective contemplation of their own depravities . . . the dissolution and emancipation of character, the absence of any passionate concentration of the will"[341]—and the formation of a serious secret society becomes wellnigh impossible.

The dedicated revolutionary who desires to carry others with him is like Moses descending from Mount Sinai and finding the children of Israel dancing around the golden calf: "Having tried, honestly but vainly, all honourable means, a young man . . . striving passionately to create at all costs a powerful and secret collective force and convinced that only the activity of such a force can liberate the people",[342] and seeing the inadequacy of the youth and the hopelessness of their uniting freely, comes to the conclusion that "they must be united involuntarily and unawares—and in order that this organisation, half-founded on coercion and deceit, should not crumble, they must be confounded and compromised to such an extent that it becomes impossible for them to withdraw."[343]

This led Nechaev, "a strong, passionate, upright and fervently sincere nature",[344] to Jesuitry. "He could see no other way out. He had either to abandon the cause entirely or adopt the Jesuit system."[345] "Since abandon it he could not, with a heavy heart he took the system to its ultimate, ugly extreme . . . pitiless impetuosity, sparing neither self nor others."[346] Nechaev appears as a crucified martyr: "This man is filled with love, and indeed cannot be otherwise. A person with love could not act with such utter self-abnegation, such a total disregard not only for his own comfort, profit, personal desires, aspirations and emotions, but even for his reputation and name. For he is willing to condemn himself to dishonour, general contempt and even to utter oblivion for the sake of the liberation of the people. It is here that his profound, highly courageous, and virginally pure integrity lies, and it is with the power of this purity and integrity that he crushes us all: whether we like it or not, if we want to be honest with ourselves we have to bow to him. . . . He is not a vain egoist or an intriguer . . . because he does not pursue his own aims, and not only would he not sacrifice a single man for his own gain, his own glory or the satisfaction of his own ambition, he would sooner sacrifice himself for every man. This man has a tender heart."[347]

But how could Nechaev have gone so far in his actions as to practise brazen lying, incessant intrigue, ruthless exploitation and deliberate compromising of his best friends? The emphasis of Bakunin is once more on Jesuitical methods within the organisation, and not in the fight against organised despotism, where he considers "stratagem" indispensable. According to Bakunin Nechaev was drawn into Jesuitry "more passionately since it was repugnant to his own nature'.[348] Because of this inner repugnance, he began with characteristic ruthlessness towards himself and towards others "and with the austerity of a religious ascetic or fanatic"[349] to root out from himself and in others "any manifestations of personal feelings, personal rectitude and all personal obligations and relationships in general, regarding them as criminal weakness . . . which hampered the cause. . . . He made himself and all his friends undergo a systematic course of re-education . . . the systematic annihilation . . . of all that is personally and socially (not secretly, but publicly and socially) sacred and dear to every man." Nechaev was looking desperately for a short cut, for ways to launch in one massive all-out effort the mortal blow to the enemy, the "immensity of the state power",[350] while being acutely conscious of "the historical backwardness, the apathy, the inarticulateness, the infinite patience and the sluggishness of our orthodox people, who could, if they realised and so desired, sink this entire ship of state with one wave of their mighty hand, but who seem still to be sleeping the sleep of the dead".[351]

The only fulcrum for toppling Russian reality seemed to Nechaev to be the youth, but saw it as "a corrupt and inane herd of jabbering doctrinaires".[352] It was the social milieu which corrupted it. Nechaev decided that youth must be uprooted from this milieu: career, family bonds, romantic attachments and vain social relationships. The possibility of a career or any other outlet had to be firmly closed. Young people must be compromised to the utmost, and their return to society made impossible; similarly all family ties must be shattered, together with all attachments of the heart and relations with society, and in this manner a "phalanx of unsparing outlaws created with a single passion in common: the passion to destroy the state and society. You must admit that this fantasy is not the product of a petty mind or a paltry soul, and it has alas!—a great deal of validity and truth."[353]

Any honest and realistic person must want to destroy existing society root and branch. "He who does not beguile himself with selfish dreams and illusions, with splendid but sterile aspirations, and idle chatter must wish for the radical destruction of this society."[354] But a special make-up is required for action in that direction. "Shall I be in a condition to give myself wholly and sincerely to the service of this destructive cause while there still exists so much of the traces of bonds of covetousness, vainglory, ambition and habitual, family and other emotional ties between myself and the society? No, I shall not. Must these bonds, then, be destroyed? Yes, they must. And if you have not the strength to destroy them, do not become involved in the revolutionary cause!"[355]

Then what was Nechaev's offence? Characteristically Bakunin speaks of the latter's "mistake", and not offence or crime. "The Baron's mistake has, in my view, consisted not in his wanting definitively to tear youth away from society and set it at loggerheads with society—this, in my opinion, is a necessity arising from the totality of the present situation in Russia—but in his impatient desire to assemble in the shortest possible time as great a force as he could. Unable, of course, to find in this era of depravity the hundreds of people who might be equal to his programme, he collected people indiscriminately and because of the absence of any real bond between them, was forced to bind them by means of deceit, compromise and coercion, and finally reached the point where he was obliged to introduce the Jesuit system into his organisation. By so doing, he corrupted it. He did not understand that, having destroyed all the social, family and emotional ties of the members of his organisation, he had to create for them a new tie, within the organisation itself, not a negative but a positive one of passionate, fraternal solidarity based on a common purpose, on reciprocal truth and trust, and on the strictest guarantees of mutual assistance.''[356]

All historic experience goes to show that these resonant generalities become pathetic irrelevancies when it comes down to brass tacks. The line of demarcation between an idealistic fighting fraternity under the strain of contending views, and an intrigue-ridden ruling clique of ambitious or headstrong pretenders and rivals is very thin. Bitter battles have to be fought out, first by argument and jockeying for position, later by psychological warfare, and in the last instance the conflicts are resolved, or rather smothered, by the only effective measures—prison, torture and physical liquidation. These practices are not however spelled out in programmes, are not taught by theoreticians, and not even explicitly prescribed in any detail by the leaders, any more than the more sordid preparations in the kitchen, such as the slaughter of the chicken by the cook, are laid down in detail or are actually supervised by the lady of the house.

Against the background of the passionate quest and bitter agonies of the earlier Russian revolutionaries, Lenin appears as their heir, the beneficiary of their experiences and executor of their will. World-shaking events enabled him to transfer ideas from doctrinal disquisition and sectarian life to the plane of global confrontation. His programme and organisation emerged out of the antinomies which plagued and destroyed the Narodniks. The revolutionaries' long work of undercutting the spiritual, and thus also social, roots of the Tsarist system, of educating men not to be afraid, to dare, to defy, made it possible for him to resolve to tear away the masses from all the remaining ties, attachments and loyalties which bound them to the regime by inciting them to disobedience at time of war. It also enabled him to turn their readiness to commit treason into a test of their ability to leap the last barrier of fear and inhibition, and to demonstrate their final emancipation and full ripeness for the revolution.

Part VI

LENIN — INTERNATIONAL REVOLUTIONARY
AND ARCHITECT OF NEW RUSSIA

Chapter One

THE FORMATIVE YEARS
(*I*) HEIR AND INNOVATOR

In "The Heritage We Renounce",[1] written in exile at the end of 1897, Lenin resolutely rejects the "narrow nationalism bordering on chauvinism"[2] of the Russian Populists.

In their belief—he goes on to say—in "Russia's exceptionalism, the Narodniks reassured themselves with the thought that although we lacked some of the features of civilised humanity,[3] . . . "we were destined to show the world new modes of economy etc. Not only was the analysis of capitalism and all its manifestations given by progressive West-European thought not accepted in relation to Holy Russia; every effort was made to invent excuses for not drawing the same conclusions about Russian capitalism as were made regarding European capitalism."[4]

Five years later in *What is to be Done?*[5] Lenin proclaims: "History has now confronted us with an immediate task which is the most revolutionary of all the immediate tasks confronting the proletariat of any country. The fulfilment of this task, the destruction of the most powerful bulwark, not only of European, but (it may now be said) of Asiatic reaction, would make the Russian proletariat the vanguard of the international revolutionary proletariat. And we have the right to count upon acquiring the honourable title, already earned by our predecessors, the revolutionaries of the seventies" (the Narodnaya Volya).[6]

Indeed, not to mention the still earlier pronouncements on the special revolutionary mission of Russia by Herzen, as early as 1861, the famous proclamation "To the Young Generation" stated: "we are a retarded people, and therein lies our salvation. . . . We believe we are destined to bring a new principle into history, to say our own word, and not to ape Europe's outlived ideas."[7] A year later the Russian Jacobin and prophet of bloody terror, Zanichevsky, was calling upon the masses to rise against "the Imperial family and the Imperial party" with the words "Kill them in the public squares, in their homes, in the streets, in the cities, in the villages and the hamlets . . . use the axe", coupling this call with the statement of Russia's destiny "to be the first to realise the great ideal of socialism".[8]

On the face of it, Lenin may appear to be denying the Russian revolutionary heritage and to be its consummation at the same time. The allegedly Russian way to socialism had been inspired by an idealised image of the Russian peasant as a socialist by his way of life in the commune and as a revolutionary by instinct. It was predicated upon an illusory conception of the village commune as an embryonic socialist society. Reviewing the works of Skaldin and Engelhardt on Russian agriculture,[9] Lenin described the *muzhiks* of the commune as bound to the soil. They were held together, especially since the establishment of the office of cantonal land-captain in 1889, not by ties of natural solidarity and by traditions of self-government, but by imposed collective responsibility for paying taxes and observing the repressive government laws. The commune was also a straitjacket on innovative initiative and improvement. Far from being animated by sentiments of kinship, the peasants had become grabbing egoists, whose dream was one day to be kulaks. So much did they begrudge the aid which they had to give to their neighbours that women would wash up only their own corner of the communal table.[10] Latent centrifugal individualism had been powerfully stimulated by the inroads of capitalism into the village. The commune was in the process of dissolution and the *mir* was being rent by class conflict between the rich peasants and the poor or, still more, landless peasants gradually drifting into urban industrial labour.

Instead of realising socialism in its own way through by-passing capitalism, the Narodnik Russia of the commune was being swept into the global process of capitalist development. The Russian working class, above all its most dynamic and rapidly growing part, the industrial proletariat, had become subjected to the dialectic of international class struggle for the emancipation of the world-proletariat.

If the Narodnik image of the undifferentiated toiling masses, with the urban workers seen as peasants working in towns, and all forging ahead together on a broad front to a Russian type of socialism, was a mirage, the vague Populist concept of the Russian people as some mystical, peculiar and self-sufficient entity had to give way to such sharply defined categories as class, class interests and class consciousness, claimed Lenin. And yet, it was the cardinal importance he gave the peasant problem in Russia, in contrast to the Western socialists' and the Mensheviks' nearly exclusive focus on industrial labour, that became the mainspring of Lenin's original contribution to Marxist thought, especially to socialist theory and practice in the backward countries outside Europe, that is to say the majority of mankind.[11] Indeed, Lenin himself was intensely alive to the possibility and the challenge of "carrying the revolutionary conflagration to Europe" after the revolutionary alliance of workers and poor peasants (the latter taking the place in Russia of the petty bourgeoisie of the West) had accomplished the radical democratic revolution in Russia through the abolition of absolutism, the liquidation of the landlord class by the distribution of their lands to the peasants, and the attainment of proletarian hegemony over the liberal bourgeoisie. The victory of the minimum programme of Russian socialism, the only one possible in the backward state of Russia, was sure to stimulate the ignited Western revolutions to proceed to a fully fledged socialist revolution, which would in turn serve as a mighty impulse to Russian developments towards a socialist order.

As if reversing Marx's view that no European revolution would be safe so long as the Russian gendarme of counter-revolution stood ready to pounce upon it, and therefore could triumph only through a victorious war against Russia waged by a Western terrorist dictatorship in the 1793 revolutionary style, Lenin seemed to proclaim that the European revolution would be set going only by a push from Russia: a variation on the Narodnik vision of Russia's messianic mission.

It was not simply because Russia was the lynchpin of the European system of alliances, or conversely the Achilles heel of world capitalism, or because it constituted such a huge chunk of humanity, that she was capable of fulfilling that role. The last will be first: the belated but also precipitated industrial revolution in backward Russia would benefit from the latest, most advanced techniques of the West, while the lack or paucity of native capital and private initiative, as well as military needs, were leading the state to step in and promote heavy and concentrated industry by resorting to foreign loans and investment. In that respect Russia was linking up with Western monopolist imperialism in a number of ways. She had become an Eldorado for Western finance, while proclaiming that she "recognised no frontiers in Asia"[12] to her expansion, and acting accordingly. With her own masses exploited by an alliance of foreign and native monopoly capitalists, Russia was determined not to be left behind by the other great powers in the oppression of conquered peoples and in the colonies. Russia was thus a distorted reflection of international imperialism. If there were doubts about the readiness of the Western proletariat for a socialist revolution, Russia was surely seething with revolution, which in the twentieth century could no longer be bottled up and isolated as a purely local political upheaval.

Lenin offered a trenchant and as it were conclusive answer to all the dilemmas and contradictions which tormented the spokesmen of the Russian revolutionary intelligentsia. He anchored the fate of the Russian revolution firmly to the global vision of the dénouement of the historic dialectic and yet reserved a special place for it. He then turned a deterministic, all-embracing faith into the instrument of the most strenuous kind of voluntarism and activism. He married a theory of objectively inevitable development and of spontaneous response to it, to a practice of the most deliberately organised action, based upon an all-encompassing faith in a final goal and upon the greatest, not to say most opportunistic, flexibility in the choice of tactics. Lenin was driven by a relentless sense of urgency which re-echoed the "now or never" slogan of the extreme Populists such as Tkachev.

The never absent feeling of being always on the eve of great events, in face of supreme chances, which might bring the promised breakthrough but if missed would cause a terrible setback, became the great and irresistible motive force of Lenin at the outbreak of the 1914 War, and still more in 1917, with the victory of the February revolution. The defeat of the Tsar and then of the ruling classes and groups which had taken over the reins of government was in his eyes sure to usher in the pre-destined revolution. Their victory, however, would enable the establishment, dominated by a military dictatorship, to drive back and suppress the revolutionary forces for no one knew how long. To work for the former eventuality implied a decision to destroy the historic Russian Empire, in the spirit of Bakunin and Tkachev, if not even Lavrov. But in the circumstances of a national war—a contingency which had not entered the forerunners' calculations—this amounted to a resolve in favour of a policy of national treason. Such a stupendous decision, which was bound to come up against the most deeply rooted traditions, instincts and inhibitions, could be taken only if it was certain that it would bring the longed-for salvation to Russia, and indeed to the world, since all mankind was poised at the edge of an abyss, facing the alternatives of socialism or barbarism.

(II) PROPHET OF WAR (LENIN) AND PROPHET OF PEACE (JAURÈS)

It has never been contested that it was Lenin who in the face of universal opposition, for a while even of almost all his closest comrades, took that fateful decision, just as throughout his whole career he had always in the end proved ready and able to impose his will and to override or drive out other wills. We are here up against another dilemma which pre-occupied the nineteenth-century Russian prophets: the role of the "new man", of the "critical personality", supposed somehow to realise his own individuality and at the same time to sacrifice it, to ride the wave of history and yet to swim against the stream.

Lenin's personality and historic role seem like a parable upon and a case story of this dichotomy. Against the background of the revolutionary camp of his day Lenin appears both to be growing out of it and yet to negate it. All believed in the historic dialectic, at the end of which was the predetermined dénouement. All believed in necessary stages of development which could not be by-passed. All held fast to the idea that history was not made by way of individual decision or deliberate contrivance, but was unfolded in accordance with objective conditions. It was not possible for Russia, any more than other countries, to skip the bourgeois democratic revolution and the capitalist phase before reaching the proletarian revolution. Another common article of faith was the notion that history was propelled by contra-dictions. The existing was always pregnant with its negation. There was however the question: whether to allow for the full gestation of the former till the inevitable maturation of the latter, or whether to hasten by every means the victory of the negating force.[13]

Lenin experienced that sense of movement, of the eternal tug of war, of unbridgeable contradictions, of the approaching crisis, with an intensity and urgency unmatched by anyone in his circle. It was said by comrades that he was truly one who dreamt of the revolution twenty-four hours a day, and that his single-mindedness was for that reason irresistible.[14] What was however most important was the fact that movement, contradiction, conflict, breakthrough, change were to him encased in an evolving totality held together by the iron-cast law of historic inevitability. The irresistible march of history could neither be affected nor could be allowed to be interfered with by human arbi-trariness, caprice, preferences, feelings, sentiments, residual inhibitions.

This unshakable consistency was most strikingly and to most people bafflingly demonstrated by the twenty-two-year-old Ulyanov when he opposed philanthropic help to the victims of famine in the province of Samara. "The famine"—he is reported to have said—"is the direct consequence of a particular social order. So long as that order exists, famines are inevitable. They can be abolished only by the abolition of that order of society. Being in this sense inevitable, famine today performs a progressive function. It destroys the peasant economy and throws peasants from village into the city. Thus the proletariat is formed, which speeds the industrialisation of the nation. . . . It will cause the peasant to reflect on the fundamental facts of capitalist society. It will destroy his faith in the Tsar and in Tsarism and will in time speed the victory of the revolution." The philanthropic reflexes of "society" were in fact an expression of bourgeois fear of disturbances and of the eventual destruction of the bourgeois order, "an expression of the saccharine sentimentality so characteristic of our intelligentsia".[15]

Lenin's vision of the historic dynamic propelled by contradiction and conflict assumed the shape of a warlike confrontation in which there was no standing still, only advance or retreat, victory or defeat. The conquering party was permanently mobilised, on the alert to turn the latent war into an actual one.

If Lenin was wholly dominated by the vision of revolution, Jean Jaurès[16] was obsessed with the ideal of peace. The most eloquent and most passionate fighter against war in the Second International, and tragic victim of nationalist-militarist frenzy, was the prophet of universal reconciliation and concord. Lenin's struggle against war was waged by a prophet of the kind who brings the sword and lives and wins by discord and strife. The two represented diametrically opposed mentalities, perhaps two different epochs. Jaurès embodied the best in pre-1914 humanism, Lenin ushered in the ice age.

The reader of the multi-volume *Histoire Socialiste de la Révolution*,[17] so highly praised by two such bitter antagonists as the great Dantonist Aulard, and the Robespierrist Mathiez, is struck not only by the illuminating discernment of the economic, social and intellectual ingredients of future socialism and by the wealth of data and quotation, but above all by the extraordinary generosity with which Jaures, who writes a "socialist" history, treats all actors in the drama; classes, parties, groups and above all, men. The author shrinks from attributing mean motives to anyone. He takes the greatest pains to explain the circumstances and compulsions which made individuals and forces act as they did, sometimes badly and wrongly, almost always, however, with good intentions. Jaurès writes a brief for socialism rather than trying to make out a case against the forces opposed to it. The same attitude may be detected in his whole political career. It is difficult to sort out the elements which went into it. There was certainly a passion for fairness. There was a strong element of that relativism which springs from vast knowledge, from fascination with the unbounded varieties of experience, and from a deep sense of the bewildering complexity of things. All these made him easily yield to inferior men with narrower horizons, more limited understanding, but greater self-assurance.

The wise old Russo-Franco-Jewish socialist Charles Rappoport, who knew Jaurès intimately and loved him deeply, says: "because he saw and knew the infinite complexity of things and of men, he had a certain inferiority—an admirable and humane inferiority—in face of men made all of one piece who go off like a bullet in the direction to which their egoism and prejudices point",[18] the more so in face of men who also had unshakable convictions such as Lenin had. Briand speaks of Jaurès' "timid temperament which dares not affront the common people".[19] Jules Romains wonders about Jaurès' inability to grasp "the essential absurdity which is the very warp and woof of life",[20] and Rappoport again suggests that "his goodness and idealism prevented him from seeing men and things in their full wretchedness and pettiness".[21] No wonder Georges Sorel, with his Leninist sympathies, chose Jaurès as his *bête noire*, as the emodiment of petty-bourgeois flabbiness, shiftiness and opportunist spinelessness. Something of the advocate who is clever and resourceful enough to argue any case may have lurked in the intellectual that was Jaurès. But it was not, it seems, lack of firm conviction: it was an extraordinary poetic capacity for empathy that gives the impression of a pantheistic comprehensiveness, or, if one prefers, of eclecticism. The marvellous quickness of sympathy and of imaginative insight combined with the unmatched gift of the word to propel Jaurès into those flamboyant rhapsodies on any subject touched by him.

Out of the depths of his all-encompassing love and compassion, Jaurès turned the historic dialectic in stark contrast to Lenin, into a canvas of constant matching opposites, of a progressively evolving harmony, a growing reconciliation, as part of a movement towards final universal concord. His vision of peace comes close to the Hebrew concept of *shalom*, denoting wholeness, healing of wounds, joining broken pieces, restoration of a pristine order of justice and amity. In Jaurès' mouth peace meant putting an end to disorder, which sprang from aggressiveness, avarice, the competitive urge, the craving for ascendancy. So socialism became to him synonymous with peace. For real peace would still all drives which made for aggression, inequality, oppression and of course war. "Your [bourgeois] violent and chaotic society, even when it wants peace, even when it seems to be in a state of repose, carries within it war, as the somnolent cloud carries the storm."[22] But socialism is "a journey . . . through truth, through reality, towards justice, towards the rule of harmony, towards the supreme beauty of agreement between men of free will. . . . The human race will only be saved by an immense moral revolution; without a great moral upheaval to restore the forces of right, equity, peace and truth, Europe will be plunged into the most disastrous events."[23] Well might a good many comrades of Jaurès murmur their doubts about whether he was really a socialist or a pacifist, and wonder what all his prophecies had to do with class war; and fear his pernicious influence.

Far from emphasising basic contradictions, Jaurès was eager to treat the conflicting elements as complementing each other in a higher unity. The campaigner for a secular society free from religious constraints, the opponent of a church allied to royalism and militarism and upholding authoritarian principles, Jaurès interpreted the concept of divinity as the synonym of spirituality and morality and saw all creation as filled with God. The adherent of the school of dialectical materialism treated idealism as the voice and instrument of economic change and the transformer of the opportunities and developments in the sphere of material culture into meaningful and benevolent arrangements. Similarly, socialism was to him in the final analysis purified and sublimated Christianity.[24] There are few more glowing apologias for capitalism than Jaurès' hymn at the end of *L'Armée Nouvelle* to "the huge capitalist sun" rising in the United States where a new society was being shaped "without irremediable ruptures and mortal dislocations . . . without breaking the essential and organic unity of human societies".[25] It is astonishing to read from the pen of a Marxist the description of the relationship between capital, labour, the nation and the army in Chapter 10 of *L'Armée Nouvelle* headed "Sources of Moral and Social Energy: Army, Nation and Proletariat": "The thing that has saved industry from senile degeneration is working class activity, working class combativeness. It has saved capitalism from the decline into which uncontrolled monopoly would have led it. What a monstrous Roman Emperor, vicious and increasingly drunken, capital would have become but for the pressure of the people from below! Luckily for capital and civilisation, the people had a conscience, an ideal, a will, a heroism, a pride both secular and made up of the accumulated forces of Christianity and the French Revolution, a great spirit of sacrifice sustained by a high hope; the resolution to struggle for its own good and the increasingly clear recognition that in struggling for itself it would be struggling for all men. During their rivalries and combats, throughout their long miseries and hatreds, capital and labour collaborated in production and technical advance in a common progress from which the two classes benefit unequally today, but from which one day the members of the two classes will benefit equally in a society where there will be no more classes and the long tremors of class-war—terrible and beneficent at the same time—will have no other function in a world of equal and reconciled individuals than to act as a spirit of emulation in work and social justice."[26]

Jaures maintained against Bernstein the radical distinction between the proletariat and the bourgeoisie. Against Kautsky he argued the necessity of contact between classes within the great human society. "We want revolution but we don't want everlasting hate." Surely the joyous fulfilment of human destiny would come "when all men finally live together". Jaurès described his socialist ideal as revolutionary evolution within the framework of democratic legality.

"No doubt, if collective ownership were imposed arbitrarily upon societies by external powers, if it were introduced according to the laws of conquest, it would crush all initiative. But if it happens by the increase of the capitalist movement and the workers' will, if it is prepared by the unconscious action of the bourgeoisie and by the conscious action of the proletariat . . . the two classes . . . whose antagonism rends the world today will be equally though diversely victorious in the achievement of communal ownership. The working class will have escaped from economic servitude, it will have won the right of co-ownership in a society which will be its final emancipation, and it will set about obtaining from the unified system of production a full degree of well-being for all. . . . But the bourgeoisie too, in its very defeat as a class will be victorious. . . . It will become conscious of the work which it was unconsciously bringing about . . . by the incessant technical revolutions with which it convulsed and strengthened industry. This capitalist concentration, which once was only the triumph of a class, will appear, after the revolution, as the germ of humanity."[27]

Jaurès defended the right to strike as a right, but not as an act intended to impose terms by means of violence. He spoke appreciatively of the noble impulses of anarchism and its fight for the untrammelled self-expression of the individual, but was horrified by its resort to assassination and by its arbitrariness in refusing to become part of and to heed the will of an organised collective body, by the stance of war against society, in brief.[28]

Jaurès will be forever remembered as the prophet of internationalism, and at the same time the poet of patriotism. The nation was conceived by him as the seed bed of individual personality.[29] Any attempt to dissolve it was tantamount to stunting man, to depriving him of all those sentiments, associations, habits, loyalties which shaped his very being, his identity, especially those of men of the people, with their deep roots in the collective soul, ancestral soil and folklore. It meant doing violence. At the same time, Jaurès considered militant nationalism as the greatest enemy of patriotism, and internationalism as the condition and accompaniment of the latter. Love, generosity, human solidarity, the will for give and take between peoples, the aspiration for international peace were the attributes of a noble nation. A people seething with aggression and xenophobia was sure to pervert human nature and it could not maintain a democratic way of life. Ultimately, only a socialist country could foster the solidarity and develop all the potentialities of the nation, since it was resolved to do away with privilege, inequality, selfishness and the rat race, and to realise national brotherhood to the full.[30]

In utter contrast to Lenin, Jaurès vehemently rejected any suggestion that the socialist revolution could or should be brought about by international war.[31] If socialism meant peace, it was unthinkable that a war should be waged to rid the world of war. The latter was too high a price for revolution. It would dangerously brutalise mankind, and make it unfit for socialism: an argument which Jaurès used against Guesdes' refusal to take sides in the quarrel between different categories of bourgeois that the Dreyfus case was to him. Every wronged person, whatever his social origins or occupation, became to Jaurès an object of concern to socialists. And if socialists were to let society be hopelessly perverted by falsehood, injustice and cruelty, it would be left without the necessary human material to build socialism.[32]

"A European war may well give birth to the revolution—and the ruling classes will do well to bear it in mind; but it may equally well give rise to a long period of counter-revolutionary crises of furious reaction, exasperated nationalism, suffocating dictatorship and monstrous militarism. And we have no wish to play at such a barbarous game of chance; we have no wish to risk on one throw of the dice of war all the certitude of the progressive emancipation of the proletariat, all the assurance of just autonomy which—above all partitions and dis-memberments—the full victory of European social-democracy offers to all peoples."[33] No less repellent to Jaurès than the spectre of what was to be called Fascism was the other possible outcome of a revolution emerging out of war—the dictatorship of a socialist minority sect.[34]

It would not be exact to say that Jaurès was a naive rationalistic believer in the goodness of man. He did believe in the possibility of sub-limating man's aggressive urges. This enabled him incidentally to achieve his famous syntheses: to acknowledge the reality of the malady and to hope for a cure, or at least a diversionary remedy. Thus on colonialism, Jaurès recognised at the London congress of the Second International the drive for colonial expansion as universal, "irresistible like a law of nature . . . a need for expansion and adventure which urges on all virile peoples today".³⁵ Any attempt to frustrate it might result in inflaming chauvinist passions in the non-democratic nations, and in transforming republican regimes into "a Caesarean regime of conquest, of noisy glory and pillage seeking".³⁶ Apart from the duty to humanise colonialism, there was the need to establish international guarantees for the free use of the great historic land routes and sea passages and the economic resources of the globe. Gradually Jaurès became more and more aware of the fundamental demoralisation caused by what he called, when observing the imperialist rat race, "a permanent Dreyfus case".³⁷ The devious scheming of the French government which brought about the first Morocco crisis in 1905 was an eye-opener to him on this, and also on the danger of Europe sliding into war in the near future. He wavered violently between fatalistic horror and hope that the vast global interests of world capitalism had become so intertwined that enlightened self-interest would restrain imperialist antagonists from an armed clash.

Most Jauresian was of course Jaurès wrestling with the dilemmas of national and international war. National defence against foreign aggression was the most sacred of tasks, indeed—with his eyes on Jacobin patriotism—the test of the moral fibre of the nation, of its love of liberty and of its will to live. Jaurès' internationalism was never anything other than a vision of a Europe of fatherlands. He had generous words for Hervé's passionate fight against chauvinism, but his rejection of national statehood and any form of patriotism as vessels of aggressive nationalism seemed to Jaurès like the Luddites breaking machines in order to stop the exploitation of workers.³⁸ Dismemberment of states would lead not to a single international community of free men, but to the imposition of a single despotic will over all by some Caesar.³⁹

L'Armée Nouvelle—Jaurès' most important book—is in fact a passionate plea for making the fatherland safe and yet for guaranteeing international peace. The pacifist tract throbs with the excitement caused to the author by the memories of the great Carnot's achievement and of the famous victories of French armies in the past. The nation in arms of the French Revolution is the model for Jaurès' "nouvelle armée". It would be free from the hierarchical features of the traditional standing armies and of the aggressive vainglorious urges driving on the professional, upper class officer corps. It would be all the more efficient and all the more formidable. It would undermine the sinister community of interests and aims of the diplomatic-military-industrial forces practising secret diplomacy. If the neutralisation of competitive and exploitative designs within the nation was a condition for their disappearance from relations between nations, the organised proletariat and socialism were the strongest guarantee of international peace and the most effective force for the prevention of war, through pressure on the respective governments as well as through international action against chauvinist militarism, and by it constituting a standing revolutionary threat to imperialist establishments.[40]

And yet, in his permanent wavering and desperate quest for means of averting the horrors of war, Jaurès could also speak approvingly—to the horror of Rosa Luxemburg[41]—of the existing alliances and alignments of the Great Powers as a mechanism protecting European peace. Early on he had a good word even for the Tsar as having been historically "the soul of the Russian people".[42] His horror however of Russian despotism and fear of France being dragged by it into war grew stronger with time. At times Jaurès showed a condescending attitude towards German social-democracy, criticising it for lack of revolutionary ardour and lamenting its lack of possibilities for revolutionary action under an authoritarian regime. Yet he was full of admiration for the marvellous theoretical and organisational resources of the SPD.[43] Jaurès displayed also a readiness to lean backwards in analysing the historic reasons for Germany's restless foreign policy. He repeatedly acknowledged the fundamentally pacific intentions of its rulers. The idea of a war for the restoration of Alsace and Lorraine was anathema to him.[44] He consoled himself with the hope that the growth of the spirit of liberty and peace on both sides of the border would secure the widest possible autonomy to the two disputed provinces. Jaurès went so far as to insist that no one should demand or expect from German socialists a policy of a renunciation of Alsace-Lorraine. No wonder French nationalists pursued Jaurès, "the Prussian Herr Jaurès", with a venom that eventually spurred a patriotic assassin to commit his awful deed, when Europe had really reached the brink. His erstwhile friend, the Catholic socialist and nationalist Charles Péguy, wrote in April 1913, when Jaurès was fighting bitterly the Bill to extend military service to three years and thundering at the famous Basle Cathedral Convention threats of an international proletarian insurrection against war-mongers: "the representative in France of the policy of imperialist, capitalist, colonising Germany . . . has fallen beneath the contempt of the lowest in the land . . . the essential traitor . . . has adorned all his capitulations with the garlands of his mock-heroics . . . a diseased mania, a monomania . . . the Convention Nationale would mean Jaurès in a tumbril and a roll of drums to drown the mighty voice".[45]

Notwithstanding all the strains which the Third Republic had to experience—such as the Panama scandal, Boulangism, the Dreyfus case, the state and church conflict and social unrest—its course confirmed Thiers' prognosis that a bourgeois republic would divide the Frenchmen least. The supreme national crisis of 1914 revealed a France more one and indivisible than ever. The hour was described by leading men of letters of various schools and convictions as the apogee of French national unity, another *fête de fédération,* the full fruition of the national idea.[46] In Russia, by contrast, those decades prepared the break-up of the centuries-old order.

It has been said that the secret of success is single-mindedness, which is another word for purposefulness. Jaurès cared most for comprehensiveness. It is possible to diagnose an anxiety complex in his fear of leaving out anything relevant to the—to him always multifaceted—matter in hand. His messianic pacifism thus lacked a definite goal in the form of a recognisable breakthrough. It was as a result vague and diffuse. As already said, Lenin was hypnotised by a most clearly articulated goal, the revolution. In order to achieve it, he was most vigilant in keeping out anything that interfered with it or could rival or even only diminish his wholehearted dedication to and full-time preoccupation with the essential. At the same time he used and harnessed everything possible for its service. He refused to give in to the softening effect of music and to his fondness for the time-consuming game of chess.[47] But he kept his body and faculties trim for the cause by regular exercise and holidays.[48] He shocked Valentinov by dismissing the writings of Mach and Avenarius as bourgeois rubbish, without even having read them, and by insisting that a revolutionary should not waste his time with irrelevancies.[49] He then sat down, studied them for many months and wrote a (feeble) book in order to fortify and immunise the minds of the faithful against them.[50]

No one can say for certain what makes a person more effective: the fully integrated personality which is able to bring its full strength and all its resources to bear upon the desired objective, or the contradictions, deprivations, sense of unfulfilment and injury, which stem from early traumas, unhappy experiences or any other unassuaged predicament and drive the victim on to overcome handicaps, to find compensation, to prove his worth, like for instance the six Prime Ministers of Britain within a span of fifty years who grew up fatherless. There can be no doubt that Lenin's extraordinary effectiveness was rooted in the former situation, if we do not count the terrible shock of the execution of his older brother for plotting the assassination of Tsar Alexander III.[51]

The real secret of Lenin's power was his fundamental modesty and his total lack of all personal vanity. Nothing was further from him than the gimmicks of a cult of personality, than pose and personal touchiness, than the wish to be in the limelight and to be approved, let alone acclaimed.[52] Lenin's approach lacked any trace of self-consciousness. He believed he was always wholly objective. He never wondered whether he was behaving correctly towards people and he never questioned his own motives: there was no lingering sense of guilt. So he could be utterly relentless. Not that Lenin did not often admit having committed an error. He would do that however without any fear of losing face. He was never worried by the accusation of being inconsistent. His monumental self-assurance was based upon an unshakable faith in the rock-like monolith of Marxist theory as the unquestionable reflection of objective reality and of the historic process.[53] The dialectical nature of the latter at the same time made possible any amount of mental zigzags and acrobatic tactics. Lenin's conviction about his own ability to decipher the needs and the imperatives of the dialectic of revolution at every turn was so innocently and monumentally free from self-consciousness that it could not be called conceit or arrogance. Just as introspection and self-doubt were alien to his nature, so was his attitude to others shaped not by their personal qualities, or by their attitude to him, but in reference to the, as it were, objective and exclusive criterion—the relevance to the Cause: it is enough to recall the manner in which Lenin overlooked the terrible things which Trotsky had been saying about him before 1917.

A personally virtuous party heretic was infinitely more despicable, more untouchable than an unscrupulous comrade who became a gigolo in order to obtain funds for the party or a Bolshevik robber practising "expropriations".[54] Most of Lenin's early comrades were incapable of such shutting off of natural impulses, sentiments and inhibitions, of a similar inhuman objectivity. They began to feel crushed by him. Vera Zasulich complained that the *Iskra* group changed from a free-loving family into a personal dictatorship soon after Lenin had joined it. Potresov felt suffocated by the total lack of youthfulness in the young Lenin.[55] Trotsky called Lenin in 1904 a Robespierre, a terrorist dictator aiming to turn the party leadership into a Committee of Public Safety.[56] In 1910 Lenin's stubbornness at the Copenhagen congress of the Second International moved Mme Krzhizhanovskaya to exclaim "He is one man against the whole party. He is ruining the party. How fortunate the party would be if he disappeared, vanished, evaporated, died!"[57] In 1914 Charles Rappoport "recognised Lenin's achievements". He went on to say "He is a man of iron will and an incomparable organiser. . . . But he regards himself as the only socialist. Whoever opposes him is forever condemned by him. . . . He sees in capital punishment the only means of assuring the existence of the Social-Democratic party. War is declared on anyone who differs from him. Instead of combating his opponents in the Social-Democratic party by socialist methods, i.e. by argument, Lenin uses only surgical methods, those of blood-letting. No party could exist under the regime of this Social-Democrat Tsar, who regards himself as a super-Marxist, but who is, in reality an adventurer of the highest order. . . . Lenin's victory would be the greatest menace to the Russian revolution . . . he will choke it."[58] Similarly Viacheslav Menzhinsky, later chief of the Soviet secret police, called Lenin in 1916 "a political Jesuit, who over the course of many years has moulded Marxism to his aims of the moment . . . this illegitimate child of Russian absolutism . . . the natural successor to the Russian throne . . . but also the sole heir of the socialist International".[59]

Lenin was moved by the unshakable conviction that the socialist goal could never be achieved by gradual reforms and by methods of mutual accommodation, give-and-take and compromise, but only by the violent imposition of the will of the conquering force, the executor of the will of history, upon the beaten enemy, in fact his annihilation as a social-political force.

This resolve arose from absolute distrust of the adversary, indeed even of any potential or possible allies in the struggle, who might have an interest and wish to go some part of the road with the army forging ahead to a total confrontation. They might be used and should be manipulated, but always in full awareness that they were strangers, even if for a while fellow travellers; that they were wholly treacherous and untrustworthy, and in the final analysis sure to prove downright hostile; and that as an obstacle to the full consummation of the enterprise they must be eliminated.

The great breakthroughs in history were not, according to Lenin, effected by parliamentary deliberations and resolutions, but by force. Fair shares, fair play, free speech, a due share to all interests and shades of opinion and accepting a majority decision—these could never be aims in themselves. This was a static view of history. Lenin's was wholly dynamic, shaped by the idea of becoming and of driving to a dénouement.

There was a great danger in all alliances for a party bent upon achieving a breakthrough. They were sure to have a debilitating effect upon its prowess and fighting resolve. A revolutionary class and still more so party, was in duty bound to fence itself off from all others, to emphasise how it differed from other parties, to maintain its independence at all costs, even when collaborating with them for tactical reasons. It must always be careful not to become their appendage, to be outwitted and betrayed by them. More than that, no alliance with others was admissible except on condition that the party was able to exercise a dominant influence, to impose its hegemony, and make its aims prevail, whether directly and openly, or indirectly by planting agents throughout the alliance. These were not only intended to prevent backsliding and to prod the allies to go as far as possible in the direction of the conquering force, but also to prepare within the "cells" the foci and cadres for the inevitable confrontation with the temporary comrades in arms. Dictatorship was in-built in the initial attitude.[60]

In polemics with Populists, and their offshoot the Socialist Revolutionaries as well as the Economists, Legal Marxists and Revisionists, and even Social-Democrats like Plekhanov, Lenin always deprecated the use of concepts and terms such as the popular masses, the toiling millions, democratic forces, fighters for liberty. They were bound to blur the fact of the singularity, individuality and vanguard nature of the proletarian class of industrial workers. Before 1861 there had been a semblance of reality about the image of popular unity: all social forces, not directly fattening upon serfdom, were being harmed by it and were against it, since it was an incubus upon the Russian economy, a dead weight on social relationships and political aspirations. The abolition of serfdom and the subsequent capitalist developments in Russia exploded the illusion that there was a common cause for all partisans of liberty.[61]

There was only one social force striving for human emancipation— the class-conscious industrial proletariat as represented by Lenin's own party. All other forces should be utterly distrusted. They had to be absorbed or eliminated.

(III) PARANOIA AND SELF-FULFILLING PROPHECY — THE STRUGGLE BETWEEN AUTOCRACY AND REVOLUTION

The early 1860's were a watershed in Russian history.[62] To most contemporaries, not excluding, as we have said, the radical opponents of the Tsarist regime, they seemed to presage a total political and social transformation in the direction of Western constitutionalism. The frustration of these hopes made a total revolution inevitable, as they destroyed the last shred of the autocracy's credibility. Lenin's obsessive suspiciousness was an excrescence of that cancerous growth in the body politic of Russia—mutual fear, distrust, bad faith and deviousness— which was the result and then again the cause of historic developments.

The political theology of the Tsarist system was founded upon the rock of autocracy by divine right as the dam holding back the flood of lurking savage anarchy. The Tsarist establishment had long realised that peasant serfdom was the root of all the evils of Russia. But it dreaded touching it lest tinkering with the very foundations of the social order might bring the whole edifice down.[63] Russia's defeat in the Crimean War revealed all the internal weaknesses of a power until then thought invincible. It compelled Alexander II to issue, after infinite deliberation, the famous Decree of Emancipation. Personal serfdom was abolished. But at a closer look it can be seen that the act of liberation was framed not simply to grant the peasants human and citizen rights and to turn them into independent owners of their allotments, but very much with an eye to safeguarding the interests and status of the landowners.[64] It contrived new forms of holding the peasants under oppressive control, so that they would not become a social-political force. The peasants were not allotted outright the land which they had cultivated for generations and which they had always regarded as their own. They were permitted to purchase about half of it in annual payments extended to 49 years. The nobles retained the remainder, the famous *otrezki*, and in addition were paid compensation out of state funds. The peasants had now to eke out a miserable existence from much smaller lots, on top of the crushing burden of the annual redemption fees. Even before 1861 the average peasant allotments kept the cultivator busy for only three days a week. The lack of capital and technical knowledge, the narrowness of the widely dispersed strips, the constant friction with the squire who claimed exclusive rights to pasture, woodland and water, the duty of the peasant to hire himself out as a day labourer working with his own horses and implements to the nobleman and to rent from him a piece of land for cash or on a crop sharing basis—all these continued after 1861 to retain the peasant in economic bondage. The more so, as rural overpopulation was increasing the land hunger to insufferable dimensions. In 1897 the peasants still constituted five-sixths of the 130 million population. In 1914 they were still 85 per cent of the 185 million souls of Russia, wage-earners in industry and commerce counting no more than 8-9 million.[65] We have to add to this the disastrous effects upon European agriculture of the opening of the vast prairies in the New World to the plough as well as the deliberate policy of the virtual dictator of the Russian economy for a whole generation, Witte, to industrialise Russia at the expense of the village by keeping bread as cheap as possible.[66]

Palliatives applied by the government to prevent a catastrophe, such as scaling down redemption fees in 1881 and 1884, then the extension of the payments arrears until the 1950's, the establishment of the State Peasant Land Bank to help the peasants with loans, eventually the total abolition of the redemption fees in 1907, and even the encouragement given to peasant emigration to and settlement in Siberia, could hardly scratch the surface of the problem. These measures were powerless to prevent the shrinkage of the average peasant allotment from 35 acres in 1877 to 28 acres in 1905.[67] Terrible famines and epidemics in the 1890's and in the first years of the twentieth century made ravages in the over-populated black-soil regions, and sent peasants to riot and to pillage the manors of the gentry. In 1897 no more than one in five peasants was literate.[68] The government felt helpless in face of this unmanageable situation, alarmed as it also was for social and political reasons by the steady impoverishment of the gentry. The State Land Bank for the Nobility (later amalgamated with the Peasant Land Bank into a unified Land Bank) was hardly able to stop the bankruptcies, which caused nobles' land to pass into the hands of the bourgeoisie and in many cases kulaks.[69] There was an additional scourge, which looked like a deliberate contrivance to squeeze the peasant dry by making him drunk, namely the state monopoly on spirits. Alcoholism became a government-vested interest. In 1914 revenue from the vodka monopoly constituted the largest single item in the state budget, a thousand million rubles out of three thousand five hundred.[70]

   In 1861 the peasants were neither made equal with the other classes nor accorded full individual freedom. They remained an inferior estate subject to discriminatory legislation. In spite of having been granted the right to own property, to marry, to go to court, they had still to pay a poll tax, the only class in the population to do so; and they continued to be subject to corporal punishment for about a quarter of a century. Though almost freed from the tutelage of the landlord, the peasant was by the new dispensation subordinated all the more stringently to the mir. For fiscal and for administrative reasons, the commune and its elders, and not the peasant, were made owner and manager of the emancipated land. The elders were empowered to fix the modes of periodic repartition of the land "from the dead to the living". They controlled the rotation of the crops and other agricultural operations and on grounds of collective responsibility for the payment of taxes were accorded the power to grant or to refuse the right to emigrate. They were most reluctant to grant such permission, since it was calculated to put a heavier tax burden on the community. They exacted therefore from those whom they allowed to do seasonal work elsewhere their share of taxation as members of the community in towns. There were special lower courts for peasants. All forms of local self-government were whittled down when the government decided to install cantonal land captains, with wide administrative and supervisory powers.[71]

It was the regime's last statesman of any high calibre, Stolypin, who had the courage and the imagination to try to save Tsarism in spite of itself, and in a ruthlessly innovative manner, reminiscent of Bach and Schwarzenburg in Austria and Bismarck in Germany. In 1906 he dissolved the communes. His intention was to create, with state help, a large independent peasant class by favouring the well-to-do and the successful, "the sober and the striving",[72] and turning the less fortunate into landless labourers or a reserve army for industry. It is one of the great ifs of history, whether another few decades of international peace and of the constitutional evolution which was started in 1905 might not have seen the rise of a rural middle class, which would have become strong enough to stand between the tenancy system and socialist revolution. The socialist revolutionaries had many reasons to fear such a course. It was natural for them to suspect an alliance between Tsarism and the *kulaks* at the expense of the poorer peasantry, on the model of the age-long alliance of Tsarism with the nobility.

The fate of the rest of Alexander II's reforms, which too looked at first like a promising instalment of constitutionalism, provided the revolutionaries with ample proof of the incurably treacherous character of the Tsarist regime, and of its determination to so manipulate the seemingly liberal arrangements as to frustrate all hopes of progress in the sphere of human rights and towards popular sovereignty. The zemstvos set up in 1864[73] were intended to give provincial assemblies a measure of responsibility for local affairs such as maintenance of roads, education, public health, economic improvement, especially agriculture. Though elective, the suffrage was so tailored that the nobility was assured of absolute hegemony over the other estates. Peasant delegates to the zemstvo assembly were appointed by the governor out of lists submitted to him, when self-government was virtually abolished by the establishment of land captains.[74] The peasants had altogether little interest in, and still less liking for, the zemstvo, since the taxes imposed by it were collected by the state police. Not a little hope was placed by the more moderate opposition upon the "third element" which was brought into being by the zemstvos: local government officials, statisticians, physicians, engineers, teachers, agricultural experts and others.[75] Vastly more important was the question whether the zemstvos were going not only to maintain their role and prestige, but also be given a chance gradually to widen their activities and to become a partner in running the government of the country, in brief, whether they were destined to evolve into a popular representation and to pave the way for a legislative assembly, and thus "crown the edifice" of the reforms of the Tsar-Liberator. The regime was determined to prevent such a development at all costs.[76] A cat-and-mouse relationship developed between the government and the zemstvos. The former were on guard not to allow deliberations on local administrative matters to spill over into the discussion of national affairs, to restrain the zemstvos from overstepping the confines of their competence, and above all to prevent any attempts of creating nationwide associations of zemstvos, even of the chairmen of their committees, lest they arrogate to themselves the status of a national representation.[77]

The sacred principle of autocracy had to remain intact. In his famous but very ambiguous memorandum on the zemstvos, Witte put his finger on the stark alternative: enlightened autocracy, or the free progressive development of the zemstvos, first into an advisory, then into a legislative, and finally into a constituent, assembly.[78] These were in fact the gradations of opinion among the zemstvo liberals, when they became vocal and organised on the eve of the 1905 revolution. In his reply to the Twer zemstvo petition the new, and last, Emperor had a decade earlier brushed aside any such dreams, which were at variance with the centuries-old tradition of Russian autocracy and its alleged "Fundamental Laws".[79]

Those morbid, but not unjustified mutual suspicions and fears, which sustained the inflexible rigidity of autocracy and exacerbated revolutionary extremism, also worked as a self-fulfilling prophecy. Each side gave the other ample cause to suspect the worst and drove it to behave accordingly. In alleviating censorship, introducing the jury system, easing restrictions on university autonomy and recognising a measure of personal liberty, on top of the two major reforms,[80] the Tsarist regime was torn between the hope that these would mitigate discontent and thus secure the substance of its power, and the panicky fear that the reforms were undermining its own foundations by revealing weaknesses and encouraging popular unrest and rebelliousness. In the eyes of the revolutionaries, the fragmentary character of the concessions was proof that the reforms were merely a tactical move intended to distract vigilance and blunt popular revolutionary energy, in brief to preserve Tsarism intact.

The obsessive suspiciousness of the polarised forces, as well as the narrowness of their base, rendered Russian liberalism utterly ineffective, distrusted, hated and despised by the protagonists on the two extremes.

Neither side believed that time could straighten things out, that compromise would be observed in good faith and develop into a give-and-take. It was still necessary to fight it out to the bitter end. This meant a kind of permanent preventive war and a strategy of deterrents and reprisals, on the part of the establishment, and a state of latent rebellion, a total denial of the legitimacy of the existing institutions and laws on the part of the revolutionary opposition.

Disappointment with the reforms of the 1860's drove the Narodnaya Volya to conspiracy and eventually to terrorist assassination, including the several attempts on the life of Alexander II. When the "dictatorship of the heart" of Loris-Melikov attempted to lift the state of siege which revolutionary terror had laid to the administration by a policy of concessions, it was answered on the very day on which Alexander II was due to sign a decree promising constitutional reform, with the assassination of the Tsar. This was followed by sustained fierce repression, which succeeded in paralysing the revolutionary movement for quite a while.[81] In an atmosphere of polarised confrontation, the weak plant of liberalism withered. Even before March 31, 1881, the liberal Chicherin was so frightened by revolutionary terror as to plead for a halt in the liberal-democratic advance.[82] Law and order had first to be restored at all cost. Free play could not be offered to nihilistic destroyers of the social order. "Orderly" repression even by a despotic government was still preferable to conspirational plotting, assassination and mob violence. No extension of liberty could be granted when terror was rampant. Progress towards a constitutional system would be resumed, the liberals believed, as soon as order had been re-established. On their part, the revolutionaries felt sure that a restoration of civil peace would also restore the autocracy's self-confidence and repression. A blow to its very heart was necessary. Lenin never forgot how the liberal friends of the family ostracised them after the execution of his elder brother for plotting to assassinate Alexander III.[83] It was perhaps then that he was filled with the seething hatred and contempt for every type of liberalism, and formed the unshakable conviction that when it came to the crunch the moderates would always prefer rallying to the establishment to making common cause with the fighters for freedom.

The radicalisation of the revolutionary movement was answered by a similar radicalisation on the extreme Right.[84] The leading latter-day spokesmen of ultra-reaction were men of much higher intellectual attainments than the reactionary hacks in the past. They were driven by self-torturing despair, which had overcome them when they became disillusioned with their early liberalism. It continued to persist throughout all their long frantic quest for faith and certainty and led them to a fantastic elaborations of the doctrine of theocratic autocracy. This was the case of Katkov, the erstwhile comrade of Herzen and Bakunin and then leading publicist of the Right, of Dostoevsky, who had as a youth passed through the traumatic ordeal of facing a firing squad, and finally of Tikhomirov, who turned from being a leader of the terrorist wing of Narodnaya Volya into the most uncompromising apologist of autocracy and repression. Pobedonostsev, the highly cultivated professor of jurisprudence, came to exercise immense influence as Procurator of the Holy Synod, intimate adviser to two Tsars and tutor to Nicolas II when heir to the throne. He raised high the banner of militant obscurantism and carried it afloat as an octogenarian beyond the 1905 revolution. Another prophet of extreme militant reaction, Leontiev, was a physician with wide scientific and literary interests. He grew into the demoniacal priest of a God of wrath, who inspired not love, but fear.[85]

All these tormented souls claimed to be striving to revitalise specific and authenticaly Russian traditions. In one way or another however they were re-echoing de Maistre's dicta that even if the dogma of papal infallibility was not doctrinally tenable, it would have had to be invented, and that the hangman was the lynchpin of society, and its saviour. Their absolutes deserve to be juxtaposed with the absolutes of the prophets at the other end of Russia's political spectrum.

(IV) THE METAPHYSIC OF A BESIEGED AND DOOMED AUTOCRACY

The theocratic reactionaries taught that the root of all evil was individualistic liberalism, nay Protestantism, the direct parent of liberalism; and even further back, Roman Catholicism, through its teachings on the separation of powers between church and state.[86] The doctrine of freedom of conscience and of different orders of truth, religious and political, doctrinal and rationalistic, undermined faith in a single absolute truth, sowed doubt, encouraged arrogance and arbitrariness, led to selfishness and bred immorality and crime. In the absence of any accepted criterion, liberty became the cause of social disintegration, despair, rebelliousness, indeed death. For man was born evil, fickle and feeble, and such he would remain forever. "Every man is a lie"— preached Pobedonostsev. "Every word said by man is an idle word of self-delusion."[87] He dreaded "the ferocious passions that lie dormant in the breasts" of that Russia that was "an icy desert and the abode of the Evil One".[88] Without faith in an omnipotent, omniscient, wrathful and punishing God, man would run amok. The denial of God made the existence of society, nation and state impossible, and rendered nihilism dominant. "Disbelief is the direct—direct!—negation of the state."[89] This had been also the conviction of the young Bakunin, before Feuerbach led him on to ferocious atheism and—as its offshoot—

extreme anarchism: "Where there is no religion, there can be no state." "Religion is the substance and the essence of the life of every state." In a sense Feuerbach's view of faith in God as a projection of man's miserable social situation found a curious confirmation in the idea of the necessity of God for the social order. The theocrats were hardly concerned with the purely metaphysical and theological problem of divinity, and certainly not with individualistic mysticism, since individual heaven-storming and quest for direct, unmediated communion with the Creator might stray into anarchical individualism. With the social-political predicament of Russia before their eyes, their object was institution-alised religion, the Orthodox church rather than God, the hierarchical structure rather than the salvation of the soul; and the representative of God on earth, the earthly embodiment of the principle of absolute authority and unity of faith, the Tsar-God rather than the Trinity. Theocratic autocracy was a moral, social and political necessity all in one. It was no personal prerogative, but a sacred duty, not an exalted position, but an onerous mission. Pobedonostsev never tired of urging upon the Emperors whom he served, that they had no right to restrict, let alone to renounce autocracy. They would be sinfully plunging society into chaos and anarchy.[90] He bemoaned the frittering away of his powers by the "pitiful and unfortunate" Alexander II, the Tsar-Reformer.[91] Pobedonostsev's pupil and disciple, the luckless Nicolas II, could never shake off his mentor's teachings. The last Tsar of all the Russias may have dug his grave when upon the accession to the throne he told the delegation of the zemstvos who came to submit their humble address of congratulations to forget the senseless dreams about the participation of zemstvo representatives in the affairs of internal government . . . "I shall preserve the principle of autocracy as firmly and as undeviatingly as did my . . . father".[92] The great conservative historian Kliuchevsky is reported to have prophesied in private a day or two after the January 17, 1895, audience that "the Romanov dynasty will end with Nicolas II. If he has a son, the son will not reign."[93]

The vagaries of Western parliamentarism; party intrigues, corruption, demagoguery and rowdy obstructionism which were rampant in the representative institutions of the constitutional regimes; the demoralising influence of the mass press—all these were cited by Pobedonostsev and his like as dire warnings. The theoreticians of absolutism did not want the Tsar to be restrained by codes of laws and the verdicts of judges. The abstract principles by which the latter were guided could become "destructive, suicidal and sinful".[94] To employ Saint-Simonist language, they thought it imperative for the Tsar to be a *loi vivante*, a court of appeal, who could adjudicate for those cases that fell outside the conventional, abstract classifications with which the written law was concerned. More than that, they held the view that sharp division of authority and a strongly departmentalised bureaucracy threatened the very nerve of Russian autocracy, its singleness of purpose in decision-making.

The extremists of the theocratic-absolutist Right lived in dread of human arbitrariness and the ineradicable perverse tendency of man towards discord and rebellion. They abhorred critical thought. It was a token of a diseased mind: the healthy never think of health. Instinct, custom, above all faith and trust were the safe guides, not logical ratiocination, permanently bogged down by the predicament of having to choose between alternatives, caught in inevitable contradictions, and weighed down by relativistic juxtaposition. They definitely deprecated education for the masses beyond religious instruction, or rather indoctrination. They valued above all the firm canalisation of time, energy and emotional needs provided by the religious calendar, rites and liturgy, and finally the patriarchal family. There was a kind of pragmatism in the view that truth had to be tested by durability and by desired results, by which they meant stability, even if it amounted to stagnation.[95]

Greek Orthodoxy was patently not a universal creed, and did not claim to be. Leontiev, who was the most Byzantine of the Russian reactionaries, not much of a Slavophile and certainly no Populist, scoffed at all ideas about general human happiness, unity, equality, perfection and contentment. This grim thinker wanted to freeze everything for fear of change, which in his view inevitably led to anarchy. Nor would he uphold faith in eternal and universal moral values based on philosophical natural law. Like Pobedonostsev he developed a kind of historical materialism: truth unfolded in historic evolution or rather in the crystallisation of life forms, and in their internalisation, so that they became unconscious automatic reflexes.

There was a deeper reason for Leontiev's implicit denial of any vision of the kingdom of God. His contempt and hatred of man was such that he was not really concerned with the salvation of man's soul, but with his punishment. Love of man was in his eyes tantamount to a rejection of God. And God was to him a God not of mercy, but of wrath, who inspired fear but not love. The horror of man led the misanthropic prophet to implacable hatred of the world, of life as such. He became a modern Tertullian. He secretly took monastic vows and subjected himself to a strenuous ascetic discipline. He never ceased thundering against the pretentions of science to explain the mysteries of creation and to turn into its master. He condemned as godless any philosophy which tended to see in man the source of ethical criteria and his own legislator.

Curiously, the latter-day Tertullian's denial of life and contempt for man, produced as a by-product a Nietzschean kind of adoration of amoral power and aesthetic brilliance. Horrified and repelled by the complacency, smugness and mediocrity which a timid and vacillating bourgeoisie was engendering—as he considered it did in for instance Switzerland, Denmark and Holland—he exclaims: "Would it not be altogether frightening and degrading if Moses' ascent to Sinai, the erection of the sublime Acropolis of the Greeks, the Punic wars of the Romans, the crossing of the Granicus and the exploits in the battle of Arbela of the gifted and handsome Alexander in his plumed helmet, the preaching of the Apostles, the torments of the martyrs, the poetry of poets, the pictures of painters, the combats of splendid knights, were to come to fruition in the French, German and Russian bourgeois in his ugly and comic dress, enjoying his 'individual' or 'collective' well-being on the ruins of all that past grandeur?"[96] The bloody wars of the Renaissance were accompanied by unsurpassed cultural splendour. The utter immorality of the power-hungry Renaissance condottieri and conquistadores in Latin America, with their overflowing, over-whelming vitality, mocked the rules, norms and opinions of the human herd. Nothing great had ever been achieved without the use of coercion and violence. "Politics have nothing to do with morality."[97] Leontiev rated socialism higher than liberalism. The former represented an organised, disciplined, collective effort to achieve high goals, whereas the latter was just a miasma. Not that he had any sympathy for the aims of socialism. He was too much influenced for that by de Maistre's gruesome vision of the universe and history as irrational to the core. History was torn by implacably contradictory forces. It was dripping with blood and groaning with suffering. Intractable men were driven to exasperation by the inevitable frustrations and disappointments and were swept on by murderous psychoses and death wishes.

By the late nineteenth century it had become difficult to keep up the pretence of mutual love and trust between Tsar and his people, only occasionally disturbed by tiny peripheral groups of Westernised perverts. Hence the open glorification of naked force by the defenders of autocracy. As innocent, genuine religious faith was replaced by a desperate will to believe, religion assumed more and more the character of a political instrument in the hand of Caesaro-papism. Leontiev spoke of the need for an "iron glove" and wanted reactionary policies to be treated and practised as an art in the same way as the revolutionaries regarded revolution as an art. Pobedonostsev was busy with plans for the deliberate stultification of the masses by denying them all secular education and by increasing religious indoctrination.

The regime was faced with tasks, responsibilities, needs, which could never be solved by freezing the status quo. It needed power, modern methods, technology, industry. The faithful nobility lacked the competence and experience to handle them. It was declining economically, and considerable parts of it were already too much influenced by liberal ideology to be trusted. The elites thrown up by modern spontaneous or government-initiated developments, were inspired by criteria, values, habits, interests and aims which were utterly at variance with the mystique of Tsarist autocracy. Pobedonostsev had no confidence in the nobility, since he dreaded the spectre of what Rousseau had called particular interests and aspirations. He could therefore put his trust only in energetic and self-made but loyal men, to serve the Tsar and hold the people in check.[98] Such an attitude was calculated to encourage unscrupulous opportunists and adventurers. The upper class became more and more alienated from the regime, just when the uprooted masses of industrial workers were losing the humble, unquestioning habit of obedience of the *muzhik*.

The identification of state with church, politics and religion, the fear of dissent and nonconformism—all these strengthened the slogan "One Faith, One Tsar, One Nation". But there was no escape from the fact that there were tens of millions among the Tsar's subjects who were sectarians, or believers in religions other than Greek Orthodoxy, not to speak of differences in ethnic origins, language, culture and aspirations. "Russia"—wrote Katkov—"needs a unitary state and a strong Russian nationality: let us create such a nationality on the basis of a common language, a common faith and the Slav *mir*. Let us abolish all that stands in our way."[99] Pobedonostsev preached that "the state recognises only one faith as true, supports exclusively the [Orthodox] church and favours it alone, whereas it regards all other churches and creeds as inferior".[100] The concomitant of these doctrines, propagated by the most influential luminaries of the regime, was brutal persecution of religious minorities, determined policies of forced russification, systematically repressive treatment of such more advanced ancient nationalities as the Poles and the Finns, and the constant whittling down of their special status and autonomy so as to denationalise them.

"He who deserts the Orthodox faith"—wrote Pobedonostsev— "ceases to be Russian, not only in his thoughts and acts, but also in his ways of living and dress . . . the church and the church alone has allowed us to remain Russian and unite our scattered strength."[101] With their ubiquitousness, intractable nonconformism, intellectual energy, bitter resentment of their inferior status and government-sponsored pogroms, and their prominent role in the revolutionary movement, the Jews appeared as the most indigestible and dangerous minority, as a standing denial of all the values and aims of Tsarist theocracy. Pobedonostsev's remedy was to bring about a situation which would cause a third of the Jewish population to die out, a third to emigrate and the remaining third to become converted.[102]

The awkward fact was that the Great Russians formed only 43 per cent of the population. The other 57 per cent embraced some eighty foreign nationalities. The problem was to become particularly acute after the jolt which the nationalities received in 1905 and after they had gained a vote in the newly formed Duma, notwithstanding all the restrictions and chicaneries practised upon them. "The Duma must be Russian in spirit"—was the official dictum—"other nationalities . . . must not and will not possess the power to be the arbiter in questions purely Russian."[103] The border areas had not been granted zemstvo institutions by the reforms of 1861, and after 1905 all kinds of jerry-mandering were employed to reduce their parliamentary representation in the Duma.[104] Since not every type of discrimination and intimidation could be promulgated by way of official *ukase*, recourse was had to whipping up nationalist-religious frenzy in the Great Russian *Lumpenproletariat* and petty bourgeoisie and in inciting them to launch pogroms.[105] Hence the various patriotic-religious leagues, especially the Union of the Russian People, patronised by the Tsar and the various Grand Dukes and lesser grandees, and the infamous "Black Hundreds", often led by priests or fanatics from among the free professions and supported from state funds. "Respectable" middle class nationalism was distrusted, since it might lead to demands for a share in shaping policies, and eventually for popular control. Following the Prussian reactionaries in the early days of the nineteenth century who thought that "Nation klingt Jakobinisch", Leontiev feared that the principle of nationality could become the seed of world revolution. Even Slavophilism smacked to him of cosmopolitanism. Pobedonostsev was not very enthusiastic about the support granted to the national liberation movements of the Slavs under Turkish rule, because of their dangerous implications for the internal situation in Russia itself. Alexander III, who was compelled to conclude an alliance with Republican France and to stand to attention with his head bare to the sounds of the "Marseillaise", bitterly reproached himself for dealing with peoples and not solely with princes.[106]

From the internal point of view colonial expansion in the Far East seemed much less perilous than intervention in the Balkans, except of course for the dream of the conquest of Constantinople. The internal political needs of Tsarism on top of economic pressures and the financial bankruptcy of the state, placed before the decision-makers of Russia the alternatives: to stem revolution by an external war, especially a military adventure in the Far East, or at all cost to avoid war and the strains it was sure to occasion, above all on the Western borders. "What we need to hold Russia back from revolution is a small victorious war"—said the all-powerful Plehve to General Kuropatkin, the designated Commander-in-Chief in the Far East on the eve of the Russo-Japanese War.[107]

In his famous memorandum of February 1914 to the Tsar, P. N. Durnovo, who had served as Minister of the Interior under Alexander III and Nicolas II, wrote: "If the war ends with victory, the pacification of the socialist movement will not, in the last resort, present any difficulties. . . . But in case of a defeat . . . the social revolution in its most extreme manifestations will be inevitable. . . . It will begin with blaming the government for all failures. A furious campaign will begin against it in the legislative institutions, as the result of which revolutionary acts will begin in the country. These latter will at once put forth socialist slogans, the only ones that have any hope of uniting the broad masses of the populace. First, there will be total confiscation, followed by general redistribution of all possessions. The defeated army, deprived during the war of its most reliable element, the officers, and seized in most of its ranks by the peasants' desire for land, will be too demoralised to maintain law and order. The legislative institutions and the opposition intelligentsia parties, deprived of any real authority in the eyes of the people, will be incapable of curbing the same unbridled masses they were the ones to raise up; Russia will be hurled into black anarchy whose outcome cannot even be imagined."[108]

This is a prognosis which Lenin might have composed, in a spirit of course of hope instead of the sentiment of dread pervading Durnovo's dire warning.

Give-and-take constitutionalism proved impossible in Russia. It lacked a natural base in a large, independent and self-assured middle class. The intelligentsia was too restricted, and partly too radicalised, to serve as a substitute. The liberals were shown to be generals without an army, orators without instruments of action. The regime realised that there was no real danger from that quarter. The redoubtable adversary was the social revolution, the socialist movement and the peasant masses. "Here the masses of the people"—wrote Durnovo in his memorandum—"unquestionably believe in the principles of unconscious socialism. In spite of the oppositionist spirit of Russian society . . . a political revolution in Russia is impossible, and every revolutionary movement will inevitably degenerate into a socialist movement. The average Russian, both peasant and worker, is not seeking political rights. . . . The peasant is dreaming of getting other people's land for nothing, the worker about the transfer to himself of all the capital and profits of the factory-owner. . . . The Russian opposition is wholly that of the intelligentsia, and that is its weakness, since between our intelligentsia and the people there is a profound abyss of mutual distrust and lack of understanding."[109]

As early as 1884, Durnovo's predecessor at the Ministry of the Interior, Count Dimitri Tolstoy, told Count (later Chancellor and Prince) Bülow: "every attempt to introduce Western-European, parliamentary forms of government into Russia is doomed to failure. If Tsarism . . . is overthrown, its place will be taken by communism, by the pure, unveiled communism of Mr Karl Marx, who died recently in London and whose theories I have studied with attention."[110]

Russian revolutionaries like Lenin, who had never had any illusions about the nature of Russian autocracy, and not the slightest thought of the possibility or desirability of any compromise, stood confirmed in their contemptuous dismissal of liberalism as a force that could be counted upon as a leading factor in a revolution, or trusted as an ally in a confrontation with the Tsarist regime. The Marxist doctrine of the inevitability of a bourgeois-democratic phase before advancing to socialism required re-thinking. There was also however, as we shall see, the sobering lesson that in spite of all the blows they had suffered in the revolutionary storm of the early years of the twentieth century, in 1904-5, the army and the bureaucracy as a whole stood firm by the Tsar, the peasantry failed to rise *en masse* and the industrial proletariat proved too weak to follow the call of the socialists and carry the revolution to a successful end.

(V) 1905—THE CURTAIN RAISER

The first half of the reign of Nicholas II was a testing time for the various political forces in Russia. To repeat, the lesson served to confirm the protagonists in their convictions. The seemingly iron-fisted despotism of Alexander III had revealed its hollowness when it proved incapable of dealing with the terrible famine which swept twenty of the most fertile southern provinces in 1891, to be followed by another famine the year after. "Society", in the first place the zemstvos, mobilised to bring aid to the suffering. The authorities tried at first to keep news of the disaster out of the press. When this became impossible, they took pains to suppress information about the voluntary help given by citizen groups.[111] In the spring of 1896 came the shock of the greatest industrial strike in Russia so far. In St Petersburg 40,000 workers, mainly in the textile industry, downed tools for economic reasons, but not without instigation and guidance by the Marxist Union of Struggle for the Liberation of the Working Class, especially its two young leaders Ulyanov (Lenin) and Martov.[112] The strike almost coincided with the ominous disaster of Khodynka which occurred during the festivities following the coronation of the new Tsar and cost thirteen hundred lives among the crowds which assembled to receive gifts, as a result of government negligence.[113] In 1901 a failure of crops, following similar failures in 1897 and 1898, resulted in widespread outbreaks of peasant unrest—pillage, arson and occasional murder which were put down by indiscriminate shooting and mass flogging. After a long period of repression the Russian students came out into the streets in 1895, in Moscow. In 1899 a student strike started in St Petersburg, spread to all Russian universities and kept the institutions of higher learning closed for half a year, after which the authorities illegally drafted large numbers of students into the army.[114] The year 1901 saw the revival of Narodnik terror by the "Fighting Organisation" of the Socialist Revolutionary party set up by the venerable veteran founder of the Narodnaya Volya, the Jewish *grand bourgeois*, the engineer Mark Natanson.[115] A terrorist campaign which claimed hundreds of victims among the highest dignitaries of state, Grand Dukes, leading ministers such as Plehve, Sipiagin, Stolypin and others, provincial governors, generals and police officers, was initiated by the assassination of the Minister of Education, Bogolepov, by the student Karpovich. The terrorist campaign of the Socialist Revolutionaries was directed by two Jewish leaders, the legendary Gershuni and the demoniacal double agent Yevno Azef.[116] In 1903, the general strike in southern Russia paralysed Russian heavy industry. It was preceded by bloody clashes between striking workers and government forces in the Urals. It was no mean shock to the government that the strikes in the south were started by government-sponsored unions under the leadership of Zubatov, whose idea had been to set up such unions in order to wean the workers away from socialism. This served to the ultras in the government as additional proof of how dangerous it was to allow any initiative from below, even under official inspiration.[117]

The reply of the supporters of autocracy was a wave of anti-Jewish pogroms, with the terrible Kishinev massacre as its climax, and increased chicanery against the revived stirrings in the zemstvo circles. Plehve went so far as to ban statistical investigation on the ground that constant intercourse with the peasants and labourers gave ill-intentioned members of the "third element" too easy opportunities for revolutionary agitation.[118]

Since the conservatives among the zemstvo people had by then come to the conclusion that Tsarist bureaucracy could not be left to govern the country without some participation of and a measure of control by the nation's elite, the authorities were scared by the consequences of allowing the zemstvos a share in the administration. On top of refusing permission to organise food supplies the government banned all regional, and of course nationwide, zemstvo consultations. Witte allowed government-sponsored provincial committees on the agrarian problem, under the chairmanship of governors (and in the counties of marshalls of the nobility), only to invite other chairmen of zemstvo boards or select members thereof, warning them not to go beyond their terms of reference and wander into general criticism of the government. This did not prevent the committees from coming out with innovative and far-reaching suggestions on the land problem such as the abolition of the special Peasant Estate, and with it of administrative tutelage over the peasantry, the dissolution of the village commune, reform of taxation, and the most striking proposal—the compulsory handing over of state, appendage and monastic lands to the peasants. In answer, the Imperial Manifesto of February 1903 restated the principle of the inviolability of the commune; yet promised aid to members who wished to quit.[119] Soon after, the government put an end to the collective responsibility of the members of communes for payment of taxes and carrying out other obligations. The word "constitution" remained banned and no hint was given on any new forms of cooperation with the zemstvos.

By that time Russian liberals had already embarked upon underground, illegal, if not revolutionary activity.[120] After a series of private zemstvo meetings, a conference held abroad in Stuttgart set up in June 1902 a party nucleus and a journal called *Ozvobozhdenie* (Liberation) under the joint editorship of the famous historian Miliukov and the ex-Marxist economist Peter Struve. The aims were the abolition of autocracy and the setting up of a constitutional regime, without specification as regards means.[121] After the preparatory conferences in St Petersburg and in Switzerland, the secret conference of the various groups of liberals of January 1904 set up an umbrella organisation under the name of The Union of Liberation. For patriotic reasons it was decided to postpone activities until after the Russo-Japanese War.[3] In the light however of the early disasters on the Far Eastern Front, the liberal elements went further. They undertook on their own or in cooperation with the authorities—in spite of Plehve's opposition—various urgent war tasks such aş care for wounded, sick and families of fallen soldiers. The assassination of Plehve on July 15, 1904, the continued misfortunes at the front, the disarray at the top, the feeble attempts of Plehve's unimpressive successor Prince Swiatopolk-Mirsky to carry out some reforms such as the abolition of flogging of peasants, and the granting of a few pardons, encouraged the opposition to shed all camouflage and come out in their true colours. This they did at the September 30-October 9 conference held in Paris and attended by all opposition groups, including the Social Revolutionaries, but boycotted by Bolsheviks and Mensheviks. There they adopted the momentous resolution to work for "a free democratic system on the basis of universal suffrage", and also recognised the right of the Russian nationalities to self-determination.[122]

It was at that conference that the future split began to mature in the liberal ranks into doctrinaire Western-minded radicals led by Miliukov—who could never shake off the hypnotic effect of memories of the French and English revolutions—and the conservative gradualists who feared a total break with Russian traditions, and the revolutionary dynamic of abstract radical principles, under Maklakov.[123] On the pre-1848 French model, the opposition decided to give public expression to its discontent and urgent desire for reform in a series of country-wide banquets. Without government sanction, the zemstvo leaders assembled for their conference in Moscow on November 6 under the chairmanship of the highly respected Shipov, whom the government had earlier vetoed several times as chairman of the Moscow zemstvo. The Eleven Theses adopted by the conference contained a programme of civil liberties, a democratic reform of the zemstvos and city Dumas, repeal of emergency laws, amnesty and, most important, the convocation of a representative legislative assembly (a compromise between a consultative and constituent assembly). This was a revolutionary challenge, although it stopped short of a demand for a constituent assembly which would have implied a call for a revolutionary, even if peaceful, change of regime by a sovereign popular assembly.[124] Although deeply outraged, the Tsar issued in reply on December 12 an *ukase* on "measures for improvement of the state order". The original draft contained an imperial promise to invite members elected by the zemstvos to the State Council. At the last moment the Tsar was persuaded by Pobedonostsev to delete the promise and to replace it with a warning to the zemstvos and the city Dumas to refrain from attempts to violate the Fundamental Laws of Russia.[125] Hardly had the shock worn off of this rebuff by a tottering regime to a popular demand voiced by moderates, when the regime and all Russia were shaken by a real earthquake—the Bloody Sunday: the shooting upon a peaceful mass demonstration carrying holy pictures and the Tsar's portraits, under the leadership of the priest Gapon, in front of the Winter Palace.[126]

In the midst of a gale of vast industrial strikes, student disturbances, assassinations and public outrages, the Imperial regime began to wobble visibly. One manifesto drafted by Pobedonostsev called upon all right-thinking elements to rally to the Tsar in defence of the ancient Fundamental Laws; another recognised the right of every subject to lodge complaints and tender advice to the Emperor, and invited such representations; still another, the most important one—the Bulygin Rescript—while proclaiming the immutability of the autocratic principle, announced the decision of the Tsar to have "elected representatives of the people to take part in the preliminary discussion of legislation". This amounted to a constitution given from above, and to the establishment of a consultative assembly.[127] It was a breakthrough. The vital problem of the location of sovereign power however remained unresolved. Rather, the Tsar continued to be its source.

The stage seemed set for the decisive battle between liberty and absolutism; not unlike the early days of the 1789 revolution. The Union of Liberation and the professional unions which had come into being joined hands to form a Union of Unions under the leadership of Miliukov, with a clear radically democratic programme. Even the zemstvos congress voiced on February 27 the demand for a legislative assembly elected on the basis of universal suffrage. On June 6 the Tsar received a zemstvo delegation, which pressed upon him the need for a legislative assembly. In reply the Tsar expressed his willingness to have a representative assembly, but stood firm on the sacredness of the historic principles of Russian statehood, which meant of course autocracy.[128] How to reconcile the two? The clarification came by the end of July on the morrow of a series of deliberations of the princes of the blood and the heads of the administration at Peterhof which reasserted the immutability of the principle of autocracy and set out the modalities of voting for the consultative assembly. They were a mockery of democratic election. The proposed system was clearly designed to split the nation, or rather prevent its coming into being, by institutionalising separate estates, voting in separate electoral colleges by indirect vote, except for the landowning class which received a direct vote. The urban workers and professional classes were virtually disenfranchised, the townspeople were subjected to a high property qualification, while the supposedly loyal peasants were secured a very high proportion of seats in the assembly. Finally, the assembly was

granted only the right to discuss projects of law and make representations to the Emperor.[129]

Coming on top of the national shame of the Odyssey of the Russian
fleet around the Cape of Good Hope, which started with the grotesque
shooting in British waters at Scottish fishermen mistaken for Japanese
and ended with the sinking of nearly the whole fleet at Tschushima, and
of revelations of criminal corruption in the highest echelons of civil and
military authority, the Imperial affront to the nation sent the people,
including this time the peasantry, into action. The newly granted
autonomy to the universities and the emergence of the network of
workers' soviets, with the soviet in the capital at their head, led by the
young Trotsky and master-minded by Parvus-Helphand,[130] and the
establishment of the Peasant's Union, with Victor Czernov as its
moving spirit, opened up channels of unrestrained public self-
expression.[131] The strike movement snowballed into a nationwide
general strike which paralysed the entire economy, while peasant riots
conjured up the spectre of a universal *jacquerie*.[132] The idea of a military
dictatorship with the Grand Duke Nikolai Nikolaievich, the Tsar's
uncle, was scotched when, so it is alleged, the candidate produced a
revolver and threatened suicide.[133] This was the background of the
famous Imperial Manifesto of October 1905.

The Manifesto looked like a constitution.[134] It granted all civil and
democratic liberties. It promised to extend the franchise to the classes
which had been deprived of it in the Bulygin Rescript. Instead of
reiterating the inviolability of the principle of autocracy, it laid down
"the immutable principle that no law may come into force without the
approval of the state Duma which controls the authorities appointed by
the Crown".[135]

The momentous question was the good faith of the Tsar. The letter
which he wrote to his mother in which he expressed his shame and
mortification at what he had done, leaves no doubt that there was
none.[136] This was guessed not only by the radical revolutionaries, but
also by Miliukov, who as if re-echoing Mirabeau proclaimed that
nothing had changed and the struggle was going on.[137] Maklakov wished
to believe that if allowed to work itself out, without violent interference by revolutionary methods, the new concessions could develop a
momentum which would lead to a conservative type of constitutionalism. It was not to be.

The battle of principles was to be fought out as a partially armed
battle for power, bedevilled by a flaring up of class war. When hunger
was extinguishing the protracted general strike, the Petersburg soviet
came out with a resolution on an eight-hour working day (instead of the

eleven and a half established in 1896). The employers, who in the main had joined the constitutional struggle and even supported the striking workers financially, answered now with a general lock-out. The strike came to an end.[138] The authorities arrested the figurehead chairman of the Petersburg soviet, Krustalov-Nosar. His successor, the Triumvirate with Trotsky at its head, issued on December 2 a call to the population to refuse to pay taxes and to withdraw deposits. A second strike proclaimed by the soviets fizzled out after three days. Provided with a good pretext—the subversive illegal manifesto of the soviet—and no longer restrained by the strike, the government took courage and arrested the whole soviet council.[139] Similarly the Peasant Union's Congress resolution on the forcible sequestration of large estates and the convocation of a constituent assembly was answered by the arrest of the entire leadership.[140] Mutinies flared up in Kronstadt and in the Baltic Fleet, in Odessa (*Potemkin*) and in Sebastopol—the *Ochakov* vessel with Lieutenant Schmidt—but the loyal government troops crushed them without difficulty.[141]

In the meantime Poland and Finland went up in flames, as their grievances, like the nationalities problem in general, were ignored in the Emperor's manifesto. The Moscow proletariat rose in a rebellion which was put down after a few days. Incited by the ultras in the Tsar's environment, and encouraged by the Emperor's declarations of support, the mobs of the "Union of the Russian People" and the "Black Hundreds" under rabble-rousers such as Dubrovin and Purishkevich came out into the streets to defend Mother Russia from Jewish domination, treasonous rebels and the foreign nations, all of whom had joined hands to murder the father of the Russian people, to destroy and dismember the Russian Empire.[142] The new-old Minister of the Interior, Durnovo, found enough strength to deport 45,000 revolutionary agitators.[143] While Finland was dealt with sparingly, Poland bore most of the brunt of government terror.

A series of new Imperial enactments confounded all those who put their trust in the Tsar's change of heart. The electoral law granted to the landowners 31 per cent of the seats in the forthcoming Duma, to the peasants 42 per cent and to the urban voters 27 per cent. The State Council was transformed into an Upper House, half of whose members were to be appointed by the Crown, and the second half by the zemstvos, the nobility, clergy, commercial and industrial interests, the universities and the Academy of Science. The two Houses were given equal legislative power. All legislative motions were in any case made subject to the Emperor's approval. The budget of the army, navy and court and state loans arrangements were reserved as an Imperial prerogative. The right of assembly and association was put under police supervision.[144] The crowning achievement was the *ukase* on the new Fundamental Laws of April 23, 1906, which proclaimed that "To the Emperor of all the Russias belongs supreme autocratic power. Submission to his power, not from fear only, but as a matter of conscience is commanded by God Himself."[145] Miliukov, who had earlier insisted that the October Manifesto should be taken as having promised a Constituent Assembly, called the new legislative enactments "a conspiracy against the people".[146] He was referring to the fact that the Tsar retained all his old prerogatives: to make war and peace, to act as the supreme authority of the Orthodox church, to summon and dissolve the Duma when he found fit, to appoint and dismiss ministers. Even a parliamentary vote of censure passed by two-thirds of the House had to be put to the Tsar's discretion. No possibility of amending these Fundamental Laws was granted to the Duma.[147]

And yet the first Duma contained no government supporters at all, unless we count as would-be collaborators the conservative-liberal Octobrists with their 12 seats, who had earlier broken away from the Constitutional-Democratic (Kadet) party, which got 180 seats. The 73 days which the first Duma was allowed to last were filled with protests against the administration. All the demands which were formulated in the Duma's address to the throne were rejected as inadmissible. They were concerned with a government responsible to the Duma, universal direct franchise, abrogation of emergency laws, abolition of the death penalty and last but not least the sequestration of large private estates.[148]

On that last point the first Duma came to grief. The government proclaimed that "the principle of the inalienability and inviolability of private property is the fundamental rule of government throughout the world".[149] The government went on to announce that it was engaged in working out a scheme of agrarian reforms. The Duma appealed to the nation to wait for a system of law to be worked out by the nation's representatives. This gave the Emperor an excuse to dissolve the Duma as punishment for illegal action. On a Sunday troops surrounded the Tauride Palace, closed the building and posted a notice of dissolution. Again imitating Mirabeau, Miliukov summoned the members of the Duma to assemble in Vyborg, in Finland. There the rump assembly threw down the gauntlet to the Tsar, calling upon the population to stop paying taxes, to withdraw deposits and to refuse recruitment into the army. The Social-Democrats on their part called for a general strike. There was no response to either.[150] There was instead a great intensification of terror and counter-terror. The former claimed 1,600 victims in 1906, and 2,500 in 1907, not counting the epidemic of political "expropriations" of banks. The military courts (without appeal, and with the power of carrying out sentences immediately) sentenced 683 people to death between September 1906 and April 1907. In the meantime, without the government having, contrary to the Fundamental Laws, fixed a date for a new election, Stolypin went ahead with his agrarian decrees which were intended, as we know, to transform land tenure in Russia: "Agrarian Bonapartism", Lenin called it. The second Duma, in which the Cadets had less than a half of their previous numbers, showed marked polarisation. The socialist parties decided not to boycott it, and they gained 65 seats, while the extreme nationalist anti-semitic Right won a substantial representation. The second Duma had its life cut short after some hundred days. It refused to suspend the parliamentary immunity of the socialist deputies who were accused on trumped-up evidence of plotting to assassinate the Tsar and foment mutiny in the army.[152] In the midst of mass demonstrations and a deluge of petitions to the Tsar by the "Black Hundreds" and other patriotic bodies, accompanied by pogroms and other acts of violence, the government issued a new electoral law, which was nothing short of a coup d'état. The landowners' representation was increased from 31 per cent to 50 per cent; that of the peasants (who had failed to display the expected loyalty) was cut from 42 per cent to 22½ per cent; of urban workers from 4 per cent to 2 per cent; and that of the nationalities, especially of the Poles and of city voters, was reduced most drastically.[153] The third Duma, elected on this franchise lived out its full term without giving much trouble to the government. In the eyes of the Left, these developments looked like a counter-revolution. The display of constitutionalism seemed to have been broken off as no longer necessary.[154]

(VI) LENIN—SPLITTER AND STRATEGIST OF REVOLUTION

Throughout the years of strenuous struggles between the socialist factions; of revolutionary storm and failures and disappointments, which led in the post-1905 period of apostasy to liberalism in the case of Struve, to religious mysticism with Berdyaev, Bulgakov and others; of weary acceptance of both the limitations and yet the modest opportunities offered by reformed Tsarism, Lenin was sustained by his unshakable faith in the historic dialectic and the destiny of the vessel of history—the revolutionary industrial proletariat led by his own party. He was not surprised by the behaviour of the liberals, any more than he was shocked by the doings of the autocracy. Nor was his faith in the ultimate victory of the Russian revolution ever shaken, since he was certain that historic inevitability, the companion of economic determinism, was on his side, whatever the momentary zigzags in the political arena. The irreversible advance of industrialisation in Russia would sweep away both small-scale farming and small-scale industry, which formed the base and the constituency of populism and liberalism, with their illusions about the rights of the individual, class collaboration, national unity, national consensus, eternal and universal values, and with them vacillation when it came to confrontation or decision. Capitalism was bringing forth ever growing numbers of class-conscious, highly organised industrial workers. They were destined to shape the world of socialism. And on their road to the final goal they were also the only genuine fighters for democracy.

The urban working class was truly revolutionary, because it was a class of uprooted individuals, not tied to existing institutions and not committed to any vested interests. It was truly radical, because unprotected but also unhampered by tradition, usages, precedents, habits, taboos. In its struggle for rights, better conditions, and weapons against exploitation, it had to fight despotic authoritarianism, hierarchical ascendancy and arbitrariness, in other words for revolutionary, democratic liberty. This made it into the vanguard of all fighters for democracy, into the only consistent upholder of the banner of liberation.[155] But its very situation—which was created by heavy industrial concentration—also turned it into the force destined to bring about the social revolution, after the liberal-bourgeois one. Unlike the scattered, petty producers on the land, in the crafts, and in small-scale industry, the workers could easily be taught by the right mentors to see beyond the present and to grasp the workings of the capitalist system as a whole, its mode of production, its organisational forms, the laws and direction of its development. They could thus be trained to act as pioneers of revolutionary socialism. A clear understanding of the all-decisive reality of class antagonism, and not just the need to shorten working hours, to gain a rise, to win a strike or to set up a union, was also bound to open their eyes to the necessity, indeed inevitability, of a total social transformation, destined to come about by a conjunction of natural developments and deliberate revolutionary assault. It was imperative to foster that all-embracing consciousness, and not to let the workers have their vision and interests restricted to immediate, trade union objectives. Not that what was called by the socialist publicists "agitation" for the concrete needs and demands of the workers should be brushed aside as unimportant and unworthy. It was vital that to agitation should be joined propaganda, that is to say the work of indoctrination, the task of which would be always to relate the particular present to the grand strategy of the social and revolutionary struggle, to the totality of the historical process leading up to the revolutionary dénouement. This was the meaning of the protracted debate on spontaneity and consciousness. The former meant trailing as it were behind matters and situations as they cropped up, and the class conflict as it evolved; the latter meant treating them as symptoms, contingencies, stages, parts and aspects in the sustained long-range war effort.[156] This distinction was also behind the polemic on the relation between the economic struggle and the political aspirations. The Economists believed that the cumulative effect of the skirmishes on economic issues and social conditions was *eo ipso* leading to political confrontation, and was calculated to develop a political consciousness and also to educate the workers into a political force. Lenin did not share that optimism. He feared the workers' sinking into an opportunist morass and petty-bourgeois mentality.[157] Nor did he have the patience to wait for long. He could not be content with piecemeal reforms and improvements. He regarded them as props to the existing order and the ruling establishment, and as a method of blunting revolutionary energy and replacing it with a mood of national and class reconciliation. There was the danger of stunting the stature, the grandeur and historic role of a revolutionary class that was destined to change the face of the earth, not because it was merely just, desirable and noble, but because it was absolutely inevitable. That faith had to be infused into men in order to make it happen.

The conception of the total process provoked by the Marxist theory "is the objective truth". "Following the path of this theory, we will approach the objective truth," writes Lenin in his *Materialism and Empiro-Criticism*, "more and more closely, while if we follow any other path we cannot arrive at anything except confusion and falsehood. From the philosophy of Marxism, cast as one piece of steel, it is impossible to expunge a single basic premise, a single essential part, without deviating from objective truth, without falling into the arms of bourgeois-reactionary falsehood."[158] "Orthodox Marxism," Lenin told Valentinov "requires no revision of any kind, either in the field of philosophy, in its theory of political economy or its theory of historical development."[159]

Since to Lenin there was in the social-political sphere only one line of demarcation, the one that divided the proletariat from the bourgeoisie, Marxism from non-Marxism, he refused to recognise anything between Marxist orthodoxy and bourgeois ideology, which was by definition opportunism, since it had no goal except maintaining the status quo, reacting to circumstances and taking advantage of what opportunity occasions.

It was this strenuous and undeviating faith that caused Lenin to be so insistent on consistency and to become so irritated, disgusted and horrified (the terms pullullate on every page of his writings) by flabbiness, hesitation, vacillation, irresolution, spinelessness and oscillation. All who disagreed with him, Narodniks, Social-Revolutionaries, Economists, revisionists, Mensheviks, above all liberals of any kind, even men in his own party like Zinoviev and Kamenev, any fluctuating opinions, were treated to that spate of epithets, against those were the hard, the resolute, the decided of his own persuasion. In a sense it all boiled down to a psychological distinction between the hard and the soft, Jacobins and Girondists. "A Jacobin who is inseparably linked to the organised class-conscious proletariat is a revolutionary Social-Democrat. A Girondist who sighs for professors and schoolchildren and fears the dictatorship of the proletariat and sighs over the absolute value of democratic demands is an opportunist."[160] Belief in the absolute and indivisible truth of Marxist theory, the equation of ideological consistency with superiority of personal character, together with the conviction that ultimately all great issues had to be resolved by force, were the cause of Lenin's unscrupulous manipulation of people, of rigging elections, packing committees with his own men, of his readiness to discredit and besmirch those who stood in his way. Valentinov for instance was horrified by Lenin's willingness to exploit the fact that a brother of Plekhanov was an officer in the Tsarist police and that there was strong physical likeness between them.[161] As we have said, men were judged solely by their relation to the cause. Heretics were thus the worst of them.

As a Marxist Lenin had to translate every quality into class terms. No wonder all his opponents became *petit bourgeois*, whatever their origins and occupation; a class that was a non-class, doomed to perish, with no compass, suspended between the proletariat and the genuine bourgeoisie, clutching at vague and abstract humanitarian illusions and alleged eternal values, like morality, justice, liberty, equality, the nation. If people were to be prevented from wavering and drifting on, things from taking their course, and situations from developing in a haphazard way, there must be a guiding hand, an organisation. "Give us an organisation of revolutionaries, and we will overturn Russia,"[162] exclaims Lenin. He recounts in *What is to be Done?* a conversation with a party comrade which seemed to confirm them in the belief that they were in complete agreement on all issues. But as soon as they reached the question of organisation they realised that in fact they agreed on nothing.[163]

Lenin's conception of a Socialist Workers' party organisation, as it was articulated in *What is to be Done?* and in the debates at the Second Congress of the Russian Social-Democratic party in Brussels and London, and elaborated, after the split, in the tract *One Step Forward, Two Steps Backward*,[164] is wholly opposed to the view held implicitly by most people. It was not to be a loose congeries of people, groups, organisations, the members of which shared common ideas and were all the time engaged in clarifying them through discussion, giving service to the cause when required and when possible while leading their lives and pursuing their interests in the world at large, sending representatives to a national (or regional) conference where leading bodies were elected, provided with instructions, and put under the control of the party as a whole, all of which realised the democratic principle that initiative came from below and executives did the will of the electors. It was conceived by Lenin as a mobilised fighting force receiving its orders from a GHQ. Once appointed by the party conference and consisting of men of proved grasp of Marxist theory—therefore of the ability to decipher the trends in history and to plan the overall strategy of the socialist revolution—the supreme body was also qualified and urgently called upon to decide upon the immediate tactics required by the shifting social-political situations in relation to the distant goal. As in an army, the GHQ was to appoint the lower authorities, to control them and to send them orders, and their duty was to carry out the orders like faithful soldiers.[165]

Such a party was a monastic order of professional revolutionaries, who were bound to the strictest discipline, a fighting commando in a state of permanent alert. Lenin considered democracy to lie in the placing of the right people in the leading bodies of the party, and not in popular control, popular initiative or the election of officers. In Russian conditions, comradely trust was indispensable and playing at democracy was impossible and harmful. It was not a mass party that was needed, but a small, tightly knit, stringently disciplined organisation "to collect and concentrate all the drops and streamlets of popular excitement"; to command the whole chain.[166]

The 1898 statement of the abortive first Social-Democratic conference, and then the *Iskra* pronouncements spoke of the need to draw clear and sharp boundaries between the army, which was laying siege to the edifice of the autocracy, and all other political forces. Martov too had at one time insisted on putting "an iron ring around the *Iskra* agents".[167] Lenin improved upon them by calling for a state of siege against "unstable and wavering elements" in the working class movement itself.[168] At the second congress Lenin and Plekhanov were still agreed in their opposition to the "Jaurèsist wording" of Martov's resolution.[169] It was only gradually that the protagonists came to realise that there was a gulf between them as regarded organisation, and so on most fundamental matters.

Lenin's opponents, like Martinov, were quick to point out that since the difference between a broad mass organisation and a narrow order of professional revolutionaries corresponded to the difference between spontaneity and consciousness, between workers' reacting to objective circumstances and receiving guidance from intellectual outsiders, Lenin's ideas about proletarian consciousness and organisation were in fact at variance with Marx's teachings on the primacy of objective conditions and developments. Dogma became more decisive than life when flesh-and-blood workers were turned into predicates and shadows of the historic process, of the dialectic, and also subjected to a group of intellectual conspirators.[170] Axelrod complained of suppression of individuality; Martov evoked the shades of Blanqui, of small underground groups cut off from the general mass of the people and oblivious of social-economic realities.[171]

Lenin kept thundering against the flabbiness, wriggling, lack of character of his opponents who had failed to understand that individuality deserved respect, indeed had meaning only when, in the midst of conflicting currents, it remained anchored to the course of historic progress.[172] Martov's definition of a member of the RSDLP was of a broad, diffuse organisation which opened doors to opportunists prepared to consider themselves as members of the party without belonging to any of the organisations of the party, but just working under its control and guidance.[173] This meant to Lenin the absence of any control and guidance. The opportunist tendency of "not building the party from above, of starting from the party congress and the bodies emanating from the latter; their tendency to proceed from below, a tendency which would allow every professor, every schoolboy and every striker to register himself as a member of the party; the hostility to the formalism which demands that a party member belong to an organisation recognised by the party"[174]—all these betokened an "inclination towards the mentality of the bourgeois intellectual who is only prepared to recognise organisational relations platonically", and has "a weakness for opportunist profundity and for anarchist phrases; a partiality for autonomy as against centralism".[175] Lenin insisted "that membership of the party must be given a narrow definition to distinguish those who work from those who talk, so as to get rid of chaos in the matter of organisation":[176] better ten workers not being admitted to the party than one chatterer passing through the sieve unnoticed.[177]

In *What is to be Done?* Lenin was most afraid of workers sliding into trade unionist opportunism, through lack of outside guidance by bourgeois intellectuals. As time went on he began to be more afraid of the tendency of intellectuals towards individualism and self-will, and to put his trust in the discipline infused into industrial workers by the factory.[178] The party was after all being prepared not as a platform for intellectual debates but for the organisation of a proletarian dictatorship. It is worth quoting here a resolution by a Bolshevik committee in the Ural region: "The preparation of the proletariat for a dictatorship—such is the important organisational task to which all others must be subordinated. The preparation consists among other things of the creation of a mood favourable to a powerful, authoritative proletarian organisation. . . . It may be objected that dictators have appeared and do appear of themselves. But this has not always been so, and it must not happen spontaneously or selfishly in the proletarian party. Here the highest degree of awareness must be combined with unchallengeable obedience—one must summon forth the other."[179]

It is unfair to say that Lenin was nothing but a commissar who believed in the exclusive and supreme efficacy of organisation and in nothing else. His conception of the Socialist party was *mutatis mutandis* close to the Catholic conception of the church. It embodied and articulated the progressive march of history. It became the Urim Vetumim of the historic dialectic, once it had, after prolonged searching and discussion, formulated its stand. This was not a matter of parliamentary majority votes or even of the view voiced by mass elections here and now. The general will conceived as the will of history was not in the contemporary articulated views of men, but in the often unperceived trend of historic development and inevitability and, what amounted to the same thing, in the unconscious, unspoken wishes of the masses. Those who were in this respect the exposed nerve of the people, the first to comprehend the direction of history, spoke for the proletariat. As if in answer to the earlier criticism by Trotsky of the principle of substitution—the nation by the class, the class by the party, the party by the Central Committee, the Central Committee by a dictator[180]—Lenin said in 1920: "Classes are led by parties, and parties are led by individuals who are called leaders . . . this is the ABC. The will of a class is sometimes fulfilled by a dictator. . . . Soviet socialist democracy is not in the least incompatible with individual rule and dictatorship. . . . What is necessary is individual rule, the recognition of the dictatorial powers of one man. . . . All phrases about equal rights are nonsense."[181]

The revolution of 1905 was to Lenin an hour of trial for the Russian people, above all its proletariat, and a test for his own ideas. It had been a triumph of spontaneity. It had been neither prepared, nor started, nor really guided by the Social-Democrats, let alone the Bolsheviks. The socialist groups joined the bandwagon, and became active in the stormy events, endeavouring with more or less success to steer them. Even the St Petersburg soviet owed its beginning rather ironically to an initiative from the establishment.[182] It was then taken over by the socialist intellectuals, Trotsky and Parvus, the former using it very effectively as his first entry into world history. Lenin at first remained cool towards the emergence of a Workers' Governing Council, and played no part in it. Its rudimentary character and the preponderant influence of the Mensheviks on it threatened to blur the independence of the Bolshevik ingredient and to turn the Bolsheviks into a "tail".[183] Nor did Lenin appreciate at the time the political potentialities of a Soviet network, in contrast for instance to Axelrod who had earlier speculated on some such eventuality.[184] It still smacked too much of a trade union organisation.

His attention was taken up with the dilemmas which a bourgeois-democratic revolution created for proletarian socialism. He adhered to the Marxist canon on the impossibility of skipping that stage and proceeding to a proletarian-socialist revolution directly. To succeed the latter required a ripe social-economic (which meant industrial) capitalist structure, and a high degree of proletarian socialist consciousness, neither of which obtained in Russia of the day. They could develop only under bourgeois-capitalist rule and in a regime which offered workers parliamentary democratic freedom to become organised and gain militant socialist consciousness. Lenin was however convinced that the feeble liberal bourgeoisie of Russia lacked the courage and human resources to rise to the occasion and carry out the bourgeois-democratic revolution, and he was also sure that from fear of the proletariat, it would when it came to the crunch prefer an accommodation with Tsarism to a common front with a determined socialist vanguard.

"All social-democrats admit that the political revolution in Russia must precede the socialist revolution: should they not therefore combine with all the elements in the political opposition to fight against absolutism and put socialism in the background for the time being?"[185] wrote Lenin.

Lenin was ready for both, but only very conditionally. The first objective being the abolition of Tsarist autocracy and the social forces supporting it, the Social-Democrats should for that purpose "support the progressive social classes against the reactionary classes, the bourgeois against representatives of privileged and feudal landownership and bureaucracy, the big bourgeois against the reactionary strivings of the petty bourgeoisie" to save small producers and halt industrial concentration and capitalist forms.[186] All this "against a particular enemy", without conceding any socialist principles. "They do not expect anything for themselves from these temporary allies and concede nothing to them."[187]

Lenin was fully conscious of the still more conditional readiness of these potential allies to make common cause with the working classes in an effort to achieve political liberty. The hostility of all other classes, groups and strata of the population towards autocracy was not absolute; their democracy always looked back. The bourgeoisie could not but realise that industrial and social development was retarded by absolutism; but it feared the complete democratisation of the political and social system and might at any time enter into alliance with absolutism against the proletariat. The petty bourgeoisie was two-faced by its very nature; on the one hand it gravitated towards the proletariat and to democracy; on the other hand "as a class of small property owners it gravitated towards the reactionary classes", giving recruits to clerical, chauvinist, anti-semitic leagues and fraternities. It was likely to conclude an alliance with the ruling class against the proletariat. Moreover the intelligentsia was being torn between hatred of obscurantist oppression and material interests, which might lead it "to sell its oppositional and revolutionary fervour for an official job, or a share in profits and dividends".[188]

The only consistent and resolute fighter for republican democracy was the proletariat: the sole "unreserved enemy of absolutism".[189] It would never make a compromise with absolutism, and will never look back. It was bound therefore to become the spearhead of the fight against absolutism, in fact to make the democratic revolution for the bourgeoisie, while maintaining its own independence. Ultimately, its success in the task was conditional on not letting its nerve be weakened by timid and reluctant allies.

Once the fortress of autocracy had been conquered, parliamentary bourgeois rule established and political liberties enacted, should the proletarian party step down, take a back seat and let the potentialities of the new regime work themselves out, as the Mensheviks claimed, or should the party of revolutionary socialists—the vanguard of the proletariat—keep up its hegemony throughout the struggle and in the course of it try to lay the foundations for an early confrontation with the liberal bourgeoisie? Marxist orthodoxy and democratic commitment dictated to the Mensheviks a policy of rigorous abstention. They would not join the revolutionary provisional government, since it would be a bourgeois establishment. But they would also do everything possible not to frighten the middle classes away and into the arms of the feudal-absolutist forces. In fact, the acme of achievement was, in Menshevik eyes, a freely elected constituent assembly on the basis of universal suffrage and the democratic, possibly republican, constitution promulgated by it. Within the framework of the latter, class conflict would be allowed to reach full fruition.[190]

Lenin did not regard liberty as a goal, even a temporary goal. In his eyes it was an opportunity: to the capitalists to exploit the working classes, and to the proletariat to brace itself and organise for a social liberation. Lenin was not afraid of frightening the bourgeoisie. He called on the proletariat to display a dynamism and tenacity that would sweep the petty bourgeoisie and the peasants away and compel the bourgeoisie to trail after the proletariat "with grinding teeth".[191] The Social-Democrats were duty bound not merely to enter the provisional government, but to gain an ascendancy over their non-socialist allies.

"The Mensheviks," wrote Lenin, "explain the process of the present struggle [well], but are incapable of giving the correct slogan for the struggle. They march well, but lead badly. They ignore the active leading and guiding part in history which must be played by parties which place themselves at the head of the advanced classes."[192]

The Mensheviks wanted the revolution of the workers to come from below: Lenin wanted it from above. The former wanted Social-Democracy to remain "the party of the extreme revolutionary opposition",[193] outside the provisional government, but not disloyal to its constitutional policies. Lenin was unable to conceive of a normalised situation. He was too obsessed with the counter-revolutionary dangers hovering over the bourgeois-democratic achievement. The greatest service to democracy, and one that could effectively be rendered only by the conscious proletarian masses, was to combat and suppress the enemies lurking against it and prevent their comeback. This could be done only by dictatorial methods, which again only a revolutionary-democratic alliance of the proletariat and an awakened peasantry could handle.

"A decisive victory of the revolution over Tsarism is the revolutionary democratic dictatorship of the proletariat and the peasantry. And such a victory will assume the form of a dictatorship that is inevitably bound to rely on military force and not on institutions established by 'lawful' means."[194] To be effective the dictatorship would have to be backed by a revolutionary army from among the workers and radical popular elements. It would have to go to the furthest limits of radical democracy such as allowing for seizure of landed estates by the peasants. "It can only be a dictatorship because the reforms necessary for the proletariat and the peasantry will call forth the desperate resistance of the landlords and the bourgeoisie. Without a dictatorship it will be impossible to break the resistance and repel the counter-revolution."[195] Here is the idea of Lenin's revolutionary democratic dictatorship of workers and peasants, which is "not a socialist dictatorship because it will not affect the foundations of capitalism" by abolishing private ownership or nationalising industry.[196] It would however go far enough in doing away with Tsarist bureaucracy, in breaking the landlord class and in inspiring the workers with conquering self-confidence and the possessing classes with fear and a sense of impotence. "We shall settle accounts with the Tsar in the Jacobin way of terror."[197]

In time of revolution, democracy meant dictatorship: "amendments are not moved in parliament, but in street demonstrations, decisive victories are scored by military operations and not by parliamentary struggles".[198] . . . "Great historical problems are solved only by force."[199]

Lenin's conception of a worker-peasant alliance was based upon an acute insight that a revolution in land tenure accomplished by the direct action of the peasantry was absolutely irreversible. He also realised that the Russian peasantry, like peasants in general, had no political ambitions. Once they had grabbed the landlord's estates and partitioned them, they would go home, and leave questions of political sovereignty to the workers' parties. The latter would then be free to mould the political realities in a revolutionary way. "They will fight together for liberty. They will not surrender to the bourgeoisie their own revolution, the democratic revolution, in preparation for further struggle for Socialism."[200]

As the prospects for the abolition of Tsardom in the "Jacobin way" were being dimmed by the October Manifesto, the arrest of the Petersburg soviet council and the Peasants Committee, Lenin and the Bolsheviks became convinced of the necessity of preparing an armed uprising, "to exterminate ruthlessly all the chiefs of the civil and military authorities".[201] The result was the Moscow uprising.

Lenin called upon the Soviets of Workers' Deputies to transform themselves from organs of the strike struggle, which was their genesis, and then organs of direct mass struggle, into organs of the general revolutionary struggle against the government, finally into organs of armed insurrection. All the same, the "soviets and similar mass institutions are not sufficient for the purpose of organising the insurrection . . . for the purpose of organising the fighting forces proper, for organising the insurrection in the most literal sense of the word";[202] only for welding the masses together and for passing on party slogans. The initiative for preparing, planning and directing the insurrection had to be taken by a separate vanguard. "Rebellion is an art . . . the principle rule of this art is that a desperately bold and irrevocably determined offensive must be waged."[203]

The idea of an armed uprising was raised by Lenin into a shibboleth of revolutionary authenticity. "Those who are opposed to armed uprising, those who do not prepare for it, must be ruthlessly cast out of the ranks of supporters of the revolution and sent back to the ranks of its enemies, of the traitors or cowards, for the day is aproaching when the force of events and conditions of the struggle will compel us to separate enemies and friends according to this principle. We must not preach passivity, not advocate waiting until the troops come over. No. We must proclaim from the housetops the need for a bold offensive and armed attack, the necessity at such times of exterminating persons in command of the enemy and a most energetic fight for the wavering troops". The Moscow uprising had inaugurated "new barricade tactics . . . of guerilla warfare", that of "mobile and exceedingly small units, units of ten, three or even two persons".[204]

"The great wars in history, the great revolutionary problems were solved only by the advanced classes returning to the attack again and again; and they achieved victory after having learned the lessons of defeat. Defeated armies learn well. The revolutionary classes of Russia have been defeated in their first campaign, but the revolutionary situation remains."[205]

But the most important lesson which the various socialist groups, Mensheviks, Bolsheviks, as well as Trotsky and Parvus, learned was that although badly battered, the edifice of Tsardom had weathered the storm of the 1905 revolution because the army and the bureaucracy stood by the Tsar, notwithstanding some minor mutinies; the peasantry failed to join the revolution; the liberal bourgeoisie proved a timid, unreliable and treacherous ally; and the working class movement lacked the strength, the tenacity and the clear resolve to bring the revolution to a victorious end. The regime survived, though changed externally. There seemed little prospect of it being toppled soon by another revolutionary wave from within Russia. Only an international gale could shake it again and give the necessary inspiration and help to the rebels inside Russia.[206]

"There is only one case," says the Menshevik conference resolution, "in which Social-Democracy on its own initiative would have to direct its efforts towards the conquest of power and keep it in its own hands as long as possible. It would be precisely if the revolution shifted into the advanced countries of Western Europe where the conditions for the realisation of socialism have already attained a certain maturity. In that case the restricted historical limitations of the Russian revolution may be substantially expanded, and the possibility of advancing on the road of socialist transformation would appear."[207] In *Two Tactics* Lenin expresses the view that the worker-peasant democratic dictatorship in Russia "may carry the revolutionary flame to Europe" where it would kindle a socialist revolution which would enable the Russian democratic dictatorship to make the leap into socialism.[208] Parvus-Helphand and Trotsky added to their theory of a permanent revolution the vital link,[209] which was never absent from Lenin's own calculation: the imperialist war, which was in the offing, was sure to hasten the collapse of the weakest link in international capitalism—Russia—and bring about a revolution there, which would be taken over by a democratic dictatorship that in turn would ignite the embers of revolution in the West and inspire the workers to make an international socialist revolution. The time lag between Russia and the West in regard to maturity for a socialist revolution would then be cancelled.

Implicitly or explicitly these speculations amounted to pinning all hopes on international war as the instrument of revolution. This became the cornerstone of Lenin's strategy in World War I. Russian defeat was the first condition. A shaken regime incapable of conducting the war, and impotent to provide the elementary needs of the population at home, would have its credibility destroyed. The failures at the front, decimation and demoralisation of the troops would deprive it of its main instrument. Under the influence of events and in response to revolutionary agitation; goaded by hunger; despairing of victory; exasperated by intolerable hardships, officer brutality and military discipline; and longing for peace, the peasant soldiers would desert en masse to seize landed estates. The army would disintegrate, the oppressed nationalities would be seized by a fervent desire for liberation and see their chance. The destruction of the main bases of Tsarism would be accomplished at a stroke. The victorious revolt of the whole nation against autocracy and for liberty would become a challenge to the most dynamic revolutionary force in Russian society to drive the revolution to the extreme limits of radical and proletarian democracy. This would stir the Western working classes, maddened by the sufferings of war, to rise, thus preventing their governments from trying to strangle the Russian revolution. When they became victorious, the socialists of the West would assist the Russian revolution to reach a socialist fruition.

Lenin had to rethink the problems of nation, war and revolution. The idea of exploiting national defeat, the disintegration of Russia's traditional society and the break-up of historic Russia by the secession of the oppressed nationalities for launching a revolution—all this demanded a confrontation with some of the deepest traditions, loyalties, instincts, inhibitions of the masses. These had first to be undermined, softened and then overcome. Liberation from them was tantamount to releasing the revolutionary energy necessary for a final assault.

In a sketch of the schema of revolution, written at the beginning of 1906,[210] Lenin takes it for granted that "the revolutionary-democratic dictatorship of the proletariat and the peasantry" would be resisted increasingly more strongly by the liberal bourgeoisie, "temporising in the third period, passive in the fourth", becoming "downright counter-revolutionary and organising itself in order to filch from the proletariat the gains of the revolution. The whole of the well-to-do section of the peasantry and a large part of the middle peasantry would also grow 'wiser', quieten down and turn to the side of the counter-revolution in order to wrest power from the proletariat and the rural poor, who sympathise with the proletariat. . . . A new crisis and a new struggle blaze forth; the proletariat is now fighting to preserve its democratic gains for the sake of a socialist revolution. The struggle would be almost hopeless for the Russian proletariat alone and its defeat would be as inevitable as the defeat of the German revolutionary party in 1849-50, or the defeat of the French proletariat in 1871, if the European socialist proletariat did not come to the assistance of the Russian proletariat. Under such conditions the Russian proletariat can win a second victory. The cause is no longer hopeless. The second victory will be the socialist revolution in Europe. The European workers will show us how to do it and then in conjunction with them, we shall bring about the socialist revolution."[211]

Chapter Two

WAR AND REVOLUTION

(I) THE SECOND INTERNATIONAL DEBATING

If the issue of nation and revolution was at the back of the internal cleavage into the reformists and radicals in the SPD, it was all the more so naturally on the international stage, in the congresses and in the conclaves of the Second International.[212] Be it the colonial question, be it the problem of socialist participation in bourgeois government coalitions (Millerandism), be it the momentous dilemma of working class attitude to war, the International was prevented by irreconcilable dissensions from passing more than tortuously phrased declarations liable to contradictory interpretations, in spite of sometimes extremist rhetoric. It was unable to formulate clear, unambiguous directives for action which would bind all national parties. While paying obeisance to general principles, it left the decision on modes of action to the national parties. This remained a lesson to Lenin when he came to draft the famous 19-21 Points of the Third International and made centralised power of decision into the cornerstone of the programme of the Comintern, to the point of refusing any autonomous status to the national parties. Perhaps still more striking was the conspicuous emergence of this very tendency in Rosa Luxemburg's outline of the New International submitted by her during the war to the Spartakist leadership.[213] As we shall see, she threw to the winds on that occasion all her past reservations about centralised leadership. Internationalism was the apple of her eye. If the global proletariat was a single entity, it had to have a firm common strategy. With all her passionate advocacy of revolutionary spontaneity, Rosa realised that declaratory inter-nationalism was meaningless. It had to be firmly institutionalised. The adversary was too powerful and too compact a force. Only she never dreamt that the GHQ of the world revolution would be situated in the capital not of a federation of proletarian communities, but in the seat of a wholly isolated socialist state, compelled or tempted to use its position as vanguard of world revolution to further its needs and interests as a great power.[214]

(a) COLONIALISM

To Rosa, Lenin and their friends the issue of monopolist capitalist imperialism had, to repeat, become the very axis of their updated Marxism, the latest and final form of class conflict within the nation; and also, as the consummation of global social-racial polarisation, the warrant of the inevitability and the imminence of world revolution. They considered opposition to militarist nationalism turned imperialism to be the most effective proletarian plank in the arena of national politics as well as in global revolutionary strategy. In contrast, the moderate "social-imperialist" spokesmen like Bernstein, David, the Fabians and for a while at least Kautsky, were able to invoke para-doxically Marx's internationalist defence of colonialism in the third volume of *Das Kapital* as support for the imperialism practised by the nation-state. "Even a whole society, a nation, or even all simul-taneously existing societies taken together," wrote Marx, "are not owners of the globe; they are only its possessors, its usufructuaries, and, like a good paterfamilias, they must hand it down to succeeding generations in an improved condition." If "the savages" don't know how to make use of their natural resources and to improve their lands, and if their natural wealth is necessary for the progress of higher civili-sation, and the well-being and progress of the undeveloped tribes requires the aid of enterprising and dynamic strangers, "higher culture should be in a position to enjoy the higher right" over the "conditional right" of the native inhabitants.[215]

Needless to say, all speakers at socialist congresses came out strongly against brutal exploitation and oppression of colonial peoples, condemned atrocities, and warned against the unscrupulous usurpation of the natural wealth and the economic opportunities in backward countries by private monopolistic interest groups which dragged their respective nations into dangerous adventures and into conflict with native and rival imperialists. But even those who branded imperialism as an expression of the urge to conquer, subjugate, exploit and plunder, drew back from the extreme theoretical and practical conclusions of Rosa. What most of them wanted was to humanise colonial activities and to keep them under stricter democratic and parliamentary control. They insisted that the duty of the imperial states was first to improve the conditions of the natives, then to prepare them for self-government and eventually to grant them independence. Out of fear of political entanglements into which governments might be involved by capitalist interests, some would even advocate non-governmental forms of colonialism such as the exploitation of natural resources by private initiative, and colonial settlement by individuals or groups that would teach the primitive populations by their example and prepare an economic infrastructure for modern independent statehood. Kautsky was at one point to go so far as to claim that imperialist exploitation of the undeveloped areas in Asia and Africa might even lead, through the intersection of international concerns and international economic agreements on the division of colonial territories and spheres of influence, to peaceful sharing out of the globe and to smooth international cooperation.

This attitude contrasted sharply with the views of the Dutch radical, van Kol, who at the 1904 Amsterdam congress of the International[216] proposed the resolution that "Colonial expansion was the inevitable accompaniment of capitalism in its latest (not last!) phase—imperialism." The latter "involved the threat of a European war, was a source of chauvinism and imposed increasing burdens on the peoples through military expenditure", which were most often paid for by the masses in indirect taxes and in high duties on imported goods of prime necessity. In her own resolution at the 1900 Paris congress Rosa called colonialism and militarism the two aspects of a new phenomenon in world politics—a phenomenon "whose paroxysms had unleashed four bloody wars during the past six years, and which threatens the world with a state of permanent war".[217] She prophesied even then that "the collapse of the capitalist system would take place not through an economic but through a political crisis, resulting from developments in the sphere of world politics", by which she meant international war which was being rendered inevitable by imperialist rivalries.

Echoes of Rosa's motion resound strongly in the resolution which was eventually adopted, namely in its references to the threat of a "permanent state of war", "the world alliance of bourgeoisie and governments for perpetual war" and "the alliance of workers of all countries for perpetual peace" and to the necessity "to organise a simultaneous and uniform movement of opposition to militarism".[218] The congress failed to follow up this radical resolution, but contented itself with a platitudinous statement affirming "the right of the inhabitants of civilised countries to settle in lands where the population is at a lower stage of development", while calling for humane treatment of the native populations, for respect of their right to eventual emancipation and for strict parliamentary control of "wealthy cliques" engaged in colonial plunder and guilty of degrading treatment of the native inhabitants.[219]

At the 1907 Stuttgart congress, Kautsky returned to the emphasis on the contradiction between the socialist concept of the right to national self-determination and colonialism of any kind, even by a socialist regime, which, though it might be a benevolent despotism, was still rule by foreign invaders. The final resolution starts with a strong diatribe against the evil features of capitalist colonialism, which by its nature gives rise "to servitude, forced labour and the extermination" of natives, under the pretext of a civilising mission that is constantly belied by systematic plunder, enslavement and atrocities. It ends with a pious wish that "in the interests of the development of the productive forces, a policy based on peaceful cultural development and one which develops the world's mineral resources in the interests of the whole of humanity" be worked out.[220] In other words, colonialism was not rejected en bloc and in all circumstances, including the one practised by nation-states. No one in fact seriously thought that it could be pursued by any other means but the state.

The arguments of socialist defenders of colonialism ranged widely. Accepting as it were the theory of their opponents that imperialism was necessary and inevitable, indeed the last phase of capitalism, they found in it a justification for intensifying colonial activity as it was bound to bring the revolution nearer. In so far as it was calculated to advance capitalism at home, the inflow of cheap raw materials and the outflow of finished goods to the colonies were sure to bring immediate benefits to the working clases as well. The extremely centralised and mono-polistic forms of capitalist economy in the age of imperialism rendered the transformation of a capitalist into a socialist economy all the easier. A ban on imperialist expansion might make sense if it was not merely accepted simultaneously by everyone in principle, but if it led the old imperial powers to divest themselves of their dominions simul-taneously. The latter was hardly to be expected: was Britain going to pull out of India, or were the Yankees prepared to return the territories of the United States to the Red Indians or to Mexico? The anti-imperialist agitation was therefore a cunning device to deprive the virile, young, overpopulated nations of their share in the bounties of the planet, and leave the field open to Britain and her like.[221]

Thus the German Revisionists, such as Gerhard Hildebrand, who was eventually expelled from the party, Schippel, Quessel, Wolfgang Heine and Eduard David, never tired of claiming that in comparison with England and France, with their early start as industrial and colonial powers, Germany was a disadvantaged country and, like the Italians, a young proletarian nation. "It would thus"—wrote Hildebrand—"be no unsocialistic step, no backsliding into nationalist tendencies, no support of capitalist special interests, if the workers of Germany and

Italy, whose colonial interests were prejudiced, were to say in the present situation: 'We are for peace, but only for peace on the platform of equality. . . . No nation that is unnaturally curtailed or threatened in its individual development need succumb without resistance to a strangulation of its economic freedom simply for the sake of peace.' "[222]

(b) BOURGEOIS COALITION GOVERNMENTS

At the turn of the century the Second International was very much pre-occupied with the question of Millerandism. The step taken by a socialist leader in joining a bourgeois coalition government, which incidentally comprised as Minister of War General Galiffet, one of the butchers of the glorious Paris Commune, appeared to fly in the face of the two basic principles of socialism—class war and internationalism. In the not too distant past a man like Guesde still had very strong objections to participating in national assemblies altogether. Even after over-coming his qualms, in his election placards he begged Messieurs les bourgeois, his class enemies, not to vote for him. Now a socialist was to sit in a Cabinet engaged in putting down strikes with the help of the army. As part of joint ministerial responsibility he would be bound to accept bourgeois majority decisions contrary to working class interests. On the plane of international relations, a socialist member of a bourgeois coalition cabinet at a time of sharply defined military alliances and armed camps plotting war against each other could not but become an accomplice of warmongers. He would thus be violating every principle of international proletarian solidarity aimed at preventing working classes being led to massacre each other. On this too the Second International adopted a resolution which, after enunciating pious generalities in the name of the purity and the international character of the proletarian struggle against international capitalism, left the decision to join or not to join coalition governments to every national party, in accordance with circumstances and local needs.[223]

It was easy to condemn Millerandism. Few of the socialists outside France grasped the nature of the dilemmas which prompted Millerand to behave as he did (with Jaurès' approval) and which were to assume extreme urgency some twenty years later all over Europe, above all in Germany. The Dreyfus case and the impending right-wing coup against the Third Republic confronted the French socialist party with these alternatives: to act on the principle of "the worse the trouble of the bourgeoisie the better for the revolution"; to let the Republic be over-thrown by a military putsch; or to hasten to the aid of the democratic

Republic. Guesde, who, as we have said, had previously justified socialist participation in parliamentary elections as "putting a socialist garrison into a capitalist citadel", prophesied that "ministerialisme" would drive the disappointed hotheads among the revolutionary socialists into the arms of anarchism or a new Caesarism, whereas Jaurès welcomed the "ouvertures de l'histoire" accorded to a virile conquering movement. Bebel, however, sensed, like Guesde, a most dangerous trap.[224]

(c) THE SPECTRE OF WAR

Of infinitely greater significance was the question of the attitude of the proletariat to the threat of international war and to war itself, once it had broken out in spite of all efforts to prevent it. The late pronouncements of Marx and Engels had prefigured the dilemmas of the Second International in the years before World War I, its terrible predicament in the last few days before the avalanche, and finally the catastrophe of August 4, 1914, when the parties of the warring nations, above all Germany, were confronted with the agonising alternative of choosing then and there, between "our nation right or wrong" fighting, in Engels' words, for its very existence, and a united international proletarian front against an imperialist war. Apart from praying for a revolution in Russia which would spare the SPD the agony of deciding to support or not to support a war against Russia, Engels had tempered his dire foreboding by reiterating his confidence that whatever happened and whatever the zigzags of history, socialism was in the end bound to win. Yet it is a very long way from Engels' enjoining the workers' representatives to vote for war credits in a war of defence, to a proletarian policy of turning the war of nations into a European civil war through resort to disobedience, a general strike, refusal to fight, sabotage and finally armed uprising.

The tendency to jettison any idea of international war as the midwife of revolution, the espousal of a policy of total opposition to war of any kind, in many cases—Hervé, Liebknecht, Rosa and Lenin and others[225]—to the point of denying the very distinction between a war of defence and a war of aggression, no doubt had something to do with a growing humanitarianism, with a clearer realisation of the horrors of modern warfare, and a consequent anxiety about the survival of civilisation and its moral values—as Bebel told the Reichstag. But it was motivated most potently, though not always quite consciously, by the dread of the test with which the working class would be confronted.

Nevertheless, as already adumbrated, not all socialists had given up the expectation that a war, if it came, in spite of proletarian opposition, might be turned into the instrument of revolution.

On the eve of 1914 Lenin, like Parvus and Rosa Luxemburg, was brooding about the opportunities which an armed clash between the great powers might offer to the proletariat. He doubted however whether Willy, Nicky and Franz Joseph, who must be aware of what was in store for them, would really oblige.[226] That the imperial rulers were conscious of the perils awaiting them, at least in Russia, we know from the astonishingly prophetic Durnovo Memorandum already referred to, warning the Tsar not to let Russia slide into a war with imperial Germany. Russia was not in a position to sustain such a struggle; and once she began to flag, not a political revolution but a flood would burst upon Russia, sweep away the throne, bring down the social order and drown the empire in a chaos of blood and fire. Durnovo also felt sure that the Hohenzollerns too would be overthrown by war, whatever its outcome.

On the face of it, all socialists professed as an article of faith the doctrine that war was inherent in the capitalist system. But this dogma was open to contradictory interpretations. One was that there was no point in trying to conjure away war, without first making an all-out effort to abolish capitalism. But those who were anxious not to commit themselves to anti-war policies, were also precisely those who opposed revolutionary action against the capitalist system.

As an international problem par excellence, opposition to war necessitated internationally concerted action. But as Kautsky was to say after August 1914, as a loose federation of national parties, with the International Socialist Bureau at Brussels being hardly more than a post box, let alone a general staff, there was just no machinery for effective leadership and rapid action in an international emergency.[227] And those who should have been most anxious to ward off the gruelling test of war, were also the least inclined to subordinate their parties to an overall international authority.

At the congresses of the Second International, German as well as French socialist spokesmen took pains not to blacken the image of their country in the eyes of foreigners. They rejected accusations of warmongering directed at the respective governments. There was a blurring of distinction between the reputation of the state and the prestige of the socialist party in it. Bebel would counter Jaurès' criticism of the lack of revolutionary impulse in the largest and best-organised Labour party, with the finest theoretical equipment in the world—the SPD—by pointing to the weakness of the French socialist movement, compared with the prospect of the SPD soon becoming a majority in the nation and on its representative bodies. When claiming with pride that the French socialists were the heirs to the Jacobin revolutionary tradition, the author of the monumental *Histoire Socialiste de la Révolution Française* was by no means ignoring the red-hot patriotism of the defenders of the République one and indivisible against the counter-revolutionary powers. Bebel in turn proudly recalled the contribution of German classical humanism and dialectical philosophy and, of course, of Marx, Engels and Lassalle to the common treasure of socialist thought. There was high drama and no little embarrassment, when Jaurès told the German comrades that while the French masses had won their franchise on the barricades, the German workers had got it as a gift from Bismarck, and Bebel shouted back: "You got it from Bismarck at Sedan."[228] The hearts of both veterans, men whose feelings and natural generosity could easily be stirred, were made to throb to the magic words of *patrie* and *Vaterland*.

There was no denying the fact that Junker-dominated Germany had far more advanced social legislation and services than Republican France and that the Reich authorities never used the army to crush strikes, whereas French soldiers were being ordered to shoot down strikers.[229] In comparison with the immense strength and wealth of the conservative German trade union movement, the French labour unions were woefully weak, notwithstanding their vociferous extremism and anti-patriotic stand. On closer scrutiny it emerges that in fact the leaders of the national parties of the Second International were concerned rather with preventing the outbreak of war and with making war impossible, than with the question of stopping it once it had broken out. That was a contingency which was too horrible to contemplate. It was a deluge against which no devices could be contrived. A large variety of ideas on how to resist the governments, the classes, interests and sentiments which were held to be working for war was being canvassed. It was thought that the abolition of permanent armies and their replacement by people's militias would sweep away military castes and traditions and insure the spread of pacific sentiments, since a people in arms were sure to have no vested interest in war and be free from chauvinist passion; and at the same time to be invincible when invaded.[230] Bernstein shrewdly objected that in those countries where a people's militia was attainable, it was unnecessary; and where it was necessary, it was not to be had in the foreseeable future.[231] The principle of refusing military and certainly war credits was accepted almost unanimously as a binding obligation upon Social-Democratic parties. Secret diplomacy and chauvinist propaganda were decried as insidious perils, to be combated by every means. The French and British socialists laid great store on the principle of international arbitration, to be made easier and more effective by gradual disarmament.[232] As usual Kautsky wavered between socialist radicalism and democratic humanism, and tried to combine the two: a United States of Europe with a common government, parliament and army would conjure away the spectre of war, and at the same time enable a united European proletariat to conquer international capitalism.[233]

It was extremely difficult to distinguish between a war of defence, which the large majority approved, and a war of aggression, which they felt bound to resist by every means. Kautsky was the most realistic, when he maintained that it was ultimately impossible to come to a firm definition in the matter: a technical aggressor might in effect be defending himself against imminent attack.[234] Bernstein went so far as to state that in modern times a country which out of deep scruples took no action to forestall an enemy and to prevent him from penetrating its territory and waging war on it, had already half lost the war.[235] Bebel contented himself with saying that you would know which was the aggressor and which was the attacked state defending itself, when you saw them.[236] The most extreme stand was taken by the French syndicalists, above all Gustav Hervé, the future ultra-chauvinist and Fascist. They refused to make any distinction between a just and unjust war. They called for armed resistance and insurrection against any government making war. Like Rosa, they refused to recognise a country which had not had a revolution as a fatherland which deserved to be defended. They held up to horror and ridicule the very notion of *patrie*, called the national flag a rag upon a dung heap and openly incited conscripts to desert.[237]

The ardent believer in international arbitration, Jaurès, wished, as we already know, to make the acceptance or refusal of arbitration into the test of a defensive or offensive war.[238] Shortly before his death, Bebel reiterated very emphatically his conviction about the socialist's duty to defend the fatherland. On that occasion he broadened the concept of national defence to include care to secure the borders in accordance with the requirements of geography and the nature of the hostile neighbour. He also dwelt on the importance of defence-mindedness and high national morale, referring with pride to the days of 1813, Gneisenau and Scharnhorst.[239] Similarly Noske claimed that far from denying the imperative of national defence, he was, for democratic and patriotic reasons, fighting for a democratised army, free from the Prussian barrack spirit and the haughtiness of Junker officers, and therefore more effective and more modern.[240]

The supreme issue in the debate on socialism and war was—to repeat—what should be done when war had broken out and all anti-war agitation, protests, demonstrations, flaming speeches, rousing resolutions and threatening warnings to the ruling classes and their mindless or selfish and perverse governments, had failed to prevent the conflagration. The ultra-Left had one reply: a general strike developing into mass insurrection. Vaillant and Keir Hardie proposed a strike at the Copenhagen congress of 1910, limiting it to war transport and war production.[241] But everybody understood that such a strike could not be halted at the point assigned to it. It would either be nipped in the bud, or would grow into a general strike and civil war.

Rosa Luxemburg was extremely far-sighted about the dangers lurking in nationalism for revolutionary socialist internationalism. "It is not for nothing"—she wrote—"that the internationalist tune vibrates so strongly in revolutionary Marxism, nor is it an accident that the opportunist way of thinking leads so naturally to national isolationism."[242]

The Stuttgart congress of the Second International in 1907 became the scene of the momentous confrontation between these stances.[243] There were motions by Bebel, by Jaurès and Vaillant, by Guesde, and finally the Rosa Luxemburg amendment, supported by Lenin and Martov. Bebel and Guesde were in fact dodging the issue by stating that war was an expression of capitalist contradictions. This could, as we have said, be interpreted as saying that the issue was really one of abolishing capitalism, and not of war. Once the former was achieved the latter would cease to be a threat. So long as capitalism continued, there was not much that the workers could do, beyond voting against military budgets and conducting pacifist agitation, and, Bebel untiringly repeated, fighting for the democratisation of the armed forces as "an essential guarantee for a lasting peace". Jaurès was quick to point out the fatalistic, defeatist and futile nature of this atitude: to prevent war meant to mobilise the workers into an army of invincible strength.[244]

The Jaurès-Vaillant resolution reaffirmed the right of any nation to wage a defensive war. As to a war of aggression, it laid stress not so much on stopping a war that had already broken out, as on the task of stopping its spread, "impeding and preventing of war . . . by the national and international action of the working class, using every means available from parliamentary intervention and public agitation to the general strike and to armed uprising".[245]

Bebel fought tooth and nail the latter operative part of the Jaurès-Vaillant resolution. He would go no further than to urge the workers and their representatives to do all in their power to prevent the outbreak of war and to bring about its termination, once it had started, "by whatever means [that] seem most appropriate".[246] That meant not only declining to offer clear directives, but also leaving the matter to the discretion of the national parties. In a passionate speech Bebel declared all references to a general strike and an armed uprising to be simply "impossible and not discussible" in German conditions, and went on to paint a lurid picture of a country which had gone through a total mobilisation with six million men (two million of them SPD members) called up ["where, then would we get the men for a general strike?"] to the accompaniment of a major economic crisis, famine, inflation. In a situation like that, could they really play about with the idea of a general strike? Their first attempt would be swept aside with derision, and if pursued would come up against the chauvinist frenzy of the nation; martial law and military courts, with their unlimited powers against traitors.[247]

Guesde, the old Leftist who was to become a minister in the French Union Sacrée coalition during the war, also came out against the general strike idea, on the grounds that it would put at a disadvantage precisely the belligerent country with the most class-conscious working class, and offer an advantage to the state with a cowed backward proletariat which would not go on strike.[248] The adopted resolution admitted that it was impossible "to lay down rightly the action to be taken against militarism by the working class in all countries, everywhere and at all times".[249] Tacked on to it was the Luxemburg-Lenin-Martov statement. While calling for the employment of "means they [the national parties] consider most effective in light of the sharpening of the class struggle", it urged the workers "to utilise the economic and political crisis created by the war to rouse the masses and thereby hasten the downfall of capitalist class rule".[250] The irony was that the resolution was adopted unanimously and no attention at all was paid by the congress and the conferences prior to August 1914 to the closing passage, which was destined to become the cornerstone of Leninism and Luxemburgism. Indeed, in his speech in Paris on his return from Stuttgart, Jaurès made no reference to it, only vaguely calling upon the masses to "crush the germ of fatal wars by parliamentary action or by social action".[251]

The Luxemburg-Lenin-Martov amendment to the Stuttgart resolution was unanimously accepted, because most of the delegates had absolutely no idea of starting a revolution. Still less did they envisage a calculated and active policy of national treason—insurrection—against their own government and armed forces waging war. As a result they simply failed to perceive that it was precisely to this that Rosa wanted them to commit themselves.

(II) THE MOMENT OF TRUTH

The agony of the Second International in the last days of July and in the first days of August 1914 revealed how feeble and irresolute was proletarian internationalism, when pitted not merely against the might of the imperialist powers bent upon war or inexorably sliding into it, but also when confronted with mass patriotism on the one hand, and the paralysing inhibitions of their leadership on the other. The leadership was wholly unprepared for the ordeal. For years it had been tossed about by panic when an international crisis flared up, and optimism when it was somehow resolved. The fact that it twice proved possible to prevent the dangerous disagreement between the great powers on Morocco from becoming a war, that quite a few colonial disputes were amicably settled, and that the Libyan war and the Balkan wars were localised and brought to a close by the Concert of Powers, lulled the socialists into a belief that the great capitalist interests fully understood their vital long-term interest in avoiding a world conflagration which would engulf them all.[252] It also encouraged the socialists to think, quite wrongly, that the volume and intensity of proletarian protest against war-mongering—and the spectre of a socialist revolution—had substantially contributed to halting the hand of bellicose governments and trigger-happy general staffs. The sardonic Victor Adler ridiculed the hysterical busybodies among the socialist anti-war agitators, who discredited socialist credibility by making so much fuss about every insignificant diplomatic incident.[253]

When the supreme test did come, the leaders of the International were unable to get any grip on the situation. Hendric de Man, who served as an interpreter at the hapless international meeting of the socialist leaders at Brussels on the very eve of the outbreak of the war, described later how "in face of stark facts and concrete responsibilities, nothing was left of all the discussions but an impression of unreal verbosity incapable of masking its own impotence".[254] In the *Dépêche de Toulouse* of July 30, 1914, Jaurès wrote: "I feel two contradictory impressions in face of the formidable threat that menaces Europe. First a sort of stupefying convulsion that is akin to despair. Can the whole progress of humanity, eighteen centuries of Christianity, the magnificent idealism of the Revolution, a hundred years of democracy, lead back to such barbarity? I find myself asking: is life worth living?"[255]

The aimless comings and goings of Labour veterans; the insistent reminder of the call of socialist duty, reiterated in so many solemn declarations and resolutions; the sense of helplessness in face of dire facts; the mounting, sweeping wave of mass enthusiasm or rather mass psychosis; the unbearable tension as world-shaking, uncontrollable events were driving to a catastrophic dénouement; the paralysing anguish—it was such a relief, when all choices and alternatives had been finally closed and it was possible, as Rosa's old comrade, Haenisch, wrote, to sing with a full throat "Deutschland, Deutschland über Alles".[256] A few days earlier Südekun had assured Chancellor Bethmann-Hollwegg that should Germany find itself at war, the Social-Democratic party and the trade union movement would not do anything to hamper the government.[257] Across the border on August 2, the old Communard and author of extreme anti-war resolutions, Edouard Vaillant, proclaimed that "a sinister fate . . . was driving us into a war of defence. In face of aggression, the Socialist will fulfil their patriotic duty."[258]

(a) THE AUGUST 1914 CATASTROPHE

On August 4 it was Hugo Haase, the Centrist leader and chairman of the Social-Democratic Parliamentary party and a Jew, one of the future founders of the USPD and its representative in the Revolutionary Directorate in November 1918, known for his anti-imperialist views, who was deliberately chosen by the party to read before the packed rows and galleries of the Reichstag the resolution of approval of the war credits and of support for the nation's war for existence. "If there ever was total agreement between the parliamentary faction of the SPD and the sentiments and thoughts of the masses, it was on August 4, that indelible day in the history of our people"—wrote Haenisch.[259] Instead of the dreaded arrests, closure of offices, ban on newspapers, the German Labour movement was for the first time given the taste of being taken into confidence, consulted, asked to cooperate and to help the state in matters of supreme importance such as the mobilisation of all the available labour force, the organisation of war production, the planning of a war economy and of the services in the rear. Some, like Scheidemann, later the first Chancellor of the Weimar Republic, visibly enjoyed the tasks, happy to forget internationalist commitments; others—notably Karl Kautsky—had to appease their consciences by resignedly recognising that history had proved that the International was a helpful instrument for peacetime cooperation between the Social-Democratic parties, but was useless once war had broken out. Germany was waging not only a war of defence, but also a crusade on behalf of the internationalist proletariat and for the world revolution: it was fighting the unspeakable Tsarist regime. Similarly, the French socialists were able to invoke the spectre of Prussian Junkerdom and militarism, the threat of a world dominated by them, with nations enslaved and a proletariat groaning under the boot of a brutal soldiery. "This time"— wrote Hervé—"all march: Royalists, Bonapartists, nationalists are as furious as we ourselves, the 'stateless' ".[260] A French syndicalist asked himself: "How is it possible that I, an anti-patriot, anti-militarist, who recognise nothing but the International, send blows to my comrades in misery and perhaps am going to die against my own cause, my proper interests, for my enemies?"[261]

The 1793 image of revolutionary France at war, and the horror of a Prussianized Germany were potent enough to turn such world-famous prophets of revolution as the two Russian exiles Plekhanov and Kropotkin, into supporters of their country's war effort. The old theoretician of monistic dialectical materialism and uncompromising class war, Plekhanov, became one of the staunchest upholders of the Burgfrieden in Russia to the point of condemning any strikes or class propaganda, while the international war lasted.[262]

Rosa's whole world seemed in ruins. She could never have brought herself to acknowledge—as a French socialist leader did, when asked why the leadership of the French party had capitulated without any resistance and had sent Guesde, Vaillant, Thomas and Sembat into the War Cabinet—that in fact the masses were so eager for war that they would have torn to pieces any of their leaders who had tried to oppose the war. Hervé, yesterday's chief propagandist of unconditional opposition to war, with no distinction between war of aggression and war of defence, turned overnight into a fanatical supporter of war, rechristening his paper, *La Guerre Sociale* as *La Victoire*.[263] To Rosa it was all treason perpetrated by an opportunist, careerist, petit-bourgeois leadership, quite in character with their behaviour in the last few years. Even if they could invoke popular enthusiasm for war, it was their duty as leaders to listen to the general will, to the historic imperatives of the proletariat, and not to yield to the passing, ephemeral moods of an ill-informed, uneducated, brainwashed, prejudiced populace.

"There is nothing more changeable," wrote the prophetess of mass spontaneity and the superiority of mass instincts, "than human psychology. The psyche of the masses contains in it always, like Thalassa, the eternal sea, all latent possibilities: the deadly stillness of the winds and the roaring gale, the basest cowardice and the wildest heroism. The mass is always what in the circumstances it must be, it is always poised for a leap to become something totally different. A fine captain would he be who fixed his course according to the momentary surge of the waves, and did not trouble to learn from the signs in the sky and in the depths of the sea about the coming storms! My little girl [she was writing to Mathilde Wurm in February 16, 1917] 'disappointment with the masses' is always the worst recommendation for a political leader. A leader of great style does not fix his tactics according to the momentary moods of the masses, but in accordance with the abiding laws of development, sticks to his tactic in the teeth of all disappoint- ments and quietly lets history bring its work to fruition."[264]

Where Lenin spoke of the traitors as the representatives of the labour aristocracy, which the imperialist phase of capitalism had thrown up, Rosa resorts to more ideological terms to explain the treason of reformist socialism. This also brings her near to psychological elitism: individual psychology, petit-bourgeois mentality, the traumatic power of nationalistic compulsions were behind the act of treason. Rosa was confirmed by Kautsky's formula in her conviction that not only the Revisionists, but the Centrists too never really had faith in and never felt the urge to employ the International as an instrument of international revolution. To them it was just a platform, and its congresses were no more than an occasion for coming together to make and to listen to platitudinous speeches and hypocritical declarations, with every national party free to pursue its policies as it wished. There had been no global revolutionary strategy at all. It was now an imperialist war, imposed upon the peoples and carried on against the international pro- letariat, that was forcing the world proletariat to evolve a new type of International, which would be the GHQ of the world proletariat in its struggle against international militant imperialism, and for world revolution: formulate global strategy, fix tactics, issue combat orders to the various national sections, which were to be considered as local fronts, and not as autonomous national parties.[265]

(b) MARTYRDOM AND REDEMPTION

Sooner than most people of any persuasion, Rosa Luxemburg was filled with the realisation of the enormity of what had happened in August 1914. It was not only the horror of the behaviour of her comrades in the Reichstag, the failure of her own line in the SPD and the collapse of the Second International; it was an overwhelming feeling that the war marked a turning point in world history, a point of no return.

Moods of that kind gradually won general dominance as the war unfolded and the undreamt-of horrors of modern warfare stood revealed: the staggering carnage, cruelty, suffering, waste, the senseless absurdity and total unpredictability of it all. What was most confusing was indeed the loss of bearings and the blow to self-confidence administered by the insatiable Moloch of war to a highly civilised society. For over a century it had not experienced a great pro-longed international war. It had been brought up in an unshakable faith in progress. It had indeed every reason to be proud of its phenomenal achievements in all fields of creative endeavour as well as in the art of living and in the rule of law. It could feel sure that it was in control of itself and its environment, that it was able to fix and carry out rational plans, weigh and assess cost and profit, ascertain cause and effect, in brief—control its instincts, shape its destiny, dominate nature and mould its surroundings. The war seemed to vindicate the warnings of the isolated, lonely prophets of wrath, like Nietzsche and Dostoevsky, who had taken such a masochistic delight in unmasking illusions and delusions, in revealing deception and self-deception, in uncovering hidden springs, in laying bare hypocrisy, and in confusing men by showing up all the antinomies, contradictions, inconsistencies, absurdities and self-destructive habits in all their beliefs and actions. Indeed, the war brought out a staggering reversal of values. Cunning, deceit, cruelty became tokens of idealistic determination and dedication, destruction was enthroned as a supreme duty, mass murder was called a sacred mission. How was it, wondered Sigmund Freud in 1915,[266] that the belligerent states were not only giving free rein to, but encouraging and glorifying those aggressive, destructive instincts, that unscrupulous art of deceit and lying, that disregard of moral restraints which were the basis of their own existence and were fostered by them so assiduously? He came to the disconcerting conclusion that "the state had forbidden to the individual the practice of wrong-doing not because it desired to abolish it, but because it desired to monopolise it, like salt and tobacco".[267]

"The six weeks' march to Paris has become a world drama," wrote Rosa Luxemburg in her flaming wartime "Junius" pamphlet, "The Crisis in German Social Democracy". "Mass murder has become a monstrous task, and yet the final solution is not one step nearer. Capitalist rule is caught in its own trap, and cannot exorcise the spirit that it has invoked. Gone is the first mad delirium. Gone are the patriotic street demonstrations, the chase after suspicious-looking automobiles, the false telegrams, the cholera-poisoned wells. Gone the mad stories of Russian students who hurl bombs from every bridge of Berlin, of Frenchmen flying over Nuremburg. . . . Business is flourishing upon the ruins, cities are turned into a shambles, whole countries into deserts, villages into cemeteries, treaties, alliances, the holiest words and the highest authorities have been torn into scraps; every sovereign by the grace of God is called a fool, an unfaithful wretch, by his cousin on the other side; every diplomat calls his colleague in the enemy country a desperate criminal; each government looks upon the other as the evil genius of its people, worthy only of the contempt of the world. Hunger revolts in Venetia, in Lisbon, in Moscow, in Singapore, pestilence in Russia, misery and desperation everywhere. Shamed, dishonoured, wading in blood and dripping with filth, thus capitalist society stands. Not as we usually see it, playing the role of peace and righteousness, of order, of philosophy, of ethics, but as a roaring beast, as an orgy of anarchy, as a pestilential breath, devastating culture and humanity—so it appears in all its hideous nakedness.''[268]

The untold suffering and waste, the unspeakable irrationality of the tragedy were too much to bear as if they were nothing but meaningless scourges. No victor's prize seemed worth that infinite cost. So resort had to be had to expectations of some ultimate messianic delivery and redemption. The unprecedented evils had to be presented as a price for some equally extraordinary good. Hence the slogans "a war to end all wars", "a war to make the world a home fit for heroes", "a war for democracy", "for the liberty of the nations", "a war for the socialist revolution". Such lofty goals were held to justify any means, the worst atrocities, especially since all efforts, ideas, hopes were focused on a single, simple breakthrough—victory—the sudden leap from a hell of horrors into a paradise of bliss. There was the terrific temptation, indeed sense of duty, to use all and any, especially the most effective, most damaging and most destructive means of murder and destruction, since they were calculated to shorten the agony of death as well as the birth pangs of the new world, and thus appeared the more humane. In this mixture of idealism and aggressiveness, all the inhibitions which had been built up throughout centuries, horror of murder, the inability to hurt, recoil from brutal lawlessness, respect for the rights, dignity and property of others, addiction to fair play were swept away in a delirious orgy of savagery.

The war brought out the massive ambivalences: ardent self-sacrificing love of country and savage hatred of a wholly diabolical enemy; heroic comradeship in the fighting unit and utter contempt for outsiders; saintly martyrdom and the crassest war profiteering. In the years of trench warfare a new type of elite came into existence: not of club, union, party, guild or school mates, but of men accidentally thrown together to face death, share a common existence, hardships and dangers, bound by all the ties of a common all-encompassing experience. In the earlier stage of the war the officer corps came from an aristocratic, almost hereditary caste. It was soon wiped out, to be replaced by men selected not by social, professional, educational, political or other more or less objective criteria, but for the elusive indefinable quality of leadership, in other words aggressive ruthlessness. There was the seedbed of the storm troops of the totalitarian movements between the two wars.

On August 5, 1914, Henry James addressed to Howard Sturgis what has become a classic account of the war's moral impact: "The plunge of civilisation into this abyss of blood and darkness by the wanton feat of those two infamous autocrats is a thing that so gives away the whole long age during which we have supposed the world to be, with whatever abatement, gradually bettering, that to have to take it all now for what the treacherous years were all the while really making for and meaning is too tragic for any words."[268a]

These shattering experiences of World War I gave rise to the ideological polarisation of the post-1918 world, to Messianic communism on the one hand, and Fascism and Nazism on the other: Lenin and Rosa Luxemburg at one pole, and Mussolini and Hitler at the opposite one.

(III) LENIN: "SOCIALISM OR NATIONALISM"

Bukharin describes Lenin's reaction to the outbreak of the war, voiced by him after he was released from prison thanks to Victor Adler's intervention, and had reached Berne: "Ilyich was striding about as mad as a tiger, an untameable one. Great sage, revolutionary prophet that he was, not for a moment did he despair, not for a moment did he helplessly fold his arms. His first slogan, an answer to the declaration of war, was a slogan for the soldiers of all armies: 'turn your guns on your officers!' This slogan was not published. Its more general form became 'Turn the imperialist war into a civil war.' I recall the long arguments carried on in our small circle, when Ilyich posed point-blank the question not only of splitting the party, but even of renouncing the very name of 'Social Democrat'! When Gregory [Zinoviev] began to talk of traditions as well as of members, Lenin remarked wrathfully and ferociously, 'Oh yes, there is plenty of dung among them' . . . and with furious energy began to expose his ideas regarding communist parties and a new International, revolutionary and insurrectionist."[269]

Posing the question in this way amounted in the circumstances of international war to the formulations adopted later by Lenin: "socialism or nationalism",[270] and "unless a struggle is waged against the social-chauvinists, the cause of socialism is hopeless".[271] "Marxism," says

Lenin, "cannot be reconciled with nationalism, be it even of the most just, purest, most refined, civilised brand."[272]

(*a*) NATION, CLASS AND THE RIGHT TO NATIONAL SELF-DETERMINATION

Unlike Rosa Luxemburg, Karl Radek, Pyatakov and others, who were anxious to deny the very reality of the phenomenon of nationalism, treating it as a deliberately invented red herring or a delusion, Lenin recognised its immense significance,[273] especially after the 1905 revolution had released nationalist ferment among the Russian nationalities, and all over Asia in revolutions in Persia, Turkey and China, and insurrectionary stirrings elsewhere. He called it "an extensive and very deep ideological trend".[274] It is however most important to quote as well his statement that "by organising production without class oppression, by ensuring the well-being of all members of the state, socialism gives full play to the 'sympathies' of the population, thereby promoting and greatly accelerating the drawing together and fusion of the nations".[275] Nationhood was not an end in itself, neither was the right to national self-determination. The self-determination of the proletariat was. The former was a function of the latter. Lenin's point of departure was in fact the denial of the concept of a single nation, in other words of the primacy of nationhood. The origins of nationalism "were closely interwoven with the interests of the land-owners and the capitalists of the dominant nations".[276] There was a fatherland of the possessing classes, and a fatherland of the deprived proletarian masses. One looked to the past, the other to the future. The whole mythology of national greatness and pride was bound up with conquest, expansionism and the domination by feudal and then bourgeois classes over subjugated peoples, as an extension of the exploitation of their own native lower orders. "National culture" meant the mores, the liberal arts, the superstructure of that feudal-aristocratic-capitalist dominion, "the culture of landlords, the clergy and the bourgeoisie".[277] The national ideology of the proletariat was encompassed within the strivings for democratic equality, for a regime of socialist justice, proletarian internationalism and, as far as its historic inspiration was concerned, based on the dreams and prophecies of such martyrs of revolution as Radishchev, the Decembrists and the later revolutionaries. Its culture was "the international culture of democracy and of the world working class movement".[278] "From each national culture," says Lenin, "we take only its democratic and socialist elements, we take them *only* and *absolutely* in opposition to the bourgeois culture and the bourgeois nationalism of *each* nation."[279] It may thus be said that "bourgeois nationalism and proletarian nationalism—these are two irreconcilably hostile slogans that correspond to the two policies of today, to the two great class camps throughout the capitalist world".[280]

(b) IMPERIALISM

The fissure between the two nationalisms had turned into a gulf when, after 1871, the bourgeoisie of Western Europe had—with the aid of the popular masses—accomplished their progressive and democratic aim of deposing feudal absolutism, of doing away with medieval privileges and distinctions, and uniting their countries under parliamentary, liberal regimes, based upon a unified industrial economy. The bourgeoisie then took up and revitalised the feudal warrior traditions of conquest and expansion by embarking upon its world-wide imperialist adventures. No sooner had the home market been fully organised than its confines became too narrow for dynamic capitalism in the quest for higher profits and new raw materials, in the need to invest and to secure cheap labour. The home economy became cartelised into trusts. A centralised economy carried with it centralised forms of government. Free trade was replaced by monopoly. A monopolist grip on the economy required putting an end to *laissez-faire* anarchy. This gave rise to planning and controls, in other words to social forms of production. But it was not so much industrial capitalism that rationalised capitalist production as it was finance capitalism—the gigantic banks, which in a parasitic form, steered its course by lending money and pocketing usurious profits. Late capitalism in its imperialist form was the highest point of its development, but also the beginning of its downfall. It thus became ripe for a take-over by victorious proletarian socialism.[282]

But the spoils of the colonies had in the meantime enabled the governing elites of the imperialist powers to bribe their working classes at home with higher wages and greater comfort. A labour aristocracy, with a stake in imperialism thus emerged and developed a pettybourgeois mentality.[283] The lower middle class became intoxicated with chauvinist pride and a vicarious sense of power and adventure, fostered by a mass yellow press and jingoist agitators.[284]

Lenin refers to Cecil Rhodes's famous statement "if you do not want civil war [between the classes], you must become imperialists".[285] An antidote to socialism and class war, imperialism was also leading to the erosion of the liberal-democratic ethos and institutions. As Marx had said, no nation which oppressed other nations could remain free.

Leaning on, or re-echoing Rosa Luxemburg and Hilferding, the socialist analyst of the workings of finance capitalism in the age of imperialism, and of course Marx's views on the Anglo-Irish problem, Lenin insisted that colonial exploitation was creating a power base for the ruling castes from which they were able to exercise total hegemony over the other classes, indeed the nation as a whole.[286] The military and naval expenditure caused by imperialist rivalry and the necessity of holding down the subjugated population overseas had become a terrible burden upon the metropolis: and also an excuse for authoritarian policies. They put arms into the hands of imperialist castes. They created a sense of national emergency which allowed the curtailment of democratic freedoms. They facilitated the bribing of ministers, politicians and the press to make them serve monopolisitic interests in the guise of high national concerns. Finally, they encouraged arrogant racism.[287]

The most important aspect of imperialism was the extension of capitalist exploitation to all parts of the world. Monopoly at home was raised to a global scale by the emergence of half a dozen great powers monopolising all the resources of the earth, and turning the most of mankind into their slaves. A whole hierarchy of conflicts developed: bitter competition between the imperialist powers; seething tension between old-timers in the colonial field—Britain, France, Russia, Holland—and hungry, resentful newcomers such as Germany and Italy; finally the racial-social rage of the plundered nations, breaking out in revolutionary social national uprisings of a bourgeois-democratic or already semi-proletarian nature against their white overlords. The colonial races had become the proletariat of the world pitted against a global capitalism in its final monopolistic stage.[288]

(*c*) THE TEST OF A REVOLUTIONARY SOCIALIST OF AN OPPRESSOR NATION

The right of oppressed nationalities to national self-determination and their right to secede from the empire of which they formed a part, is advocated by Lenin not as an abstract, natural principle of law and as an extension of man's right to liberty, but as a right to resist oppression as well as a device to equalise the status and situation of all sections of society so as to make domination of one over the other and exploitation by one of the other impossible. More than that, the real aim of Lenin is to use the liberating principle to weaken, undermine and destroy the power of the oppressing imperialist establishments to practise social and national oppression of the underprivileged of whatever kind, be they proletarians at home, be they natives in the colonies. Russian absolutist feudalism was guilty on both counts, more than any other power.

Not unlike Rosa Luxemburg, Lenin is fully conscious of the nature of nationalist resentment and aspiration as a powerful irritant which diverts attention from the common international struggle against capitalist oppression and for socialism, and inhibits the working classes of the deprived peoples from fighting their own bourgeoisie with enough vigour. Lenin nevertheless differs fundamentally from Rosa, who is out to deny the reality of national sentiment and to treat it as an invention of bourgeois intellectuals or as a delusion. Rosa's approach— Lenin claims—meant abstract generalisation inadmissible to a Marxist. The concrete objective and subjective circumstances in which an oppressed nationality found itself were vital to a Marxist analyst of the social situation and the prospects of revolution.[289] But Lenin is not prepared at all to give a blank cheque, a promise of unconditional recognition of and support to any ethnic group which may wish to break away from a larger state unit and establish an independent state of its own. Divorce may be a right, but it is not a duty, and since it has social implications, it shall not be granted on demand to all and sundry.[290] As a good Marxist, Lenin repeatedly voices his conviction that the progress of civilisation, and with it that of socialism, required and was leading to larger political units; that particularism and tiny tribal states were a reactionary medieval relic. He is sure that a separate political existence by breaking away from a larger unit would not be desired at all by the proletarian masses, once the stigma of humiliation and sting of oppression had been taken out of their situation through the recognition of their right to secede from the majority nation; certainly not when the latter had become a socialist society.[291]

The right to self-determination and secession were thus in the final analysis not an end in themselves, but a necessary precondition and stage on the way to socialist fraternity and fusion, the global socialist society, just as the dictatorship of the proletariat was a stage that could not be skipped on the way to a socialist classless society freedom.[292] Lenin's fierce opposition to cultural-national autonomy advocated by Austro-Marxists, and the federal principle defended by the Bund and other ethnic social-democratic parties of Russia, was motivated by the deep conviction that these tendencies affirmed precisely the principle of the eternity of nationalist isolationism, and were weakening international proletarian unity.[293] Needless to say, the attitude of the Polish Social Democratic party, which reduced its contribution to the common struggle against Tsarism to the fight for the national independence of Poland, was stark petty-bourgeois nationalism, and a denial of socialist doctrine. To repeat: socialists would consider every demand for self-determination and secession only from the point of view of proletarian needs and revolutionary strategy.[294]

The real point in Lenin's theory is not so much the stand taken by the oppressed nationality, or rather proletariat, as the attitude taken by the socialists of the oppressing nations. He repeats again and again that it was incumbent upon the latter to insist on the right of the former to break away, while it would be expected of members of the oppressed nationalities to be unwilling to make use of the opportunity.[295] The Great Russians must on no account appear to act as chauvinists. "The most difficult and most important task is . . . to unite the class struggle of the workers of the oppressor nations with that of the workers of the oppressed nations."[296] There was no more drastic and more telling test of international revolutionary socialist faith than the readiness or reluctance of socialists of dominant nations to let subjugated nationalities depart, reducing thus the historic patrimony of the powerful nation. In the case of Russia, with its 57 per cent of population of alien stock, it was a matter not merely of securing or weakening Russia's status as one of the great powers, and of safeguarding or removing their power base from the ruling classes, but of the continuation or disintegration of the Russian state. Lenin speaks of "the bourgeois methods of fooling the masses, such as frightening the petty bourgeoisie and the peasants with the spectre of the 'disintegration of the state',[297] and deluding them with phrases about people's freedom and historic tradition".[298]

The issue touched revolutionary socialists on the raw. It had proved to be the gravest stumbling block in the relations between Polish insurgents and Russian revolutionaries in the nineteenth century. The Poles passionately refused to recognise the legitimacy of any of the partitions, and insisted on a return to the 1772 borders. To the Russians that meant a Russia driven out of Europe to the vicinity of Smolensk and beyond the Dnieper. They claimed that the territories acquired by Russia in the first and second partitions were inhabited by vast masses of White Russian, Ukrainian and Lithuanian peasants, and by only a thin crust of Polish, or even only Polonised, aristocracy and gentry, not counting the Jews. To this the Poles answered that the Russian claim to rule them was hardly better than that of the Poles. Herzen was, apart from Bakunin, the only Russian revolutionary of note who was prepared to support the Polish case openly in the 1863-4 uprising. By that time Ukrainian separatism was just beginning to stir (but not yet Byelo-Russian and Lithuanian nationalism). But even he became open-mouthed when the possibility of Kiev's separation from Russia was suggested: "but Kiev is as Russian as Moscow and St Petersburg are".[299]

Cession of a part of national territory had always been regarded as high treason, even in the case of an absolute monarch: a violation of the fundamental, organic laws of the realm. In Germany, the Secretary-General of the SPD, Ignaz Auer, proclaimed the issue of Alsace and Lorraine closed. August Bebel swore not to renounce an inch of German soil.[300] Jaurès rebuked his compatriots for demanding from German socialists a declaration of intent to return the disputed provinces. As we saw, he himself, like German socialist leaders, would not go beyond demands for greater autonomy for them, and expressions of hope that with the growth of internationalism, the question of which side of the border they were on, would become irrelevant.[301]

The 1914-18 war put the question on the agenda in a most painful way. Lenin decided to spare no susceptibilities, but to force men to stand up and be counted. As early as 1893 Plekhanov declared, in his capacity as rapporteur on the question of socialism and war at the Zürich congress of the Second International, that a war against the Tsar might become the hour of emancipation for the Russian popular masses.[302] Similarly in 1904, he demonstratively shook hands with the Japanese delegate to the International Socialist Congress amidst general acclaim.[303] Lenin considered the defeat of the Tsarist army at the hands of Japan as a blow to Tsarism and Russian aristocracy but not to the Russian people.[304]

The Jewish socialist, the Bundist Litvak, described his incredulity when hearing Lenin in August 1914: "We were amazed that Lenin advocated cutting away Russia's peripheral provinces, the Ukraine, the Baltic provinces and the rest. When I said that he must have been jesting, that he might have meant autonomy and federation, but surely not cutting Russia off from the Baltic and Black seas, the arteries of Russian economy, he replied that he was in deadly earnest".[305]

The war brought to the surface as a touchstone for all socialists the question: defencism or defeatism; participation in the war effort, be it only in the form of passively bearing it, or the desire for the defeat of one's country and its government, and consequently action to bring it about, in conjunction with like-minded socialist comrades of other lands, acting in a similar manner against their own governments, and thus joining an international civil war.[306]

"Whoever justifies participation in the present war," wrote Lenin, "perpetuates the imperialist oppression of nations. Whoever advocates taking advantage of the present embarrassments of the governments to fight for the social revolution champions the real freedom of really all nations, which is possible only under socialism."[307]

Lenin was quite pitiless towards social-democrats of the belligerent nations like Kautsky, Renaudel, Turati, Henderson, Vandervelde and of course his Russian compatriots like Plekhanov, Potresov and in the early days of the war even Trotsky and Martov, who ventured into eloquent generalities about a democratic peace with no annexations, but became very vague and hesitant when it came to particulars, like the future borders of their own country, Turati going even so far as to demand strategically defensible borders, whatever the ethnic composition of the disputed territory, for future Italy: "the rectification of the Italian frontiers in regard to what is indisputably Italian and corresponds to guarantees of a strategical character".[308]

Resistance to the enemy was to Lenin a slope hurling one down to imperialism: "What is most important, basic, significant and closely connected with practice is one's attitude to the nation that is oppressed by one's own nation, a matter which Martov preferred to gloss over or forget. . . . The Russian social-democrat who recognises the self-determination of nations more or less as it is recognised by Messrs Plekhanov, Potresov & Co., i.e. without bothering to fight for the freedom of secession for nations oppressed by Tsarism, is in fact an imperialist and a lackey of Tsarism. No matter what the subjectively good intentions of Trotsky and Martov may be, their evasiveness objectively supports Russian social-imperialism. The epoch of imperialism has turned all the great powers into the oppressors of many nations, and the development of imperialism will inevitably lead to a sharper difference of opinion over this question in international social-democracy too."[309]

(d) FROM AN INTERNATIONAL TO A CIVIL WAR

The Great War had polarised mankind into slave-owning governments and enslaved peoples, into predatory states fighting for the spoils of war and oppressed races as well as deluded proletarian masses; into social chauvinists clinging to the historic national patrimony and trying to enlarge it at the expense of other peoples, and genuine socialist revolutionaries determined to turn the imperialist war into an international civil war, a world-wide proletarian uprising to administer a final blow to a criminal, obsolete and tottering system of oppression, and to bring about the emancipation of all the underprivileged of the world. More insidiously dangerous than the avowed social-chauvinists were, in Lenin's view, the hidden lackeys of imperialism camouflaged as pacifists, as well as those who deluded themselves that they were serving the cause of a democratic peace by preaching an international settlement without annexation, and without reparations.[310]

The programme of their spokesmen in the Zimmerwald and Kiental conferences, as well as in the Independent German Social-Democratic party which broke away from the SPD, implied leaving the existing state formations and their class structure intact, in other words the class state as it was. They would adopt the principle of national self-determination in one form or other, pledge themselves not to resort to war, to accept international arbitration and mutually disarm.[311] Those who sponsored these aims, claimed Lenin, were oblivious or too committed to social-patriotism, or not enough of genuine international revolutionaries, to grasp that the class-states system simply could not in the age of imperialism carry on without colonial possessions, imperialist rivalry, heavy armament and sooner or later war. It was mockery to believe that imperialist states would relinquish territories into which they had invested millions, and which were their power bases. No democratic peace was possible between imperialist powers on the basis of a capitalist status quo.[312] Only socialism, achieved by a revolution sweeping away the whole system of powers and imperialist aims and policies, and making all nations free and equal, could secure a genuinely democratic peace. It is no exaggeration therefore to say that Lenin's aim was not peace in the sense of cessation of hostilities and an international arrangement between states, but an international revolution in the form of an international civil war between the possessing classes and the revolutionary forces with the aim of dismantling all existing states with their present structures. Lenin indeed never ceased to proclaim that he was no pacifist, and that socialism was not pacifism.[313]

There was little difference between Lenin and Rosa Luxemburg and her friends in the asessment of the revolutionary challenges and possibilities opened by the war. They parted company from there on. In her anxiety to launch an all-out global assault on the fortress of imperialism, and in her revulsion from and fear of any national deviation, Rosa refused to have any truck with or to allow for any alliance with nationalist aims and movements, to the point of opposing the dismemberment of existing states, the grant of independence to their ethnic components, and the restoration of territories annexed during the war. That was a trap,[314] sheer waste, if not indeed a dangerous diversion. All peoples were called upon to march straight to a socialist world community, with no border sign-posts, as Pyatakov put it.[315] Lenin branded such an approach not only as utopianism, but also as opportunism. The simultaneous march of all mankind was, in view of the uneven development of its various parts, a delusion. The neutralisation of nationalist insurgency against the multi-national and colonial empires meant failure to make use of a powerful weapon against them, which might make all the difference between enabling them to survive or bringing them down. Rosa's policies played into the hands of imperialist oppressors. If they prevailed, a revolutionary weapon and a challenge to immediate and sustained action would be thrown away in favour of opportunist waiting upon events.[316]

Rosa Luxemburg taught that no nation could be really free and no people could wage a war of national liberation so long as imperialism continued to exist. She opposed futile adventures. In the eyes of Lenin, such a view was like saying that as long as the revolution had not established a socialist order, there was no point in fighting for immediate rights to strike, to organise unions, to demonstrate and agitate.[317] Even a bourgeois movement of national liberation in a colony acted as a division attacking the common enemy—imperialism. It also had social significance as participating in a struggle against a foreign exploiter and representative of universal finance capitalism. Moreover, a victorious national liberation movement in which the local pro-letariat took part and which would usher in a bourgeois-democratic regime, would automatically give a start to class war between the local bourgeoisie and its working classes, with the socialist revolution as its distant, but predestined aim.[318]

"To imagine," wrote Lenin on the occasion of the Irish Easter Rising, "that social revolution is conceivable without revolts by small nations in the colonies and in Europe, without revolutionary actions by a section of the petty-bourgeoisie with all its prejudices, without a movement of the politically non-conscious proletarian and semi-proletarian masses against oppression by the landowners, the church and the monarchy, against national oppression etc.—to imagine all this is to repudiate the social revolution. . . . Whoever expects a 'pure' social revolution will never live to see it. Such a person is paying lip-service to revolution, without understanding what revolution is. The socialist revolution in Europe cannot be anything other than an outburst of mass struggle on the part of all and sundry oppressed and discontented elements. Inevitably, sections of the petty bourgeoisie and of the backward workers all participate in it—without such participation, mass struggle is impossible, without it no revolution is possible—and just as inevitably will they bring into the movement their prejudices, their reactionary fantasies, their weaknesses and errors. But objectively they will attack capital, and the class-conscious vanguard of the revolution, the advanced proletariat expressing this objective truth of a variegated and discordant, motley and outwardly fragmented mass struggle, will be able to unite and direct it, capture power, seize the banks, expropriate the trusts which all hate (though for different reasons!) and introduce other dictatorial measures which in their totality will amount to the overthrow of the bourgeoisie and the victory of socialism, which, however, will by no means immediately purge itself of petty-bourgeois scum."[319]

The Great War and imperialsim confirmed Clausewitz' statement that war was a continuation of diplomacy by other means. The same relationship obtained between civil war and class struggle. The imperialist world war had inaugurated the period of civil war between the forces of revolution and the camp of capitalism.[320] The civil wars, which were indeed wars, could be avoided only by the simultaneous universal victory of all the working classes of the world. There was, however, once more, no possibility of such a dramatic dénouement, in view of the time lag and differences in the development of nations. There was no escape from a transitional period of civil wars designed to crush the resistance of the bourgeoisie wherever possible. From the point of view of socialism these would be wars of defence, patriotic wars.[321]

"Socialism cannot achieve victory simultaneously in all countries. It will achieve victory first in one or several countries, while the others will remain bourgeois or pre-bourgeois for some time. This will create not only friction, but a direct striving on the part of the bourgeoisie of the other countries to crush the victorious proletariat of the socialist state. In such cases a war on our part would be a legitimate and just war. It would be a war for socialism, for the liberation of other nations from the bourgeoisie . . . defence of the victorious proletariat against the bourgeoisie of other countries."[322]

This sounds very much like the French Revolution declarations of November 19 and December 15, 1792, on the right and duty of the French Revolution to hasten to succour revolutionary patriots who had risen against despotism wherever they be, and on the treatment of liberated populations refusing the gift of liberty as enemies of France. The class-conscious vanguard of the revolution, the advanced proletariat, appears in the midst and then at the head of the motley of heterogeneous rebellious forces as representing the general will of them all, and as its executor.

Lenin seems to transfer the *Problematik* of the revolutionary general will from the confines of a given society or area onto the global plane. Moreover, the premise that the conscious workers of one country were sure to want fusion with the victorious proletariat of the neighbouring nation, in contrast to the nationalist separatism of the bourgeois class, taken together with the duty of hastening to aid a proletariat defending itself against its own bourgeoisie and endeavouring to crush it, offered the Red Army a reason and a right for preventing the secession of the border lands from Russia, and even for a world campaign for proletarian liberation.

(*IV*) 1917

The crucial issue in Russia between the February and the October revolutions was that of "defencism" and "defeatism". All the important questions, of dual power, land reform, indeed even economic difficulties, hinged upon it.

(*a*) DEFENCISM AND DEFEATISM—THE CRUCIAL ISSUE OF THE REVOLUTION

The main argument of the critics of the Tsarist government in the Duma on the eve of the February Revolution—like that of the pre-1789 "revolution of the nobility" in France—was that the autocracy had failed in the conduct of the nation's war. The supreme task of national defence has therefore to be taken over by the nation itself—that is to say its elected representatives. The fulminating speeches of Miliukov, Kerensky and others against defeatism and treason in high places, with their clear hints at the Tsarina, read very much like the utterances of Vergniaud on the eve of August 10, 1792—when the Jacobin dictatorship was already at the gate—against the court and Marie Antoinette. Now it was the famous Declaration of April 18 by Miliukov as Foreign Minister in the newly appointed provisional government that unleashed the first storm of the young Republic. The Minister spoke for those to whom the change of regime did not mean any deviation from the defence and promotion of what they regarded as the abiding interests and historic aspirations of Russia, including the planting of the Holy Cross on the St Sophia cathedral in Constantinople; and on a more mundane plane, but of decisive importance, the capture of the Straits. The way in which the two fugitive German ships *Emden* and *Breslau* had sneaked into the Dardanelles in the first days of the war and after a while compelled Turkey to enter the war on the side of the Central Powers,[323] thus cutting off nearly all of Russia's exports and imports, without which she was unable to wage war or to sustain her population, brought home the utter vulnerability of Russia's position of a gigantic land-locked mass. Miliukov also wished to reassure Russia's allies and to pledge the honour of the liberated nation to them.[324] Whether they had a direct share in the destruction of the autocracy or not, France and England were heartened by the February Revolution. Rejuvenated Russia would now fight—they believed—a truly national war. Moreover, the stigma of being allied to a despotic-feudal regime, which worried so many progressives in the West and was made so much of by German propaganda, now seemed removed.[325]

On the other side, as early as March 14, the Petrograd Soviet issued an "Appeal to all Peoples of the World" in favour of a democratic peace, without annexations and without indemnities. While, however, voicing the firm resolve to oppose any annexationist plans on the part of the new rulers of Russia, it also patriotically vowed that "the Russian Revolution will not flinch in face of the bayonets of conquerors and will not let itself be crushed by a foreign military power".[326]

Up to Lenin's arrival on April 3 and the publication of his famous Theses, even the leading Bolshevik spokesmen of the hour, such as Kamenev, took great pains to reiterate their support for the national war effort. The more perceptive leaders of the provisional government quite early realised the close connection between the fortunes of the war and the future social-political developments at home. They received with alarm the famous Order Number One adopted by the Soldiers' Soviet by which elected soldier committees were put above the officers.[327] It was a resounding act of vengeance upon the brutal conditions in the old Tsarist army. But in time of war, the politisation of the army and a general loosening of discipline, it was a lethal blow to the army's fighting capacity, indeed to its very existence, as well as to national unity and the whole social order. Miliukov tried to hope that fighting would undo the damage. "Perhaps something will be preserved as a result of war; without the war everything would break up more quickly"[328]—he is reported to have told Nabokov in order to counter voices suggesting a separate peace with Germany.

Notwithstanding the strains and stresses inherent in the existence of a system of dual power, the arrangement might have continued more or less satisfactorily as long as the war effort was accepted by both sides as a national cause. Against a background of such a national consensus, the soviets might have been presented as a compensation for previous mass disenfranchisement, as a platform of the unrepresented in the Duma, as the voice of the grass roots, indeed even as a helpmate to a provisional government, which in the midst of a vast social-political upheaval had to make do with an inherited apparatus of doubtful loyalty and proven inefficiency. The war could have been relied upon to inhibit attempts to rock the boat, at the helm of which was the provisional government. Given the universally accepted axiom that a constituent assembly would

possess unquestioned legitimacy and unlimited power to shape a new
Russia, it was also possible to postpone—in the name of the patriotic
duty to preserve national unity and fighting capacity—decisions on such
most pressing issues as the peasant drive to seize land from the landlords
or the calls for independence from the nationalities on the borders of
Russia. Demands for the nationalisation of industries, too, could have
been deferred. The war had in any case put the economy under state
control, and the urgent question was to make it function rather than to
restructure the system of ownership.

Lenin's April Theses were calculated to make dual power impossible
by putting all the emphasis upon the necessity to end hostilities. The war
which Russia had inherited from the Tsarist government had not—he
proclaimed—been turned into a war of the nation by the new rulers. It
was still an alliance of the predatory imperialist governments to subjugate and plunder the weaker nations and the colonial peoples, as well
as to intensify the exploitation of the European proletariat duped by its
labour aristocracy—the lackeys of the ruling castes and of war
profiteers. The new rulers of Russia were the capitalist-aristocratic
heirs of the bureaucrats of the autocracy.[329] A Duma elected by an out-
rageously undemocratic franchise and the provisional government
emerged from it, were thus not the representatives and plenipotentiaries of the nation, but agencies of anti-popular interests and
accomplices of an international conspiracy. Hence the slogan "All
power to the soviets". The soviets constituted the genuine representation of the toiling masses, therefore of the nation as such.

Lenin offered an alternative foreign policy. Once the soviets had
come into power, they would propose an immediate peace to all the
belligerent states, and, over the heads of governments, to their peoples.
Such an offer was sure to be hailed by the war-weary and starved masses
of all the countries as a deliverance from universal carnage. The governments would be forced by their peoples to heed the call. Should they
refuse to listen, the masses would answer with disobedience culminating
in riot and revolution. The international war would thus be transformed at a stroke from a latent into an actual international civil war.[330]

To bring this about, the Russian popular masses, the workers,
peasants and soldiers organised in the soviets were called upon to bring
down the provisional government by every means, from a systematic
effort to undermine the power and prestige of the state institutions to an
armed uprising. The most important immediate task was to discredit the
"defencists" in the soviets themselves, the Mensheviks and Social
Revolutionaries, as tools of the imperialist establishment and seducers of
the proletariat. For did not the Father of Russian Marxism turned

patriot, Plekhanov, preach civil peace and cessation of class struggle and strikes for the duration of the war?[331] Nothing could have served Lenin's plans better than the entry of the socialists into the reconstituted provisional government in the second part of May, after the resignation of Miliukov and his colleague at the War Ministry, Guchkov. The non-Marxist socialist [Trudovik] Kerensky became Minister of War and virtual head of the government.[332]

It was once more the issue of war that changed the destinies of the revolution some two months later. In the hope of galvanising the nation into single-minded patriotic fervour, the new coalition government launched its ill-fated July offensive. The attack was preceded by Kerensky's speaking tour of the fronts like a second Danton preaching "de l'audace, et encore de l'audace, et toujours de l'audace!" Once the offensive ended in failure, it was clear that the provisional government had reached an impasse.[333]

Lenin's stand on war and his programme to disorganise the provisional administration in the midst of war by direct action from below, were at first greeted by his own uncomprehending comrades with embarrassed silence and raised eyebrows. His socialist opponents responded with sneering laughter or furious protests. He looked to them like a reincarnation of Bakunin. He sounded like a Blanquist. Lenin's ideas struck them as the ravings of an obsessed anarchist, with no sense of reality or responsibility, who was preaching chaos for chaos' sake.[334] They themselves were too hampered by their anxiety for law and order, too inhibited by their instinctive patriotism and too weighed down by their horror of violence to grasp what Lenin was after. Their commitment to democratic and parliamentary legality made them impervious to Lenin's fundamental argument, which he had learnt from the Jacobins, Babeuf and of course Marx, that great decisions and vast social transformations were not realisable by means of ballot, but by rendering a possessing class impotent and thus harmless, in other words by liquidating it as a social-political force. And that moreover, by direct action, before any national vote had been taken. The call to the peasants to resort to such direct action and through the instrumentality of elected committees to seize the land from the landlords was calculated to take away the latter's possessions and power as a class. Defeatist anti-war propaganda was intended to encourage the peasant-recruits, who constituted the core of the army, to desert in order to secure a share in the seized lands. The disintegration of the army was of course tantamount to felling another pillar of the establishment, the officer class and—more still—the armed fist of the bourgeois-landlord class regime. Lenin's plan to stop war profiteering by the arrest, trial and execution of some dozens or hundreds of speculators—a measure which made his hostile listeners clamour that he was a cynical rabble-rouser, ignorant of elementary economic laws[335]—was meant to incite the masses to view the economic crisis not as the outcome of objective circumstances, but as the result of the deliberate doings of a band of robbers, who had thus forfeited their right to their possessions. In line with this was Lenin's insistence on the immediate nationalisation of the state banks and of banks in general, as well as on the socialisation of the great syndicates—cartels such as, for instance, the sugar industry.[336] That the war effort would be dangerously affected by such strains and dislocation did not worry Lenin, to whom war was the root cause and epitome of all evils and the predestined opportunity. At a time of shortage and famine such actions could in any case be presented as emergency steps made inevitable by war.

Good Marxist that he was, Lenin was also able to argue that the imperialist war had prepared the conditions for a vast economic-social transformation. Mobilisation, labour conscription and workers' direction, the virtual nationalisation of war industries, strict state control of production, finally rationing—all these measures had already paved the way to a system of planning from above and to the sub-ordination of private economic interests to the national needs. But so long as the wartime state direction of production and distribution was exercised by capitalists, who also ran the industries for their own profit, social control was sure to be used by vested interests as an opportunity for fleecing the population all the more effectively and for making colossal gains out of a national misfortune. The nation, the popular masses represented in the soviets, was called upon to step in and take over the task of running the national economy in the interst of the nation as a whole: workers' control.[337]

(b) A DELIBERATE SCHEME AND THE FORCE OF CIRCUMSTANCES—BOLSHEVIKS AND JACOBINS

Lenin continued to claim that in their campaign to deprive the ruling classes of their possessions, privileges and power, to disarm the bour-geoisie and arm the workers and to set up a revolutionary government by revolutionary means and direct action, the Bolsheviks were by no means trying to set up a doctrinaire socialist system then and there.[338] In language re-echoing pronouncements by Robespierre, Saint-Just and other Montagnards, Lenin insisted that the Bolsheviks were acting under the stress of concrete developments, grappling with a situation which had evolved objectively, and had not been contrived according to some blue-print or dogma. The steps taken were new, unprecedented, unplanned, as was the revolution itself.[339] They were intended to save the masses from exploitation and distress, but also to prevent the return of the oppressors and parasites to unlimited power. Improvised in response to desperate needs, those actions, while not undertaken as part of a deliberate plan of establishing socialism, were by their very nature indeed leading to socialism. They were not however in themselves socialism.[340]

In arguing thus Lenin was restating his famous early saying that a Social-Democrat was a Jacobin joined to socialism, that revolutionary freedom from oppression as well as from the fears, passivity, egoism and evil habits resulting from stultifying bondage which the Jacobins were compelled to try to secure with the help of a reign of virtue (or terror), appeared unattainable in the twentieth century without public ownership of the basic branches of production and an overall direction of the economy. Indeed, capitalism itself had prepared the conditions, nay created the necessity, for collective ownership and centralised production. It had also forged the necessary tools in the form of banking, accounting and effective control. Moreover the war had enormously accelerated the process.[341] The Jacobin dictatorship, especially its economic dictatorship, had failed precisely because the age knew only scattered, small-scale production, lacked experienced central machinery, not to mention technological means and was too ignorant, too prejudiced and too timid even to envisage a systematic and permanent nationwide economic organisation with teeth. The Bolsheviks had railways, cars, telegraph and telephone, electricity and gas, huge industrial concerns and cartels at their disposal, but above all an unfailing guide, the economic theory of Marxism—all of which the Montagnards had lacked.

Lenin was driven by the same vision as Robespierre, who proclaimed that he and his friends were determined "in a word, to fulfil the will of nature, accomplish the destinies of mankind, realise the promises of philosophers, absolve providence of the long reign of crime and tyranny".[342] The vagueness of this early Jacobin version of the final salvationist stage of history was now given substance—the latter-day Jacobin was absolutely convinced—with concrete contents of irrefutable scientific validity and with proofs of historic inevitability. Robespierre had had to pray and to prepare, with the help of terror, a reign of virtue for that vision to come true. Lenin had an unfailing analysis of objective reality and laws of history and economics to be guided by.

(c) REVOLUTION POLARISES

In spite of his slogan "All power to the soviets", Lenin was in the early days careful to acknowledge that his own party was a minority in comparison with the mass following of the Mensheviks and Social Revolutionaries.[343] He disclaimed any Blanquist designs by the Bolsheviks to seize power by a coup.[334]

Lenin was confident that the Bolsheviks would be able—as Marx had expected the communists to be in 1850—to prod and goad their moderate senior allies to take action beyond their original intentions, drive them to more and more radical policies, and then put themselves at the head. Lenin kept urging upon his followers the need to assure his enemies of his resolve to wait patiently until proletarian and peasant opinion had veered round in favour of Bolshevik policies.[345] This was predicated upon the Jacobin tenet that a desperate political-social struggle, especially in the middle of a national war combined with civil war, was bound to polarise the nation progressively. It was sure to create a tug of war which either extreme wing had to win, carrying with it all the moderate, hesitant, undecided, inhibited, and therefore passive and pliable elements. The débâcle of the July offensive seemed to some Bolshevik leaders to have already brought about such a polarisation. The Bolsheviks had been the sole consistent and uncompromising opponents of war. They alone stood out against the broad alliance of socialists and liberals, which planned and waged the disastrous offensive. The failure of the Bolshevik insurrection on the morrow of the defeat proved that the Bolsheviks had made an exaggerated estimate of the public mood and of their own strength. Defencism was not yet wholly bankrupt. The government was still able to count on the patriotic feelings of the population.[346] It worked up the courage to launch a counter-offensive by denouncing Lenin and his associates as paid German agents, traitors to the nation—forcing Lenin, Zinoviev and others to go underground or to escape into hiding in Finland—and arrested Trotsky.[347]

These measures caused the Bolsheviks to abandon the slogan "All power to the soviets", since the rival socialist parties of the coalition (and of the soviets) had clearly gone over to the enemy. Not only did they bear responsibility for the criminal military adventure, but by persecuting the Bolshevik leaders, closing their newspapers and turning people against them, they had begun to destroy the most faithful and dynamic representative of the proletariat.[348] The replacement of the slogan "All power to the soviets" by the call for a revolutionary democratic dictatorship of the workers and the poor peasants was an open bid for the transfer of exclusive power to the Bolshevik party as the leader of the deceived and betrayed masses. It was reminiscent of the Montagnard campaign to oust the Girondins from the Convention on the morrow of the defection of General Dumouriez, Brissot's protégé, to the enemy, culminating in the risings of May 30-June 2, 1793.

It was the Kornilov affair that brought about the complete polarisation for which Lenin had been waiting and working. A Tsarist general, defying the provisional government, and marching upon the capital to crush and disperse the "anarchists", compelled all devotees of the Revolution to close ranks and to frustrate the counter-revolutionary conspiracy by direct action. Railway workers simply stopped the trains and the soldiers melted away, under the eyes of the disorientated, discredited and powerless Kerensky government.[349] Not all workers switched over at once to Bolshevism. The followers of Menshevism and Populism, until then hesitating, vacillating, irresolute—in Lenin's favourite words—had simply no more conviction or strength to resist the furious energy and resolve of the Bolsheviks.[350] The bourgeoisie, which had hailed Kornilov, the head of the "Savage Division" at the Democratic Conference as the saviour of Russia,[351] faded out as a political force. It was then that Lenin again felt justified in resuming the slogan "All power to the soviets", although the Bolsheviks had not yet gained the desired majority. Their moral ascendancy over the moderates in the soviets was assured, because the tide was rapidly flowing in their direction. They were and behaved as a fighting vanguard, bullying their confused rivals, who had lost their self-assurance. Soon they secured majorities in the soviets in the two capitals, Petrograd and Moscow.[352]

(*d*) THE GENERAL WILL AND THE REVOLUTIONARY PROLETARIAT

Would the Bolsheviks be able to assume responsibility for governing the country, while still a negligible minority in the nation as a whole? Lenin had no hesitation on this score. If a quarter of a million landlords could, the more or less equal number of card-bearing Bolshevik party members, fired with zeal, highly organised and most disciplined, certainly could.[352] It was not only that, since February and under the impotent and inept provisional government, Russia was in fact ruled by nobody, except the determined groups of activists—whether soviets, peasant committees or party cells. It was they who rushed into a vacuum, in the absence of an effective middle class, of institutions of local self-government, of focuses of responsible citizenry and forms of popular initiative and public control, a system of checks and balances, let alone ways and means of resistance to irresponsible and arbitrary rule from above.

In the Russian condition of total severance between government and people, Marx's description of the state and its institutions as simply a congeries of instruments of coercion such as army, police, bureaucracy, courts, priesthood and hired scribes appeared plausible.[354] For these institutions could not be regarded in Russia as the sinews of a historically and democratically constructed nation. By throwing them off, the people would be able to come into its own. Given the insignificance of the Russian bourgeoisie, the toilers in factories, workshops and on the land could be presented as a single undifferentiated mass, an entity with a common interest, a single will; and this with greater relevance still than in Jacobin France of 1793. They were called to govern themselves directly, free of the tutelage imposed by exploiters, to deliberate and to legislate on their common business in their popular assemblies—the soviets—with no delay or reservation, to carry out their own decisions, to sit in justice as people's courts, and finally to overawe through sheer mass and armed might all counter-revolutionaries and class enemies by swift and exemplary punishment.[355] They were inspired and guided by enlightened pioneers and tried and hardened veterans of the struggle for the people's rights and emancipation, the members of the Communist party, which was the most articulate and wholly incorruptible spokesman of the proletariat, with no interests and aspirations of its own. Its formulations of the true interests and innermost wishes of the indivisible people of toilers were sure to be recognised by the masses as their true general will, once they had been freed from inhibitions, fears, ignorance and confusion, and become immunised against the influence of misguided, perverse and selfish elements.

The urban, more precisely the advanced, conscious industrial proletariat was the most exposed, sensitive nerve of the people and carried the greatest responsibility for the well-being of the masses because of their proximity to the arteries of power and social organisation. The peasants' mission was, as said earlier, that of disorganisation. Their essentially individualistic, fragmentary mode of production and existence was in any case not conducive to endowing them with the ability or desire to act as a political class with aspirations to seize power and mould the social-political order. After having seized and divided the land of the landowners, they would go home. The urban workers would be left and called upon to shape the new society.[356]

It was the intuition and the might of the people that in the last resort stood against all the obstacles and perils on the way to revolutionary victory. As the real sovereign the people was not bound by any institutionalised procedures, precedents or checks in exercising its powers, as were its elected plenipotentiaries in the legislative chambers. The people's cause and will had at the same time to be envisaged as stretching beyond the actual and immediate, and the here and now. It embraced a vision of things distant in time and place. Its standard bearers were motivated by deep, massive reasons and large perspectives, however momentarily clouded by the actual and the particular. Where these universal aims were at stake, and global historical strategy was in question, present numerical majorities or minorities could not be the final sanction. Nor could the true self-expression of direct democracy be constrained and distorted by accidental majorities. It was part of a vast historic process, brought to consciousness and fruition upon a huge gradually unfolding canvas.

Lenin might wait until the Bolsheviks got their majority in the Petrograd and Moscow soviets. But he waited not so much in order to reassure himself, as to make others, friends and foes, admit that the two most important nerve centres and most authoritative outposts of the proletarian struggle had offered a clear mandate to the Bolsheviks. In contrast to Kamenev and Zinoviev,[357] and even Trotsky,[358] Lenin had little or no use for formal authorisation and accepted codes of behaviour, no need for some mandate from an institutionalised body such as the All-Russian Congress of soviets or any other assembly or committee. He heard voices from above, that is to say from history. From his hiding place in Finland, which had become a kind of sanctuary, a Holy of Holies of history, Lenin bullied his timid comrades. Their incomprehension of the titanic powers that moved him and their awed stepping back from the brink caused them to file away his thunderous admonitions, that history would never forgive them their inaction and their timidity. It was the hour of destiny, the hour to dare, because the masses and the political elites had reached a peak of disorientation and vacillation, had lost their bearings; power was in the streets waiting to be picked up by somebody who wanted it and knew what to do with it. This is the reason behind his threat to resign and the resolve to act on his own, if his colleagues refused to launch the October coup.[359] Likewise Lenin would not be daunted—any more than the Jacobins—by the non-Bolshevik majority at the Constituent Assembly.[360] History had already evolved a more advanced, more democratic, more unfailing vessel of popular self-expression, in the image of the Paris Commune of 1871—

the soviets.[361] That form of direct democracy was going to do away with all forms of government of man by man, depersonalised institutions, class-structured representation, gradual procedures of election and delegation of powers intended to deform the real and direct will of the masses.

(e) PROLETARIAN DICTATORSHIP AND CLASSLESS UNANIMITY

At first it looks baffling that, just as in 1793 the Reign of Terror was preceded by the hasty promulgation of the most democratic constitution history had yet known—according to which 10 per cent of the voters in half of France's Départments plus one were enabled to invalidate a law adopted by the Legislative Assembly—the establishment of the most dictatorial regime in modern history should have been ushered in by such an ultra-democratic, not to say anarchist and utopian tract as the "State and Revolution" composed by Lenin in the summer of 1917, while he was in hiding.[362] Was this a piece of hypocrisy? Was it an apologia and extenuation got out by Lenin before imposing himself as dictator upon a vast empire? Could so shrewd, realistic and personally honest a man describe in the same breath the dictatorship of the proletariat as an instrument for the merciless suppression of the bourgeoisie and all counter-revolutionary forces, and at the same time as the most advanced form of democracy? Did Lenin seriously believe that a modernised and industrialised state of such vast dimensions and diversities could be ruled by a direct democracy of largely illiterate masses through workers' direct control, and still be more democratic than the system of bourgeois democracy in a pluralistic society with its checks and balances? Is it possible to imagine Lenin really envisaging the disappearance of all hierarchical arrangements in an intricate modern society with a centralised economy so that every need for imposed discipline and coercion would cease, and in the end the coercive institutions of the state and the state itself would die out?[363]

How was so perspicacious a person as Lenin able to reduce all complex human and social relationships to no more than consequences of the system of private property and—in theological language—of capitalist greed, and to believe that after the expropriation of the possessing classes and the transfer of the direction of the entire national economy into the hands of the amorphous people broken up into small communes, the affairs of society could be administered by a girl who knew some elementary arithmetics and could read and write—under the eyes of a unanimous nation?[364] And that crime would almost vanish from a society freed from deprivation and exercising an inhibiting effect on it just by stern disapproval of the assembled righteous people?[365]

It is not enough to say that such a vision of utopian harmony and bliss was calculated to make the provisional terrorist dictatorship of the proletariat look as indeed a small price, and, to justify its stringency, even cruelty, as a way of shortening the birth pangs. The key to the riddle is the fact that only through a genuine belief in the possibility, indeed inevitability and imminence of the great fulfilment were the vanguard of the messianic revolution able to feel entitled to claim that they expressed the true will of the people and to act as the instrument of history, when resorting to coercion and usurping unlimited dictatorial powers. Otherwise they would have had to be utter hypocrites or cynics in their own eyes. And this they were not, at least at the start, notwithstanding all the hypocrisy, self-deceit, trickery and unscrupulous cruelty and tyranny they were in due course to practise. In brief, the messianic vision was not an afterthought and an excuse. It was the point of departure. The inevitable frustrations became the cause of all the later perversions. So high a vision was however bound to bring those bitter frustrations which led to the distortions. Any expectation of unanimity, to repeat it once more, postulates, knowingly or not, the imposition of a single will. The fanatical certainty that unanimity was the eventual frame of mind of all decent people had to breed utterly impatient intolerance, hatred and contempt for dissidents, and a resolve to put an end to "abnormality"—the phenomenon of people who seem to refuse to be rational and free. A hypnotic faith in ultimate harmony was the cause of the claim that dictatorship was only a transitional phase. It would last only so long as men refused to be free and rational. As soon as they had become rational, that is to say unanimous, there would be no need and no place for coercion, therefore for the state itself.

(f) NATIONAL-REVOLUTIONARY DEFENCISM

As an instrument of coercion in the hands of the exploiting class the state was a historical and passing phenomenon. The bourgeois nation-state had come into existence at a certain juncture, when the rising bourgeoisie became interested in a wide market, and therefore in the abolition of feudal distinctions. In a classless society in which all citizens served in the people's militia, the need for a special police would almost cease, since the people as a whole would do the watching, judging and punishing. There would be active participation of all citizens in legislation by rotation, as well as in the administration of community affairs, and superimposed officialdom would become superfluous. All this suggests not merely the withering away of the state in the abstract, but also of the nation-state. The history of the nation and nation-states had, for good or ill, consisted throughout the centuries not merely of the story of economic development and changing habits, but also of political life; constitutional struggles; foreign relations, including war, myths and aspirations; a panorama of ideas and a gallery of heroes. Those together formed the distinct history, the fate, the destiny, the historic personality of the nation. If in the future, societies—let us call them nations—were to become so one-dimensional, indeed merely sections of a homogeneous, one-dimensional mankind, what would the right of self-determination signify? Surely, it would be of no relevance. Just as in a classless society no one would have reason to complain of being unfree and wish to assert his independence, so in a socialist world no nation would have any reason or possibility to oppress another, and thus none would have cause to complain of being oppressed.

Lenin's thinking on the nationalities problem[366] indeed paralleled his syllogistic reasoning on democracy, proletarian dictatorship and the withering away of the state. There was of course an element of opportunism in his seemingly liberal stand on the right of national self-determination, since Lenin was always more concerned with the fact that the denial of it was an irritant impeding wholehearted devotion to the cause of the international revolution than with national independence as an end in itself. It was still more of a tactical measure than the identification of the dictatorship of the proletariat with democracy, since to Lenin democracy never meant fair distributive justice, which would accord to each segment of the nation a due share in shaping the national policies, but invariably designated the rise and victory of the underprivileged over the privileged. All the same, just as there is no ground to impugn the sincerity of Lenin's starry-eyed belief in eventual unanimity in the single community, so there is no reason to question the sincerity of his conviction about the eventual willingness of all socialist nationalities to join and to fuse into a federal structure and then a world commonwealth of socialist communities.

Geo-political data, the burden of history and, paradoxically, the circumstances of the revolution itself combined to frustrate Lenin's vision of an early coming together of socialist nations to form a single socialist world. Still, to a larger degree than the Germans and Hungarians in the Habsburg monarchy, the Great Russians were the master race in the multi-racial empire of all the Russias.[367] With the exception of the Kingdom of Poland, created by the Congress of Vienna, and Finland, allotted to Russia at that time, in both of which the Russians exercised only political supremacy, in all the other provinces of the colossal empire—with all its enormous variety of geographical setting, climate, social-economic conditions, cultural development and national consciousness, the Great Russians formed either the landlord class, or the bourgeoisie, or the main urban dwellers and indeed often also the bulk of industrial workers. From the utterly primitive, illiterate tribes in Siberia, through the Mahometan principalities and nomads of Central Asia, even in the Baltic countries, in advanced Ukraine, as well as in White Russia and in the countries of old and original culture in the Caucasus, the growth of national consciousness had been much retarded, and its pace was kept slow after it had awakened. In the Ukraine, in White Russia and in Lithuania the nobility was either Russian or Polish, and the urban population largely Jewish, Russian or Russified. In Latvia and Estonia the larger cities had been built and ruled mainly by Germans, with Jews forming a large part of its inhabitants, while the landlord class was composed of Russians or Germans (the Baltic barons). Only the peasantry in those regions was authentically native. The intelligentsia was again either Russian, Russified or Jews. The educated elements of the population which had escaped or resisted Russification to become the spearhead of nationalism formed a small, almost marginal minority. They had thus only a narrow social base and shallow roots in the popular masses. A substantial number of those nationalists spoke and wrote in Russian, and hardly knew the languages, some with a very scant literature, which they wished to revive and make dominant. The entrepreneurial class in the cities of Central Asia and much of the Caucasus consisted again of Great Russians. A large proportion of the industrial workers in the Ukraine were Great Russians.[368] The cultivable land in Siberia had been put under plough by the land hungry peasants from Great Russia, and the cities of Siberia were built and populated mainly by Great Russian migrants and exiles. Against this background Lenin was not far off the mark when he identified national-political with social-economic oppression.

While patriotic Russians shrank from the idea of breaking up their national patrimony, Lenin regarded it as the fruit of class robbery and as the mainstay of the robbers' power. He looked to the aspirations of oppressed nationalities for help in bringing down the edifice of despotic autocracy and national-social exploitation. But it was precisely the Revolution that was destined to check the trend to secession, without weakening Great Russian hegemony; in fact it only transformed and strengthened it.

So long as the war had not come to an end, the civil war continued and the Western powers had not yet given up their interventionist activities, any province seceding or wishing to secede from Russia was bound or was likely to come under the occupation or influence of a foreign power hostile to revolutionary Russia. [At the height of the civil war Russia was indeed reduced to the territories inherited by Ivan the Terrible.[369]] The Bolsheviks had every reason to regard such a province as enemy country. The Bolsheviks dubbed any national liberation movement which was not communist "bourgeois nationalism". It could be conditionally supported by communists if it was actually or potentially, or even temporarily, an ally against a common imperialist enemy. There was always the hope that the temporary bourgeois-proletarian alliance would be terminated by a revolutionary class struggle as soon as the goal of political independence had been achieved. Otherwise the proletariat would be left prey to the capitalist class, and the new class-state would be set free to join the imperialist states. And a revolutionary proletarian Russia was in honour and duty bound to offer every aid to the proletariat of a neighbouring state.

It was in the Ukraine that all these dilemmas came to the fore.[370] Lenin had no thought of not letting Poland and Finland secede.[371] Those nations had too distinct a history, culture and national consciousness, which neither the Ukrainians nor any other nationality in Russia had. The Ukraine was the granary of Russia; and a large part of Russian coal, iron, oil and other natural wealth came from the Donetz region. Much of Russia's most advanced industry was concentrated there. The German army had planted itself in the Ukraine, supporting successive puppet nationalist governments and plundering the country's wealth. After the German collapse, the Ukrainian nationalists found protectors in the French and in the British, and most incongruously in 1920 in the Poles, who got as far in their invasion of the Ukraine as Kiev. Much of the most dangerous and longest fighting in the civil war took place in the Ukraine. There were thus overriding economic, strategic and ideological reasons for not allowing an enemy outpost to be established near the heart of Russia. The largely Great Russian local Bolsheviks in the towns rose in any case in revolt against the Ukrainian bourgeois nationalists, as part of the common revolutionary endeavour. The Ukrainian peasants for their part feared that the White generals would bring back the landlords. They therefore withheld help from the Ukrainian Rada. Moreover, the Ukrainian nationalists feared a total victory by the counter-revolutionary Russian forces, who dreamt of restoring the unity of the Empire and Great Russian rule over it. So the Red Army was defending both Russian soil and the Soviet revolution. It was obliged to help the newly proclaimed communist government of the Ukraine to shake off the yoke of the native capitalist class, and at the same time compelled to prevent the Ukraine from becoming the spearhead of the array of hostile forces besieging the fatherland of socialism.[372]

Since most of the war against the counter-revolutionary generals and the Western expeditionary forces was waged in the border territories by a Red Army recruited and officered by Great Russians, the myth of the civil war became a combination of ideological communist and Great Russian nationalist motives. The necessities of reconstruction and the growth of centralisation accompanying it put the Great Russians and Jews in positions of responsibility all over Russia. They were the best-educated and were nearest to the central arteries of power. The Soviet government also had no choice but to avail itself of the services of members of the Tsarist bureaucracy, the old officer corps and bourgeois experts and technicians, to many of whom the cause of the unity and glory of Mother Russia meant more than their private or class interests. Most of the leading Bolsheviks of the ethnic minority groups who were active in the governing elite of Soviet Russia or in positions of influence in the autonomous regions were more ardent centralists than the Great Russian Bolsheviks themselves, either out of deep internationalist conviction—to be internationalist meant in the circumstances to desire Great Russian hegemony—or because of lack of backing in their own ethnic communities.[373]

The evolution of the attitude of Soviet Russia towards the minority nationalities in the border areas bears some comparison with the evolution of policies in the French Revolution—from the promise of November 19, 1792, of liberation and aid for subjugated populations to shake off serfdom and to gain the conditions for choosing freedom, to the famous December 15, 1792, decree ordering the liberated populations to choose freedom, that is to say the republican institutions of revolutionary France, under the threat of being treated as enemies of France. The way in which at the end of World War II the USSR imposed communist regimes on all the countries which it reconquered from Nazi Germany is similarly reminiscent of the policy adopted by post-Thermidorian France, which had by that time already lost her proselytising enthusiasm, in surrounding herself with a chain of sister republics whose governments were appointed by, or at all events made dependent on, the French. It was by then difficult to say whether France still cared for the diffusion of the ideas of the rights of man, popular sovereignty and the secular state or was solely concerned with her own security and her international influence.[374]

The October revolution was undertaken by Lenin in the unshakable faith that the example of Russia would be immediately followed by the toiling masses in country after country in a Europe reeling under the horrors of war and seething with revolutionary unrest. Russia was at the head of a whole procession. Furthermore, as Lenin and his associates repeatedly admitted, they would never have dared to embark upon so bold and dangerous a venture, had they not been sure that the inevitable counter-revolutionary crusade of the imperialist governments— German or Allied—would be strangled by the newly created revolutionary proletarian governments, determined to secure the survival of the Soviet regime and eager to help it on the way to socialism. Lenin saw already in the February revolution, and in the social unrest and rebellious stirrings which he believed to discern (and which he vastly exaggerated) in all the belligerent countries, the start of an era of international civil war. About its outcome he had no doubts. This faith served as an anchor to the Bolsheviks when their fortunes were at their lowest ebb in the days of Brest-Litovsk and afterwards during the civil war.

Lenin, Trotsky, Radek, Zinoviev, Pyatakov and all the rest, whose consciousness of the universal character of the communist message was especially keen, did not in the early days think at all of settling down to the ancient game of diplomacy between sovereign, scheming, grasping, suspicion-ridden rival states. It is enough to recall Trotsky's jibe, when appointed Commissar for Foreign Affairs, that he was just going to draft a few revolutionary proclamations to the workers of the world, publish the secret treaties concluded by the Tsarist governments and the Entente on the division of spoils after the war, and then shut up shop.[375] An outbreak of the revolution in the two warring camps of imperialist powers at the same time was a necessary article of faith. Without such synchronisation, Bolshevik Russia stood in danger of being overrun and destroyed by the forces which had remained capitalist.

Such was the bitter dilemma in the days of Brest-Litovsk. A separate Soviet peace with Germany looked like insuring the triumph of Prussian militarism over the Western democracies. It was also an indelible disgrace to a proletariat which had just won its revolutionary victory— on behalf of the proletarians of the world—to start its career by submitting to a draconian and humiliating peace dictated by an imperialist power which at that moment seemed to be winning the war against the Western democracies and becoming free to strangle the Russian revolution in its cradle. What an encouragement to German chauvinists and what a disheartening disappointment to the workers of Europe, indeed to a world straining for a revolutionary breakthrough.[376]

This was the *prima facie* unanswerable argument of the opponents of the Brest-Litovsk peace who clamoured for a people's revolutionary war on the pattern of the Jacobin *levée en masse* in 1793. Throughout the passionate polemics with defencists, who had accused Lenin of lacking a shred of that Jacobin patriotism which the revolutionary tradition had so glorified, he countered the taunt with solemn vows and eloquent incantations about a revolutionary patriotic war *à l'outrance*, once the ·proletarian masses had wrested their country from the hands of Russian imperialist bandits in league with the imperialist robbers in the West, and had turned it into a real fatherland of the working classes—the true nation—to be loved, cherished and defended. The armed people would then display wonders of heroism in the defence of their country against capitalist invaders.[377]

Lenin was too much of a realist to fancy that a demoralised and dissolving army, an exhausted and politicised population in a ruined country could ever resist the might of the German Imperial army. Not for him Trotsky's eccentric proposal neither to surrender nor to fight: neither peace nor war, as a way out of the dilemma. Although Lenin was beginning to have doubts about the ripeness of the revolution in the West—only a pregnancy compared with the baby already born in Russia[378]—and came out decidedly for the peace of surrender—he had to cling desperately to the hope of an imminent German revolution, while at the same time half-heartedly trying to woo President Wilson as a kindred spirit in his adherence to the principle of self-determination and the idea of a democratic peace.[379]

Part VII

THE GENERAL WILL OF THE GLOBAL PROLETARIAT — UNIVERSAL TOTALITARIAN DEMOCRACY

THE GENERAL WILL OF THE GLOBAL PROLETARIAT
—UNIVERSAL TOTALITARIAN DEMOCRACY

The Brest-Litovsk negotiations were presented by Trotsky and others as a platform from which to bring home to the masses of the world the titanic nature of the confrontation between predatory imperialism and a nation embodying the cause of world revolution, and thus to make them put irresistible pressure upon the Allied governments to respond to the Russian appeal to join the negotiations.[380] Were the Bolsheviks nevertheless to be left alone and forced to yield to brute force, the Prussian *Diktat* would goad the German workers to revolt.

(*a*) THE NATIONAL AND THE INTERNATIONAL REVOLUTION

From the day of the famous "Decree of Peace", issued on the morrow of the October coup, the Bolsheviks continued to describe themselves as the vanguard of the world revolution.[381] The word "Russia" does not appear in the official designations and documents. Not only members of national minorities, like Caucasians and Letts—not to mention the considerable number of Jews among the highest decision-makers—but such men as Rakovsky, half-Roumanian, half-Bulgarian; Karl Radek, who in a chameleon-like manner could switch over from representing the Bolshevik party to acting as spokesman for the Social-Democratic party of Poland and Lithuania, as he had earlier been exchanging Austrian socialism for German Social-Democracy; and Poles like Dzierzhinski and Marchlewski—were in the inner councils of the party-cum-government. Attempts were also made to create International Brigades out of prisoners of war in Russian lands.[382] Radek proclaimed: "we are no longer Muscovites, citizens of Sovedepia, but the advance guard of the world revolution".[383]

The Bolsheviks insisted at Brest-Litovsk on both, at the same time, the right to self-determination and the international character of the socialist revolution. Their breath was taken away, when General Hoffman unfolded the map with the famous blue line, to the left side of which were the vast territories over which the German occupation troops were in his words pledged to defend their right to self-determination.[384] When Trotsky started a lecture on the Prussian boot trampling over the freedoms of peoples, the shrewd German general gave him back in kind asking what right the Bolsheviks had to speak of respecting the free wishes of a population.[385] The exchange happened to take place on the day of the dispersal by the Bolshevik sailors of the freely elected all-Russian Constituent Assembly. Contemptuously shrugging their shoulders, the Germans nevertheless promised not to transfer troops from Russia to the Western front, so as to spare the susceptibilities of the Bolshevik conscience about helping one set of imperialist robbers against another, and agreed to "organised contacts" to foster amity between the Russian and German armies as a substitute for the facilities for fraternisation between soldiers which the Bolsheviks had demanded.[386]

The working class in the west, above all the German proletariat, failed to budge, even when the German troops resumed their lightning offensive on February 18, 1918, against an unresisting, almost non-existent Russian army.[387] Lenin's peace motion won its sad victory at the end of a most dramatic series of contradictory and inconclusive votes in the highest councils of the party.[388] So the Bolsheviks discovered the reality of nation-states. Instead of treating all capitalist and belligerent states as one single and undifferentiated reactionary mass, with whom no truck was allowed, they tried to play off the Western Allies against the Central Powers, in order to squeeze (in Lenin's words) potatoes and ammunition out of one band of robbers against another one, and even at the cost of toning down temporarily the propaganda against imperialism and of invoking Russian national interests instead of the imperatives of the socialist revolution. Not only Bolsheviks of extreme internationalist persuasion, but also Martov, saw in that a return to the policies of Miliukov.[389]

The Third International came into existence, or rather was hastily stitched together, as if to catch up with the attempt to revive the Second International at the conference convened for January 27, 1919, at Berne.[390] On January 24 an invitation was issued by Lenin, Trotsky and representatives of East European and Balkan communist parties or groups to "all parties opposed to the Second International" to attend a congress in Moscow.[391] The list of the invited, and then of the attending parties, was reminiscent of the procedures of nineteenth-century revolutionaries like Mazzini and Bakunin, and to some extent Marx, in putting on paper names of representatives of parties which did not in fact exist, except in the hopes of the organisers, in appointing themselves or associates to speak for countries in which there was no one willing or able to join them, and in granting recognition to tiny local groups to represent parties in the process of emerging.[392] Disturbed communications, government chicanery and lack of proper organisation, all of which paralysed action by the splinter groups, embryonic parties and the as yet undecided pro-communist factions, were the cause of the unrepresentative character of the rump assembly that came together in Moscow in March 1919. The object of the congress was to create "a general fighting organ for permanent coordination and systematic leadership of the movement, the centre of a communist International, subordinating the interests of the movement in each particular country to the interests of the revolution on its international scale, in the immediate seizure of state power by the national parties in their respective countries."[393] The conference was wholly dominated by the Russian delegation, consisting of the Soviet top leadership: Lenin, Trotsky, Stalin, Zinoviev, Bukharin and Chicherin.[394] Thirty-five delegates represented communist parties or groups in nineteen countries, but with doubtful mandates. For instance Reinstein, who was residing in Russia, was made to represent the United States, Fineberg of Great Britain, who also lived in Moscow, was given a consultative status only. Eberlein, the delegate from Germany, actually had a clear mandate to demand a postponement of the creation of the Comintern, conditions not being yet ripe for it. He spoke in that spirit and nearly won the day. He was then however silenced and neutralised by the Austrian delegate's clarion call announcing an imminent general explosion in all central Europe. The countries of Western Europe— Belgium, Italy and France, England, Spain and Portugal—were in actual fact absent from the founding congress.[395]

The manifesto "To the Proletarians of the Whole World" issued by the newly established Third International was intended to constitute "a second Communist Manifesto".[396] It was followed by an appeal, "To the Workers of All Countries", to support the Soviet Union and to combat interventionist policies of their governments.[397]

There is no reason to doubt the sincerity of Zinoviev, the first president of the Comintern (with Radek appointed, but Angelica Balabonova, the Zimmerwald veteran, acting, though only for a short while, as secretary), of Trotsky and of course of Lenin—who described the new International as "the forerunner of the international republic of Soviets".[398] Nor were they hypocritical when saying that the Soviet communists would have been much happier to establish the head-quarters of the Comintern in Paris or Berlin, instead of Moscow, for that "would mean the complete triumph of the proletarian revolution in Europe and, probably, in the whole world".[399]

This being as yet impossible, the Russian communists found them-selves in a situation not unlike the Montagnards a century and a quarter earlier as defined by Robespierre in his great speech on the doctrine of revolutionary government: "The two opposite genii . . . contesting the empire of nature are in this great period of human history locked in mortal combat to determine irretrievably the destinies of the world, and France is the stage of this redoubtable struggle. Without, all tyrants are bent upon encircling you, within, all the friends of tyranny are banded in a conspiracy: they will go on plotting until all hope has been wrested from crime. We have to strangle the internal as well as the external enemies of the republic, or perish with her."[400]

The Bolsheviks put much stronger emphasis than the Jacobins upon the universal character of their message. Their expectation of an immediate response from other countries was much livelier because in the first place Marxism was fundamentally more internationalist than Jacobinism. "In the question of foreign policy," said Lenin, "two fundamental lines confront us—the proletarian line which says that the social revolution is dearer than anything else and above anything else, and that we must take into account whether it is likely to arise quickly in the West or not, and the other, the bourgeois line, which says that for me the status of a great power and national independence are dearer than anything else and above everything else."[401] "He is no socialist who has not proved by deeds his readiness for the greatest sacrifices on the part of 'his own' country, if only the cause of the social revolution can be really advanced. . . . The peace of surrender signed at Brest-Litovsk was our sacrifice for the world-wide workers revolution . . . we said [then]: if you are a socialist, you must sacrifice your patriotic feelings in the name of the international revolution which is coming, which has not yet come, but in which you must believe if you are an internationalist."[402]

The international revolution was however not only a challenge but, as already said, was regarded as a condition for Soviet survival. The Jacobins did not look for salvation to revolutionary movements outside. They prayed for it ardently, but when they supplanted the Girondists the hope of spontaneous revolutions elsewhere had grown dim. "It is not open to the slightest doubt," said Lenin, "that the final victory of our revolution, if it were to remain alone, if there were no revolutionary movements in other countries, would be hopeless. . . . Our salvation from all these difficulties, I repeat, is in an all-European revolution. . . . Anglo-French and American imperialism will inevitably strangle the independence and freedom of Russia unless world-wide Bolshevism triumphs."[403]

In order however that revolutions in the West should break out and succeed, and provided that communism did not altogether die out there, Soviet Russia must survive at all costs and be helped by foreign communists to remain afloat by whatever means possible. The Communist party Manifesto proclaimed: "By upholding Soviet power we render the best and most powerful support to the proletariat of all countries in its unprecedently difficult and onerous struggle against its own bourgeoisie. There would be no greater blow now to the cause of socialism than the collapse of Soviet power in Russia. . . . We have been defencists since October 25, 1917, we have won the right to defend the fatherland. We are not defending the secret treaties, we have torn them up, we have revealed them to the whole world, we are defending the fatherland against the imperialists. We defend, we shall conquer. We do not stand up for the state, we do not defend the status of a great power. Of Russia nothing is left save Great Russia. These are not national interests; we affirm that the interests of socialism, the interests of world socialism, are higher than national interests, higher than the interests of the state. We are defencists of the socialist fatherland.''[404]

The manifesto of the Third International launched on March 10, 1919, four days after the ending of the inaugural Moscow congress, under the signatures of Lenin, Trotsky, Zinoviev, Rakovsky and Fritz Platten from Switzerland (all participants of the Zimmerwald conference which went into liquidation by merging with the Third International) is a blueprint for a universal communist revolution, which was designed precisely to do away with national states.[405] Its basic assumption is the conclusion drawn from the collapse of the Second International in World War I, that opportunistic reformism upheld by labour aristocracy, the mainstay of capitalism in the age of imperialism, was indissolubly bound up with bourgeois nationalism, with the inevitable concomitant of war. The most important imperative of revolution was in this respect the prevention of nationalist deviation. The Third International as the instrument of world revolution was thus put under a most stringently centralised leadership, which was to act indeed as a GHQ of the global camp of revolution in the life-and-death struggle against the camp of imperialism. Hence the relentless insistence, as first condition of belonging, on the expulsion of anyone tainted with social-chauvinism: Kautsky, Turati, Henderson, Snowden, Longuet, Thomas and their like; and the Leninist precept on policies of ruthlessly splitting these Western parties, in which Left, Centre and Right retained a comradeship based on mutual consideration, democratic tradition and the memory of common origins and past experiences.[406] But there was also another reason for turning the fight for the elimination of reformist social-chauvinists into a condition *sine qua non* of belonging to the Third International. Like the Bolshevik party the Comintern was conceived not as a comprehensive democratic organisation designed to reflect and offer an opportunity for self-expression to the widest diversity of views, but as a fighting con-fraternity engaged in a ceaseless battle under the direction of a centralised leadership on a global scale. Any type of deviationism, particularly the nationalist variety, was more dangerous than the foreign enemy, when a global confrontation was the goal. The remarkable thing, which some analysts found difficult to explain, is that in contrast to the primacy accorded by Lenin to the Bolshevik party in Russia, the manifesto entirely ignores the communist national parties,[407] and exalts the Council of Workers, Peasants and Soldiers as the workers' sole instrument for gaining power, transforming the economy and establishing a true proletarian democracy.[408]

It was precisely the fear of insubordination and deviation that dictated the policy of demoting the national parties. But there may have been more to it: a national party presupposed the nation-state as a stable entity. Arising out of and caring primarily for the basic needs of working men as such, which were held to be everywhere the same and to which national historic boundaries were irrelevant, the soviets were intended to by-pass the question of national-territorial unity, to be free from the vested interests, traditions, mystifications and delusions connected with it. The workers', peasants' and soldiers' councils seemed best suited for the task of "transforming the whole world into one cooperative commonwealth and bringing about real human brotherhood and freedom".[409] The direct democracy embodied in the soviets also appeared to be less exposed to the accusation of being non-democratic than the Communist party; it was however precisely the direct democracy of the soviets that made them the unfailing instruments of the dictatorship of the proletariat. The more stringently that proletarian dictatorship acted towards the old order and old ruling classes, the sooner it would enthrone a true democracy, make itself superfluous and disappear. "As the opposition of the bourgeoisie is broken, as it is expropriated and gradually absorbed into the working groups, the proletarian dictatorship disappears and finally the state dies and there is no more class distinction . . . a classless communist commonwealth."[410]

There was furthermore no contradiction but the closest relationship between a more and more centralised structure and "the constant drawing [of] ever increasing elements of the working people into the immediate control of government".[411] For the people was one and indivisible. The proletariats-become-peoples were sure to possess incomparably more freedom than the nations in the present small national states. The economic developments of late capitalism had made them "too narrow for the development of the powers of production".[412] They had long ago lost their indepndence to the stronger and more industrialised powers and to the international imperialist forces. Their parliamentary institutions, parties and press had been corrupted and rendered illusory by capitalist interests, imperialist pressures and bribery. The devastations of war and the ravages brought by inflation and famine had confirmed with a vengeance the accuracy of the doctrine of increasing misery of the masses and of the imminent death of capitalism.[413] The war had finally transformed the monopolistic cartels and trusts, which had grown out of free competition, into tools of a wholly militarised establishment. "All these basic matters of the world's economic life are no longer regulated by free competition, nor yet by combinations of national and international trusts, but through the direct application of military force. Just as the complete subordination of the state's power to the purposes of finance capital has, through the mass slaughter entirely militarised not only the state, but also finance capital itself, so it [finance capital] can no longer carry on its essential economic functions except by means of blood and ruin."[414]

Only the proletarian revolution was able to secure the existence of the small nations, for it would be a revolution which freed the productive powers of all countries from the restrictions of the national states, "which unites all people in the closest economic cooperation on the basis of a universal economic plan, and enables the smallest and weakest peoples freely and independently to carry on their national culture without detriment to the united and centralised economy of Europe and of the whole world".[415]

Like that of individuals, the liberation of peoples became a reality only through making them economically secure, independent of stronger partners, in contrast to the abstract or formal equality preached by bourgeois liberalism. [416] This was possible only with the help of universal planning of production whereby differences in natural wealth, human resources and stages of development could be levelled out without the stronger units dominating and exploiting the weaker partners.[417] The principle of classlessness in the single socialist community must be made to prevail in the community of nations. The world of nations would thus be replaced by a world of economically classless and politically undifferentiated communities.

It was the undoing of the Second International, says the manifesto of 1919, that the centre of gravity of the workers' movement during that period remained wholly on national soil, wholly within the framework of national states, founded upon national industry and confined within the sphere of national parliamentarism.[418] The restriction of activity to national boundaries fed reformism and opportunism, which were inevitably engendered by the need for adaptation to the realities, interests and procedures of the bourgeois state and its parliamentary institutions. "Decades of reformist organisational activity created a generation of leaders the majority of whom recognised in words the programme of social revolution, but denied it by their actions; they were bogged down in reformism and in adaptation to the bourgeois state . . . parties which had become transformed into subsidiary organs of the bourgeois state."[419]

The common interest of the world proletariat was not the sum total of the particular interests of each component of the totality, nor were its true will and destiny to be found and fixed by compounding the partial wills of the various elements. Overall planning was designed to bring the partial interests into harmony with general well-being and to combat sectionalism, even the one produced by workers' unlimited control of the enterprise in which they worked. Partial interests had to be subordinated to the workings and needs of the totality. The general interest was articulated by the general will of the whole, of the unified world proletariat in the same way as in the single nation. The doctrine of totalitarian democracy was thus transplanted on a global scale in both phases of the messianic fulfilment: by the revolutionary struggle under the guidance of the global general staff, and then in the creation and maintenance of a single world economy and world polity.

Federation (such as realised in the USSR) was a transitional form towards the complete union of the working people of all nations. "Such a union will however become possible only after communist education has eradicated all forms of race-hatred and mutual suspicion between races, after it has liberated the colonial and backward peoples not only from the yoke of imperialism but also from the legacy of distrust and resentment against the oppressor races (including their proletariats), sentiments which have been exacerbated by their having to serve as cannon-fodder and slaves of the war machines of the Great War."[420] In order to hasten the process, "it becomes all the more urgent to transform the dictatorship of the proletariat from a national dictatorship (i.e. a dictatorship existing in one country alone, and incapable of conducting an independent world policy) into an international dictatorship (i.e. a dictatorship of the proletariat in at least a few advanced countries, which is capable of exercising decisive influence in the political affairs of the entire world)."[421]

It is difficult not to discern here the shadow of Big Brother. True internationalism, it is claimed, lies not simply on the free give-and-take between nominally equal sovereign states, but in the universality of the liberationist grand design, which demands that the weaker brethren jettison their self-interest, and that the already liberated elder and stronger brethren make sacrifices on behalf of their still enslaved or naturally weaker kinsmen.

"Petty-bourgeois nationalism calls the mere recognition of the equality of nations internationalism, and (disregarding the purely verbal character of the recognition) considers national egoism inviolable. Proletarian internationalism on the other hand demands: (1) subordination of the interests of the proletarian struggle in one country to the interests of the struggle on a world scale; (2) that the nation which achieves victory over the bourgeoisie shall display the capacity and readiness to make the greatest national sacrifices in order to overthrow international capitalism."[422] But then elitist self-sacrificing altruism so easily slides into dictation by those who have sacrificed and done so much.

(b) THE BOLSHEVISATION OF THE THIRD INTERNATIONAL

Soviet proselytising internationalism went through a series of ups and downs in the first three years after October. There were the high hopes in the closing weeks of the war, with revolutions sweeping Germany and Austria, the rise of communist regimes in Bavaria and Hungary, the spread of social unrest and mutinies in the victorious Western democracies. The euphoria at the end of the war was dashed by the failure of the Spartakists, and the death of Rosa Luxemburg, Karl Liebknecht and Leo Jogiches in Germany, the split in the German Communist party, with the sectarian KAPD carrying off half the membership,[423] and by the rapid collapse of the communist governments in Bavaria and Hungary. By the middle of 1919 the Soviet-dominated part of Russia was encircled by the White Guard armies, which seemed to be closing in on Moscow while receiving supplies from the West and active backing from Western expeditionary forces on all the peripheries of the empire. Karl Radek, Paul Levi and Klara Zetkin voiced the resigned view that even on a European scale, "the revolution will be a prolonged process",[424] and official Soviet pronouncements reassured the Western powers, and more immediately the Poles, that the Bolsheviks were merely defending the national interest and "their own soil", and had no intention of spreading communism and forcing it upon nations which were not yet ready for it.[425]

Soviet proselytism was then electrified by the Polish invasion of the Ukraine in the spring of 1920, the ensuing rout of the Polish forces and the rapid advance of the Red Army to the outskirts of Warsaw—in Lenin's words "the last bulwark against Bolshevism"[426] on the way to Berlin and to the "centre of world imperialism which rests on the

Versailles Treaty".[427] The Bolsheviks were also immensely heartened by the decisions of the majorities in the socialist parties in France, Italy, Norway and Bulgaria to join the Third International and by the fusion of the majority of the USPD, by then not much smaller a party in membership than the reformist SPD,[428] with the KPD.

Thrilled by watching on huge maps the lightning advance of the Red Army westwards and by the news of the formation of a Polish Soviet government, the Second Congress of the Third International felt inspired to proclaim the cause of Soviet Russia as its own. "The international proletariat will not sheath the sword until Soviet Russia becomes a link in a federation of Soviet Republics of the whole world" and the Comintern "a single communist party having branches in different countries", not a "letterbox" like the Second, but a "strong centralised institution".[429] The victorious young commander of the Soviet armies conquering Poland, Tukhachevsky, went so far as to suggest setting up a general staff to lead the international proletarian army which would set out to make the revolution victorious in the near future.[430] The general was re-echoing Trotsky's statement made to the first congress of the Comintern "that the communist workers who form the real kernel of this [soviet] army regard themselves not only as the forces defending the Russian socialist republic, but also as the Red Army of the Third International".[431]

In spite of the Russian setback in Poland, Soviet successes in destroying the White armies and freeing Russian territory from foreign troops, and the failure of Western communists to revolutionise their countries, led to the bolshevisation of the Third International. The October revolution began to be presented as a model to all communist movements. Just as throughout the nineteenth century revolutionaries had the compulsive need to generalise the states and stages of the French Revolution into a kind of anatomy of every revolution, so now the dates of the 1917 calendar, the February revolution, Lenin's April Theses, the July events, the Kornilov affair and above all October, were raised to the dignity of parts in an inevitable pattern which would be followed in every revolution.

The Theses on the Basic Tasks of the Communist International adopted by the Second Congress on July 19, 1920;[432] the Statutes of the Communist International[433] of August 4, followed two days later by the Conditions of Admission to the Communist International;[434] Lenin's pronouncements in the course of the congress[435] and his "Infantile Disease of Left Communism"[436]—all breathe a spirit of utter self-righteousness and intolerance. The adoption of the Manifesto of 1919 and of the new enactments, and the expulsion of opportunist social-chauvinists who are named, were made into a primary condition for admission to the Comintern of every candidate party, in which the struggle between extremists and moderates was not yet resolved. They were sternly enjoined to follow the example set by the Bolshevik party in systematically getting rid of heretics or timid fellow-travellers, and in preferring a cohesive small fighting party to a comprehensive camp.[437] Equally uncompromising was the insistence on endorsing the principle of the dictatorship of the proletariat, including terrorist coercion and suppression and on the absolute renunciation of any ideas on gradual and peaceful advance towards socialism. Parliamentarism received reiterated condemnation as an expression of bourgeois hypocrisy and reformist cretinism.[438]

There arose the dilemma whether the party was to become a sect and in its adherence to immaculate revolutionary purity eschew participation in national parliaments, general trade unionism, cooperatives and municipalities—or was it to strive to act as a church militant within existing working class movements and institutions, in order to undermine the influence of opportunists and to make communist ideas in them prevail?[439] Lenin came out decisively against Leftist sectarianism.[440] The solution proposed was a mixture of legal and illegal activity within the state and within all the organisations which the communists were well advised to join or succeeded in infiltrating.

In his "Infantile Disease of Left Communism", Lenin strongly urged his followers in the West to resist all efforts of opportunist majorities to oust communists from the trade unions.[441] He taught them "to resist all this, to accept any and every sacrifice, even in case of necessity to resort to every kind of trick, cunning, illegal expedient, concealment, suppression of the truth, in order to penetrate into the trade unions, to remain in them, to conduct communist work in them, at whatever cost".[442]

The communist parties were ordered to create secret cells in all organisations and institutions and to exercise the strictest control over communist representatives in them, above all in parliaments.[443] Similar emphasis was laid upon sustained supervision and censorship of publications and writings by members of the party.[444]

(c) EAST AND WEST

The communists in the various countries were thus ordered to put their loyalty to the world revolution above loyalty to their own country, and to treat their own governments and official institutions as enemies, in the same way as the Russian revolutionaries had behaved under the

Tsar. Western delegates bridled. The clashes on this point between them and their Russian mentors serve to reveal the fundamental chasm between the partners from the East and the West.

Lenin called upon the Western communists, especially the British delegation, to offer all support to the national liberation movements in India and other colonies, even of the "national-revolutionary variety, as a way of undermining British imperialism and bringing down the capitalist regime in Britain."[445] The British delegate, Quelch, roundly declared that a majority of the British working class would "regard support of the revolutionary struggle of the colonies against British imperialism as treason", and would applaud the suppression of colonial uprisings.[446] Radek reacted by saying that the British proletariat would never be free of the capitalist yoke unless it supported the colonial revolts. The quality of British communism would be measured precisely by the number of arrests from among its members who risked their lives to help the colonial insurgents.[447]

Lenin's "Theses on the National and Colonial Question" adopted by the Second Congress laid down that the soviet form of organisation was entirely suited to feudal and semi-feudal peasant conditions . . . "for pre-capitalist conditions".[448] They no longer stipulated the necessity for the backward countries to go through a period of capitalist development before embarking upon a socialist revolution. "If the victorious revolutionary proletariat organised systematic propaganda and the soviet governments give them all the help they can, it is incorrect to assume that such peoples must pass the capitalist stage of development." Bukharin said: "If we propound the solution of the right of self-determination for the colonies . . . we lose nothing by it . . . the most outright nationalist movement is only water for our mill against British imperialism."[449]

With their Russian background, their experience of Tsarism and their messianic mentality, the Bolsheviks were quite incapable of understanding Western comrades' qualms, which stemmed from the fact that notwithstanding all abstract rhetoric, they did not feel so entirely alienated from their countries, and their institutions and traditions, and could not bring themselves to feel so crushed and suffocated by their governments as to regard as legitimate every means and action to destroy them. When an anarchist deputy in the All-Russian Soviet Executive Committee in 1918 pointed out that the Western proletariat "feels itself as the bearer of a fragment of power and as a part of this same state which it is at present defending", Lenin pounced upon him, exclaiming that this was a view "so stupid that I do not know how it could be more so".[450]

Some glimmer of understanding, mixed with contemptuous pity, can however be discerned in a later pronouncement by Lenin: "In Western Europe there are hardly any people who have lived through revolutions that are at all serious; the experience of the great revolutions is almost entirely forgotten there; and the transition from the desire to be revolutionary and from conversations (and resolutions) about revolution to real revolutionary work is difficult, slow and painful."[451]

Zinoviev reacted similarly to Hilferding's argument at the Halle Congress[452] that revolutionary slogans from outside would not be able to rouse the masses, without the objective social-economic conditions driving them on to revolt,[453] by saying that the "fear of revolution . . . runs like a red thread through your whole policy", the fear of "dislocation", "hunger" and of "what we have in Russia".[454]

With the failure of the German communist uprising in 1923, the normalisation of the political and social situation as a result of the stabilisation of the currency, the beginnings of the New Economic Policy, and the resigned adoption of the slogan of "socialism in one country", the communists outside Russia found themselves in the situation of "nationalists of a foreign power", as Leon Blum put it. Soviet Russia, on its part, was able to invoke the right, indeed duty, to extend help to any uprising against the existing capitalist order, as to an actual or potential part of the world revolution.

(d) THE EWE LAMB—THE EAST EUROPEAN NATIONS UNDER THE RED SHADOW

Serious as this matter was for the Western states, it was a major and immediate concern to the newly created or the reshaped but precarious nation-states on the borders of the USSR. Their peoples had for generations borne the yoke of Russian domination or lived in its shadow. Their newly won national independence was the poor man's little sheep—a very unsafe possession. Their parliamentary and democratic institutions had no roots, and the heritage of economic backwardness and social injustices clogged all their early steps. The danger from the side of the Russian colossus was by no means diminished by the universal creed of post-Tsarist Russia. In a sense, it grew more insidious and more pressing. The Soviet rulers could with a good conscience claim not to be out to conquer, but to liberate, while depriving the weaker nations not only of their independence, but also, in the name of the socialist world revolution, of their historic personality and distinct traditions.

In an unpublished and unfinished article, printed only in 1928 in the

Grünberg Archiv under the title "Fragment on War, the National Question and Revolution", Rosa Luxemburg tried in the last days of her life to raise the alarm about developments in and around Soviet Russia. The emergence of the new national states in central and Eastern Europe, and the enthusiastic support given to them by the socialist parties of those countries and by that part of the international proletariat, which had entirely adopted the bourgeois Wilsonian peace programme of yesterday's imperialists, implied class reconciliation under the banner of national resurrection, renunciation of class war in the spirit of August 4, 1914, and the rescue of the bourgeois order from bankruptcy.

"The idea of class war capitulates here before the national idea. Class harmony in every nation appears as the precondition and completion of the harmony of nations as in the League of Nations." "Nationalism is at this moment the victor. On all sides nations and national groups are ganging up to claim their rights to create their own states. Mouldering corpses emerge from centuries'-old graves . . . historyless peoples, who have never formed states, are filled with a fierce drive for statehood. Poles, Ukrainians, Byelorussians, Lithuanians, Czechs, Yugoslavs, ten new nations in the Caucasus . . . the Zionists are already establishing their Palestine ghetto, for the time being in Philadelphia. . . ."[455]

That old pedant Kautsky was hailing the rise of the new nation-states on the ruins of the defunct empires as the victory of democracy, as if he was still living in the age of the Risorgimento, and not in the age of imperialism. Rosa Luxemburg takes the Bolsheviks to task for their fatal mistake in adopting the principle of national self-determination and in recognising the right of secession from Russia. It was the immortal service of the October revolution to have put the social revolution on the agenda of history, to have irretrievably polarised the classes into a war for life or death, and to have exploded the humbug of class cooperation, parliamentary procedures; to have ruined the *modus vivendi* between socialism and capitalism; and to have turned socialism from a harmless electoral slogan for the distant future into the serious bloody problem of the present, and to have made another June 1848 impossible. The Bolshevik revolution had filled the international bourgeoisie with fear and terror and with pitiless hatred of the spectre of proletarian dictatorship. "These sentiments constitute today the innermost kernel of the nationalist delirium in the capitalist world."[456] "They form the objective historic content . . . of all nationalisms."[457] The bourgeoisie of the new nation-states had found legitimation for its class rule, and for the strangulation of proletarian revolutionary awakening and action, in their common horror of the ancient national enemy and oppressor—

Russia, and in their fear of the threat of cosmopolitan ideology to the independence and authenticity of national existence. The feasts of national resurrection and brotherhood in the "small nations" were in fact linking the imperialists of various countries, while the brotherhood of nations in the League of Nations concealed the imperialist conspiracy against the USSR and the international proletariat.

But at the same time—and this is what the bourgeoisie of all countries sensed—"behind its back its nemesis is ripening: the giant spectre of the socialist world revolution, which silently moves onto the back of the stage . . . the historic necessity of socialism and the inevitability of the world revolution . . . the dictatorship of the proletariat".[458] The upheaval of war, the exasperation of the deceived mass armies, the bankruptcy of all states, the loss of all moral authority by their leaders, had created conditions for a seizure of power such as no class had ever been granted by history before. The difficulty was solely in the immaturity of the proletariat and of its parties and leaders. The proletariat recoiled from the immensity of the task. "But it must, it must . . . from night and horror . . . into the light of liberation."[459] Because history had decided: socialism or barbarism.

The Bolsheviks had themselves reared their most dangerous enemy. With their slogan of national self-determination they had offered legitimisation to the secession of the Finns, Poles, Ukrainians (their nationalism before October "was naught, a soap bubble, a fraud, perpetrated by a dozen professors and lawyers, who could not themselves speak Ukrainian")[460] and to the creation of bourgeois class states, which could not survive without implacable enmity to a Bolshevik Russia. By their emergence, those new states were weakening and threatening the very existence of the socialist state. Since the latter would not be able to sustain the losses incurred by the secession of vital areas and to tolerate imperialist plotting in them, Bolshevik Russia would be compelled to embark upon a campaign of suppression. And this would force the Soviet leaders to stop "the general chase after nationalism and the League of Nations. The socialists must now go to school to learn the ABC again—in practice, but in an abridged form."[461] The peace programme of bourgeois society was not feasible. Here was the historic guarantee of the imminence of the revolution and victory. But the Soviet state would be compelled to resort to coercion and to adopt terrorist measures against the secessionist nationalities, and these would inexorably strengthen the incipient terrorist trend in Russia itself.

The Second International adopted the post-war formula of its creed
"Political System of Socialism" at its congress in Geneva in July 1920,[462]
almost at the same time as the Third International restated its articles of
faith in Moscow. Its essential difference from the communist formulations was the stand on the reality and supremacy of the nation as a
whole and as such—"the community as a whole"—and as embodied in
parliament, which represented "all the popular aspirations and desires
from the standpoint of the community as a whole".[463] "The government of the nation will be its executive." Arrogation by any "factious"
minority group of a special revolutionary mission and of a right to direct
action and terrorist violence to carry it out and "to bring popular liberty
to naught" was sternly condemned.[464] "Any tendency to convert an
industrial strike automatically into political revolution cannot be too
strongly condemned."[465] Moreover, labour was broadly defined to
include not only independent craftsmen, and of course peasant
cultivators, but also "all those who cooperate by their exertions in the
production of utilities of any kind", that is to say even managers and
employers.

The platform looked forward to the creation of a socialist commonwealth "by the conquest by labour of governmental power", but only
by democratic means, never by the use of dictatorial powers. Its very
raison d'être and "historic mission" was to "carry democracy to
completion".[466]

All forms of syndicalism were given short shrift. "It will be for
parliament to determine the general lines of social policy and to make
the laws; it will decide to what industries and services the principle of
socialisation shall be applied under what conditions; it will exercise
supreme financial control", while granting all facilities to trade
unions.[467] The document spoke vaguely of the possibility of setting up a
National Industrial Council composed of representatives of the various
organisations of trades and professions. It was however to be only an
advisory body to parliament.

The schism in the world-wide working class movement was thus
completed: into believers in a messianic world revolution through a
violent breakthrough, and the devotees of the nation-state based on
democratic reformism.

Part VIII

FROM GEORGES SOREL TO BENITO MUSSOLINI

Chapter One

THE LEGACY OF GEORGES SOREL — MARXISM, VIOLENCE, FASCISM

Georges Sorel lived long enough to see and to hail the Bolshevik revolution as a great fulfilment, and long enough if not to congratulate Mussolini on the accomplished march on Rome, at least to express his fascinated interest in and keen admiration for rising Fascism. There is the story that in the same week, in the late 1920's, the director of the Bibliotheque Nationale in Paris was approached by the ambassadors of Soviet Russia and Fascist Italy, on behalf of their respective governments, with offers of sums of money for the repair of the tombstone on Georges Sorel's grave. True or apocryphal as the story may be, Sorel did utter shortly before his death the prayer to which adherents of either ideology could have responded with a fervent amen—"to be allowed, before descending into the grave, to see the humbling of the proud bourgeois democracies, today so cynically triumphant. . . ."[1]

If Benedetto Croce spoke of Georges Sorel as one of "the two sole original thinkers thrown up by socialism"[2] (the other was Karl Marx), Wyndham Lewis, the grim hater of philistinism, a ferocious kill-joy and one of the first intellectuals in the West to hail Hitler with a special book, saw in Sorel "the key to all contemporary political thinking".[3] Mussolini repeatedly acknowledged Sorel as his master: "What I am, I owe to Sorel."[4]

And Sorel, in turn, called Mussolini "a man no less extraordinary than Lenin . . . of a greater reach than all the statesmen of the day . . . not a socialist from the bourgeoisie; he has never believed in parliamentary socialism".[5]

Notwithstanding Lenin's dismissal of Sorel as a muddle-headed mischief-maker,[6] Sorel described Lenin as the greatest theorist socialism had had since Marx, and a head of state whose genius recalled that of Peter the Great—in his efforts to orientate Russia "towards the constitution of a republic of producers, capable of encompassing an economy as progressive as that of our capitalist democracies". Although he modestly stated that he "had no reason to suppose that Lenin may have

451

accepted my ideas,"[7] Sorel was proudly sure that his "syndicalism was a slope inclining towards Bolshevism".[8]

In the light of these statements, one need not be startled by the opinion of the French Fascist, Ramon Fernandes, expressed in 1937, that "Georges Sorel directly inspired the totalitarian régimes".[9] Recent scholarship has been increasingly more inclined to focus attention on that strange encounter just before 1914 between the ageing Sorel and some of his Syndicalist disciples on the one hand, and, on the other, a few youthful ultra-Rightist nationalists in France and Italy, as a kind of curtain-raiser to post-1918 Fascism. And it is impossible not to be struck by similarities of thought and speech between the young New Left radicals of today and the author of the *Réflexions sur la violence* seventy years ago.

(1) THE HEROIC LEAP

Sorel was a seeker. His restless and easily discouraged questing, his tentative enthusiasms and bitter disillusionments, epitomise the spiritual biography of his age, the pathetic pilgrimage of modern man who had lost the past certainties. Sorel was fascinated by the legend of the Wandering Jew—"the symbol of the highest aspirations of mankind condemned to be forever travelling, without reaching any goal".[10] In his vehement rejection of the eighteenth century's facile and optimistic substitute for the religious Theodicea and in his revulsion from the bourgeois civilisation based on it, Sorel joins the ranks of the nineteenth century's great prophets of wrath—de Maistre, Carlyle, Schopenhauer, Burckhardt, Nietzsche, Dostoevsky, Ibsen, among others.

Born in 1847 into a royalist bourgeois family in Normandy (he was a cousin of the historian Albert Sorel, author of the monumental work, *L'Europe et la Révolution Française*): Georges Sorel was destined to take his first bearings in the world just as France was going through the ordeal of national defeat and civil war—the Commune—in 1870-71, and then to follow the anguished post-mortem to which such conservative thinkers as Taine, Renan, Le Play and others had submitted the history of France, making the Revolution of 1789 responsible for that zig-zag course of revolution, anarchy, terror, Bonapartist dictatorship and restoration, vast conquest and terrible defeat, the triumph of liberty and its demise. The arrival of the masses filled these writers with dread. As for the universal suffrage which the Third Republic—a pathetic caricature of the great revolution—seemed to have enthroned forever, had it not in 1848 swept Louis Napoleon Bonaparte into power, and enabled him, as both the elect of the masses and the defender of bourgeois property against the Red Revolution, to strangle liberty? The vagaries of the blind multitude and its associated demagoguery could no longer be held in check by any of the proposed dams—a restored monarchy, religion or state authority.

Nothing shows better the impact that this national self-questioning had on Sorel than his frequent reference to Ernest Renan's anguished question—"On what will the future generations live?" after the inherited Christian habits of thought and conservative inhibitions had lost their grip completely (as they clearly were losing it all the time).[11]

It was in order to sort out these bewildering things for himself that the civil engineer (roads and bridges) left government service at the age of 45 and retired on a small pension with the ribbon of the Légion d'honneur, into a Paris suburb, to study, meditate and write. He frequented intellectual circles composed of very young men, mostly disciples on the Left Bank, attended regularly the lectures of Henri Bergson at the Collège de France, and worshipped the memory of his deceased (apparently illiterate) wife, who died childless in 1897. Sorel, incidentally, never tired of extolling chastity as the virtue of virtues, as the sign of moral health and social cohesion, and of stigmatising the lack of it as proof of sickness and degeneracy.

The very titles of his earliest books—*Contribution à l'etude profane de la Bible* (1889), *Le procès de Socrate* (1889) and *La ruine du monde antique* (1898)—betray Sorel's preoccupation with the phenomena of integration and disintegration, decadence and rebirth. While the tract on the Bible is an attempt to bring into relief the naively heroic tone of the biblical stories, and their educational value as antidotes to utilitarianism and revolutionary ideology,[12] *Procès de Socrate* is an essay on the freewheeling intellectual who, by questioning and criticising the ways of men from an abstract stand, undermines the instinctive certainties, the massive traditions, the life-sustaining prejudices and the inherited institutional framework of the nation. Socrates stands condemned for arrogantly trying to replace the earthly, concrete, "social" reality of family by the abstract ideal of the "fictitious moral family", the organically and historically structured state with an essentially "ecclesiastic" conception of society, based on pure reason and spiritual values, and for inspiring moods of ecstatic and orgiastic intoxication that invite the imposition of both revolutionary and tyrannical solutions.[13]

La Ruine du monde antique is a study in disintegration and decline. The late Roman Empire had its strength, its very life, all the values and institutions which had made it great, sapped by too much self-consciousness and by other-worldly spirituality. The victory of Christianity had been prepared by the spread of oriental cults and introspective philosophies which "sowed everywhere the seeds of despair and death",[14] by putting personal salvation above country, family and social ties, holiness above law, poverty above the productive effort, renunciation above responsibility, contemplation above virile struggle, the heavenly fatherland above the city. "Le moyen âge peut commencer; il n'y a plus de cité, plus de droit."[15] At a later date Sorel portrayed early Christianity as the most powerful impulse towards spiritual and social rebirth in the midst of total decay. A naive, narrow, but heroic message, it enabled its believers to raise themselves to the heights of a strenuous, new beginning—the *ricorsi* of Vico. This juxtaposition of decomposition and reintegration, decadence and rebirth expresses Sorel's deepest and most abiding sentiments: his aggressive and overwhelming pessimism and his yearning for deliverance. "This pessimism is a metaphysic of ethics rather than a theory of the world." It stems from "the experimental knowledge which we have acquired of the obstacles which oppose the satisfaction of our imaginations" and from "the profound conviction of our natural weakness".[16] The pessimist regards the prevailing social conditions as "constituting a system held together by an iron law", which must either be supported as a whole as something inevitable, or made to disappear "through a catastrophe carrying all with it". Do not therefore blame any particular persons for the evils that be, and do not engage in partial reforms.[17]

In language very reminiscent of de Maistre, Schopenhauer, Burckhardt and Nietzsche, Sorel poured scorn upon all those who promised easy solutions and rapid improvement, and who proclaimed happiness as our right and pleasure as man's legitimate aim. Pain and suffering riveted us to life; its reality, dignity and depth; pleasure-seeking marked an escape from it, a sliding away from its inexorable course. Decadence fascinated Sorel, as, incidentally, it did so many philosophers of history and culture, from whom the extreme Right derived much of its inspiration. The natural tendency towards dissolution and decay was to him a universal law. Civilisation was a most precarious possession, and was maintained by the skin of its teeth. Any sign of relaxing was soon followed by rot, collapse and ruin. Barbarism was always creeping into the weak ramparts built against it. What gave meaning and grandeur to our life was the state of tension and unyielding struggle to ward off the forces of decay and destruction, and above all the yearning and striving for deliverance. Sorel did not see this "deliverance" in the ease of relaxation, or in Schopenhauer's loving communion with art in an all-embracing Nirvana; or in Burckhardt's vision of a secular neo-

monasticism as a refuge for the chosen few; he saw it rather in the spirit
of Nietzsche, in the elation which came from tearing oneself out of the
maze of snares and the miasma of feebleness: the heroic leap into a new
and immensely strenuous discipline which had been resolutely chosen,
without ever looking back or sideways—a monastic order, the early
Puritan communities, the Grande Armée.

This faith—pessimism linked to a vision of deliverance—was a
doctrine "without which nothing truly great has ever been accomplished in this world".[18] This is clearly a religious frame of mind. Sorel
was never a believer; he never used the word "God"; but he never
ceased to be fascinated by religion and to write on religious problems.
Sin and purification, guilt and redemption, self-willed arrogance and
objective certainty, right and force, legitimacy and revolution—these
speculations are at the source of his quest.[19]

(II) THE REVOLT AGAINST POLITICS

By 1893-4 Georges Sorel had become a fully-fledged Marxist. As he
writes: "I hold the theory of Marx to be the greatest innovation introduced into philosophy for centuries. . . . All our ideas are bound today to
congregate around new principles posed by scientific socialism. . . . The
human spirit refuses to be content with the old economic scepticism . . .
with the registering of facts, with reasoning about the balance of
profits, with comparing the increase of prosperity in the various
countries."[20]

The accent is clearly not upon the evils of capitalism or the
sufferings of the poor, but upon objective certainty and impersonal
necessity, in contrast to the "subjective personal and crude notions of a
philosophy delivered to accident", emotional preferences or speculative conjecture. The Archimedean point of Marxist philosophy was
according to Sorel the conception of man as "tout entier comme
travailleur", never separated "from the instruments with which he
earns his living", in other words the constant and intimate relationship
between men and the machine; between the free and creative freedom
of the worker as tool-maker, *homo faber*, manipulator of inert matter on
the one hand and the inexorable determinations thrown back by the
medium and the tools on the other. In comparison with this, the abstract
ideologism of intellectuals and the would-be metaphysical eternal
moral principles of philosophers represented vague conjectures,
imaginings or emotional states. Sorel goes so far as to maintain that the
great theoretical advances in science had in most cases been nothing but

generalisations of technological inventions. This quest for certainty and abhorrence of arbitrariness and vagueness caused Sorel, from the first, to envisage integral trade unionism as the expression of all authentic values, and to view socialist party politics as a sign and a danger of corruption. Sorel expected the syndicates to become a separate and self-sufficient kingdom of God, bearers of a new morality and a new civilisation. The idea of secession, of total separation from the surrounding world, was not yet worked out at this stage by Sorel, but the tutelage exercised by the professional politicians at the head of the political labour parties was already bitterly assailed by him.[21]

Before Sorel had an opportunity to develop those ideas, he became deeply involved in the tremendous experience that at the turn of the century shook France to its foundations.

In becoming a Dreyfusard Sorel was not really concerned with destroying the power of the church, the army or militant chauvinism as an end in itself. He gave himself soul and body to a mystique pitted against another mystique: the fight for abstract justice and the pure truth against the supposedly life-giving and power-sustaining forces of national myth, prejudice and tradition, represented by "les autorités sociales" of bygone days. In a sense Sorel took the side of the Socratics whom he had earlier so bitterly condemned. Sorel's hopes for a purifying *ricorsi* soon gave way to disillusionment. In the words of another significant figure who went through a somewhat similar experience, Charles Péguy, the Dreyfus *mystique* degenerated into *politique*. The Dreyfus affair and its aftermath, says Sorel, "produced an extraordinary accumulation of accidents, very much like those which sometimes enable the physicist in his laboratory to see suddenly in a wholly unexpected manner, and under an almost transparent veil, laws which had long escaped methodological investigation".[22]

The consequences of the affair revealed "the inadequacy of the socialist teachings of the day". In joining the non-proletarian forces in a struggle for not distinctly proletarian aims, the workers lost their own identity and the clarity of their proletarian purpose. Anti-clericalism proved in fact to be only a springboard for power-thirsty demagogues of both varieties, the bourgeois radical and the socialist politicians. The Marxist principle of class war was "definitely submerged in the democratic ocean of the unity of the people".

Sorel goes on to draw a momentous lesson from this failure: "The parliamentary socialists lost a great deal of their prestige; men of violence covered themselves with glory."[23] The affair revealed the vital importance of sustained direct action "with its very frequent accompaniment of acts of violence", as a method distinct from sporadic acts of violence, which were no more than "simple accidents which come to trouble the normal advance" of a movement. This discovery called for a revision of Marxism or, rather, a return to its authentic tradition. Sorel's reappraisal of socialist teachings was carried out not only under the impression of the *affaire*, but, no less important, under the impact of and in direct reference to the great "revisionist" controversy, begun by Eduard Bernstein at the turn of the century.[24]

Sorel's reaction to the revisionist heresy should be considered along-side the violent responses of Lenin, Mussolini (the first communist in Europe in that he forced the reformists out of the party), Rosa Luxemburg and Parvus-Helphand. Theirs was a passionate reassertion of revolutionary voluntarism and élitism, and of the early revolutionary and universalist messianism of Marx, in opposition to Bernstein's tendency to turn the socialist parties into a left wing of parliamentary democracy and an integral part of the national body politic. The revulsion from the revisionist renunciation of revolution propelled others in a quite different direction. One of the Italian theoreticians of syndicalism (he later became a prophet of the corporate state and a close collaborator of il Duce), Sergio Pannunzio, traces the beginning of his evolution from socialism to Fascism to the shock administered to him by the "revisionist heresy". Unlike the above-mentioned anti-revisionists, Sorel accepted the whole of Bernstein's social economic critique of orthodox Marxism, but drew diametrically opposite political conclusions from those of Bernstein.

In his *Décomposition du Marxisme* (1908)[25] Sorel agrees with the thesis (indeed states it more emphatically than Bernstein himself) that capitalism had not failed at all. More than that, the progress of capitalist production and of its inevitable concomitant, trade unionism, had not only raised the workers' standard of life but had blunted the edge of class war, since collective bargaining had turned the workers into partners of management rather than enemies thereof. In the early days of the industrial revolution it was the financiers and usurers, totally ignorant of the problems of technology, who laid down the law for industrialists and engineers; while at the same time the workers, stupid brutes, snatched from the plough or the workshop, had to be kept in line by brutal methods. But in the meantime technologically trained employers had come into their own, and workers had learned to handle the machine and even to like it. Capitalism had evolved sufficient powers of adjustment to cope with passing crises. There were, thus, no technological or social-economic reasons for interfering with the workings of capitalism, not even in the sphere of salaries and wages, since a rough kind of justice of reward proportionate to contribution was being realised by capitalism. Socialism was not going to change that, because in this respect, Marxism, Sorel claims, was closer to the Manchester school than to the "justice"-obsessed utopians of the earlier days (who thought in terms of fool-proof blueprints and perfect egalitarian justice, consciously and artificially contrived, and not of the workings of the mechanism of production).[26]

If this be so, then why revolution at all? The question is especailly insistent as Sorel has no sympathy at all with what he regards as the modern version of a *jacquerie*—the envious desire of the poor to redistribute property for the sake of equality. And if the revolution is an absolute imperative, for moral or other reasons, are we not thrown back upon the idea of a violent seizure of political power for the purpose of imposing the socialist order by violence—in a word, "Blanquism"? Sorel will not give up the revolution, but he will reject Blanquism, and this on quite original (though mistaken) grounds. Blanquism—he claims—did not really envisage the uprising of a class, but the assumption of the revolutionary mission by a political party, in fact by bourgeois intellectuals, who shared neither the needs and the way of life nor the real aspirations of the genuine workers. Here we reach the nodal point already foreshadowed in Sorel's theory of revolutionary syndicalism based on the idea of violence. Sorel sees the proletariat—organised in syndicates—not as paupers fighting for a larger share of the cake but as a force predestined by history to enthrone a new civilisation and a heroic morality on the ruins of the decaying bourgeois world. The authenticity of this force and singleness of its purpose were vitiated and distorted by professional politicians, by intellectuals, and by the corrupting effects of parliamentary party politics. Sorel believes he is fighting for a return to the true Marx. He tries to depict Marx as a prophet of the embattled class and the enemy of party politics. He fails to mention the relevant passages in the Communist Manifesto as well as the famous Article 7a of the General Rules of the International—"the proletariat can act as a class only by constituting itself as a distinct political party". But he quotes with fervent approval the concluding passage in *The Poverty of Philosophy*, Marx's famous tract against Proudhon: "The antagonism between the proletariat and the bourgeoisie is a struggle of a class against class, a struggle which carried to its highest expression is a total revolution . . . the clash of body with body, as its final dénouement . . . combat or death: bloody struggle or extinction. . . . It is in this form that the question is inexorably put."[27]

Sorel then makes much of the International's circular (in which Marx's share is rather uncertain) against Bakunin's "Alliance of Socialist Democracy and the International Working Men's

Association". This ridicules the idea of putting a vanguard of men recruited from the privileged classes above the masses ("cannon fodder"), to act "as intermediaries between the revolutionary idea and the popular instincts", in order to bring to the fore "lawyers without briefs, doctors without treatments and without science, students of billiards, shopkeepers and others employed in commerce, and especially journalists of the petty press . . . who discovered, in the International, a career and a cause".[28]

Sorel quotes with glee Engels' description of the political struggle in the modern (bourgeois) state: "a body of intellectuals invested with privileges and possessing so-called political means to defend itself against the attacks of other groups of intellectuals and to acquire the profits of public offices. Parties are organised for the acquisition of these public posts."[29] Sorel not only refuses to draw any distinction between bourgeois politicians and socialist politicains; all his scorn is directed against the latter—because of their greater hypocrisy.

These were two entirely different things: the revolutionary élan of a class acting from instinct and in full simplicity, also a class that had finished its apprenticeship, evolved a system of ideas and values, a juridical framework of its own, and reached full awareness of its historic mission to install a new civilisation and a new moral order; and the connivance of professional party politicians, banking on the revolution to deliver to them "the object of their cupidity", the state. Sorel also refers with approval to Bernstein's exposure of the cant which, under the guise of formal popular sovereignty, makes civil servants, professional politicians and newspaper owners run the show, and to his definition of the dictatorship of the proletariat—"the dictatorship of club orators and literati".

Fundamentally, we are faced here with a problem which has never ceased to perplex mankind—the question of the very legitimacy of politics. Its utter vagueness and elusive character, the mixture of abstract principle and crass ambition, of objective goals and sheer histrionics, of rational argument and squalid bamboozling; its seeming remoteness from the concrete, measurable, and truly necessary things— all this leads to the despairing conclusion that whatever the politicians, men of no particular training, ultimately dilettanti, say or do is only a mask and pretence for the desire for power, power for its own sake. "Politics!" exclaims Paul Valéry, "at the word I am struck dumb. . . . I regard the political necessity of exploiting all that is lowest in man's psyche as the greatest danger of the present time." Sorel would add bourgeois politics, but he means democratic politics: the competition for power or rather for the favour of the people who held the prize of power. Politics of this type emerged—Sorel claims—in Europe, more precisely in France, only at the end of the eighteenth century, as a function of a new *Weltanschauung*. This leads him to undertake a fundamental reappraisal of the eighteenth-century tradition. He rejects it, root and branch, as a colossal derangement, an alienation; and so it justifies his prophecy of its imminent demise at the hands of the victorious proletariat.

"All our efforts," Sorel writes, "should aim at preventing bourgeois ideas from poisoning the class which is arising; that is why we can never do enough to break every link between the people and the literature of the eighteenth century . . . to demolish this whole scaffolding of conventional falsehoods and to destroy the prestige still enjoyed by those who vulgarise the vulgarisations of the eighteenth century."[30]

One is reminded of Mussolini's boast in 1926, for which many parallels could be found in statements by Fascist and Nazi spokesmen: "We represent a new principle in the world; we represent the exact, categorical, definitive antithesis of the whole world of democracy, plutocracy, freemasonry, in short the whole world of the immortal principles of 1789."[31]

In this utter repudiation of eighteenth-century values and the conscious endeavour to replace them by different, indeed contrasting, principles, Sorel parts company not merely with the liberal-democratic tradition of the modern era, but in the last analysis also with every shade of socialism known hitherto.

(III) FORCE, TERROR AND RENEWAL

"Les Illusions du Progrès" is the central issue on which Sorel takes up his fight against the eighteenth-century tradition: that belief in some final salvationist stage of the historic process, the preordained resolution of all contradictions and conflict into a state of concord, harmony, resulting from the final victory of the basic rationality and social nature of man over all the disturbing and corrupting influences of bygone ages—ignorance and selfishness, oppression and evil teachings. The essential features of this religion of progress were its abstract universalism and its humanitarian optimism. Sorel proclaims his bitter enmity to this religion of peace and concord, in the name of a religion of struggle and war. He considered the opposition between the two approaches fundamental.[32] Sorel's most faithful disciple, Edouard Berth, put his finger on it, invoking Nietzsche's uncompromising challenge ("are you pacific, or are you warrior-like?") and Proudhon's famous disquisition on the place of war in the scheme of civilisation (its role as the inspiration of all the great values). It was either the one or the other. Each of the two basic attitudes determined a system of values, a morality, a pattern of behaviour quite irreconcilable with the ones shaped by the other; in brief, of concord on one side, and violence on the other, of universal reconciliation or the victory of the best. Sorel entirely ignores the eighteenth-century humanist and universalist ingredients in both the original impulse and the ultimate vision of socialism.

The facile optimism of the rationalists rouses Sorel to a fury of contempt. He takes a malignant pleasure in the resistance, recalcitrance and intractableness of things; he is hypnotised by insoluble contradictions and conflict. Sorel despises Descartes, the philosopher of clarity and harmony, and adores Pascal, the tormented prophet, weighed down by the mystery of evil and consumed by a yearning for salvation. The former epitomises the "small science" of smug positivism and automatic mechanism, the latter represents the "great science"— true vision suspended over unfathomable abysses.[33] To take a characteristic instance, Sorel is scathing about the social Catholicism of the Modernist movement in the church of Leo XIII, and its attempt to explain away the mysteries, absurdities and irrationalities of revealed religion as parables and symbols of rational truths and liberal social ethics. Needless to say, he prefers a tough, wholly indigestible religion.

Humanitarian rationalism seems to Sorel a colossal lie which has had a most stultifying and corrupting effect, breeding an arrogant and capricious desire to obtain full gratification quickly and cheaply, to make a cowardly escape from the realities of life and the lessons of history. It simplifies the mysteries of nature and the complexities of existence into encyclopaedias and digests, glib rhetoric and castles in the air, and fosters an unprincipled readiness to compromise and bargain. Conflict and war are the fathers of all true morality and manly responsibility.

We need not be detained by Sorel's critique, at times acute, at times quite fanciful, of the roots of the eighteenth-century philosophy. More important for us is Sorel's connection with the far-reaching and lasting course of the rationalist ideology.

For the French Revolution produced the strange type of the fanatical would-be saviour in a hurry who sees himself justified in forcing everybody to be free. Universal happiness would follow the extermination of all evil recalcitrants, or at any rate deviants, who were doomed by history. The more usual breed of "the religion of progress", however, has been the professional politicians or intellectuals in politics who banded together in political parties ostensibly to serve and guide the people in the direction of the desired state of social happiness, but in fact to cajole the people with promises, blandishments and tricks into giving them power. Their progressive ideology had little real relevance. Rhetoricians, sophists, adventurers, speculators, clowns all rolled into one, neither coping with real problems, nor rooted in any ancient group loyalties, nor part of historic institutions: they were all ultimately parasites. They gambled on the frustrations and envious dissatisfactions of men. They encouraged indolent craving for easy gratification. Their weapons were ruse and cunning.

As against "bourgeois deceit and decadence" (of which socialist politicians had become an integral part), the arrival of the proletariat presages a purifying *ricorsi*. The proletariat comes to bring war and not peace; to add burdens, not to alleviate them; to heighten tension, and not to offer a détente. It struggles on in the full consciousness of its destiny to inherit the earth: not to come to an accommodation with the existing establishment, but to eradicate it entirely. Its heroes are warriors, and not politicians, diplomats or negotiators.[34]

A new, revolutionary and all-transforming principle associated with the modern industrial effort—the communion with the machine—is an instrument of creative freedom, a warrant of integrity, an educational discipline, a vantage point for seeing things in their full concreteness and interaction, in contrast to the vagueness, the abstractness, and indeterminacy as well as the moral laxity and selfish arbitrariness of liberal-democratic and socialist politics, indeed of bourgeois society in general.

Sorel's terms of reference, metaphors and similes are all taken from religious movements and war. The most frequent words are honour and glory, sublimity, heroism, virility and loftiness. The comparison is between the syndicates and their impending general strike and the early Christians or the extreme Protestant sects waiting for a Second Coming or the monastic orders which arose to purify the Church.[35] Sorel says again and again that the fact that these historic expectations were never fulfilled did not matter. All that mattered was that in each case the myth had enough vitality to sustain the believers' resolve and to turn them into little kingdoms of God, with an ethos, a high morality, indeed a culture of their own, in strenuous opposition to the rotten world around them. The proud self-awareness of representing a higher civilisation and morality was bound to inspire the workers with puritan virtues: love of the job for its own sake, precision and loyalty, care for the heritage of the future heirs of the earth. The redeemed proletariat would be marked above all by the heroic selflessness and disinterestedness peculiar to crusades and soldiers of liberty.

To keep themselves pure and resolute it was absolutely essential for the workers to cut themselves off entirely from the unregenerate world. This meant in the first place shaking off the tutelage of politicians and intellectuals, with all their machinations and corrupt practices. In the second place, it meant class war à l'outrance: no truck with the employers. The more isolated the syndicates were, the more they would have to fall back upon their own resources; the more intensely would they become aware of their own identity and high calling; the richer and deeper and more authentic would their own values become. In the form of direct action and strikes, the struggle would also gradually shape a new and wholly autonomous juridicial system, which would be based on the morality of a confraternity at war. War—as in Proudhon's vision— would beget the virtues of heroism, total devotion, a sense of solidarity, right and honour. The strikes were sure to engender and sustain new conceptions and new patterns of relationship between the leaders and the led (the former embodying the true general will, and not the mystical general will of Rousseauist democracy). Occupying factories would accustom the workers to seeing themselves as the legitimate owners and managers of social wealth. The physical clash with employers, state authorities and strike-breakers would educate the strikers in the use of violence. Sustained by the spirit of a revolutionary army, the workers would not be moved by envy, by a craving for revenge or a vision of spoils, let alone self-pity. They wanted a clean fight—a judgement of God—in the heroic tradition of medieval chivalry. But their campaign was also conceived in the spirit of a Napoleonic resolve to annihilate the enemy.[36]

It was the vision of the general strike that was to inspire and sustain the proletariat in their heroic struggle. The General Strike was the great myth, but it was most emphatically not a vision of utopia. Utopia, according to Sorel, was an intellectual proposition, a description of a desirable state of affairs which would be an improvement upon the existing one. Myth, however, was not a truth to be analysed and taken to pieces, but a power that stirred the soul, an ensemble of images that satisfied and propelled all our faculties.[37] Upon it were focused all our urges and drives, dreams and hopes. It was a vision of life turned drama, a convulsion of final fulfilment, like the revolutionary breakthrough, or the Second Coming, the arival of the Messiah or the last war of liberation.

The myth presupposed man to be not a creature of reason, but a suggestible being, whose intuitive grasp of and reaction to an uplifting heroic vision would raise him out of himself into that élan vital which opened to him the domain of creative freedom. He would then cease to be a link in the chain of natural causality, and (in the spirit of Henri Bergson) make a new start towards a unique destiny.[38] The general strike signified the triumph of violence at the end of a series of clashes.

Sorel's eloquent pages read like a poetic evocation, a prophecy rather than a prognosis or a blueprint. We are left in the dark as to how the great drama of violence would really unfold. We are told that its essence would not be in much bloodshed or acts of brutality, in a large number of victims or untold destruction. These would be few; they would bear rather the character of a warning. What Sorel seems to have had in mind is the overwhelming will to win, the supreme confidence of conquerors, the iron determination to go to the bitter end, in the face of which the adversary reels, because he lacks the conviction and the self-assurance of those who embody manifest destiny and know it.

"A social policy founded on middle class cowardice, which consists in always surrendering to the threat of violence, cannot fail to engender the idea that the middle class is condemned to death, and that its disappearance is only a matter of time. Thus every conflict which gives rise to violence becomes a vanguard fight, and nobody can foresee what will arise from such engagements. . . . Each time they come to blows the strikers hope that it is the beginning of the great Napoleonic battle. . . . In this way the practice of strikes engenders the notion of a catastrophic revolution."[39]

At a later date Sorel defined violence as "an intellectual doctrine, the will of powerful minds which know where they are going, the implacable resolve to attain the final goals of Marxism by means of syndicalism. Lenin has furnished us a striking example of that psychological violence."[40]

The determination of the assailants and the faltering of the attacked conditioned each other. The capacity and readiness to resort to violence became the test of faith and of belonging to the elect. " . . . en se regardant comme le grand moteur de l'histoire . . . il a le sentiment très net de la gloire . . . son rôle historique et de l'héroisme. . . . La mesure de sa valeur."[41] Sorel resorts in this connection to the vocabulary of stern determinism. The final act of violence in the victorious strike would be "no more than the necessary effort to make the old withered branches fall to the ground". The fall would be like the final crush of the glacier tearing itself away from its old base, "after having been attacked by the sun for centuries".[42]

An apologia for "violence"? Sorel devotes quite a few pages to the distinction which later would become a commonplace among ideologists of violence of all kinds. Force was an instrument for maintaining existing power (what would nowadays be called the establishment).

"The object of force is to impose a certain social order in which the minority governs, while violence tends to the destruction of that order. The middle class have used force since the beginning of modern times, while the proletariat now reacts against the middle class and against the state with violence."[43]

It was hidden and camouflaged, operating not so much with weapons of direct coercion as by manipulating the levers of power, insidiously blocking all attempts at a change or cunningly denuding them of any real effectiveness, while making much of form and ritual.

"Thus we see that economic forces are closely bound up with political power, and capitalism finally perfects itself to the point of being able to dispense with any direct appeal to the public force, except in very exceptional cases...."

Sorel gives an interesting slant to the Marxist description of the bourgeois state as the executive of the exploiting classes (and to Engels' denunciation of parliamentary "cretinism") by substituting intellectuals and politicians for capitalists and their stooges: "There is a great resemblance between the electoral democracy and the Stock Exchange; in both cases it is necessary to work upon the simplicity of the masses, to buy the co-operation of the most important newspapers, and to assist chance by endless trickery. There is not a great deal of difference between a financier who puts high-sounding concerns on the market which come to grief in a few years, and the politician who promises endless reforms to the citizens which he does not know how to bring about, and which resolve themselves simply into an accumulation of parliamentary papers.... Democrats and businessmen have quite a special science for making deliberative assemblies approve of their swindling; parliaments are as packed as shareholders' meetings... profound psychological affinities resulting from these methods of operation; democracy is the paradise of which unscrupulous financiers dream."[44]

In brief, the regime of bourgeois liberalism rested on force: on cunning and make-believe. Sorel proclaimed the violence preached by him to be noble and chivalrous because it was open and direct and constituted a full and unequivocal commitment, without subterfuge, reservations or convenient avenues of retreat.

As for terror, it was always just a question of inspiring fear or self-confidence by demonstration. Andreu calls "extraordinary" the sentence in which Sorel asked himself—"whether in liquidating so large a number of literati and ideologues the Terror had not rendered a service to France. Perhaps Napoleon would not have consolidated his administration so easily had his regime not been preceded by a great purge...."[45]

Violence in effect was the token of authenticity. The revulsion from hypocrisy (which was just another way of putting the quest of "authenticity") led to the glorification of instinct and force, and to a contempt for devious men, especially intellectuals. The greater the contempt for conventional "falsehood", the greater the glory of violence. Sorel pondered over the difference between the severity with which old heroic societies punished deceit and fraud (while being lenient towards crimes of violence) and the heavy punishments meted out to crimes of violence (coupled with the indulgent treatment of crooks) in modern commercial society. He upbraided the rude justice meted out to offenders by primitive societies in accordance with their ancient notions of honour. Surely a knife-thrust by an honest but violent man would have less serious moral consequences than theft and deceit, or the excesses of lust. For barbarism, Sorel complained, tends to be replaced by cunning.[46]

On the eve of World War I we find Sorel speculating on the two possible ways of arresting bourgeois decadence and the socialist demoralisation that accompanies it. At the end of the *Insegnamenti sociali della economica contemporanea*, he writes that "a great international war (which he regards as not very likely) may have as its effect the suppression of the causes which tend today to favour the taste for moderation and the desire for social peace". It would certainly bring to power "men with the will to govern". Sorel's other hope is "a great extension of proletarian violence, which would make the bourgeoisie see the revolutionary reality and fill it with disgust for the humanitarian platitudes with which Jaurès has been lulling them to sleep".[47]

Indeed, Sorel wants the capitalists to fight, to believe in themselves and in their class interests, to be like the early captains of industry or American robber barons. Let them mind their own business, and not act as philanthropists with a social conscience, always ready to conciliate, to give in. This softness was a sign of effeminacy, and it demoralised the workers. By being what history has meant them to be—harsh and ruthless taskmakers—the employers would deploy their potentialities to the full, keep their workers on their tiptoes as fighters, and thus hasten the day of confrontation.

"When the governing classes, no longer daring to govern, are ashamed of their privileged position, are eager to make advances to their enemies, and proclaim their horror of all divisions in society, it becomes much more difficult to maintain in the minds of the proletariat this idea of division without which socialism cannot fulfil its historical role."[48]

Reformist socialists who wished to act as conciliators, who work for "social peace" and national unity, were traitors to the working class, and destroyers of morality. "Finally . . . anti-patriotism becomes an essential element in the syndicalist programme . . . an inseparable part of socialism."[49]

In words reminiscent of Lenin's elitism, Sorel says that the syndicates must search less for the greatest number of adherents than for the organisation of the vigorous elements; revolutionary strikes were excellent for effecting a solution by weeding out the pacifists.[50]

(IV) BETWEEN MARX AND MUSSOLINI

What would be the state of affairs on the morrow of the victorious General Strike? What kind of society was desirable or likely to emerge? On this Sorel is maddeningly vague, and he has many excuses. He had rejected utopianism from the start. He believes in the unpredictable Bergsonian creativeness of the *élan vital*. He was prepared to endorse Mussolini's famous slogan: "Every system is an error, every theory is a prison." But what Sorel does say on the subject reminds one very much of Lenin's Old Left conceptions in *State and Revolution* and of contemporary New Left notions. Sorel rejects the idea of any guidance, supervision or control from outside and from above, (Those supervisors would always be thinking of the next election). And he could not conceive of tribunals or penalties or prisons to coerce the victorious proletariat. There would be no need for anything of the kind. Steeled in revolutionary ideology and tempered by the fire of strikes, the workers would, in the manner of true soldiers of liberty (or, perhaps, warriors of God), have developed a superb blend of dignity, pride, individualistic self-reliance and an enthusiastic readiness and capacity to engage in co-operative effort. They would thus be totally free in their utter unanimity. The key phrases here are "heroic exploits . . . extra-ordinary enthusiasm . . . ardour takes the place of discipline . . . the greatest possible zeal . . .", etc.[51]

A few lines later Sorel drops the very revealing remark that as a result of his fierce individualism on the one hand and his keen sense of responsibility on the other, the soldier of the revolutionary armies, "felt no pity for the generals or officers whom he saw guillotined after a defeat on the charge of dereliction of duty. . . . In his eyes failure could only be explained by some grave error on the part of his leaders . . . made him approve of rigorous measures against men who . . . caused it to lose the fruit of so much heroism".[52]

Obviously, where absolute perfection is postulated as predetermined, any failing appears malevolent, perverse and treasonable. Where unanimity—unanimity which is constantly renewed—is considered inevitable, any dissent must seem arbitrary and selfish. Unanimity must be made manifest by every means. The road from perfectionist anarchy to democratic centralism (perhaps better called totalitarian democracy) is not a very long one.

And yet, numerous and close as are the points of contact between Sorel and Bolshevism, the spirit and temper that pervade his writings are utterly uncongenial to the proletarian mentality, and alien to Marxist philosophy and socialist values. It was not for nothing that on being asked whether he had been influenced by Sorel's work one syndicalist leader replied, with a shrug of the shoulders, that he only read Alexandre Dumas! Reality was different. The real workers could hardly be expected to lend an ear to appeals to heroic self-abnegation in order to enthrone someone else's lofty morality, or to entertain the idea that they should make superhuman efforts on behalf of some mythology.

In spite of Sorel's insistent claim to be remembered as "the faithful servant of the proletariat", he decisively parts company with socialism and comes close to Fascism. It is true that Lenin, like Marx before him, struck many elitist notes; he belaboured the bourgeoisie (and the Mensheviks and Social Revolutionaries) for their philistinism, flabbiness and hypocrisy, and extolled the resoluteness and determination of his own revolutionary fighters. Yet to him heroic qualities were never an end in themselves, but only a means of arriving speedily at a final regime of social justice; at most, they were tokens of devotion. The display of vitality or the achievements of glory are not values in themselves. The socialist revolution is not made to create a superior breed of man. The institutions of the socialist system are sure to beget better men: better, above all, for being less rapacious and more co-operative, more rational and more civilised; but certainly not for being inspired by a combative urge for self-expression as members of some superior elite or master race. Nothing is more alien to socialism than Nietzscheanism. Thus one can hardly call the teachings of Sorel socialism. What they are in fact is a Nietzschean repudiation of bourgeois mediocrity and deceit and a Nietzschean philosophy of the elite applied to the proletariat. Sorel turned the tables on Nietzsche. Whereas the prophet of *The Will to Power* denounced socialist ideology as slave ethics, Sorel expected a revaluation of all values and the enthronement of a heroic civilisation to come from the proletariat. Its syndicates were called upon to assume the social leadership,[53] given in the past by the ruling families of an aristocracy. The impulse of both thinkers was (to repeat) the same: revulsion from the shabbiness, the hypocrisy, the meanness and mediocrity of bourgeois society in the nineteenth century. A resurgence of heroic virtues was an end in itself to both prophets. It is scarcely true to say that Sorel's aim was to replace the political authoritarian state of the bourgeois intellectuals by "a network of free syndicates". This new type of social organisation had, in his eyes, no value in itself except as an instrument for the new heroic morality. In spite of Sorel's preoccupation with juridical concepts and institutions, his concern was really with a change of heart and not with a new institutional order. Sorel's glorification of the sense of manifest destiny, of the will to conquer and the joy of struggle as the begetters of all heroic virtues, transformed these from means into ends in themselves. Heroic for what? It does not, in the last analysis, much matter for what purpose. After all, Sorel spoke with deep admiration of the heroic qualities of the bourgeoisie in its prime, and he enjoined the proletariat to be fierce and uncompromising so that even their effeminate philanthropic employers might recover the kind of militant virtues which characterised the early captains of industry.[54]

Sorel opted for the heroic proletariat and not for the re-born bourgeoisie—as he might well have, and as indeed some of his followers did—because, it seems, he had the Hegelian sense that the next phase of history belonged to the proletariat. It was not because he wanted to redeem the proletariat as an oppressed class. He spoke with the same admiration of the heroism of the Spartans, the early Christians, the apocalyptic Protestant sects, the monastic orders, the soldiers of the Grande Armée and the followers of Mazzini. "In the total ruin of institutions and of morals there remains something which is powerful, new and intact, and it is that which constitutes, properly speaking, the soul of the revolutionary proletariat. Nor will this be swept away in the general decadence of moral values, if the workers have enough energy to bar the road to the middle-class corrupters, answering their advances with the plainest brutality. . . . The bond which I pointed out in the beginning between socialism and proletarian violence appears now in all its strength. It is to violence that socialism owes those high ethical values by means of which it brings salvation to the modern world."[55]

"Proletarian violence . . . appears a very beautiful and heroic thing . . . in the service of the primordial interests of our civilisation. . . . [It] may save the world from barbarism. . . . Let us salute the revolutionaries just as the Greeks saluted the Spartan heroes who defended Thermopylae and thus contributed to maintaining light in the ancient world."

The turn soon came for syndicalism to be rejected by Sorel as "hyper-demogoguery"—as socialism had been before it, also for its

"demogoguery" and "stupidity". Sorel stumbled upon (or rather was
lured into) a new view of historic opportunity: the extreme nationalist
royalist Right as candidates for a revival of virility and heroism. He
gave his blessing to a bizarre flirtation between a handful of young
enthusiasts of the syndicalist Left and of the extreme Right. It was not
really, so far as Sorel himself was concerned, a joyous espousal of the
royalist-nationalist cause; rather a half-hearted, uneasy relationship,
hampered by a certain sense of incongruity. But the young disciples who
came from syndicalism, as well as those who came from integral
nationalism, and who had as yet no past to live down, were able to enjoy
the affair with undisturbed relish.

A signal event in Sorel's rapprochement with the Right was his
article on Charles Péguy under the title "Le Réveil de l'âme française, le
Mystère de la Charité de Jeanne d'Arc" (1910). In it he hailed the proud
and defiant resurgence of traditionalist Catholic French patriotism and
militarism as the revenge of the anti-Dreyfusards upon the "dregs of the
humanitarianism" of the Sorbonne (and democracy in general).[56] Sorel
prophesied that these old-new ideas were destined to direct contemporary thought.

The programmatic declaration of the *Cité Française*, the still-
born organ of the syndicalist-nationalist alliance, was signed by Sorel
(who drafted it), his two disciples Georges Valois and Edouard Berth
and the two royalists Pierre Gilbert and Jean Variot (author of the
Propos de Georges Sorel. The aim of the editors was to "liberate French
intelligence from all those ideologies . . . which dominated Europe in
the last century".[57] Whatever the differences dividing them, they were
perfectly united in the opinion that "for any solution of the problems of
the modern world . . . it is absolutely necessary to destroy the democratic institutions . . . as the greatest social peril to all classes of the community, in the first place the working classes. Democracy mixes up the
classes, in order to enable a few bands of politicians, associated with
financiers or dominated by them, to exploit the producers." The editors
pledged themselves to foster the self-awareness of every social class by
weaning it away from the stultifying teachings of democracy, and to
restore to it its original virility and sense of mission.

For some years Sorel was a regular contributor to the nationalist
L'Indépendence; he also emerges as the somewhat reluctant patron saint
of the "cercle Proudhon", where his disciples and the young Rightist
enthusiasts (Henri Lagrange, Gilbert Maire, René de Maranes, André
Vincent) were trying with the blessing of Maurras, Barrès and other
nationalist luminaries, to evolve a type of French national socialism—
Proudhon against Marx—which would fight democracy, "the stupidest

of dreams . . . the mortal error". Capitalism was also the enemy: "the capitalist regime which destroys in the community what the democratic ideas destroy in the domain of the spirit, that is the nation, the family, the way of life, substituting the law of gold for the law of the blood".[58]

(V) NIHILISM: FROM SOREL TO VALOIS

The man who used Sorel as the foundation stone for a genuine and full-blooded Fascist philosophy was Georges Valois. Valois has been called the French Mussolini *manqué*,[59] who in 1925 tried to emulate the Duce's triumphant march on Rome (but failed to reach Paris). He started out as one of the wildest young Leftists on the Left Bank, and then wandered for years across the globe, to South-East Asia, Russia and other distant places. On his return to Paris, Valois was smitten by a revelation—the idea of elitist authority. He wrote a book entitled *L'Homme qui vient; Philosophie de l'Autorité*, and dedicated it to the "young, energetic men, whose intelligence has been stultified and whose muscles have been rendered flabby by voluptuousness", as a result of a philosophy of moral anarchy which for generations had been teaching the abolition of all restraints. Valois defines his new ideal as "work, and its condition: authority and the state". He intends to confound the "horde juive triomphante" in the Dreyfus affair.[60] Valois proclaims war on the three prophets who "wrought ruin upon the modern world . . . three great criminals, three great impostors, fathers of lies. . . . J. J. Rousseau, the false man of nature, Immanuel Kant, the false man of duty, and Karl Marx, the false man of necessity".

Valois identifies his own prophets: in the first place, Sorel; then Charles Maurras, Carlyle, Kipling, H. G. Wells; the now forgotten scientist René Quinton; the old masters (de Maistre, Bonald, Auguste Comte and Taine), but above all Nietzsche.

"I owe my liberation to Nietzsche. At a time when we were stuck in the democratic humanitarian swamp . . . wasting our energies in an effort to solve irrelevant problems . . . Nietzsche . . . forced us to consider with true sincerity the real problems . . . to see ourselves without pity . . . the liberator of our energy."[61] In fact, Valois' whole theory is nothing but a smudged, coarse-grained and petulant variation on Nietzsche and Sorel.

Sorel's elitist conception of the proletarian syndicates and their revivalist mission is transformed by Valois into a vision of the rule of born masters, "holders of the whip", over the slavish, indolent, swinish multitude. The masters are no longer a hereditary social class like an ancient aristocracy—something quite impossible in the twentieth century—or an elite of brains, but men endowed with the undefinable gifts of leadership who prove themselves in a Darwinian struggle and rivalry. You recognise them when you see them coming, these men at the top, the successors to the medieval barons, the famous condottieri and the great capitalists. Their success is their title to legitimacy. The "strongest will reveal himself incontestably . . . no one will doubt his qualifications, once he had defeated all the others". Never mind the means. Without a ruthless, uninhibited urge for power and leadership no one would ever get to the top.[62] It was the impotent but envious and cunning demagogues of democracy who spoke of "rights" and "justice" and flattered the masses.

Sorel's earliest concern was with authenticity, certainty and social cohesion. He sought them first in the realities of organic historic tradition, then successively in Marxist teaching, in the inexorable determinations of productive effort, in the condition of the proletariat, finally in the life-giving collective myth. He never ceased to fear and hate self-willed arbitrariness and intellectual vagrancy. Georges Valois goes far beyond his master when he raises the instinctive will-to-power of the individual and the visceral ties of the community of blood—"la verité charnelle"—to the dignity of absolutes.

It was instincts that mattered most, and not the intellect. Man's mission was not to know the world or to learn to know himself, but to fight. "The means which you wish to employ for knowing yourself—intelligence—subordinate it and do not use it for tasks for which it was not made. . . . It is a gift which was given to you not that you may know yourself, nor that you may know our raison d'être, but to enable you to understand, with the aid of experience and instinct, in what way the things surrounding you may serve and contribute to your growth."[63]

We are faced here with the fear of thought and analysis, the dread of choosing between alternatives and a craving to be propelled mindlessly by powerful instincts or, for that matter, the force of habit. "False sages and liars!" exclaims Valois, "To say that one is led by his intelligence is an error and a lie. Man is guided by his instincts. . . . What is the brain? An organ like his foot, his hand, his eye, used by his instinct. . . . Who commands in living nature? It is the instinct of life." The power to act was superior to the ability to think. "Intellectuals!" cries Valois, "if you are true leaders, speak in the name of your energy, do not ask for power, take it. If you are strong, the people will recognise you as leaders." All creative force came from instinct, and this is why "the master of life, the aristocrat, will never be an intellectual but a doer, the one whose life instinct had the greatest strength".[64] The supreme fact of life—of men as well as of nations—was war.

"All the things that we call the pacific blessings of civilisation are the creations of war; civilisation itself is the fruit of war. . . . The nations . . . working today to develop a civilisation of peace, were themselves formed by war and maintain their work of peace, of solidarity and of brotherhood thanks to nothing but war. War is the primary law of life, and for the species it is the only way of achieving the highest plane of its life instinct. . . ."[65]

This truth did not have to express itself in actual fighting. Warlike rivalry was also present in the accumulation of so much power that all dangers from within and from without would be staved off without going to war. War is "a happy necessity for civilisation".[66] It was also an instrument for realising social justice among the nations, by wresting lands and resources which indolent and incompetent nations did not know how to make use of, and thus "abuse their sovereign rights over them."[67]

The democratic politicians—a breed that emerged in the French Revolution—represented a kind of anti-elite of the déclassé of all classes. "The democratic regime is in the full sense an organised, systematic disorganisation of the nation, and carries with it its own ruin. . . ." As for socialism, it was only a new form of parliamentary exploitation which has simply changed the electoral formulae, but it "pursues the same aim as the other parties—the conquest of power in order to obtain the wealth which that conquest provides. . . ."[68]

Behind the anti-elite of democratic and socialist politicians, a loose congeries of adventurers who come and go, there stood an anti-elite acting from behind the scenes, but of the most distinct identity, cohesion and continuity—the Jews.[69] The politicians were no more than the puppets or agents of that Jewish power. The Jews were an anti-elite *par excellence*: few and physically weak, with no aristocratic tradition or martial qualities, intellectuals and reasoners, they could succeed and obtain the power that they craved not by imposing themselves in an elemental irresistible way, but through manipulation and scheming. They represented and embodied everything that was not instinctive and concrete, but was abstract and universal. Cut off from the land and its pursuits for so long, with no country of their own, with no share in the hard productive effort, they had developed two weapons which had no particular home or race: ideas and money. These became the instruments with the help of which these aliens could worm their way into French society and overcome the natural resistance and healthy egoism of a deeply rooted, idiosyncratic nation. Against French in-stinctive certainties, traditions and customs, the French conception of justice, they proclaimed and fostered an abstract universal natural law, the idea of Man *per se*, eternal ideal justice. Their promised land was pitted against authentic native French patriotism: the French were seduced into adopting the abstract ideology of revolution as their national ideology. The alien Jews could thus appear as most excellent Frenchmen, while remaining a closely knit separate entity. Finance capitalism, *laissez-faire* liberalism, rationalism, even socialism founded on class war—all were Jewish devices to sap the self-assurance, the cohesion, the unity and the authenticity of the French nation.[70]

Parliamentary democracy became a convenient façade for the wire-pullers. Apparently an expression and guarantee of popular sovereignty, it was just a camouflage for hidden but real powers. Sorel had already drawn attention to the close similarity, and indeed the link, between speculators who gambled on the stock exchange and parasitic democratic politicians who gambled for power. He did that without specifically mentioning the Jews. However, Sorel the Dreyfusard eventually developed into a bitter anti-semite, calling upon Europe to defend itself against the Jewish peril in the same way as America fought the Yellow peril; he blamed the Chekist terror on the Jewish members of the Bolshevik party. The Jews (Valois claims) had their agents in all parties, but they had lately concentrated their attention on the socialists: for the sake of a better disguise, and in order to make sure that they became the heirs of the expropriated French bourgeoisie on the morrow of the revolution which they were plotting. Once the revolutionary general strike succeeded in paralysing all production, the ensuing chaos could be overcome only with the help of ready cash—gold. The Jewish financiers would have kept it in their safes; they would then appear as saviours, offer help, but extort a heavy price, namely complete domination over the economic and political life of the French nation. "It is probable that a terrible anti-semitic movement will then develop and it will manifest itself through the most beautiful massacre of Jews in history."[71] The Jews would then call in foreign troops to rescue them, in order that Jews and foreigners together might share the spoils. Some of the participants in the debate on "The Monarchy and the Working Class", initiated and analysed by Valois, saw the Jews as working for the enemies of France—for England, Germany and Italy. Others depicted the Jew as the enemy of every authentic nation, and called for an international alliance against the common Jewish danger. Georges Valois himself coined the slogan "L'or juif contre le sang français", Jewish gold against French blood.

The Jew thus appears as the lynchpin of the whole theory, resolving the contradiction between socialism and nationalism.

Chapter Two

MUSSOLINI AND THE FASCIST DENOUEMENT

Georges Sorel was better known in Italy than in France. Some of his writings appeared first or even only in Italian. He kept up an extensive correspondence with leading Italian thinkers such as Croce and Pareto. Every publication of his was widely commented upon by writers of the most diverse views. Every newspaper and weekly in Italy, whatever its political orientation, went to great lengths to secure an interview with the celebrated author of the *Reflections on Violence*.[72]

Sorel was bitterly abjured by his erstwhile devotee, Benito Mussolini, when he started his flirtation with the extreme nationalist Right in France;[73] all the more striking is the fact that the movement which the extreme socialist revolutionary eventually enthroned as the dictatorial regime of Fascism was indeed a synthesis of syndicalism and nationalism. Without rushing to the facile conclusion of naming Georges Sorel as the father of it all, one can hardly dispute the fame his name had gained in Italy. Some particular affinity with Sorel's ideas and sentiments must have been in the air, waiting to be articulated and systematised.

No country in the aftermath of World War I shows up so sharply the dilemmas and stresses of a society going through a great social and ideological travail in face of the contradictory challenges of world revolution and the other nationalist self-assertion.[74] In stark contrast with Russia, with which she showed not a few similarities, it was nationalist and dictatorial Fascism that won in Italy.

(I) THE PECULIARITIES OF ITALY'S PAST — ABSENCE OF AN ITALIAN NATIONAL MYTH

The baffling paradox of Italy's history has been the fact that although seemingly marked out by geography and history to constitute a political unit, Italy had never up to 1861 been a nation-state, despite the tremendous common cultural heritage, the single religion of its inhabitants, the relative absence of racial minorities and the blessings of

475

natural borders. Of course there were the vast natural differences between north and south, regional peculiarities and very diverse local traditions. But these were surely no greater than in some larger neighbouring countries, in which a strong dynasty, a centralised government, economic needs and a unifying ideology had proved potent enough to overcome centrifugal factors and tendencies.

The single strongest impediment to Italian unity was the Christianised myth of Rome embodied in the papacy. Italy did not as it were belong simply to her inhabitants. Her very heart was also the heart of universal Christendom. The Italians held it in trust on behalf of mankind. Powerful foreign invaders—German emperors and French kings—were hypnotised by the primacy which direct influence upon the papacy gave them, on top of the facilities which a foothold in Italy could give for gaining mastery of the Mediterranean and vast openings in the Middle East.

There was another factor which stood in the way of unification. The Italian elite had an enormous field at its disposal in which to realise its potentialities and ambitions, first in Christendom at large, then as the trustees and active continuers of the richest, oldest, most unbroken cultural tradition in Europe. Gifted Italians left their unmistakable and lasting imprints as artists, architects, writers, scholars, scientists, educators, sailors and discoverers of continents, royal advisers, diplomats, ministers, spouses of mighty kings, in many places bankers and generals, in every European country from Lisbon to Moscow.

These facts encouraged and facilitated other far-reaching developments. The great coastal city-republics and famous commercial and artistic centres like Florence turned all their attention to overseas ventures, trade and colonisation, to the cultivation of their strong municipal and communal traditions with the bitter class strife, party struggles, family rivalries and condottieri exploits that these entailed. They became almost oblivious of the immediate Italian hinterland, but remained extremely conscious of the eternal need to compete with each other.

It was the massive presence of the papacy and the ubiquitousness of its spiritual challenge that gave a special twist to the Italian movement of national liberation and unification—the Risorgimento. Since it pitted itself against the very embodiment and symbol of transcendental and universal authority, and at the same time against the countries of the ancien regime, it had to become revolutionary, republican and anticlerical. But the myth of the unique and at the same time universal significance of Rome was so deeply embedded in the Italian mind that the claim to secular, national self-determination seemed a poor, inadequate, indeed demeaning challenge in comparison with the myth of the universal church, the heir of the imperial myth.

(II) THE RISORGIMENTO—A "MUTILATED" DREAM

That is why the dream of the rebirth of the Italian nation developed into a vision not merely of a political nation, but of a new spiritual community, a universal message of purification and revival, a Third Rome at the head of the liberated, united and redeemed nations, each expressing the deepest and most authentic values of its own, and together forming a new universal church of confraternities-nations pursuing a universal goal. So high an office and calling demanded means and methods suited to them. The noble awakening of a great people, the generous trustee of a universal promise, would not stoop to the use of shady stratagems, diplomatic ruses, selfish immorality. It would gain its ends through an appeal to idealistic hearts, and in open combat waged by self-sacrificing heroes and martyrs.[75]

Unfortunately there was an abysm between pretence and reality. The national liberation and unification movement of Italy was very much a minority aspiration—of the student youth, the intelligentsia and a part of the bourgeoisie. The vast peasant masses, especially in the south, were untouched. The millions of Catholics were held back by their religious convictions. Many of the aristocracy preserved their feudal loyalties towards the dynasties. The undeveloped urban proletariat was unimportant. Nor were there those powerful economic interests and tendencies which caused the upper middle class elsewhere to strive for large markets, customs unions and parliamentary institutions. Deprived of the basic natural requisites of industrial capitalism, coal, iron and oil, the country was hardly on the way to an industrial revolution. Finally, in comparison with the high claims made for abstract national unity, the local constitutions, traditions and loyalties proved to have far greater staying power and appeal than idealists and doctrinaires were prepared to concede.

Dismal unpreparedness and military inadequacy having brought humiliating failure on the battlefield, it was left to the liberal-conservative Cavour to "diplomatise" the national liberation movement by hitching the cause of Italy to the chariot of Napoleon III; in the eyes of Mazzinians and Garibaldists a most awkward and ambiguous ally. United Italy came into being not as the result of a spontaneous, universal uprising throughout the Italian nation, but as the fruit of an intrigue master-minded by Cavour with like-minded people in the other Italian states, designed to put the latter under the government of Piedmont and to offer a share to the popular revolutionary element at the same time.[76] There were only twenty-four Sicilians in Garibaldi's Thousand who liberated Sicily. United Italy then had the galling experience of being thoroughly beaten at Lissa and Custozza by the Austrians in 1866. She received Venice from the hands of her victorious Prussian allies. She came into the possession of her capital, Rome, only at the demise of Napoleon III's Second Empire. Not daring to provoke disapproving Catholic world opinion, and the powers which refused to recognise Rome as the capital of united Italy, King Vittorio Emanuele made no triumphant entry, but sneaked into his newly recovered capital, the Eternal City, as if to console its population just badly hit by a flood, read out the proclamation of Rome as capital and speedily returned the same day to Turin.[77]

The manner in which the Italian nation achieved its unification left behind it a haunting sense of non-fulfilment, of missed greatness, of a painfully embarrassing gap between aspirations and realities, pretence and substance, the sonorous rhetoric, flamboyant posture and pathetic performance. These gaping ambiguities and ambivalences goaded the Italians to bridge them, to show to the world and prove to themselves their real worth.

After Italy was united, the Italians made the discovery that the Italian nation had still to be made. It had by no means sprung forth ready made, all of a piece, from a great revolution, nor from the crucible of war. The great ideal had not lifted men above themselves. The grim poet of disenchantment, remorse and wrath, Oriani, lamented "the heroes who became soldiers, the martyrs changed into clerks".[78] Italy was made by the "heroic imposition of the few". Thinking Italians became painfully aware of how little of an organic nation Italy really was. From the social-economic point of view she had two Irelands, one in the south, Sicily, the other in the north, Emilia–Romagna. She had hardly a political tradition to fall back upon, in spite of a multitude of myths: nothing like a British constitution of slow and organic gestation, no monarchy to be idealised, as the Bourbons still were in republican France by nostalgic royalists, not much of an army with a roll of honour of memorable feats of arms and victories and unmistakable identity. "Italy too easily crushed," wrote Oriani, "during the revolutions of 1821 and 1831; defeated in 1848 through its cities and countryside, barely victorious in 1859, miserably beaten in 1866 on the fatal plains of Custozza and in the waters of Lissa, Italy, into which Garibaldi could not breathe his courage, Mazzini his genius or Cavour his good sense, which entered Rome in 1870 on the sly."[79]

The Risorgimento was a revolutionary-democratic movement which exalted the principle of popular sovereignty above everything. This was the title to legitimacy which it invoked vis-à-vis the papacy and other transcendental and authoritarian principles. But its idealised image of Westminster aroused more expectations which could not be fulfilled in Italy. The Italian parliament became a byword for lack of principle, shady dealings and makeshifts and lack of responsibility. It was based for quite a while upon an exceedingly narrow franchise, some 2 per cent of the population. Universal suffrage had to wait until 1912. Only about half the voters usually bothered to avail themselves of their right.[80] A single constituency system without proportional representation turned parliamentary seats into holdings of local magnates and patrician families, all of which worked against the formation of large modern parties with a fixed programme and party discipline, and invited manipulation by skilful politicians at the centre, like Giolitti.[81]

(III) IN QUEST FOR A MYTH AND POWER

Contempt for the elected government bred a longing for something better outside the institutionalised framework. Italy was too sophisticated for crude populism. The nation was also much too differentiated for that. Speculative minds searching for the real, the true Italy took refuge in nebulous philosophies, on some Rousseauist general will, deeply buried in the soul of the uncorrupted masses, yet articulated and realised by an elite and even a legislator of genius—the dream of Carlo Pisacane[82]—no mean equation to solve. Some delved into Hegelian conceptions of the state as a repository of universal rationality, impersonal aspirations and objective moral will.[83] Germany had the Prussian king, with his nobles and bureaucracy; but an alliance of throne and altar, glorified by French counter-revolutionary thought, was not to be thought of in an Italy which had come into existence in the teeth of papal opposition. It was revulsion from empty rhetoric, verbosity, lack of grip on things and a nostalgic respect for medieval communal traditions that early on gave rise to speculations about some form of a corporate state: a network of economic, professional and business organisations to replace or to exist alongside the purely political parliamentary bodies.[84]

Given Italian traditions, the hold of Machiavelli on Italian thinking and the developments which were still in store for Italy, it is not surprising that the best-known elitist thinkers of Europe at the turn of the century were Italians: Pareto, Mosca, Michels and others.

In so far as they treat statecraft, the acquisition and exercise of power as a morally neutral phenomenon and a problem of techniques and not as an instrument, condition or preparation for the realisation of objectively desirable values, the Italian theorists of elitism follow the tradition inaugurated by Machiavelli. The author of *The Prince* was hypnotised by ways and means of performing great astonishing deeds of lasting effect. He was not concerned with sacred principles, but with how to hold and increase power and make its grip wider and deeper, and thus more indispensable and more impregnable, and, if secure existence be a goal in itself in a world always on the brink of anarchy—ultimately beneficial.[85] A victorious self-made prince-conqueror may in the natural course of events be led to consistency in his behaviour towards his subjects, to keep his promises to them, to respect their possessions and rights, since these modes of conduct are calculated to solidify and stablise his rule. But ultimately he will act in that way only out of prudential considerations. He may for instance decide that if it proves impossible or impolitic to exterminate or expel newly conquered populations, the wisest thing will be to spare them resentment. If the usurper has to liquidate some magnates, he will take care not to confiscate the goods which the prospective heirs had hoped to inherit. For they will forgive the killing of their relatives, but not the usurpation of the property they thought due to them.[86]

There is undeniably something cynical and something despairing—the politics of cultural despair—in the cogitations of Pareto, Mosca and Michels, not on the ideal goals to be pursued, but on the circulation of governing elites, the ways in which they arrive, keep themselves in power, prove themselves effective, then begin to lose grip and self-confidence, provoke disrespect and rebelliousness among the governed, to be eventually replaced by the new elite waiting in the wings.[87] Michels makes much of the inertia and indifference of ordinary party and union members and considers the emergence and self-perpetuation of bureaucratic oligarchies as a law of nature.[88] More subtle and insidious is the approach of Pareto, and to a lesser extent the empirical observations provided by Mosca.[89]

Pareto's theory of residues has as its point of departure the view that human, and for that matter political, behaviour is shaped in various degrees by compulsive drives, inherited, habitual modes of response and ritualistic remnants or residues of basic primitive mentality. For example, the deep-seated need to preserve aggregates, that is to say associations of ideas and responses, is the characteristic feature of conservatives. The urge to temper and tinker with them, the inclination to criticise, oppose, rebel, dismantle, try out new combinations and introduce innovations is the root of rebelliousness. The two attitudes alternate as public moods: a swing of the pendulum. Those who came to power in one or other period were men in whom the respective inclinations were present and active in a more condensed manner, and who therefore became more pugnacious, more persevering and freer from inhibition in giving expression to them. That measure of intensity gave them a chance to secure ascendancy and effectiveness. In brief, they achieved goals and realised aims not because they strove for them as ends in themselves, but because of their ability to respond to the mood of the public, to yield to one or other set of residues at the given moment.[90]

The straining for and eventually the cult of effectiveness which came to dominate so much of Italian political thinking, of its literary and artistic preoccupations and of its general climate—D'Annunzio, Papini, Marinetti—may be seen as an education for Fascism.

Both the extreme Left and the extreme Right were fascinated by defiance, force, violence, action, confrontation and breakthrough. On the extreme Left this mood was represented on the eve of 1914 by Mussolini, the revolutionary syndicalists like Bianchi, de Ambris, the future leading henchmen of the Duce; and on the extreme Right by the Italian nationalist literati such as Corradini, Federzoni, Coppolo, Prezzolini and others.[91] Both currents represented a reaction against the positivist trend and mechanical forms of reasoning which had driven out the romanticism of the Risorgimento and insisted on the exclusive validity of analytical thinking, while deprecating any sweeping generalisations about metaphysical connections, ultimate goals, eternal verities and transcendental values.

Oriani voiced his longings for the tempests of Hegel's thought and the storms of Napoleon's wars. He wished to "scale the peaks of metaphysics with Hegel, while the air thins and the bravest companions suffocate and fall to the earth".[92] In literature this mood glorified the Byronic hero and his revolt against bourgeois mediocrity, the hypocrisy of the *juste milieu*, the low cunning of democratic politicians, the pedestrian character of life around. The smugness and complacency of humanitarian ethics, petty utilitarianism and the abhorrence of hazard, risk, adventure and cruelty were condemned or ridiculed as signs of decadence. Starting, like Maurice Barrès, as narcissistic priests in the temple of the *culte de moi*, Oriani, Corradini and of course D'Annunzio shifted from disdain of the crowd and the *hoi polloi* into a Promethean posture. On the far peaks of inspiring leadership the hero remains alone, yet how artistically creative in manipulating the crowd, in turning amorphous human dust into the instrument of great decisive actions, in moulding and channelling the energy of the nation.[93]

Italian pioneers of expressionism and prophets of futurism spread their fascination with violent outbursts of instinctual forces, the cult of sex, virility, speed, modern technology, sheer size and shocking novelty, mad deeds and vast mass pageants.[94] These were re-echoed in the imperialists' bombastic evocations of battle, conquest and colonial adventure with its release from the constraints and malaise of modern city life and communion with the elements, the desert and savage primitivism.[95] Many voices began to call for a baptism of fire and blood to reunite and cement the Italian nation, to test it and purify it for the fulfillment of its manifest imperial destiny, of which the Risorgimento was only a first and not wholly successful instalment.

(*IV*) THE MANIFEST DESTINY OF ITALY

This was of course largely an expression of frustration and of the continuing sense of unfulfilment. In the late nineteenth and early twentieth century destiny was manifested in imperial expansion and the mastery of the oceans.[96] Italy had come too late to the banquet. Conceded grudgingly and mockingly the status of a great power *honoris causa*, Italy did not count in the council of powers. Her military weakness was a subject for derision, and her unreliability and unscrupulous manoeuvering—the fate of the weak—and invariably lean and hungry look rendered her contemptible. Italy had the unique distinction of suffering a crushing defeat from the hands of African natives—the Ethiopians—at Adowa in 1896. The swarming superfluous poor of the south, whose natural place of settlement was, Italians believed, Africa, were being packed off to the United States, Latin America and elsewhere, there to become detribalised and to bring the name of Italy to ridicule and calumny by their low occupations and their prominent part in the Mafia. The vision of Roman eagles reconquering Africa, Roman legions trudging the ancient Roman roads all over the coasts of the Mediterranean, laying the foundation for a restored Roman Empire, rescuing the Italian nation from its plight as a proletarian nation held down by satiated, plutocratic decadent races such as England and France, flashed again across the sky when on the eve of the Great War Italy embarked upon the conquest of Libya. Flamboyant rhetoric broke all restraints and modesty.[97] The adventure appeared all the more pathetic when it began to look like a failure. The Italians occupied barely the coast. Inside, the Arabs remained unsubdued. There was no land for European settlement. Most galling of all—Libya's tremendous oil wealth remained undiscovered till after World War II.

There is something jarring in the hymns to force, violence and a relentless Darwinian struggle for survival and power coming from representatives of a militarily unsuccessful nation. D'Annunzio was full of envy for the "German instinct for supremacy" and for the way in which England was "opening its jaws to devour the universe".[98] In his review *Regno*, Corradini bewailed "all the signs of decrepitude sentimentalism, doctrinarism, immoderate respect for fleeting life and for the weak and lowly . . . displayed in the intellectual life of the Italian class which rules and governs".[99] Papini improved upon the prophet of nationalism, mocking the soft-headed bourgeois respect for the sanctity of life. "Human life", he scoffed, "is sacred; the breath of some insignificant creature more precious than an empire; the lives of a few thousand savages of greater import than the power of a nation. Fear of blood has become the incubus of modern men, who are pursued like so many women, little nineteenth-century Lady Macbeths, by the spectre of death . . . the principle of right to life is utterly without justification. The word right is a verbal travesty. I have a right to do something when I *can* do it, when I have the means, the *power* equal to the deed."[100]

"Give me a few men who feel and understand what I wish to do, and with their contagion they will change the moral climate of the country, and the contagion will change the world," reads Papini's quasi-promise of Fascism. "Rome has always had a universal and ruling mission"[101]—he exclaims.

Where will the like-minded men be found? Above all not in the legal government, the legislative chambers, for as Prezzolini put it, there could be no "greater liberation of the fatherland, no greater conquest . . . than the awareness of the evil of parliament".[102] Not from those sickly, weak, opportunist, cynical politicians and lawyers will they come, but from among the real producers . . . those courageous industrialists of Milan, the port workers of Genoa, the agricultural labourers of Romagna and Venetia, the contadini of Puglia.[103]

(V) WAR AS REVOLUTION

The nationalists, at first no more than a literary clique, reluctant to enter political life as a party among parties for fear of losing their distinct character as bearers of a revivalist message unlike any other in Italian public life, eventually organised themselves into a party and on the eve of the Great War gained a modest parliamentary representation.[104]

Among the groups which they discerned as a vital force, convertible to their own way of thinking and methods, were the extreme revolutionary socialists, whom Mussolini, the young socialist Duce—as he was already beginning to be called—represented. Never mind their obsession with class war, with anti-militariam, their anti-patriotism, their vision of a total international revolution. They had the fire, the nerve, the decisiveness, the anti-bourgeois passion, above all the will to conquer, the courageous self-assurance and freedom from inhibiting doubt and they were moved by a sense of mission. They were poised for action, lived as it were on the eve of some great violent breakthrough. The nationalists dreamt of a rebirth through the imperialist deed, above all war; the syndicalists of a revival through the baptism of bloody revolution. War—the nationalists taught—partook of the nature of a revolution. It was therefore war or revolution. Indeed, the syndicalist Angelo Olivero had proclaimed "a people which cannot make war cannot make revolution".[105]

"We are the proletarian people in respect to the rest of the world. Nationalism is our socialism. This established, nationalism must be founded on the truth that Italy is morally and materially a proletarian nation"—read the manifesto published in December 1910 by the just founded Nationalist Association in Florence under the leadership of Corradini, Scipio Sighele, Maurizio Maraviglia, the (sole) anti-semite Francesco Coppola, Federzoni and others.[106]

Discussing the Italian edition of Sorel's *Reflections on Violence*, Corradini elaborated the reasons why in spite of doctrinal differences, nationalism and syndicalism could nevertheless join together. "A doctrine, any doctrine, exists not so much in its programme as in the power of action which its programme can release. . . . This being accepted, we can then imagine a syndicalism which stops at the nation's shores and does not proceed farther, which ceases to operate internationally, but instead works on the national level. The workers unite, no longer on a world-wide basis, but within the confines of the nation. They unite to win power not throughout the world but nationally. If then, this were to happen, the principal point of opposition between the two doctrines would be suppressed."[107]

What mattered was the urge to conquer, expand; in brief the will to power that was common to syndicalists and imperialists. That meant that violence was the method which was assumed by both, in other words direct mass action, which again required maximum cohesion, concentration of forces, iron discipline and utter ruthlessness. It was easy to substitute soldiers for workers, war for mass action, the destruction of the national enemy and the seizure of his patrimony for the capitalist class order. Once more, the will to power on the part of those who felt the urge and the capacity to wield it—this was the decisive factor. Here was an experience, a discovery that was tormenting Europe, a universal doctrine, a token of the "rebirth of the collective values of existence": this "unrelenting will to domination . . . this tragic imperialism of man over nature".[108] The plenitude of this experience put the nationalist imperialists as well as the syndicalists in "strict and absolute opposition to everything which is representative of that Italy of which we disapprove and from which we wish to remove ourselves",[109] an Italy effeminate, soft, pacific, humanitarian, petty-minded, timid, taking refuge in law and order and makeshifts. In short, the two trends represented the spirit of renewal through revolution or war in Italy.

It becomes difficult to decide whether the Italian imperialist nationalists professed a doctrine as an objective truth and an end in itself or were on the look-out for a myth like Sorel, which would stir up, absorb and goad men to become supermen, to transcend their natural mediocre humanity. Pure imperialism, perhaps as more than an instrument to provide for Italy's surplus population and to answer the desire for a place and status among the nations, seemed to offer the necessary myth.

(VI) MUSSOLINI'S SOCIALIST CREED—REVOLUTION AND VIOLENCE

The distinct feature of young Mussolini's Marxism was, still more than with his like-minded contemporaries abroad—Guesde, Rosa Luxemburg, Lenin, Hervé and the radical Dutchmen—revolutionism. Mussolini's very wide reading, his journalist's urge to impart his knowledge to his readers at once, and his propagandist's need to make converts to his ideas, on top of his astonishing impressionability, led him on to touch upon a wide range of questions: inevitably, economic doctrine, such as surplus value, the falling rate of profits, agrarian socialism, and problems which the professional trade union struggle occasions.[110] But he clearly had less stomach and understanding for them than the other revolutionary socialists.

He was a product of the conspiratoral and insurrectionary traditions of his native province, Romagna-Emilia, and the son of his father, who in his youth was active in Bakuninist circles. Benito Mussolini's attention was focused on ways and means to bringing down capitalism by immediate insurrection. Strikes, electoral activities, demonstrations, the struggle for better conditions, were just skirmishes in preparation for the catastrophic confrontation, which would be triggered off by the general strike. Parliamentary idiocy was no way to revolution. It blunted revolutionary energy and fostered illusions about gradual reform. War à l'outrance, a sustained struggle between two mutually exclusive worlds—one conquering, the other doomed—this was the image of socialism which Mussolini had in mind[111] when he spoke of the socialism of his day, of the Latin nations, as taught by Georges Sorel "which offers a much firmer grasp of Marxism than the unrecognisable one which was being imported from Germany:[112] . . . a barbaric socialism".[113]

Like the radicals in other countries, Mussolini believed that in the early twentieth century the myth of the nation-state, had become the mainstay of the bourgeois. It was the task of revolutionary socialists to cut that nerve. Patriotism was an antidote to class war. The so-called national interest was a cover for the interests of the ruling classes. The imperatives of foreign policy, which required armed strength, were the state secrets of the capitalist regime. The myth of the nation-state, with patriotic mystification and militarism as its prop, had to be fought constantly and relentlessly in proportion to the depths of the roots which they had struck in the popular mind. Hence the Hervéist and syndicalist slogan adopted by Mussolini about the national flag as "the rag on a dung heap", his incitement to desertion, his ridicule of the army and its symbols.[114] War was used by the rulers to unite the classes into a single nation and to sow discord among the proletariat of the various nations.

"Those nationalisms were only attempts, diversions by the bourgeoisie to delay the great event which will mark the end of mankind's prehistory by one year, by a single day."[115] In 1910 Mussolini wrote: "Monarchy, Army, War!—these are the three spiritual-ideological lighthouses around which flutter the moths of Italian nationalism—late developers. Three words, three institutions, three nonsenses!"[116] The bourgeoisie wants war, sings hymns to wars, because it fondly believes it will liberate it from socialism.[117] Mussolini never tires of repeating the Marxist commonplace on the fiction that was the idea of fatherland: "there were only two international fatherlands, of the exploiting and of the exploited classes". "Woe unto the reformist socialists to whom it has become a fetish, and a trap." "We admit our heresy. We are unable to grasp patriotic socialism." He knows only "an all-human and universal socialism".[118]

Good Leninist doctrine this was. "If war breaks out, instead of rushing to the frontiers, we will unleash an uprising from within."[119] And as the bourgeoisie was about to escalate colonial war ventures to a world conflagration, "we hope to be ready for it then".[120]

At the time of the Libyan War, Mussolini proclaimed the Arab and Turkish proletarians to be brothers, and the bourgeois Italians enemies of the Italian working classes.[121]

In view of the growing economic, political and cultural inter-dependence of nations, and of growing proletarian internationalism, "the outbreak of a socialist revolution in one country will cause the others to imitate it or so to strengthen the proletariat as to prevent its national bourgeoisie from attempting any armed intervention".[122] In an article published on April 11, 1909, Mussolini depicts the clash between nationalist militarism and socialist internationalism as the very axis of the struggle between bourgeois capitalism and revolutionary socialism. "The cause of economic depression and of general scarcity is to be sought in the foreign policy of the Austrian court and in the wars between the various nationalities in the empire. The vast millions which should have been assigned for the people's welfare, are swallowed up by the army, on the pretext of the need for military preparedness. Militarism! Here is the monstrous leech that is incessantly sucking the blood of the people and its best energy! Here is the target for our attacks! We must put an end to barbarism, proclaim that the army is now a highly organised school of crime and that it exists solely to protect bourgeois capital and profits. We must not be deterred from proclaiming ourselves international socialists. We recognise no borders and no flags, we hate all steel, every institution that exists to kill men, waste energy, strangle the advance of the workers",[123] the chief victims of war, in which they are forced "to shed their blood after having shed their sweat in the factory".[124]

But it was not just a question of preventing or stopping war by a general strike. "War is nearly always the prelude to revolution"[125]— proclaims Mussolini, echoing Lenin, Guesde and Rosa Luxemburg. On June 25, 1909, in a debate in the Camera del Lavoro in Trento, Mussolini fixes priorities for the period of the outbreak of the war: "The socialists will have a single duty: the war on the frontier must become a signal for the general strike, insurrection, a civil war."[126] In late September 1911 Mussolini tried to put this doctrine to the test on the outbreak of the Italian war against Turkey for the conquest of Libya. As secretary of the party at Forli he proclaimed a general strike, which was accompanied by acts of sabotage. It petered out after a few days, and Mussolini landed in prison. After his release in March 1912, it was this episode that enabled him to launch a violent campaign against the reformists in the party, Bissolati and Bonomi, for causing the collapse of the strike, to force them out—and then in November of that year to be elected unanimously editor of the chief party organ *Avanti*, with a seat on the central committee.[127] Not so long ago an obscure starving vagabond, an army deserter, and a storming socialist agitator with a schoolmaster's diploma, busy among Italian workers in Switzerland, young Mussolini was now well on the way to becoming the undisputed leader of the Italian Socialist party.[128]

It could be said that the mark of adherence to Marxist socialism was, notwithstanding the voluntarist and even heroic accents in Marx and Engels, the emphasis on inevitable developments; and that therefore the greater the stress on subjective behaviour, the further from genuine Marxism.[129] The dichotomy looms large in Lenin, in his theory of (the revolutionary) vanguard and in his uncompromising verdict upon reformist leadership in the West and upon non-Bolshevik Russian socialism—opportunists,   time-servers,   in   the   final   analysis liquidators—all of them petty-bourgeois in spirit. The qualities of heroism, self-sacrifice, audacity are terms singled out by Lenin for authentic proletarian fighters. But he would never go so far as to claim that these could or should be manipulated from outside.

The famous Red Week, which began in June 1914 just on the eve of the Sarajevo crisis and snowballed into a general strike all over Italy—as indeed the first general political strike in history—looked, to Mussolini, who played a decisive part in it, "almost a revolution".[130] In an article in his theoretical journal *Utopia* Mussolini all the same called the events inevitable. Why? Because there was too much electricity in the air. He ascribes this accumulation not to natural conditions, but to a revolutionary state of mind, the desire and the expectation of seeing something new; and, in distinct Sorelian language, "this ardent expectation—quasi-mystical—felt by Young on his travels in France on the eve of the Revolution".[131]

On July 22, 1913, Mussolini spoke in Milan: "This proletariat wants a blood bath."[132] A year later, on June 12, 1914, à propos the Red Week, he wrote in *Avanti*: "We record these events with some of that justifiable joy which an artist feels when he contemplates his creation. If the Italian proletariat is in the act of acquiring a new mentality, freer and wider than of old, this is due to our newspaper."[133] This is hardly the language that Lenin would use. It is already the language of the future Duce.

The reformist socialist, Bonomi, whom Mussolini had forced out of the party, describes Mussolini in June 1914: "Nothing matters to him now except to win. What matters is to triumph over timidity, fear and prudence which impede and arrest the revolutionary advance of the proletariat."[134] Dynamic activism becomes a goal and the highest criterion.

Mussolini's heroic tone, his contempt for bourgeois decadence, his faith in the reinvigorating effect of proletarian pugnacity, his glorification of sacrifice, even of bloodshed as the fertiliser of heroic progress, the call for military discipline in the conquering army of socialism, his vision of the expanding personality and of enhanced life, after the revolution and classless society has given the lie to ascetic Christianity and revealed the hollow hypocrisy of a puritanism preached by avaricious capitalism—all these Nietzschean accents could, as Nolte argues,[135] have been partly reconciled with Marx and Lenin, so long as the sublime heroism of the superman of the future—constantly tested and hardened in struggle—was not made into an end in itself, and history was not represented as an eternal combat between the Roman ideal of *imperium* and the Judean morality of priests and slaves, the ethics of self-denial and of hatred of life.

Mussolini crosses the Rubicon to reach Fascism, and even racism, when he abandons the concept of humanity, even though it be identified with and reduced to the proletariat on the way to universal redemption, and espouses the vision of eternal war between masters and slaves, the hard and the soft, the warlike and the sheep-like, the dynamic elite and the inert static majority.[136]

In an essay, "Finis Europa?", on the danger of a new barbarian invasion of Europe from Asia, Mussolini writes in reference to the widespread dread of decadence: "So let there be conquest, destruction and renovation. Just as the confrontation between the barbarians and the Roman Empire did not prove a danger to the species, so it is probable that the clash between continents, which will elevate the race through the annihilation of the weak, will prove beneficial for the future development of the plant man [a favourite Nietzschean term]."[137]

(*VII*) THE BREAK WITH INTERNATIONALISM

In the first week of August 1914 Mussolini was left without a cause and without a programme. In the light of the choice made by the working classes in all belligerent countries, the doctrine of resisting war by a general strike, turning it into an insurrection which was then to escalate into an international civil war and ultimately world revolution, now sounded quite hollow. Quite soon Mussolini admitted that a general strike was possible only if it broke out simultaneously in all the belligerent countries. Otherwise, as Guesde taught, the most revolutionary proletariat would have to pay a dire price, and indeed fail.[138] There was no strike in any country. The only important country which was not swept off its feet into war was Italy. Although like most

Italians, and above all the Socialist party, Mussolini at first took Italian neutrality for granted, many Italians felt that it was a singularly unheroic role. As the war proceeded and assumed the dimensions of a colossal combat and unprecedented tragedy, a man like Mussolini could not but realise the force of a mystique which drove millions to make the supreme sacrifice and others to bear untold suffering. Such an upheaval was surely pregnant with vast changes and revolutionary potentialities. At the end of the war nothing would ever be the same again. A new world would arise. It was demeaning to a great country, with the tradition of Risorgimento, and for men professing a dynamic view of history, to stand aside and be content with being onlookers. Moreover, everyone was conscious that secret negotiations were going on with both belligerent coalitions and that Italy was hawking about her entry into the war, determined to sell herself to the highest bidder.

Even if, after having taken the plunge, Mussolini did accept money from interested sources, there is every indication that it was not bribery that decided him, and that there was infinite hesitation, vacillation and pain behind his *volte face* in favour of joining the Entente.[139] Apart from his inability to be an onlooker, Mussolini, like many Italians, was conscious that if Italy stayed out of the war to the end, it would forfeit any chance of having a say in the postwar international settlement. If the Central Powers won, Austria would undoubtedly be in the strongest possible position to refuse Italy any territorial concessions out of her own possessions, in Trentino, Trieste or Dalmatia, especially to an Italy which had deserted the Austro-German alliance. It was possible to extort from France and England no end of promises at somebody else's expense: in Europe, Asia Minor and Africa. The war effort was also sure to precipitate an industrial revolution in Italy, to stimulate modernisation and democratisation, as total war did everywhere.[140]

Was Mussolini still feeling like an internationalist at that juncture? As we shall see, he had by then shed all illusions about international revolutionary solidarity, but he had not yet evolved into a chauvinist and believer in *egoismo sacro*. Like many radical democrats and socialists, Mussolini was convinced that a German victory would throw back the general advance towards democracy, socialism and freedom in general, although he was at the same time quite emphatic about not regarding France and England, in spite of their tradition, as spearheads of international democracy, let alone revolutionary socialism.[141]

Mussolini had certainly not yet become a nationalist in the sense in which Corradini was a gut nationalist. In the shipwreck of the great universal hope, the cause of the single nation seemed to be emerging as the most real, and as it were the most innocent, at least in so far as it did not infringe the rights of others. In 1914 Mussolini was still insistent on the need to respect the rights of the Slav neighbours and to avoid creating an *irridenta* in reverse.[142] He was still some way from the religion of nationalism. But the road led through disenchantment with internationalism.

Mussolini's contribution to the theoretical journal *Utopia* in autumn of 1913 already attests a growing crisis of faith. "Militarism"—he writes—"is the incubus of contemporary Europe. Disarmament or international war—this is the tragic dilemma."[143] For reasons of principle as well as tactics socialism was called upon to make the struggle against militarism its main cause: for indeed it was a case of either nationalist militarism or revolutionary socialism. "Socialism will not be strong enough to oppose a violent military coup."[144] By embracing reformism and thereby recognising the primacy of the national community, the Socialist party establishment had become hostages of legality, *ergo* nationalist-militarist policies. They could no longer resort to direct action, and paper resolutions were of no avail. Their theoretical opposition to nationalism was not only politically, but also psychologically and morally undermined. In such circumstances, the endeavour of revolutionary socialists to play the card of anti-militarism in the hope that a general strike would paralyse the belligerent states and lead to civil war, was fraught with heavy risks. If the theoretical conviction and the sentiments behind such a stand were not strong enough, the bourgeoisie might be tempted into starting a war as an opportunity to discredit and strangle revolutionary socialism for many a day.[145] From there Mussolini is led to begin to wonder whether a "modern international socialism" was not an entirely meaningless phrase. There was in fact no single gospel of socialism for all nations. The undisputed hegemony of German Social-Democracy had created an illusion of a general consensus. But who in the SPD really believed in the general strike? "Only Rosa Luxemburg, a Polish Jewess", an outsider and a heretic.[146] The SPD had long ago become an ally of Kaiserdom.

By the end of August 1914 Mussolini's views hardened. In a requiem for the Second International signed by him with his old pen name, "L'homme qui cherche", he writes: "The Socialist International is dead. . . . But has it ever lived? . . . It was an association, not a reality. It had an office in Brussels and published a sophorous bulletin in three languages twice a year. . . . The Trade Union International lived for one year and published a single bi-weekly."[147] Theoretically 6-7 million workers were organised in the International. "How many of them had internationalist convictions? Very few." The bankruptcy of the

International was not only in that it failed to prevent the war, and that the socialists had decided temporarily—because of genuine love of country or for lack of any alternative—to fuse with the nation. Its roots lay in the absence of a common view on the causes of the war and on the question of responsibility for it, which meant—in theory in general.[148]

A violent swing of the pendulum becomes discernible from revulsion against fictitious internationalism to the affirmation of the primary reality of national interest. In answer to the challenge which Libero-Tancredi threw out to Mussolini—"the only man in the leadership of the Socialist party capable of independent thought"—in the conservative *Resto del Carlino*[149] Mussolini writes on October 8, 1914, that he cannot bring himself to join in the superficial exaltation of the tripartite war effort as a revolutionary, democratic or socialist war.[150] As to the rationale of Italian intervention, the question should be examined from a purely and simply national point of view. And what is the purely national point of view? The challenge and opportunity for Italy to behave like a great power.[151]

A few days later, Mussolini reiterates his preference for national considerations over instinctive, sentimental or ideological sympathy for the country of the French Revolution.[152] But, he adds significantly, that preference does not exclude the national point of view as being "the proletarian one".[153] Here we have a hint of the future adoption by Mussolini of the theory of Italy as a proletarian nation. In Mussolini's pronouncements following the break with the party we can watch an awakening to the enormity of ignoring, as the Leftist socialists had done, the intense reality of the national sentiment, the imperative of the defence of the fatherland. Could one condemn the French and Belgian socialists for having in an hour of supreme national emergency merged with or subordinated their class consciousness to national solidarity? "If so, then there was in the world only one original, true and pure type of socialism: Italian socialism"—a piece of *hubris* Mussolini emphatically rejects.[154]

"The root of our psychological weakness was this: We socialists have never examined the problems of nations. The International was never concerned with it. The International is dead, paralysed by events. Ten million proletarians are today on the battlefield."[155]

The leading party in the International, the SPD, did nothing to stop the war. It was not merely indifferent to the national problem. It felt drawn to reformism, consequently nationalism and imperialism ("a dangerous theory").[156] Bebel had proclaimed: "we are Germans first, and socialists afterwards". The SPD never found a "basis for a compromise between the nation, which was a historic reality and the class, which was a living reality".

Human progress had not yet skipped the stage of nations. Look at Austria, which was to serve as laboratory for the first experience in internationalism. "The experiment failed completely because of the national question. The national sentiment exists, it is impossible to ignore it! The old anti-patriotism has been eclipsed . . . To proclaim, like Turati, the duty to defend a fatherland under attack means admission of the need for militarism."[157]

And so power and force impose themselves as supreme categories. It was no accident that Mussolini provided mottoes for his new journal *Il Popolo d'Italia*: from Blanqui "Qui a du fer a du pain", and from Napoleon, "Revolution is an idea armed with bayonets."

In this spirit Mussolini writes that "the war will reveal Italy to the Italians. It will above all wipe out the base legend that the Italians are no fighters. It will wipe out the shame of Lissa and Custozza. It will prove to the whole world that Italy is capable of making war, a great war, we repeat—a Great War."[158]

(*VIII*) THE SEARCH FOR A MISSION—FROM SOCIAL MESSIANISM TO IMPERIALISM

"If the revolution of 1789, which was both a revolution and a war"— proclaimed Mussolini—"opened up the world to the bourgeoisie after its long and secular novitiate, the present revolution which is also a war, seems to open up the future to the masses and their novitiate of blood and death in the trenches. . . . May 1915 was the first episode of the revolution, its beginning. The revolution continued, under the name of war, for forty months. It is not yet over. It may or may not follow this dramatic and striking course. Its tempo may be quick or slow. But it goes on. . . . As to methods, we have no prejudices; we accept whatever becomes necessary, whether legal or so-called illegal. A new historic epoch is beginning, an epoch of mass politics and democratic inflation. We cannot stand in the way of this movement. We must guide it towards political and economic democracy."[159]

Revolutionary messianism had also affected conservatives. On November 20, 1918, Orlando called the war "the greatest social-political revolution recorded by history, surpassing even the French Revolution".[160] Salandra opined: "Yes, the war is a revolution, a great, a very great revolution. It is the hour of youth. Let no one think that a peaceful return to the past will be possible after this storm."[161]

All parties in Italy were speaking of the necessity of convening a constituent assembly.

At the end of 1921 it looked for a brief moment as though a left-wing coalition pledged to put an end to Fascist violence might emerge. Mussolini sensed danger. "To-morrow"—he declared—"Fascists and communists, both persecuted by the police, may arrive at an agreement, sinking their differences until the time comes to share the spoils. I realise that though there are no political affinities between us, there are plenty of intellectual affinities. Like them, we believe in the necessity for a centralised and unitary state, imposing an iron discipline on everyone, but with the difference that they reach this conclusion through the idea of class, we through the idea of the nation."[162]

On the morrow of the armistice of 1918, Mussolini spoke the language of messianic revolution. The proletarian masses had arrived on the wings of a war which was also a revolution, as the French Revolution had done.[163] The author and beneficiary of the present revolution did not make the revolution by resisting war or turning it into civil war, but by riding the war in the direction of revolution. The national war was still presented by Mussolini in class terms as far as its nature and goal were concerned.

"The war has brought the proletarian masses to the fore. It has broken their chains and freed their courage. The people's war ends with the triumph of the people".[164] . . . In fact, the future of Italy was seen as part of an international movement: the fall of the four empires, the emergence of new states, the reshaping of some old ones, the Bolshevik revolution and revolutionary transformations in a number of other countries—all these national developments required the formulation of new social contracts.

If as late as the end of 1918 it was primarily a social revolution that Mussolini had in mind, albeit confined to a single nation, how did it happen that nationalism eventually got the upper hand in the struggle for the soul of the Italian people? At the bottom of this development was the sense of disappointment and humiliation throughout the Italian nation, when—as they believed—they were cheated out of the fruits of victory and deprived of the reward for suffering. "This sense of injustice and loss was cold-bloodedly exploited to a pitch of frenzy by Mussolini and was perhaps the most important of the psychological factors", writes A. Rossi in his admirable *Rise of Italian Fascism, 1918-1922,* "contributing to the success of Fascism . . . in wounded national feelings the most efficacious method of clinging to power and carrying on the struggle against the democratic revolution".[165]

The image of an injured proletarian nation straining to regain its rightful place became Mussolini's answer to the doctrine of socialist revolution. It came to constitute the axis of the totalitarianism of the Right, the source of its dialectic and the justification of all its bewildering opportunism—a similar role to that played by revolutionary strategy in the service of communism.

The original programme adopted by the founding conference of the Fasci in the Piazza San Sepolcro in Milan on March 23, 1919, contains all possible democratic whitewash—universal suffrage with proportional representation and votes for women; abolition of the Senate; a constituent assembly; national technical councils à la Kurt Eisner in Bavaria; an eight-hour day; a minimum wage; participation of workers in the management of industry—compulsory retirement at fifty-five; replacement of the regular army by a militia, with short periods of training; nationalisation of arms and munition factories; far-reaching progressive taxation, including an extraordinary levy on capital amounting to a partial expropriation of all wealth; an 85 per cent levy on wartime profits; acceptance of the League of Nations principles; rejection of imperialism; and reaffirmation of the integrity of every nation.[166]

The clauses formulating a democratic foreign policy are however immediately negated not only by the insistence that the principle would be realised in the case of Italy "in the Alps and the Adriatic through her claim for Fiume (ethnically Italian, but not accorded to Italy at the London Treaty of 1915) and Dalmatia"[167] (conceded, but overwhelmingly non-Italian in its ethnic composition), which would have meant annexing very large non-Italian populations. They are totally incompatible with the ringing declaration by Mussolini, added to the programme:

"We have a population of forty millions in an area of 287.000 square kilometres, bisected by the Apennines, which reduce still further the cultivable land at our disposal. In six to twenty years we shall be sixty millions, and we have only a million and a half square kilometres of colonies, of which the greater part is desert and quite unsuitable for settling our excess populations. But if we look round we find England, with a population of 47,000,000 and a colonial empire of 55,000,000 kilometres; and France with a population of 38,000,000, has an empire of 15,000,000 kilometres. And I have figures to prove that every nation in the world has a colonial empire, which it is far from ready to give up. . . . Imperialism is the basis of life for any nation seeking economic and spiritual expansion. We say that either everyone must become an idealist or no one. Let us seek our own interests. We want our place in the world, because we have a right to it. Let us be frank: the League must not become a trap set for the proletarian nations by the wealthy as a means of perpetuating the present conditions of the world balance of power."[168]

Thus conservative and Right-wing premises become the point of departure for revolutionary or, if one prefers, counter-revolutionary attitudes. The historic, impersonal, objective, all-determining datum of the nation-state and the acceptance of the postulate of an international order—the League of Nations—give place to a revisionist stance which rebels against the existing law of nations as codified in the status quo and in international covenants. It denies the legitimacy of the existing international order, and implicitly invokes the revolutionary right of resistance to oppression and injustice, just as the French and Bolshevik revolutions did. Only this is done in order to justify imperialism as the manifest national destiny of Italy. We shall see that simultaneously and as a condition for imperialism, or as a corollary of it, totalitarianism is proclaimed as a revolutionary (counter-revolutionary) negation of individualism, liberalism, democracy and socialism—as their grave-digger and successor.

(*IX*) "THE DOCTRINE OF FASCISM" [169]

The famous "Doctrine of Fascism" composed by the Duce of Fascist Italy in 1932 as the ripe fruit of Fascist self-knowledge begins with Mazzini's arguments; it could also be said with Hegelian categories—no doubt Gentile's contribution—as adapted by the prophet of the Risorgimento to the circumstances of Italy. This Mazzinian-Hegelian introduction is then grafted upon ideas which hail from a very different universe. The author was clearly writing with an eye to classes in political philosophy and history seminars. He was anxious to display the comprehensiveness of his grasp, and the profundity of his message, and to claim for it at one and the same time both revolutionary novelty, and respectability. All in all, Mussolini's most potent motive force was the unremitting need (also characteristic of that other world-saviour and usurper, Napoleon) to prove himself *stupor mundi*. The artistry of this was of course much more important than its accuracy.

The nation was the primary datum. The nation was not the fruit of a social contract between individuals, an ever-renewed plebiscite. It was not the sum total of its components. It was a superior, super-personal reality, but not in the biological sense. It was a moral law, a tradition, a mission binding together generations past, present and future, and all the individuals in so far as they had succeeded in tearing themselves away from the limitations of the present and of their immediate private contingencies and interests.

The individual was expected to make himself into an instrument, a means. His life was duty, dedication, service, sacrifice. This view of nationhood and of the individual in relation to it was an ethical conception which covered the whole of reality. Life therefore, as conceived by the Fascist, "is serious, austere, religious":[170] a Mazzinian religious calling.

Mussolini contrasted this with the individualistic abstractions of the eighteenth century, such as individual rights, liberty of choice, personal good, the materialistic ideas of happiness, as well as with the utopias and innovations designed to secure individual and general well-being in some final state of harmony and bliss. The rights and liberties of the individual were realised in the dignity of service to the national cause, in other words to the state, in man's ability to identify himself with the institutionalised rational liberty which the state embodied and enforced. "If liberty is to be the attribute of the real man, and not of that abstract puppet envisaged by individualistic liberalism, Fascism is for liberty."[171] Everything was contained and shaped by the state; nothing that could be called human or spiritual was outside the nation-state. "In this sense Fascism is totalitarianism, and the Fascist state, the synthesis of unity of all values, interprets, develops and gives strength to the whole life of the people."[172] It was not just a nightwatchman or guarantor of civil peace, as the liberal state was.

The mission and tradition, the supreme law and the historic general will of the generations were not a collection of elusive flabby sentiments and noble intentions. They were upheld by a compact code of behaviour enforced by the state. The emphasis was upon the fountainhead of organised power and not upon natural evolution, that is upon the state and not upon its people.

"It is not the nation that generates the state . . . rather the nation is created by the state, which gives to the people, conscious of its own moral unity, a will, and therefore an effective existence."[173] As we have said, the Italians had never been a unitary state and Italy had for centuries been dismembered, dominated by foreigners, made to serve alien causes, while nursing a variety of discordant traditions. The Italian nation could therefore hardly be regarded as a repository of a tradition, the bearer of a mission, and upholder of a general will. The state of Italy born in 1861 was certainly still too young, too weak, too unsure of its identity and destiny and too pathetically ineffective on the international stage for that. Where could Mussolini discover the general will, the tradition, the peculiar national principle of existence? While abjuring his former phobias and rather grudgingly conceding religion and the monarchy a place in the national pantheon, he is unambiguous about rejecting de Maistre's ideas on the Pope as the supreme sanction, and of any royalist mystique. As we have already observed, Italy had no political class to fall back on as the repository of a historic tradition, a national will, the knowledge of how to govern, like the Prussian Junkers and bureaucracy. Mussolini curtly dismisses any nostalgia for the pre-1789 hereditary castes. The French Revolution had made that impossible. What then remained, apart from the nation, the sovereign people? But this was not Mussolini's stand.

"The state . . . is not to be thought of numerically as the sum total of individuals forming the majority of the nation." Fascism would not equate the nation with the majority, "lowering it to the level of that majority".[174] "Fascism is opposed to democracy of numbers." It was searching not for the approval of the many or of the majority, but for the certainty of discerning and willing the general will: "the most powerful idea (most powerful because most moral, most coherent, most true) which acts in the nation as the conscience and the will", even though only a few people know it, even only one ("Mussolini is always right"— the Tenth Commandment of the Fascist Decalogue).[175]

Neither race nor territory were decisive for the formation of that conscience and will, but "the will to existence and to power: consciousness of itself and personality". "The purest form of democracy" emerged when the nation was "conceived . . . qualitatively and not quantitatively . . . as it should be"; not in just being, but in realising its distinct ethos and destiny.[176]

The Fascist Italian state came into being precisely so, as "we pushed the country into the war and we led it to victory".[177] It was not born as a fully-fledged doctrine but as a fighting elite. From the ideological point of view it was at first only "a series of suggestions, of anticipations, of admonitions".[178] If it had an adversary, it was that socialism which was guilty of opposition to the war, of facile, irresponsible slogans, as well as of a technical and spiritual regression,[179] and of course of class selfishness. At the same time Fascism had never intended to be a "lightning conductor" for the bourgeoisie. It was born out of the need for action, as "a movement against all parties".[180] Fascism evolved as a national doctrine in the process of combating "liberal, democratic, socialist . . . demagogic doctrines".[181] It came into shape and consciousness as a confraternity, an organisation of its own, as a master elite. While the battle was raging—in punitive expeditions[182] against labour strongholds, chambers of Labour, municipalities, headquarters—armed commandos consisting of war veterans were absorbed into the older and wiser part of the nation. Thus they became the bearers of the nation's general will and conscience, its mentors and the trustees of its destiny.

Here indeed was a moral phenomenon, foreshadowed in the spheres of thought and propaganda, but not in action, by the extreme monarchist-nationalist Action Française. A minority group that in principle glorified the values of law, order, tradition, social cohesion and national solidarity assumed the right to rebel against a legitimate, democratically elected government, condemning it as inept and—worse still—disloyal to those categorical imperatives of the nation's history which the elitist vanguard pretended to embody. The message of a restorative revolution was preached in the form of a curious perversion of the right to resist oppression, a licence for anarchy in order to impose a regime of authority and obedience. A page seems to have been taken out of the book of the predetermined social revolution, which invoked the right to overthrow the existing order in the name of a universal social revolution.

The first test of the successful revolutionary coup from the Right in Italy was the *coup d'état* of May 1915. A conspiracy of the King and his leading ministers, and demonstrators of various descriptions, nationalists, revolutionary syndicalists, big business and excited literati, imposed their will by direct action on a pacificist parliamentary majority, and indeed most Italians, and forced them to enter the Great War, without the clauses of the Protocol of London—the conditions for Italian intervention—having been made known (this was not done until 1920). The second instalment was D'Annunzio's operatic dictatorship in Fiume. It was the curtain-raiser to graver things. A motley collection of regular soldiers, idealists, freebooters, adventurers and bohemians took the law into their own hands, acting in opposition to their lawful government and the expressed will of the community of nations—all in the name of an allegiance due to a higher dispensation: the categorical imperative of national destiny. They improvised a kind of revolutionary-collectivist utopia, inspired by the exclusive, true general will of the nation: they unfolded a new style of politics—a mixture of patriotic cult, civil religion and artistic licence. This sustained act of rebellion was supported and glorified by large parts of the Italian nation on the ground that although anarchical, rowdy, eccentric and dangerous as a precedent, the Fiume fighters and rebels deserved respectful, indeed awed sympathy, since the motives behind the movement were patriotic, something like a response to the challenge of *"patrie en danger, sauve qui peut"* and an act of defiance in face of an international conspiracy against them.

(X) THE INADEQUACIES OF DEMOCRACY
AND FAILURES OF SOCIALISM

The inadequacies and failings of the democratic regime, the vagaries and makeshifts of its short-lived majorities, the inept handling of the grave problems of a shaky national economy in transition from a crippling war through the uncertainties of a period of readjustment to peace, above all the cowardly inability to stand up to bullying foreign powers—all these appeared to offer legitimacy to rebellion. If Fascism indeed put an end to liberal democracy in Italy, it is no less true to say that a ramshackle parliamentary regime in a state of dissolution invited a Fascist coup.

It was not difficult for nationalist veterans of the war to make out a plausible case for laying most of the responsibility for the dysfunction of the social system on the socialist unions, who had imposed their tyrannical will upon producers and encouraged the sabotage of the national economy. They had not rallied to the war effort, and their propaganda denied the justice of Italy's case. They were in the forefront of those who strove to insult war veterans, especially officers, who had shed their blood for their country, and debar them from influence on the country's future.[183]

Yet the Italian Socialist party, with its impressive gains in the 1919 election, was the only political force that could offer an answer to the messianic longings of the masses. It seemed to be the sole and natural alternative to the existing regime. It was the only socialist party outside Russia to have remained untainted with responsibility for and participation in the war.

Like German Social-Democracy, the highly organised Italian party, with its Chambers of Labour, agrarian associations, co-operatives and labour-dominated municipalities, constituted a state within the state. At the end of the Great War both parties were called upon to carry out a democratic revolution in their respective countries. The SPD set out to fulfil the mission, but faltered and succumbed to totalitarian Nazism just over a dozen years later. The Italian party did not even attempt to put itself at the head of the democratic forces and play the part of the Third Estate of 1789, that of the national party of the hour. A profoundly reformist party, the Italian socialists lacked both the appetite for power and the messianic sense of mission. This was true for all the three branches into which it split after the war: the reformists, maximalists and the communists. For all of them doctrinal commitment was a rationalisation of the failure to seize the initiative. Turati, Treves, Modigliani and their friends would counter the advances of the old liberal wizard Giolitti by repeating that the party was unwilling to help the bourgeoisie which had plunged Italy into war. The maximalists, like the German USPD, found it difficult to steer a course between the mystique of revolution and respect for parliamentary forms. Nor could it bring itself to overcome comradely scruples and expel tried veterans at Moscow's command. It was still less inclined to enter the arena along-side bourgeois parties and make alliances and compromises in order to achieve attainable goals. The maximalists firmly believed in the principle of the worse the better. Practical steps to topple the reactionary mass of the bourgeois parties had to wait for the vaguely defined revolutionary situation out of which the proper instruments of action would emerge—the workers' and peasants' councils.

Such revolutioary noises as they dared to make, the Soviet-like rhetoric, the closed-shop methods of intimidation, practised especially by the agrarian associations in the Po valley, the waves of strikes, above all the seizure of factories by the workers, finally the lamentable general strike proclaimed a little while before the march on Rome, were not enough to inspire fear, but sufficient to cause exasperation. The steps taken by labour did not look like measures resorted to by a determined and irresistible force, but like a compulsive going through the motions. They fed a resolve among victims and opponents to do away with a squalid and demoralising nuisance. It gave the opportunity to Mussolini's *squadristi* to step in as defenders of law and order, and the country's economy, especially as the government seemed to be impotent. Moreover many of its functionaries and parts of the armed forces and the police showed an active sympathy with the self-appointed defenders of the country's national interests and of the liberties of citizens threatened by the monopolistic power of strongly entrenched and well organised socialist forces.[184]

(X) IMPERIUM

Fascism presented itself not only as an alternative, but also as the heir to socialism. The original revolutionary dynamism of socialism was inspired by a universal creed poised to achieve an international revolu-tionary breakthrough. Once it succumbed to reformism, its inter-nationalism changed from a militant crusade designed to change the world into simple bourgeois pacifism to be blown to the winds when emotional, idealistic and practical movements storm the hearts of peoples. Its brand of historical materialism then reduced the idea of happiness to the prospect of economic prosperity, in Mussolini's words—"degraded in consequence to a merely physical existence . . . that of being well-fed and fat".[185] Far-sighted Social-Democrats like Bebel and Guesde had often expressed their apprehension that reformism might drive the more ardent elements in the labour movement into the arms of a Caesarism and Bonapartism—their word for Fascism.

The revolutionary dynamism which the radical elements, above all the revolutionary syndicalists, were unwilling and unable to give up, found an outlet in the mystique of a national war. Fascism believed "neither in the possibility nor in the utility of perpetual peace . . . renunciation of the struggle", seeing in them "an act of cowardice in the face of sacrifice".[186] War was necessary for stretching man to the utmost limit. The tension and risks of war brought out the noblest qualities. Fascism "is education for combat, the acceptance of risks in life as duty, ascent, conquest . . . noble and full . . . [involving] educational severities . . . differentiations and distances".[187]

By glorifying war as the expression of sublime living and heroism, Fascism anchored itself to the values of authority, discipline, hierarchy and obedience. It "attacks the whole complex of democratic ideologies",[188] the idea of human equality, the rule of the majority, government by periodic consultation, universal suffrage, which was a cover for the rule of irresponsibility and secret forces. "But if democracy can be understood in other ways, that is, if democracy means not relegating the people to the periphery of the state", then Fascism could be defined as an "organised, centralised, authoritarian democracy".[189] In other words, if it was properly organised by placing every man in his right place, and by drawing out the best in him, and if all parts of the nation were mobilised and activised as intended by "Nationalism, Futurism, Fascism",[190] the twentieth century could be turned into a century of authority . . . of collectivism and of the state, as the nineteenth had been of "socialism, liberalism and democracy . . . of the individual".[191] "Fascism is not reactionary, but revolutionary."[192] Its aim was not to establish a police state of tutelage, restriction and coercion for their own sake in the manner of pre-1789 absolutism. Fascism was totalitarian, as it strove to make citizens imbibe fully the essence and the values of the state, "founded on millions of individuals who recognise it, feel it, and are ready to serve it".[193] In the Fascist state, the individual "is not suppressed, but rather multiplied"[193] like a soldier in a regiment. Individuals and groups in it were thinkable and real only in so far as they existed within the state, within "the immanent conscience of the nation".[194] They had no existence outside them as abstract atoms. The Fascist state limited the useless and harmful liberties, but preserved those that were essential. But "it cannot be the individual who decides this matter, only the state".[195]

The Fascist state is exalted not only as the guarantor of internal and external security, discipline and purposefulness, but also as the guardian and the transmitter of the spirit of the people throughout ages past, present and future, and primarily as the conscience of the nation. The contents of the state's message remain however singularly elusive. Ultimately, it boils down to the will to power, to the Roman tradition which is "an idea that has force",[196] "a will to power and to government (imperium)",[197] to the tendency to expand, spread and deploy vitality, in contrast to the liberal-bourgeois decadent wish to stay at home.

The Fascist doctrine of empire is presented by Mussolini not as merely a territorial, military or mercantile enterprise, but above all as a spiritual or moral phenomenon. He invokes the myth of the Roman Empire. It is not however the mission to unify nations and tribes into a single humanity of equal citizens, with no regard for race, religion and history, all equally inspired by and realising the universal natural law. What is envisaged is the repeated exercise of imposing government through a disciplined and sustained collective effort. Its purpose was to enhance the quality of a people rising again after many centuries of neglect or enslavement and thirsting for a plce in the sun. It was to answer the imperial urge which throbbed in the hearts of all dynamic nations. This called for "discipline, co-ordination, duty and sacrifice", and for the severity towards those who opposed those "great experiments of political and social transformation . . . the peoples thirst for authority . . . for leadership, for order . . . for a faith".[198]

We thus find the imperial idea—carried beyond the nation's boundaries—projecting political and organisational patterns back into the internal arena: a mobilised nation geared for the deployment of vitality and power was to be led by a new kind of nobility, men endowed not with ancestry, wealth, education or even intellectual conviction, but with the unfathomable gifts of dynamic leadership. This urge for leadership and power became wholly unscrupulous. The struggle lasted as long as the state of mobilisation and emergency of the imperial endeavour required it.

Part IX

THE GERMAN REVOLUTION OF 1918 AND
HITLER IN THE WINGS

Chapter One

THE DILEMMAS OF THE GERMAN REVOLUTION OF 1918

(*a*) A RESENTFUL NATION

After the surrender of 1918 and the Treaty of Versailles, Germany was filled with resentment. To a generation which had been brought up to consider the country's military might invincible, and had this belief confirmed by the way in which the Reichswehr had stood alone against the world for more than four years, the defeat appeared undeserved and unnatural; not really a failure, but the result of having been tricked by a cunning adversary into an armistice on false pretences—Wilson's Fourteen Points, promises of general disarmament, the right to national self-determination; the result of a stab in the back by a malevolent internal foe. Those who had not identified themselves with the old regime vented their frustrations upon the vanquished establishment, charging it with incompetence, *hubris*, class interest and conservatism.

Yet even those who looked for guilty men in yesterday's system and traditional elite were by no means prepared to recognise the Treaty of Versailles as an arrangement entered upon by free parties, or as a just retribution.

The first chancellor of the republic, the Social-Democratic leader Scheidemann, who on November 9 had taken it upon himself to proclaim the republic from the steps of the Reichstag, cursed the hand which would sign the shameful *Diktat* and not wither. He preferred resignation to putting his own name to the treaty.[1] It proved very difficult to find men willing to make the journey to Versailles to accept on behalf of Germany what they regarded as a shameful and suicidal act of surrender.[2]

In the last analysis, almost all parties regarded the Treaty of Versailles as illegitimate, not morally binding. Its obligations were to be evaded and circumvented wherever and whenever possible. In the eyes of men bearing responsibility for running the government, compliance with this or that restrictive condition was permissible only in order to blunt the edge of some other prohibition or imposition or in order to

507

make the victors feel benevolent and trusting.[3] Those few and ineffective men who went so far as to advocate complying with the treaty, did so only out of anxiety not to disturb the slow and gradual emergence of a peaceful system of international relations in which a cooperative Germany would be granted her rightful place and the chance of recouping her worst losses. Some dreaded another world catastrophe, of which the Germans would be the first victims.

The universal mood of resentment shaped the various attitudes to the revolutionary change of regime. When the two war-lords Hindenburg and Ludendorff first voiced to wholly unprepared and unreceptive civilian leaders the urgent need to obtain a cessation of hostilities (and then adopted their highly ambiguous attitude) their immediate concern was to enable the Reichswehr to return home from the conquered foreign territories in full military order as a functioning entity.[4] In the current emergency the army was to serve as the symbol and instrument of the Reich's survival in face of social disintegration and revolution. These considerations also determined the generals' consent to the introduction of a democratic parliamentary regime and the abolition of the monarchy, and conditioned their willingness to cooperate with the rulers of a German republic. Just as, after France's disaster of 1870, Thiers considered that a conservative republic would divide the French least and would bring about political and social stabilisation more speedily than any other alternative, so the defeated rulers of the Second Reich regarded an SPD-dominated government as in the circumstances the most promising hope for moderation.

(*b*) A PROBLEMATIC DEMOCRACY

The German revolution was not the predestined dénouement of a historic dialectic, the victory of a mature revolutionary class rising to inherit the earth and fashion the national community in its own image. It was, rather, an accident, the by-product of a national disaster. In a sense it was the condition for remaining afloat, since the victors would not treat with the Emperor and the Prussian militarists. If the republic could be tolerated, even by those who did not believe in it, as a means of rescuing the German state from the wreckage, it could in different circumstances be made responsible for Germany's defeat and disgrace.

The Social-Democratic party was the obvious alternative to the old ruling caste. Circumstances forced it to become its heir too. The role of the SPD as the temporary keeper of Germany's destiny was however bedevilled by heavy ambiguities. German social-democracy appeared to be confronted by these alternatives: to carry out the socialist programme on the ruins of a bankrupt feudal-absolutist regime and as part of the post-war international revolutionary wave, or to rescue the ship in distress that was the German nation and steer it to harbour, where the process of recuperation would begin. The choice was never in any doubt. It was a question of a revolutionary dictatorship of the pro- letariat, based on the Soviet councils of workers, peasants and soldiers, versus a parliamentary regime with a national assembly chosen by all and sundry citizens of Germany and vested with the powers and duties of a constituent assembly. The provisional revolutionary coalition government, known as the Council of Peoples Representatives, and composed of three representatives of the SPD and three USPD leaders, came into being on the revolutionary wave initiated by the Kiel sailors who refused to sail out onto the high seas for a suicidal encounter with the British Navy, and by the network of councils that emerged spon- taneously all over Germany, and the Kurt Eisner revolution in Munich.[5] It was on the face of it a popular revolutionary creation, which took over power on behalf of the insurgent masses. But it was also intended as a brake upon the anarchical potentialities of a radicalised leaderless mass movement. In addition to its revolutionary legitimacy, it also became a national government carrying on constitutional legality and continuity, when the last Chancellor of the Empire, Prince Max von Baden, handed over the seals of office to Friedrich Ebert, to the accompaniment of a pathetic exchange: the prince impressing upon the ex-saddler that the fate of Germany now depended on his conscience, and the SPD leader promising the liberal prince that having lost two sons in the father- land's war, he would know how to discharge the trust.[6] Moreover, Ebert made no secret of the fact that he hated revolution like sin.[7] No less decisive was the resolution of the Berlin councils to endorse the government's decision to hold elections to a National Assembly, and subsequently to disband and to leave the state legislature and the executive emanating from it alone in the field.[8] Thus the potential leaders of the international revolution in Germany abdicated in favour of the principle of historic continuity and pluralistic nationhood. It was a clear-cut decision.

The success secured by the SPD in the first general election of the Republic should have given it the courage to act as the national party of the Weimar Republic.[9] Instead, the party soon disappeared from the coalition governments for nearly ten years, while supporting them from outside. Nevertheless it has been held by contemporaries, as well as by historians, to be primarily responsible for the republican experiment. It was indeed identified by them with it, although the party was not at the helm of the ship for most of the time, and in the light of the constantly shrinking number of its seats in the Reichstag, was rather the victim of the Republic than its beneficiary.

From the second Reichstag election onwards, the forces of the Right were in almost uninterrupted ascendancy. But this was not the sole cause for the SPD's reluctance to discharge its historic responsibility. The SPD suffered from an inability to commit itself fully to a single cause. It was too national and too patriotic, too scrupulously democratic and too unsure of itself and its title to embark upon a genuinely socialist programme. Neither could it shake off its social-democratic commitments and fall in with the USPD when the latter found it impossible to countenance the suppression of workers' activism.

It was scarcely possible for the mobilised radical revolutionary elements to behave as if the revolution which they believed they had brought about had not happened, or had already come to an end, while the changes effected fell so short of their vision of revolution. Few could have hoped to conquer power by force in the new future. A good many wished to keep up revolutionary unrest in order to provoke the right-wing socialists into more radical action, so as to discredit them when they failed to do so. Most of them rioted, both as propaganda and to keep in practice for the revolutionary opportunity when it occurred, what with private armies parading in the streets, partisans capturing strategic points and activists seizing presses to print their newspapers.[10] Mass meetings of the radical Left erupted into demonstrations, which in turn grew into attempts at a coup. The Social-Democratic government found itself compelled (or thought it least troublesome) to make use of the available Praetorian Guard—the nationalist Freikorps—to subdue left-wing rioting. Once this cooperation was achieved, they were trapped into conniving, gladly or resignedly, at such brutalities as the murders of Rosa Luxemburg and Karl Liebknecht. Somebody had to act the part of the *Bluthund*—Noske defined his own position in the process.[11]

The regime had no roots, lacked prestige, was vulnerable to the accusation of having been born out of a national catastrophe, was devoid of myth and pomp and faced the humiliating and laborious task of obeying the stern dictates of Germany's conquerors. In the circumstances the army's backing was indispensable. Since the restoration of the Kaiser was unthinkable, the army could tolerate a Social-Democratic or a bourgeois republican government, which tried sincerely to preserve a peaceful German state until better days came. To the generals this was a marriage of convenience. Once the army became convinced that the Republic was failing to fulfil its part, the army, which regarded itself as the true trustee of Germany's destiny, would withdraw its support from the regime. In any event, the preservation of the army with its unity and morale intact was more important in the eyes of the generals than the maintenance of republican institutions and prestige. "Our forces will not attack each other", was Seeckt's famous slogan.[11] Ultimately, the Reichswehr alone was to judge whether, when in difficulties from enemies at home, the Republic was or was not able to maintain its position as the guardian of state unity and national sovereignty. In theory, the government of the Republic was bound to assert its sovereign power against a recalcitrant, let alone a mutinous army. But would it have the courage and the strength to act not only without the help of the armed forces, but against them?

(c) RIGHT OR WRONG—MY REVOLUTION

If August 4, 1914, was a searing disappointment to Rosa Luxemburg, the days that followed the victory of the German Revolution were no less traumatic. In the two months of freedom before her assassination she led the existence of a hunted animal, refused accommodation by every hotel, spending every one of her mostly sleepless nights in a different place. Neither she nor Karl Liebknecht was accorded a seat on the Workers' Delegates Council, and at a workers' meeting Liebknecht had the galling experience of being nearly bayoneted by a soldier.[12]

The lack of revolutionary resolve and energy in the masses was shattering to a believer in the instinct of the masses, in mass spontaneity, in free collective self-expression as more genuinely revolutionary than the contrivances of socialist leadership.

Rosa's famous article of 1904 against Leninist ultra-centralism, which in a cryptic way was also aimed at the SPD leadership, has often been cited as the formulation of a democratic—and humane—socialism. She naturally preached the dictatorship of the proletarian class, but deprecated its usurpation by a central committee. This was only to be expected from the great romantic of revolution, enamoured of the vision of both an inexorable, inevitable process, and of the spontaneous eruption of the masses, when they sense a crisis. In her article, "Organisational Questions of Russian Social Democracy", written in 1904 against Lenin's conception of a rigidly centralised party guided by an all powerful central committee, she says: "The unconscious comes before the conscious. The logic of the historic process comes before the subjective logic of human beings who participate in the historic process."[13] With her eyes on German conditions she adds: "The tendency is for the directing organs of the Socialist party to play a conservative role. Experience shows that every time the labour movement wins new ground those organs work it to the utmost. At the same time they transform it into a kind of bastion which holds up advance on a wider scale." Attacking Lenin personally, Rosa says: "Lenin is full of the sterile spirit of the overseer . . . not so much to make the activity of the party more fruitful as to control the party—to narrow the movement rather than to develop it, to bind rather than to unify it."[14]

Viewing the unfolding of the socialist revolution as a process, as a prolonged siege, with assaults and retreats, Rosa regarded the zigzags, trial and error, failures and mistakes as parts of the proletariat's growth to maturity. Unlike Blanquism, social-democracy did not teach the art of staging a coup by a handful of conspirators in conditions of utter secrecy, who admitted the people only after they had won. It reflected the advance of a vast class. "Historically, the errors committed by a revolutionary movement are infinitely more fruitful than the infallibility of the cleverest central committee."[15]

Lenin was afraid of the opportunism, the anarchical individualism, undisciplined spiritual vagabondage of intellectuals, in contrast to the discipline learnt by the workers in the factory. Rosa was against any obedience imposed from above, directly or indirectly, by despotic authority. She glorified the self-discipline of conscious socialists. The Russian phenomenon of opportunism was due not to the absence of a firm guiding central committee, but—she claimed—to the absence of a large compact core of conscious proletarians, which was able to assimilate the historic lessons and re-educate the waverers. Of course an omniscient and omnipotent central committee would, like the parliamentary parties of the West, attract petty-bourgeois intellectuals escaping from a decaying class and hungry for power, influence and a career. In Russia the intellectual joined the party by renouncing his ego. He was impelled by an urge for self-sacrifice, a wish to expiate. "We can conceive of no greater danger to the Russian party", wrote Rosa, "than Lenin's plan of organisation. Nothing will more surely enslave a young labour movement to an intellectual elite hungry for power than this bureaucratic straitjacket, which will immobilise the movement and turn it into an automaton manipulated by a central committee."[16]

No wonder that fourteen years later Rosa was at first appalled by the dispersal of the Russian Constituent Assembly by the Bolsheviks. Although she had so often voiced her reservations about parliamentarism as conducive to opportunism, careerism and nationalism, and paraded on every occasion her contempt for parliamentary idiocy and hypocrisy, she just could not conceive of mass participation in politics without freedom of the press, of association and assembly and above all free elections. Without a free struggle of opinion "life dies out in every public institution, becomes a mere semblance of life, in which only the bureaucracy remains as the active element. Public life gradually falls asleep, a few dozen party leaders of inexhaustible energy and boundless experience direct and rule . . . not the dictatorship of the proletariat, however, but only the dictatorship of a handful of politicians . . . an elite of the working class is invited from time to time to meetings where they applaud the speeches of the leaders, and approve proposed resolutions unanimously—basically just a clique . . . such conditions must inevitably cause the brutalisation of public life: attempted assassinations, the shooting of hostages, etc."[17] Nothing could be more thrilling to the heart of a liberal than Rosa's stirring apologia for freedom for all and everybody: "Freedom only for the supporters of the government, only for the members of one party—however numerous— is no freedom at all. Freedom is always and exclusively freedom for the one who thinks differently. Not because of any fanatical concept of justice, but because all that is instinctive, wholesome and purifying in political freedom depends on this essential characteristic, and its effectiveness vanishes, when freedom becomes a special privilege."[18]

This hymn to democratic liberties is however wholly negated when Rosa comes face to face with the concrete question of the stand a convinced revolutionary should adopt towards a revolution which has been carried out successfully by a resolute minority, no matter what "irregularities" attended its birth and beginnings. The more so, if it continues to be harassed and threatened with defeat by counter-revolutionary and endangered by immature, selfish or perverse elements and sections. It was unthinkable to Rosa that a successful revolution should be abandoned out of regard to formal democracy and in disregard of the hopes and imperatives of social liberation. Socialism had not come into being in order to offer equal opportunities for political self-expression to all and sundry. The goal was to break the resistance of the possessing classes to the emancipatory endeavour of the oppressed working classes "in the most energetic, most tenacious way, defying all other considerations, in other words by exercising a dictatorship". What else could the Bolsheviks have done when on the morrow of the October revolution, "all the middle class, bourgeois intellectuals and lower bourgeoisie . . . boycotted the Soviet government for months, paralysing the railways, the postal service, telegraph, schools, the administrative apparatus, and in so doing put themselves in revolt against the workers' government"?[19] "Surely, all measures of repression became necessary, and imposed themselves: the withdrawal of political rights, of the means of economic existence—to break their resistance with a mailed fist. The dictatorship of the proletariat must not shrink from using force . . . in the interest of the whole . . . to enforce or prevent particular measures."[20] Rosa Luxemburg is careful not to countenance the proscription of whole groups of people for an indefinite period. She is anxious to limit Draconian measures to concrete cases for a definite period—so long as active resistance continues.[21]

However, from depriving whole classes and groups of their political rights as punishment for boycotting the workers' government, it was only a short step to the barbarous punitive expeditions against peasants hiding their produce and withholding it from the townspeople; to the building up of the Cheka, which was indeed set up originally in answer to attempts on Lenin's life and the assassinations of Uritsky and of the German Ambassador Count Mirbach, and to other counter-revolutionary acts of terror; to the consolidation of bureaucratic, centralised direction of the national economy "in the interest of the whole" which evolved when the original principle of workers' control of every single factory and plant threatened anarchy and famine.[22] Government terror is hardly ever propounded as a part of a programme, a principle for its own sake. It is at most suggested as a deterrent against racalcitrant elements. It eventually emerges, takes shape and is systematised pragmatically and cumulatively.

The prophetess of free expression for all came in the last few weeks of her life to defend the forced closure of bourgeois counter-revolutionary newspapers and the seizure of their printing presses by left-wing activists. Surely the revolution, in the midst of a bitter life-and-death struggle, could not allow its implacable enemies to engage with impunity in poisoning the minds of the people, and in slandering its leaders.[23] The proletarian revolution was not a seminar in political science, but the determined action of the oppressed classes to shake off the yoke of the exploiters by a knock-out blow.

At a closer look too, Rosa's image as the foe of centralism and champion of mass spontaneity begins to dissolve. Under the shock of the failure of communist armed demonstrations in the first few days of January 1919, on the very eve of her death, she emerges as an ardent advocate of centralised leadership. On January 11 she writes: "the present situation—absence of direction, the non-existence of a centre charged with the task of organising the working class of Berlin—has become untenable. . . . Concentration of the revolutionary energy of the masses and the creation of adequate bodies to direct them in their struggle—these are the most burning tasks of the hour in which we live, and the most important lesson of the last five days."[24] Finally, Rosa, who had been so shocked by the dispersal of the Russian Constituent Assembly, becomes the fervent defendant of the supremacy of the German workers and soldiers councils, and the opponent of a national constituent assembly, which she considers an obsolete idea, intended to perpetuate bourgeois rule. When the question is resolved by the councils themselves in favour of the assembly, she advocates participation in it in the teeth of her party majority's wish to boycott it, but of course yields to their decision.[25]

On the other hand Rosa insisted that the revolution would become a reality only when the time was ripe and the vast majority of the people wanted it. Then of course there would be no need for terror. But instead of waiting to let things come in their own good time, she was always calling on the masses to act, to display revolutionary energy and daring, usually without specifying the precise objectives and methods. She knew that the partisan improvisations by small minorities were futile, and she usually tried to stop acts of revolutionary adventurism at the last minute. But once the activists had moved into action, she could not stay out, still less disavow them. This is what actually happened in the adventure which she first opposed and then found her death in.[26] There was the propaganda value of constant revolutionary activity. Moreover, the revolution was destined to win only after a long series of defeats. But there was also the risk of squandering forces and of provoking the class enemy into using the premature and futile attempts of the revolutionaries to paralyse their organisation and to put them out of action altogether. Inactivity however was the greatest sin.

Chapter Two

HITLER IN THE WINGS

(*a*) DAMNOSA HEREDITAS: THE VIENNESE "GRANITE FOUNDATION" OF
HITLER'S WELTANSCHAUUNG

"In this period", writes Hitler about his years of study and suffering in
Vienna, "there took shape within me a world picture and a philosophy
which became the granite foundation of all my acts. In addition to what
I created then, I have had to learn little; and I have had to alter
nothing."[27]

What were the components of that *damnosa hereditas*, the awful
legacy which doomed Austria bequeathed through Hitler to the
German nation and through the instrumentality of Germany inflicted
upon the world? A few pages earlier Hitler sums up two early
"outstanding acquisitions" as a "particularly significant" part of it:
"first: I became a nationalist [a little further on he boasts "I became a
fanatical German nationalist"]; second: I learned to understand and
grasp the meaning of history".[28] Here as in Marxism we have striking
confirmation of the view that a philosophy of history has been the
matrix of every modern ideology. As we can see from the juxtaposition
of the two formative lessons learned by Hitler, for him the fundamental datum of history was the nation and race, in most cases used
interchangeably. What were the facts that suggested this idea? Hitler
gives us the key in immediately following up the admission quoted
above with the statement that the old Austria was a "state of nationalities".[29]

The outstanding fact was that for centuries the German minority in
the Ostmark, 10 million at the turn of the century, had ruled and
imprinted its stamp upon a nation numbering by that time about 52
million. That feat was due to the Austrian German having been "of the
best blood".[30] To Hitler the decisive test of the prowess and superiority
of a nation or race was in its ability to gain mastery not over nature, but
over other nations and races. Unlike Mussolini and the ancient
Romans, however, he considered that the secret of that particular gift

516

was not just a special aptitude, long training or an inherited continuous tradition, but the mystery of the blood.

The other important feature of Hitler's philosophy of history was his vision of the Germans of superior blood in Austria finding themselves all through their history in the position of an embattled nationality locked in "the eternal and merciless struggle for the German language, German school and a German way of life . . . forced to fight for one's nationality . . . the poison of foreign nations gnawing at the body of our nationality".[31] The recent disloyalty of the Habsburg dynasty to the Germans and their alliance with the Slavs, presaged "the slow extermination of the Germans".[32] And so, paradoxically, the members of a master-race were being driven to becoming rebels, and Hitler "became a little revolutionary".[33] This development took place primarily in answer to an ideology which proclaimed itself and was seen by others as revolutionary par excellence: Marxist socialism.

Hitler was challenged to a revolutionary response by the Marxist ideology's rejection of the "nation as an invention of the capitalistic classes; the fatherland as an instrument of the bourgeoisie for the exploitation of the working class; the authority of the law as a means of oppressing the proletariat, the school as an institution for breeding slaves and slaveholders; religion as a means of stultifying the people and making them easier to exploit, morality as a symbol of stupid, sheeplike patience etc".[34] Hitler was gripped by horror at the sight of the masses seduced by socialism. "They no longer belonged to their people . . . swelling to a menacing army."[35]

The observations and concerns imposed by the Austrian situation were elaborated by Hitler into a metaphysic—buttressed by the most literal reading of Darwin, Nietzsche and Houston Stuart Chamberlain—of racism and elitism. In the beginning was the race and not the individual. The latter was merely a sample or a particle of the former. He received all his characteristics, aptitudes and culture from the fact of having been born into the race and having been endowed with its blood. The isolated individual was, moreover, wholly impotent in the face of the paramount reality of the eternal struggle between racial entities for ascendancy, power and a share of the cosmic life-force and in the bounties of nature. Clearly, the supreme imperative was the self-preservation of the race.

In the natural selection that took place in the course of the struggle of races, the weak and unfit races were sent by nature to the grave. Similar treatment was meted out to the individual members of the struggling race. This was not a punishment, but an education. Through the relentless struggle for the survival of the fittest and the destruction of the feeble and the botched, Nature "keeps the race and species strong, in fact raises them to the highest accomplishments".[36] Hitler scoffed at those who were hysterically concerned that "once a being is born it should be preserved at any price".[37] Only the strongest and healthiest races and individuals deserved to be preserved. "A stronger race will drive out the weak, for the vital urge in its ultimate form will time and again burst all the absurd fetters of the so-called humanity of nature."[38]

Now the German nation had been multiplying at a rate which raised the urgent question of finding food for the newcomers. When that need had turned into distress, the German nation would have the "moral right to acquire foreign soil" by force. "The sword will become Germany's plough", and "from the tears of war the daily bread of the future generations will grow".[39] Surveying alternative ways of expansion to meet the growing need for food, Hitler gave absolute priority to the colonisation of conquered lands at Germany's doorstep, with emphatic preference for the Ukraine.[40] He dismissed internal colonisation, that is to say industrialisation and urbanisation, as a way of supplying the needs of the growing population. Industrial civilisation, the evils of urban life, social friction and the general demoralisation accompanying them were bound to have a debilitating effect upon the quality of the race.[41] Colonial expansion overseas would result in Germans becoming cut off from the mother country, their members exposed to climatic and morally and culturally detribalising influences.[42] "For Germany, the only possibility therefore for carrying out a healthy territorial policy lay in the acquisition of new land in Europe itself."[43] The most precious reservoir of pure German blood and Teutonic authenticity was the peasantry living in compact settlements and away from alien influences. Was there a right to conquer foreign lands?

"Nature knows no political boundaries."[44] She watched the nations competing, and "then confers the master's right on her favourite child, the strongest in courage and industry. . . . The soil exists for the people which possess the force to take it and the industry to cultivate it".[45]

Nature knew only the aristocratic principle.[46] She disapproved of the application of modern democratic notions to the relations between races so that numerically stronger races might rule, and the soil be shared out in accordance with numbers. "The laws of the natural order of force . . . [determine that] . . . the peoples of brutal will will conquer, and . . . not the nations of self-restraint."[47] Hitler prophesied "that the world will some day be exposed to the severest struggles for the existence of mankind".[48] In the end, the stronger urge for self-preservation would conquer, and "so-called humanity, the expression of a mixture of stupidity, cowardice and know-it-all conceit, will melt like snow in the March sun".[49] "Mankind", wrote Hitler, "has grown great in the eternal struggle, and only in eternal peace does it perish."[50] War was the mother and the crucible of all real values: the law of self-preservation was therefore the supreme imperative. Anything that strengthened that will was positive. Anything that weakened and distracted it was harmful, indeed deadly. Pacifist nonsense, "peaceful economic" conquest, world peace—all such ideas were poisonous drugs.[51] And so were abstract concepts and norms of allegedly unconditional validity, such as state authority, democracy, international solidarity:[52] they caused vital national needs to be judged exclusively from their standpoints, with no reference to the only thing that really mattered.[53] No less pernicious was objectivism, weighing the rights, claims and needs of ourselves and our antagonists, instead of acting spontaneously, unreflectingly and unhesitatingly from a pure instinct of self-preservation.

"Let the German people be raised from childhood up with that exclusive recognition of the rights of their own nationality and let not the hearts of children be contaminated with the curse of our objectivity."[54]

The theory of the primacy of economics was pernicious since it led to giving a premium to the individual's selfishness.[55] It was thereby bound to weaken the species' instinct for self-preservation, since the primacy accorded to earthly goods and profit was also sure to sap the individual's heroic readiness to sacrifice himself for the totality. The great heroic states like Prussia proved that "not material qualities, but ideal virtues alone make possible the foundation of a state . . . the inner strength of a state only in the rarest cases coincides with so-called economic prosperity".[56]

The state came into being not as a series of contracts for the fulfilment of economic tasks, but as "the organisation of a community of physically and psychologically similar beings for the better facilitation of the maintenance of their species".[57] State-forming and state-preserving qualities were not connected with economics. Economics was only one of the instruments in preserving the state and the species. In the spirit of List, Hitler considered economics a function of politics. Economic strength and prosperity were a function of political, that is to say military, power. The wealth of militarily weak nations was always precarious and in danger from aggressive neighbours.

"Prussia, the germ-cell of the Empire, came into being through resplendent heroism and not through financial operations or commercial deals, and the Reich itself in turn was only the glorious reward of aggressive political leadership and the death-defying courage of its soldiers. How could this very German people have succumbed to such sickening of its political instincts?"[58] It was the outcome of "a continuous stream of poison . . . into the outermost blood-vessel . . . inducing progressively greater paralysis of sound reason and the simple instinct of self-preservation".[59]

As a permanently mobilised entity engaged in an unrelenting struggle, in which superior prowess won, the nation was not a society which came together for the purpose of handing out equitable shares, or an association run by inert numerical majorities, or managed by clever manipulators. Like all great deeds, important discoveries, historic breakthroughs, which had always been the achievement of individual genius, and were never put together, bit by bit, or evolved by inert multitudes, so the establishment and leadership of states were the pre-rogative and triumph of individual genius. "Is not every deed of genius in the world a visible protest against the inertia of the masses?"[60] The struggle of a nation called for a central authority to assume individual supreme responsibility. "Is not the very idea of responsibility bound up with the individual?"[61] If that be so, then the principle of parliamentary majorities must lead "to the demolition of any idea of leadership".[62] Leadership was being swamped by mediocrity, anonymity, hypocrisy and the cowardly evasion of all responsibility. The idea of leadership by the grace of nature was incompatible with the flattery of a mob of nonentities and the role of a political gangster. "By rejecting the authority of the individual and replacing it by the members of some momentary mob, the parliamentary principle of majority rule sins against the basic aristocratic principle of nature."[63] Authority that imposed itself irresistibly and a readiness to shoulder responsibility absolutely alone—these were the basic elements of true leadership.[64]

"The truly Germanic democracy is characterised by the free election of a leader and his obligation fully to assume all responsibility for his actions and omissions. In it there is no majority vote on individual questions, but only the decision of an individual who must answer with his fortune and his life for his choice."[65] The leader was elected, but he was chosen once and for all, unconditionally, and there was no machinery to supervise, control, criticise or depose him. He had advisers, but no partners. He called assemblies together to commune with them, but received no orders from them.[66]

The leader was not someone who argued amicably with his consti-tuency. He did not conduct seminars with his hearers. He conquered them by his hysterical fanaticism (Hitler's favourite expression) and overflowing passion, more directly through the "magic power of the word". "The power which has always started rolling the greatest religious and political avalanches in history has from time immemorial been the magic power of the spoken word, and that alone. Particularly the broad masses of the people can be moved only by the power of speech. And all great movements are popular movements, volcanic eruptions of human passions and emotional sentiments, stirred either by the cruel Goddess of Distress or by the firebrand of the word hurled among the masses; they are not the lemonade-like outpourings of literary aesthetes and drawing-room heroes. Only a storm of hot passion can turn the destinies of peoples, and he alone can arouse passion who bears it within himself."[67]

(b) NEUROSIS BECOMES MURDEROUS MADNESS

In the chapter of *Mein Kampf* on the lessons bequeathed by the two Austrian anti-semitic leaders, Lueger, head of the Austrian Christian-Social party, and Schönerer, founder of the racist pan-German movement in Austria, Hitler writes: "In general the art of all truly great national leaders at all times consists among other things primarily in not dividing the attention of a people, but in concentrating it upon a single foe. The more unified the application of a people's will to fight, the greater will be the magnetic attraction of a movement and the mightier will be the impetus of the thrust. It belongs to the genius of a great leader to make even adversaries far removed from one another seem to belong to the same category, because in weak and uncertain characters the knowledge of having different enemies can only too readily lead to the beginning of doubt in their own right. Once the wavering mass sees itself in a struggle against too many enemies, objectivity will put in an appearance, throwing open the question whether all others are really wrong and only their own people or their own movement are in the right. And this brings about the first paralysis of their own power. Hence a multiplicity of different adversaries must always be combined so that in the eyes of the masses of one's own supporters the struggle is directed against only one enemy. This strengthens their faith in their own right and enhances their bitterness against those who attack it."[68]

In a later chapter of *Mein Kampf* on propaganda in the Great War, Hitler says: "The broad mass of a nation does not consist of diplomats, or even professors of political law, or even individuals capable of forming a rational opinion; it consists of plain mortals, wavering and inclined to doubt and uncertainty. As soon as our own propaganda admits so much as a glimmer of right on the other side, the foundations for doubt in our own right has been laid."[69]

Should we therefore, in the light of these cynical avowals of deliberate and systematic lying, consider Hitler's monomaniac and paranoiac anti-semitism as a clever pragmatic device? It could never have become so murderously effective had it been only that. He believed in it. In his political testament written only hours before his suicide in the bunker in burning Berlin, the man who brought all that infinite evil and suffering upon the world could still write . . . "centuries will pass, but the ruins of our cities and monuments will repeatedly kindle hatred for the race ultimately responsible, who have brought everything down upon us: international Jewry and its accomplices";[70] and to conclude the document with a call to "the leaders of the nation and all followers to observe the racial laws scrupulously and to implacably oppose the universal poisoner of all races, international Jewry".[71]

We see thus a centuries'-old neurotic inability to take even the existence of the Jews for granted, and a stubborn disposition to consider the Jew a priori as somehow guilty, culminating in a demoniac and murderous madness. From a different angle, we also see the apparently perennial need of mankind to assume the existence of an ultimate single source of evil, and Satan embodied in a whole people.

As one of the "ten million Germans condemned to death" by the Austrian state, it dawned upon Hitler very early that Social-Democracy was a mortal threat to the survival of the German nation in the Ostmark. He was "overcome by gloomy foreboding and malignant fear" of that doctrine, "comprised of egotism and hate, which can lead to victory pursuant to mathematical laws, but in so doing must put an end to humanity".[72] By 1913-14 Hitler was trying to convince his newly made German friends in Munich that "the questions of the future of the German nation was the question of destroying Marxism".[73] Hitler's greatest transformation, which cost him months of battle between reason and sentiment, until "sentiment followed reason and from then on became its most loyal guardian and sentinel", came when he discovered that "only knowledge of the Jews provides the key with which to comprehend the inner and consequently real aims of Social-Democracy".[74] "The scales dropped from my eyes":[75] the Jew was its leader.

The starting point of Hitler's *Weltanschauung*, amounting to and in fact presented by Hitler himself as the refutation of Marxist socialism, and ultimately as the antithesis of Judaism—was his condemnation of the Jewish belief, "truly Jewish in its effrontery as it is stupid!" that man's role was to overcome nature. Man was simply an extension of nature and, exclaimed Hitler, had never yet conquered nature in any-thing.[76] At most he discovered some laws and secrets of nature "to lord over those other living creatures who lack this knowledge".[77]

The immediate consequence of that "Jewish nonsense" was the Jewish-Marxist denial of the aristocratic principle of nature",[78] and the replacement of "the eternal privilege of power and strength by the mass of numbers and their dead weight".[79] Judaism (Hitler dares not add Christianity and the secular creeds reared by them) rejected the obvious imperative of nature that those whom nature had endowed with higher strength, she had thereby also designated to higher positions. Judaism refused to acknowledge the irreversible natural data "nationality and race" and the inequality of races. By rejecting the hierarchical order fixed by nature, Judaism made "any order intellectually conceivable to man" impossible and deprived humanity of the basic condition for "its existence and its culture".[80] The mishmash of races and individuals of different aptitudes, inclinations and mentalities was bound to issue "only in chaos and then the detruction of the inhabitants of this planet".[81]

"If, with the help of his Marxist creed, the Jew is victorious over the other peoples of the world, his crown will be the funeral wreath of humanity and this planet will, as it did thousands ["millions" in the second edition] of years ago, move through the ether devoid of men."[82] The prophet of wrath proclaims his mission: "Hence today I believe that I am acting in accordance with the will of the Almighty Creator: by defending myself against the Jew, I am fighting for the work of the Lord."[83] In another place Hitler enjoins his readers to consider the day in which they had not been reviled by Jews a wasted day.[84]

Hitler is at pains to resolve the contradiction between the Jewish categorical rejection of the nation and its racial contents, and the amazing staying-power of the Jews as an entity and their deter-mination to persevere as such, which seems stronger than that of any other race. At the same time, the Jews lacked any of the attributes of a religious or national entity. They had no religion, only functional devices to gain material advantages. They had never had a state, because any form of idealism was beyond them. Their solidarity was simply the huddling together of a herd in danger; when the danger had passed they would again be at each other's throats. For culture they preyed on others. Hitler explains the mystery by the fact that the Jews were noth-ing but a standing conspiracy against the nations, indeed mankind, aim-ing to subjugate all non-Jews to the dominion of the Jews.— Their way to world mastery was through the systematic denationalisation of nations, by diluting racial integrity, compactness and instinctive self-assurance.[86] This had been done by the desecration and mongrelisation of the race by the infusion of foreign and inferior blood—to lower the capacities of and disorient the bastardised race; materialistic utilitarianism and teachings on the paramount importance of economics—to undermine idealistic self-sacrifice upon which nations and states were founded; cosmopolitan pacifism—to disarm, debilitate and deliver the brave nations to the cunning races; democracy and parliamentarism—to sow anarchy and chaos; the Jewish press—to stultify the gullible and deprave the vulgar.[87]

In the past the Jews had used the bourgeoisie as their tool against feudalism, and liberal ideology as their battering ram against deep-rooted traditions.[88] They had succeeded in thoroughly saturating the middle classes of Europe with Judaic materialistic and cosmopolitan values. They then decided to make the workers their dupes in order to disinherit the bourgeoisie. They found in Marxism a most effective tool to subject the national economies to Jewish international finance, and to the slavery of interest. After having wormed their way into national societies and led to their disintegration with the aid of liberal democratic ideas and institutions, the Jews realised that class war, socialist internationalism, revolution and the dictatorship of the proletariat would serve their purposes better.[89] They would make the world of nations ripe for being taken over by an international Jewish dictatorship. "As a shock and storm troop, Marxism is intended to finish off what the preparatory softening up . . . has made ripe for collapse."[90]

"Now begins the great last revolution. In gaining political power the Jew casts off the few cloaks that he still wears. The democratic peoples' Jew becomes the blood-Jew and tyrant over peoples. In a few years he tries to exterminate the national intelligentsia and by robbing the peoples of their natural intellectual leaders makes them ripe for the slave's lot of permanent subjugation."[91] Karl Marx had prepared a "concentrated solution for the swifter annihilation of the independent existence of free nations on this earth . . . Marxism itself systematically plans to hand the world over to Jews".[92] The most insidiously dangerous weapon of Marxism was internationalism, since it was the most potent solvent of races and nations. Against that plot the Aryan Germans must create "an instrument . . . for the folkish world view to enable it to fight, just as the Marxist party organisation creates a free path for internationalism".[93]

As applied to Germany, this quintessential summary of history contained the following lesson on the most recent misfortunes of that nation: "If we pass all the causes of the German collapse in review, the ultimate and most decisive remains the failure to recognise the racial problem, and especially the Jewish menace."[94] The German people of the Second Reich had been subjected to systematic poisoning which robbed the Germans of their political and moral instincts, forces which alone made nations capable and hence worthy of existence. German blood was allowed to become contaminated, and the German mind to be depraved. "The lost purity of the blood alone destroys inner happiness forever, plunges man into the abyss for all time, and the consequences can never be eliminated from body and spirit."[95] August 1914 was "the last flicker of the national instinct of self-preservation in face of the progressing pacifist-Marxist paralysis of our national body".[96]

In this respect the defeat was a deserved punishment, but also a salutary shock. Under its impact a movement had arisen which had sworn not merely to halt the decline of the German people, but to create the "granite foundation" for a state, which "represents not an alien mechanism of economic concerns and interests, but a national organism":[97] "a Germanic state of the German nation",[98] in which the cultivation of racial purity and of the genius of the race was the supreme goal. A start was to be made with the solution of the Jewish question, "without whose solution all other attempts at a German reawakening and resurrection are and remain absolutely senseless and impossible".[99] The national resolve of Germany to solve that important question became a springboard for an international mission, as Hitler went on to proclaim that just as it was to the German nation this was also "a vital question for all humanity, with the fate of all non-Jewish peoples depending on it".[100]

(c) BEYOND NATIONALISM?

"The German Reich as a state", writes Hitler, "must embrace all Germans [to "the very last German" proclaims the opening page of *Mein Kampf*][101] and has the task, not only of assembling and preserving the most valuable stock of basic racial elements in this people, but slowly and surely raising them to a dominant position[102] (after they had been reared in special border areas and studs). The socialist aim of National Socialism is described by Hitler as "to give the German worker back to his people and to tear him away from the international delusion", to free him from social distress[103] "caused by an employer who conducts his business in an inhuman exploiting way, misuses the national labour force and makes milions out of his sweat".[104] The worker in turn is warned against making extortionate demands upon the employer, and thus harming the national economy in a similar way as the wicked employer.[105] There is of course no suggestion of abolishing wage labour, let alone of public ownership of the means of production. All that is promised are efforts to be made by the Germanic state "to raise them [the workers] out of their cultural misery and lead them to the national community as a valuable, united factor, national in feeling and desire".[106]

On closer scrutiny we are no longer here in the orbit of modern nationhood and nationalism. "The national community" is not conceived as a partnership of equals, which in a vague form is the basic premise of all modern nationalism. It recalls rather medieval and reactionary romantic ideas about the "organic community" presided over by a hereditary nobility, and linking together the various estates. In the ultimate Nazi (especially Himmler's) vision the possessors of the best blood, who were to be raised to "a dominant position", were not to be confined to ethnic Germans alone, but to comprise particularly fine Nordic specimens from other nations as well. Their "dominant position" was presumably to be made hereditary as befits a nobility. The "valuable factor", the workers, would be taught to love their station in life, and their reward would be "feeling" and "desiring" in a national way.

Racist nationalism is also seen as a step beyond the concrete and—as in the case of every European nation—pluralistic cultural tradition, towards some sort of Aryan or Nordic internationalism. The enlarged racial unit is of course envisaged as dominated by the German ingredient. It would however be drawing its inspiration from the common mythical or archaic sources of pre-Christian Germanism. One wonders what would be left of the national heritage of any European nation if the whole Judeo-Christian legacy and all that had been built upon it throughout the ages were to be cut away. A foretaste of that was offered by the spectacle of yesterday's arch-patriots ganging up in World War II to hawk their services as Quislings and collaborators to the hereditary German enemy, invader of their countries and oppressor of their nations.

But an obsessive insistence on the adoption of exclusively national forms and contents, a warlike stance towards all other nations, and strenuous *Gleichschaltung* policies, surely amount to a return to tribalism. It would not be too far-fetched not only to compare national exclusiveness with the Marxist-Soviet commitment to an all-encompassing exclusive philosophy, but also to compare the future "dominant position" of the members of the best racial stock with the role of the members of the Communist party in its leading echelons in a communist country.

In comparison with the vague, elusive, imprecise, malleable

character, and yet Latin transparence, of Italian Fascism, Nazism is anchored to a relentless quasi-scientific, impersonal determinism and is at the same time shrouded in Teuton-Wagnerian vapours of myth and legend, and haunted by an all-damning fatalism. If Italian Fascism appears to be an aspiration, Nazism embodies a colossal *hubris*. Both were characterised by blasphemous arrogance, one to begin a new calendar from the march on Rome, the other to promise a thousand-year-Reich; one harking back to Caesar, the other to Arminius. If the *hubris* was infinitely greater on the part of the Nazis, so was also their *Angst*, the baffling fear of contamination, the compulsive Wagnerian communion with death, the haunting sense of the vulnerability of the foundations of their whole enterprise and of the nihilism gnawing at its heart and on its flanks.

National Socialism claimed to be carrying out a revolution. It was really meant to be in medieval parlance a Renovatio. The vision did however combine four characteristics of a total modern revolution: rejection of the values and institutions, if not the social-economic order, of the previous society; an image of ultimate reality; terror against foes within the country; and the resolve to conquer and expand abroad.

(*d*) THE LED AND THEIR LEADER

Given the character of the Nazi revolution as a defiant rejection of ancient, cherished sanctities and certainties, the most painful question is not what made the man Hitler think and act as he did, but how an ancient and great nation like Germany, an essential part of European civilisation, could have come to be led by a person like the author of *Mein Kampf*— like a tribal chieftain, who once elected will share power with no one, will brook no control, will suffer no criticism and be religiously obeyed and venerated.

The German nation was, moreover, ravished by a mountebank who, while rhapsodising on the excellence of the German blood and the potentialities of that German "herd unity" (had the Germans had it in the past, "the German Reich today would doubtless be mistress of the globe"),[107] was pouring out in acres of print his utter contempt for the German masses and for masses in general. Denying them rational understanding, judgement, will-power and mental balance, he composed an astonishingly shrewd *vade-mecum*: how to bamboozle them with hysteria and incitement, oversimplification and repetition, stunts and tricks, parades and ceremonials. Brooding morbidly over its lost glory, and wallowing in an ecstasy of self-pity, a defeated Germany offered a uniquely propitious target for the possessed demagogue to cast his spell and hypnotise its masses: he and they shared the same resentment of defeat and foreign dictation. There was, true, a difference in intensity: theirs was indignation, his was all rage. The difference in degree evinced immediate and powerful response, had a liberating and intoxicating effect. The seemingly absolute determination and irresistible force swayed the timid, the hesitant, the irresolute, the unsure into yielding and into ignoring the less congenial ideas and sentiments which surrounded the main thrust of the relentless attack on Versailles.

Driven by compulsive memories of his youth in Vienna, it became possible for Hitler to present the Versailles Treaty, the League of Nations, the loss of territory, the reduction of the Reichswehr to 100,000 soldiers and above all the reparations and the war guilt, as parts of a systematic policy to hold down and eventually strangle the German people, as the Slavs in alliance with the Jews and Habsburgs had set out to do to the Germans in the Ostmark.

The regime of the "November criminals", with its alleged policy of fulfilment, could be condemned, if not as an enterprise of wilful traitors to the fatherland, certainly as presided over by weak-kneed, cowardly nonentities, who lacked the conviction, the guts and the will to stand up to foreign oppressors.

The leaders of the Weimar Republic and their supporters were indeed unable to command the self-assurance, the conviction, the strength of character to resist, let alone silence that barrage effectively, because they shared the fundamental premise: the unshakable faith in the horrible wrong done to the German people and in the illegitimacy of the constraints imposed upon it. There is no telling to what extent a wiser and more liberal understanding of the difficulties of the Weimar regime by the Allies might have straightened the backs of its fumbling leaders and taken the wind out of the sails of Hitler, Hugenburg, Helfferich and other nationalists. Nazi and other nationalist propaganda never tired of clamouring that inflation, as well as any other economic difficulties and every type of social unrest, were the direct consequence of reparations, and of a deliberate Franco-British plan not to let the German economy recover. That was the burden of the sustained nationalist campaign against the acceptance of the Young plan. When the 1929 crisis broke out, and the number of unemployed began to swell into millions, those arguments seemed in very many eyes to gain plausibility. The Weimar regime appeared to be crumbling—the victim of incompetence and feebleness both at home and abroad, shaky coalitions of the same type following each other at short intervals.

The regime also seemed to be disavowed by the nation, when on the flanks of the Weimar coalition the anti-parliamentary forces pledged to destroy the Republic came to outnumber its supporters, and the constitution had to be virtually suspended and the country run by presidential decree.[108]

The relentless and rowdy pressure of the Nazis, who had by then become a state within a state, disposing of a private army, presiding over a network of associations and institutions, professing allegiance to the Fuhrer alone, spread the impression that here was a historic force which was irresistible. If it could not be halted, it must be allowed a chance, and either it would fail and the air would be cleared, or it would be tamed by more moderate partners—the hard-nosed representatives of massive earthly interests.[109]

Those who allowed the Nazis to win, as distinct from the total devotees, did so out of exasperation or because they saw no alternative. They neither really knew nor did they comprehend or indeed pay heed to its daunting doctrine and its frightening implications.

We spoke before of the difference in intensity between the ordinary people's indignation and Hitler's obsessive rage in relation to Versailles. There was a similar gap between the more or less pragmatic considerations of the non-Nazis—and perhaps even of a good many Nazis—and the pseudo-messianic message and demoniacal resolve of Hitler. The same would apply to the problem of anti-semitism. Probably only the hard core of Nazi fanatics were driven by the burning conviction that the Jewish question—as the concrete quintessence of the racial theory—was the key to all history, that the Jews were the collective Satan destroying all other nations with injections of humanitarian pacifism and then—like imperialism in late Marxism—sending them to butcher each other; that Marxism and class war were really instruments of Jewish finance out to dominate the world; that all the evils afflicting societies and nations could be traced back to Jewish machinations; and that the satanic spirit of Judaism was so ubiquitous, so potent and so irresistible that its members had to be exterminated bodily, men, women and children. The bulk of the German people had however been so conditioned by age-long prejudices and images and then by the spite and malice of monomaniac writers like Fritsch, or the more sophisticated prophets Treitschke, Lagarde, Langbehn, Chamberlain and others, so disposed to view the Jews as alien, harmful, indeed sinister throughout history, that a state of deep frustration and exasperation made them morbidly susceptible to the "Jewish stimuli".

If not ready and eager to swallow all that they were told by monomaniacal anti-semites, they were nevertheless no longer able to master enough conviction or strength, not to speak of humanity and courage, to voice disapproval of, let alone to resist, the sustained campaign to deprive Jews of rights, human dignity and possibilities of existence and in the end to exterminate them. The revolution of 1918, so widely regarded as the seal on Germany's defeat, had brought a good many Jews to the fore and put them into conspicuous positions, and their enemies could point a finger with glee at the misfortunes of Germany coinciding with the rise of the Jews. There were the venerable Haase and Landsberg (who as one of the plenipotentiaries actually refused to sign the Versailles Treaty) in the Provisional Government; Preuss, who drafted the Weimar Constitution; then of course Walter Rathenau, the Foreign Minister who concluded the Rappallo pact, to be assassinated by nationalists; and Hilferding, the eminent economist of the USPD, who was for a while Finance Minister.

Before them, there was the hapless, naive Kurt Eisner, who in Catholic, conservative Bavaria set out a day or two before the Berlin revolution to play the role of a Leftist d'Annunzio. When ignominiously defeated in the general election, he was assassinated while driving to submit his resignation—a messianic revolutionary who abhorred violence and believed in the sanctity of parliamentary majorities, and was so misguided as to publish secret diplomatic documents proving German war guilt, in the hope of convincing the victorious Allies that the Germans had become converted to democracy and internationalism and should therefore be absolved of any guilt and punishment.[110]

There was of course Rosa Luxemburg, actually so ineffectual, and yet so frightening; and then some of the members of the short-lived Bavarian communist government which followed the death of Eisner. In the days of wrath, when the Jews were hunted to death, most Germans looked away, and as German police documents show were rather unpleasantly taken aback, when the decree compelling Jews to wear the yellow star revealed that there were so many still about, while they had thought that all had already been evacuated to the East.[111] Uneasy consciences preferred them to be out of sight and out of the way. Hitler countered the various expressions of protest against or reservation about annihilating Jews, instead of employing them as a much needed labour force, with the reply that no economic considerations should interfere with carrying out the final solution.[112]

In the famous *Denkschrift* of 1936 on the tasks of the Four-Year Plan, Hitler laid down that: "Since the French Revolution the world has been driven at an increasing pace towards a new confrontation, the most extreme outcome of which would be Bolshevism, the contents and goal of it being solely the elmination and replacement of the existing ruling social groups of mankind by internationally spread Jewry. No state can withdraw from or stay away from that confrontation." The victory of Bolshevism would be "the most horrible catastrophe for the nations . . . since the extinction of the world of antiquity. . . . In the face of the necessity of defending ourselves against this danger all other considerations must be relegated into the background as wholly irrelevant! The victory of Bolshevism over Germany would lead not just to a Versailles Treaty, but to the total destruction, the annihilation of the German nation."[113]

(e) THE DISTANT FOUNDATIONS

The function of an exacting dogma, the fruit of a historic situation and of a concatenation of exceptional circumstances, the various German attitudes in the Nazi period, were nevertheless also an extreme expression and climax of certain abiding German tendencies, patterns and traditions which had long set Germany apart from her Western neighbours.[114]

What in Western mouths might sound like a casual remark or an empirical statement somehow becomes in the German language, through the tendency to over-emphasis and the need for systematisation, an eternal truth, often the linchpin of a schema. Thus the syllogism "all against Germany, Germany against all" carries an infinitely heavier charge and more menacing overtones than the French Revolutionary myth of "le complot de l'étranger"—a foreign conspiracy.[115]

From being a definition of a current state of affairs it reaches out into the distant past, to some pristine condition, and then takes in all time, past, present and future. It no longer dwells on tangible, immediate differences of interests or clashes of ideologies and temperaments; it sweeps whole worlds, histories, destinies, mentalities of races and nations into perennial, insoluble conflict.

The resistance of parts of the German population to Napoleon was thus raised from the natural response of an invaded country to the dignity of another act in the timeless saga of the defence of German identity against the levelling, cosmopolitan, rationalistic tendencies of an unformed and shallow nation brought up on the facile worship of natural law: a repetition of the Homeric combat between Arminius and the Roman legions. And so Fichte, the ex-Jacobin and would-be spiritual citizen of revolutionary France, whence the light beckoned to all enlightened men the world over, was led under the impact of Jena to proclaim the Germans the sole European aboriginals. They were the only truly original and creative nation thanks to having preserved their own language, while those indolent and superficial nations, the Italians, French, Spaniards and the rest, had adopted Latin and turned it into a jargon. The German learned to feel and to think in deep Faustian travail, while the parasitic nations just played with borrowed sentiments and ideas. Tacitus *Germania,* whether intended as a tract on the noble savage or as a cryptic castigation of Roman decadence, proved to be heady wine for German stomachs.

The Second Reich witnessed a proliferation of patriotic leagues, pan-German, colonial, naval, national, preaching strenuous social Darwinism and expansionism,[116] and youth movements striving to restore man's communion with the vital natural forces and to regain a sense of wholeness.[117] The air of the Weimar Republic was thick with prophecies of doom like those of Oswald Spengler, with oracular messages on the coming of Third Reich, the books of Moeller van den Bruck on the coming of a redemptive conservative revolution,[118] Ernst Jünger's exaltation of violence, of the "drunken orgy" of war, of face to face battle in the trenches, of "passions too long dammed up by society and its laws, become once more uniquely dominant and holy and the ultimate reason".[119] Elitist groups such as the June Club and the Tat Circle, national associations like the upper class Thule Gesellschaft at one end and the plebeian Schutz and Trutz Bund at the other end, propagated Moeller's slogan "There is only one Reich, as there is only one Church", in which the individual is wholly immersed in "the Prussian style", or—in the words of Spengler—in a socialism of *Preussenthum,* the antithesis of flabby and corrupt liberalism and greedy selfish bourgeois capitalism as well as materialistic Marxism: a proto-Nazi version of the Prussian myth.[120]

Cultural and literary modes of thought and imagery were transferred into the domain of historic and political conflict. The romantic apotheosis of authenticity, spontaneity and originality engendered the cult of vital elemental forces bursting forth as it were straight from the spring, of demoniacal, possessed types and phenomena of frightening originality and daring, genius soaring above all conventions, constraints and laws of men and nature. The licence granted to extraordinary individuals was accorded all the more readily to nations, each considered a unique personality, with contents, compulsions, aspirations and laws of its own, pitted against other nations in mortal combat in order to express and assert its uniqueness, with no judge above them. They were all driven by the will to power, the urge to deploy their vitality and potentialities, in brief the *Dämonie der Macht*, or in Spengler's words "the unalterable necessity of destiny".

There seemed to be an unfathomable mystery and a fateful inevitability about the eternal conflict between the *Dämonie der Macht* and the precepts of ordinary morality, as in the case of Frederick the Great or Bismarck. Some of the historic heroes came out victorious, after having made the tragic sacrifice of their private consciences; others go under in the midst of awful tragedy, like the giants of Wagnerian operas. Too many eminent and humane German historians have succumbed to the fascination of those implacable antinomies.

By one of the greatest ironies of history, the last poet of this awful enigma was the most squalid practitioner of mass murder for the glory of the race, Heinrich Himmler. Speaking of the liquidation of the Polish élite, he says: "They had to go, there was no choice. . . . I can tell you, it is hideous and frightful for a German to have to watch such things [executions]. . . . It is, and if we did not find it hideous and frightful, then we should no longer be Germans. Hideous though it is, it has been necessary and in many cases will continue to be necessary. . . . Because if we now lose our nerve, our children and grandchildren will have to pay for our loss of nerve. [Therefore] let us not weaken. Let us never become soft, but grit our teeth and carry on."[121]

In the Poznan speech of October 4, 1943, before SS leaders, Himmler called the extermination of the Jews, a "glorious page of our history". "I want to tell you about a very grave matter in all frankness. We can talk about it quite openly here, but we must never talk about it publicly. . . . I mean the evacuation of the Jews, the extermination of the Jewish people. . . . Most of you will know what it means to see 100 corpses piled up, or 500, or 1,000. To have gone through this and . . . to have remained decent, that has made us tough. This is an unwritten, never to be written, glorious page of our history."[122]

The most hideous and most horrifying case of consistency growing into monstrosity.

(f) "ROME AND JUDAEA"

From the "meta-historical" point of view, the Nazi holocaust thus transcends the dimensions of just another wave of anti-Jewish persecution, of a dire warning of where racism combined with ultra-modern technology may lead, even of a manifestation of genocide in all its horror. It assumes the character of a grandiose confrontation between the two Nietzschean moralities, of Rome and Judaea: on one side the will to imperium, power, conquest, dominion; and on the other, the ethics of slaves and priests, with their ascetic values of humanity, self-restraint and mutuality; on one side the aim to bring forth superior specimens in the crucible of rivalry, struggle and war; and on the other the vision of a Theodicea, the dénouement of history in reconciliation, retribution, and harmony.

"The two opposing values . . . have fought a dreadful, thousand-year fight in the world," we read in Nietzsche's *The Genealogy of Morals*; " . . . the future of the fight is still indecisive . . . in the meantime it has become more and more intense . . . 'Rome against Judaea, Judaea against Rome'. Hitherto there has been no greater event than that fight, the putting of *that* question, *that* deadly antagonism. Rome found in the Jew the incarnation of the unnatural, as though it were its dia-metrically opposed monstrosity, and in Rome the Jew was held to be convicted of hatred of the whole human race", because of the Roman association of the "well-being and the future of the human race to the unconditioned mastery of the aristocratic values, of the Roman values". "The Jews, conversely, were that priestly nation of resentment par excellence, possessed of a unique genius for popular morals." Judaea has been victorious "not only in Rome, but over almost half of the world, everywhere where man has been tamed or is about to be tamed—to three Jews and one Jewess", with the help of the "oecumenical synagogue" called the "Church". When in the Renaissance, ancient Rome was beginning to stir beneath "Judaised Rome", immediately Judaea triumphed again thanks to that fundamentally popular (German and English) movement of revenge, which is called the Reformation." Three centuries later "Judaea proved yet once more victorious over the classical ideal in the French Revolution . . . a victory more crucial and even more profound". Nietzsche concludes with a cryptic question, whether the destruction of Napoleon, the last blinding flicker of "the terrible and enchanting counter-war-cry of the prerogative of the Jew", "the aristocratic ideal in itself . . . that synthesis of Monster and Superman", signified that "the greatest of all antitheses of ideals [was] thereby relegated *ad acta* for all time? May there not take place at some time or other a much more awful, much more carefully prepared flaring up of the old conflagration? Further, should not one wish *that* consummation with all one's strength? Will it one's self? Remind it of one's self? He who at this juncture begins, like my readers, to reflect, to think further, will have difficulty in coming quickly to a decision."[123]

CONCLUSIONS

This quest, which was started in *The Origins of Totalitarian Democracy*, was carried on in *Political Messianism—the Romantic Phase*, and is now brought to a close in the present work, was originally triggered by a rather personal response to certain shattering contemporary events. In 1937-8, when the minds of so many, and especially the young, were being deeply exercised by the terrible enigma of the Moscow trials, I happened to be working on an undergraduate seminar paper on the ultra-democratic French constitution of 1793 as seen against the background of the Jacobin terrorist dictatorship. The analogy between An II and what was happening in 1937-8 struck one most forcibly. Who had so criminally betrayed the Russian Revolution—the accused or the accusers? In either case, how could such vast evils, whether committed by one group or the other of the makers of the October revolution and the builders of the Soviet Union, be reconciled with the message of universal salvation upheld by both sides? But why the analogy? Surely, it could not be just the same eternal and incurable human wickedness or merely a similar concatenation of untoward circumstances that had brought about both sets of developments. The parallel seemed to suggest the existence of some unfathomable and inescapable law which causes revolutionary salvationist schemes to evolve into regimes of terror, and the promise of a perfect direct democracy to assume in practice the form of totalitarian dictatorship.

The Jacobin phase of the French Revolution, where that great ironic law was first demonstrated, bequeathed a hypnotic model and a myth, and above all started a continuous tradition. The experience of the French Revolution was soon universalised by its devotees into a vision of a preordained revolutionary breakthrough to the consummation of the historic process in the form of a final and perfect social order. According to the myth, this new order was willed by all men of good will in their heart of hearts, but would inevitably have to be enthroned by a vanguard of the enlightened and the brave, with the help of coercion, a total restructuring of society, and a sustained effort of far-reaching and all-embracing re-education.

The numerous versions of the religion of revolution and the various groups that sprang up to propagate them, including the one which proved to be the most important and the most effective of all—Marxism in all its diversity—should therefore be regarded not as self-contained doctrines and entities, but rather as different rationalisations of a

535

primary semi-religious impulse and as successive elaborations and applications of a single sustained endeavour in the light of changing circumstances and new lessons.

The basic assumptions, values and hopes, and the very thrust of the messianic expectation were, to be sure, part of that general emancipatory drive—of men, classes, peoples and races—for liberty, equality and self-expression, which has been such a vast and mighty force in the last two hundred years, indeed in the eyes of many the proof and the essence of "the unmistakable surging march of history" in the modern era. The totalitarian-democratic wing of the messianic movement, however, broke away from the general body of believers in the religion of continuous progress towards liberation and became inimical to and even destructive of the more comprehensive trend, not out of disbelief in the common tenets, but as the result of an exaggerated faith in the inevitability and imminence of the complete realisation of the creed in all its parts and aspects. Its representatives were seized by a strenuous resolve to make men free and happy here and now, and if the objects of their ministrations proved racalcitrant and perverse, to remake them—"dénaturer" in Rousseauist language—following upon the elimination of those—individuals, groups and classes—who showed themselves wholly incapable of regeneration.

Reformed men in a totally reshaped society were sure to realise themselves in a manner wholly consonant with perfect social cohesion, and the dichotomy of liberty and equality would be resolved by men having learned to will unanimously the common good, in other words the general will. For being unanimous they would become both free and equal. So the longing for an emancipatory release from constraints evolved into an ardent passion for deliverance.

It was the fanatical determination of saviours-in-a-hurry, intent on fitting an imaginary new man into an artificially contrived, or as it came to be held, an inevitably evolved ultimate social harmony, that became the source and motive of all the contradictions, paradoxes, casuistry, hypocrisy, ruse and tyranny displayed in the Jacobin dictatorship, and several generations later in the Bolshevik regime, the Soviet purges and the Stalinist era.

The impact of the Fascist-Nazi phenomenon proved to be still more traumatic. Even before their murderous intent had fully unfolded there was the profoundly bewildering spectacle of a defiant rejection by the leadership of a great nation of the axioms and values of liberal democracy, and indeed of the Judeo-Christian tradition, which had been thought for so long self-evident and irreversible. They had been perverted and violated earlier by messianic totalitarian democracy, but hardly ever denied explicitly and in principle. Brutal transgressions and crimes were explained by their perpetrators as inescapable necessities yielded to for the sake of warding off mortal perils and achieving lofty goals. The suspension of constitutional guarantees was presented as only a temporary emergency measure, to be amply compensated for by an eventual total lifting of all constraints and all forms of dependence. Freedom could not be granted so long as men disagreed—as if liberty would have any meaning if no one was left to dissent.

No wonder that there was much uncertainty about the nature of the relationship of those two dynamic and demoniacal historic trends which reached their climax in totalitarian dictatorships. If they were branches from the same trunk, what was it that made them take different courses? If their origins and development were wholly disparate, whence the striking similarities in patterns of thought and modes of operating as churches militant and then triumphant? Were those similarities solely due to the nature of the instruments and techniques provided by the age, and to the challenges presented by the given phase of historic development? If the ideology of the extreme Left was to be regarded as in the final analysis a heresy growing out of the common Western heritage, where should we look for the roots and antecedents of the extreme Right? If the former was conceived in the Enlightenment and born in the French Revolution, where should we locate the beginnings of the latter?

On deeper scrutiny the extreme Right came to be seen as an ideology that emerged originally as a reaction to the victory of the religion of progress in the French Revolution. This reaction was fully confirmed in this century in Hitler's description in *Mein Kampf* of his political evolution as the gradual discovery of an answer to Marxist socialism, as well as in what we know of Mussolini's road to Fascism via his conflict with his erstwhile Socialist party.

Why should we not consider counter-revolutionary thinking at the turn of the eighteenth and nineteenth centuries as a simple continuation of the ideology of the *ancien régime*? If ideology is to be treated, as we prefer, not as the rationalisation and justification of established interests, but as a programme for changing or at least deliberately shaping reality in accordance with some professed principles, we should be forced to conclude that the *ancien régime* just had no ideology, and moreover that there were no ideologies in pre-revolutionary society in the sense of deliberately formulated comprehensive alternatives to the traditional social-political order. Such an alternative was put on the agenda for the first time on the eve of the French Revolution.

Founded on appeal to divine sanction, resting upon tradition and precedent, upheld by the general acceptance of the sanctity of hierarchy and of the naturalness of a society based on status, the *ancien régime* might welcome and benefit from the theorising of Filmer and Bossuet in the same way as it was helped by pamphleteers commenting on current affairs, and of course by the mystery, awe, pomp and circumstance surrounding royalty. But it had no need to defend or justify its very title, which if one excludes millenarian fringe groups, was hardly questioned, even though this or that abuse, one action or another, a particular failing or failure might be criticised and even opposed. Nor did the exercises in political philosophy by thinkers of what might be called the theoretical opposition and their quest for underlying principles, amount to an ideology, a practical alternative to the existing order.

Opposition, rebellion and revolution in the early modern era were all uprisings against abuses, usurpations, distortions and violations of the good old laws, and of movements calling for a restoration of an earlier and allegedly more just state of affairs, even if the momentum of the movement carried men beyond their initial intentions. On the extremes of those movements of protest were the outbursts of elemental rage in the peasant *jacqueries* on the one hand, and the dreams of a Second Coming and the restoration of a state of nature, and apostolic purity, by the millenarians on the other. It is uncertain whether the utopian writings of those times were intended as anything more than a critique and satire on existing society, and whether at any point they set out seriously to outline an alternative programme.

Hints and anticipations of a genuine confrontation between traditional and ideological attitudes glimmer at us from the Puritan Revolution. Standing before his judges and questioning their right to sit in judgment over him, Charles I argued that without a king no one would have any right to call anything his own. This did not deter Cromwell from threatening to cut off the King's head with the crown on it. In the Putney debates however radical Leveller spokesmen provoked Cromwell and his son-in-law Ireton to an astonished, indeed uncomprehending protest against views which, as they put it, had never been heard of since England was England. Men with no stake in society wished to arrogate to themselves the right and power to decide how to remake England by simply invoking abstract reason and a pretended natural law, which, after all, any casually assembled group of men might interpret in their own arbitrary way. Moreover, they wished to ignore all the ancient laws and traditions which had made England; even to despising Magna Carta as "that beggarly thing".

Yet whatever traces puritan radicalism may have left on the fringes or in the undercurrents of English life, it did not give rise to a continuous and, what is more, a general European tradition, notwithstanding the attempts of internationally minded Puritan republicans to establish and maintain contacts with like-minded Protestant groups on the Continent. The first real alternative was formulated and tried out in the French Revolution, thus opening a new era in world history. The very word "idéologie" was first used in print in 1796 by Destut de Tracy, and soon after the term "ideologue" became an expression of mocking opprobrium in the mouth of Napoleon Bonaparte. These expressions were destined never to disappear from human discourse.

The fundamental issue between the *ancien régime* and French Revolutionary ideology, one may say modern ideology *tout court*, was the question of hereditary status, of inherited privilege. Divine right monarchy, patrimonial feudalism, society divided into estates—all these rested on the principle of hereditary succession. So did the particularistic features of the medieval and early modern state, with its jumble of provincial liberties, municipal immunities, the special privileges of localities, social or professional groups, often indeed families. Once granted or recognised and confirmed, they were passed on from generation to generation as a type of property, an integral part of the patrimony. Burkean prescription does not signify only respect for the ways of old, which had proved their worth and were hallowed by time; it implies sanctification of the legacy of one's ancestors, primarily property.

The old order did not consider the individual man as the first and basic component of society. There was no abstract man as a lawgiver to himself or to society, no individual person endowed with a right to abstract liberty. For religious, cultural, and social reasons a solitary creature was not held fit for self-determination. He needed the aid and cover of authority, church, tradition, the past, his superiors, the class and group to which he belonged. Nor was any generation of men free to throw overboard all that had gone before and to start from scratch, as upon a *tabula rasa*, in accordance with its own ideas and desires. In this sense it may be said that enlightened despotism, with its reliance on geometry rather than on mythology and with its passion for rationalisation and modernisation, undercut the branch upon which it sat and indeed opened the floodgates of revolution.

Counter-revolutionary spokesmen found themselves challenged by the revolution to rationalise the traditional order, which precisely lacked rational criteria at its source, and at the same time to confront revolutionary ideology with arguments operating within the terms of reference of revolutionary philosophy.

Rationalistic abstract universalism, based upon the idea of man *per se* and of his goodness and perfectibility within a society made rational, was countered by Joseph de Maistre with the grim conception of human nature as utterly depraved, feeble and perverse, and thus hopelessly ensnared in a universe that was irrational at its core and was wallowing in the blood of crime and expiation. The hangman was the linchpin of human societies. The Pope was their anchor and final arbiter. If he did not exist, he had to be created.

The emancipatory drive was met by Haller and Bonald with an equally universalistic theory of patrimonial authority as the natural principle of all societies and the essence of all social ties. Novalis' and Chateaubriand's visions of a revivified and poeticised Christianity and of a restored unity of European Christendom might have inspired the Holy Alliance monarchs to pledge themselves to be guided by the teachings of the Gospel and to apply them in their dealings with each other and with their subjects: an answer to the revolutionary appeal to objective reason as the sole criterion, and to the view that the brotherhood of free and equal men was a guarantee of international peace.

Edmund Burke's great apologia for conservatism, which inspired Gentz, Adam Müller, Bonald and early German Romantics, was a flaming protest against the doctrinaire intent of revolutionary ideology to destroy all the historic and peculiar traditions and institutions in order to impose abstract and levelling patterns. The revolution threatened implicitly to deprive flesh-and-blood creatures of instinct, reflex, habit and affections, of their authenticity and spontaneity, and to take away from historically evolved societies their distinctly differentiated and integrated personalities. German romantic populists offered a radical version of this philosophy by exalting German or even Germanic uniqueness, denying the existence of objective and universal natural law, and initiating the cult of archaic modes of self-expression.

In contrast to ultramontane and Holy Alliance universalism, the two latter strands of reactionary thinking contained nationalist ingredients. In its sweeping condemnation of any and all forms of opposition to the hereditary principle, legitimism however made no distinction between vindication of constitutional rights, social protest and movements of national liberation and unification. Any concession to demands for freedom of self-expression or for limitation of the power of established authority and for a popular share in government, in defiance of those ancestral ways and historic institutions which embodied the allegedly natural order of society, was in legitimist eyes a descent towards anarchy and war of all against all. The final outcome would be the tyrannical Bonapartist usurpation of unlimited power, and the creation of a centralised state all of a piece and a nation one and indivisible, unprotected by the obstacles to despotism that were provided by inherited rights and privileges pertaining to provinces, estates, corporations and guilds in an organic, historically evolved society.

Rigid legitimists regarded liberalism as the road not only to anarchy but also to communism. Together they led to tyranny. The massive attack on the hereditary principle on the grounds that man had a right to be wholly untrammelled by inherited handicaps, or conversely should not be allowed the aid of any inherited privilege in his pursuit of that happiness which was everyone's due, was bound to result in the denial of the right to inherit property. In the light of the practical impossibility of maintaining a society characterised by absolute equality, the demand for total social-economic equality would sooner or later lead to a call for a community of goods, while the slogan of the right to work was sure to enthrone a dictator who would take over the national economy as the only way of realising this principle.

Liberalism found itself attacked not only by legitimists, but also by socialists. The former accused the liberals of loosening the dams holding back the waters of anarchy, the latter of negating the idea of the rights of man and equality—which they themselves had vouchsafed—by proclaiming property sacred. The conservation of inherited property not only meant the perpetuation of inequality, it amounted to the restoration of a type of feudalism. Both liberals and socialists agreed that the right to property was essential for safeguarding all other civil rights. Therefore, the liberals claimed, it must not be touched. To be deprived of property, the socialists maintained, meant in practice not possessing any of the other rights. The bourgeois liberals argued that the desire for property was the sole effective incentive to effort, and thus a condition of general prosperity. Socialists condemned such a view as a regression to the injurious libels on human nature which had for centuries been spread by clerical obscurantists and feudal exploiters. These pessimistic views of human nature now became a pretext for a restricted franchise, so as to prevent the allegedly ignorant and uncouth from misusing or even selling their votes. The real motive however, was the wish to rob the poor of any possibility of exercising an influence on government in the direction of social change and of breaking the political monopoly of the haves.

The conviction of being held down by an alliance of conservatives and liberals, aristocracy and bourgeoisie, in other words non-proletarian society, fostered the belief that the fundamental division of mankind was not into nations or races, but into haves and have nots, privileged and deprived, oppressors and oppressed, exploiters and exploited. The proletariat had no fatherland. Workers of all nations were called upon to unite.

A testing year for this dichotomy as well as for the hereditary principle in general, 1848, also put on trial that multitude of messianic and all-contradictions-resolving schemes of history, which the age of revolutionary changes and romantic visionaries so deeply cherished and which it believed to be near practical realisation. What did those salvationist hopes not promise: the coming of eternal peace, the total unfolding of a self-knowing and self-willing Spirit (or Reason) incarnate, the triumph at last of a genuinely spiritual and authentically social New Christianity, the emancipation of the most numerous and poorest class in a classless society, and what concerns us most here—the liberation of all peoples, and the emergence of a brotherhood of regenerated nations. In the event, all expectations were eclipsed by the failure of the last to come to fruition.

In a manner not dissimilar to the fission that in 1789 rent the seamless robe of the Third Estate upon the secession of the Fourth Estate, the revolutionary fraternity of 1848 was violently severed by the separatist attitudes of the "unhistoric" nations, which had for so long lived beside or in the midst of, at all events under the tutelage of, the "historic" nations, absorbed their culture, and passively acquiesced in their dominion. It was a particularly bewildering and upsetting experience to the Germans, Hungarians and Poles of the radical-democratic persuasion to be stabbed in the back, while fighting the despotic-feudal dynasties, by a Vendée which invoked the right to free self-expression, and yet supported the Holy Alliance governments.

Democratic principles came to be violated in the name of the highest form of democracy. The "historic" nation at the moment of its rebirth felt itself bound by both the imperatives of liberty and the traditions of its people to gather in all the scattered members of the race, and all partners in the nation's culture and speech, who centuries earlier had been torn from the body of the nation by dynastic accident, superior force, or feudal particularism; to incorporate into the fatherland those areas upon which the genius of the nation had at one time or another imprinted its indelible mark; and to secure to future generations defensible borders and the indispensable assets that past generations had placed at the disposal of the nation on the wide open frontiers.

For their part, the "unhistoric nations" became acutely aware that their inferior economic-social situation and backwardness were the result of centuries-old national-political subjugation. Disabused of their faith in the natural alliance of all freedom-loving nations against the unified forces of counter-revolutionary reaction, they decided that social emancipation hinged on national liberation. National liberation assumed the character of an uprising against oppression and degradation, and as the ageing Marx began to perceive, became a challenge to the honour and idealism of the best elements of a subject nationality, capable of hindering them from throwing themselves unreservedly into the cause of the international socialist revolution. The humiliations and injuries of a persecuted nation had greater immediacy and urgency than the more abstract cause of the international proletariat, as distinct from the concrete grievances of the workers, especially when compared with the relatively privileged position of the working class of the dominant nationality.

The way out of the dichotomy was for the socialist parties of the oppressed races to become the spearhead in the struggle for national liberation, that is to say to become what Marx had called the national party of the deprived nationality. They would thus emerge as the avenger of all the discontents, taking political independence as their first objective, while determined to press on, upon the achievement of national liberation, for the promised emancipatory social-economic transformation.

And so was born the doctrine of the national liberation movement as the form of the revolutionary crusade, with the socialist programme as its content. Experience was however to show that more often than not socialist-revolutionary leaders in the struggle for national liberation would, as the saying in central Europe went, hasten to alight from the tramway of history upon reaching the station "Independence," sometimes tolerating, but more frequently stopping, others from continuing the journey to the socialist terminal. Independence seemed again so much more urgent and more absorbing.

In due course, too, international rivalry between the long-established and prosperous powers and the emergent, poor, but striving nations became charged with social dynamite. The dissatisfied rising peoples came to look upon the satiated old states as guilty of having acquired the wealth of the globe by force by keeping the weaker claimants out of the race, taking advantage of their immaturity and internal troubles. To the possessing nations these representations by late-comers sounded like the threats of upstarts and usurpers guilty of flouting the international order and imperiling peace. This was the background for the future definition of nationalism as socialism confined to one country, and of the division of Europe, and eventually the world, into plutocratic powers and proletarian nations. The spokesmen of the better-off workers in the wealthy empires would argue the inadmissibility of lowering the living standards won by a national proletariat the hard way. Inequalities and rivalries between nations were thus made to appear as a sublimation of class war within a single nation-state.

The second part of the nineteenth century witnessed an acceleration of the process of the nationalisation of the masses, as the nation-state grew more prosperous, more centralised, in every way active and powerful. The rising birth rate, rapid industrialisation and urbanisation, mass production, the phenomenal growth of international trade and the development of international finance—all these were riveting the individual to the state, whatever his class, by ties stronger than the divisive interests, tensions and conflicts resulting from sectional and class antagonisms. In an era of universal suffrage, parliamentary government, municipal activity and democratic procedures, politics ceased to be the preserve of kings, ruling castes and even of the propertied classes. Spreading literacy and a mass circulation press were causing vast multitudes to come to share the same concerns, anxieties, often humiliations and disasters, to be swept by collective excitements, pride, arrogance, to yield to the contagion of aggressive passions and irrational panic, to labour under common grievances and obsessions.

It is no exaggeration to say that in the growingly prosperous and more stable West the spectre of revolution was being replaced by the nightmare of international war and, given the new technology and the realities of mass society, total war at that, with no distinction between front and rear, soldier and civilian, labourer and bourgeois. Shortly before his death, as we saw, Marx voiced his deep anxiety—apropos the situation of a restlessly ambitious, yet deeply scared Germany, wedged in between an implacably revanchist France and a seemingly incurably barbaric Russia—that in any future war every nation would be fighting for its very existence, and socialists would be confronted with the dreadful dilemma of choosing between international proletarian solidarity and their country right or wrong.

The general and increasing preoccupation with the nation's rights, needs and grievances, the brooding over its identity and its past, its fate and its manifest destiny, the reflections on its moments of glory and its failures and defeats were in every case a journey into bygone ages, a reckoning with ancestors, a communing with the myth of the nation. No wonder the century produced such a flowering of the historical sciences and of a literature and art that set out to serve as a mirror to the nation's soul and a portrait of its modes of existence. National cults grew up and spread, replete with myths, symbols, rites, liturgy, commemoration, and heroes and saints' days, parades and displays, artistic effects and hypnotic suggestiveness.

All these tendencies fed upon and in turn promoted the far-reaching change in the image of man from that bequeathed by the Enlightenment. Far from constituting the basic element and goal of society, from being his own autonomous lawgiver and free and equal partner to the social contract, as he was seen in the eighteenth century, man was made to appear more and more a function of collective forces, past traditions, the social setting, the organisational framework, the spirit of the nation, the *Zeitgeist*, the milieu, group mentality, finally the race. No longer a free agent in making choices, the individual was shown to be in the grip of compulsive urges and aversions, automatically re-enacting ingrained modes of behaviour and reflexes. In brief, the individual was portrayed as the plaything of the unconscious and the hereditary, a mere abstraction when pitted against the collective forces deposited in the whole to which he belonged, above all in the nation. Not man, therefore, but the nation, was the measure of all things, and the dominion of the dead was depicted as infinitely more potent than the deliberate decisions of the living. Indeed, this state of affairs was made the condition of social cohesion, political stability and the health of the nation.

If the individual was a fiction, the idea of the oneness of mankind was an illusion. From the biological, historical, cultural and social point of view the impact of the nation appeared infinitely more effective than the influence of either the individual or the ideal of a unified mankind. There was therefore no point in applying to the concrete, palpitating reality of the nation abstract, objective, universal criteria, derived from atomistic and mechanical patterns of thinking.

Every nation was a world of its own, a unique blend. Since it fashioned countless men and determined their fate and well-being, the nation's interests, the imperatives of its particular situation, the conditions favouring its survival, cohesion, strength and influence contained its truth, morality and justice. The latter were perspectives, not objective data.

It was only a short step from this type of integral nationalism, tinged with Darwinism, to race theory. The elusive, ineffable and vague concepts of *Volksgeist* and *Volkstum* had ceased to satisfy seekers after scientific precision and metaphysical certainty. German addicts to system-building, and other fundamentalists on the Right who, like the saviours-in-a-hurry on the Left, were thirsting after absolute consistency, eagerly seized upon the concept of race. It claimed fool-proof scientific validity, and yet resounded with mystical overtones. It was a most tangible and ineluctable datum of nature, and at the same time capable of determining the most refined and most rarified expressions of the spirit and artistic genius. It satisfied and brought into coherence all the postulates and expectations of integral nationalism, while presenting itself as a science. Above all the new science showed the Germans to be the superior example of he superior species of man, in a universe of unchangeably unequal races.

With the aid of Darwinism, racism set the seal upon the doctrinal denial of the reality of both the individual and mankind. The struggle for survival and a share of cosmic power was waged by species and races. Each of these had its truth, morality, culture and political traditions determined and shaped by the exigencies and circumstances of the struggle, as a function of self-adaptation; it may therefore be said as weapons of war and tools of power.

No man was born and no nation came into existence with any natural rights or inalienable claim to objective justice. The title to rights was in the power that had become strong enough to wrest them and in the strength accumulated by generations to hold them against the envious rapacity of rival races.

As Tocqueville had never tired of repeating, in post-revolutionary Europe no party defending institutionalised hereditary inequality and inherited privilege had a chance. It was however an entirely different matter if the hereditary principle was raised to the plane of relations between nations and races and sublimated into collective possession and common experience. In this form the conservative principle proved strong enough to carry with it most of the other values of the extreme Right such as the organic society, hierarchical relationships, tradition and loyalty, discipline and obedience. It was moreover able to hitch to its wagon the knightly ideals which contemporary intellectual and artistic trends exalted, such as overflowing vitality, aristocratic non-chalance, spontaneity, heroic virtues, dangerous living, love of adventure and the will to power, intuition and imagination; and to prop these up with dutiful, humble hard work on the part of the lower orders.

This defiant reassertion of the aristocratic principles of heredity and hierarchy combined extreme élitism with a popular appeal, an authoritarian temper with a revolutionary élan. Nationalist-racist self-idolisation had an intoxicating effect upon multitudes sunk in anonymous, impersonal ineffectiveness. There was much compensation to a populace treated as an amorphous and irrational mob in serving as clay and tools in the hands of the allegedly compact, well-formed, masterly specimens of the race, out to perform great deeds. The élitists of the extreme Right preached a national revolution. They set out to roll back the ideas and forces let loose upon the world by the Enlightenment and the French Revolution, which under the name of liberty, equality, fraternity, popular and parliamentary sovereignty, individualism and liberalism, social mobility and *laissez-faire*, loosened all moral and social ties, enthroned greed and corruption, debilitated the nation and made it prey to alien Jewish exploiters and foreign powers. The national revolution was to restore the nation to the state of pristine authenticity, simplicity, wholeness and integrity which modern solvents had destroyed. It was the glorification of instinctual spontaneity and immediacy, in contrast to the cunning and hypocrisy of the bourgeoisie and the hesitations of the intellectuals, and the aggressive contempt for liberal-democratic procedures that offered licence to violence. More than that, the élitists of the new extreme Right were not able to invoke the legitimacy of an inherited status. They neither possessed it, nor would it have been accepted had they claimed it. Their only title was the claim to be born to leadership, and this could be demonstrated only by wholly uninhibited insolence and ruthlessness. The rowdy bands of the new extreme Right before 1914, in France, Austria and elsewhere, became the pioneers of the storm troopers of the period between the two wars.

The progeny of integral nationalism, imperialism and its companion, racism, stimulated the devotees of total world revolution, who were losing their battle against the nationalist heresy and its concomitant reformist deviation in the ranks of Social-Democracy, to refurbish their extreme version of internationalist Marxism and to revitalise the vision of world revolution. Imperialism became their blanket term for all the evils telescoped into their abstract Manichean adversary. Racist imperialism did not try to hide, camouflage, explain away, gloss over, or offer hypocritical apologies for its will to power, dominion, conquest and loot. The theory of a mankind divided into born masters and breeds destined to be ruled by superiors, was the corner-stone of the creed of racist imperialists.

To the extreme Left the important feature of racist imperialism was, however, not the theory of racial distinctiveness, nor that of the inequality of races, but rather the universal character of the phenomenon of imperialism as it spread in the wake of the unification of the world into a single economic unit. The result was the transplantation of class war from the nation-state to the global plane, the face-to-face confrontation between a world-wide capitalist camp and a global proletariat.

Imperialism also seemed to be reaffirming the basic early tenet of Marxism that oppression was indivisible. The political subjugation of the colonial races was an expression and an extension of economic exploitation. The somewhat battered theory of the growing mono-polistic concentration of ownership of the means of production in the hands of the upper bourgeoisie and the corresponding pauperisation of the masses could now be restated in the form of a Marxist theory of imperialism. The concentration of all the world's wealth and power in the hands of the ruling castes of the few great powers was turning the vast majority of mankind, above all the coloured races, into their slaves, and their weaker neighbours in Europe into their satellites and cannon fodder, thus bringing nearer the global Day of Judgment. For all its immense expansion and power, the highest and final variant of capitalism had become all the more vulnerable. Wholly dependent on raw materials, cheap colonial labour, and the new overseas markets, the imperialist governments were compelled to maintain a state of emergency, to whip up mass fears and collective passions in order to raise the money for the vast armies and navies that were needed to keep out rivals, secure established positions, and hold down the countless milions groaning under an economic yoke and seething with nationalist rage.

The new Marxist theory of imperialism was calculated to infuse a new dynamic spirit into the proletarian parties' ranks. Instead of waiting for the economic contradictions and the recurrent crises to bring down the capitalist edifice of the nation, the faithful were now enjoined to act in a revolutionary manner. As in 1848 the emphasis of revolutionary strategy shifted from purely social-economic calculations to political-military considerations, but this time on a global scale. The concomitants of this shift were systematic anti-militarist and anti-patriotic agitation designed to unmask the class character of imperialist policies, the incitement of colonial populations to revolt, and preparations to turn the inevitable war between the imperialist powers into an international civil war, in which the united front of the as yet uncorrupted European proletariat and the colonial races would administer the final coup to the imperialist-capitalist order.

The sentiments and ideas analysed in this work might have remained merely the mood of this or that marginal group or a subterranean influence, or perhaps fizzled out altogether, if the Great War had not intervened and enthroned them as major, indeed dominant, creeds. There can however be little doubt that the myth of the race, the religion of nationalism, social Darwinism, the glorification of war as a prelude to rebirth or the fatalistic acceptance of its inevitability, the wish to ward off social revolution by resorting to nationalist and imperialist policies, and, as the consequence of these, the sense of now or never, had become massive, powerful forces well before 1914. In July and August of that year they exercised a powerful influence on statesmen, opinion makers, and indeed on the population in general, far beyond those small groups of committed doctrinaires and true believers who were the direct bearers of the tradition.

The fact, too, that at the other pole of the political spectrum all Social-Democratic parties rallied to the national colours in August 1914, but a few years later, in the wake of the Bolshevik Revolution, major parts of quite a number of them joined the Third International, was due not merely to the sufferings inflicted by war, but to the example of the triumph of a creed that seemed to be able to move mountains. It revitalised the messianic dream of world revolution, which nationalist sentiment had all but extinguished.

The mood of exasperation caused by the Great War, the gnawing doubts about the future of civilisation, deepening all the time under the impact of inflation, the great Depression and mass unemployment, and the resulting loss of nerve and self-confidence in the centre—all these combined to bring the extremes to the fore, and to make bewildered multitudes receptive to the rantings of those terrible simplifiers, the standard bearers of world revolution at one end, and the guardians of national destiny at the other.

So there took shape the life-and-death confrontation between the two exclusive all-embracing ideologies of totalitarianism, so similar, yet so different.

Both types of totalitarianism were based on the assumption that there is a single, all-embracing and exclusive truth in politics, and both ideologies, in the final analysis, recognised only one plane of existence—the political. If the Left derived its doctrine from the belief in the deterministic primacy of matter, the changing modes of production, and the corresponding forms of class war, the Right gradually evolved its reply by proclaiming the deterministic and decisive significance of the natural data of race and blood. Each of the two ideologies anchored itself to a vision of a history destined to reach a salvationist consummation, a resolution of social contradictions via a revolutionary breakthrough, or the restoration of a pristine authenticity by cleansing the racial substance of distorting and debilitating diluents. Both creeds adhered to a Manichean view of history. By being convinced of the possession of the all-embracing and all-healing truth, each believed that whatever promoted its goals was right and good, and what hampered its advance was evil. There being no middle ground, what was not Marxist was bourgeois, just as what was not Nordic was Jewish.

The Left was seemingly concerned with removing injustice and securing rights, while the Right considered rights to be a function of power. On closer scrutiny, however, the Left appears divided on this issue. From the point of view of the historic dialectic, the workers were destined to inherit the earth not because they deserved to be compensated for wrongs, but because social-economic conditions, and they themselves in tune with them, were mature enough for the socialist transformation, the older forms and former holders of power having spent their force and outlived their usefulness. The Right treats rights—not entirely dissimilarly—as the measure of power and of adaptive achievement in the eternal struggle.

The Left sees history as shaped by objective forces, and man as a function of these. The peculiarities of individual leaders in history are bound to cancel themselves out by pulling in opposite directions. Personal leadership thus plays no part at all in the doctrine as such. Yet owing to the deterministic view of historic development held by Marxism and to its insistence that there is a solely valid interpretation of the direction of history at every juncture, the task of oracle became in practice lodged exclusively in the mind and the will not even of the van-guard of the brave and the dedicated, but in the infallible wisdom of the personal leader and in the bureaucratic centralised apparatus. The armies of the Right, on the other hand, without the benefit of a rigorous dialectic, had to be guided by voices from above heard by the leader-seer, aided by an élite which laid claim to be the quintessence of the racial substance.

A form of democratic participation was preached by both movements. In totalitarian democracy the individual was held to have already achieved or to be on the way to acquiring a self-identification with the general will, brought about by the historic process, the social transformation, and thorough indoctrination. The conclaves of the party were a form of direct democracy. The unanimous vote of the Supreme Soviet, elected from a single slate, was both a public demon-stration and an educational device. Unanimity secured both freedom and equality. In the racist state, willing of the general will was ensured since all its members shared the common blood, and consequently values, ideas, interests. To both the alleged permanent state of emergency, as in a beleaguered city, also guaranteed and justified forced unanimity.

The Left was riveted to the vision of a classless society, in which there was no dominion of class over class and no government of man over man. The Right reverted to the medieval concept of the organic society which, together with the idea of the mystical community of blood, enables it to portray classes as limbs in an organism and to treat class differences as of no consequence in comparison with the spiritual partnership. The facts of class exploitation are attributed to the selfish rapacity of alien forces. Social protest is also seen as caused by such forces or as artificially fomented by subversive factors of alien provenance in alliance with or serving the interests of the anti-national exploiters. The aim of the national revolution was to liberate the workers from those oppressive and divisive forces, to incorporate them into the ideal national community, and to instil in them a proud sense of belonging. Fascist-Nazi totalitarianism stopped short of "nationalising" the economy not because it was the last rampart of a besieged and tottering capitalism or because the debt it owed to big business. Its Darwinist élitism made it treat the great captains of industry as fine specimens of a warior race. The alliance with those ruthless and eager conquerers was expected to provide the sinews of war and imperialist expansion.

The presupposition of the scientific nature of the Marxist doctrine on one side, and the axiom of the unerring instinct of blood on the other, were supposed to ensure infallibility. Hence the horror, common to both sides, of divisive influences and deviations. All these had to be attributed to alien factors, in the one case to petty-bourgeois heresies or imperialist intrigue, in the other to the sinister Jewish presence.

The baffling obsession with the Satanic ubiquitousness and malignant effectiveness of the Jews was more than the modern outcrop of a perennial Christian neurosis. It was an inescapable consequence of the indispensable need to uphold the faith in the originally immaculate and perfect quality of the Teutonic race. All failings and inadequacies had to be traced back in tune with race thinking, to the evil influence of another race. The Jews, outsiders and insiders at the same time, seemed to fit the role of the anti-race. Aliens to the ancestral soil and tradition, given to abstract and cerebral preoccupations, with a penchant for critical analysis, on top of their ubiquitous presence they were a standing threat to the distinctness, compactness, potency, unerring instincts and fighting prowess of every nation or race. Cosmopolitan characterlessness, individualistic atomisation, exploitative capitalism, materialistic mentality, revolutionary agitation, humanitarianism and pacifism were thus branded as weapons employed by Jewry with the calculated intention of emasculating, confusing, and denationalising the peoples, in order to spread Jewish dominion over them all.

The metaphysical effort to extend the role of the evil spirit alleged to be incarnate in the Jewish anti-race back into the most distant beginnings and forward to the end of days focused, in the final analysis, on the messianic vision of theodicy with its roots in the idea of the oneness of mankind and the brotherhood of men. At the end of history such unity would be realised, thus proving God's ways to be just and right. This vision, which originated in Judaism, was shared by Christiantity, the Enlightenment, liberalism, democracy and socialism, not to speak of pacifism. Indeed, the ultimate difference between messianic totalitarian democracy and Nazi-Fascist totalitarianism hinged upon this point. All violations of the values of the Western heritage were defended by the Left as speeding up the realisation of that predestined social harmony. The modern extreme Right defiantly and uncompromisingly rejected that vision, seeing in it the very negation of its own image of history as the stage upon which superior specimens asserted their superiority in the crucible of rivalry and battle. Even if this rather theoretical distinction between the two types of totalitarianism makes little difference in practice, it is nevertheless not without significance.

The violent refutation of that basic common tenet of the various Western creeds highlights the paradoxical transformation undergone by an ideology that began by identifying itself as the guardian of Christian values and the traditions of legitimacy. From this starting point it developed into a pagan, anti-Christian force of revolutionary usurpers, whose ruthless dynamism attracted a great many disillusioned Left revolutionaries, to whom the tamed policies of parliamentary, reformist socialism failed to offer an outlet, and believed it found it in nationalist self-assertion, with anti-semitism as an ersatz internationalism. It was a "universalist" racist anti-semitism which in World War II led these arch nationalists to commit national treason as Quislings and collaborators of the invaders of their countries and tormentors of their peoples.

No less paradoxical has been the dialectic which shaped the development of the extreme Left. Its response to the nationalisation of the masses and to the corresponding embourgeoisement of Social-Democratic ideology was the shift of emphasis in the direction of the universalist, fundamentally political idea of world revolution. The day of judgment was to be ushered in by the essentially political upheaval of international war rather than by the predetermined decomposition of the capitalist economy. The triumphant Russian Revolution gave wings to the revitalised creed far beyond Russia. The consequences were however different from those that were intended. The fact that the Soviet regime remained confined to a single country turned the would-be-internationalists in the West into nationalists of a foreign power. It caused the Comintern to place the strongest emphasis on promoting national liberation movements in the colonies as a way of undermining the power of Western imperialism, the arch-enemy of Russia. The nationalist mystique which spread to all the colonial peoples, overshadowing social-economic considerations, deserves to be recognised as a confirmation of our thesis that the messianic salvationist drive released by the French Revolution, and not the Marxist doctrine, was the primary impulse of the liberation movements of this century.

The role of midwife to national liberation movements assumed by Soviet Russia placed great-power political strategy at the top of her priorities. This made Russia forfeit much of her moral standing as standard-bearer of the world socialist revolution. It exposed her rigid centralised and bureaucratised dictatorship to the charge of being a mere self-perpetuating power apparatus. This disillusionment became one of the most important causes for the emergence of the neo-anarchist revolutionary and terrorist movements in so many countries. Other outcomes have been the schisms which have been tearing asunder the seamless robe of communism—such as Titoism, insurrectionary outbursts in Poland and Hungary, Euro-Communism in the West and above all the secession of China. In all these cases the drive for freedom and free self-expression is hardly distinguishable from nationalist self-assertion.

A case can similarly be made for regarding the socialist self-identification and measures of the recently created states in Asia and Africa as devices to replace tribalism with a nation-building myth of a common endeavour to carry out an industrial revolution and establish a centralised regime on the basis of equal citizenship.

Paradoxically on the morrow of the crushing defeat of murderous racism and the almost voluntary exodus of the white man from the vast expanses of Asia and Africa, it is the race problem that has—more spectacularly than the nuclear threat and the ecological situation—emerged as the most intractable issue of our era. Before our eyes the social cleavage into bourgeois and proletarians is being replaced by the contrasts, tensions and conflicts between prosperous societies and guest workers, old imperialist nations and immigrant ex-colonial subjects ("we are here because you were there"), whites and blacks in the United States, European and Indian in Latin America, and on a global scale between the rich (and white) north and the poor (and colonial) south.

Western imperialism and its shadow, political messianism, have stirred up the spirit of rebellion in the East and South and stimulated the mood of rising expectations. They have caused upheavals of extreme violence, with none of the inhibiting factors of the Western legacy. They have at the same time left the West with a deep sense of guilt towards the coloured races and about its own prosperity to the point of being incapable of making any use of its might to secure the life blood of its economy and of not daring to resort to the good socialist argument about the need to (inter-)nationalise the vital means of production of mankind. There is yet no guarantee against a resurgence of various forms of militant totalitarian racism in the West in reaction to the mounting wave of aggressively anti-Western self-assertion of religious, cultural and political nativism—on the one hand, and in response to the murderous ideological and tribal confrontations in Asia and Africa, which together with growing overpopulation and misery threaten to result in increasingly larger multitudes of desperate "boat people" heading for more fortunate continents—on the other.

The rampant anti-imperialist mystique is placing the U.S.S.R. and China in highly ambiguous situations. In spite of advancing embourgeoisement, the growing nationalism of the ethnic minorities in Russia—about half the population—is compelling the great Russian establishment to raise high the banner of Marxist internationalism, and with it of a revolutionary interventionism which is hardly distinguishable from sheer Great Power expansionism. Out of fear of the Soviet Union, a schismatic China, in the role of a virtual ally of the United States, seems at a loss to fix its destiny—of a reformed eternal China, a model of genuine Marxism, or spearhead of the underprivileged coloured races forging ahead. All these paradoxical phenomena are the ironical outcome of the fusion of the myth of the nation and the vision of salvationist universal revolution.

NOTES

Introduction (pp. 1-18)

1 The following is a select list of works on the subject of nationalism:

B. Akzin, *Nations and Nationalism in the Twentieth Century*, London 1961

Edward H. Carr, *Nationalism and After*, London 1945

Karl Deutsch, *Nationalism and Social Communication*, Cambridge (Mass.) 1966

Raoul Girardet (ed.), *Le nationalisme français, 1871-1914*, Paris 1966

Carlton J. H. Hayes, *The Historical Evolution of Modern Nationalism*, New York 1931;

Carlton J. H. Hayes, *Nationalism: A Religion*, New York 1960

Paul Henry, *Le problème des nationalités*, Paris 1949

Ghita Ionescu and Ernst Gelner (eds.), *Populism, its Meaning and National Characteristics*, London 1969

Eugene Kamenka (ed.), *Nationalism: the Nature and Evolution of an Idea*, Canberra 1973

Elie Kedourie, *Nationalism*, London 1969

Hans Kohn, *Nationalism: its Meaning and History*, Princeton 1965

Hans Kohn, *The Idea of Nationalism; A Study in its Origins and Background*, New York 1967

Hans Kohn, *Prophets and Peoples, Studies in Nineteenth Century Nationalism*, New York 1966

Alexandre Koyré, *La philosophie et le problème national en Russie au début du 19ème siècle*, Paris 1929

Eugen Lemberg, *Nationalismus*, Hamburg 1964

Kenneth R. Minogue, *Nationalism*, London 1967

George L. Mosse, *The Nationalization of the Masses*, New York 1975

Jacques Ploncard d'Assac, *Doctrines du nationalisme*, Paris (n.d.)

Ch. Pouthas, *Le problème des nationalités dans la première moitié du XIXe siècle*, Cours de Sorbonne 1950

Boyd C. Schafer, *Faces of Nationalism*, New York 1972

Leonard B. Schapiro, *Rationalism and Nationalism in Russian Nineteenth Century Political Thought*, New Haven 1967

Anthony D. Smith, *Theories of Nationalism*, London 1971

Jerzy Szacki, *Ojczyzna, Naród, Rewolucja*, Warsaw 1961

Jacob L. Talmon, *Romanticism and Revolt, Europe 1815-1848*, London 1967

Jacob L. Talmon, *The Unique and the Universal, Some Historical Reflections*, London 1965, ch. I: "The National Brotherhood and the International Confraternity" pp. 11-63

2 Isaiah Berlin, *Vico and Herder: Two Studies in the History of Ideas*, London 1976

Alfred Cobban, *Edmund Burke and the Revolt against the Eighteenth Century; A Study of the Political and Social Thinking of Burke, Wordsworth, Coleridge and Southey*, London 1960

Alfred Cobban, *Rousseau and the Modern State*, London 1964

Friedrich Meinecke, *Weltbürgertum und Nationalstaat; Studien zur Genesis des Deutschen Nationalstaats*, München 1922

Jacob L. Talmon, "Herder and the German Mind", in his: *The Unique and the Universal*, pp. 91-118

3   Georges Lefebvre, *Quatre-vingt-neuf*, Paris 1970; English translation, *The Coming of the French Revolution*, translated by R. R. Palmer, Princeton, New Jersey, 1973, pp. 169-181

Alphonse Aulard, *Histoire politique de la révolution française*, Paris 1901, pp. 39-48

4   Jacques Droz, *L'Allemagne et la révolution française*, Paris 1949

Georges Lefebvre, *La Révolution française*, Paris 1951, pp. 198 ff

Albert Sorel, *L'Europe et la révolution française*, Paris 1922, vol. I pp. 537-552; vol. II pp. 144 ff, 154 ff

Studies on the Social Problem in the French Revolution

5   Albert Soboul, *The Parisian Sans-Culottes and the French Revolution 1793-1794*, Oxford 1964

Albert Soboul, *La Ière République, 1792-1804*, Paris 1968, pp. 35 ff, 124 ff

Jean Jaurès, *L'Histoire socialiste de la révolution française*, ed. A. Mathiez, Paris 1922, vol. V

Albert Mathiez, *La Vie chère et le mouvement social sous la terreur*, Paris 1927

Albert Mathiez, *La Révolution Française*, Paris 1925 vol. II pp. 130 ff, vol. III pp. 65-77, 147 ff

6   Jacob L. Talmon, *The Origins of Totalitarian Democracy*, London 1952, pt. III

7   Jacques Droz, *Le romantisme politique en Allemagne*, Paris 1963

Reinhold Aris, *History of Political Thought in Germany 1789-1815*, London 1936

Friedrich Meinecke, *Das Zeitalter der Deutschen Erhebung 1789-1815*, Bielfeld 1906

Franz Schnabel, *Deutsche Geschichte im neunzehnten Jahrhundert*, Freiburg im Breisgau 1947, vol. I, pp. 283-315

8   Studies on pre-1848 Radicals and nationalism:

John Plamenatz, *The Revolutionary Movement in France, 1815-1871*, London 1952

Georges Weill, *L'Eveil des nationalités et le mouvement libéral 1815-1848*, Paris 1930

Maurice Dommanget, *Les Idées politiques et sociales d'Auguste Blanqui*, Paris 1957

Alan B. Spitzer, *The Revolutionary Theories of Louis Auguste Blanqui*, New York 1957

Samuel Bernstein, *Blanqui*, Paris 1970

Guiseppe Mazzini, *Scritti editi ed inediti*, Imola 1906-1943, 94 vols.

Guiseppe Mazzini, *Life and Writings*, London 1864-1870, 6 vols.

G. Salvemini, *Mazzini*, London 1956

Hans Kohn, *Prophets and Peoples*, New York 1966

Jacob L. Talmon, *Political Messianism, The Romantic Phase*, London 1960 pt. II: "Messianic Nationalism"

Jehuda Tchernoff, *Le Parti Républicain sous la Monarchie de Juillet*, Paris 1901

9   Utopian socialism and nationalism:
    Henri Saint-Simon *Selected Writings,* edited and translated by F. M. H.
    Markham, Oxford 1952
    Henri Saint-Simon, *Nouveau Christianisme,* London 1834
    Maxime Leroy, *Le socialisme des producteurs; Henri de Saint-Simon,* Paris 1924
    Frank E. Manuel, *The New World of Henri Saint-Simon,* Cambridge (Mass.)
    1956 ch. 14 "The Reorganization of Europe"
    S. Charléty, *Histoire du Saint-Simonisme,* Paris 1931
    Jacob L. Talmon, *Political Messianism,* pp. 279 ff
    Pierre Joseph Proudhon, *La Fédération et l'unité en Italie,* Paris 1862
    Pierre Joseph Proudhon, *Nouvelles observations sur l'unité italienne,* Paris 1865
    Pierre Joseph Proudhon, *Du Principe Fédératif et de la Nécessité de Reconstituer le
    Parti de la Révolution si les Traités de 1815 ont céssé d'exister,*
    Paris 1868
    Pierre Joseph Proudhon, *La Guerre et la paix,* Paris 1927
    Victor Considerant, *Destinée sociale,* Paris 1835-1844
    Victor Considerant, *Principe du socialisme; Manifeste de la démocratie au XIX
    siècle,* Paris 1847
    Victor Considerant, *Le Socialisme devant le vieux monde, ou le vivant devant les
    morts,* Paris 1848

Part I. Marx, Engels and the Nation (pp. 19-66)

1   For the writings of young Marx and Engels see: *Marx Engels Werke (MEW),*
    Berlin 1958-68, 41 Vols. Ergänzungsband, Schriften bis 1844, Erster Teil,
    pp. 467-591
    Karl Marx/Friedrich Engels, "Die heilige Familie", (1845) *MEW* Bd. 2, pp.
    3-223
    Marx/Engels, "Die deutsche Ideologie" (1845-46), *MEW, Bd. 3,* pp. 9-530
    Karl Marx, *Grundrisse der Kritik der Politischen Ökonomie,* Erstveröffentlichung
    Moskau 1939-41, 2 vols., Neue Ausgabe, Ostberlin 1953
    Siegfried Landshut (ed.), *Karl Marx: Die Frühschriften,* Stuttgart 1964
    Secondary sources:
    Maximilien Rubel, *Karl Marx: essai de biographie intellectuelle,* Paris 1957
    Auguste Cornu, *Karl Marx et Friedrich Engels: leur vie et leur oeuvre,* Paris
    1955-62, 3 vols.
    Thilo Ramm, "Die künftige Gesellschaftsform nach der Theorie von Marx
    und Engels", *Marxismusstudien II,* Tübingen 1957
    David McLellan, *Marx before Marxism,* London 1970
    Shlomo Avineri, *The Social and Political Thought of Karl Marx,* Cambridge 1968
    Louis Althusser, *Pour Marx,* Paris 1968
    Richard Schlacht, *Alienation,* New York 1970
    Iring Fetscher, *Karl Marx und der Marximus; Von der Philosophie des Proletariats
    zur proletarischen Weltanschauung,* München 1967
    Gustav Mayer, *Friedrich Engels, Eine Biographie,* Den Haag 1934, 2 vols.

Works on Marx, Engels and the Nations:

R. N. Berki, "On Marxian Thought and the Problem of International Relations", *World Politics*, Vol. XXIV, Oct. 1971

S. F. Bloom, *The World of Nations. A Study of the National Implications in the Work of Karl Marx*, New York 1941

Horace B. Davis, *Nationalism and Socialism, Marxist and Labor Theories of Nationalism to 1917*, New York 1967

2 Marx/Engels, "Ideologie", *MEW*, Bd. 3, p. 33

3 *Ibid.*, p. 35

3a *MEW* Bd. 26, pt. 3, *Theorien über den Mehrwert*, (Vierter Band des "Kapitals"), p. 441

4 Marx/Engels, "Manifest der Kommunistischen Partei" (February 1848), *MEW*, Bd. 4, p. 466

5 Marx/Engels, "Die deutsche Ideologie," *MEW*, Bd. 3, p. 60, pp. 36-37

6 Marx/Engels, "Manifest", *MEW*, Bd. 4, p. 479

7 Marx/Engels, "Ideologie", *MEW*, Bd. 3, p. 35

8 Marx to Engels (8.10.1858), *MEW*, Bd. 29, p. 360

9 Marx to P. W. Annenkow (28.12.1846), *MEW*, Bd. 4, p. 547ff

10 Marx/Engels, "Ideologie", *MEW*, Bd. 3, pp. 69-70

11 Marx/Engels, "Manifest", *MEW*, Bd. 4, p. 479

12 *Ibid.*

13 Engels, "Das Fest der Nationen in London", *MEW*, Bd. 2, p. 614

14 *Ibid.*, p. 613

15 Marx, "Reden uber Polen" (29.11.1847), *MEW*, Bd. 4, p. 417

16 Engels, "Das Fest der Nationen", *MEW*, Bd. 2, p. 613

17 Engels, *ibid.*, p. 611

18 Talmon, *Political Messianism—The Romantic Phase*, London 1960, pp. 210-214

19 Marx/Engels, "Ansprache der Zentralbehörde an den Bund vom Marz 1850", *MEW*, Bd. 7, p. 252

20 Marx/Engels, "Programme der radikal-demokratischen Partei und der Linken zu Frankfurt", *MEW*, Bd. 5, p. 42

21 Engels, "Der Schweizer Burgerkrieg", *MEW*, Bd. 4, pp. 396-397

22 Marx/Engels, "Ansprache an den Bund vom Marz 1850", *MEW*, Bd. 7, pp. 246-248

23 Talmon, *Political Messianism*, pp. 213-214

24 The 1848 Revolutions:

Roman Rosdolsky "Friedrich Engels und das Problem der geschichtslosen Völker" (Die Nationalitätenfrage in der Revolution 1848-1849 im Lichte der *Neuen Rheinischen Zeitung*), *Archiv fur Sozialgeschichte*, Bd. IV, Hannover 1964, pp. 87-282

Miklos Molnar, *Marx, Engels et la Politique internationale*, Paris 1975, pp. 17-20

Gustav Mayer, *Friedrich Engels*, vol. I, chs. XI, XII

Jacques Droz, *Les Révolutions allemandes de 1848*, Paris 1957

Veit Valentin, *Geschichte der deutschen Revolution von 1848-49*, Berlin 1930-31

Rudolf Stadelmann, *Soziale und politische Geschichte der Revolution von 1848*, München 1948

25 Engels, "Einleitung zu Karl Marx 'Klassenkämpfe in Frankreich 1848-1850' von 1895", *MEW*, Bd. 22, p. 512
26 Talmon, *Political Messianism*, pp. 423-455
27 Stadelmann, p. 153; Talmon, *Political Messianism*, Part V
28 Stefan Kieniewicz, *Historia Polski 1795-1918*, Warsaw 1975, pp. 25ff, 105ff, 132ff
29 Marx to Engels, 2.12.1856, *MEW*, Bd. 29, p. 88
30 Engels, "Die Polendebatte in Frankfurt", *MEW*, Bd. 5, p. 334
31 Marx/Engels, "Reden auf der Gedenkfeier in Brussel", *MEW*, Bd. 4, p. 521
32 Marx, *Manuskripte über die polnische Frage (1863-1864)*, hrsg. von Werner Conze und Dieter Hertz Eichenrode, 'S-Gravenhage 1961, p. 124
33 Lewis B. Namier, *1848: The Revolution of the Intellectuals*, London, 1944; Namier, "1848: Seed-Plot of History", *Avenues of History*, London 1952, pp. 45-56
34 Engels, "Die Polendebatte in Frankfurt", *MEW*, Bd. 5, p. 334
35 Namier, *1848: The Revolution of the Intellectuals*, London 1944, p. 88
36 Engels, "Die Polendebatte in Frankfurt", *MEW*, Bd. 5, pp. 319-326, 344
37 Engels, "Po und Rhein", (1859) *MEW*, Bd. 13, p. 267; Shlomo Na'aman, *Lassalle*, Hannover 1970; Hermann Oncken, *Lassalle, eine politische Biographie*, Stuttgart/Berlin 1923; Gustav Mayer, *Friedrich Engels*, translated by Gilbert and Helen Highet, New York 1969, pp. 168 ff
38 Benoît P. Hepner, *Bakounine et le Panslawisme révolutionnaire*, Paris 1950; Max Nettlau, *Bakunin, eine biographische Skizze*, Berlin 1901; E. H. Carr, *Michael Bakunin*, London 1937; Anthony Masters, *Bakunin, the Father of Anarchism*, London 1974
39 Franco Venturi, *Roots of Revolution*, New York 1966, ch. 2, pp. 36-63
40 Hepner, *Bakounine et le Panslawisme révolutionnaire*, esp. pp. 277 ff
41 Molnar, *Marx, Engels et la Politique internationale*, p. 85; Rosdolsky, *Archiv fur Sozialgeschichte*, Bd. IV, p. 89
42 Engels, "Der Prager Aufstand", *MEW*, Bd. 5, pp. 81-82
43 Engels, "Die auswärtige deutsche Politik und die letzten Ereignisse zu Prag", *MEW*, Bd. 5, p. 202
44 Engels, "Der demokratische Panslawismus", *MEW*, Bd. 6, pp. 279-280
45 *Ibid.*, p. 285
46 *Ibid.*
47 *Ibid.*, p. 286
48 Marx to Engels (2.7.1858) *MEW*, Bd. 29, p. 336; Marx to Engels (8.8.1858) *ibid.*, p. 349; Marx to Engels (25.2.1859), *ibid.*, pp. 401, 442; Marx to Engels (9.2.1860) *MEW*, Bd. 30, p. 29; Marx to Engels (26.6.1860) *ibid.*, p. 71
49 E. Silberner, *Sozialisten zur Judenfrage*, Berlin 1962, p. 128
50 Engels, "Der Magyarische Kampf", *MEW*, Bd. 6, p. 176
51 *Ibid.*, p. 173; Rosdolsky, *Archiv fur Sozialgeschichte*, Bd. IV, pp. 103-104
52 *Die Neue Rheinische Zeitung*, Nr. 114, 12.10.1848, in *MEW*, Bd. 5, pp. 417-8; Nr. 235, 2.3.1849, in *MEW*, Bd. 6, pp. 315-19; Nr. 158, 2.12.1848; Nr. 226, 19.2.1849; in Rosdolsky, pp. 104-105

53 Engels, "Der Dänisch-preussische Waffenstillstand", *MEW*, Bd. 5, p. 394
54 Engels, "Der Magyarische Kampf", *MEW*, Bd. 6, p. 168
55 *Ibid.*, p. 174
56 Engels, "Der demokratische Panslawismus", *MEW*, Bd. 6, p. 275
57 *Ibid.*, p. 270
58 Molnar, *Marx, Engels et la Politique internationale*, p. 57
59 Engels, "Der demokratische Panslawismus", *MEW*, Bd. 6, p. 278
60 *Ibid.*, p. 279
61 Engels to Marx (23.5.1851) *MEW*, Bd. 27, pp. 266-267
62 Engels to Joseph Wedemeyer (12.4.1853) *MEW*, Bd. 28, pp. 575-582
63 Engels to Marx (23.5.1851) *MEW*, Bd. 27, p. 267
64 *Ibid.*, pp. 267-268
65 Engels, "Revolution und Konterrevolution in Deutschland", (1852), *MEW*, Bd. 8, p. 52
66 Engels, "Der demokratische Panslawismus", *MEW*, Bd. 6, p. 273
67 *Ibid.*, p. 274
68 Shlomo Avineri (ed.), *Karl Marx on Colonialism & Modernization*, New York 1969; George Lichtheim, *Imperialism*, New York 1971, chs. 6, 7, 8; Molnar, *Marx, Engels et la Politique internationale*, chs. IV, V
69 Engels to Karl Kautsky (12.9.1882) *MEW*, Bd. 35, p. 358
70 Molnar, *Marx, Engels et la Politique internationale*, p. 23
71 Chimen Abramsky and Henry Collins, *Karl Marx and the British Labour Movement; Years of the First International*, London 1965, pp. 52 ff, 112 ff
72 Karl Marx, "Inauguraladresse der Internationalen Arbeiter-Assoziation," *MEW*, Bd. 16, p. 13
73 *Ibid.*, pp. 5-13
74 Davis, *Nationalism and Socialism*, ch. 2, pp. 39-51
75 *Ibid.*, p. 45ff; Abramsky and Collins, *Karl Marx and British Labour*, pp. 106 ff
76 Engels to Karl Kautsky, *MEW*, Bd. 35, p. 271
77 Marx to Sigfried Meyer and August Vogt (9.4.1870) *MEW*, Bd. 32, pp. 667-668
78 Berthold F. Hoselitz and Paul W. Blackstock (eds.), *The Russian Menace to Europe*, a collection of articles, letters and new dispatches by Karl Marx and Friedrich Engels, Glencoe 1952, pp. 29 ff
79 Marx/Engels, "Für Polen", *MEW*, Bd. 18, p. 574
80 Engels to Karl Kautsky (7.2.1882) *MEW*, Bd. 35, p. 270
81 *Ibid.*, p. 272
82 Engels to Eduard Bernstein (22.2.1882) *MEW*, Bd. 35, p. 279
83 Engels to Karl Kautsky (7.2.1882) *MEW*, Bd. 35, pp. 272-273
84 *Ibid.*, p. 272
85 *Ibid.*, p. 273
86 Engels, "Ergänzung der Vorbemerkung von 1870 zu 'Der deutsche Bauernkrieg'" (1.7.1874), *MEW*, Bd. 18, pp. 515-517; Marx/Engels, "Brief an den Ausschuss der Sozialdemokratischen Arbeiterpartei" (22.-30.8.1870), *MEW*, Bd. 17, p. 270
87 Marx, "Zweite Adresse des Generalrats uber den Deutsch-Französischen Krieg," *MEW*, Bd. 17, p. 276

88 Marx, "Kritik des Gothaer Programms April – Mai 1875'', *MEW*, Bd. 19, p. 24

89 *Ibid.*, p. 24

90 Marx, "Der Burgerkrieg in Frankreich'', *MEW*, Bd. 17, p. 361

91 Marx to Friedrich Adolph Sorge (27.9.1877) *MEW*, Bd. 34, pp. 296-297

92 Engels, "Was soll aus der europäischen Turkei werden?'', *MEW*, Bd. 9, p. 33

93 Ferdinand Lassalle, *Der italienische Krieg und die Aufgabe Preussens*, Berlin 1859; Hermann Oncken, *Lassalle*, Berlin 1923, pp. 154-168

94 Maximilien Rubel, *Karl Marx devant le Bonapartisme*, Paris 1960

95 Engels to August Bebel (22.12.1882) *MEW*, Bd. 35, p. 416

96 Engels, "Die auswärtige Politik des russischen Zarentums'', *MEW*, Bd. 22, p. 13

97 Engels to Ion Nadejde (4.1.1888) *MEW*, Bd. 37, p. 5

98 *Ibid.*, p. 6

99 Engels, "Die auswärtige Politik des russischen Zarentums'', *MEW*, Bd. 22, p. 48

100 Engels, "Der Sozialismus in Deutschland'', *MEW*, Bd. 22, p. 255

101 Davis, Nationalism and Socialism, p. 49

102 Engels to August Bebel (13.10.1891) *MEW*, Bd. 38, pp. 175-176

103 *Ibid.*, p. 176

104 Engels to Eduard Bernstein (9.8.1882) *MEW*, Bd. 35, pp. 349-350

Part II: The Emancipation of the Proletariat and the National Destiny—Wilhelmine Germany (pp. 69-130)

1 The fullest collection of Rosa Luxemburg's works is the *Gesammelte Werke* in four volumes (1/1, 1/2, 2,3) covering the period up to July 1914, published in the seventies by Dietz Verlag in East Berlin. Additional selections of her writings are:

Rosa Luxemburg, *Politische Schriften*, edited by K. Flechtheim, Frankfurt/M. 1966-1968, 3 Vols.

Rosa Luxemburg, *Gesammelte Werke*, hrsg. c. Zetkin und A. Warski, 3 vols., Berlin 1923-8

Rosa Luxemburg, *Selected Political Writings*, edited by Dick Howard, New York 1971

Rosa Luxemburg, *Selected Political Writings*, edited by Robert Looker, translated by W. D. Graf, London 1972

There is no edition of collected works by Eduard Bernstein. We shall refer to his writings whenever appropriate.

1a Karl Radek, *Rosa Luxemburg, Karl Liebknecht, Leo Jogiches*, Hamburg 1921

Henriette Roland-Holst—van der Schalk, *Rosa Luxemburg, Haar leven en werken*, Rotterdam 1935 (In German: *Rosa Luxemburg, Ihr Leben und Wirken*, Zurich 1937)

Paul Frölich, *Rosa Luxemburg, Gedanke und Tat*, Paris 1939 (English translation: *Rosa Luxemburg, Ideas in Action*, translated by Joanna Hoorweg, London 1972)

2   V. I. Lenin, "Notes of a Publicist" (1922), *Collected Works,* Moscow/London 1966, vol. 33, p. 210

3   J. V. Stalin, "Some Questions Concerning the History of Bolshevism" (1931), *Works,* Moscow/London 1955, vol. 13, pp. 88-89

4   Gilbert Badia, "La place de Rosa Luxemburg dans le mouvement socialiste", *Revue Historique,* Juillet-Septembre 1974 (No. 511), p. 107

5   Rosa Luxemburg, *Sozialreform oder Revolution?,* Leipzig 1899, p. 74

6   The main studies on Rosa Luxemburg are:
    Gilbert Badia, *Rosa Luxemburg, Journaliste, Polémiste, Révolutionnaire,* Paris 1975, a model of exhaustive treatment.
    Lelio Basso, *Rosa Luxemburg, Dialektik der Revolution,* Frankfurt/M 1969
    Paul Frölich, *Rosa Luxemburg, Gedanke und Tat,* Paris 1939
    Peter J. Nettl, *Rosa Luxemburg,* London, 1966, 2 vols; also abridged in one volume, Oxford University Press, 1969. (Here the 2 volume edition is used.)
    Fred Oelssner, *Rosa Luxemburg, Eine kritische biographische Skizze,* Berlin 1951
    Annelies Laschitza and Gunther Radczun, *Rosa Luxemburg, Ihr Wirken in der Deutschen Arbeiterbewegung,* Frankfurt/M 1971
    Norman Geras, *The Legacy of Rosa Luxemburg,* London 1976 (A view from the Left ably presented).
    Main studies on Eduard Bernstein and Revisionism:
    Pierre Angel, *Eduard Bernstein et l'évolution du socialisme allemand,* Paris 1961
    A. Joseph Berlau, *The German Social Democratic Party, 1914-1921,* New York 1950
    G. D. H. Cole, *A History of Socialist Thought,* vol. II, part 2, London 1963
    Peter Gay, *The Dilemma of Democratic Socialism, Eduard Bernstein's Challenge to Marx,* New York 1952
    George Lichtheim, *Marxism,* London 1967
    Erika Rikli, *Der Revisionismus, Ein Revisionismusversuch der deutschen Markxistischen Theorie 1890-1914,* Zurich 1936

7   Eduard Bernstein, *Die Voraussetzungen des Sozialismus und die Aufgaben der Sozialdemokratie,* Reinbek bei Humburg 1969, p. 53

8   *Ibid.,* p. 200

9   *Protokoll uber die Verhandlungen* des Parteitages der SPD abgehalten in Stuttgart, vom 3 – 8.10.1898, Berlin 1898, pp. 99-100, 118

10   Angel, *Eduard Bernstein,* p. 158

11   Karl Kautsky, *Bernstein und das socialdemokratische Programm,* Stuttgart 1899, p. 22

12   Karl R. Popper, *The Open Society and its Enemies,* vol. II, London 1966, ch. 25
     Karl R. Popper, *The Poverty of Historicism,* London 1963
     Isaiah Berlin, *Historical Inevitability,* London 1954

13   Bernstein, *Voraussetzungen,* pp. 95-111

14   Luxemburg, *Sozialreform,* p. 66

15   *Ibid.,* p. 82

16   G. D. H. Cole, *A History of Socialist Thought,* vol. III, London 1956, pp. 276-284

Eric Roll, *A History of Economic Thought*, London 1973, pp. 266-273

Bernard Shaw, ed., *Fabian Essays in Socialism*, London 1908, pp. 12-18

17 Bernstein, *Voraussetzungen*, pp 36, 75-79
18 Luxemburg, *Sozialreform*, pp. 45-46
19 Bernstein, *Voraussetzungen*, pp. 147-163
20 Luxemburg, *Sozialreform*, p. 78
21 Luxemburg, *Sozialreform*, pp. 80-85
22 Bernstein, *Voraussetzungen*, p. 199; Luxemburg, *Sozialreform*, pp. 54-55, 57-60
23 Luxemburg, *Sozialreform*, p. 61
24 Luxemburg, *Internationalismus und Klassenkampf, Die polnischen Schriften*, ed. Jurgen Tentze, Berlin 1971, p. 259
25 Luxemburg, *Sozialreform*, p. 94
26 *Ibid.*, p. 93
27 *Ibid.*, p. 96
28 Letter to Luise Kautsky (15.4.1917) in *Bulletin of the International Institute of Social History*, Amsterdam, VIII, pp. 103-104
29 Luxemburg, in a letter to Klara Zetkin (9.3.1916) Institut des Marxismus-Leninismus Berlin, NL 5/91 p. 123
30 Luxemburg, *Gesammelte Werke*, Hersg. Paul Frölich vol. IV, "Die Akkumulation des Kapitals", Berlin 1923 p. 638
31 Luxemburg, "Organisationsfragen der russischen Sozialdemokratie", *Gesammelte Werke*, Berlin (Ost), 1972, 1/2 p. 422

Letters of Rosa Luxemburg:

32 *Briefe aus dem Gefängnis*, Berlin 1920
    Briefe an Karl und Luise Kautsky (1896-1918), Berlin 1923
    Briefe an Freunde, Hrsg. Benedikt Kautsky, Hamburg 1950
    Rosa Luxemburg, *Listy do Leona Jogiches-Tyszki*, ed. Feliks Tych, Warsaw 1968-71, 3 vols. (for German version see note 34)
    Rosa Luxemburg, *Vive la lutte! Correspondence 1881-1914*, edited by Georges Haupt, Paris 1975
33 Rosa Luxemburg, *Die Akkumulation des Kapitals. Ein Beitrag zur ökonomischen Erklärung des Imperialismus*, 1913
34 Rosa Luxemburg, *Briefe an Leon Jogiches* (with an introduction by Feliks Tych) Frankfurt/M. 1971, pp. 143, 151, 155
35 quoted in Nettl, *Rosa Luxemburg*, p. 371
36 *Briefe an Leon Jogiches*, p 150
37 *Ibid.*, p. 91
    Cecil Roth, *Benjamin Disraeli*, New York 1952, p. 36
    André Maurois, *Disraeli, A Picture of the Victorian Age*, London 1948, p. 66
38 Max Adler, quoted in Paul Frölich, *Rosa Luxemburg, Gedanke und Tat*, pp. 196-7
39 Emil Vandervelde, quoted, *ibid.*, p. 39
40 Letter to Luise Kautsky (15.4.1917) in *Bulletin of the International Institute of Social History*, Amsterdam VIII

41 Nettl, *Rosa Luxemburg*, p. 115 (Summer 1889—"Sächsische Arbeiterzeitung")
    Badia, *Rosa Luxemburg*, pp. 595, 783 (October 1905, when editor of "Vorwärts")
42 Letter dated 5.1.1902, No. 162, quoted in Nettl, *Rosa Luxemburg*, p. 188
43 See note 32 for editions of Rosa Luxemburg's letters
44 Zdzislaw Leder, Leon Jogiches-Tyszka, *Centrale Archiwum Ruchu Robotniczego*, Vol 14 (Warszawa 1976) pp. 194-339
45 Israel Getzler, *Martov*, Cambridge 1967, ch. 2
46 Nettl, *Rosa Luxemburg*, p. 780; Frölich, *Rosa Luxemburg, Gedanke und Tat*, p. 301
47 Nettl, *Rosa Luxemburg*, p. 779
48 Charles Rappaport, "The Life of a Revolutionary Emigrant" (in Yiddish) YIVO, *Studies in History*, vol. III, Wilno 1939; p. 299
49 *Ibid.*, p. 301
50 *Ibid.*, p. 310
51 Rosa Luxemburg: *Listy do Leona Jogichesa-Tyszki*, ed. F. Tych, 2 Vols. (Warsaw 1961) vol. I, Introduction p. vii
52 *Briefe an Leon Jogiches*, pp. 29-32, 94, 101, 134
53 Quoted by Tych, in *Briefe an Leon Jogiches*, p. 222 n. 6
54 Studies on SPD:
    Carl E. Schorske, *German Social Democracy 1905-1917, The Development of the Great Schism*, New York 1972
    Gerhard A. Ritter, *Die Arbeiterbewegung im Wilhelminischen Reich*, Berlin 1959
    Hans J. Steinberg, *Sozialismus und Deutsche Sozialdemokratie, zur Ideologie der Partei vor dem Ersten Weltkrieg*, Hannover 1967
    G. D. H. Cole, *A History of Socialist Thought*, vol. II part 2, London 1956
    George Lichtheim, *Marxism*, London 1967 pp. 259-276
    P. Domann, *Sozialdemokratie und Kaisertum unter Wilhelm II*, Wiesbaden 1974
55 Studies on German social-economic history:
    Rolf Engelsing, *Sozial-und Wirtschaftsgeschichte Deutschlands*, Göttingen 1976
    Moderne deutsche Sozialgeschichte, Hrsg. Hans-Ulrich Wehler, Berlin 1970
    Moderne deutsche Wirtschaftsgeschichte, Hrsg. K. E. Born, Koln/Berlin 1966
56 The dilemmas of SPD:
    Michael R. Gordon, "Domestic Conflict and the Origins of the First World War: The British and German Cases", *Journal of Modern History* vol. 46, June (1974), pp. 191-226;
    William Maehl, "The Triumph of Nationalism in the German Socialist Party on the Eve of the First World War", *Journal of Modern History*, vol. 24 (1952), pp. 15-41
    Jurgen Kuczynski, *Die Geschichte der Lage der Arbeiter unter dem Kapitalismus*, Band 3, Berlin 1962
57 Gustav Mayer, *Friedrich Engels—Eine Biographie*, Den Haag 1934, vol. II p. 498
58 *Protokoll über die Verhandlungen* des Parteitages der SPD abgehalten zu Erfurt vom 14 – 20.10.1891, Berlin 1891, p. 172
59 "Einige Briefe Rosa Luxemburgs und andere Dokumente", *Bulletin of the International Institute of Social History*, 1952, VII, p. 10

60 Bebel to Kautsky (4.9.1901) quoted in Z. Zeman and W. Scharlau, *The Merchant of Revolution*, London 1965, p. 46

61 *Protokoll über die Verhandlungen* des Parteitages der SPD abgehalten in Lubeck 1901, Berlin 1901, p. 165

62 Studies on Parvus-Helphand: Winfried B. Scharlau, *Parvus-Helphand als Theoretiker in der deutschen Sozialdemokratie und seine Rolle in der ersten russischen Revolution 1867-1910*, Diss. Münster Universität 1964
Winfried B. Scharlau and Zbynek A. Zeman, *Freibeuter der Revolution. Parvus Helphand. Eine politische Biographie*, Köln 1964. (in English: *The Merchant of Revolution*, London 1965)

63 Scharlau and Zeman, *Freibeuter der Revolution*, pp. 334-340

64 Angel, *Eduard Bernstein*, p. 151

65 Eduard Bernstein, "Ignaz Auer, der Führer, Freund und Berater", *Sozialistische Monatshefte*, 1907, I, pp. 345-346

66 Eduard Bernstein, *Aus den Jahren Meines Exils*, Berlin 1917
Angel, *Eduard Bernstein*, pp. 103-109
Gay, *The Dilemma of Democratic Socialism*, pp. 107-109

67 Schorske, *German Social Democracy*, pp. 79-87
Steinberg, *Sozialismus und Deutsche Sozialdemokratie*, pp. 109-111

68 quoted in Eduard Bernstein, *Der Revisionismus in der Sozialdemokratie*, Amsterdam 1909, p. 39

69 Julius Braunthal, *Victor and Friedrich Adler*, Wieu 1965, pp. 114-117

70 *Protokoll über die Verhandlungen* des Parteitages der SPD abgehalten in Dresden, 1903, Berlin 1903

71 The Second Reich:
Volker R. Berghahn, *Germany and the Approach of War in 1914*, London 1973
Erich Eyck, *Das Persönliche Regiment Wilhelm II*, Zürich 1948
Eckart Kehr, *Der Primat der Innenpolitik*, Berlin 1970
Arthur Rosenberg, *Imperial Germany*, London 1966
Kopel S. Pinson, *Modern Germany, Its History and Civilization*, New York 1966
Fritz Hartung, *Deutsche Geschichte 1871-1919*, Bonn 1924

72 Von Puttkammer, "An den Vater, Mai 1859", p. 15, quoted in Kehr, *Der Primat der Innenpolitik*, p. 65

73 Friedrich Meinecke, *Weltbürgertum und Nationalstaat*, München 1962
Helmut Boehme, *Deutschlands Weg zur Grossmacht: Studien zum Verhältnis von Wirtschaft und Staat während der Reichsgründungszeit 1848-1881*, Köln/Berlin 1966

74 Heinrich von Sybel, *Die Begründung des Deutschen Reiches durch Wilhelm I*, München 1889 – 1894, 7 vols.

75 Otto Hintze, *Die Hohenzollern und ihr Werk*, Berlin 1915

76 Peter Domann, *Sozialdemokratie und Kaisertum unter Wilhelm II*, Wiesbaden 1974, p. 34

77 *Ibid.*, p. 23

78 *Ibid.*, p. 174

79 *Ibid.*, p. 141

80 Kehr, *Der Primat der Innenpolitik*, p. 101

81 R. Ensor, *England 1870-1914*, Oxford 1941, pp 87-90, 414-421
    Cecil S. Emden, ed. *Selected Speeches on the Constitution*, London 1939, vol. I,
    pp. 30-37, 174-180
82 Roy Jenkins, *Asquith*, London 1964
83 Schorske, *German Social Democracy*, pp. 227-233
84 Ritter, *Die Arbeiterbewegung*, pp. 177-187
    Erich Eyck, *Bismarck and the German Empire*, London 1958, pp. 174-179
85 Rainer Wahl, "Der preussische Verfassungskonflikt und das konstitutionelle
    System des Kaiserreichs", *Moderne deutsche Verfassungsgeschichte 1815-1918*,
    ed. Ernst Wolfgang Böckenförde, Köln 1972, pp. 171-188
    Pinson, *Modern Germany*, pp. 156-172
86 Fritz Stern, *The Failure of Illiberalism*, Chicago 1971, Part II
    Berghahn, *Germany and the Approach of War*, ch. 2
    Ludwig Dehio, "Um den deutschen Militarismus", *Historische Zeitschrift* 180,
    1955, pp. 43-64
    I. Geiss, "The Outbreak of the First World War and German War Aims",
    Journal of Contemporary History, July 1966, pp. 75-91
87 Max Weber, "Politik als Berufung", *Gesammelte Politische Schriften*, Stuttgart
    1958, pp. 493-584
    Federico Federici, *Der deutsche Liberalismus*, Zürich 1946, pp. 351-372
    John L. Snell, ed., *The Nazi Revolution, Germany's Guilt or Germany's Fate?*
    Boston 1959
    Theodor Heuss, *Friedrich Naumann*, Stuttgart/Tübingen 1949, pp. 126-133
88 1914-1918 War:
    Berghahn, *Germany and the Approach of War*, pp. 29-31
    Fritz Fischer, *Griff nach der Weltmacht. Die Kriegszielpolitik des kaiserlichen
    Deutschlands*, Düsseldorf 1962, pp. 110-128
    Wolfgang Schieder, Hrsg. *Erster Weltkrieg. Ursachen, Entstehung und
    Kriegsziele*, Köln 1969
    D. Groh, "The 'Unpatriotic Socialists' and the State", *Journal of Contemp-
    orary History*, Oct. 1966, pp. 151-177
    W. J. Mommsen, "The Debate on German War Aims", *Journal of
    Contemporary History*, July 1966, pp. 47-72
    Gerhard Ritter, "Das Problem des Militarismus in Deutschland", *Historische
    Zeitschrift*, 177, 1954 pp. 21-48
89 Domann, *Sozialdemokratie und Kaisertum*, p. 93
90 *Ibid.*, p. 177
91 *Ibid.*, p. 179
92 Berghahn, pp. 165-169
    Erich Eyck, *Das Persönliche Regiment Wilhelm II*, Zurich 1948, pp. 705-718
    Fritz Fischer, *Griff nach der Weltmacht*, Düsseldorf 1962, pp. 15-55
    Kehr, *Der Primat der Innenpolitik*, pp. 176-183
93 Gordon, *Journal of Modern History*, Vol. 46, p. 212
94 *Ibid.*, p. 226
95 Fritz Stern, "Bethmann Hollweg and the War: The Limits of
    Responsibility", *The Responsibility of Power; Historical Essays in Honour*

of Hajo Holborn, New York 1967, p. 265
96 *Ibid.,* p. 257
97 Rohan D'O. Butler, *The Roots of National Socialism, 1783-1933,* London 1941
Heinrich von Treitschke, *Politik,* Vorlesungen gehalten an der Universität zu
Berlin, Leipzig 1899-1900. (Here used the English translation, *Politics,*
London 1916, 2 vols.)
Friedrich Meinecke, *Die Idee der Staatsräson in der neueren Geschichte,* München
1928
K. S. Pinson, *Modern Germany,* pp. 308 ff
98 Treitschke, *Politics,* pp. 12-13
99 *Ibid.,* p. 13
100 *Ibid.,* p. 14
101 *Ibid.,* p. 43
102 *Ibid.,* p. 42-43
103 *Ibid.,* p. 15
104 *Ibid.,* p. 19
105 *Ibid.*
106 *Ibid.,* p. 21
107 *Ibid.,* p. 33
108 *Ibid.,* pp. 65-66
109 *Ibid.,* p. 66
110 *Ibid.,* p. 67
111 *Ibid.*
112 *Ibid.,* p. 68
113 Maehl, *Journal of Modern History,* Vol. 24, pp. 23-25
Heinrich Potthoff, *Die Sozialdemokratie von den Anfängen bis 1945,* Bonn 1974,
pp. 47-50
114 Domann, *Sozialdemokratie und Kaisertum,* p. 42
115 Steinberg, *Sozialismus und Deutsche Socialdemokratie,* p. 43
Domann, *Sozialdemokratie und Kaisertum,* pp. 39-44
Gerhard A. Ritter, *Die Arbeiterbewegung,* pp. 87-90
116 Karl Kautsky, *Der Weg zur Macht,* Berlin 1910
George Lichtheim, *Marxism,* Part V, ch. V
Cole, *History of Socialist Thought,* vol. III, Part I, pp. 249-322
117 Domann, *Sozialdemokratie und Kaisertum,* p. 88
118 Bebel, quoted in: Berlau, *The German Social Democratic Party,* pp. 46-47
Rikli, *Der Revisionismus,* pp. 111-113
Herman Heidegger, *Die Deutsche Sozialdemokratie und der nationale staat,*
1870-1920, Göttingen 1956, pp. 61-63
119 Hans Kohn, *Die Idee des Nationalismus,* Frankfurt/M. 1962, pp. 381-392
Pinson, *Modern Germany,* pp. 16, 18
120 Talmon, *Political Messianism,* pp. 199-200
Talmon, *The Unique and the Universal,* pp. 29-30
121 Karl Severing, *Mein Lebensweg,* Köln 1950, Bd. I, p. 147
122 Engelbert Pernerstorffer, quoted in Heidegger, *Die Deutsche Sozialdemokratie,*
pp. 62 ff

123 Bernstein, *Voraussetzungen*, p. 174
124 *Ibid.*
125 Ferdinand Lassalle, "Fichtes politisches Vermachtnis und die neueste Gegenwart", *Gesammelte Reden und Schriften*, hrsg. von E. Bernstein, Band 6, Berlin 1919, pp. 98-102; m"Die Philosophie Fichtes und die Bedeutung des Deutschen Volksgeistes", *ibid.*, pp. 134-152
H. Oncken, *Lassalle, Eine Politische Biographie*, Berlin, 1923, pp. 168-179; S. Na'aman, *Lassalle*, Hanover 1970, pp. 305 ff., 352 ff., 394 ff
126 *Protokoll über die Verhandlungen* des Parteitages der SPD, 1919, Berlin 1919, pp. 241-242
127 August Bebel, in: *Protokoll über die Verhandlungen* des Parteitages der SPD, abgehalten in Stuttgart 1907, Berlin 1907, p. 254
128 Rikli, *Der Revisionismus*, p. 112
129 Eduard Bernstein, "Sozialdemokratie und Imperialismus" *Sozialistische Monatshefte* IV, 1900, pp. 238-251
Gay, *The Dilemma of Democratic Socialism*, pp. 271-276
Pinson, *Modern Germany*, pp. 291-312
130 Gordon, *Journal of Modern History,* Vol. 46 pp. 214-226
Maehl, *Journal of Modern History*, Vol. 24 pp. 35-41
Schorske, *German Social Democracy*, chs. 9, 10
131 Badia, *Rosa Luxemburg*, ch. II
Paul Frölich, *Ideas in Action*, pp. 113-125
Nettl, *Rosa Luxemburg*, pp. 345-360
Luxemburg, Briefe an Karl und Luise Kautsky, pp. 89-180
132 Badia, *Rosa Luxemburg*, pp. 789-790
Nettl, *Rosa Luxemburg*, pp. 378-384
133 Letter to Henriette Roland-Holst (3.7.1905) in George Haupt (ed.) Rosa Luxemburg, *Vive la Lutte! Correspondance 1891-1914*, pp. 227-229
Luxemburg, *Briefe an Karl und Luise Kautsky*, p. 109
Letter to Emanuel and Mathilde Wurm (18.7.1906) in *Briefe an Freunde*, p. 44
Z. Kormanowa and Walentyna Najdus, eds., *Historia Polski*, vol. III, Part II, 1900-1914, Warsaw 1972, pp. 334-561
134 Karl Kautsky, "Ein Sozialdemokratisches Katechismus", *Die Neue Zeit*, 1893/94, I, pp. 368-403
135 Rosa Luxemburg, *Massenstreik, Partei und Gewerkschaften*, in: *Politische Schriften, I.* edited by K. Flechtheim, vol. I, pp. 135-228 (in English, *The Mass Strike, The Political Party and The Trade Unions*, London 1971)
For the impact of the 1905 Revolution on Rosa see:
Badia, *Rosa Luxemburg*, pp. 81-126
Frölich, *Ideas in Action*, pp. 77-123
Annelies Laschitza and Günter Radczun, *Rosa Luxemburg*, pp. 145-165
Fred Oelssner, *Rosa Luxemburg*, pp. 37-54
H. Schürer, "The Russian Revolution of 1905 and the Origins of German Communism", *The Slavonic and East European Review*, vol. 39, 1960-61, pp. 459-471

Maria Szlezinger, "Teoretyczne podstany Koncepcji spontanicznosci procesu rewolucyjnego w doktrynie R. Luksemburg", *Studya Socjologiezno Polityczne 1959*, no. 3, pp. 135-153

136 Luxemburg, *Mass Strike*, pp. 29-35
137 Talmon, *Political Messianism*, pp. 212-214
138 G. D. H. Cole, *British Working Class Politics, 1832-1924*, London 1946, pp. 11-21
Beatrice and Sydney Webb, *The History of Trade Unionism*, London 1920, pp. 117-118, 157-168
139 Luxemburg, *Mass Strike*, pp. 64-66
Luxemburg, *Wybór Pism*, Warsaw 1959, vol. I, p. 599; speech at 5th Congress of S.D.P.R.R. in London, May 1907
140 *Protokoll über die Verhandlungen* des Parteitages der SPD, abgehalten in Mannheim, 23 – 29.9.1906, Berlin 1906, pp. 289-305
Schorske, *German Social Democracy*, pp. 48-53
141 Gerhard A. Ritter, pp. 170-175
142 Schorske, *German Social Democracy*, p. 38
Luxemburg, *Mass Strike*, p. 46
143 Schorske, *German Social Democracy*, pp. 53-58
Steinberg, *Sozialismus und Deutsche Sozialdemocratie*, pp. 72-75
Berlau, *The German Social Democratic Party*, ch. II
144 Luxemburg, *Mass Strike*, pp. 70-73
145 Socialist theories of imperialism:
Parvus, *Die Gewerkschaften und die Sozialdemokratie*, Dresden 1896
Parvus, *Marineforderungen, Kolonialpolitik und Arbeiterinteressen* Dresden, 1898
Luxemburg, *Die Akkumulation des Kapitals oder Was die Epigonen aus der Marxschen Theorie gemacht Eine Antikritik*, Leipzig 1921
J. A. Hobson, *Imperialism*, London 1902
Rudolph Hilferding, *Das Finanzkapital*, Wien 1909
Karl Radek, *Der deutsche Imperialismus und die Arbeiterklasse*, Bremen 1912
J. Karski, *Zusammenbruch und Revolution*, Leipzig 1911
146 Luxemburg, *The Accumulation of Capital*, London 1963, with an introduction by Joan Robinson, pp. 13-28
Badia, *Rosa Luxemburg*, pp. 484-539 (esp. pp. 486-487)
Nettl, *Rosa Luxemburg*, pp. 530-536
147 Imperialism and Militarism:
Karl Kautsky, *Sozialismus und Kolonialpolitik*, Berlin 1907
Karl Kautsky, "Der Imperialismus", *Neue Zeit 1913-1914*, Bd. 2, p. 908 ff.
148 Luxemburg, *Sozialreform*, pp. 56-61;
Luxemburg, "Miliz und Militarismus", *Politische Schriften* Leipzig 1970, pp. 100-125
B. Semmel, *Imperialism and Social Reform*, London 1960, chs I-III
Lichtheim, *Imperialismus*, ch. 6, 7; R. Koebner, *Imperialism*, Cambridge 1964
V. G. Kiernan, *Marxism and Imperialism*, London 1974, pp. 9-27
149 Karl Erich Born, "Der soziale und wirtschaftliche Strukturwandel

Deutschlands am Ende des 19. Jahrhunderts'', *Moderne deutsche Sozialgeschichte,* Hrsg. Wehler, pp. 271-284

150 *Rosa Luxemburg im Kampf gegen den deutschen Militarismus,* Berlin (Ost) 1960 (Articles and speeches from 1913-1915 against German Militarism).

151 The permanent Revolution:
     Leon Trotsky, *Die permanente Revolution,* Berlin 1930
     Isaac Deutscher, *The Prophet Armed, Trotsky, 1879-1921,* New York/London 1954, ch. VI
     Parvus, Introduction to Trotsky's pamphlet, *Do Dewjatogo Janwarya,* (Till the 9th January), Genève 1905
     Parvus, ''Woina i Rewoljuzijy'' (War and Revolution) *Iskra,* 1904, nr. 59
     Parvus, ''Naschi Sadatschi'', *Natschalo,* 1905, Nr. 1
     Baruch Knei-Paz, *The Social and Political Thought of Leon Trotsky,* Oxford 1978, ch. IV

152 Karl Liebknecht, *''Militarismus und Antimilitarismus'',* 1907, in *Gesammelte Reden und Schriften,* Berlin 1958, Bd. I pp. 276-278

153 *Internationaler Sozialistenkongress zu Stuttgart,* 18. – 24.8.1907, Berlin 1907, p. 102

154 Badia, *Rosa Luxemburg,* pp. 161-166
     Laschitza/Radczun, *Rosa Luxemburg,* pp. 223-225
     Oelssner, *Rosa Luxemburg,* pp. 72-104
     Schorske, *German Social Democracy,* pp. 187-196

155 Badia, *Rosa Luxemburg,* p. 183
     The letter was published by Rosa Luxemburg in *Leipziger Volkszeitung,* 24.7.1911
     Laschitza/Radczun, *Rosa Luxemburg,* pp. 256-278
     Schorske, *German Social Democracy,* pp. 197-201
     Nettl, *Rosa Luxemburg,* pp. 446-450
     Protokoll über die Verhandlungen des Parteitages der SPD, abgehalten in Jena, 10 – 16.9.1911, Berlin 1911, pp. 204-218

156 Jan Kancewicz, ''Rosa Luxemburg, eine glühende Internationalistin'', Beiträge zur Geschichte der Arbeiterbewegung, vol. 13, 1971, pp. 407-409
     A. Ciolkosz, *Roza Luksemburg a rewolucja rosyjska* (Rosa Luxemburg and the Russian Revolution) Biblioteka ''Kultury'' LXII, Paris 1961

157 *Protokoll uber die Verhandlungen des Parteitages der SPD,* abgehalten in Chemnitz 1912, Berlin 1912, p. 427; This was exactly the view of Lenin in 1908 (with special emphasis upon ''the revolutionary democratic struggle in Asia''); see D. H. Gankin and H. H. Fisher, *The Bolsheviks and the World War,* Stanford 1940, pp. 65-66

158 *Chemnitz Parteitag,* p. 119

159 Maehl, *Journal of Modern History,* Vol. 24, p. 38

160 Schorske, *German Social Democracy,* pp. 276-284

161 Kancewicz, p. 411-412

162 Rosa Luxemburg, ''Dem Andenken des Proletariat'', *Gesammelte Werke,* Berlin (Ost) 1972, vol. 1/2, p. 313

163 Luxemburg im Kampf, p. 97

164 Luxemburg, *Wybór Pism*, vol. II, p. 119 ff; *Internationaler Sozialistenkongress zu Paris, 23 – 27.9.1900*, Berlin 1900, p. 27

165 For the fullest presentation in English of Rosa's views on the national question, see: *The National Question, Selected Writings by Rosa Luxemburg*, edited with an introduction by Horace B. Davis, New York 1976; for the views of SPD see Hans Ulrich Wehler, *Sozialdemokratie und Nationalstaat*, Würzburg 1962, especially ch. VI: "Die deutsche Sozialdemokratie und die preussischen Polen".

166 Jozef Feldman, "Ignacy Daszynski", *Polski Slownik Biograficzny*, Krakow 1938, vol. IV pp. 448-454
     Luxemburg, *Wybór Pism*, vol I, pp. 446 ff

167 Luxemburg, *Wybór Pism*, vol. II, pp. 128 ff

168 *Ibid.*, vol. I, pp. 56 ff

169 *Ibid.*, vol. I, pp. 73 ff
     Historia Polski, vol. III, pt. 1, pp. 370 ff, pt. 2, pp. 43 ff, 106 ff, 163 ff

170 Luxemburg, *Wybór Pism*, vol. I, pp. 64 ff

171 *Ibid.* vol. II, p. 126

172 *Ibid.*, vol. I, p. 383

173 *Historia Polski*, vol. III, pt. 2, pp. 298 ff; pt. 3 "Revolution in the Kingdom of Poland, 1905-1907"

174 *Ibid.*, vol. III, pt. 1, pp. 483 ff

175 *Ibid.*, pp. 472 ff; pt. 2, pp. 307 ff

176 Badia, *Rosa Luxemburg*, p. 452

177 *Briefe an Leo Jogiches*, p. 82

178 Parteitag der SPD in Mainz 1900, in Rosa Luxemburg, *Gesammelte Werke*, Berlin 1972, Band 1/1, pp. 797-798

179 Jürgen Hentze (ed.), Rosa Luxemburg, *Internationalismus und Klassenkampf; Die polnischen Schriften*, Berlin 1971, p. 178
     Rosa Luxemburg, in *Die Internationale, eine Monatsschrift für Theorie und Praxis des Marxismus*, Berlin 1915, p. 75

180 Luxemburg, *Polnische Schriften*, p. 169

181 *SDKPil Materjaly i Dokumenty 1914-1918*, Moscow 1936, pp. 372, 169

182 Luxemburg, in *Die Internationale*, p. 71

183 Luxemburg, "Die polnische Frage und die sozialistische Bewegung", *Polnische Schriften*, p. 261-262

Part III: "The Witches' Kitchen" and its brew—the nationalities problem in Austria (pp. 133-165)

General Bibliography:

Victor Adler, *Der Parteimann, Reden und Aufsätze*, hrsg. von Dr Gustav Pollatschek, Wien 1929

Julius Braunthal, *Victor und Friedrich Adler*, Wien 1965

Otto Bauer, "Die Natonalitätenfrage und die Sozialdemokratie", *Marx-Studien II*, Wien 1907

Heinrich Benedikt, "Die Wirtschaftliche Entwicklung in der Franz-Joseph Zeit", *Weiner Historische Studien* 4, Wien 1958

Ludwig Brügel, *Geschichte der Österreichischen Sozialdemokratie*, Wien 1923

G. D. H. Cole, *A History of Socialist Thought*, III, Pt. I: *The Second International 1889-1914*, London 1960

Werner Conze, "Die Strukturkrise des östlichen Mitteleuropas vor und nach 1919", *Vierteljahreshefte für Zeitgeschichte*, I, 1953

J. Feldmann, "I. Daszynski", *Polski Slownik Biograficzny*, IV, Krakau 1938

Ernst Fischer, *Der grossdeutsche Gedanke und die österreichische Arbeiterbewegung*, Wien 1946

Charles A. Gulick, *Austria from Habsburg to Hitler*, Berkeley, Los Angeles, 1948

Walter F. Hahn, "The Socialist Party of Austria; Retreat from Marx", *Journal of Central European Affairs*, XV, 1955

Hugo Hantsch, *Das Nationalitätenproblem im alten Österreich. Das Problem der konstruktiven Reichsgestaltung* (Wiener Historische Studien 1), Wien 1953

Oskar Jaszi, *The Dissolution of the Habsburg Monarchy*, Chicago 1929

James Joll, *The Second International 1889-1914*, London 1955

Robert A. Kann, *The Multinational Empire, Nationalism and Reform in the Habsburg Monarchy 1848-1914*, 2 vols., New York 1950

Karl Kautsky, "Nationalität und Internationalität", *Die Neue Zeit*, Erg. Heft I, Berlin 1908

Karl Kautsky, *Nationalstaat, imperialistischer Staat und Staatenbund*, Nürenberg 1915

Denis A. Kogan, "The Social Democrats and the Conflict of Nationalities in the Habsburg Monarchy", *Journal of Modern History*, XXI, 1949

Erik v. Kuehnelt-Leddin, "The Bohemian Background of German National Socialism", *Journal of the History of Ideas*, IX, 1948

Eugen Lemberg, *Die Geschichte des Nationalismus in Europa*, Stuttgart 1950

Edward Marz, "Some Economic Aspects of the Nationality Conflict in the Habsburg Empire", *Journal of Central European Affairs*, XIII/2, 1949

Erich Mathias, "Kautsky und der Kautskyanismus. Die Funktion der Ideologie in der deutschen Sozialdemokratie vor dem ersten Weltkrieg", *Marxismusstudien*, I, 1957

Arthur May, *The Habsburg Monarchy 1867-1914*, Cambridge 1951

Erwin Mayer-Löwenschwerdt, *Schönerer, der Vorkämpfer*, Wien 1938

Hans Mommsen, *Die Sozialdemokratie und die Nationalitätenfrage im Habsburgischen Vielvölkerstaat*, Wien 1963 (a precious quarry of a book)

Éduard Pichl, *Georg Schönerer und die Entwicklung des Alldeutschtums*, Berlin 1938

Karl Renner, *Staat und Nation*, Wien 1899

Karl Renner, *Der deutsche Arbeiter und der Nationalismus*, Wien 1913

Hans Rothfels, "Grundsätzliches zum Problem der Nationalitat", *Historische Zeitschrift*, 174, 1952

Hans Rothfels, "Zur Krise des Nationalstaates in Mitteleuropa", *Vierteljahreshefte für Zeitgeschichte*, I, 1953

Theodor Schieder, "Nationalstaat und Nationalitätenproblem", *Zeitschrift für Ostforschung*, I, 1952

Theodor Schieder, "Das Problem des Nationalismus in Osteuropa", *Osteuropa und der Deutsche Osten*, Reihe I, Buch 3, 1956

Theodor Schitlowsky, "Der Sozialismus und die Nationalitätenfrage", *Deutsche Worte*, XIX, 1899

Heinrich Schnee, *Georg Ritter von Schönerer, Ein Kämpfer für Alldeutschland*, Reichenberg 1941

R. W. Seton-Watson, *A History of the Czechs and Slovaks*, London 1943

Kurt L. Shell, *The Transformation of Austrian Socialism*, New York 1962

Edmund Silberner, "Austrian Social-Democracy and the Jewish Problem", *Historica Judaica*, XIII, 1951

Zdenek Solle, "Die tschechische Sozialdemokratie zwischen Nationalismus und Internationalismus", *Archiv für Sozialgeschichte*, Bd. IX, 1969, pp. 181-266

Zdenek Solle, "Die Sozialdemokratie in der Habsburger Monarchie und die tschechische Frage", *Archiv für Sozialgeschichte*, Bd. VI-VIII, 1966/67, pp. 315-390

Joseph Strasser, *Der Arbeiter und die Nation*, Reichenberg 1912

Leo Valiani, *The End of Austria-Hungary*, London 1973

A. J. P. Taylor, *The Habsburg Monarchy 1809-1918*, New York 1973

Andrew Whiteside, *Austrian National Socialism before 1918*, The Hague 1962

Andrew Whiteside, "Industrial Transformation, Population Movement and German Nationalism in Bohemia", *Zeitschrift für Ostforschung*, X, 1961

Otto Wittelshöfer, "Politische und wirtschaftliche Gesichtspunkte in der österreichischen Nationalitätenfrage", *Preussische Jahrbücher*, 76, 1894

Reinhard Wittram, *Das Nationale als europäisches Problem*, Göttingen 1954

Fran Zwitter, *Les problèmes nationaux dans la monarchie des Habsbourg*, Belgrade 1960

1   Victor Adler, *Der Parteimann*, p. 377

2   Charles A. Gulick, *Austria from Habsburg to Hitler*, Berkeley, Los Angeles, vol. I, ch. 2

Arthur J. May, *The Habsburg Monarchy 1867-1918*, Cambridge 1951, ch. I

A. J. P. Taylor, *The Habsburg Monarchy, 1809-1918*, chs. I, II

3   François Fejto (ed.), *The Opening of an Era 1848*, New York 1966, pp. 1-49; 253-280; 414-427

Robert A. Kann, *The Multinational Empire*, vol. II, ch. XV

Lewis B. Namier, *1848, The Revolution of the Intellectuals*, London 1944

Charles H. Pouthas, *Démocratie et capitalisme (1848-60)*, Paris 1961, pp. 46-54; 83-98

Priscilla Robertson, *Revolutions of 1848*, New York 1952, pp. 187-309

Taylor, *The Habsburg Monarchy*, chs. V, VI

4   Kann, *The Multinational Empire*, vol. II, chs. XVIII, XIX

Taylor, *The Habsburg Monarchy*, ch. VII

Hugo Hantsch, *Wiener Historische Studien*, I, Wien 1953, ch. IV

Hans Rothfels, *Vierteljahreshefte fur Zeitgeschichte*, I, 1953, pp. 138-152

Theodor Schieder, *Osteuropa und der deutsche Osten*, Reihe I, Buch 3, 1956

5   R. W. Seton-Watson, *The Czechs and Slovaks*, ch. 13
6   C. A. Macartney, *The Habsburg Empire 1790-1918*, London 1968, ch. XI
    Taylor, *The Habsburg Monarchy*, ch. XI
    Leo Valiani, *The End of Austria-Hungary*, ch. I
7   May, *The Habsburg Monarchy*, ch. II
8   Carlton Hayes, *Nationalism: A Religion*, New York 1960, chs. 7, 8
    Eugen Lemberg, *Nationalismus*, Hamburg 1964, vol I, Pt. II, ch. E
    P. Renouvin, *Le XIXe siècle, de 1815-1871, L'Europe des Nationalités et l'éveil de Nouveaux Mondes*, Paris 1954, ch. XVIII
    Seton-Watson, *History of the Czechs and Slovaks*, pp. 220-223
    Taylor, *The Habsburg Monarchy*, ch. XIII
    Fran Zwitter, *Les Problèmes nationaux*, pp. 86-113
9   Walter F. Hahn, "The Socialist Party of Austria, Retreat from Marx", *Journal of Central European Affairs*, XV, 1955, pp. 115-133
    Hans Rothfels, "Zur krise des Nationalstaates in Mitteleuropa", *Vierteljahreshefte für Zeitgeschichte*, pp. 138-152; and also his "Grundsätzliches zum Problem der Nationalität", *Historische Zeitschrift*, 174, 1952, pp. 339-358
    Theodor Schieder, "Nationalstaat und Nationalitätenproblem", *Zeitschrift für Ostforschung*, I, 1952.
10 Hans Mommsen, *Die Sozialdemokratie und die Nationalitätenfrage im Habsburgischen Vielvölkerstaat*, Wien 1963, p. 6
11 V. Adler to Engels (13.7.1895), in: *Aufsätze, Reden, Briefe*, ed. F. Adler, Wien 1922, Heft I
12 Mommsen, *Die Sozialdemokratie*, p. 4
13 Gustav Mayer, *Bismarck und Lassale, ihr Briefwechsel und ihre Gespräche*, Stettin 1928
    Hermann Oncken, *Lassale, Eine Politische Biographie*, Heidelberg 1923, pp. 374-403
    Shlomo Na'aman, *Lassale*, Hannover 1970, pp. 623-634
14 Zdenek Solle, "Die Sozialdemokratie in der Habsburger Monarchie und die tschechische Frage", *Archiv fur Sozialgeschichte*, VI, 1966-67, pp. 323-327
15 Mommsen, *Die Sozialdemokratie*, pp. 188-189
    Parteitagsprotokoll 1891, p. 175
16 Mommsen, *Die Sozialdemokratie*, p. 188
17 Brügel, *Geschichte der österreichischen Sozialdemokratie*, Bd. I p. 92
18 *Ibid.*, p. 122
19 *Der Radikale*. Sozialdemokratisches Organ der Arbeiter Nordböhmens, Reichenberg, 2.10.1884, quoted in Mommsen, *Die Sozialdemokratie*, p. 84
20 Solle, "Die Sozialdemokratie", *Archiv fur Sozialgeschichte*, VI 1966-67, pp. 317-318
21 Karl Marx, *Revolution und Konterrevolution in Deutschland*, Stuttgart 1896, introduction by Karl Kautsky, pp. 21-22
22 *Ibid.*, p. 30
23 Benedikt, *Die Wirtschaftliche Entwicklung*, pp. 133-153
    Marz, *Journal of General European Affairs*, 1949, pp. 123-135, esp. p. 129

Whiteside, *Zeitschrift für Ostforschung*, X, 1961 p. 50 ff
Wittelshöffer, *Preuss. Jhb*, 1894, pp. 461-484

24 Mommsen, *Die Sozialdemokratie*, p. 35
25 *Ibid.*, p. 35
Marz, *Journal of Central European Affairs*, 1949
Wittelshöfer, *Preuss. Jhb*, pp. 491-493
26 Jaszi, *The Dissolution of the Habsburg Monarchy*, Part IV, ch. 4
Seton-Watson, *A History of the Czechs and Slovaks*, ch. 13
Zwitter, *Les Problèmes nationaux*, pp. 129-147
Hayes, *Nationalism, A Religion*, ch. VIII
27 Mommsen, *Die Sozialdemokratie*, p. 329
28 Taylor, *The Habsburg Monarchy*, pp. 171-172
Jaszi, *The Dissolution of the Habsburg Monarchy*, p. 292
29 Seton-Watson, *A History of the Czechs and Slovaks*, pp. 221-222
30 Valiani, *The End of Austria-Hungary*, p. 8
31 Jaszi, *The Dissolution of the Habsburg Monarchy*, p. 290
Mommsen, *Die Sozialdemokratie*, pp. 272-276
32 Valiani, *The End of Austria-Hungary*, p. 29
33 Zdenek Solle, "Die tschechische Sozialdemokratie", *Archiv fur Sozialgeschichte*, IX, 1969, 181-189
34 Mommsen, *Die Sozialdemokratie*, p. 32
May, *The Habsburg Monarchy*, p. 202
35 Mommsen, *Die Sozialdemokratie*, p. 39
36 Eduard Benès, *Le problème Austrichien et la question Tschèque*, Paris 1908, p. 307
37 Solle, "Die Sozialdemokratie", pp. 221-226
38 Valiani, *The End of Austria-Hungary*, p. 3
39 Mommsen, *Die Sozialdemokratie*, pp. 35-39
Ernst Fischer, *Der grossdeutsche Gedanke und die österreichische Arbeiterbewegung*, Wien 1946
Andrew G. Whiteside, "Nationaler Sozialismus in Osterreich vor 1918", *Vierteljahreshefte fur Zeitgeschichte*, IX, 1961, p. 333 ff
40 Seton-Watson, *A History of the Czechs and Slovaks*, p. 234
41 Mommsen, *Die Sozialdemokratie*, p. 121
42 *Ibid.*, p. 26
Marz, "Economic aspects", *Journal of Central European Affairs*, XIII/2 1949, p. 130
43 Gulick, *Austria from Habsburg to Hitler*, vol. I, ch. 2
Hantsch, *Das Nationalitätenproblem*, ch. IV
Mayer-Löwenschwerdt, *Schönerer*, chs. IV-VII
Pichl, *Georg Schönerer*, ch. VI
Schnee, *Georg Ritter von Schönerer*, pp. 12-77
Whiteside, *Austrian National Socialism Before 1918*, ch. I.
44 Mommsen, *Die Sozialdemokratie*, pp. 346-352
Julius Braunthal, *Victor und Friedrich Adler*, pp. 122-123
Carl E. Schorske, "Politics in a New Key: An Austrian Triptych", *Journal of Modern History*, vol. 39, 1967, pp. 345-386

45 History of Socialist thought:
Cole, *The Second International 1889-1914*, vol. III, Pt. II, pp. 531-542
Kogan, *Journal of Modern History*, vol. XXI, 1949, pp. 204-217
Hahn, *Journal of Central European Affairs*, XV, 1955, pp. 115-119
Kann, *The Multinational Empire*, vol. II, pp. 154-179
Kurt L. Shell, *The Transformation of Austrian Socialism*, New York 1962, pp. 7-11

46 May, *The Habsburg Monarchy*, p. 63
Cole, *A History of Socialist Thought*, vol. III, pt. II, p. 530

47 *Ibid.*, p. 527
Mommsen, *Die Sozialdemokratie*, p. 107

48 Brügel, *Geschichte der Österreichischen Demokratie*, pp. 308; 340-343

49 Mommsen, *Die Sozialdemokratie*, pp. 381-439
May, *The Habsburg Monarchy*, pp. 337-339

50 Mommsen, *Die Sozialdemokratie*, pp. 171-178; 362-370
Hahn, *Journal of Central European Affairs*, pp. 115-119

51 Shell, *The Transformation of Austrial Socialism*, pp. 7-11

52 Mommsen, *Die Sozialdemokratie*, pp. 167-172
Taylor, *The Habsburg Monarchy*, pp. 164-168

53 Victor Adler, *Briefwechsel mit August Bebel und Karl Kautsky*, ed. Friedrich Adler, Wien 1954, p. 233

54 Mommsen, *Die Sozialdemokratie*, pp. 173-175; 366-369

55 *Ibid.*, pp. 174-175

56 Ibid., pp. 161-170

57 Adler, *Der Parteimann*, p. 328

58 Mommsen, *Die Sozialdemokratie*, pp. 314-315
Hantsch, *Das Nationalitätenproblem*, pp. 69-80

59 Hugh Seton-Watson, *The Decline of Imperial Russia 1855-1914*, New York 1961, pp. 231-245
Oscar Janowsky, *Nationalities and National Minorities*, New York 1945, pp. 19-22

60 Mommsen, *Die Sozialdemokratie*, pp. 384-388
R. W. Seton-Watson, *A History of the Czechs and the Slovaks*, pp. 241-244

61 Josef Feldman, ''I. Daszynski'', *Polski Slownik Biograficzny*, Krakow 1938, vol. IV, pp. 448-454

62 Solle, *Die tschechische Sozialdemokratie*, *Archiv für Sozialgeschichte*, IX (1969), pp. 201-210
Mommsen, *Die Sozialdemokratie*, pp. 401-422

63 *Ibid.*, pp. 417-421

64 Victor Adler, *Aufsätze, Reden, Briefe*, Wien 1926, Heft VIII, P. 94

65 Solle, ''Die tschechische, Sozialdemokratie'', *Archiv für Sozialgeschichte*, IX (1969), pp. 210-213
Mommsen, *Die Sozialdemokratie*, pp. 441-442
Cole, *A History of Socialist Thought*, Vol. III, pt 2, pp. 532-535

66 Cole, *ibid.*, pp. 546-558
Hahn, *Journal of Central European Affairs*, XV, 1955, pp. 115-133

Shell, *The Transformation of Austrian Socialism*, pp. 126-137
Kann, *The Multinational Empire*, vol. II, pp. 154-178
Norbert Leser, *Zwischen Reformismus und Bolschewismus*, Wien 1968, pp. 249-262
Karl Renner (pseud. Rudolf Springer), *Der Kampf der österreichischen Nationen um den Staat*, Wien 1902

67 Otto Bauer, "Die Nationalitätenfrage und die Sozialdemokratie"
68 *Ibid.*, pp. 120-138
    Renner, *Der Kampf*, pp. 29-31
69 Bauer, *Die Nationalitätenfrage*, pp. 146-164
    Renner, *Der Kampf*, pp. 26-32
70 Bauer, *Die Nationalitätenfrage*, pp. 353-381
71 *Ibid.*, pp. 83, 92
72 *Ibid.*, pp. 101-109
73 *Ibid.*, pp. 314-323
74 *Ibid.*, pp. 507-521
    Renner, *Der Kampf*, pp. 168-173
75 Bauer, *Die Nationalitätenfrage*, pp. 353-366
76 *Ibid.*, pp. 324-353
    Renner, *Der Kampf*, pp. 42-44
77 *Ibid.*, pp. 72-92
78 Bauer, *Die Nationalitätenfrage*, pp. 334-339
    Renner, *Der Kampf*, pp. 35-36
79 Bauer, *Die Nationalitätenfrage*, pp. 274-282
    Renner, *Der Kampf*, pp. 71-73

Part IV. The Jewish Dimension (pp. 169-234)

1 The Attorney-General of the Government of Israel *versus* Adolf Eichmann, In the District Court of Jerusalem, Criminal Case No. 40/61, Session 13, 24.4.1961
2 Louis B. Namier, *Avenues of History*, London 1952, pp. 4-5
3 Salo W. Baron, *Social and Religious History of the Jews*, New York 1937, vol. I, pp. 132-133
   Menachem Stern, "The Time of the Second Temple", *History of the Jewish People*, ed. H. H. Ben-Sasson (Hebrew), Tel-Aviv 1969, vol. I, pp. 268-270
   Michael Grant, *The Jews in the Roman World*, New York 1973, Introduction p. 11
4 Grant, *Jews in the Roman World*, p. 59
5 Tacitus, *Histories*, Book V, 1-5
   Menachem Stern, *Greek and Latin Authors on Jews and Judaism*, Jerusalem 1977, vol. I, p. 409
   Emil Schürer, *A History of the Jewish People in the Time of Jesus*, New York 1961, p. 206

6   Stern, "The Time of the Second Temple", p. 280
    Stern, *Greek and Latin Authors*, p. 389 ff
6a Fr. Nietzsche, *The Genealogy of Morals*, First Essay, §8, "The Philosophy of
    Nietzsche, the Modern Library, New York 1954, pp. 644-645
7   Matthew Arnold, "Hebraism and Hellenism", in *Culture and Anarchy*,
    Cambridge 1935, pp. 129-144
8   Joseph Klausner, *The Messianic Idea* (Hebrew), Tel Aviv 1950
    Gershom Scholem, *The Messianic Idea in Judaism and Other Essays on Jewish
    Spirituality*, London 1971
    Abba-Hillel Silver, *A History of Messianic Speculation in Israel from the 1st through
    the 17th Centuries*, New York 1927
9   James Parkes, *The Conflict of the Church and the Synagogue*, London 1934
10 St Bernard of Clairvaux, *Letters*, trans. Bruno Scott-James, London 1953, pp.
    462-463 (see also in J. Prawer, *A History of the Latin Kingdom of Jerusalem*,
    (Hebrew) Jerusalem 1963, vol. I, pp. 262-264)
11 N. McLean, "Marcionism" in *Encyclopaedia of Religion and Ethics*, ed. J.
    Hastings, New York 1916, vol. VIII, pp. 407-409
12 S. Safrai, "The Times of the Mishna and the Talmud", in H. H. Ben-Sasson
    (ed.) *History of the Jewish People*, p. 301 ff; for "Minyan", see: *Encyclopaedia
    Judaica*, Jerusalem 1971, vol. XII, p. 67
13 Jean Juster, *Les Juifs dans l'Empire Romain*, Paris 1914
14 Henri Pirenne, *Medieval Cities*, Princeton 1939, esp. chs. V-VIII
15 H. H. Ben-Sasson, "The History of the Jews in the Middle Ages" in: *History
    of the Jewish People*, vol. III, pp. 22-23
16 Yitzhak Baer, *A History of the Jews in Christian Spain*, Philadelphia 1966, esp.
    vol. II, ch. XV, pp. 437-439
17 Selma Stern, *The Court Jew*, trans. R. Weiman, Philadelphia 1950
18 Arthur Herzberg, *The French Enlightenment and the Jews*, New York 1968
19 Samuel Ettinger, "Jews and Judaism as seen by the English Deists of the 18th
    Century", in: *Zion*, vol. XXIX (1964), pp. 182-207, (Hebrew)
20 Simon Dubnov, *History of the Jews*, transl. M. Spiegel, New York 1971, vol.
    IV, pp. 512-514
    Bernhard Blumenkranz (ed.) *Colloque "Les Juifs et la Révolution Francaise"*,
    Toulouse 1976
21 Jacob Katz, *Emancipation and Assimilation: Studies in Modern Jewish History*,
    Farnborough 1972
    Jacob Katz, *Out of the Ghetto; The Social Background of Jewish Emanci-
    pation, 1770-1870*, Cambridge, Mass. 1973
22 Maurice Liber, "La Révolution, les Juifs et le Judaisme", *Univers Israëlite*, 25
    Août – 1 Sept. 1939
23 Bruno Bauer, *Die Judenfrage*, Braunschweig 1843, pp. 24-45, 75-79
    Nathan Rotenstreich, "For and Against Emancipation: The Bruno Bauer
    Controversy", *Leo Baeck Institute Yearbook IV*, London 1959
24 James Joll, "Rathenau", in: *Intellectuals in Politics*, London 1960
    on Namier see: Talmon, *The Unique and the Universal*, London 1965, ch. 10
25 A. Toussenel, *Les Juifs, rois de l'époque. Histoire de la féodalité financière*, Paris

1845-1847, pp. 73-74

26 Moses Hess, *Briefwechsel*, ed. E. Silberner, The Hague 1959, p. 80; see also Dubnov, *History of the Jews*, Vol. IV, p. 514

27 Zygmunt Krasinski, *Nie-Boska Komedia*, Paris 1862

28 Hannah Arendt, *Rahel Varnhagen: Lebensgeschichte einer deutschen Jüdin aus der Romantik*, München 1959

29 Karl Dietrich Bracher, *The German Dictatorship*, transl. J. Steinberg, London 1973, pp. 42-43

Koppel Pinson, *Modern Germany*, New York 1954, p. 66 ff

30 R. Stadelmann, *Soziale und Politische Geschichte der Revolution von 1848*, München 1948, pp. 45-46

V. Valentin, *Geschichte der Deutschen Revolution 1848-49*, 2 vols. Berlin 1930-31

Jacques Droz, *Les Révolutions allemandes de 1848*, Paris 1957

F. Fejtö (ed.), *The Opening of an Era: A Historical Symposium*, New York 1966

Jacob Touri, *Turmoil and Confusion in the Revolution of 1848* (Hebrew), Tel-Aviv 1968

31 Touri, *Turmoil and Confusion*, pp. 68, 72

32 *Ibid.*, pp. 118-119

33 Benjamin Disraeli, *Life of George Bentinck*, London, 1905, ch. XXIV, "The Jewish Question"

34 J. L. Bernays, Articles in: *Israel's Herald*, 4.5.1849, 18.5.1849. I wish to thank Prof. Jacob Touri of the University of Tel-Aviv for placing the journal at my disposal

35 Cecil Roth, *Disraeli*, New York 1952, p. 143 ff

Robert Blake, *Disraeli*, London 1966, pp. 194-6

36 W. F. Monypenny and G. E. Buckle, *The Life of Benjamin Disraeli*, London 1920, Vol. VI, pp. 10 ff

37 Bernays, see note 34

38 Edmund Silberner, *Moses Hess*, Leiden 1966, p. 29; Hess "Tagebuch", 13 July 1835

39 Disraeli, *Life of George Bentinck*, ch. XXIV

40 *Ibid.*

41 Talmon, *The Unique and the Universal*, p. 83

42 K. Grunwald, "Europe's Railways and Jewish Enterprise", *Leo Baeck Institute Yearbook* XII (1967)

L. Landes, *Bankers and Pashas*, London 1958

43 L. D. Easton and K. H. Guddat, *Writings of the Young Marx on Philosophy and Society*, New York 1967 pp. 245-247

44 George Lichtheim, "Socialism and the Jews", *Dissent*, July – August 1968, pp. 314-342

Edmund Silberner, *Western European Socialism and the Jewish Question, 1800-1918*, Jerusalem 1955 (Hebrew)

Talmon, *Political Messianism*, London 1960, p. 207

45 Bauer, *Die Judenfrage*, p. 14

46 Fritz Stern, *Gold and Iron; Bismarck, Bleichröder and the Building of the German*

Empire, London 1977

47 Walter Frank, *Demokratie und Nationalismus in Frankreich der Dritten Republik*, Hamburg 1933

48 Paul W. Massing, *Rehearsal for Destruction. A Study of Political anti-Semitism in Imperial Germany*, New York 1946
P. G. Pulzer, *The Rise of Political Anti-Semitism in Germany and Austria*, New York 1946 (for statistical data see pp. 9-11)
Fritz Stern, *The Politics of Cultural Despair*, New York 1965
Léon Poliakov, *Histoire de l'antisemitisme*, Paris 1955-77, 4 vols.
Léon Poliakov, *The Aryan Myth; a History of Racist and Nationalist Ideas in Europe*, translated by Edmund Howard, London 1979

49 Jaques Chastenet, *Histoire de la Troisième République*, Paris 1952-56, Vol. II, ch. IX, p. 177 *ff*
Adrien Dansette, *Le Boulangisme*, Paris 1946

50 Zeev Sternhell, *La Droite révolutionnaire 1885-1914: les origines française du fascisme*, Paris 1978, pp. 33 ff

51 Hannah Arendt, *The Origins of Totalitarianism*, New York 1968, p. 242
Jean-Paul Sartre, *Anti-Semite and Jew*, transl. G. J. Becker, New York 1974, (French: *Reflexiones sur la question juive*, Paris 1946)

52 On the French Right after 1870 see:
Raoul Girardet (ed.), *Le Nationalisme français 1871-1914*, Paris 1966
Réné Rémond, *La Droite en France de la première restauration à la Cinquième République*, 3ème ed., Paris 1968
Eugen Weber, *Action Française*, Stanford 1962

53 Maurice Barrès, *Scènes et doctrines du nationalisme*, Paris 1902
Zeev Sternhell, *Barrès et le nationalisme français*, Paris 1972
Zeev Sternhell, *Les idées politiques et sociales de Maurice Barrès, 1884-1902*, Paris 1969

54 Heinrich von Treitschke, *Ein Wort über unser Judentum*, Berlin 1881; English transl.: *A Word About Our Jewry*, transl. H. Lederer, Cincinnati 1958

55 Walter Frank, *Hofprediger Adolf Stöcker und die Christlich-Soziale Bewegung*, Berlin 1928

56 Pulzer, *The Rise of Political Anti-Semitism*, ch. 12, p. 108 ff

57 Erich Eyck, *Bismarck*, 3 vols. Zürich 1941-44, vol. III, p. 287 ff

58 Fritz Stern, *Gold and Iron*, ch. 18, pp. 494 ff, esp. pp. 517-531

59 Eyck, *Bismarck*, vol. III, pp. 252 ff

60 Frank, *Hofprediger Adolf Stöcker*, p. 118 ff

61 Fritz Stern, *Gold and Iron*, pp. 516 ff, 529

62 *Ibid.*, pp. 470 ff

63 Bina Garncarski, *The Industrial Region of Warsaw in the years 1865-1914, and the Role of Jews in its Development*, (Hebrew, unpublished Ph.D. Dissertation in the Hebrew University, Jerusalem 1971)

64 Zana Kormanowa and Walenty Najdus (eds.), *Historia Polski*, Polish Academy, Institute of History, vol. III, 2, Warsaw 1972, p. 327

65 Andrew G. Whiteside, *The Socialism of Fools: Georg Ritter von Schönerer and Austrian Pan-Germanism*, Berkeley, California 1975

66 Pulzer, *The Rise of Political Anti-Semitism*, pp. 3-17
67 *Ibid.*, For growth of Jewish population in Vienna see: "Vienna" in: *The Universal Jewish Encyclopaedia*, (New York, 1943), Vol. 10, p. 417; in: *Encyclopaedia Judaica* (Jerusalem, 1971), Vol. 16, p. 124
68 Whiteside, *The Socialism of Fools*, pp. 33, 38, 112
69 Kurt Skalnik, *Dr Karl Lueger: der Mann zwischen den Zeiten*, Wien 1954
70 'Friedrich Engels', *Briefwechsel mit Karl Kautsky*, ed. B. Kautsky, Wien 1955, p. 125
71 *Ibid.*, p. 159
72 Heinrich Schnee, *Georg Ritter von Schönerer*, Reichenberg 1941, pp. 18-19
73 Whiteside, *The Socialism of Fools*, pp. 95-97
74 Theodor Mommsen, *Auch ein Wort über unser Judentum*, Berlin 1880
75 George L. Mosse, *The Nationalization of the Masses*, New York 1975, p. 97; p. 136
76 Uriel Tal, *Christians and Jews in Germany; Religion, Politics and Ideology in the Second Reich 1870-1914*, transl. N. J. Jacobs, Ithaca 1975
   Uriel Tal, *Religious and Anti-Religious Roots of Modern Anti-Semitism*, New York 1971
77 Treitschke, *Ein Wort*, p. 3
78 Friedrich Nietzsche, *Beyond Good and Evil*, sec. 251
79 Frank, *Stöcker*, p. 118
80 Alfred Bäumler, *Bildung und Gemeinschaft*, Berlin, 1942, p. 81
81 Richard Wagner, *Juden in der Musik*, Leipzig 1850
82 Henry C. Plaine (ed.), *Darwin, Marx and Wagner — a Symposium*, Columbus, Ohio 1962
   Leon Stein, *The Racial Thinking of Richard Wagner*, New York 1950
   Robert W. Gutman, *Richard Wagner*, London 1969
83 Jacques Droz, (ed.), *Le romantisme politique en Allemagne*, Paris 1963
   J. L. Talmon, *Romanticism and Revolt*, London 1967, pp. 135 ff
84 Houston Stewart Chamberlin, *Die Grundlagen des XIX Jahrhunderts*, 9th ed. 2 vols. München 1909, English trans. by J. Lees: *Foundations of the 19th Century*, 2 vols. New York 1914
   Erich Voegelin, *Rasse und Staat*, Lübingen, 1933
   George Mosse, *Towards the Final Solution*, London 1978, pp. 105-108
85 Allan Bullock, *Hitler: A Study in Tyranny*, New York 1962, pp. 80 ff
   Bracher, *The German Dictatorship*, pp. 30, 165
   Joachim Fest, *Hitler*, London 1974, pp. 55 ff, pp. 200 ff
86 Dietrich Eckart, "Der Bolshevismus von Moses zum Lenin", in: Ernst Nolte, *The Three Faces of Fascism*, New York 1965, pp. 329 ff, p. 406
87 G. Himmelfarb, *Darwin and the Darwinian Revolution*, New York 1968, ch. VI
88 Nietzsche, *Beyond Good and Evil*, transl. Walter Kaufmann, sec. 257 ff
89 Raoul Girardet, (ed.), *Le Nationalisme Français*, 1871-1914, Paris 1966, pp. 143-146; "La France Juive", pp. 146-149—Conquête Juive et problème social, by Edouard Drumont
90 Fritz Stern, *Gold and Iron*, p. 503
91 Nolte, *Three Faces of Facism*, pp. 329 ff

92 Nietzsche, *The Dawn*, sec. 205
93 Pulzer, *The Rise of Political Anti-Semitism*, p. 219 ff
93a Quoted in Pulzer, *The Rise of Political Anti-Semitism*, pp. 185-187
94 *Historia Polski*, III, 2, pp. 325 ff, 416, 428
95 Georges Haupt, "Les Socialistes et la Campagne Antisémite en Pologne en 1910: un épisode inédit", *Revue du Nord*, Tome LVII, No. 225 (1975) p. 185
96 Eugen Weber, *L'Action Française*, Stanford, 1962, p. 229
97 Schnee, *Georg Ritter von Schönerer*, pp. 207-211
98 Sigmund Freud, *Works*, trans. into Hebrew by Ch. Issak and A. Baer, Tel-Aviv 1966
99 Rosa Luxemburg, *Briefe an Freunde*, Hamburg 1950, pp. 48-49
100 Rosa Luxemburg, *Vive la Lutte! Correspondance 1891-1914*, Paris 1975, pp. 105-106
101 *Ibid.*, p. 106
102 Julius Braunthal, *Victor und Friedrich Adler*, Wien, 1965, ch. 14, p. 189 ff
103 K. Kautsky, "Rzeź w Kiszyniowie i kwestja Zydowska" *Przegląd socjaldemokratyczny*, V (1903), Nr. 5, pp. 170-175
104 Rosa Luxemburg, *Briefe an Karl und Luise Kautsky, 1896-1918*, Berlin 1923, p. 69
105 "Gewalt ai wai geschriehen" (Parvus, Rosa Luxemburg), *Listy*, vol. I, p. 442
106 Edmund Silberner, *Moses Hess*, p. 27
107 Gustav Noske, *Aufstieg und Niedergang der Deutschen Sozialdemokratie*, Zürich 1947, p. 27
108 Leopold L. Haimson, *The Russian Marxists and the Origins of Bolshevism*, Boston 1955, p. 60
109 Leon Trotsky, *Moya zhizn*, Berlin 1930, vol. I, pp. 110-111
110 Georg Lucács, *Geschichte und Klassenbeurnstsein, Studien über Marxistische Dialektik*, Berlin 1923, p. 56
111 Talmon, *Political Messianism*, p. 65 ff
112 *Ibid.*, p. 71
113 *Ibid.*, p. 72
114 Silberner, *Moses Hess*, p. 27
115 Braunthal, *Victor und Friedrich Adler*, pp. 30-31
116 Rosa Luxemburg, *Vive la Lutte!*, p. 61
117 Carl E. Schorske, "Politics and Patricide in Freud's 'Interpretations of Dreams'", *American Historical Review*, vol. 78 (1973), pp. 328-347
118 On the part played by Jews in the Russian Revolutionary Movement see:
Israel Getzler, *Martov*, Cambridge 1967
Leonard Schapiro, "The Role of the Jews in the Russian Revolutionary Movement", *Slavonic and East European Review*, vol. XL (1961-1962)
F. Venturi, *Roots of Revolution*, New York 1960
A. Yarmolinsky, *Road to Revolution*, New York 1962
Abraham Ascher, *Pavel Axelrod and the Development of Menshevism*, Cambridge Mass. 1972
Robert S. Wistrich, *Revolutionary Jews from Marx to Trotsky*, London 1976

119 E. Tscherikover, *Jews in Time of Revolution*, (Hebrew), Tel-Aviv 1957, pp. 209-210
120 *Ibid.*, p. 217
121 *Ibid.*, pp. 217-218
122 *Ibid.*
123 Shlomo Na'aman, *Ferdinand Lassale: Deutscher und Jude*, Hannover 1968
124 Lichtheim, "Socialism and the Jews", *Dissent* (July-August 1968), pp. 317, 319-323
     E. Silberner, "Proudhon's Judeophobia", *Historia Judaica*, X, 1948
     "The Revolutionary Jew-hatred of M. A. Bakunin", *ibid.*, XIV, 1952
125 Lichtheim, "Socialism and the Jews", p. 322
126 *Ibid.*
127 *Ibid.*
128 Tscherikover, *Jews in Times of Revolution*, pp. 200 ff
129 *Ibid.*, p. 395
130 On this subject see:
     Edmund Silberner, "Antisemitism and Philosemitism in the Socialist International", *Judaism*, vol. II, (1953), pp. 117-122
131 Lucy Dawidowicz (ed.), *The Golden Treasury*, New York 1967, pp. 406-410
     see also: A. Ascher, *Pavel Axelrod*, p. 107, n. 1
     Tscherikover, *Jews in Time of Revolution*, pp. 393-394
132 E. Silberner, "Antisemitism in French Revolutionary Syndicalism", *Jewish Social Studies*, vol. XV, 1953
     Eugene Weber, *The Nationalist Revival in France 1905-1914*, Berkeley 1959
     H. Arendt, *The Origins of Totalitarianism*, pp. 228-229
133 Tscherikover, *Jews in Time of Revolution*, p. 214
134 *Ibid.*, pp. 237-241 (on Zundelevich)
135 *Ibid.*, p. 225
136 Th. Herzl, *Diaries*, ed. by M. Lewenthal, London 1958, p. 395
137 Zeev Ivianski, *Individual Terror: Theory and Deed* (Hebrew) Tel-Aviv 1977, pp. 241-242
138 Michael Cherniavsky, *Prologue to Revolution*, Englewood Cliffs (New Jersey), 1967, pp. 56-58
139 Richard Charques, *The Twilight of Imperial Russia*, Oxford 1958, pp. 167-168
140 I wish to thank Mrs Dvora Barzilai-Jager for kindly letting me see the memorandum on the meeting in the Weizmann Archives, Rehovot.

Part V. Russia—Holy, Profaned and Pre-destined (pp. 235-332)

1 F. L. Carsten, *Revolution in Central Europe 1918-1919*, Berkeley and Los Angeles 1972, "A Revolution Defeated", pp. 323-335
2 Michael T. Florinsky, *Russia: A History and Interpretation*, Oxford, New Haven 1955
   Richard Pipes, *Russia under the Old Regime*, New York 1974
   Hugh Seton-Watson, *The Russian Empire, 1801-1917*, Oxford 1969

B. H. Sumner, *Survey of Russian History*, London 1961
3 Thomas Masaryk, *The Spirit of Russia*, 2 vols., London 1961
   Nikolai Berdyaev, *The Origin of Russian Communism*, Ann Arbor 1962
   Tibor Szamuely, *The Russian Tradition*, London 1974
   Edmund Wilson, *To the Finland Station*, New York 1972
   The Russian Intelligentsia, *Journal of the American Academy of Arts and Sciences,
   Daedalus*, 1960
   E. J. Simmons, (ed.), *Continuity and Change in Russian and Soviet Thought*,
   Cambridge, Mass. 1955
   Jerzy Plechanow, *Historia Rosyiskiej Mysli-Spolecznej*, 3 vols., Warsaw 1967
4 George Katkov, Ervin Oberländer, Nicolas Peppe and George von Rauch
   (editors), *Russia enters the Twentiety Century 1894-1917*, London 1971 —
   Harry Willetts, The Agrarian Problem, pp. 120-121
5 Andrezej Walicki, *The Slavophile Controversy: History of a Conservative Utopia
   in XIXth Century Russian Thought*, Stanford 1975

2. The Birth of a Revolutionary Ideology — Belinsky and Herzen
1 G. Plekhanov, *Izbrannye filosoficheskie sochineniya*, Moscow 1956-1958, vol.
   IV, pp. 541-542
2 Quoted in I. Berlin, *Russian Thinkers*, London 1978, p. 150
3 *V. G. Belinsky, Polnoye sobranie sochinenii*, Moscow 1953-1959, XII, p. 23:
   Letter to Botkin (1.3.1841)
   (In succeeding references this edition will be referred to as V. Belinsky); I
   was greatly helped by *Wissarion Bielinski, Pisma filozoficzne*, 2 vols. (in
   Polish), ed. by Andrzej Walicki, Warsaw 1956. Besides I. Berlin, the
   secondary studies most utilised were H. E. Bowman, *V. Belinsky 1811-1848,
   A Study in the Origins of Social Criticism in Russia*, Cambridge, Mass. 1954;
   Jerzy Plechanow, *Historia Rosyjskiej Mysli spolecznej*, vol. III, Warsaw 1967
4 *V. Belinsky*, vol. XI, p. 282, Letter to Bakunin 10.9.1838
5 *Ibid.*, p. 283
6 *Ibid.*
7 *Ibid.*, p. 318, Letter to Bakunin (12 – 24.10.1838)
8 *Ibid.* pp. 176-181. Letter to Bakunin (16.8.1837)
9 *Ibid.* p. 320
10 *Ibid.*, p. 174, Letter to Bakunin (16.8.1837)
11 *Ibid.*, vol. XII, P. 66, Letter to Botkin (8.9.1841)
12 Bielinsky (ed. Walicki), p. 142. Letter to Ivanov (7.8.1837)
13 Belinski, Vol. II., p. 240
14 *Ibid.*, Vol. XI, p. 152
15 H. E. Bowman, *V. Bielinski*, pp. 55-6
16 Belinsky, Vol. XI, p. 146
17 *Ibid.*, p. 148; see also Plechanow, III, 205; Walicki, (ed.), *Wissarion Bielinski,*
   vol. I, p. 145
17a *Ibid.*, pp. 148-9
18 *V. Belinsky*, vol. XI, p. 150; Plechanow, *Historia*, vol. III, pp. 206-208

19   *V. Belinsky,* Vol. XI, p. 150
20   *Ibid.,* p. 151
21   *Ibid.,* p. 153
21a *Ibid.,* Plechanow, *Historia,* vol. III, pp. 207-208
22   *Belinsky,* vol. XI, p. 281, Letter to Bakunin, 10.9.1838
23   *Ibid.,* p. 283
24   *Ibid.,* p. 285
25   *Ibid.,* p. 286
26   *Ibid.,* p. 318, Letter to Bakunin, 12 – 24.10.1838
27   *Ibid.,* p. 286, Letter to Bakunin, 10.9.1838
28   *Ibid.,* pp. 385-386, Letter to Stankevich, 29.9. – 8.10.1839
28a Walicki (ed.), *Bielinski,* p. 170
28b *Ibid.,* p. 192
28c *Ibid.,* p. 194
28d Bowman, *Bielinsky,* pp. 113-114
29   *V. Belinsky,* vol. XI, p. 577, Letter to Botkin 10 – 11.12.1840
30   *W. Belinski,* vol. XII, p. 22, Letter to Botkin 1.3.1841
31   *Ibid.,* p. 23
32   *Ibid.,* p. 23
33   *Ibid.,* pp. 69-70, Letter to Botkin 8.9.1841
34   V. Belinsky, vol. XI, pp. 556, 558, Letter to Botkin 4.10.1840
35   *Ibid.,* vol. XII, p. 52, Letter to Botkin 27 – 28.6.1841
36   *Ibid.,* p. 66, Letter to Botkin 8.9.1841
37   *Ibid.,* p. 70
38   *Ibid.,* pp. 70-71
39   *Ibid.,* pp. 71-72
40   *Ibid.,* pp. 70, 72
41   *Ibid.,* vol. VI, p. 96
42   *Ibid.,* vol. XI, p. 528, Letter to Botkin 13.6.1840
43   *Ibid.,* vol. XII, P. 49, Letter to Botkin 27 – 28.6.1841
44   *Ibid.,* vol. XI, p. 527, Letter to Botkin 13.6.1840
45   *Ibid.,* p. 577, Letter to Botkin 10 – 11.12.1840
46   *Ibid.,* vol. XII, p. 67, Letter to Botkin 8.9.1841
47   *Ibid.,* p. 68
48   *Ibid.,* vol. XII, 576-7, Letter to Botkin, 10-11.11.1840
49   *Ibid.,* p. 527, Letter to Botkin 13.6.1840
50   *Ibid.,* vol. XII, p. 66, Letter to Botkin 8.9.1841
51   *Ibid.,* vol. XI, p. 529, Letter to Botkin 13.6.1840
52   A. I. Herzen, *Sobranie sochinenii v tridtsati tomakh,* Moscow 1954-56, vol. IX,
     p. 23; Alexander Herzen, *My Past and Thoughts,* New York 1968, vol. II,
     p. 403.
        In addition and alongside the Russian edition of the Collected Writings
     to be referred to as Herzen, *Sobranie,* we utilized the English translation of
     Herzen's Selected Philosophical Works, Moscow 1956, and the excellent Polish
     version of the Philosophical Works edited by Andrzej Walicki, *A. Hercen,*
     Pisma filozoficzne, 2 vols., Warsaw 1965-66. The English version will be

referred to as *"Herzen, Selected,"* the Polish as *"Hercen, Pisma."*
The studies most frequently consulted have been the Polish translation of George Plekhanov's *History of Russian Social Thought,* Jerzy Plechanow *Historia rosyjskiej myśli społecznej,* 3 vols., Warsaw 1967; Isaiah Berlin, *Russian Thinkers,* London 1978; M. Malia, *Alexander Herzen and the Birth of Russian Socialism,* New York 1965; E. Lampert, *Studies in Rebellion,* London 1957; Franco Venturi, *Roots of Revolution,* New York 1960; Andrzej Walicki, *Rosyjska Filozofia i Myśl społeczna, od Oswiecenia do Markiszmu,* Warsaw 1974

53 *Herzen, Sobranie,* vol. III, pp. 5 – 88; *Selected,* pp. 15-96
54 *Herzen, Sobranie,* vol. IX, p. 23; *My Past,* vol. II, p. 403
55 *Herzen, Pisma,* vol. II, p. 643, entry Diary of 15.8.1842; H. Malia, *Alexander Herzen and the birth of Russian Socialism,* 254
56 E. H. Carr, *Michael Bakunin,* New York 1961, pp. 76-85; N. Pirumova, *Mikhail Bakunin, Zhizn i deyatelnost,* Moscow 1966, p. 21
57 Plechanow, *Historia rosyjskiej,* vol. III, pp. 235, 420-427, 430, 424
58 L. Greenberg, *The Jews in Russia,* Yale University Press 1965, vol. I, p. 34
59 *Ibid.,* p. 32
60 *Ibid.*
61 *Ibid.,* p. 35
62 Herzen, *My Past,* vol. I, pt. II, pp. 159-220, vol. II, pt. IV, pp. 426-469
63 *Herzen, Sobranie,* vol. VI, pp. 14-15; *From the Other Shore,* London 1956, pp. 12-13
64 *Herzen, Sobranie,* vol. II, p. 240; Malia, *Alexander Herzen,* p. 305; Plechanow, *Historia,* vol. III, 319-320
65 *Herzen, Selected,* pp. 51 ff; Plechanow, *Historia,* vol. III, 438 ff
66 Herzen, *Pisma,* vol. II, pp. 643-644 (entry into Diary 15.8.1842)
   Herzen, Selected, 57 ff, p. 80, p. 18
67 *Herzen, Selected,* pp. 80-81
68 *Herzen, Sobranie,* vol. II, p. 336; *Pisma,* vol. II, p. 703, Diary entry of 21.2.1844
69 Herzen, *Pisma,* vol. II, p. 703
70 Herzen, *From the other Shore,* pp. 101-102
71 *Ibid.*
72 *Ibid.,* pp. 144-146
73 *Ibid.,* p. 57
74 *Ibid.,* p. 95
75 *Ibid.,* pp. 134-135
76 *Ibid.,* p. 136
77 *Ibid.*
78 *Ibid.,* p. 148
79 *Ibid.,* pp. 132-133
80 *Ibid,* p. 114
81 *Ibid.,*pp. 36-37
82 *Ibid.,* p. 62
83 *Ibid.,* pp. 62-63

84 *Ibid.*, pp. 63-64
85 *Herzen, Sobranie*, vol. VII, p. 309; *From the other Shore*, p. 167 (An Open Letter to Jules Michelet)
86 Herzen, *From the other Shore*, p. 183
87 *Ibid.*
88 *Ibid.*, p. 177
89 *Ibid.*, p. 175

3. Loosening the Spiritual arcana imperii—Chernyshevsky and Dobrolyubov

90 E. H. Carr, *Romantic Exiles*, London 1968
91 Malia, *Alexander Herzen*, p. 389
91a Herzen, *Pisma*, Warsaw 1966, vol. II, pp. 393-399
92 D. I. Pisarev, *Sochineniya v czetyrekh tomach*, Moscow 1956, vol. IV, p. 8
93 Quoted in E. Lampert, *Sons against Fathers*, p. 223
94 *Ibid.*
95 N. G. Chernyshevsky, *Polnoie sobranie sochinenii v piatnadtsati tomach*, Moscow, vol. I, 1939, p. 777
96 William F. Woehrlin, *Chernishevsky, the Man and the Journalist*, Cambridge, Mass., 1971, p. 326
97 N. Valentinov, *Encounters with Lenin*, London 1968, pp. 63-68
    N. Valentinov, *Tschernychewski et Lénine*, I-II, *Contrat Social*, vol. I, 1957, pp. 101-110; 162-172.
    We also utilized frequently Jerzy Plechanow, *Historia Rosyjskiej Myśli spolecznej*, vol. II, which is wholly devoted to Chernyshevsky; Avrahm Yarmolinsky, *Road to Revolution*, New York 1968, and the English translation of Chernyshevsky's *Selected Philosophical Essays*, Moscow 1953, referred to as Chernyshevsky, *Selected*
98 Valentinov, *Tschernychevski*, vol. I, 101
99 *Ibid.*
100 Chernyshevsky, *Polnoie sobranie sochinenii*, vol. I, pp. 27-28
101 *Ibid.*, p. 358
102 *Ibid.*, p. 483
103 T. A. Bogdanovich, *Liubov Liudei shestidesiatych godov*, Leningrad 1929, p. 132; W. F. Woehrlin, *Chernishevskii, the Man and the Journalist*, pp. 73-86
104 Chernyshevsky, *Polnoie sobranie*, vol. I, p. 535
105 *Ibid.*, p. 500
106 *Ibid.*, p. 418, Plechanow, *Historia*, vol. II, pp. 42 ff, Lampert, *Sons against Fathers*, pp. 182 ff, A, Yarmolinsky, *Road to Revolution*, pp. 114 ff; Woehrlin, *Chernishevsky*, pp. 31-34, 53-55
107 For Chernyshevsky's indebtedness to earlier thinkers, see his *Polnoie sobranie sochinenii*, vol. I, pp. 929-930 (Hegel); 248 (Feuerbach); 385 (Helvetius); 178, 182-183 (Fourier), IV, 5-221 (Lessing), VII, pp. 229, 39-40 (J. St. Mill). I wish to thank Mr Alex Dan for permission to use the materials collected by him for his Ph.D. dissertation on the genesis of Chernyshevsky's ideas (Hebrew University, Jerusalem)

108 T. Masaryk, *The Spirit of Russia*, vol. II, p. 8
109 Chernyshevsky, *Polnoie sobranie*, vol. VII, pp. 38-39, 415; vol. IV, pp. 841-842; Plechanow, *Historia*, vol. II, pp. 135 ff, 197 ff, 212-214, 262; Lampert, *Sons against Fathers*, pp. 197 ff
110 Chernyshevsky, "The Anthropological Principle in Philosophy," in his *Selected Philosophical Essays*, p. 115
111 *Ibid.*, 114-115
112 *Ibid.*, p. 94; see also: Plechanow, *Historia*, vol. II, pp. 111, 314, 315-316
113 Chernyshevsky, *Selected*, p. 70; Plechanow, *Historia*, vol. II, pp. 106-109
114 Chernyshevsky, *Selected*, p. 122; Plechanow, *Historia*, vol. II, pp. 135 ff
115 Chernyshevsky, *Selected*, pp. 125-132; Plekhanow, *Historia*, vol. II, pp. 139, 144, 147-148
116 Chernyshevsky, *Polnoie sobranie*, vol. X, p. 916
117 *Ibid.*, p. 910
118 Chernyshevsky, *Selected*, p. 92
119 Chernyshevsky, *Izbrannye Filosoficheskie sochineniia*, edited by M. M. Grigorian, Moscow 1950-51, III, 202-203 contains a fuller version than the *Collected Works*, vol. VII, 253-254; See Woehrlin, *Chernishevsky*, 134-135, n. 16 (p. 372)
120 Chernyshevsky, *Polnoie sobranie sochinenii*, vol. II, pp. 271, 273-274, 514-516
121 *Ibid.*, vol. V, p. 166
122 *Ibid.*, vol. II, pp. 85-86, II, 10-14; see also: Woehrlin, *Chernyshevsky*, pp. 144-186; Plechanow, *Historia*, vol. II, pp. 271-367, Lampert, *Sons against Fathers*, pp. 208-225
123 Chernyshevsky, *Polnoie sobranie*, vol. II, 24-26, 177-179
124 *Ibid.*, vol. II, p. 86; III, 302; Plekhanow, *Historia*, vol. II, pp. 286-305; A. Walicki, *Rosyjska filozofia i mysl spoteczna od oswiecenia do Marksizmu*, pp. 282 ff
125 Called by E. Lampert, *Sons against Fathers*, pp. 261-271, "a literary Robespierre"
126 Woehrlin, *Chernyshevsky*, pp. 251 ff
127 Herzen, *Sochinenia*, Moscow 1958, vol. VII, pp. 347-348; *Kolokol* Nr. 44 (1859); Herzen, *Pisma*, vol. II, pp. 393 ff, Introduction by A. Walicki, p. 37; Woehrlin, *Chernyshevsky*, pp. 256 ("axes"); 252, 254 ("very dangerous"), 109, 256
128 Chernyshevsky, *Polnoie sobranie*, vol. I, p. 419; vol. VI, p. 418
129 Plechanow, *Historia*, vol. II, p. 61 n
130 On Herzen's role see Woehrlin, *Chernyshevsky*, p. 119; on Manifesto, Chernyshevsky, *Selected Philosophical Essays*, p 11; Walicki, *Rosyjska filozofia*, pp. 279 ff
131 Woehrlin, *Chernyshevsky*, p. 103
132 Chernyshevsky, *Polnoie sobranie*, vol. V, pp. 668-669; Plekhanow, *Historia* vol. II, pp. 433-436, 440-441
     The most characteristic pronouncements on the subject were Chernyshevsky's distinction between liberals and democrats in his article on "Party struggles in France under Louis XVIII and Charles X", in

Sovremennik ("Contemporary") 1858, Nos. 8 and 9, *Polnoie sobranie,* vol. V, 215-216; and above all Dobrolyubov's "What is Oblomovitis?" and "When will the Real Day come?" (a review of Turgenev's *On the Eve,* both published in Ralph E. Matlaw (ed.), *Belinsky, Chernyshevsky and Dobroliubov, Selected Criticism,* New York 1962, pp. 133-175, 176-226

133 N. Dobrolyubov, *Sobranie sochinenii,* Moscow-Leningrad, 1962-1964, vol. 4, pp. 336-337; on Dobrolyubov see A. Walicki, *Rosyjska filozofia,* Warsaw 1973, pp. 300 ff

134 Lampert, *Sons against Fathers,* p. 83

135 Yuri Steklov, *N. G. Chernyshevsky—jego zhizn' i deyatelnost,* Moscow—Leningrad 1928, 2 vols.

136 Lampert, *Sons against Fathers,* p. 84

137 *Ibid.*

138 Chernyshevsky, *Polnoie sobranie,* vol. V, pp. 316-317

139 *Ibid.,* vol. VII, 223

140 Chernyshevsky, *Ibid.,* Plechanow, *Historia,* vol. II, 167

141 Chernyshevsky, *Polnoie sobranie,* vol. XIV, p. 48; Plechanow, *Historia,* vol. II, pp. 218-222

142 See for example Chernyshevsky, *Polnoie sobranie,* vol. I, pp. 121-122; Plechanow, *Historia,* vol. II, pp. 251 ff

143 Chernyshewsky, *Pisma Filozoficzne,* Warsaw, vol. II, pp. 383-384

144 *Ibid.,* pp. 426-427; see also Walicki (ed.), *Filozofja spoleczna narodnictwa rosyjskiego, Wybor Pism,* Warsaw 1965, vol. I, p. LX

145 Chernyshevsky, *Polnoie sobranie,* vol. V, p. 69

146 Woehrlin, Chernyshevsky, pp. 189; Chernyshevsky, *Polnoie sobranie,* vol. XIII, 187-188

147 See for example, Chernyshevsky, *Polnoie sobranie,* vol. V, pp. 65-107, 500-570; Plechanow, *Historia,* vol. II, 53-55, 423-427, 436, 415-419; Woehrlin, Chernyshevsky, 189-202

148 Chernyshevsky, *Polnoie sobranie,* vol. V, pp. 737, 734

149 *Ibid.,* vol. X, pp. 90-114

150 *Ibid.,* p. 114

151 See for example, *Ibid.,* vol. V, pp. 703-704

152 Yu. G. Oksman (ed.), *N. G. Chernyshevsky v vospominaniakh sovremennikov,* Saratov 1958-1959, vol. II, pp. 72-73; Walicki (ed.), *Filzofja,* vol. I, p. LXI

153 Chernyshevsky, *Polnoie sobranie,* vol. V, p. 217

154 Chernyshevsky, *Polnoie sobranie,* vol. IV, p. 713, vol. V, pp. 577-578, 589-590; Woehrlin, *Chernyshevsky,* pp. 202 ff; Plechanov, *Izbrannye filosofskie proizvedenia v piati tomakh,* 1956-1958, vol. IV, pp. 309-317; *Historia,* vol. II, 199, 435-436, 443

155 Lampert, *Sons against Fathers,* p. 190

156 Chernyshevsky, *Polnoie sobranie,* vol. VII, p. 36

157 *Ibid.,* vol. IV, p. 713

158 *Ibid.,* p. 744

159 *Ibid.,* vol. V, pp. 363, 387-390

160 Lampert, *Sons against Fathers,* pp. 193-194

161 Chernyshevsky, *Pisma filozofiuzne*, vol. I, p. 90; Walicki (ed.), *Filozofja*, vol. I, p. LX

162 Chernyshevsky, vol. I, pp. 356-357, 418

163 *Ibid.*, pp. 372-373; Lampert, *Sons against Fathers*, pp. 182, 183-184

164 *Ibid.*

165 Chernyshevsky, vol. VII, pp. 922-923

166 Chernyshevsky, vol. XI; English translation, "What Is to Be Done?" trans. Benjamin R. Tucker, revised and abridged Ludruilla B. Timkevich, New York 1961. On the famous proclamation of 1860-1861 attributed to Chernyshevsky, which was used as the main incriminating charge at his trial, "To the Landlords' Peasants," vol. XVI, pp. 947-953, see Woehrlin, *Chernyshevsky*, 274 ff

167 *Ibid.*; R. Hare, *Pioneers of Russian Social Thought*, Oxford 1951, pp. 195 ff

168 Chernyshevsky, *Polnoie sobranie*, vol. XI, p. 210; Hare, *Pioneers of Russian Social Thought*, pp. 196-7

169 Chernyshevsky, *Polnoie sobranie*, vol. IV, pp. 5-221; Plechanow, *Historia*, II, 278

170 Chernyshevsky, *Polnoie sobranie*, vol. IV, p. 6

171 *Ibid.*, vol. III, p. 357

172 *Ibid.*, vol. VII, pp. 429-433

173 Herzen, *Sobranie Sochinenii*, Moscow 1955-1959, vol. VIII, p. 381

174 N. Berdyaev, *Istoki i smysl russkovo kommunisma*, Paris 1955, p. 43

175 Chernyshevsky, *Polnoie sobranie*, vol. XI, p. 145; Valentinow, *Tschernyshevsky et Lénine*, vol I, pp. 101-110, 162-172

176 Chernyshevsky, *Polnoie sobranie*, vol. X, pp. 737-772; Plechanow, *Historia*, vol. II, 175-176, 181, 187

4. The Antinomies — Bakunin and Lavrov

177 As representative texts may serve the two *Programmes* of Zemlya i Volya, and the article by the radical Populist turned extreme reactionary L. A. Tikhomirow, "What may be expected of the Revolution?"—all contained in the two massive volumes of texts on Russian Populism published by Andrzej Walicki, *Filozofja spoleczna Narodnictwa rosyjskiego*, Warsaw 1965, vol. I, pp. 117, 119, 120-121, 121-122, and vol. II, pp. 552-558. See also the "Four Anarchist Programmes" composed by Bakunin in the years 1968-1972, to be found in Michael Bakunin, *Selected Writings*, edited and introduced by Arthur Lehning, London 1973, pp. 166-177, especially the fourth "The programme of the Slav section in Zurich." See also G. P. Maximoff: *The Political Philosophy of Bakunin, Scientific Anarchism*, Ch. IX (pp. 409-415) — "On the Morrow of the Social Revolution."

The most detailed treatment of Russian populism utilized was by Franco Venturi, *Roots of Revolution*, London 1960, and Maria Wawrykowa, *Rewolucyjne Narodnictwo w latach siedemdziesiatych XIX go wieku*, Warsaw 1963; Philip Pomper, *Peter Lavrov and the Russian Revolutionary Movement*, Chicago and London 1972

178 See the able Introduction by the English translator and editor James P.

Scanlan of Peter Lavrov, *Historical Letters,* Berkeley and Los Angeles, 1967, pp. 52, 58 (in contrast to the views of Plekhanov and M. Ostrogorsky, to Yuri Steklov Lavrovism was "the original Russian Marxism"); Wawrykowa, p. 194; Pomper, *Peter Lavrov,* 126-127

179 Lavrov, *Historical Letters,* pp. 211, 135 ff, 329

180 Walicki (ed.), *Filozofja spoleczna Narodnictwa Rosyjskiego,* vol. I, p. 180

181 *Ibid.,* p. 181

182 *Ibid.,* p. 50; see also Lavrov, *Historical Letters,* p. 111

183 Selections in Walicki (ed.), *Filozofja,* vol. I, pp. 409-602

184 *Ibid.,* pp. 411-426, 525-527

185 *Ibid.,* pp. 449-493

186 Lavrov, *Historical Letters,* Third Letter, pp. 115 ff

187 Lavrov, *Historical Letters,* pp. 97ff, 324 ff

188 *Ibid.;* Pomper, *Peter Lavrov,* pp. 88-89, 103

189 Walicki, (ed.), *Filosofja,* vol. I, pp. 5-19

190 Quoted in Venturi, *Roots of Revolution,* p. 439; see Grinter Grützner, *Die Pariser Kommune, Macht und Karriere einer Legende,* Köln und Opladen, 1963

191 M. Bakunin, *Selected Writings,* pp. 195-213 — "The Paris Commune and the Idea of the State"; Venturi, *Roots of Revolution,* p. 454; Pomper, *Lavrov,* pp. 119 ff, 202-203; G. P. Maximoff, *The Political Philosophy of Bakunin,* p. 235—"Federation . . . ignoring . . . national differences and State Boundaries . . . French proletariat . . . State patriotism is all in the past," p. 272 — "it wanted the unity of the nation, of the people . . . not . . . of the State")

192 Venturi, *Roots of Revolution,* pp. 439-441

193 Lavrov, *Historical Letters,* p. 251; Szamuely, *The Russian Tradition,* pp. 308-309; Wawrykowa, *Revolucyjne Narodnictwa,* pp. 196 ff, 203, 210 ff

194 Lavrov, *Historical Letters,* pp. 59, 235 ff, 296 ff; Venturi, *Roots of Revolution,* p. 455

195 Venturi, *ibid.*

196 Venturi, *Roots of Revolution,* p. 455

197 Michael Confino (ed.), *Daughter of a Revolutionary, Nathalie Herzen and the Bakunin/Nechayev Circle,* London 1974, p. 250; Bakunin, *Selected Writings,* p. 182

198 Bakunin, *Selected Writings,* p. 189

199 Quoted in Venturi, *Roots of Revolution,* p. 456; Wawrykowa, *Rewolucyjne,* pp. 158 ff; Pomper, *Lavrov,* pp. 52, 139, 147 ff — on Lavrov's article on "Knowledge and Revolution"

200 Bakunin in Maximoff, *Political Philosophy of Bakunin,* pp. 351-358 — "The Rationale of Revolutionary Tactics"

201 H. Confino, *Daughter of a Revolutionary,* p. 256

202 *Ibid.,* p. 259 ff

203 *Ibid.,* p. 241

204 *Ibid.,* p. 266

205 *Ibid.,* p. 250

206 Bakunin, *Selected Writings,* p. 183; Confino, *Daughter,* pp. 250-251

207 Confino, *Daughter*, p. 258; Bakunin, *Selected Writings*, p. 183
208 Confino, *Daughter*, p. 259
209 *Ibid.*
210 Confino, *Daughter*, p. 259; Bakunin, *Selected Writings*, p. 191
211 Confino, *Daughter*, p. 259
212 Bakunin, *Selected Writings*, p. 192
213 Confino, *Daughter*, p. 260
214 Confino, *Daughter*, p. 260; Bakunin, *Selected Writings*, p. 192
215 Confino, *Daughter*, p. 260; Bakunin, *Selected Writings*, pp. 192-193
216 Confino, *Daughter*, p. 261; Bakunin, *Selected Writings*, pp. 193-194
217 *Ibid.*
218 Confino, *Daughter*, pp. 261-262; Bakunin, *Selected Writings*, p. 194
219 Confino, *Daughter*, p. 263
220 *Ibid.*, p. 262
221 Confino, *Daughter*, p. 255; Bakunin, *Selected Writings*, pp. 186-187
222 Quoted in Venturi, *Roots of Revolution*, p. 458
223 *Ibid.*, p. 459
224 *Ibid.*, p. 461
225 *Ibid.*, pp. 463-464
226 Szamuely, *The Russian Tradition*, p. 310
227 Quoted in Venturi, *Roots of Revolution*, p. 464
228 Wawrykowa, *Rewolucyjne*, p. 162
228a Walicki (ed.), *Filozofja*, vol. I, pp. lxxxviii-lxxxix
229 Quoted in Szamuely, *The Russian Tradition*, p. 311
230 *Ibid.*, p. 312
231 *Ibid.*, pp. 293-294

5. A Russian Version of Totalitarian Democracy — Tkachev

232 Most of Tkachev's works are to be found in the B. P. Koznin's selected works on social-political themes, *Izbrannyye sochineniia na sotsialno—ekonomicheskie temy*, edited originally in four volumes in the years 1922-1923 (Moscow). Two further volumes were added in the years 1935 and 1937. We were greatly helped by the considerable selections contained in Walicki (ed.), two-volume anthology, *Filozofja spoleczna Narodnictura Rosyjskrego*, the two monographs on Tkachev, Albert L. Weeks, *The First Bolshevik, a Political Biography of Peter Tkachev*, New York-London 1968; Deborah Hardy, *Peter Tkachev, The Critic as Jacobin;* the lengthy chapters on Tkachev in the comprehensive works already cited by Venturi, Szamuely, Walicki, Wawrykowa and Yarmolinsky

233 G. V. Plekhanov, *Sochinenia*, vol. XXIV, Moscow Leningrad, 1927, pp. 154-155

234 V.I. Lenin, *Sochinenia*, 4th edn., Moscow, vol. V, 1946, p. 477

235 Quoted in Szamuely, *The Russian Tradition*, p. 318; A. L. Weeks, *The First Bolshevik, a Political Biography of Peter Tkachev*, p. 5

236 Szamuely, *The Russian Tradition*, p. 318

237   Ibid., see also M. N. Pokrovsky, Izbrannye proizvedeniya, Moscow, 1967, vol.
      4, pp. 378, 380
238   P. N. Tkachev, quoted in Walicki (ed.), Filozofja spoleczna, vol. I, p. 283;
      Wawrykowa, Rewolucyjne; D. Hardy, Peter Tkachev, pp. 239-40, pp. 183,
      228 (concept of truth), pp. 80-84, 161, 178-180 (progress)
239   Tkachev, vol. II, pp. 206-207
240   Tkachev, vol. V, p. 178; Walicki (ed.), Filozofja spoleczna, vol. I, pp.
      353-355; Venturi, Roots of Revolution, p. 406
241   Tkachev, vol. I, pp. 326-327; Wawrykowa, Rewolucyjne., pp. 237 ff
242   Tkachev, I, p. 328
243   Tkachev, vol. III, pp. 64-65; Walicki (ed.), Filozofja spoleczna, vol. I, pp. 384-
      394; Hardy, Peter Tkachev, pp. 254 ff
244   Tkachev, vol. I, pp. 69-70; Wawrykowa, Rewolucyjne, p. 226
245   Tkachev, I, p. 132
246   Tkachev, vol. I, p. 131
247   Tkachev, I, pp. 276-277;Venturi, Roots of Revolution, p. 406; Wawrykowa,
      Rewolucyjne, pp. 234 ff; Hardy, Peter Tkachev, 230 ff
248   Tkachev, vol. II, pp. 181-182, 188-193, 196-197, 212, 204, 206, 208; vol. V,
      pp. 300-302, 306-307
249   Tkachev, vol. III, p. 225, vol. II, p. 139; Walicki (ed.), Filozofja spoleczna,
      vol. I, pp. 295, 311-312, 318-320
250   Tkachev, vol. III, pp. 312-313; Walicki (ed.), Filozofja spoleczna, vol. I, pp.
      385-402; Hardy, Peter Tkachev, pp. 240-244, 252, 262, 272
251   Tkachev, vol. II, pp. 192-194
252   Tkachev, vol. II, pp. 203-204; Walicki (ed.), Filozofja spoleczna, I, pp.
      330-331; Hardy, Peter Tkachev, p. 181
253   Tkachev, vol. I, pp. 404-407; Walicki (ed.), Filozofja spoleczna, vol. I,
      pp. 265-268
254   Quoted in: Venturi, Roots of Revolution, p. 402
255   Tkachev, vol. III, pp. 264-268
256   Walicki (ed.), Filozofja spoleczna, vol. II, pp. 496-512, Weeks, The First
      Bolshevik, pp. 113-116
257   Szamuely, The Russian Tradition, pp. 295, 298; Tkachev, vol. III, p. 459
258   Tkachev, vol. III, pp. 88-98; Hardy, Peter Tkachev, pp. 203-211
259   Tkachev, vol. III, pp. 91-92
260   Ibid., pp. 69, 219, 273; Walicki (ed.), Filozofja spoleczna, I, 393-394, 395-405
261   Tkachev, vol. III, pp. 69-70; see Hardy, Peter Tkachev, pp. 196-208, 247-286
262   Tkachev, vol. III, pp. 92-93, 272-273, 275
263   Ibid., p. 263, Walicki (ed.), Filozofja spoleczna, I, p. 538
264   Ibid., p. 396
265   Ibid., p. 387
266   Ibid., p. 388
267   Tkachev, vol. III, p. 265
268   Ibid.
269   Ibid.; Walicki (ed.), Filozofja spoleczna, I, 388
270   Tkachev, vol III, pp. 265-266; Walicki (ed.), Filozofja spoleczna, p. 389

271 Tkachev, vol. III, pp. 266-267; Walicki (ed.), *Filozofja spoleczna*, pp. 390-391
272 Tkachev, vol. III, p. 268; Walicki (ed.), *Filozofja spoleczna*, p. 392
273 Tkachev, *ibid.*, Walicki (ed.), *ibid.*
274 Tkachev, *ibid.*, Walicki (ed.), *Filozofja spoleczna*, p. 394
275 Tkachev, vol. III, pp. 225-226; Venturi, *Roots*, p. 419
276 See for example: Tkachev, vol. III, pp. 252-255, 277-318, 325, 362-363
277 *Ibid.*, pp. 223-224
278 *Ibid.*, p. 224; see Hardy, *Peter Tkachev*, pp. 256-257, 258-264, 264-270
279 Tkachev, vol. III, p. 227; Walicki (ed.), *Filozofja spoleczna*, vol. II, pp. 97 ff; vol. II, pp. 87-106
280 Tkachev, vol. II, pp. 205-206; see Hardy, *Peter Tkachev*, pp. 169-176, 180
281 Tkachev, vol. II, p. 207; Hardy, *Peter Tkachev*, p. 181
282 Walicki (ed.), *Filozofja spoleczna*, vol. II, p. 99; Tkachev, vol. III, p. 227
283 Tkachev, vol. III, p. 250
284 *Ibid.*, p. 251
285 Tkachev, vol. I, p. 174
286 *Ibid.*, p. 208

6. When "Consistency Reaches the Point of Monstrosity"
— Nechaev and Bakunin

287 Quoted in Venturi, *Roots of Revolution*, p. 359
288 *Ibid.*, pp. 361-363; see also: Szamuely, *The Russian Tradition*, p. 252; Michael Confino, *Violence dans La Violence*, Paris 1973, pp. 43 ff
289 Confino, *Violence*, p. 64
290 Venturi, *Roots of Revolution*, p. 362; Confino, *Violence*, p. 68
291 Confino, *Violence*, pp. 39-51
292 Confino, *Daughter*, pp. 230
293 Quoted in Venturi, *Roots of Revolution*, p. 368
294 *Ibid.*
295 Confino, *Daughter*, p. 225
296 *Ibid.*
297 *Ibid.*
298 *Ibid.*, p. 226
299 *Ibid.*
300 *Ibid.*, p. 227
301 *Ibid.*, p. 228
302 *Ibid.*, p. 228
303 *Ibid.*, p.229
304 *Ibid.*
305 *Ibid.*
306 *Ibid.*
307 *Ibid.*
308 *Ibid.*
309 *Ibid.*, pp. 229-230
310 *Ibid.*, p. 230

311   *Ibid.*, p. 232
312   *Ibid.*, p. 233
313   *Ibid.*, p. 234
314   *Ibid.*
315   F. M. Dostoevsky, *The Devils*, transl. by D. Magarshack, Penguin, 1968
      Joseph Conrad, *The Secret Agent*, London 1928
316   E. H. Carr, *Michael Bakunin*, London 1975, pp. 375 ff
317   Zeev Ivianski, *Individual Terror: Theory and Deed*, (Hebrew), Tel-Aviv 1977
318   See M. Prawdin (Charol), *The Unmentionable Nechaev; A Key to Bolshevism*,
      London 1961, p. 46
319   Anthony Masters, *Bakunin the Father of Anarchism*, London 1974, pp. 163-164,
      195-196
320   Confino, *Daughter*, p. 290
321   *Ibid.*, pp. 243-244. Letter from M. Bakunin to Sergey Nechaev, June 2, 1870,
      first published in Russian by M. Confino in *Cahiers du monde russe et
      soviétique*, 1966, No. 4, and also in *Violence dans La Violence*, pp. 106-149
322   A. Masters, *Bakunin, the Father of Anarchism*, pp. 198 ff
323   Confino, *Daughter*, pp. 238-280
324   *Ibid.*, pp. 291-300
325   *Ibid.*, p. 243
326   *Ibid.*, pp. 243-244
327   *Ibid.*, p. 239
328   *Ibid.*, p. 244
329   *Ibid.*, pp. 244-245
330   *Ibid.*, p. 246
331   *Ibid.*, p. 277
332   *Ibid.*, p. 264
333   *Ibid.*, p. 265
334   *Ibid.*, p. 268
335   *Ibid.*
336   *Ibid.*, p. 268
337   *Ibid.*, p. 292
338   *Ibid.*, pp. 292-293
339   *Ibid.*, pp. 293-294
340   *Ibid.*, p. 294
341   *Ibid.*, pp. 294-295
342   *Ibid.*, p. 295
343   *Ibid.*, p. 295
344   *Ibid.*
345   *Ibid.*
346   *Ibid.*
347   *Ibid.*, p. 296
348   *Ibid.*
349   *Ibid.*p. 297
350   *Ibid.*, p. 297
351   *Ibid.*

352 *Ibid.*
353 *Ibid.*, p. 298
354 *Ibid.*
355 *Ibid.*
356 *Ibid.*, p. 298-299

Part VI.

Lenin—International Revolutionary and Architect of New Russia (pp. 335-430)

The following editions of Lenin's writings were used:
V. I. Lenin, *Selected Works*, New York 1967, 3 vols., referred to as *Selected Works* (New York)
V. I. Lenin, *Selected Works*, London 1944, 12 vols. referred to as *Selected Works* (London)
V. I. Lenin, *Collected Works*, Moscow 1964, referred to as *Collected Works*

I: THE FORMATIVE YEARS

1 V. I. Lenin, "The Heritage We Renounce", *Selected Works* (New York), vol. I, pp. 54-90
2 *Ibid.*, p. 71
3 *Ibid.*, p. 75
4 *Ibid.*, p. 75
5 Lenin, "What Is to Be Done", *Selected Works*, (New York), pp. 97-255
6 *Ibid.*, p. 120
7 David Shub, *Lenin*, Pelican Books, 1966, p. 21
8 *Ibid.*, p. 22
9 Lenin, "The Heritage . . .", *Selected Works*, (New York), pp. 55-71; p. 889 (on Skaldin); p. 872 (on Engelhardt)
10 *Ibid.*, p. 67
11 David Mitrany, *Marx against the Peasant: A Study in Social Dogmatism*, Chapel Hill 1951, 57-59; E. H. Carr, *The Bolshevik Revolution 1917-1923*, London 1954, vol. I, ch. III; Adam B. Ulam, *The Bolsheviks*, New York 1969, pp. 214-216
12 Richard Charques, *The Twilight of Imperial Russia*, London 1968, p. 89
13 Leopold H. Haimson, *The Russian Marxists and the Origins of Bolshevism*, Boston 1955, ch. 7, 8; J. L. H. Keep, *The Rise of Social Democracy in Russia*, Oxford 1963, ch. IV; E. H. Carr, *The Bolshevik Revolution*, vol. I, ch. 2; Leon Trotsky, *The Russian Revolution*, New York 1959, ch. I; Jonathan Frankel, ed., *Vladimir Akimov on the Dilemmas of Russian Marxism*, Cambridge 1969, pp. 43-75; Theodore Dan, *The Origins of Bolshevism*, London 1964, ch. 9
14 Carr, *The Bolshevik Revolution*, vol. I pp. 34 ff
15 Shub, *Lenin*, p. 39
16 On Jean Jaurès see:
J. Hampden Jackson, *Jean Jaurès, His Life and Work*, London 1943; Milorad M.

Drachkovitch, *Les Socialismes français et allemand et le problème de la guerre* (1870-1914), Genève 1953; H. Goldberg, *The Life of Jean Jaurès*, Madison 1962; Felicien Challaye, *Jaurès*, Paris 1948

17 Jean Jaurès, *L'Histoire socialiste de la revolution française*, ed. Albert Mathiez, Paris 1922-1924, 8 vols.

18 J. H. Jackson, *Jean Jaurès, His Life and Work*, p. 159; Ch. Rappoport, *Jean Jaurès, l'homme, le penseur, le socialiste*, Paris 1915, pp. 201 ff, 221 ff

19 Jackson, *Jean Jaurès*, p. 159

20 *Ibid.*, p. 159

21 *Ibid.*, p. 159

22 Jean Jaurès, *Textes Choisis*, vol. I, "Contre la guerre et la politique coloniale", intro. Madeleine Reberioux, Paris 1959, p. 88

23 M. M. Drachkovitch, *Les socialismes français et allemand*, pp. 104-105

24 Jackson, *Jean Jaurès*, p. 101

25 Jean Jaurès, *L'Armée Nouvelle*, Présentation par Madeleine Reberioux, Paris 1970, pp. 187, 204

26 Jackson, *Jean Jaurès*, pp. 143-144

27 *Ibid.*, pp. 195-196

28 *Ibid.*, pp. 69-70

29 *Ibid.*, pp. 64-65

30 Drachkovitch, *Socialismes*, pp. 175-180; *Jaurès Textes*, pp. 187-191

31 Drachkovitch, *Socialismes*, p. 108; *Jaurès Textes*, pp. 95-102, 126-131

32 Jackson, *Jean Jaurès*, p. 76

33 *Ibid.*, p. 125

34 Jaurès, *Textes*, p. 131

35 *Ibid.*, p. 98

36 *Ibid.*, p. 99

37 Drachkovitch, *Socialismes*, p. 88; *Jaurès, Textes*, p. 38

38 Drachkovitch, *Socialismes*, pp. 102-105

39 *Ibid.*, pp. 187-191

40 Jackson, *Jean Jaurès*, pp. 142-145

41 Rosa Luxemburg, The Junius-Pamphlet, in: *Gesammelte Werke*, Berlin 1972, vol. III, pp. 70-71

42 Drachkovitch, *Socialismes*, p. 72

43 Jackson, *Jean Jaurès*, pp. 149-150, pp. 181-182

44 Drachkovitch, *Socialismes*, p. 109

45 Jackson, *Jean Jaurès*, pp. 175-176

46 Annie Kriegel et Jean-Jacques Becker, *1914 — La Guerre et le mouvement ouvrier français*, Paris 1964, pp. 21-38

47 Shub, *Lenin*, pp. 48-50

48 *Ibid.*

49 Nikolai Valentinov, *Encounter with Lenin*, New York 1968, pp. 251-252

50 Lenin, "Materialism and Empiro-Criticism", *Collected Works*, vol. 14

51 Shub, *Lenin*, pp. 13-16

52 Angelica Balabanoff, *Impressions of Lenin*, Michigan 1968, pp. 4-5

53 Edmund Wilson, *To the Finland Station*, London 1960, pp. 364-376; Carr, *The*

Bolshevik Revolution, vol. I, pp. 3-25; Alan Basançon, *Les Origines intellectuelles du Leninisme*, Paris 1977

54 Shub, *Lenin*, pp. 123-131

55 *Ibid.*, pp. 74, 40-41

56 Isaac Deutscher, *The Prophet Armed, Trotsky 1879-1921*, London 1954, pp. 91-96

57 Shub, *Lenin*, p. 137

58 *Ibid.*, pp. 153-154

59 *Ibid.*, p. 180

60 L. H. Haimson, *The Russian Marxists and the Origins of Bolshevism*, pp. 198-208; J. L. H. Keep, *The Rise of Social Democracy in Russia*, ch. VI; T. Dan, *The Origins of Bolshevism*, pp. 322-336; Robert Conquest, *Lenin*, London 1974, pp. 54-79; Georg Lukacs, *Lenin*, Berlin 1969, pp. 22-35; Harold Shukman, *Lenin & Russian Revolution*, New York 1966, ch. VII

61 Lenin, "What the Friends of the People Are," *Selected Works*, (London), vol. I, pp. 389-455

62 Charques, *The Twilight of Imperial Russia*, ch. I; Michael T. Florinsky, *Russia A History and an Interpretation*, New York 1955, vol. II, ch. XXXIII; Chamberlin, *The Russian Revolution*, ch. I; Franco Venturi, *Roots of Revolution*, New York 1966, ch. 19; Cyril E. Black (ed.), *The Transformation of Russian Society*, Cambridge (Mass.) 1960, Part III; Tibor Szamuely, *The Russian Tradition*, London 1979, ch. 3; Hugh Seton-Watson, *The Decline of Imperial Russia*, New York 1962, ch. II

63 H. T. Florinsky, *Russia, A History*, p. 777; Harry Willets, "The Agrarian Problem", in George Katkov, Errin Oberländer, Nicolas Peppe and George von Rakch (eds.), *Russia Enters the Twentieth Century, 1897-1917*, London 1971, pp. 111 ff

64 Florinsky, *Russia*, ch. XXXIII; Geroid Tanquary Robinson, *Rural Russia under the Old Regime*, New York 1932, pp. 64-93

65 Charques, *The Twilight*, p. 198; G. T. Robinson, *Rural Russia*, pp. 97 ff: Karl C. Thalheim, *Russia's Economic Development*, pp. 85-110

66 Charques, *The Twilight*, pp. 61-62; H. Willets, The Agrarian Problem, pp. 125 ff

67 Charques, *The Twilight*, pp. 63, 136

68 Florinsky, *Russia, A History*, p. 1235

69 *Ibid.*, pp. 1217-1218

70 Charques, *The Twilight*, p. 199

71 Florinsky, *Russia, A History*, pp. 888-906; Robinson, *Rural Russia*, ch. VII

72 Charques, *The Twilight*, p. 178; Hugh Seton-Watson, *The Decline of Imperial Russia*, pp. 271-277

73 Florinsky, *Russia, A History*, p. 897; Charques, *The Twilight*, pp. 26-29

74 Charques, *The Twilight*, pp. 31-32; Florinsky, *Russia, A History*, 897-900

75 Charques, *The Twilight*, p. 29; Florinsky, *Russia, A History*, pp. 900-901; Seton-Watson, *The Decline*, p. 144

76 *Ibid.*

77 Charques, *The Twilight*, pp. 32-33

78 Charques, *The Twilight*, p. 56; Seton-Watson, *The Decline*, p. 139; Florinsky,

Russia, A History, p. 900; C. E. Black, The Transformation of Russian Society, pp. 93-110

79 Florinsky, Russia, A History, p. 1156; Charques, The Twilight, p. 54

80 Florinsky, Russia, A History, pp. 1152-1155

81 Ibid., pp. 1083-1085

82 Leonard Schapiro, Rationalism and Nationalism in Russian XIXth Century Political Thought, New Haven 1967, pp. 94 ff

83 Shub, Lenin, pp. 13-16, 36

84 Robert F. Byrnes, "Pobedonostsev on the Instruments of Russian Government," in Ernest J. Simmons (ed.), Continuity and Change in Russian and Soviet Thought, Cambridge (Mass.) 1955, pp. 113-128

85 Thomas Masaryk, The Spirit of Russia, London 1961, 2 vols., vol. Ii, p. 209 ff; Robert F. Byrnes, Pobedonostsev, His Life and Thought, Indiana Univ. Press 1968; Hans Kohn, Prophets and Peoples, New York 1961

86 Nicolas Berdaev, les sources et le sens du communisme russe, Paris 1951, pp. 7-29; E. J. Simmons, Continuity and change in Russian and Soviet Thought, pp. 359-369

87 Robert F. Byrnes, "Pobedonostsev on the Instruments of Russian Government, in Simmons (ed.), Continuity and Change, p. 114

88 Ibid., p. 115

89 Bakunin: Scientific Anarchism, edited by G. P. Maximoff, Glencoe 1953, ch. X; F. Venturi, Roots of Revolution, p. 37
T. Masaryk, The Spirit of Russia, vol. II, pp. 221 ff

90 Byrnes, Pobedonostsev, in Simmons (ed.), Continuity and Change, pp. 118-120; Masaryk, The Spirit of Russia, vol. I, pp. 156-158

91 Byrnes, Pobedonostsev, in Simmons (ed.), Continuity and Change, p. 120

92 Charques, The Twilight, p. 54

93 Ibid.

94 Byrnes, Pobedonostsev, in Simmons (ed.), Continuity and Change, pp. 120-121

95 Simmons (ed.), Continuity and Change, pp. 359-377

96 T. Masaryk, The Spirit of Russia, vol. II, p. 216

97 Ibid.

98 Byrnes, Pobedonostsev, in Simmons (ed.), Continuity and Change, p. 121

99 Thomas G. Masaryk, Russland und Europa. Studien über die geistigen Stromungen in Russland, Jena 1913, vol. II, p. 198

100 Byrnes, Pobedonostsev, in Simmons (ed.), Continuity and Change, pp. 124-125

101 Ibid., p. 124

102 Ibid., p. 126

103 Charques, The Twilight, p. 173

104 Charques, The Twilight, p. 173; Florinsky, Russia, A History, p. 1202

105 A more nuancé view is presented by Hans Rogger, "Russian Ministers and the Jewish Question", 1881-1917, in California Studies, vol. III, 1975, pp. 15-76, and in his "Jewish Policy of Late Tsarism, A Reappraisal", The Wiener Library Bulletin, 1971, vol. 25, Nos. 1 & 2

106 Charques, The Twilight, p. 47

107 Ibid., p. 87

108 Dan, *The origins of Bolshevism,* pp. 399-400
109 *Ibid.,* p. 399
110 *Ibid.,* pp. 398-399
111 Charques, *The Twilight,* p. 32; Florinsky, *Russia, A History,* p. 1148
112 Charques, *The Twilight,* p. 77; B. D. Wolfe, *Three Who Made a Revolution,* Boston 1955, pp. 124-126; Israel Getzler, *Martov,* Cambridge 1967, ch. II
113 Charques, *The Twilight,* pp. 54-55
114 *Ibid.,* pp. 67-68
115 Dan, *The Origins of Bolshevism,* pp. 266-267; Chamberlin, *The Russian Revolution,* vol. I, pp. 35-41
116 Charques, *The Twilight,* pp. 70-71; Chamberlin, *The Russian Revolution,* vol. I, pp. 40, 43
117 Charques, *The Twilight,* pp 79-82; Keep, *The Rise of Social Democracy in Russia,* pp. 102-105
118 Charques, *The Twilight,* pp. 84-85
119 *Ibid.,* p. 75
120 Florinsky, *Russia, A History,* p. 1168; Charques, *The Twilight,* pp. 84-87
121 Charques, *The Twilight,* p. 85; Keep, p. 73; Shmuel Galai, *The Liberation Movement in Russia 1900-1905,* Cambridge Univ. Press 1973, especially Pt. II
122 Florinsky, *Russia, A History,* pp. 1169-1170
123 Michael Karpovich, "Two Types of Russian Liberalism, Maklakov and Miliukov," in Simmons (ed.), *Continuity and Change,* pp. 129-143
124 Florinsky, *Russia, A History,* pp. 1169-1171; Charques, *The Twilight,* pp. 108-109
125 Charques, *The Twilight,* pp. 109-110
126 Chamberlin, *The Russian Revolution,* vol. I, pp. 48-49
127 Charques, *The Twilight,* p. 114
128 *Ibid.,* p. 118
129 *Ibid.,* p. 122
130 Florinsky, *Russia, A History,* pp. 1176-1178
131 Florinsky, *Russia, A History,* pp. 1173-1176; Charques, *The Twilight,* pp. 137-138
132 Florinsky, *Russia, A History,* pp. 1176-1177
133 Charques, *The Twilight,* p. 128
134 *Ibid.,* pp. 128-129
135 *Ibid.,* p. 129
136 *Ibid.*
137 *Ibid.,* p. 131
138 *Ibid.,* p. 134
139 *Ibid.,* p. 135
140 Florinsky, *Russia, A History,* p. 1181
141 *Ibid.,* p. 1182
142 Florinsky, *Russia, A History,* pp. 1175-1176; Charques, *The Twilight,* p. 133
143 Charques, *The Twilight,* p. 142
144 Florinsky, *Russia, A History,* pp. 1186-1187; Charques, *The Twilight,* pp. 144-145

145 Charques, *The Twilight*, p. 148
146 *Ibid.*, p. 149
147 Charques, *The Twilight*, pp. 151-152; Florinsky, *Russia, A History*, pp. 1190-1191
148 Charques, *The Twilight*, pp. 154-155
149 *Ibid.*, p. 154
150 *Ibid.*, pp. 158-159
151 *Ibid.*, pp. 161-163
152 *Ibid.*, pp. 168-172
153 Florinsky, *Russia, A History*, pp. 1197-1198
154 *Ibid.*, pp. 1199-1201
155 V. I. Lenin, "Two Tactics of Social Democracy", chs. 5-6, *Selected Works*, New York, vol. I; Keep, *The Rise of Social Democracy*, ch. III; Haimson, *The Russian Marxists*, ch. VI; Shub, *Lenin*, ch. 7; Alfred G. Meyer, *Leninism*, New York 1963, ch. VI
156 Keep, *The Rise of Social Democracy*, pp. 88-91; Haimson, *Russian Marxists*, pp. 132-139
157 Lenin, "What Is to Be Done", *Selected Works*, (New York), vol. I, p. 130
158 Lenin, "Materialism and Empiro-criticism," *Collected Works*, Moscow 1962, vol. 14, p. 326
159 Nikolai Valentinov, *My Talks with Lenin*, New York 1948, p. 325
160 Lenin, "One Step Forward, Two Steps Back", *Selected Works*, (New York), vol. I, p. 412; see also: Keep, *The Rise of Social Democracy*, pp. 143-147; Dan, *The Origins of Bolshevism*, pp. 249-263; Conquest, *Lenin*, ch. 3; Lukacs, *Lenin*, pp. 12-35
161 N. Valentinov, *My Talks with Lenin*, pp. 199-201
162 Lenin, *Selected Works*, (New York), I, p. 202
163 *Ibid.*, p. 189
164 Keep, *The Rise of Social Democracy*, pp. 141-148; Haimson, *Russian Marxists*, pp. 189-194; Ulam, *Lenin and the Bolsheviks*, pp. 176-216; A. G. Meyer, *Leninism*, ch. V
165 Werner Hahlweg, "Lenin und Clausewitz, Ein Beitrag zur politisehen Ideengeschichte des 20. Jahrhunderts," *Archiv fur Kulturgeschichte*, vol. 36 1954, pp. 30-59
166 Lenin, *Selected Works*, (New York), p. 161
167 Haimson, *Russian Marxists*, p. 132
168 Haimson, *Russian Marxists*, p. 180; Dan, *The Origins of Bolshevism*, p. 252
169 Second Congress Proceedings, quoted in Keep, *The Rise of Social Democracy*, pp. 120-121
170 Jonathan Frankel, *Vladimir Akimov on the Dilemma of Russian Marxism 1895-1903*, Cambridge 1969, pp. 43-73
171 Keep, *The Rise of Social Democracy*, pp. 127-129; Haimson, *Russian Marxists*, pp. 174-175
172 Keep, *The Rise of Social Democracy*, pp. 127-130; Dan, *The origins of Bolshevism*, pp. 244-246
173 Haimson, *Russian Marxists*, p. 175

174 Lenin, "One Step . . .", *Selected Works* (New York), vol. I, p. 260
175 *Ibid.*, p. 261
176 *Ibid.*, pp. 304-310
177 Keep, *The Rise of Social Democracy*, p. 129
178 Lenin, "One Step," *Selected Works* (New York), vol. I, pp. 417-419
179 Dan, *The Origins of Bolshevism*, p. 254
180 Leon Trotsky, "Our Political Tasks," August 1904, Geneva, quoted in I. Deutscher, *The Prophet Armed*, Trotsky 1879-1921 p.90
181 Shub, *Lenin*, p. 88
182 Chamberlin, *The Russian Revolution*, vol. I, pp. 46-57; Carr, *The Bolshevik Revolution*, vol. I, pp. 45-48; Keep, *The Rise of Social Democracy*, pp. 175-182
183 Shub, *Lenin*, pp. 95-106
184 Dan, *The Origins of Bolshevism*, pp. 294-298
185 Lenin, "The Tasks of Russian Social Democrats," *Selected Works*, (London), vol. I, p. 502
186 *Ibid.*
187 *Ibid.*, pp. 502-504
188 *Ibid.*, p. 504
189 *Ibid.*
190 Dan, *The Origins of Bolshevism*, p. 287; Carr, *The Bolshevik Revolution*, vol. I, pp. 38-44
191 Dan, *The Origins of Bolshevism*, p. 287
192 Lenin, "Two Tactics of Social-Democracy in the Democratic Revolution," *Selected Works*, (New York), vol. I, p. 481
193 *Ibid.*
194 *Ibid.*, pp. 491-492
195 *Ibid.*, p. 492
196 *Ibid.*
197 *Ibid.*, pp. 493-494
198 *Ibid.*, pp. 480 ff
199 Lenin, *Selected Works* (London), vol. III, p. 305
200 Lenin, "On the High Road," *Selected Works* (London), vol. IV, pp. 3-12
201 Lenin, *Selected Works* (London), vol. III, p. 350
202 *Ibid.*, p. 379
203 *Ibid.*, p; 351
204 *Ibid.*
205 *Ibid.*, vol. IV, p. 7
206 Winfried B. Scharlau and Zbynck A. Zeman, *Freibeuter der Revolution, Parvus Helphand, eine politische Biographie*, Köln 1964, pp. 110-133; Deutscher, *The Prophet Armed*, pp. 145-163
207 Dan, *The Origins of Bolshevism*, pp. 335-336
208 Lenin, "Two Tactics . . .", *Selected Works* (New York), vol. I, p. 492
209 Scharlau and Zeman, *Freibeuter der Revolution*, pp. 139-142; Deutscher, *The Prophet Armed*, pp. 158-159
210 Lenin, "The Stages, Trends and Prospects of the Revolution", *Selected Works* (London), vol. III, pp. 134-135
211 *Ibid.*, pp. 134-135

2: WAR AND REVOLUTION
(I) The Second International Debating

212 James Joll, *The Second International 1889-1914*, London 1968
213 Rosa Luxemburg, "Entweder—Oder" (Illegal Pamphlet of the Spartakus Bund, 1916), in *Ausgewählte politische Schriften*, Frankfurt/M 1971, Bd. 3
214 See notes 455 ff
215 J. Braunthal, *History of the International*, (London 1966), pp. 306-309; Karl Kautsky, *Sozialismus und Kolonialpolitik*, Berlin 1907; Gustav Noske, *Kolonialpolitik und Sozialdemokratie*, Stuttgart 1914; Karl Kautsky, "Der Imperialismus," *Neue Zeit*, 1913-1914, vol. 2, p. 908; Karl Kautsky, "Nochmals die Abrustung," *Neue Zeit*, 1911-1912, vol. 2, pp. 844-850; Karl Kautsky, *Sozialismus und Kolonialpolitik*, pp. 43-44; V. G. Kernan, *Marxism and Imperialism*, London 1974, pp. 6-17; Shlomo Avineri (ed.), *Karl Marx on Colonialism & Modernization*, New York 1969, pp. 39-44; Karl Marx, *Kapital*, III, 2, p. 309, quoted in Bernstein, *Voraussetzungen*, p. 180
216 *Internationaler Sozialistenkongress zu Amsterdam*, 14 – 20.8 1904, Berlin 1904, pp. 23-24
217 *Internationaler Sozialistenkongress zu Paris*, 23 – 27.9.1900, Berlin 1900, p. 27
218 *Ibid.*, p. 28
219 *Ibid.*, pp. 28 ff
220 *Internationaler Sozialistenkongress zu Stuttgart, 1907*, Berlin 1907, p. 39
221 James Joll, *The Second International*, pp. 123-125; Milorad M. Drachkovitch (ed.), *The Revolutionary Internationals 1864-1943*, Stanford 1968, pp. 95-116; Maehl, "The Triumph of Nationalism in the German Socialist Party on the Eve of the First World War", *Journal of Modern History*, vol. 24 (1952), pp. 28-30
222 Gerhard Hildebrand, *Sozialistische Auslandspolitik*, Jena 1911, pp. 61-62; Joll, pp. 85-87, 94-99
223 E. Dolleans, *Histoire du Mouvement Ouvrier*, Paris 1946, vol. II, Part II, ch. I; Georges Lefranc, *Le Socialisme sous la Troisième République*, Paris 1963, pp. 105-117
224 M. Drachkovitch, *Les Socialismes*, p. 24
225 Merle Feinsod, *International Socialism and the World War*, Harvard University Press, 1955 pp. 15-20; Drachkovitch (ed.), *The Revolutionary Internationals*, pp. 108-116; Georges Haupt, *Socialism and the Great War*, Oxford 1972
226 Shub, *Lenin*, p. 156
227 Karl Kautsky, *Die Internationale*, Wien 1920, pp. 6-7
228 *Internationaler Sozialistenkongress zu Amsterdam*, p. 43
229 *Ibid.*, pp. 41-42
230 Julius Braunthal, *Geschichte der Internationale*, Bd. I, pp. 340-347
231 Quoted in Drachkovitch (ed.), *The Revolutionary Internationals*, p. 253
232 *Ibid.*, pp. 112-114
233 Karl Kautsky, *Die Vereinigten Staaten Mitteleuropas*, Stuttgart 1908
234 *Protokoll über die Verhandlungen des Parteitages der SPD*, abg. zu *Essen*, vom, 15 – 21.9.1907, Berlin 1907, p. 261
235 Drachkovitch, *Socialismes*, p. 254

237 Drachkovitch, *Socialismes,* pp. 87-92
238 Jaurès, *Textes Choisis,* pp. 148-163; Jackson, *Jean Jaurès,* pp. 126-128
239 Drachkovitch, *Socialismes,* p. 265
240 *Protokoll,* Essen, pp. 229-231
241 *Internationaler Sozialistenkongress zu Kopenhagen,* 23.8 – 3.9.1910, Berlin 1910, p. 32; Joll, pp. 140-142; Drachkovitch, *Socialismes,* pp. 333-338
242 Rosa Luxemburg, "Organisationsfragen der russischen Sozialdemokratie," *Politische Schriften,* Frankfurt/M, 1966-68, vol. III, p. 83
243 *Internationaler Sozialistenkongress zu Stuttgart,* 1907, Berlin 1907; O. Gankin and H. H. Fisher (eds.), *The Bolsheviks and the World War,* pp. 50-66
244 *Stuttgart-Kongress,* p. 89
245 *Ibid.,* p. 86
246 *Ibid.*
247 *Ibid.,* p. 100
248 *Ibid.,* p. 86
249 *Ibid.,* p. 102
250 *Ibid.*
251 Jaurès, *Textes,* p. 150

(II) THE MOMENT OF TRUTH

252 Julius Braunthal, *Geschichte der Internationale,* Bd. II, pp. 17-21
253 Drachkovitch, *Socialismes,* p. 346
254 *Ibid.*
255 Quoted in Jackson, *Jean Jaurès,* p. 179
256 Carl E. Schorske, *German Social Democracy 1905-1917,* New York 1972, p. 290
257 Schorske, pp. 291-294; H. Feinsod, *International Socialism,* pp. 23-29; Joll, *The Second International,* pp. 166-167
258 Drachkovitch, *Socialismes,* pp. 129-130
259 Drachkovitch, *Socialismes,* p. 291
260 Hervé, "La Patrie en danger," p. 93, quoted in Drachkovitch, *Socialismes,* p. 179
261 Drachkovitch, *Socialismes,* p. 153
262 Carr, *The Bolshevik Revolution,* vol. I, p. 66; Samuel Baron, *Plekhanov, the Father of Russian Marxism,* Stanford 1963, ch. XVII
263 Drachkovitch, *Socialismes,* p. 92
264 Rosa Luxemburg, *Briefe an Freunde,* Hamburg 1950, p. 47
265 Braunthal, *Geschichte der Internationale,* pp. 55-63
266 Sigmund Freud, "Thoughts for the Times on War and Death," *The Standard Edition of the Complete Works of S. Freud,* vol. XIV, trans. James Strachey, London 1957, pp. 257-288
267 *Ibid.,* p. 279; Paul Fussel, *The Great War and Modern Memory,* London 1975
268 Rosa Luxemburg, The Junius Pamphlet, *The Crisis in the German Social Democracy,* February-April 1915, Colombo 1967, pp. 1-2
268a Quoted in: F. W. Dupee, *Henry James,* New York 1965, pp. 248-249

(III) LENIN: "SOCIALISM OR NATIONALISM"

269 Shub, *Lenin*, p. 160

270 Lenin, "Socialism and War," *Collected Works*, vol. 21, p. 325; Mary Holdsworth, "Lenin and the Nationalities Question," in L. Schapiro and Reddaway (eds.), *Lenin the Man, the Theorist, the Leader*, London 1967, pp. 265-294

271 Lenin, "Socialism and War", *Collected Works*, vol. 21, p. 325

272 Lenin, "Critical Remarks on the National Question", *Ibid.*, vol. 20, p. 34

273 Lenin, "On the National Pride of the Great Russians", *Selected Works*, (New York), vol. I, p. 664

274 *Ibid.*

275 Lenin, "The Discussion on Self-Determination Summed up," *Collected Works*, vol. 22; Horace B. Davis, *Nationalism and Socialism*, New York 1967, ch. VIII

276 Lenin, *Selected Works*, (New York), Vol. I, p. 664

277 Lenin, *Collected Works*, Vol. 20, p. 24

278 *Ibid.*, p. 22

279 *Ibid.*, p. 24

280 *Ibid.*, p. 26

281 Lenin, "Imperialism, the Highest Stage of Capitalism," *Selected Works*, (New York), Vol. I, pp. 673-777; V. G. Kiernan, *Marxism and Imperialism*, ch. I; Shlomo Avineri (ed.), *Karl Marx on Colonialism & Modernization*, Introduction

282 Lenin, "Imperialism . . . *Selected Works*, (New York), Vol. I, pp. 761-772

283 *Ibid.*, p. 683, pp. 753-758

284 *Ibid.*, pp. 760-763

285 *Ibid.*, p. 737

286 Belfort Bax, quoted in Lenin, "Notebooks on Imperialism," *Collected Works*, Vol. 39, p. 590 quoted in Kiernan, *Marxism and Imperialism*, pp. 7-8; H. B. Davis, *Nationalism and Socialism*, pp. 188-189

287 Rudolf Hilferding, *Das Finanzkapital*, Wien 1909; Kiernan, *Marxism and Imperialism*, pp. 14-17

288 Lenin, "Imperialism . . .", *Selected Works*, (New York), vol. I, pp. 735-744; Kiernan, *Marxism and Imperialism*, pp. 37-60

289 Lenin, "The Right of Nations to Self-Determination," *Selected Works*, (New York), Vol. I, pp. 601-608

290 *Ibid.*, pp. 624-5

291 *Ibid.*, pp. 625-626

292 Lenin, "State and Proletarian Dictatorship," *Selected Works*, (London), Vol. VII, pp. 223-233

293 Lenin, "Critical Remarks . . .", *Collected Works*, vol. 20, pp. 17-52; "The Socialist Revolution and the Right of Nations to Self-Determination," *Collected Works*, Vol. 22, pp. 143-156; J. V. Stalin, "The National Question and Social Democracy, *Prosvescheniye*, no. 3, 4, 5, 1913

294 Lenin, "The National Question in our Programme," *Collected Works*, vol. 6, pp. 454-63

295 *Ibid.,* vol. 21, pp. 407-414: "The Revolutionary Proletariat and the Right of Nations to Self-Determination"

296 Lenin, "The Socialist Revolution and Self Determination," *Collected Works,* vol. 22, p. 151

297 Lenin, "The Right of Nations," *Selected Works,* (New York), vol. I, p. 625

298 *Ibid.*

299 Herzen, *Kolokol,* Nr. 147, 15.10.1862, p. 1214, quoted in Roman Rosdolsky, "Der Streit um die polnisch-russischen Staatsgrenzen anlasslich des polnischen Aufstandes fon 1863," *Archiv fur Sozialgeschichte* 9, 1969, p. 170

300 Hans Ulrich Wehler, *Sozialdemokratie und Nationalstaat,* Wurzburg, 1962; Drachkovitch (ed.), *The Revolutionary Internationals 1863-1943,* pp. 95-113

301 Jaurès, *Textes Choisis,* pp. 82-95; Jackson, *Jean Jaurès,* pp. 123-124

302 Dan, *The Origins of Bolshevism,* pp. 185-186

303 Joll, *The Second International,* p. 106

304 S. R. Tompkins, *The Triumph of Bolshevism: Revolution or Reaction?* University of Oklahoma Press 1967, p. 168

305 Shub, *Lenin,* p. 160

306 Merle Feinsod, *International Socialism and the World War,* pp. 13-84; Lenin, "Socialism and War," *Collected Works,* Vol. 21, pp. 295-338

307 Lenin, *Collected Works,* Vol. 21, pp. 305-6

308 Lenin, "Bourgeois Pacifism and Socialist Pacifism," *Collected Works,* Vol. 23, p. 184

309 Lenin, "Discussion on Self-Determination Summed Up," *Collected Works,* Vol. 22, pp. 359-360

310 Lenin, "The Conference of the RSDLP Groups Abroad," *Collected Works,* Vol. 21, pp. 158-164; Lenin, "The Collapse of the Second International," *Collected Works,* Vol. 21, pp. 205-259; Lenin, "Socialism and War," *Collected Works,* Vol. 21, pp. 295-338

311 Feinsod, *International Socialism,* op. cit., pp. 63-85; Angelica Balabanoff, *Impressions of Lenin,* Michigan 1964, pp. 36-44

312 Lenin, *Collected Works,* Vol. 21, pp. 158-164, 205-259

313 *Ibid.,* pp. 158-164

314 Gilbert Badia, *Rosa Luxemburg,* Paris 1975, pp. 443-483; Nettl, *Rosa Luxemburg,* London 1966, Appendix — The National Question

315 Lenin, "Speech on the National Question," *Collected Works,* vol. 24, pp. 297-9, April 29, 1917

316 Lenin, *Selected Works,* (New York), Vol. I, pp. 643-653

317 Lenin, "The Revolutionary Proletariat and the Right of Nations to Self-Determination, *Collected Works,* Vol. 21, pp. 407-414

318 *Ibid.*

319 Lenin, "The Discussion on Self-Determination Summed Up," *Collected Works,* Vol. 22, pp. 355-356

320 Stefan Thomas Possony, *A Century of Conflict,* Chicago 1953, pp. 20-23

321 Lenin, "The Military Programme of the Proletarian Revolution," *Collected Works,* Vol. 23, pp. 77-87

322 *Ibid.,* pp. 78-79

(IV) 1917

323 Barbara Tuchman, *The Guns of August,* New York 1970, ch. X
324 Chamberlin, *The Russian Revolution,* Vol. I, pp. 142-147
325 See note of Foreign Minister P. N. Milyukov to the Governments of the Allied Powers May 1, 1917, *ibid.,* p. 444
326 *Ibid.,* p. 433
327 *Ibid.,* pp. 429-430, pp. 85-88
328 *Ibid.,* p. 107
329 Lenin, "The Task of the Proletariat in the Present Revolution," *Selected Works,* (New York), Vol. II, pp. 13-20
330 *Ibid.,* pp. 31-32; "The Seventh (April) All-Russia-Conference of the RSDLP (B)", *ibid.,* Vol. II, pp. 69-75, pp. 85-89; Jonathan Frankel, "Lenin's Doctrinal Revolution in April 1917", *Journal of Contemporary History,* Vol. IV (1969), pp. 117-142; Stanley W. Page, *Lenin and World Revolution,* New York chs. II and III
331 Samuel Baron, *Plekhanov, the Father of Russian Marxism,* London 1963
332 Chamberlin, *The Russian Revolution,* Vol. I, p. 149; Leon Trotsky, *The Russian Revolution,* translated by N. Eastman, Ann Arbor (Michigan), 1957, ch. XVIII
333 Chamberlin, *The Russian Revolution,* Vol. I, pp. 163-165
334 Shub, *Lenin,* pp. 218-222; Chamberlin, *The Russian Revolution,* Vol. I, pp. 170-172; Trotsky, *The Russian Revolution,* pp. 235-237
335 Shub, *Lenin,* pp. 230-231; Lenin, *Selected Works* (New York), Vol. II, pp. 90-92, pp. 142-145
336 Lenin, *Selected Works,* (New York), Vol. II, pp. 37-38, 113-115
337 Lenin, "The Seventh All-Russian Conference . . .", *Selected Works,* (New York), Vol. II, pp. 113-118, 140-150
338 Lenin, "The Task of the Proletariat in our Revolution," *Selected Works,* (New York), Vol. II, pp. 23-43
339 Jacob L. Talmon, *The Origins of Totalitarian Democracy,* London 1952, pp. 137-138
340 Lenin, *Selected Works,* (New York), vol. II, pp. 140-150
341 *Ibid.,* pp. 113-115, pp. 246-254
342 Charles Vellay, *Discours et Rapports de Robespierre,* Paris 1908, p. 326 (see also: Talmon, *The Origins of Totalitarian Democracy,* p. 80)
343 Lenin, "Lessons of the Revolution," *Selected Works,* (New York), Vol. II, p. 187
344 Lenin, "The Eighteenth of June," *ibid.,* p. 151; Trotsky, *The Russian Revolution,* p. 264
345 Lenin, "On Compromises," *Selected Works* (New York), Vol. II, pp. 201-205; "Draft Resolution on the Present Situation," *ibid.,* pp. 207-212
346 Shub, *Lenin,* pp. 237-242; Chamberlin, *The Russian Revolution,* Vol. I, pp. 166-179
347 Shub, *Lenin,* p. 242; Trotsky, op. cit., p. 264
348 Lenin, "On Slogans," *Selected Works,* (New York), vol. II, pp. 174-180

349 Chamberlin, *The Russian Revolution*, vol. I, pp. 192-200

350 Podvoysky, quoted in Shub, *Lenin*, p. 260

351 Deutscher, *The Prophet Armed*, pp. 279-280; Chamberlin, *The Russian Revolution*, Vol. I, p. 203

352 Shub, *Lenin*, pp. 260-263; Trotsky, *The Russian Revolution*, pp. 265-270; Lenin, "To the Central Committee of the RSDLP," *Selected Works*, (New York), Vol. II, pp. 196-200; Deutscher, *The Prophet Armed*, p. 286

353 Lenin, "Can the Bolsheviks Retain State Power?", *Selected Works*, (New York), Vol. II, p. 402

354 Marx, The Civil War in France, quoted in Lenin, "The State and Revolution," *Selected Works*, (New York), vol. II, pp. 296-298

355 *Ibid.*, pp. 300-304

356 Lenin, "The Impending Catastrophe and How to Combat It," *Selected Works*, (New York), Vol. II, pp. 217-254; Trotsky, *The Russian Revolution*, pp. 315-316

357 Chamberlin, *The Russian Revolution*, Vol. I, pp. 293-295; Carr, *The Bolshevik Revolution*, Vol. I, pp. 93-98

358 Trotsky, *The Russian Revolution*, pp. 281-285

359 Lenin, "The Bolsheviks Must Assume Power," *Selected Works*, (New York), Vol. II, pp. 362-364

360 Lenin, "Marxism and Insurrection", *ibid.*, pp. 365-370

361 Carr, *The Bolshevik Revolution*, Vol. I, pp. 93-95; Trotsky, pp. 281-283

362 Lenin, "The State and Revolution", *Selected Works,* (New York), Vol. II, pp. 263-362

363 *Ibid.*, pp. 330-345

364 *Ibid.*, p. 299

365 *Ibid.*, pp. 329-330

366 Carr, *The Bolshevik Revolution*, Vol. I, pp. 418-428; Baruch Knei-Paz, *The Social and Political Thought of Leon Trotsky*, Oxford 1978, p. 547; Schapiro and Reddaway (eds.), *Lenin: the Man, the Theorist, the Leader*, London 1967, pp. 265-294; Richard Pipes, *The Formation of the Soviet Union: Communism and Nationalism, 1917-1923*, Cambridge (Mass.), 1954, pp. 34-49

367 R. Pipes, *The Formation of the Soviet Union*, pp. 1-8; Carr, *The Bolshevik Revolution*, Vol. I, pp. 255-256

368 Carr, *The Bolshevik Revolution*, Vol. I, pp. 253-258, 290-292

369 *Ibid.*, p. 253

370 Carr, *The Bolshevik Revolution*, Vol. I, p. 265; Chamberlin, *The Russian Revolution*, Vol. I, pp. 373-377; Pipes, *The Formation*, pp. 50-73

371 Lenin, "The Sixth Prague All-Russian Conference of the RSDLP, 5 – 17.1.1912", *Collected Works*, Vol. 17, p. 485; "Finland and Russia", *ibid.*, Vol. 24, pp. 335-338; "Mandates to Deputies of the Soviet-elected at Factories and Regiments", *ibid.*, pp. 354-356; "Speech on the National Question", *ibid.*, pp. 297-303

372 Carr, *The Bolshevik Revolution*, Vol. I, pp. 289-307

373 *Ibid.*, pp. 278-280

374 Albert Sorel, *L'Europe et la revolution française*, Paris 1922, vols. IV, V; Georges Lefebvre, *The French Revolution*, London 1962-64, 2 vols., especially vol. I, ch. II

375 Chamberlin, *The Russian Revolution*, Vol. I, p. 363

376 Carr, *The Bolshevik Revolution*, Vol. III, pp. 20-42, pp. 50-58

377 Lenin, "A Painful but Necessary Lesson", *Selected Works*, (New York), Vol. II, pp. 559-562; "Strange and Monstrous", *ibid.*, pp. 564-570

378 Lenin, "Extraordinary Seventh Congress of the RCP (B), 6 – 8 March, Political Report of the Central Committee, March 7", *Selected Works*, (New York), Vol. II, pp. 573-592

379 Carr, *The Bolshevik Revolution*, Vol. III, pp. 10-11

Part VII. The General Will of the Global Proletariat (pp. 433-448)

380 Chamberlin, *The Russian Revolution*, Vol. I, pp. 356-357, pp. 389-408; J. W. Wheeler-Bennett, *Brest Litowsk: The Forgotten Peace*, London 1938, pp. 193-195

381 *The Communist International, 1919-1943*, Documents edited by Jane Degras, Oxford 1956; Bunyan and Fisher, *The Bolshevik Revolution, 1917-1918*, Stanford 1943

382 Carr, *The Bolshevik Revolution*, Vol. III, pp. 15-16

383 *Ibid.*, p. 16

384 *Ibid.*, pp. 31-32

385 Chamberlin, *The Russian Revolution*, Vol. I, pp. 394-396

386 Carr, *The Bolshevik Revolution*, Vol. III, pp. 27-29

387 Chamberlin, *The Russian Revolution*, Vol. I, pp. 401-402

388 Chamberlin, *The Russian Revolution*, pp. 402-404; Carr, *The Bolshevik Revolution*, Vol. III, pp. 38-39; Shub, Lenin, pp. 337-338

389 Carr, *The Bolshevik Revolution*, Vol. III, p. 71

390 G. D. H. Cole, *Communism and Social Democracy 1914-1931, A History of Socialist Thought*, Vol. IV, Part I, London 1938, pp. 290-291

391 G. D. H. Cole, *Communism and Social Democracy*, pp. 299-300; Carr, *The Bolshevik Revolution*, Vol. III, p. 118

392 Carr, *The Bolshevik Revolution*, pp. 119-120; Cole, *Communism and Social Democracy*, pp. 301-302

393 Carr, *The Bolshevik Revolution*, Vol. III, p. 119

394 *Ibid.*, pp. 119-120

395 Cole, *Communism and Social Democracy*, pp. 301-304

396 *Ibid.*, p. 305

397 "Manifesto of the Communist International to the Proletariat of the Entire World", *The Communist International, 1919-1943*, Docum. ed. by Jane Degras, pp. 38-47

398 Carr, *The Bolshevik Revolution*, Vol. III, p. 125

399 *Ibid.*, p. 124

400 Vellay, *Discours et Rapports de Robespierre*, p. 332
     Talmon, *The Origins of Totalitarian Democracy*, p. 119

401 Lenin, quoted in Carr, *The Bolshevik Revolution,* Vol. III, p. 53
402 *Ibid.*
403 *Ibid.*
404 Lenin, "A Painful but Necessary Lesson", *Selected Works,* (New York), Vol. II, pp. 560-561
405 Degras (ed.), *Documents on the Communist International,* pp. 38-47
406 Cole, *Communism and Social Democracy,* pp. 300-301
407 Carr, *The Bolshevik Revolution,* Vol. III, pp. 125-126; Degras, *The Communist International,* pp. 38-47; Cole, pp. 305-306
408 Cole, *Communism and Social Democracy,* p. 306
409 *Ibid.*
410 *Ibid.,* pp. 309-310
411 *Ibid.,* p. 309
412 Degras, *The Communist International,* p. 42
413 *Ibid.,* p. 43
414 Cole, *Communism and Social Democracy,* p. 313
415 *Ibid.,* p. 314
416 Degras, *The Communist International,* p. 139
417 Cole, *Communism and Social Democracy,* p. 309
418 Degras, *The Communist International,* p. 46
419 *Ibid.*
420 *Ibid.,* pp. 141-144
421 *Ibid.*
422 *Ibid.,* p. 143
423 Carr, *The Bolshevik Revolution,* Vol. III, pp. 132-138
424 *Ibid.,* p. 140
425 *Ibid.,* pp. 157-161
426 *Ibid.,* p. 212
427 *Ibid.*
428 *Ibid.,* pp. 194-195; for the best study of the most important party on the Continent see Annie Kriegel, *Aux Origines du Communisme Français, 1914-1920,* 2 vols., Paris 1964
429 *Ibid.,* pp. 189-190
430 *Ibid.,* p. 211
431 *Ibid.,* p. 210; see also: Michael Florinsky, *World Revolution and the U.S.S.R.,* New York 1933, Ch. II, "The Period of Sturm and Drang, 1918-1920"
432 Degras, *The Communist International,* pp. 113-127
433 *Ibid.,* pp. 161-166
434 *Ibid.,* pp. 166-167
435 Carr, *The Bolshevik Revolution,* Vol. III, pp. 188-196
436 Lenin, "Infantile Disease of 'Leftism' in Communism" (Left-Wing Communism, an Infantile Disorder), *Selected Works,* (New York), Vol. III, pp. 333-419
437 Carr, *The Bolshevik Revolution,* Vol. III, pp. 191-195
438 Lenin, *Selected Works,* (New York), Vol. III, pp. 339-341
439 Carr, *The Bolshevik Revolution,* Vol. III, pp. 201-205

440 Lenin, *Selected Works,* (New York), Vol. III, pp. 346-353
441 *Ibid.,* pp. 359-367
442 *Ibid.,* p. 366
443 "Theses on the Basic Tasks of the Communist International Adopted by the Second Comintern Congress", Degras, *The Communist International,* pp. 120-121
444 *Ibid.,* pp. 122-123
445 Carr, *The Bolshevik Revolution,* Vol. III, pp. 235-237
446 *Ibid.,* p. 256
447 Lenin, "Second Congress of the International", *Selected Works,* (New York), Vol. III, pp. 457 ff
448 *Ibid.,* p. 459
449 Carr, *The Bolshevik Revolution,* Vol. III, pp. 235-236
450 *Ibid.,* pp. 219 ff
451 *Ibid.,* p. 222
452 USPD: *Protokoll uber die Verhandlungen des Ausserordentlichen Parteitags zu Halle,* quoted in Carr, *the Bolshevik Revolution,* Vol. III, p. 220
453 *Ibid.,* p. 188
454 *Ibid.,* pp. 148-149
455 Rosa Luxemburg, "Fragment uber Krieg, nationale Frage und Revolution", in *Politische Schriften,* edited by Ossip K. Flechtheim, Frankfurt/Main 1968, Vol. III, p. 143
456 *Ibid.,* 147
457 *Ibid.*
458 *Ibid.,* p. 149
459 *Ibid.*
460 *Ibid.,* p. 145
461 *Ibid.,* p. 142
462 Cole, *Communism and Social Democracy,* pp. 323-324
463 *Ibid.,* p. 325
464 *Ibid.,* p. 326
465 *Ibid.,* p. 325

Part VIII. From Georges Sorel to Benito Mussolini (pp. 451-502)
1. The legacy of Georges Sorel—Marxism, Violence, Fascism

1 Pierre Andreu, *Notre maître G. Sorel,* (Paris, 1935), p. 306; Georges Sorel, *Réflexions sur la violence,* 4th edition (Paris, 1919), Appendix 3, "Plaidoyer pour Lénine", p. 454; *Reflections on Violence,* tr. Hulme & Roth. Introduction by Edward Shils (New York 1961), "In defense of Lenin", p. 286
2 B. Croce, *Pagine Sparse,* p. 227
3 Wyndham Lewis, *The art of being ruled,* London 1926, p. 128
4 Jean Variot, *Propos de G. Sorel,* Paris 1935, p. 219; James H. Meisel, *The Genesis of G. Sorel,* Ann Arbor, Mich. 1951

5   Georges Pirou, *Georges Sorel,* Paris 1927, pp. 55-56. See also: R. Humphrey, *Georges Sorel, Prophet without Honour,* Cambridge, Mass. 1951, p. 22; Meisel, *The Genesis of G. Sorel,* pp. 226, 230

6   Lenin, *Collected Works,* New York 1929, Vol. XIII, p. 249; Pirou, p. 49; Humphrey, p. 24

7   Sorel, *Réflexions,* pp. 442, 451

8   Sorel, *Lettres à Paul Delesalle 1914-1921,* Paris 1947, p. 234

9   *Revue de Paris,* 1 March 1937, p. 150; quoted in: Variot, p. 57, Meisel p. 219

10 Sorel, *Réflexions,* p. 24

11 Michael Freund, *Georges Sorel, Der revolutionäre Konservatismus,* Frankfurt a/M, 1932, p. 17

12 Andreu, pp. 46-48

13 Freund, *Georges Sorel,* pp. 18, 34

14 Andreu, *Notre Maître G. Sorel,* p. 203

15 Freund, *Georges Sorel,* p. 69

16 Sorel, *Réflexions,* p. 17

17 Sorel, *ibid.,* p. 18

18 Sorel, *ibid.,* p. 13

19 Sorel, *ibid.,* p. 22 ff

20 Sorel, "Science et Socialisme", *Revue Philosophique,* (1895), pp. 509-554

21 Sorel, "Avenir socialiste des syndicates", *Humanité nouvelle,* (Mars-Avril, 1898); "Mes Raisons du Syndicalisme" (1910), both articles included in: *Matériaux d'une Théorie du Proletariat,* (Paris, 1910). See also: Sorel, *D'Aristote à Marx,* (Paris, 1935), pp. 263 ff

22 *Matériaux,* pp. 283-284

23 *Matériaux,* pp. 283-285

24 *Ibid.,* p. 285

25 Translated into English by Irving L. Horowitz as an appendix to his *Radicalism and Revolt against Reason: The Social Theories of Georges Sorel,* (1961), pp. 207-254

26 *Ibid.,* p. 240

27 *Ibid.,* p. 231

28 *Ibid.,* p. 246 (Marx's letter of April 5, 1872 on Bakunin's Alliance)

29 *Ibid.*

30 G. Sorel, *Les Illusions du progrès,* 5th edition, 1947, pp. 285-286; 275-276

31 B. Mussolini, *Opera Omnia,* Vol. XXI, p. 109

32 G. Sorel, *Les Illusions du progrès,* pp. 316-317; Edouard Berth, *Les Méfaits des Intellectuels,* (Paris 1926), p. 65 ff; also under the pen-name of Jean Darville, in: *La Monarchie et la classe ouvrière: une enquète,* (ed. G. Valois, 1914), pp. 1030 ff

33 Sorel, *Illusions,* 1 ff; 41 ff

34 *Ibid.,* 9 ff, 54 ff, 80 ff, 135 ff, 146 ff, 184 ff

35 *Ibid.,* pp. 224-225

36 Sorel, *Réflexions,* pp. 161-163

37 *Ibid.,* p. 49

38 *Ibid.,* 172 ff, 176-177, 179 ff

39 *Ibid.*, pp. 32, 41, 46-47, 78, 81, 89, 91, 109, 114, 118-119, 168, 193, 201, 172 ff
40 Variot, *Propos de G. Sorel*, pp. 55 ff
41 *Réflexions*, pp. 249, 433 ff, 319-320
42 Variot, *Propos de G. Sorel*, p. 43; Sartre, *Georges Sorel*, (Paris, n.d.), p. 191
43 *Réflexions*, pp. 257 ff
44 *Ibid.*, pp. 341-342
45 Andreu, *Notre maître G. Sorel*, p. 192
46 Andreu, *ibid.*, p. 183; *Réflexions*, p. 142
47 Andreu, *Notre maître*, p. 388; *Réflexions*, p. 110
48 *Réflexions*, p. 279 (English trans., 208)
49 *Ibid.*, p. 281 (Eng. trans. 210)
50 *Ibid.*, pp. 428-430
51 *Ibid.*, pp. 371-376
52 *Ibid.*, p. 381
53 *Ibid.*, p. 367
54 *Ibid.*, pp. 109-110
55 *Ibid.*, p. 388-389 (Eng. trans. 277-278)
56 Andreu, *Notre maître G. Sorel*, pp. 71-72
57 *Ibid.*, p. 178
58 *Ibid.*, p. 67; Appendix XVII pp. 327-328; *Ibid.*, p. 84; Meisel, *The Genesis of G. Sorel*, p. 183 ff
59 Ernest Nolte, *Three Faces of Fascism*, London 1966, p. 473; Eugen Weber, "Nationalism, socialism and national socialism in France", *French Historical Studies*, Vol. II, N.3 (Spring 1962); Yves Guchet, "Georges Valois, ou l'illusion fasciste", *Revue Française de Science Politique*, (Vol. XV, 1965); Zeev Sternhell, *La Droite Révolutionnaire en France, 1885-1914*, Paris 1978, pp. 364 ff, 385 ff
60 G. Valois, *L'Homme qui vient, Philosophie de l'Autorité*, 2nd ed., Paris 1909, pp. VIII-IX
61 *Ibid.*, Introduction
62 Valois, *L'Homme qui vient*, pp. 20-22
63 *Ibid.*, p. 145
64 *Ibid.*, pp. 150-154
65 *Ibid.*, p. 168
66 *Ibid.*, p. 177
67 *Ibid.*, pp. 173, 177, 180
68 G. Valois, *La Monarchie et la classe ouvrière*, (Paris 1914)
69 *Ibid.*, p. 18
70 *Ibid.*, pp. 38 ff
71 *Ibid.*, p. 41

2. Mussolini and the Fascist Dénouement

72 G. Megaro, *Mussolini in the Making*, Boston, New York 1938, pp. 232-233; J. J. Roth, "The Roots of Italian Fascism: Sorel and Sorelism", *Journal of Modern History*, Vol. 39, n. 1, 1967; E. Santarelli, "Le Socialisme national en Italie: précédents et origines", *Le Mouvement Social*, n. 50, Jan.-March 1965

73 Megaro, *Mussolini in the Making*, pp. 234-235

74 Post-1918 Italy:
   P. Nenni, *Sei anni di guerra civile*, (Milano-Roma, 1945/) Denis Mack Smith, *Italy, a Modern History*, (Ann Arbor. Mich. 1969), pp. 307 ff
   Gaetano Salvemini, *The Origins of Fascism in Italy*, (New York 1973)
   Nino Valeri, *La lotta politica in Italia dall'unità al 1925: idee e documenti*, Firenze 1966: "Guerra e dopoguerra", 469 ff; "Socialisti", 517 ff
   Seton-Watson, *Italy from Liberalism to Facism*, (London 1967), p. 505 ff

75 The myth of the Risorgimento:
   G. Salvemini, "Mazzini" (London 1956) Hans Kohn, *Prophets and Peoples: studies in 19th century nationalism*, ch. 3
   S. J. Woolf, *The Italian Risorgimento*, (London 1969)
   Walter Maturi, *Interpretazioni del Risorgimento*, (Torino 1962)

76 Denis Mack Smith, *Cavour and Garibaldi 1860: a study in political conflict*, (Cambridge 1954)

77 John A. Thayer, *Italy and the Great War*, Madison and Milwaukee 1964, p. 9

78 A. Oriani, *La rivolta ideale*, (2nd ed. Naples, 1908), pp. 70-84, quoted by Thayer, p. 53

79 A. Oriani, *Fino a Dogali*, (Bologna 1923), p. 355 in Thayer, p. 136

80 Thayer, *Italy and the Great War*, p. 46
   G. Salvemini, "Fu l'Italia prefascista una democrazia?", *Il Ponte*, Jan-March 1952, pp. 14-20

81 N. Valeri, *La Lotta politica in Italia*, Il Trasformismo, pp. 141 ff
   Guiliano Procacci, "Appunti in tema di crisi dello stato liberale e di origini del Fascismo", *Studi storici*, Vol. VI, (1965)

82 Thayer, *Italy and the Great War*, p. 35

83 *Ibid.*, pp. 128-130

84 *Ibid.*, 124 ff, 223 ff
   Guido De Ruggiero, "The History of European Liberalism": *Italian Liberalism*, pp. 275-343, (Boston 1959)
   B. Croce, *A History of Italy*, 1871-1915 (Oxford 1929)

85 Friedrich Meinecke, *Machiavellianism; the doctrine of raison d'Etat and its place in modern history*, London 1957
   Federico Chabod, *Machiavelli and the Renaissance*, London 1958, pp. 79-105
   Felix Gilbert, *Machiavelli and Guicciardini; Politics and History in Sixteenth Century Florence*, (Princeton 1965)

86 Niccolò Machiavelli, *The Prince*, (London 1938), Ch. XVII ff

87 Robert Michels, *Political Parties*, (N.Y. 1959)

88 *Ibid.*

89 Gaetano Mosca, *The Ruling Class*, New York 1939
   Vilfredo Pareto, *The Mind and Society*, 4 vols., New York 1963; *International Encyclopaedia of Social Sciences*, vol. XI, 1968, "Pareto's Contributions to Sociology", pp. 411-415

90 "Elites" in *International Encyclopaedia of Social Sciences*, Vol. V, 1968, pp. 26-29

91 Thayer, *Italy and the Great War*, pp. 198; 203; 216-218; 237
   Roberto Vivarelli, "Il dopoguerra in Italia e l'avvento del Fascismo (1918-1922), (Napoli 1967), Vol. I, pp. 262-263

92 Thayer, *Italy and the Great War*, p. 135

93 G. L. Mosse, The poet and the exercise of political power: Gabriele D'Annunzio, *The Journal of General and Comparative Literature*, 1976, pp. 35-36
   G. L. Mosse, *The Nationalization of the Masses*, (N.Y. 1975)

94 *Ibid.*

95 Thayer, *Italy and the Great War*, pp. 256 ff

96 William Langer, *The Diplomacy of Imperialism*, (N.Y. 1956), Ch. III
   Elie Halévy, *A History of the English People in the Nineteenth Century,* Vol. V, "Imperialism and the rise of labour (1895-1905)": The Triumph of Imperialism, p. 67 ff

97 Thayer, *Italy and the Great War*, pp. 233 ff
   N. Valeri, *La Lotta politica in Italia*, (La guerra libica e il nazional-ismo), pp. 327 ff

98 Thayer, *Italy and the Great War*, p. 193

99 E. Corradini, Editorial, *Il Regno*, I, No. 1, (November 29, 1903), quoted by Thayer, p. 194

100 G. Papini, "Per la vita contro la vita", *Il Regno*, I, No. 4, (December 20, 1903) in Thayer, p. 194

101 Gian Falco (Papini), "La cultura e la vita italiana, *Leonardo* (October-Dec., 1905) in Thayer, pp. 196-197

102 G. Prezzolini, "La menzogna parlamentare", *Il Regno*, I. No. 29 (June 5, 1904), in Thayer, p. 197

103 *Il Regno*, I, No. 48 (Oct. 23, 1904), the Editorial on "Le elezioni" quoted by Thayer, p. 197

104 Federico Chabod, *A History of Italian Fascism*, p. 34

105 Thayer, *Italy in the Great War*, p. 203

106 *Ibid.*, p. 207

107 *Ibid.*, p. 217

108 *Ibid.*, p. 218

109 *Ibid.*

110 Ernst Nolte, *Der Faschismus in seiner Epoche* (Munchen, 1963), pp. 200 ff
    E. Nolte, "Marx und Nietzsche in Sozialismus des jungen Mussolinis", *Historische Zeitschrift*, Vol. 191, (1960), pp. 249-335
    Roberto Vivarelli, "Benito Mussolini dal socialismo al fascismo", in: *Rivista Storica Italiana*, Vol. 79, 1967, pp. 445-447

111 G. Megaro, *Mussolini in the Making*, pp. 104-107, 126, 218-221, 233, 281-293

112 Benito Mussolini, *Opera Omnia*, eds. E. & D. Susmel, 35 vols., Firenze 1951-1963, Vol. 2, p. 167

113 Megaro, *Mussolini in the Making*, p. 218
Max Gallo, *L'Italie de Mussolini*, Paris 1964, p. 22ff

114 Megaro, pp. 81-86

115 Mussolini, *Opera Omnia*, III, p. 281

116 Mussolini, *Ibid.*

117 *Ibid.*, IV, p. 234

118 *Ibid.*, IV, p. 155

119 *Ibid.*, II, p. 170

120 *Ibid.*, IV, p. 59

121 *Ibid.*, p. 130; Nolte, *Marx und Nietzsche*, p. 296

122 Mussolini, *Opera Omnia*, V, p. 180; Nolte, *Marx und Nietzsche*, p. 296

123 Mussolini, *Opera Omnia*, II, p. 7

124 *Ibid.*, IV, p. 234

125 *Ibid.*, IV, p. 74

126 *Ibid.*, II, p. 170

127 Renzo De Felice, *Mussolini il Rivoluzionario*, Turin 1965, pp. 127, 133-135
Michael Ledeen, Renzo de Felice and the Controversy over Italian Facism, *Journal of Contemporary History*, Vol. XI, Nr. 4 October 1976

128 G. Megaro, *Mussolini in the Making*, p. 344
De Felice, *Mussolini il Rivoluzionario*, pp. 249-335

130 Mussolini, *Opera Omnia*, VI, p. 256

131 *Ibid.*

132 Salvemini, *The Origins of Fascism in Italy*, p. 72

133 Mussolini, *Opera Omnia*, VI, pp. 219-220

134 Bonomi, Gli avvenimenti recenti e il socialismo italiano, in: *Azione socialista",* June 20, 1914
De Felice, p. 128 (Discourse of Mussolini on July 18, 1912) "Il congresso socialista di Reggio Emilia dev'essere invece interpretato come un tentativo di rinascita idealista. L'anima religiosa del partito (ecclesia) si é scontrate ancora una volta col pragmatismo realistico . . . Ci sono i termini del l'eterno conflitto tra l'idealismo e l'utilitarismo, tra la fede e la neces- sità. Che importa al proletariato di capire il socialismo come si capisce un teorema? E il socialismo é forse riducibile a un teorema? Noi vogliamo crederlo, noi dobbiamo crederlo, l'umanità ha bisogno di un credo. E' la fede che muove le montagne, perché da l'illusione che le montagne si muovono. L'illusione é forse l'unica realtà della vita".

135 Nolte, *Marx und Nietzsche*, pp. 269-277

136 *Ibid.*, 304 ff

137 Mussolini, *Opera Omnia*, II, pp. 246-247; Nolte, *Marx und Nietzsche*, p. 322
Zibordi, Critica sociale, 1 – 15/8/1914, in: De Felice, p. 216: "Col prestigio irresistibile della sua combattività aspra, ma elevata, che trascina le folle senza essere – in barba alla etimologia – volgarmente demamogiga, con alcune doti personali di credente e di milite, egli fa ingoiare alle masse tutto quel che vuole".

Nenni, *Sei anni di guerra civile*, p. 39: "Tra lui e il mondo di fronte – il mondo dei borghesi, il mondo ufficiale – vi era un abisso. Le considerazioni mondane e sentimentali non contavano per lui. Plebeo era e voleva restare, ma senza amore per le plebi. Negli operai ai quali parlava non vedeva dei fratelli, ma una forza, un mezzo del quale potrebbe servirsi per rovesciare il mondo

138 Mussolini, *Opera Omnia*, VI, p. 321
139 Salvemini, *The Origins of Fascism in Italy*, pp. 100 ff
De Felice, *Mussolini il Rivoluzionario*, p. 271 ff
140 *Ibid.*, pp. 228-239; Mussolini, VII, pp. 171-173, 229-231; 238-240
141 Mussolini, VI, pp. 383, 391-392
142 Mussolini, *Opera Omnia*, VII, p. 310; De Felice, *Mussolini il Rivoluzionario*, pp. 310-311
143 Mussolini, *Opera Omnia*, VI, p. 7
144 *Ibid.*, VI, p. 6
145 *Ibid.*, IV, p. 234
146 *Ibid.*, VI, p. 263
147 *Ibid.*, p. 321
148 *Ibid.*, (VI, p. 321)
149 Massimo Rocca (Libero Tancredi) "Il Direttore dell'Avanti! amascherato. Un uomo di Paglia. Lettera aperta a Benito Mussolini" (Il Resto del Carlino,7.10.1914) quoted by De Felice, p. 255
150 Mussolini, *Opera Omnia*, VI, p. 382-383
151 *Ibid.*, VI, pp. 383-384
152 *Ibid.*, pp. 391-392
153 *Ibid.*, p. 392
154 *Ibid.*, p. 401
155 *Ibid.*, p. 427
156 *Ibid.*, p. 428
157 *Ibid.*
158 *Ibid.*, VII, p. 197
159 A. Rossi, *The Rise of Italian Fascism 1918-1922*, N.Y. 1966, pp. 10-11
160 *Ibid.*
161 *Ibid.*
162 *Ibid.*, p. 171
163 *Ibid.*, p. 10
164 *Ibid.*
165 *Ibid.*, pp. 31-32
166 De Felice, *Mussolini il Rivoluzionario*, p. 506 ff, 742 ff, Rossi, *op. cit.*, 33-36
167 Rossi, *The Rise of Italian Fascism*, p. 35
168 *Ibid.*, pp. 35-36

The Doctrine of Fascism

169 Dottrina del Fascismo in: Mussolini, *Opera Omnia,* Vol. 34, pp. 115-138;
     Enciclopedia Italiana, Milano 1932, Vol. 14, pp. 847-851; English Trans. by
     M. Oakeshott, The Social and political doctrines of contemporary Europe
     (N.Y. 1950), pp. 164-186; 190-197
170 *Dottrina del Fascismo,* I (Fundamental ideas), para. 4
171 *Ibid.,* I, para. 7
172 *Ibid.*
173 *Ibid.,* I, para. 10
174 *Ibid.,* I, para. 9
175 *Ibid.*
176 *Ibid.*
177 *Ibid.,* II (Political and Social Doctrine), para. 1
178 *Ibid.*
179 *Ibid.*
180 *Ibid.*
181 *Ibid.,* II, para. 2
182 *Ibid.*
183 De Felice, *Mussolini il Rivoluzionario,* p. 422 ff
     Rossi, *The Rise of Italian Fascism;* Salvemini, op. cit., 160 ff; Luigi Ambrosoli,
     Né aderire né sabotare, 1915-1918, Milano 1961; Leo Valiani, ''Il Partito
     socialista italiano dal 1900 al 1918'', in *Rivista storica italiana'', 1963*
     Robert Paris, *Histoire du fascisme en Italie; I des origines à la prise du pouvoir,*
     (Paris, 1962), pp. 169 ff
184 Rossi, *The Rise of Italian Fascism,* 82 ff; De Felice, *Mussolini il Fascista,*
     Turin 1966, pp. 25-35
185 *Dottrina del Fascismo,* II, para. 5
186 *Ibid.,* II, para. 3
187 *Ibid.*
188 *Ibid.,* II, para. 6
189 *Ibid.,* II, para. 7
190 *Ibid.,* II, para. 8
191 *Ibid.,* II, para. 9
192 *Ibid.,* II, para. 11
193 *Ibid.*
194 *Ibid.,* II, para. 10
195 *Ibid.,* II, para. 11
196 *Ibid.,* II, para. 13
197 *Ibid.*
198 *Ibid.*

Part IX. The Dilemma of the German Revolution 1918
and Hitler in the Wings (pp. 507-534)

1   Erich Eyck, *A History of the Weimar Republic,* Cambridge (Mass.) 1962,
    2 vols. Vol. I, pp. 101 ff
2   *Ibid.,* pp. 102-105
3   *Ibid.,* pp. 103-105
4   *Ibid.,* pp. 30-32
5   *Ibid.,* pp. 47 ff
6   *Ibid.,* p. 45
7   *Ibid.,* p. 50
8   *Ibid.,* p. 51
9   *Ibid.,* p. 61
    See also:
    Erich Matthias, "Die Sozialdemokratie und die Macht im Staate", *Der Weg
    in die Diktatur 1918-1933,* München 1963, pp. 73-93
    Karl Dietrich Bracher, Wolfgang Sauer and Gerhard Schulz, *Die National-
    sozialistische Machtergreifung* Köln/Opladen 1960, pp. 32-33
    Werner Kaltefleiter, *Wirtschaft und Politik in Deutschland,* Köln/Opladen
    1968, p. 30
10 Robert G. L. Waite, *Vanguard of Nazism, The Free Corps Movement in
    Postwar Germany 1918-1923,* New York 1969, esp. ch. IV
    Eyck, *A History of the Weimar Republic,* Vol. I, p. 52
11 Eyck, *The Weimar Republic,* Vol. I, p. 150
12 Peter J. Nettl, *Rosa Luxemburg,* London 1966, 2 vols., p. 499
13 Rosa Luxemburg, *The Russian Revolution and Leninism or Marxism?* intr. by
    Bertram D. Wolfe, Michigan 1961, p. 93
14 *Ibid.,* p. 94
15 *Ibid.,* p. 94
16 *Ibid.,* p. 102
17 *Ibid.,* pp. 71-72
18 *Ibid.,* p. 69
19 Gilbert Badia, *Rosa Luxemburg, Journaliste, Polémiste, Révolutionnaire,* Paris
    1975, p. 302
20 *Ibid.,* pp. 302-303
21 *Ibid.,* p. 303
22 William Henry Chamberlin, *The Russian Revolution 1917-1921,* New York
    1954, vol. II, pp. 42-65
    Isaac Deutscher, *The Prophet Armed, Trotsky: 1879-1921,* London 1954,
    pp. 398-428
23 G. Badia, *Rosa Luxemburg,* p. 303
24 *Ibid.,* p. 386
25 *Ibid.,* pp. 365-368
26 *Ibid.,* pp. 387-390
27 Adolf Hitler, *Mein Kampf,* translated by Ralph Manheim, Boston 1943, p. 22
28 *Ibid.,* p. 10

29 *Ibid.*
30 *Ibid.*, p. 11
31 *Ibid.*, pp. 11, 15
32 *Ibid.*, p. 15
33 *Ibid.*
34 *Ibid.*, p. 40
35 *Ibid.*, p. 41
36 *Ibid.*, p. 131
37 *Ibid.*, p. 132
38 *Ibid.*
39 *Ibid.*, p. 3
40 *Ibid.*, p. 140
41 *Ibid.*, pp. 133-139
42 *Ibid.*, pp. 139-140
43 *Ibid.*, p. 139
44 *Ibid.*, p. 134
45 *Ibid.*
46 *Ibid.*, p. 81
47 *Ibid.*, p. 135
48 *Ibid.*
49 *Ibid.*
50 *Ibid.*
51 *Ibid.*, p. 143
52 *Ibid.*, p. 111
53 *Ibid.*
54 *Ibid.*, p. 113
55 *Ibid.*, pp. 150-151
56 *Ibid.*, p. 152
57 *Ibid.*, p. 150
58 *Ibid.*, p. 154
59 *Ibid.*
60 *Ibid.*, p. 80
61 *Ibid.*, p. 79
62 *Ibid.*, p. 80
63 *Ibid.*, p. 81
64 *Ibid.*, pp. 81-82
65 *Ibid.*, p. 91
66 *Ibid.*, pp. 344-345
67 *Ibid.*, p. 107
68 *Ibid.*, pp. 118-119
69 *Ibid.*, p. 183
70 Joachim C. Fest, *Hitler*, New York 1975, p. 746
71 *Ibid.*, p. 746
72 Adolf Hitler, *Mein Kampf*, p. 51
73 *Ibid.*, p. 155
74 *Ibid.*, p. 55, p. 51

75 *Ibid.*, p. 60
76 *Ibid.*, p. 287
77 *Ibid.*, p. 287
78 *Ibid.*, p. 65
79 *Ibid.*
80 *Ibid.*
81 *Ibid.*
82 *Ibid.*
83 *Ibid.*
84 *Ibid.*, p. 352
85 *Ibid.*, pp. 301-302
86 *Ibid.*, pp. 306-307
87 *Ibid.*, pp. 314-318
88 *Ibid.*, p. 319
89 *Ibid.*
90 *Ibid.*, p. 320
91 *Ibid.*, p. 326
92 *Ibid.*, p. 382
93 *Ibid.*, p. 384
94 *Ibid.*, p. 327
95 *Ibid.*
96 *Ibid.*, p. 329
97 *Ibid.*
98 *Ibid.*
99 *Ibid.*, p. 113
100 *Ibid.*, p. 120
101 *Ibid.*, p. 398
102 *Ibid.*
103 *Ibid.*, p. 340
104 *Ibid.*
105 *Ibid.*
106 *Ibid.*
107 *Ibid.*, p. 396
108 Bracher, Saur and Schulz, *Die Nazionalsozialistische Machtergreifung*, pp. 34-35
109 *Ibid.*, pp. 40-44
110 Erich Eyck, *The Weimar Republic*, Vol. I, pp. 57-58; 78
111 Otto Dov Kulka, "The Churches in the Third Reich and the 'Jewish Question' in Light of Secret Nazi Reports on German Public Opinion", Lecture delivered at the Congress of the Commission Internationale d'Histoire Ecclésiastique Comparée (C.J.H.E.C.), Warsaw July 1978
112 The final solution:
     Andreas Hillgruber, "Die 'Endlösung' und das deutsche Ostimperium als Kernstück rassenideologischen Programms des Nationalsozialismus", *Vierteljahreshefte für Zeitgeschichte*, Jg. 20 (1972), pp. 133-153
     Martin Broszat, "Hitler und die Genesis der 'Endlösung'," *ibid.*, Jg. 25 (1977), pp. 739-775

113 "Denkschrift Hitler über die Aufgaben eines Vierjahresplans (1936)'', *ibid.,* Jg. 3 (1955), pp. 204-205
On the significance of this key document and its place in research literature see Otto Dov Kulka, *"The Jewish Question" in the Third Reich; Its Significance in National Socialist Ideology and Politics,* Diss. The Hebrew University of Jerusalem 1975, pp. 208-210, notes 37-43

114 Edmond Vermeil, "The Origin, Nature and Development of German Nationalist Ideology in the Nineteenth and Twentieth Centuries'', *The Third Reich,* London 1955, pp. 3-111
Gerhard Ritter, "The Historical Foundations of the Rise of Nationalism'', *ibid.,* pp. 381-416

115 Jacob L. Talmon, *Political Messianism, The Romantic Phase,* London 1960, pp. 177-201
Karl Dietrich Bracher, *The German Dictatorship: The Origins, Structure and Effects of National Socialism,* New York 1970, pp. 20-28

116 Dirk Stegmann, *Die Erben Bismarcks, Parteien und Verbände in der Spätphase des Wilhelminischen Deutschlands,* Berlin 1970

117 Walter Z. Laqueur, *Die deutsche Jugendbewegung, Eine historische Studie,* Köln 1962
George L. Mosse, *The Crisis of German Ideology: Intellectual Origins of the Third Reich,* New York 1964
Kurt Sontheimer, "Antidemokratisches Denken in der Weimarer Republik'', *Der Weg in die Diktatur 1918-1933,* München 1962, pp. 49-69
Kurt Sontheimer, "Der Tatkreis'', *Von Weimar zu Hitler 1930-1933,* Hrsg. von Gotthard Jasper, Berlin 1968, pp. 197-228
Karl Dietrich Bracher, *The German Dictatorship,* pp. 28-45
Moeller van den Bruck, *Das Dritte Reich,* Hamburg 1931, quoted in Gordon A. Craig, *Germany 1866-1945,* Oxford 1978, p. 492

118 Armin Mohler, *Die Konservative Revolution in Deutschland 1918-1932,* Grundriß ihrer Weltanschauungen, Stuttgart 1950
Klemens von Klemperer, *Konservative Bewegungen. Zwischen Kaiserreich und Nationalsozialismus.* München; English trans. *Germany's New Conservatism,* Princeton 1957, pp. 155 ff

120 *Ibid.,* p. 488
Oswald Spengler, *Preussenthum und Sozialismus,* München 1934
Uwe Lohalm, *Völkischer Radikalismus.* Die Geschichte des Deutschvölkischen Schutz — und Trutz-Bundes 1919-1923, Hamburg 1970

121 Bracher, *The German Dictatorship,* p. 523

122 *Ibid.*

123 Friedrich Nietzsche, *Genealogy of Morals,* trans. by Walter Kaufmann, 1. Essay, Sec. 16-17

INDEX